About IFPRI

The International Food Policy Research Institute (IFPRI), established in 1975, provides research-based policy solutions to sustainably reduce poverty and end hunger and malnutrition. IFPRI's strategic research aims to foster a climate-resilient and sustainable food supply; promote healthy diets and nutrition for all; build inclusive and efficient markets, trade systems, and food industries; transform agricultural and rural economies; and strengthen institutions and governance. Gender is integrated in all the Institute's work. Partnerships, communications, capacity strengthening, and data and knowledge management are essential components to translate IFPRI's research from action to impact. The Institute's regional and country programs play a critical role in responding to demand for food policy research and in delivering holistic support for country-led development. IFPRI collaborates with partners around the world.

About IFPRI's Peer Review Process

IFPRI books are policy-relevant publications based on original and innovative research conducted at IFPRI. All manuscripts submitted for publication as IFPRI books undergo an extensive review procedure that is managed by IFPRI's Publications Review Committee (PRC). Upon submission to the PRC, the manuscript is reviewed by a PRC member. Once the manuscript is considered ready for external review, the PRC submits it to at least two external reviewers who are chosen for their familiarity with the subject matter and the country setting. Upon receipt of these blind external peer reviews, the PRC provides the author with an editorial decision and, when necessary, instructions for revision based on the external reviews. The PRC reassesses the revised manuscript and makes a recommendation regarding publication to the director general of IFPRI. With the director general's approval, the manuscript enters the editorial and production phase to become an IFPRI book.

The Economics of Teff: Exploring Ethiopia's Biggest Cash Crop

Edited by Bart Minten, Alemayehu Seyoum Taffesse, and Petra Brown

A Peer-Reviewed Publication

International Food Policy Research Institute
Washington, DC

International Food Policy Research Institute, 1201 Eye Street NW, Washington, DC 20005, USA Telephone: 202-862-5600

Cover Design: Jason Chow/IFPRI
Project Manager: John Whitehead/IFPRI
Book Layout: BookMatters
Cover photos: (top) A. Davey/Flickr; (bottom-left) Robin Hammond; (bottom-middle) Andrew McConnell/Panos; (bottom-right) Robert E. Brown.

Contents

Figures and Tables

Figures

Tables

DOI: https://doi.org/10.2499/9780896292833

Library of Congress Cataloging-in-Publication Data

Names: Minten, Bart, editor.
Title: The economics of teff : exploring Ethiopia's biggest cash crop / edited by Bart Minten, Alemayehu Seyoum Taffesse, and Petra Brown.
Description: Washington, DC : International Food Policy Research Institute, 2018. | Includes bibliographical references and index. | Description based on print version record and CIP data provided by publisher; resource not viewed.
Identifiers: LCCN 2017039651 (print) | LCCN 2017048355 (ebook) | ISBN 9780896292840 (ebook) | ISBN 9780896292833 (pbk. : alk. paper)
Subjects: LCSH: Teff—Ethiopia. | Teff industry—Ethiopia.
Classification: LCC SB191.T43 (ebook) | LCC SB191.T43 E36 2018 (print) | DDC 338.1/73110963—dc23
LC record available at https://lccn.loc.gov/2017039651

Foreword

Ethiopia, one of Africa's most populous countries, relies heavily on agriculture. For almost 80 percent of the population, agriculture is the main source of livelihood. Understanding the functioning of this agricultural economy and exploring what can be done to improve its performance will provide a crucial stepping stone toward transforming the agriculture sector and, more broadly, Ethiopia's rural and overall economy.

In Ethiopia's economy, teff is one of the most important, and intriguing, commodities. Teff is both the country's most frequently grown staple food and its biggest cash crop, but so little research has been conducted on teff that it is sometimes called an "orphan crop." This neglect may reflect the fact that teff is not widely grown outside of Ethiopia and Eritrea or the belief that, because of low yields, teff has little potential to address Ethiopia's food security problems.

The Economics of Teff: Exploring Ethiopia's Biggest Cash Crop begins to fill this knowledge gap. The book's contributors explain the production and consumption aspects that make teff unique and use an impressive range of datasets and models to understand the teff value chain and assess the impacts of different investments. The authors show that as the leading cash crop, teff contributes considerably to the income of many agricultural producers in Ethiopia, particularly that of poor smallholders. Given the fast economic growth that Ethiopia is experiencing and the rapid increase in urbanization (the urban population consumes significantly more teff than the rural one), the importance of teff in the country's food system is expected to increase further in the near future. With this potential, teff cannot continue to be ignored. However, increasing teff production involves challenges. The authors look carefully at these issues and make sensible recommendations for teff value chains. Overall, the book makes a vital contribution to the evidence base on teff that will help decision makers improve the performance of this critical sector in Ethiopia.

Shenggen Fan
Director General, IFPRI

Acknowledgments

This study benefited from the comments and suggestions of many people. They are too many to mention, but we are particularly thankful to Paul Dorosh for his guidance, to Mahlet Mekuria and Nahume Yadene for their support throughout this process, and to Indra Lamoot and Todd Benson for their careful reading and editing of large parts of the book. We would further like to acknowledge the Debre Zeit Agricultural Research Center; the Ethiopian Institute of Agricultural Research; the World Bank, which funded the Agricultural Growth Program datasets; and the Central Statistical Agency for giving us access to the multiple datasets that were used for this analysis; as well as the enumerator teams, farmers, and traders who participated in the different surveys. We are also very thankful to the Publications Review Committee of the International Food Policy Research Institute (IFPRI) and its Chair Gershon Feder and to two anonymous reviewers for their critical and valuable comments and suggestions. We gratefully acknowledge the editing and design of this book by IFPRI's Editorial Services and Visual Design and Production teams, particularly John Whitehead, and the great support of IFPRI's Communications and Public Affairs division, led by Rajul Pandya-Lorch.

Preliminary results of this book were presented at a conference on "Improved Evidence towards Better Policies for the Teff Value Chain" held on October 10, 2013, in Addis Ababa. We would like to thank the participants in that conference for their valuable feedback. We would further like to thank our partner institution in the Ethiopia Strategy Support Program (ESSP), the Ethiopian Development Research Institute, for all the assistance given in helping to complete this work. The ESSP is financially supported by the

United States Agency for International Development; the United Kingdom, Department for International Development; and the European Union—we would like to acknowledge that support. We further note that the research presented in this book was conducted as part of the CGIAR Research Program on Policies, Institutions, and Markets, which is led by IFPRI.

Chapter 1

INTRODUCTION

Bart Minten and Alemayehu Seyoum Taffesse

Ethiopia is one of the most populous countries in Africa with the agricultural sector playing an important role in the country. It is estimated that in 2011 the agricultural sector contributed about 45 percent to gross domestic product (GDP). More important, it is a major source of employment in the country, with almost 80 percent of the population making a livelihood in the sector (World Bank 2014a). Understanding the complex linkages in agriculture, and identifying opportuntities and challenges to improve its performance, is therefore fundamental. Moreover, while Ethiopia has made important strides in the reduction of poverty and the improvement of food security over the past decades, poverty and food insecurity levels remain high. At the forefront, government policies and stakeholders have made enormous efforts to improve the functioning of the agricultural sector and of staple food sectors in particular, along with attempts to understand what policies and investments are likely to have the most impact.

However, given the heterogeneous nature of agriculture and its spatial spread over very diverse agroecological regions, there is often a dearth of updated and representative evidence and analysis on the agricultural sector. In addition, appropriate and updated information on the functioning of food and agricultural value chains is often insufficient for policy makers and other stakeholders to make informed decisions. Given that different crops within the agricultural sector often have specific characteristics related to soils, temperature, moisture, labor, harvest and postharvest management, marketing, and preferences by consumers, analysis at the crop level to assist policy making is often considered the most relevant level. This has therefore given a boost to the analysis of crop value chains, internationally as well as in Ethiopia, to improve decisions on investments and policies. In an effort to contribute to better knowledge, which has developed from evidence-based improvements of the agricultural sector in the country, this book in particular focuses on the most grown staple food and most important cash crop in Ethiopia: teff (*Eragrostis tef*).[1]

Compared with other cereals, teff is hardy and able to withstand adverse weather conditions and is therefore considered a lower risk crop (Fufa et al. 2011). Teff is mostly grown at middle elevations between 1,800 and 2,200 meters above sea level and in regions where there is adequate rainfall. These characteristics, together with it being easy to store, seemingly explain the sustained importance of teff in the country. Its grain is mainly used for making injera, a spongy flatbread, Ethiopia's (and Eritrea's) main national dish. Teff is also valued for its fine straw, which is used for animal feed as well as for other purposes, such as mixing with mud for building.

By any standards, teff is an important crop, for farm income as well as food security in Ethiopia. It counts for 22 percent of the cultivated area; and in 2013/2014 it was estimated that about 6.6 million smallholders were involved in the production of teff—that is, 43 percent of all farmers in the country (Chapter 2). On the consumption side, teff makes up as much as 12 percent of all food expenditures and is therefore for consumers the leading food crop in their consumption basket. Teff is the most important cash crop in the country, and it contributes considerably to income generation for a large number of agricultural producers. Moreover, the production is mostly in the hands of poor smallholders whose livelihoods are likely to have significantly changed with the important changes seen recently in teff supply chains, documented throughout this book. To cite some examples, increasing consumption in urban areas and improved market performance are aspects likely to have had an influence on poverty reduction in Ethiopia. Moreover, the World Bank (2014b) has recently shown that agricultural growth (in particular, cereal growth) has been a major contributor to fast poverty reduction in the country.

Why This Book?

This book affords the title *The Economics of Teff: Exploring Ethiopia's Biggest Cash Crop* for two main reasons. First, most of the analysis documents economic fundamentals of the sector and shies away from the more agronomic

---

1 The word teff is written in one of three forms: teff, tef, and t'ef. Throughout this book the spelling of the word teff has been adopted for consistency. Some references may include an alternative spelling.

insights. These can be found in *Achievements and Prospects of Tef Improvement* by Assefa, Chanyalew, and Tadele (2013). Second, by area, teff is the single most important cultivated crop. Moreover, when the commercial surplus of teff was valued at producer prices in 2013/2014, its total value for producers (as high as US$750 million) is significantly more important than any other crop—even coffee, which is Ethiopia's main export crop—and it is estimated that the income generated by farmers from teff is as important as the income generated from all other cereals combined.

This book makes three main contributions to the international literature. First, teff is often called an "orphan" crop (Fufa et al. 2011). Teff receives little attention from international agricultural research centers (CGIAR). Primarily, this is because teff falls outside the mandate of these centers that are structured along such major international crops as maize, wheat, and rice. Also, the Ethiopian government has devoted little attention to the crop, likely because of its desire and emphasis to ensure enough food supply in the country. Given the low yields of teff compared with other crops, teff is often viewed as a low-priority crop. For these reasons, there is relatively little known on the production and marketing of teff, and hence one of the objectives of this book is to address this gap. This is especially important given the high-income elasticity of teff and the fast growth of Ethiopia's population, which is likely to elevate teff's importance in the country's agricultural and food economy.

Second, the diverse datasets applied throughout the book in this research of teff, and the methods engaged in the analyses, are unique in their breadth and diversity. They include the Agricultural Sample Survey of a number of years collected by Ethiopia's Central Statistical Agency (CSA); a large household survey fielded in high-potential agricultural areas (the Agricultural Growth Program areas) in 2011; the Social Accounting Matrix (SAM) of Ethiopia; several waves of the national Household Income, Consumption and Expenditure Survey (HICES) as well as panel data on urban consumers; price data collected by CSA on a number of retail and producer markets, as well as wholesale market prices collected by the Ethiopian Grain Trade Enterprise (EGTE). In addition, a unique large-scale survey dataset fielded at different levels of the teff value chain is investigated that explores the market functioning from major commercial teff areas to the biggest city in the country, Addis Ababa. Table 1.1 gives an overview of the different datasets used in the research described in different chapters in the book. To analyze these diverse datasets, a number of different methods are employed, including productivity and efficiency analysis, spatial analysis, market and price analysis,

TABLE 1.1 Datasets used for empirical analysis

Chapter	Dataset	Who collected?
Chapter 2	Ethiopia's Central Statistical Agency (CSA) Agricultural Sample Survey	CSA
	Household Income, Consumption and Expenditure Survey (HICES)	CSA
Chapter 3	Literature review	
Chapter 4	CSA Agricultural Sample Survey	CSA
	Seed distribution	Ministry of Agriculture and Natural Resources
	Agricultural Transformation Agency (ATA) Baseline Survey	International Food Policy Research Institute (IFPRI)
Chapter 5	ESSP row-planting survey	Ethiopia Strategy Support Program (ESSP)
Chapter 6	CSA Agricultural Sample Survey	CSA
	Geographic Information Systems (GIS) data	Different sources
Chapter 7	Agricultural Growth Program (AGP) Baseline Survey	CSA
Chapter 8	CSA Agricultural Sample Survey	CSA
Chapter 9	ESSP teff value-chain survey	ESSP
Chapter 10	Social Accounting Matrix (SAM)	ESSP
Chapter 11	ESSP teff value-chain survey	ESSP
Chapter 12	Ethiopia Grain Trading Enterprise (EGTE) wholesale price survey	EGTE
	Market survey	ESSP
	CSA retail and producer prices	CSA
Chapter 13	ESSP teff value-chain survey	ESSP
Chapter 14	Ethiopian Urban Socio-economic Survey (EUSS)	Addis Ababa University/ University of Gothenburg
Chapter 15	Literature review	
Chapter 16	Literature review	

Source: Authors.
Note: ESSP is a joint program of IFPRI and the Ethiopian Development Research Institute.

consumption and demand analysis, and Computable General Equilibrium (CGE) modeling.

Third, a value-chain approach is used to analyze different issues upstream, midstream, and downstream in the value chain. In contrast to other value-chain studies that mostly rely on case studies or rapid rural appraisal methods, access to large-scale datasets at each level of the value chain has the added advantage that it allows researchers and analysts with reasonable confidence to make a fair assessment of the functioning of the teff value chain, which is representative for large parts of the country.

Questions Addressed in This Book

The structure of this book follows the teff value chain from producers to consumers, upstream to downstream. Each of the three major sections—upstream, midstream, and downstream—poses challenging questions to try to tackle many of the issues surrounding the policy implications for developing the teff market in Ethiopia. These questions are the following:

Upstream

- What are agronomic characteristics of the teff crop, and what has been the role of agricultural research toward improving its performance?
- What are the adoption rates of improved practices, including improved seed varieties, and what is their link in real-world settings to gain higher productivity levels?
- What are the determinants of these adoption rates and differential productivity levels?
- To what extent are the missing or malfunctioning input markets constraining efficiency?
- How do producers change their production and marketing behavior and technology adoption based on market access, access to extension agents (and the type of extension advice), and household characteristics?
- What is the role of price incentives in production decisions?
- What are determinants of prices obtained by farmers?
- How is the rollout of major extension programs perceived (such as row planting of teff), and what are the impacts?
- How does adoption of improved practices, such as chemical fertilizer use, differ over space?
- What would be the expected impact of extending production of teff on Ethiopia's economy, and how might the impact differ with other cereals?

Midstream

- How do farmers interact with markets—that is, when do they sell, what prices do they obtain, who do they sell to, and how does their marketing behavior change over space?
- What is the prevalent structure of the teff value chain, and what are the opportunities to improve efficiencies?
- What is the share of different value-chain agents in the final price paid by consumers?
- What is the willingness to pay for quality at different levels in the value chain?
- How are transport arrangements and the milling sector of teff organized?
- How does the teff value chain function, and how is it changing over time?
- What is the role of seasonality in marketing and in prices?
- How well are teff markets integrated and to what extent are measures of agricultural performance and marketing margins changing over time?

Downstream

- What is the role of different market outlets (traditional versus modern) in urban markets and to what extent are some vertical integration and coordination mechanisms being used?
- What is the role of the milling sector in teff distribution, and how is their role changing over time?
- What are overall consumption levels, and how are these changing over time?
- What are consumption levels of teff by income level, by region, and by urban-rural divide, and how are these changing over time?
- How do different types of teff vary in importance with respect to consumption?

Overview

Figure 1.1 gives an overview of the book. The first part of the book presents research findings upstream in the value chain, covering the production

FIGURE 1.1 Overview of the book

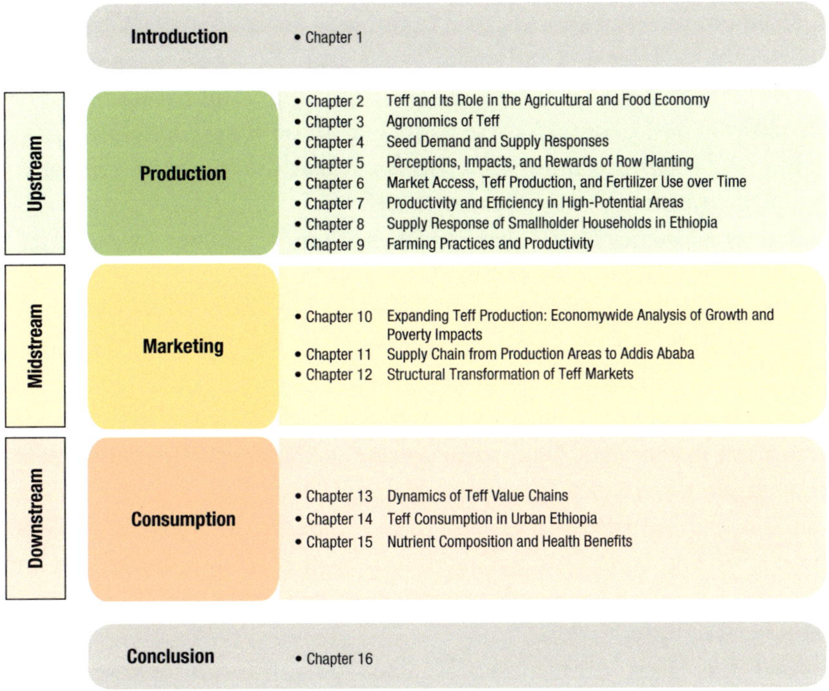

Source: Authors.

environment as well as farmers' output marketing. The second part examines and describes the issues encountered midstream in the value chain, along with the functioning of markets and the important transformations that are happening in this area. The third part focuses on consumption patterns in the downstream part of the value chain and discusses nutrition issues and health benefits of teff.

Chapter 2 discusses the role of teff in Ethiopia's agricultural and food economy. It uses production datasets to evaluate teff's importance in area and production as well as in the number of smallholders involved in its cultivation. On the consumption side the chapter assesses the level of consumption of teff, the forms of teff consumed, and consumption patterns by region, by wealth levels, and along the rural-urban divide. Chapter 3 provides an overview of the agronomics of teff. Teff is a unique crop with specific agronomic characteristics, such as small seeds and a weak stem leading to important issues with lodging. These factors strongly determine the environment in which teff can flourish, and what possible constraints exist around improving productivity of the crop. Two important input factors that can significantly contribute to improved productivity are examined in the subsequent chapters. Chapter 4 discusses the seed demand and supply responses in Ethiopia's teff seed system. As for any crop, seed systems are extremely important to improve production performance. Chapter 5 presents an analysis on the potential and impact of a new and promising innovation that has recently been promoted by the Ethiopian government: row planting of teff.

Chapter 6 looks at spatial characteristics of production and input use in the teff sector; temporal changes in these areas are also examined. Ethiopia is characterized by a very diverse agroecology that results in different agricultural production and consumption patterns across the country and in spatial specialization. It also has a rapidly improving road network. This particular aspect has hampered the adoption of improved technologies and access to output markets in the past. The chapter uses detailed maps and spatial techniques to investigate these issues. Chapters 7, 8, and 9 cover analyses on teff productivity and its determinants. Different datasets attempt to evaluate the contribution of various input factors that potentially increase teff productivity and efficiency. Also given is a detailed overview on prevalent farming practices in commercial teff production.

The Ethiopian government is committed to significantly increase teff production. In Chapter 10 a Computable General Equilibrium (CGE) model of Ethiopia is used to analyze the impact such increases might have on growth and poverty in the country. Growth in teff production is compared with the impact that growth has in other cereal sectors, including wheat and maize. The next three chapters (11, 12, and 13) analyze the teff value chain midstream. A detailed analysis in Chapter 11 examines the structure of the teff value chain between major production areas and the largest city in the country, Addis Ababa. Chapter 12 documents important changes that are happening in teff marketing systems. The drivers for these changes are identified as well. Chapter 13 looks at developments in production, marketing, and consumption practices, both in major commercial zones and in the market system to Addis Ababa.

Finally, the last two chapters look at consumption aspects. Chapter 14 documents teff consumption practices in urban areas, where consumption of teff is significantly higher than in rural areas. Chapter 15 gives an overview of the nutrient composition of teff and looks at its health benefits. In the conclusion, Chapter 16, the major findings from each chapter are drawn together, followed by a discussion of the implications these findings have for policies and investments in Ethiopia.

References

Assefa, K., S. Chanyalew, and Z. Tadele. 2013. *Achievements and Prospects of Tef Improvement.* Addis Ababa: Ethiopian Institute of Agricultural Research (EIAR); Bern, Switzerland: University of Bern.

Fufa, B., B. Behute, R. Simons, and T. Berhe. 2011. *Strengthening the Tef Value Chain in Ethiopia.* Mimeo, Agricultural Transformation Agency (ATA), Addis Ababa.

World Bank. 2014a. *Ethiopian Economic Update: Strengthening Export Performance through Improved Competitiveness*, 3rd ed. Washington, DC: World Bank.

———. 2014b. *Ethiopia: Poverty Assessment.* Report AUS6744. Poverty Global Practice. Africa Region, World Bank. Washington, DC: World Bank.

Chapter 2

TEFF AND ITS ROLE IN THE AGRICULTURAL AND FOOD ECONOMY

Ibrahim Worku Hassen, Mekdim Dereje Regassa, Guush Berhane, Bart Minten, and Alemayehu Seyoum Taffesse

To fully appreciate the transformation of the Ethiopian agricultural and food economy, and to illustrate the role teff plays in this, this chapter explores rapid changes since 2003 in the agricultural sector (on the production side) and food economy (on the consumption side). During this period Ethiopia's economy has been characterized by high economic growth rates, making the country one of the fastest-growing economies in the world (World Bank 2014). Considering this, important implications on its agricultural and food economy become apparent.

The chapter first discusses the role of teff on the production side. Ethiopia is an extremely diverse country, with large variation in ecosystems and agricultural potential, ranging from pastoralist areas to moisture-reliable lowlands and highlands as well as drought-prone highlands and lowlands (Chamberlin and Schmidt 2012). Moreover, there is large variation in population density and access to markets. These factors contribute to a diversified agricultural economy with spatial specialization of agricultural activities and very diverse livelihood strategies. Next, the chapter analyzes teff consumption. Data are analyzed from national consumption surveys over a 15-year period to illustrate the extent to which transformation in consumption patterns is occurring (for an overview of patterns in nutritional transition in developing countries overall, see Popkin [2003]) and what exactly the role is of teff in Ethiopia's changing food economy. To better understand that transformation, the link between food demand and income levels in particular is examined later in the chapter. This might give an indication of the trend in food consumption patterns, especially within a country where urbanization is encouraged and mid-income status is set as a goal by the year 2025 in several policy documents.

Data

We use production and consumption data collected by Ethiopia's Central Statistical Agency (CSA). We chose to use these data because they are the only ones that are systematically available over time and because they are representative at the national and regional levels. Ethiopia is blessed with such datasets, and although the quality of CSA data has been challenged by some authors (for example, Dercon and Hill 2009; Gollin 2011; Mandefro and Jerven 2015), they are nevertheless considered to be among the best in Africa. These datasets should therefore allow us big picture overviews in this area.

Data on agricultural production information is collected annually through an agricultural sample survey implemented by the CSA. This survey is typically fielded in more than 2,000 enumeration areas, and more than 40,000 farmers are visited. For example, in 2010/2011, almost 45,000 agricultural households were interviewed. The survey collects data, among others, on area allocation, production levels, yields, use of harvest, and land management practices. The sample is set up in such a way that the results are representative of the regional and zonal levels. The annual data from these surveys for the period 2003/2004–2013/2014 are used in the analysis.

The consumption analysis relies on the Ethiopian Household Income, Consumption and Expenditure Survey (HICES) dataset from the past four rounds—that is, 1995/1996, 1999/2000, 2004/2005, and 2010/2011. These data were also collected by the CSA. In total, 11,678, 17,320, 21,560, and 27,831 households were interviewed over the four periods, respectively. The survey contains detailed information on consumption and expenditures of both food and nonfood items. The number of calories contributed by each of the consumable items is also available within the dataset. These data are explored to analyze trends in the consumption of different food categories over these periods.[1] In particular, the focus is on quantity consumed, expenditures, and calorie contribution of the three varieties of teff (white, mix, and red) and of injera. It is to be noted that there have been some differences in data collection methods over the years, and some caution in the interpretation over time is warranted (Stifel and Woldehanna 2014). In addition to the HICES dataset, the retail price dataset of the CSA is used to account for inflation over this period.

1 Note that since a different cleaning procedure was followed before statistics were calculated, there are slight differences with the national estimates.

Teff in Ethiopia's Agricultural Economy

Using a number of indicators, teff is estimated to be the most important crop in Ethiopia's agricultural economy. In 2013/2014 it was estimated by the CSA that teff made up 22 percent of all the cultivated area by private smallholders in the meher season, covering about 3 million hectares, and that it was grown by 6.6 million farmers.[2] As there are a total of 15.3 million farmers in Ethiopia, this implies that 43 percent of all Ethiopian farmers grow teff. The second most important crop is maize at 15 percent of all cultivated land, followed by sorghum accounting for 12 percent. Teff makes up 31 percent of all the cultivated land in the cereal sector. This sector is the most important in Ethiopia's agricultural economy, accounting for 72 percent of all cultivated land.

Figure 2.1 shows how the area allocated to teff and other major crops has evolved over time. While the teff area has grown by 50 percent over 10 years—from 2 million hectares in 2003/2004 to 3 million hectares in 2013/2014—the share of teff in total area cultivated has stayed relatively stable over time. It was as high as 21.3 percent in 2003/2004, and it even slightly increased to 22.1 percent in 2013/2014. The share of other crops also remained surprisingly stable over time, with seemingly no important diversification in Ethiopia's agricultural economy during the meher season to date. For example, the share of cereals in total area cultivated during the meher season was as high as 75 percent in 2003/2004. Although it declined over time, it remained as high as 72.1 percent in 2013/2014.

Although teff is the most important single crop by total cultivated area in Ethiopia, its importance in agricultural production is far less. This is due to the relatively low yields of teff compared with most other crops, especially other cereals. The total national production of teff in 2013/2014 (4.4 million metric tons) was lower than maize (6.5 million metric tons) but higher than wheat (3.9 million metric tons) and sorghum (3.8 million metric tons) (Ethiopia, CSA 2014b). The average yield of teff that year was 1.46 metric tons per hectare, less than half the yield of maize (3.25 metric tons per hectare).

However, prices paid per kilogram of teff are considerably higher (Table 2.1). When considering the production value of teff in 2013/2014 and comparing it to other cereals, teff production is found to be valued at

---

2 Taffesse, Dorosh, and Gemessa (2012) show that smallholders generate 95 percent of the total production of the main crops in Ethiopia, and that 97 percent of the total crop production is in the meher season. The second season (belg) is therefore relatively less important.

FIGURE 2.1 Share of different crops in total cultivated area (private peasant holdings; meher season)

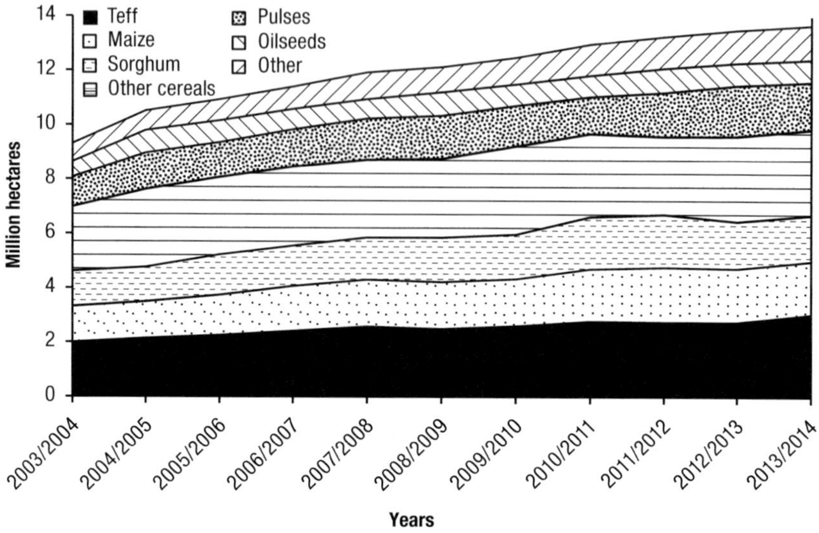

Source: Authors' calculations, CSA Agricultural Sample Surveys, 2003/2004–2013/2014.
Note: This includes private peasant holdings during the meher season.

US$2.5 billion, Ethiopia's crop of highest value.[3] Figure 2.2 shows the value of other cereals. Maize and wheat are each valued above US$1.5 billion (US$1.59 billion for maize and US$1.57 billion for wheat), while sorghum at US$1.27 billion and barley at US$0.69 billion are significantly lower. Overall, teff makes up 32 percent of the total value of the cereal sector.

If the commercial surplus (that part of production that is sold) is considered, its value for teff in 2013/2014 was estimated to be US$750 million. Within the cereal sector, teff is the most commercialized crop, with an estimated 30 percent of the production sold (Ethiopia, CSA 2014a). The value of the commercial surplus of teff makes up half of the value of total commercial surplus of the cereal sector and therefore equals the commercial surplus of all other cereals combined in the country, as shown in Figure 2.2 and in

3 To value production, the following methodology was used: The median retail price collected by CSA in all the surveyed markets in the country over the period July 2013–June 2014 was calculated. The prices of the following types in the CSA's dataset were used as an approximation of the price of the product: mixed teff, white wheat, white barley, white maize, white sorghum, millet, oats, and imported rice. The exchange rate of January 2014 of 19.33 Br (Ethiopian birr) per US$ to convert birr is used. For calculations of commercial surplus, the number published for the year 2013/2014 (Ethiopia, CSA 2014a) is relied upon.

FIGURE 2.2 Production value and use of cereals, 2013/2014

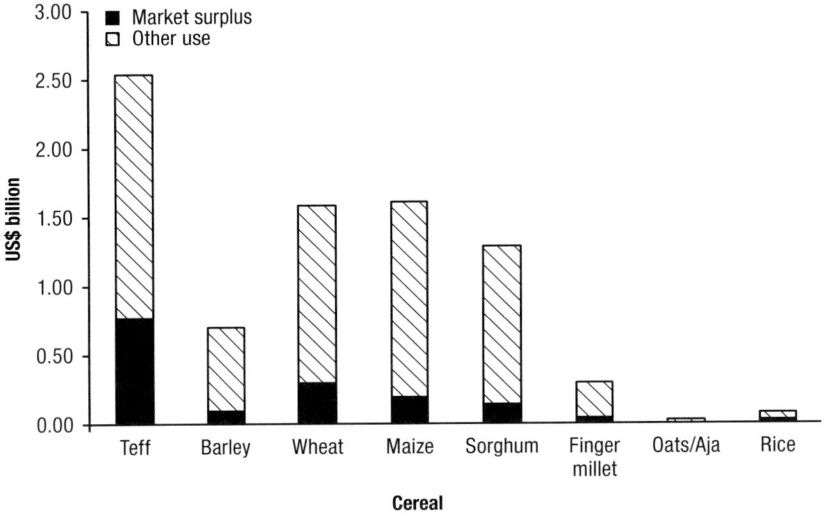

Source: Authors' calculations, CSA Agricultural Sample Surveys, 2013/2014.

TABLE 2.1 Production and commercial surplus of cereals, coffee, and sesame, 2013/2014

	Quantities (million metric tons)		Price	Values (US$ billions)	
Food item	Production	Market surplus	(birr per kilogram)	Production	Market surplus
Teff	4.42	1.31	11.03	2.52	0.75
Barley	1.91	0.24	6.95	0.69	0.09
Wheat	3.93	0.72	7.71	1.57	0.29
Maize	6.49	0.72	4.75	1.59	0.18
Sorghum	3.83	0.39	6.42	1.27	0.13
Finger millet	0.85	0.10	6.57	0.29	0.03
Oats	0.06	0.01	7.03	0.02	0.00
Rice	0.09	0.02	9.70	0.05	0.01
Total cereals	**21.58**	**3.52**	**n.a.**	**8.00**	**1.48**
Coffee	0.39	0.20	55.03	1.12	0.56
Sesame	0.22	0.15	32.41	0.37	0.26

Source: Authors' calculations, CSA Agricultural Sample Surveys, 2013/2014.

Note: n.a. = not applicable.

Table 2.1. The value of the commercial surplus of teff is also approximately equal to the value of coffee exports from Ethiopia during the same period (which amounted to US$714 million from July 2013 to June 2014). However, when the cash value accrued by farmers from the sales of teff is compared with the income gained through the sale of the two other major export crops from the country, income from teff is 34 percent higher than income from coffee, and almost triple the income that farmers make from the sales of sesame. Teff is thus by far Ethiopia's most important cash crop.

The role of teff in agricultural production between regions exhibits significant differences, partly driven by climatic suitability but also due to producer and consumer preferences. Figure 2.3A shows the share of different regions in total teff production in Ethiopia in 2013/2014. Oromia is the most important teff-producing area in the country, and its share in total national production is estimated to be as high as 48 percent. The second highest is Amhara with 39 percent. The other regions are relatively less important, with Southern Nations, Nationalities, and Peoples' (SNNP) region at 7 percent, Tigray at 5 percent, and the other regions combined at less than 1 percent. When the share of teff is examined as a proportion of total cereal area in each of the four major regions, relatively few differences are noted (Figure 2.3B). The share of teff in cereal area is highest in Amhara, where it reaches almost 35 percent. However, it drops to less than 25 percent in Tigray.

To understand the associates of growth in teff production since 2003, the level of production, area allocated, and yield is equated to 100 for the agricultural year 2003/2004. As Figure 2.4 illustrates, teff production has increased by 163 percent since 2003/2004, a combination of both area and yield increases of 50 percent and 73 percent respectively. Yield growth has thus been the main contributor to production growth. During the first half of the decade, yield and area growth were at similar levels (for the period 2003–2007). The gap between the two growth rates has, however, become wider since. Figure 2.4 also shows that the number of teff farmers has increased significantly since 2003/2004: an increase of 44 percent. As the area increase was of similar magnitude as the number of teff farmers, there has been no significant change in the area of teff cultivated per farmer over this period.

Table 2.2 further shows the relation of farm size and area allocation of all land, as well as teff land over the past decade. Based on the CSA data, 22 percent of total area in 2013/2014 was cultivated by farms that are 1 hectare or smaller. This compares to 32 percent for farm sizes between 1 and 2 hectares. In this same period (2013/2014), 46 percent of cultivated land was in the hands of farmers with farms larger than 2 hectares. The share of farmers

FIGURE 2.3 Share of the different regions in national teff production, 2013/2014

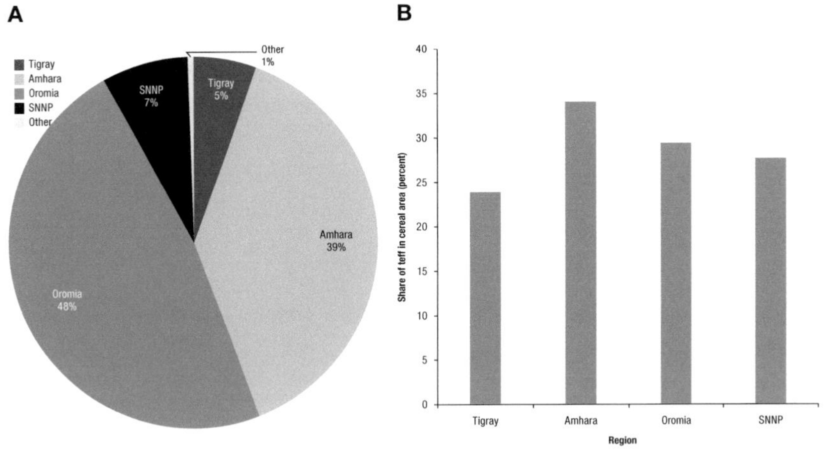

Source: Authors' calculations, CSA Agricultural Sample Surveys, 2013/2014.

FIGURE 2.4 Changes in teff production, area, yield, and number of producers, 2003/2004–2013/2014 (private peasant holders, meher season)

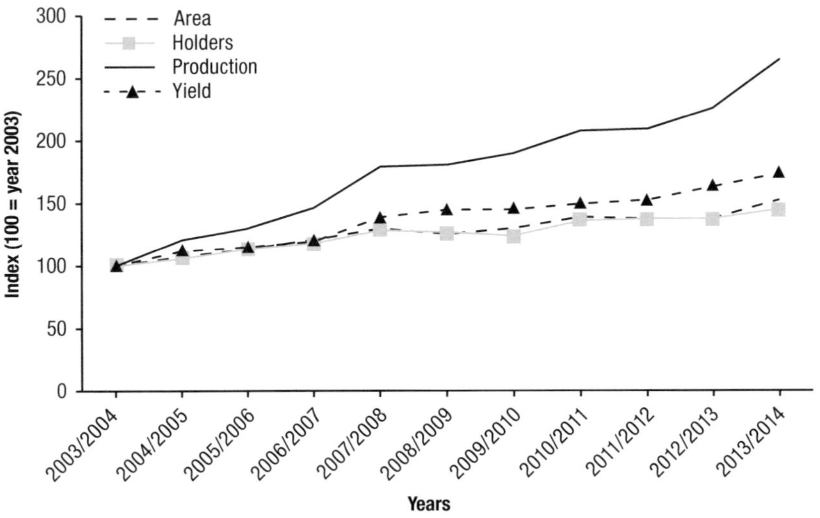

Source: Authors' calculations, CSA Agricultural Sample Surveys, 2003/2004–2013/2014.

TABLE 2.2 Size of holdings and teff area, 2003/2004 and 2013/2014

Farm size (in hectares)	Total area (millions of hectares)	Share (%)	Teff area (millions of hectares)	Share (%)	Number of teff producers (millions)	Share (%)
2003/2004						
0–0.5	0.89	8	0.09	5	0.65	14
0.5–1.0	1.91	17	0.28	14	1.12	25
1.0–1.5	2.13	18	0.38	19	1.01	22
1.5–2.0	1.82	16	0.34	17	0.68	15
2.0–3.0	2.38	21	0.47	24	0.69	15
3.0–4.0	1.20	10	0.23	11	0.24	5
> 4.0	1.25	11	0.19	10	0.14	3
Total	**11.58**	**100**	**1.98**	**100**	**4.53**	**100**
2013/2014						
0–0.5	1.30	7	0.12	4	0.88	13
0.5–1.0	2.72	15	0.40	13	1.61	24
1.0–1.5	2.98	17	0.52	17	1.40	21
1.5–2.0	2.68	15	0.51	17	1.00	15
2.0–3.0	3.62	20	0.70	23	1.03	16
3.0–4.0	1.94	11	0.35	12	0.39	6
> 4.0	2.69	15	0.42	14	0.31	5
Total	**17.93**	**100**	**3.02**	**100**	**6.61**	**100**

Source: Authors' calculations, CSA Agricultural Sample Surveys, 2003/2004 and 2013/2014.

with farms larger than 2 hectares in total land area has stayed relatively stable over the years but increased slightly in 2013/2014 compared to 2003/2004. In the latter period, cultivated land of 2 hectares or larger was held by 42 percent of farmers. In the case of teff, almost half of all teff land (49 percent) was held by farmers with farms of 2 hectares or larger. This compares to 27 percent of teff farmers that actually have farms that are larger than 2 hectares. On the flip side, 73 percent of the teff farmers (the ones with farms smaller than 2 hectares) therefore cultivate half of the teff land. This ratio changed very little over the decade. The magnitudes of these shares illustrate the small size of the farms in Ethiopia overall but also the relatively equitable distribution of land.

Teff in Ethiopia's Food Economy

This section considers consumption patterns and their changes over time using four rounds of HICES datasets, covering the period from 1996 through

2011. To ensure comparability over time in this analysis, expenditures are deflated using the national Consumption Price Index (CPI) and values are expressed in constant 1996 birr, implying a lowering of nominal prices from later HICES rounds through a division by this CPI. Quantities consumed per capita were calculated as well.[4] The results of this exercise, presented in Table 2.3, illustrate a number of interesting findings. First, the share of non-food items in the total consumption basket increased significantly over time, especially since 2000. In 2000 the share of nonfood consumption expenditures accounted for 36.4 percent of the total. Over the following decade, this type of expenditure grew rapidly, and its share in total household expenditures surged to 52.8 percent in 2011. Such increases of nonfood expenditures in total consumption aggregates are typical of transforming and improving economies, implying significant improvements in welfare in the country (World Bank 2014; Ethiopia, MoFED 2012). As a consequence of greater income, people's expenditures shift from food to nonfood products.

Second, an important increase of the total quantity of food consumed per capita is seen (at the bottom of Table 2.3). Consumption increased from 229 kilograms per capita per year in 1996 to 353 kilograms, an increase of 54 percent. The quantities of cereals consumed have shown much less growth, especially in the last 10 years. Here, consumption of cereals grew from 132 kilograms per capita in 2000 to 143 kilograms per capita in 2011, an increase of 8 percent. Moreover, expenditures on food have grown in real terms in the last two surveys conducted compared to 2000. Per capita food expenditures in 2011 were 19 percent higher than in 2000.

Third, some important patterns and shifts are noted within the food basket. Overall, the share of cereals in total food expenditures is declining. While the share made up 43.4 percent of expenditures in 2000, it had declined to 35.5 percent 10 years later. Most growth in the noncereal food categories was recorded in the "other food" category that grew from 9.7 percent to 15.4 percent from 2000 to 2011. There is also an increasing importance of animal products over time. Although the share of animal products is still relatively low, it has grown from 9.9 percent of the food basket in 1996 to 12.9 percent in 2010. These patterns are a reflection of Bennett's law that describes a relative decline in starchy staples and an increase in animal proteins with income (Bennett 1941). Ethiopia is generally characterized by a lack of diverse diets (Headey 2014), but over time this seems to be slowly changing.

4 To convert injera to kilograms of teff, it was multiplied by a conversion factor of 0.325.

TABLE 2.3 Food consumption and real per capita expenditures, by category, 1996–2011

	1996		2000		2005		2011	
Food item	Birr	Share (%)	Birr	Share (%)	Birr	Share (%)	Birr	Share (%)
Real per capita expenditures (birr per capita per year)								
Food								
White teff	16	2.6	18	3.0	17	2.6	18	2.5
Mixed teff	22	3.6	28	4.6	18	2.8	19	2.6
Red teff	31	5.0	32	5.2	22	3.4	19	2.6
Injera	5	0.8	5	0.8	9	1.4	34	4.7
Total teff	73	11.9	82	13.4	67	10.3	90	12.4
Wheat	44	7.2	53	8.7	57	8.8	56	7.7
Barley	28	4.6	23	3.8	41	6.3	18	2.5
Maize	63	10.2	70	11.5	40	6.2	57	7.8
Sorghum	43	7.0	37	6.1	52	8.0	37	5.1
Five major cereals	251	40.8	265	43.4	257	39.7	258	35.5
Other cereals, pulses, and oilseed	87	14.1	89	14.6	85	13.1	121	16.6
Vegetables, fruits, roots, and tubers	100	16.3	132	21.6	96	14.8	143	19.7
Animal products	61	9.9	63	10.3	73	11.3	94	12.9
Other foods	115	18.7	59	9.7	136	21.0	112	15.4
Total food	**615**	**100.0**	**610**	**100.0**	**648**	**100.0**	**727**	**100.0**
Food versus nonfood								
Food	615	51.5	610	63.6	648	54.3	727	47.2
Nonfood	579	48.5	349	36.4	546	45.7	812	52.8
Total	**1,194**	**100.0**	**959**	**100.0**	**1,194**	**100.0**	**1,539**	**100.0**
Food Item	**Kg**	**Share (%)**	**Kg**	**Share (%)**	**Kg**	**Share (%)**	**Kg**	**Share (%)**
Consumption (kilograms per capita per year)								
White teff	5	2.2	6	2.0	7	2.2	8	2.3
Mixed teff	8	3.5	11	3.7	8	2.5	9	2.5
Red teff	11	4.8	13	4.3	10	3.1	10	2.8
Injera	2	0.9	3	1.0	3	0.9	7	2.0
Total teff	25	10.9	31	10.3	27	8.3	29	8.2
Wheat	21	9.2	25	8.3	30	9.3	25	7.1
Barley	14	6.1	10	3.3	24	7.4	10	2.8
Maize	34	14.8	43	14.3	25	7.7	51	14.4
Sorghum	17	7.4	23	7.7	32	9.9	28	7.9
Five major cereals	111	48.5	132	44.0	138	42.6	143	40.5
Other cereals, pulses, and oilseed	30	13.1	28	9.3	27	8.3	29	8.2

	1996		2000		2005		2011	
	Kg	Share (%)	Kg	Share (%)	Kg	Share (%)	Kg	Share (%)
Vegetables, fruits, roots, and tubers	54	23.6	114	38.0	105	32.4	114	32.3
Animal products	15	6.6	14	4.7	17	5.2	17	4.8
Other foods	20	8.7	12	4.0	37	11.4	49	13.9
Total food	229	100.0	300	100.0	324	100.0	353	100.0

Source: Authors' calculations based on HICES and CSA.
Note: Kg = kilograms.

While still low, there were on average more diverse consumption expenditures in 2011 than 10 years earlier.

Fourth, cereal expenditures make up 35.5 percent of the total consumption basket, but they make up 40.5 percent of the quantity consumed. This indicates that the relative cost of cereals is lower. In contrast, animal products constitute 12.9 percent of expenditures and 4.8 percent of the quantities consumed. These animal products are the most expensive in the consumption basket. On the opposite side of the price spectrum, the category "vegetables, fruits, roots, and tubers" is considered a relatively cheap food category in the consumption basket.

Fifth, the most important crop within the cereal expenditures of the food basket is teff, which accounted for 12.4 percent of food expenditures in 2011. This compares to 7.8 percent for maize, 7.7 percent for wheat, and 5.1 percent for sorghum. Over time some minor shifts within the consumption of cereals are observed. For example, the share of expenditures on sorghum in cereal expenditures was 6.1 percent in 2000 and 8.0 percent in 2005, but it declined to 5.1 percent in 2011. Compared to 2000, the share of maize in cereal expenditures has decreased as well. Sorghum and maize are both characterized by low income elasticities, and it seems that the growing average incomes in Ethiopia might lead consumers to retreat from consuming these crops (Berhane et al. 2012).

Sixth, some important changes are noted within the teff category. While red teff made up 5.0 percent and 5.2 percent of food expenditures in 1996 and 2000 respectively, this share declined to half that level in 2011.[5] Expenditures on red teff in 2011 were only 2.6 percent of all food expenditures. Expenditures on white teff were consistently lower than those on red and mixed teff in 1996 and 2000, but they were at an equal level in 2011. Hence there is a notable shift away from the cheap red teff to the more expensive white teff. The

5 Red teff is also referred to as "black teff."

most important change within the teff expenditures is, however, the quick emergence of injera as an important food item in the food basket. It represented 4.7 percent of expenditures in 2011—a significant increase compared to 0.8 percent of total food expenditures in 1996 and 2000. This seems to follow the pattern that as consumers become richer and opportunity costs of women's time in the household are on the rise, ready-to-eat foods become more readily part of the consumption basket (Kennedy and Reardon 1994; Dibley, Boughton, and Reardon 1995).[6]

Seventh, total teff consumption over the years has remained at similar levels. It was as high as 31 kilograms per capita in 2000, dropped to 27 kilograms in 2005, and then increased again to 29 kilograms in 2011. Within the teff categories the same trends are seen in teff expenditures. The quantities consumed of white teff and injera are on the rise. On the one hand, white teff consumption increased from 5 kilograms in 1996 to 8 kilograms in 2011, and injera consumption increased in the same period from 2 kilograms to 7 kilograms. On the other hand, red teff consumption (from 13 kilograms in 2000 to 10 kilograms in 2011) and mixed teff consumption (from 11 kilograms in 2000 to 9 kilograms in 2010) decreased over time.

Table 2.4 further illustrates the differences in consumption patterns between rural and urban areas. It shows that the average per capita expenditures are significantly higher in urban areas than in rural areas, and the share of nonfood expenditures is also significantly higher in urban areas (62.3 percent) than in rural areas (48.8 percent). Compared to the rural areas, urban food expenditures are also relatively higher: rural food consumption expenditures are only two-thirds of the urban food expenditures (669 birr versus 1,017 birr respectively). Although the food expenditures are significantly higher in urban areas, the actual quantities consumed are slightly lower (366 kilograms in rural areas versus 319 kilograms in urban areas), likely because of the higher prices paid in urban areas for food but also possibly because of lower calorie requirements in these urban settings (Deaton and Drèze 2009).

Interestingly, there are almost no differences in the share of cereals in the food consumption basket, and the quantities consumed of cereals are also at similar levels. However, consumption of animal products is significantly higher in urban areas. Within the cereal category, though, consumption patterns differ significantly. Rural consumers consume significantly more sorghum (32 kilograms versus 12 kilograms) and maize (58 kilograms versus

6 However, some caution in the interpretation of injera consumption might be required given that rural consumption seems low and that injera can be made from different cereals.

TABLE 2.4 Food consumption and per capita expenditures in 2011, urban versus rural

	Urban		Rural		Total	
Food item	Birr	Share (%)	Birr	Share (%)	Birr	Share (%)
Real per capita expenditures (birr per capita per year)						
Food						
White teff	45	4.4	13	2.0	18	2.5
Mixed teff	60	5.9	11	1.6	19	2.6
Red teff	25	2.5	17	2.6	19	2.6
Injera	93	9.1	23	3.4	34	4.7
Total teff	223	21.9	64	9.5	90	12.4
Wheat	98	9.6	48	7.1	56	7.7
Barley	9	0.8	20	3.0	18	2.5
Maize	24	2.4	63	9.4	57	7.8
Sorghum	16	1.5	41	6.2	37	5.1
Five major cereals	370	36.3	236	35.3	258	35.5
Other cereals, pulses, and oilseeds	176	17.3	109	16.4	121	16.6
Vegetables, fruits, roots, and tubers	191	18.8	133	19.9	143	19.7
Animal products	169	16.6	79	11.8	94	12.9
Other foods	111	10.9	112	16.8	112	15.4
Total food	**1,017**	**100.0**	**669**	**100.0**	**727**	**100.0**
Food versus nonfood						
Food	1017	37.7	669	51.2	727	47.2
Nonfood	1684	62.3	639	48.8	812	52.8
Total	**2,701**	**100.0**	**1,308**	**100.0**	**1,539**	**100.0**
Food Item	Kg	Share (%)	Kg	Share (%)	Kg	Share (%)
Consumption (kilograms per capita per year)						
White teff	19	5.8	6	1.6	8	2.2
Mixed teff	28	8.6	5	1.4	9	2.5
Red teff	13	3.9	9	2.5	10	2.7
Injera	23	7.1	4	1.1	7	2.0
Total teff	81	25.5	24	6.6	34	9.4
Wheat	35	11.1	23	6.3	25	7.0
Barley	4	1.1	11	3.0	10	2.7
Maize	18	5.7	58	15.7	51	14.3
Sorghum	12	3.6	32	8.7	28	7.9
Five major cereals	150	47.0	147	40.3	148	41.3
Other cereals, pulses, and oilseeds	30	9.5	29	7.9	29	8.2

(continued)

TABLE 2.4 Continued

	Urban		Rural		Total	
Food Item	Kg	Share (%)	Kg	Share (%)	Kg	Share (%)
Vegetables, fruits, roots, and tubers	83	26.1	121	33.0	114	32.0
Animal products	21	6.4	17	4.6	17	4.8
Other foods	35	10.9	52	14.2	49	13.7
Total food	**319**	**100.0**	**366**	**100.0**	**358**	**100.0**

Source: Authors' calculations based on HICES and CSA.
Note: Kg = kilograms.

18 kilograms). In contrast, the share of teff in the urban food consumption basket is significantly higher than in rural areas—more than twice as high. Moreover, urban consumers eat 81 kilograms of teff per person per year—more than three times the level in rural areas. Urban teff consumers consume mostly mixed teff (28 kilograms out of 81 kilograms), whereas with rural consumers, it is mostly red teff (9 kilograms out of 24 kilograms). While red teff makes up 11 percent of all teff consumption expenditures in urban settings, this contrasts to 27 percent in rural areas. The share of injera and mixed teff is higher in urban than in rural areas, and urban consumers spent 9.1 percent of all food expenditures in the form of injera.

If teff consumption is disaggregated by region (Table 2.5), distinctive patterns become apparent. As indicated, the highest teff consumption appears in Ethiopia's major cities, with Addis Ababa in the lead (101 kilograms per capita), followed by Harar (40 kilograms) and Dire Dawa (38 kilograms). The country's major production zones also show relatively higher per capita consumption levels, 36 kilograms in Amhara, 35 kilograms in Oromia, and 38 kilograms in Tigray. Consumption levels are relatively low in the southern (a region known for consumption of root crops) and western parts of the country (a region where maize is commonly consumed)—that is, 19 kilograms in SNNP, 17 kilograms in Gambela, and 3 kilograms in Somali. Injera is consumed more in urban areas both in relative and absolute terms. Except for Addis Ababa, the Amhara region is the only region where white teff consumption exceeds 10 kilograms per capita per year.

Quantities consumed were further converted to calories per adult equivalent using the standard conversion rates in vogue in Ethiopia (Table 2.6). A consistent increase in the per capita calorie consumption is seen over the years, reflecting the country's improving food security situation. Average calorie consumption was only 2,200 kcal per day per adult equivalent in 1996, but this measure reached 3,000 kcal in 2011. Cereals are the major contributors

TABLE 2.5 Teff consumption by region in kilograms per capita per year, 2011

	Type of teff				
Region	White	Mixed	Red	Injera	Total
Tigray	8	9	16	5	38
Afar	9	10	1	9	30
Amhara	11	8	10	8	36
Oromia	7	9	13	6	35
Somali	1	0	0	2	3
Benishangul-Gumuz	3	3	12	4	22
Southern Nations, Nationalities, and Peoples' (SNNP) region	6	5	2	6	19
Gambela	3	4	1	9	17
Harari	6	12	7	15	40
Addis Ababa	18	45	9	29	101
Dire Dawa	6	9	4	19	38
Total	**8**	**9**	**10**	**7**	**34**

Source: Authors' calculations based on HICES and CSA.

to total calorie consumption. They contributed 58.7 percent of all the calories in the food basket in 2011. Although their absolute level of consumption has increased over time, their share in total consumption has come down from 62.1 percent in 1996.

The total quantities of teff consumed have remained stable over the years. They were at a level of 402, 354, and 380 kcal per adult equivalent per day in 2000, 2005, and 2011 respectively. However, the share of teff in total calorie consumption has gone down. It contributed almost 15 percent of all calories in 1996, but that share declined to 12.7 percent in 2011. While the share of mixed teff and red teff are decreasing in total expenditures compared to white teff and injera, the former products still contribute significantly to calorie consumption, mostly because of their lower prices. Mixed teff and red teff contributed 3.7 percent and 3.9 percent respectively of calorie consumption in 2011.

By comparing expenditures on food with consumption of calories, prices per calorie can be calculated. Table 2.7 shows that the price per calorie differs significantly between food groups. When the prices for 2011 are considered, prices of cereals are significantly lower than those of any other category. These other crops are therefore usually called "high-value" crops. Animal products

TABLE 2.6 Daily calorie consumption per adult equivalent, 1996–2011

	1996		2000		2005		2011	
Food item	Kcal	Share (%)	Kcal	Share (%)	Kcal	Share (%)	Kcal	Share (%)
White teff	66	3.0	73	2.7	84	2.9	97	3.2
Mixed teff	96	4.3	136	5.0	104	3.7	110	3.7
Red teff	141	6.4	163	6.0	129	4.5	116	3.9
Injera	22	1.0	30	1.1	38	1.3	57	1.9
Total teff	325	14.7	402	14.7	354	12.4	380	12.7
Wheat	260	11.8	316	11.6	364	12.8	304	10.1
Barley	129	5.8	85	3.1	219	7.7	121	4.0
Maize	440	19.9	555	20.3	330	11.6	605	20.2
Sorghum	217	9.8	289	10.6	363	12.7	353	11.8
Five major cereals	1,371	62.1	1,647	60.4	1,630	57.2	1,763	58.7
Other cereals, pulses, and oilseeds	369	16.7	351	12.9	339	11.9	424	14.1
Vegetables, fruits, roots, and tubers	199	9.0	536	19.6	466	16.4	549	18.3
Animal products	109	4.9	94	3.4	127	4.5	75	2.5
Other foods	159	7.2	101	3.7	287	10.1	189	6.3
Total food	2,207	100.0	2,728	100.0	2,849	100.0	3,001	100.0

Source: Authors' calculations based on HICES and CSA.

carry the highest price for calories, with a calorie price that is eight times as high as the average price paid for cereals. The price for other foods is also significantly higher than the average. Within the cereal category the lowest calorie prices are found for maize and sorghum. These prices are half the level that consumers pay per calorie for teff products. The prices for wheat and barley fall in between maize or sorghum and teff.

Notably, the shift that is seen over time in food preferences shows a reduction in consumption of low-priced calories, while there is an increase in consumption of more expensive ones. The average price that consumers pay per calorie has increased by 8 percent between 2000 and 2011. This is mostly driven by a shift to more expensive commodities. For example, Table 2.7 shows that prices paid for calories of basic staples have consistently decreased over time, and real prices paid for calories from cereals were 20 percent lower in 2011 than the price paid in 1996. The real prices of other food categories have mostly gone up, but especially so for the period between 2005 and 2011. Similar trends are seen within the teff category. Cheapest calories are obtained from red and mixed teff, while the highest prices are obtained for

TABLE 2.7 Real price per kcal paid, 1996–2011

Food item	1996	2000	2005	2011
White teff	0.66	0.68	0.55	0.51
Mixed teff	0.63	0.56	0.47	0.47
Red teff	0.60	0.54	0.47	0.45
Injera	0.62	0.46	0.65	1.63
Total teff	0.62	0.56	0.52	0.65
Wheat	0.46	0.46	0.43	0.50
Barley	0.59	0.74	0.51	0.41
Maize	0.39	0.35	0.33	0.26
Sorghum	0.54	0.35	0.39	0.29
Five major cereals	0.50	0.44	0.43	0.40
Other cereals, pulses, and oilseeds	0.65	0.69	0.69	0.78
Vegetables, fruits, roots, and tubers	1.38	0.67	0.56	0.71
Animal products	1.53	1.84	1.57	3.43
Other foods	1.98	1.60	1.30	1.62
Total food	**0.76**	**0.61**	**0.62**	**0.66**

Source: Authors' calculations based on HICES and CSA.

white teff and injera. As with cereals in general, however, there is a shift away from the cheap to the more expensive calories available within teff products.

Income and Its Link with Food and Teff Consumption

Significant research has been conducted in agricultural economics to understand the link between income and food consumption patterns. The parameters resulting from such research are important as they allow for economic modeling to assess impacts on consumption of food policy changes, as well as projecting food requirements in the future, given reasonable assumptions on income growth. There have been significant methodological advances. While demand for food items was previously analyzed in single-equation models, these estimates often led to inconsistencies in parameters when total food baskets were considered. To address this issue, a methodology called the Almost Ideal Demand Systems (AIDS) was developed. This method is widely used to estimate parameters as part of complete food demand systems (Deaton and

Muellbauer 1980). Researchers have also tried to improve their understanding of transforming food systems in economic development and associates with changes in consumption (for example, Reardon and Timmer 2007). A number of food consumption patterns can be distinguished with increasing income and economic development: (1) processed and ready-to-eat foods take off; (2) cereals become less important; and (3) the share of high-value crops such as fruits and vegetables, dairy and animal products, and fish in food consumption baskets increase. Comparing the differences in consumption patterns of richer and poorer households is often indicative of how transformation of food systems will shape food economies in a particular country.

In an effort to understand these patterns in Ethiopia, all households in the HICES survey of 2011 were ranked by wealth quintile, from the poorest quintile 1 to the richest quintile 5. The shares of different consumption categories were then calculated. As expected (for example, Subramanian and Deaton 1996; Bouis 1994; Bouis and Haddad 1992; Pingali 2007), strong differences in the composition of consumption baskets are seen over poverty quintiles. While food expenditures make up 54.3 percent of total consumption expenditures for the poorest quintile, this declines to 38.0 percent for the richest one. The five major cereals make up 37.7 percent of the poorest quintile, and this surprisingly only declines minimally for the richest quintile to 32.2 percent (Table 2.8). Notably, the share is relatively stable for the poorest three quintiles and drops off only for quintiles 4 and 5, suggesting that transformation in the food basket has only started to occur in the richest two quintiles. The food budget for animal foods for the richest households comprises 20.4 percent, yet this is only 7.9 percent for the poorest ones. As for cereals, the higher consumption of animal products is especially noted for the richest quintiles 4 and 5 (see also Tafere and Worku Hassen 2012).

The share of cereals in total food consumption is relatively stable over poverty quintiles, but there are large differences within this category by poverty quintile. Maize and sorghum are the two cereals that are typically consumed more by the poor than by the rich; 13.5 percent of all food expenditures of the poor goes toward maize. This compares to 2.5 percent for the rich. These numbers are 7.4 and 1.8 percent respectively in the case of sorghum. The consumption of barley is low overall, but its share also decreases when incomes increase. There is relatively little variation in wheat, based on the poverty level; however, it is consumed slightly more by the rich.

Teff consumption also shows a distinctive pattern by poverty level. It increases consistently over poverty quintiles, and teff only makes up 6.9 percent of the food expenditures of the poorest quintile. By contrast, teff

TABLE 2.8 Share of expenditures by poverty quintile, 2011

Food item	(Poorest) Q1	Q2	Q3	Q4	(Richest) Q5	Total
White teff	1.1	1.6	2.2	2.7	4.1	2.5
Mixed teff	1.3	1.9	2.5	3.0	3.6	2.6
Red teff	2.0	2.5	3.2	3.0	1.9	2.6
Injera	2.6	2.6	3.0	4.3	9.1	4.7
Total teff	6.9	8.6	10.8	13.0	18.8	12.4
Wheat	6.6	7.0	8.0	8.4	7.9	7.7
Barley	3.2	3.3	2.9	2.3	1.3	2.5
Maize	13.5	11.1	9.4	6.3	2.5	7.8
Sorghum	7.4	6.8	6.5	4.9	1.8	5.1
Five major cereals	37.7	36.8	37.6	35.0	32.2	35.5
Other cereals, pulses, and oilseeds	15.7	17.2	17.2	17.3	15.5	16.6
Vegetables, fruits, roots, and tubers	22.9	21.4	18.9	19.4	17.4	19.7
Animal products	7.9	9.0	10.0	13.2	20.4	12.9
Other foods	15.8	15.6	16.3	15.2	14.5	15.4
Total food	**100.0**	**100.0**	**100.0**	**100.0**	**100.0**	**100.0**
Food versus nonfood						
Food	54.3	53.8	51.8	48.0	38.0	47.2
Nonfood	45.7	46.2	48.2	52.0	62.0	52.8
Total	**100.0**	**100.0**	**100.0**	**100.0**	**100.0**	**100.0**

Source: Authors' calculations based on HICES and CSA.

comprises 18.8 percent of all food expenditures of the richest quintile. Teff is therefore clearly a preferred food of the rich. Moreover, within the teff category there are a number of other further distinctive patterns. Red teff makes up 28 percent of the teff expenditures for the poorest households (quintile 1), but this decreases to 10 percent for the richest ones. Expenditures on injera drop from 48 percent for the richest quintile to 38 percent for the poorest one, likely driven by the significantly higher prices per kilogram or per calorie for injera as seen in Table 2.6.

Figure 2.5 shows to what extent total food consumption and total food expenditures vary by income. This figure illustrates an upward trend in both lines, indicating that the richer consumers become, the more they spend on food and the more food they consume. It also shows that the gradient of the expenditures is steeper than that of the quantity consumed, indicating a shift from lower-priced food to higher-priced food on becoming richer. Figure 2.5B

FIGURE 2.5 Food consumption and spending on food and price per calorie by income level, 2011

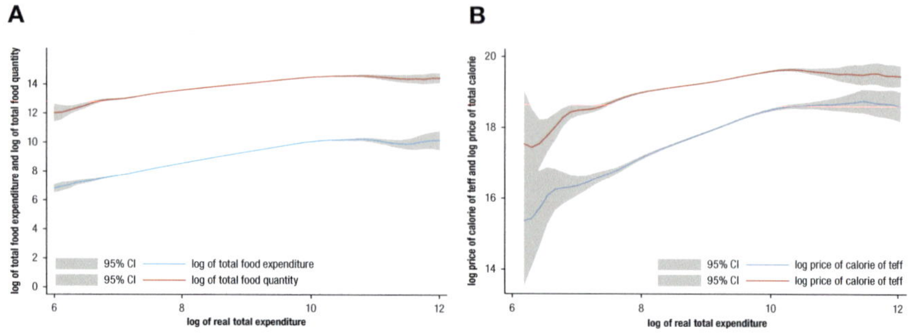

Source: Authors' calculations based on HICES and CSA.
Note: CI = confidence interval.

further shows the extent to which prices paid per calorie increase by income level. This trend exists for the food consumption basket overall as well as for teff in particular.

In a more complete quantitative approach, Tafere, Taffesse, and Tamru (2010) use an AIDS model to estimate income elasticities from the HICES data of 2004/2005. As predicted from the previous tables, animal products have the highest income elasticity of all the food product categories considered (Table 2.9). A doubling of income leads to a 172 percent increase in animal expenditures in urban areas and a 198 percent increase in rural areas. Animal products are therefore an economically superior product (for example, Berhane et al. 2012; Delgado et al. 1999; Delgado 2003). Teff also shows high income elasticities (1.2 in rural and 1.1 in urban areas), indicating that a doubling of income increases expenditures by 120 percent and 110 percent respectively. Other cereals show much lower elasticities. Sorghum even has a negative income elasticity in urban areas, indicating that it is an economically inferior commodity in this urban environment. When households become richer, the consumption of such goods is reduced. The importance of sorghum as a food is therefore likely to reduce, and the importance of teff is likely to increase with the rise in income over time, as Ethiopia becomes wealthier and more urbanized.

To further explore patterns of consistency between quintiles and changes in consumption behavior patterns, Figure 2.6A illustrates how the share of food in the total consumption basket has evolved over time by quintile. The figure illustrates that the reduction in the food share has been consistent over quintiles. Although food expenditures made up 71 percent of total

TABLE 2.9 Own price and income elasticity of demand for selected food items, 2004/2005

	Urban		Rural	
Food item	Own price elasticity	Income elasticity	Own price elasticity	Income elasticity
Teff	−0.92	1.10	−0.92	1.20
Wheat	−1.00	0.78	−0.94	1.19
Maize	−0.93	0.37	−0.70	0.82
Sorghum	−0.93	−0.36	−0.71	0.51
Pulses and other cereals	−0.88	0.90	−1.03	0.74
Animal products	−0.91	1.72	−0.94	1.98
Fruit, vegetables, and other root crops	−0.99	1.22	−1.01	1.18
Other foods	−0.92	0.66	−0.92	0.92

Source: Tafere, Taffesse, and Tamru 2010.

FIGURE 2.6 Share of food in total consumption expenditures and share of cereals in food expenditures, 2000–2011, by quintile

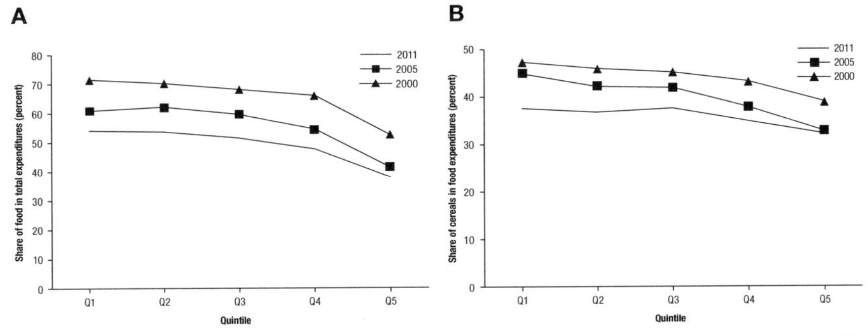

Source: Authors' calculations based on HICES and CSA.

expenditures of the poorest quintile in 2000, this came down to 54 percent in 2011. Similar reductions over time are seen for all quintiles. In Figure 2.6B the share of cereals in food expenditures is shown for the five quintiles over the last three surveys. The share of cereals for the poorest quintile was 47 percent in 2000, but it declined to 38 percent in 2011. Again, there has been a consistent decrease of the share of cereals for all quintiles in the consumption basket, even though the average quantities consumed increased over time. Overall, these findings seemingly indicate that the growth in Ethiopia from 2000 to 2011 has been equitable and has benefited the majority of the population (World Bank 2014).

FIGURE 2.7 Share of teff in food expenditures and teff consumption per person per year, 2000–2011, by quintile

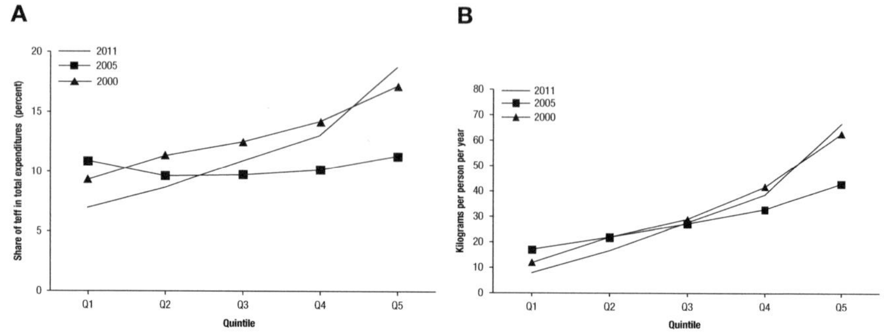

Source: Authors' calculations based on HICES and CSA.

Finally, when the share of teff in food expenditures in particular is investigated (Figure 2.7A), and when trends between 2000 and 2011 are compared, the poorest quintiles are seen to have reduced their consumption of teff while the richest quintiles display higher levels of consumption, if measured in shares of their food expenditures. Similar trends show up when quantities of teff consumed per capita are examined (Figure 2.7B).

Exports

Global interest in teff from Ethiopia is increasing. This is seemingly driven by two factors. First, teff is gluten-free and is therefore suitable to prepare food products for people who suffer from celiac disease (see Chapter 15). It is also rich in amino acids, and it has even been dubbed by some as the new superfood (Secorun 2016). The rapid international growth of the quinoa market—a gluten-free cereal mostly produced in Peru and Bolivia—has stimulated the Ethiopian government to revise its export ban of teff and open teff export markets to the increasing global demand. However, as the government is conscious of local price increases by opening these export markets, it has currently only allowed a limited number of commercial farmers to start producing teff to fulfill this export demand. Second, exports of injera are rapidly increasing. Figure 2.8 shows how the value of injera exports from Ethiopia has evolved over time. Official exports of injera in 2015 were valued at about US$10 million. While the Middle East was the traditional region to which injera was exported, North America received the largest share of injera exports in 2015. Injera exports to Europe are also on the rise. It seems that these

FIGURE 2.8 Injera exports from Ethiopia, by value, 2008–2015

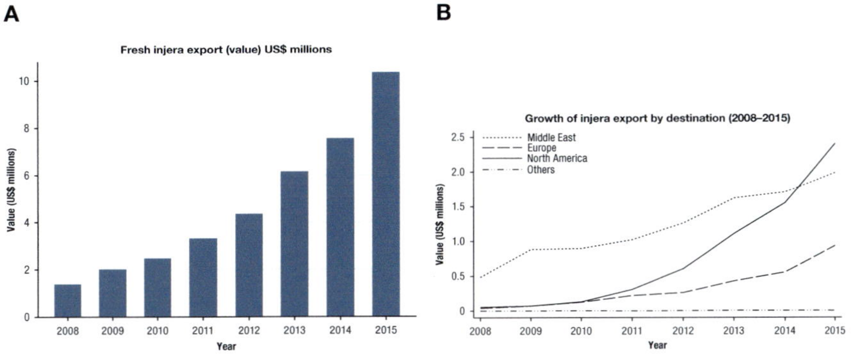

Source: Authors' calculations based on data from the Ministry of Trade.

exports are especially driven by demand from immigrant Ethiopians in these areas who remain attached to the culinary culture of their homeland.

The rapid take-off of injera exports is seemingly linked with the increased number of direct flights from Addis Ababa to a number of international destinations. As injera is highly perishable, short travel times are required, which makes air travel the only option for international trade. As Ethiopian Airlines has been rapidly expanding its international flight destinations, injera exports have followed along the lines of these destinations. For example, in 2012/2013 Ethiopian Airlines served 76 international destinations, rising from 54 destinations five years earlier—an increase of 41 percent. Moreover, Ethiopian Airlines doubled the frequency of their flights to these destinations.

Conclusion

The analysis in this chapter illustrates the importance of teff in Ethiopia's agricultural and food economy. On the production side it is estimated that teff is Ethiopia's most important single crop, making up 22 percent of its cultivated area during the most important meher season. Teff is grown by 6.6 million farmers. The production value of the crop was estimated in 2013/2014 to be as high as US$2.5 billion. Moreover, it is shown that teff is the most important cash crop in the country. The value of income generated for farmers from teff is estimated to be more important than that from coffee, the most important export product of Ethiopia. The value of the commercial surplus of teff is as high as the commercial surplus of all the other cereals in the country combined. Since 2003, further significant increases have occurred in the production of teff, driven by area expansion as well as yield improvements. However, teff yields are still significantly lower than yields of other cereals.

This chapter has reviewed important transformations that characterize Ethiopia's agricultural and food economy. Average quantities and calorie consumption per capita have consistently and significantly improved over the past 15 years. The past decade has seen a shift from the least preferred yet lower cost foods to more costly and more preferred food options. The consumption of high-value foods is therefore on the rise. While the quantities of cereals slightly increased over the past decade, the share of the lower-priced cereals in the total food consumption basket has declined, from 43 percent of the average consumer in 2000 to 35 percent in 2011. Important changes are seen within the cereal sector, with the shares of maize and sorghum relatively declining in importance, while the share of teff remains stable. Within the teff sector, ready-to-eat injera and the more expensive white teff are on the rise, while the cheap red and mixed teff are on the decline.

Teff is consumed more by urban households than by rural households. Urban consumption per capita is as high as 81 kilograms per year based on national household consumption data. In comparison, this figure is only 24 kilograms per capita per year for rural areas. Teff is further characterized by high income elasticities, evaluated at 1.10 in urban areas and 1.20 in rural areas. These figures demonstrate that teff is an economically superior commodity, implying that an increase in income leads to a disproportional increase in teff consumption. Teff will continue to be a product that is consumed in greater quantities by the rich, in mostly urban areas, than by the poor. The lower consumption by the poor is partly explained by the high prices of teff, which are typically twice as high as the cheapest cereal—that is, maize.

Finally, we note an increasing interest for teff exports. While teff exports were banned in the past because of fears of price rises, this policy has recently been changed, with a number of commercial farmers being identified and permitted to export from Ethiopia. The increasing demand for teff globally is driven by its gluten-free characteristic, which makes it a suitable product for the increasing health-conscious consumers in Western countries. Exports of prepared injera is also on the rise, with large demands from Ethiopian diaspora living abroad. The rapid expansion of flight routes by Ethiopian Airlines, adding to the already good connections of Ethiopia with a number of these countries in which these diasporas reside, has facilitated the market. Given the fast economic growth that Ethiopia is experiencing and the rapid increase in urbanization, as well as export demand, the importance of teff in food systems is expected to increase in the near future. Therefore, ensuring appropriate investments to deal with the increasing demand of teff products is a priority for agricultural and food policy in Ethiopia.

References

Bennett, M. K. 1941. "International Contrasts in Food Consumption." *Geographical Review* 31: 365–374.

Berhane, G., L. McBride, K. Tafere Hirfrot, and S. Tamru. 2012. "Patterns in Food Grain Consumption and Calorie Intake." In *Food and Agriculture in Ethiopia: Progress and Policy Challenges*, edited by P. Dorosh and S. Rashid, 190–218. Philadelphia: University of Pennsylvania Press.

Bouis, H. E. 1994. "The Effect of Income on Demand for Food in Poor Countries: Are Our Food Consumption Databases Giving Us Reliable Estimates?" *Journal of Development Economics* 44 (1): 199–226.

Bouis, H. E., and L. J. Haddad. 1992. "Are Estimates of Calorie-Income Elasticities Too High? A Recalibration of the Plausible Range." *Journal of Development Economics* 39 (2): 333–364.

Chamberlin, J., and E. Schmidt. 2012. "Ethiopian Agriculture: A Dynamic Geographic Perspective." In *Food and Agriculture in Ethiopia: Progress and Policy Challenges*, edited by P. Dorosh and S. Rashid, 21–52. Philadelphia: University of Pennsylvania Press.

Deaton, A., and J. Drèze. 2009. "Food and Nutrition in India: Facts and Interpretations." *Economic and Political Weekly* 44 (7): 42–65.

Deaton, A., and J. Muellbauer. 1980. "An Almost Ideal Demand System." *American Economic Review* 70 (3): 312–326.

Delgado, C. L. 2003. "Rising Consumption of Meat and Milk in Developing Countries Has Created a New Food Revolution." *Journal of Nutrition* 133 (11): 3907S–3910S.

Delgado, C. L., M. W. Rosegrant, H. Steinfeld, S. K. Ehui, and C. Courbois. 1999. *Livestock to 2020: The Next Food Revolution*. Vol. 61. Washington, DC: International Food Policy Research Institute (IFPRI).

Dercon, S., and R. V. Hill. 2009. "Growth from Agriculture in Ethiopia: Identifying Key Constraints." Paper prepared as part of a study on agriculture and growth in Ethiopia by the United Kingdom, Department for International Development (DFID). Accessed October 5, 2017. http://users.ox.ac.uk/~econstd/Ethiopia%20paper%203_v5.pdf.

Dibley, D., D. Boughton, and T. Reardon. 1995. "Processing and Preparation Costs for Rice and Coarse Grains in Urban Mali: Subjecting an Ipse Dixit to Empirical Scrutiny." *Food Policy* 20 (1): 41–50.

Ethiopia, CSA (Central Statistical Agency). 2014a. *Agricultural Sample Survey 2013/2014. Crop and Livestock Production Utilization (Private Peasant Holdings, Meher Season).* Addis Ababa: CSA.

———. 2014b. *Agricultural Sample Survey 2013/2014. Report on Area and Production of Major Crops (Private Peasant Holdings, Meher Season).* Addis Ababa: CSA.

Ethiopia, MoFED (Ministry of Finance and Economic Development). 2012. *Ethiopia's Progress Towards Eradicating Poverty: An Interim Report on Poverty Analysis Study (2010/2011).* Photocopy. Addis Ababa.

Gollin, D. 2011. *Crop Production in Ethiopia: Assessing the Evidence for a Green Revolution.* Technical report, International Growth Centre, London, UK.

Headey, D. 2014. *An Analysis of Trends and Determinants of Child Undernutrition in Ethiopia, 2000–2011.* Ethiopia Strategy Support Program (ESSP) Working Paper 70. ESSP, Addis Ababa.

Kennedy, E., and T. Reardon. 1994. "Shift to Non-traditional Grains in the Diets of East and West Africa: Role of Women's Opportunity Cost of Time." *Food Policy* 19 (1): 45–56.

Mandefro, H., and M. Jerven. 2015. "GDP Growth and Poverty Decline in Ethiopia: Who Owns the Numbers?" *Addis Standard* (March 3): 12–14.

Pingali, P. 2007. "Westernization of Asian Diets and the Transformation of Food Systems: Implications for Research and Policy." *Food Policy* 32 (3): 281–298.

Popkin, B. M. 2003. "The Nutrition Transition in the Developing World." *Development Policy Review* 21 (5): 581–597.

Reardon, T., and C. P. Timmer. 2007. "Transformation of Markets for Agricultural Output in Developing Countries since 1950: How Has Thinking Changed?" In *Handbook of Agricultural Economics,* vol. 3, edited by R. E. Evenson and P. Pingali, 2808–2855. Amsterdam: Elsevier Press.

Secorun, L. 2016. "Teff Could Be the Next Quinoa As Ethiopia Boosts Exports." *The Guardian,* October 14. https://www.theguardian.com/sustainable-business/2016/oct/14/teff-quinoa-ethiopia-boosts-exports-food-africa.

Stifel, D., and T. Woldehanna. 2014. "Utility-Consistent Poverty in Ethiopia, 2000–11: Welfare Improvements in a Changing Economic Landscape." WIDER working paper 2014/125. Helsinki, Finland: United Nations University World Institute for Development Economics Research (UNU-WIDER).

Subramanian, S., and A. Deaton. 1996. "The Demand for Food and Calories." *Journal of Political Economy* 104 (1): 133–162.

Tafere, K., A. S. Taffesse, and S. Tamru. 2010. *Food Demand Elasticities in Ethiopia: Estimates Using Household Income, Consumption and Expenditure (HICE) Survey Data.* Addis Ababa, Ethiopia.

Tafere, K., and I. Worku Hassen. 2012. *Consumption Patterns of Livestock Products in Ethiopia: Elasticity Estimates Using HICES (2004 / 05) Data.* Addis Ababa, Ethiopia.

Taffesse, A. S., P. Dorosh, and S. A. Gemessa. 2012. "Crop Production in Ethiopia: Regional Patterns and Trends." In *Food and Agriculture in Ethiopia: Progress and Policy Challenges,* edited by P. Dorosh and S. Rashid, 53–84. Philadelphia: University of Pennsylvania Press.

World Bank. 2014. *Ethiopia: Poverty Assessment.* Report no. AUS6744. Poverty Global Practice, Africa Region, World Bank, Washington, DC.

Chapter 3

AGRONOMICS OF TEFF

Kebebew Assefa and Solomon Chanyalew

This chapter gives an overview of the agronomics of teff primarily focusing on the major biophysical aspects of the teff plant and its husbandry in Ethiopia. The first section elaborates on the major peculiar features that constitute the reasons for the sustained extensive cultivation of the crop in Ethiopia. An understanding and appreciation of the relative merits of the crop in cultivation and use are vital for government policy makers, researchers, development partners and donors, and the public at large for agrarian transformation in Ethiopia to be achieved. Notably, the focus on research and development of teff has given rise to considerable attention of this crop's significance and meritorious features. In the subsequent sections, other salient aspects are covered, including brief insights into the genetic resources to improve the crop, the improved varieties released so far, and the agronomic and pest management methods used in teff husbandry. The chapter concludes with a summary of the practical implications of the major issues covered, followed by remarks on the prospects of teff research and development in Ethiopia.

Significance of the Teff Crop in Ethiopia

In Ethiopia the cultivation of teff predates historical records, and it existed even before the introduction of wheat and barley in the country. Despite its low productivity (current national average is about 1.3 metric tons per hectare), the Ethiopian farmers who engineered domesticating the crop have continued growing teff over the millennia with its acreage increasing through time. Hence, an important question to consider is, Why have Ethiopian farmers continued growing teff? The teff crop exhibits a multitude of relative merits to both husbandry and use (Ketema 1993; Tefera and Ketema 2001; Assefa 2003; Assefa et al. 2012) as discussed below.

Relative Merits in Husbandry

The major relative merits of teff over the other crops in terms of husbandry include its (1) broad adaptation to a range of altitudes from below sea level up to 3,000 meters above sea level and to varied agroecological and edaphic conditions; (2) reasonable tolerance to both low (drought) and high (waterlogging) moisture stresses; (3) importance as a reliable and low-risk catch crop at times when other crops (such as maize and sorghum) fail due to natural calamities such as drought, pests, and diseases; (4) adaptability to various cropping systems and crop rotation schemes; (5) relative resilience from serious epidemics of pests and diseases in at least the country's major teff production regions; and (6) minimal postharvest losses since the grains suffer less from damage by storage pests (such as weevils) and diseases.

Relative Merits in Use

In addition to its merits in farming, the sustained cultivation of teff is also prompted by its relative merits in terms of its use over other crops. These major relative merits include the following: First, the grains of teff give the best quality and most consumer-preferred injera (traditional fermented Ethiopian pancake) in terms of water-holding capacity, long shelf-life, unique flavor (slightly sour but pleasant), pliability, and smooth and glossy texture. Second, the grains yield high returns in flour upon milling of 99 percent, compared to 60–80 percent from wheat (Ebba 1969). In other words, if 100 kilograms of wheat are used for milling, the usable flour yield is 60–80 percent and the rest is bran, while 100 kilograms of teff gives 99 percent flour yield. Upon baking, teff flour produces a large amount of injera due to its high water-holding capacity. Third, teff entails minimal postharvest losses and high storage longevity of the grains even under traditional storage conditions. Fourth, the straw is important mainly as fodder for cattle and as a binder of mud used for plastering walls of local houses. Fifth, teff offers cash crop value for farmers owing to the high market prices of both the grains and the straw.

Teff is a very nutritious cereal grain. Its nutritional content is generally comparable to that of the major world cereals like wheat, barley, rice, maize, and sorghum (Table 3.1). In fact, teff is superior in many aspects, particularly in such minerals as iron, calcium, magnesium, and zinc. In recent years teff has become popular as a health and performance food in the global market. Since the grains are gluten-free, it is useful as food for humans suffering from the gluten protein allergy ailment known as celiac disease (Spaenij-Dekking, Kooy-Winkelaar, and Koning 2005). Its low glycemic index characterized

TABLE 3.1 Nutritional composition (%) of teff grains compared with other major world cereals

Nutritional item	Teff	Wheat	Rice	Maize	Sorghum	Barley
Protein	11.0	11.0	9.7	9.4	8.6	8.5
Fat	2.6	1.9	1.6	4.4	3.8	1.5
Fiber	3.5	1.9	5.8	2.2	1.9	4.5
Carbohydrates	73.0	69.3	64.7	69.2	71.3	67.4
Mineral ash	3.0	1.7	5.0	1.3	2.4	2.6

Source: Modified from Agren and Gibson (1968).

by slow-release-type starches make it particularly suitable for diabetic people. Moreover, its high iron content is associated with the low prevalence of hook worm (Ethiopian Nutrition Survey 1959) and pregnancy-related anemia in people consuming teff as a staple food. Further details on the nutritional aspects of teff are covered in Chapter 15.

Botany of Teff

Taxonomy

Teff belongs to the Grass Family, Poaceae (formerly Gramineae), subfamily Chloridoide (Eragrostoidae), tribe Eragrostidae, subtribe Eragrosteae, genus *Eragrostis*. As one of the biggest genus in the grass family, the genus *Eragrostis* contains over 350 species (Watson and Dallwitz 1992). Of these species, about 43 percent are considered to have originated in Africa, 18 percent in South America, 12 percent in Asia, 10 percent in Australia, 9 percent in Central America, 6 percent in North America, and 2 percent in Europe (Costanza 1974). Among the 54 species found in Ethiopia, 14 are endemic to the country (Cufodontis 1974). Teff and finger millet (*Eleusine coracana* (L.) Gaertn.) constitute the sole species in the subfamily Chloridoidae cultivated as a cereal crop for human consumption.

Various nomenclatures have been given to teff by several authorities at different times. These synonymous binomial nomenclatures are summarized in Table 3.2. However, the most accepted binomial nomenclature for teff is *Eragrostis tef* (Zucc.) Trotter. In this nomenclature "Zucc." stands for Zuccagni, the taxonomist who gave the species epithet "tef"; "Trotter" stands for the name of the taxonomist who proposed the binomial name *Eragrostis tef* in 1918 based on the species epithet first given by Zuccagni.

TABLE 3.2 Various binomial nomenclatures given to teff by authorities in different years

Suggested name	Year
Poa tef Zuccagni	1775
Poa abyssinica Jacquin	1781
Poa cerealis Salisb	1796
Cynodon abyssinicus (Jacq.) Rasp.	1825
Eragrostis abyssinica (Jacq.) Link	1827
Eragrostis pilosa (L.) P. Beauv. subsp. *abyssinica* (Jacq.) Aschers and Graben	1900
Eragrostis tef (Zucc.) Trotter	1918
Eragrostis pilosa (L.) P. Beauv. var *tef* (Zucc.)	1923

Source: Modified from Ebba (1975) and Ketema (1993).

Genetics

The species in the genus *Eragrostis* generally range from diploid (2x = 2n = 20) to hexaploid (2x = 6x = 60). Teff is an allo-tetraploid species (2n = 4x = 40) originating from the hybridization of two distinct species followed by diploidization. Through cytological examinations the formation of 20 bivalents in the meiotic Metaphase I in both the interspecific and intraspecific hybrids provides evidence of it being an allotetraploid hybrid (Tavassoli 1986). In support of this, other genetic studies further depicted disomic inheritance patterns for some qualitative characters, including panicle form and branching pattern as well as glume/lemma and caryopsis color (Berhe et al. 1989a, 1989b, 1989c).

Although the putative ancestral diploid progenitor species for teff are not fully known, based on morphological and cytological evidences, Ponti (1978) and Tavassoli (1986) suggested that the following species are closely related to teff: *Eragrostis aethopica* (2x), *E. pilosa* (4x), *E. mexicana* (6x), *E. barrelieri* (6x), *E. minor* (2x, 4x), and *E. cilianensis* (2x, 4x, 6x). Recent DNA-based studies (Ayele 1999; Ayele et al. 1999; Ayele and Nguyen 2000; Bai et al. 1999, 2000; Ingram and Doyle 2003) confirmed that *E. pilosa* is the closest relative and presumably one of the intermediate wild progenitors of teff.

As revealed from the karyotype analyses of 15 *Eragrostis* species, the chromosomes of teff are minute even by the standards of the genus, with the largest and smallest chromosomes of teff measuring from 1.6–2.9 and 0.8–1.1 micrometers (μm) respectively. The range in each of these two size groups is due to differences in condensation (Tavassoli 1986). This implies that the largest chromosome of teff is approximately three times smaller than the smallest (1D) wheat chromosome (Gugsa, Belay, and Ketema 2001). Unlike that of some of its related wild *Eragrostis* species, the presence of chromosomal races and aneuploidy is not known in teff.[1] Indeed, flow cytometric analysis revealed that the tetraploid nuclear genome size of teff is about 730 megabase pair (Mbp), and no significant teff genotype differences were noted (Ayele et al. 1996; Hundera, Arumuganathan, and Baenziger 2000). This indicates that the genome size of teff is roughly 50 percent larger than the rice genome, and the equivalent diploid teff genome size is about 75 percent the size of the rice genome (Kantety et al. 2001). Notably, two of the three major world cereals (wheat, rice, and maize) are large genome size polyploids, with wheat being an allopolyploid (6x = 16,000 Mbp) and maize being an ancient tetraploid (4x, 2,500 Mbp).

Morphology and Physiology

Teff plants rarely root from nodes above the base, with the roots growing 4–8 centimeters deep in a very thin, fibrous (threadlike) root system under field conditions (Ebba 1975). Generally, teff plants grow to 20–156 centimeters high, of which the culm or stem (11–82 centimeters) and the panicle (10–65 centimeters) comprise 47–65 percent and 35–53 percent, respectively (Assefa et al. 2001). The stems are mostly erect, rarely creeping or bending or elbowing (geniculate) in few cultivars. They are jointed with hollow internodes separated by nodes. The culm internodes normally increase in length and decrease in thickness toward the tip (acropetal), often being short and thick at the basal part and long and thin at the uppermost internodes.

The teff leaves consist of a basal light green to dark purple sheath distinctly shorter than the corresponding culm internode, a very short and ciliated ligule and a blade or lamina. The latter are slender, narrow, flat, and nearly linear or linear-lanceolate with elongated acute tips. The blades vary in color and in size, generally measuring 2–55 centimeters long and 2–10 millimeters wide at the broadest part (Ebba 1975).

The inflorescence of teff is paniculate, which varies in form from very compact with the panicle branches appearing fused to the rachis forming a whip-like structure to very loose types of open and laterally spread branches. The color of the lemmas, which is important in the classification of teff cultivars, can be grayish olive, yellow green, green, dark purple, dark red, grayish yellow

1 Aneuploidy is a form of polyploidy where certain chromosomes are duplicated as opposed to the duplication of the whole chromosome set.

green, or variegated with red or purple tips and margins of yellow green, greenish yellow, grayish olive, or green basal color backgrounds. In these variegated cultivars, the mix of colors is not all over the lemmas but rather across the tips and the margins. The seed are very small (100 kernel mass = 10–38 milligrams), generally ovoid or oblong to ellipsoidal, and opaque or lustrous, and their embryo marks facing the lemmas are about five-sevenths the size of the grain. The grains range in color from dark brown to orange white (Ebba 1975).

Teff generally takes 25–81 days to emerge the panicle tips, 60–140 days to mature, and 29–76 days for the grain filling period (Assefa et al. 2001). It is a C4 plant having Kranz-type leaf anatomy with the vascular bundles surrounded in a circular manner bundle, with sheath cells consisting of high concentrations of chloroplasts, and depicting low CO_2 compensation of leaves, which is typical of C4 as opposed to C3 species (Kebede, Johnson, and Ferris 1989).

Breeding

Historical Milestones

Scientific research in teff improvement started in the late 1950s at the former Jimma Technical and Agricultural High School, as it was known, in Jimma. The research was moved in 1960 to the then Central Experiment Station, now the Debre Zeit Agricultural Research Center. With regard to the overall history of teff breeding, the following three interrelated phases are distinguished:

- Phase I (1956–1974) was characterized by: (1) germplasm enhancement (collection/acquisition, characterization and evaluation, systematics and conservation); (2) genetic improvement relying entirely on mass and/or pure-line selection directly from the existing germplasm; and (3) initiation of induced mutation techniques.
- Phase II (1975–1995) featured: (1) the discovery of the chasmogamous floral opening behavior of teff flowers (from about 6:45–7:30 am) and thereby the artificial crossing technique by Berhe (1975); and (2) incorporation of intraspecific hybridization in the genetic improvement program following the discovery of the crossing technique.
- Phase III (1995–to date) is characterized by: (1) initiation of molecular/genomics approaches involving development of molecular markers and

genetic linkage maps and analyses of molecular genetic diversity; (2) incorporation of in vitro culture techniques and interspecific hybridization; (3) reappraisal of induced mutagenesis particularly for lodging and leaf rust disease resistance; and (4) strengthened use of participatory breeding approaches (Belay et al. 2006; Belay et al. 2008).

Objectives of the Teff Breeding Program

The overall objectives of the teff breeding program are the following: (1) to enrich and improve the germplasm resource base; (2) to develop suitable varieties for different agroecologies and cropping systems; and (3) to generate basic scientific information on the crop species. To reach these objectives, attention has focused on the following: (1) high productivity in terms of both grain and straw yield; (2) tolerance to low moisture stress; (3) improved lodging resistance; and (4) desirable grain quality mainly in terms of most farmer and consumer-preferred caryopsis color (often white).

Breeding Methodology

Figure 3.1 illustrates the process of the teff breeding methodology. The first step generally involves germplasm enhancement through mainly collection/acquisition, characterization and evaluation, hybridization (intraspecific and interspecific) and induced mutation techniques.

Ethiopia is the center of both origin and diversity of teff (Vavilov 1951). In the absence of influences from abroad regarding breeding materials, the crop's genetic improvement relies heavily on the indigenous genetic resources. Table 3.3 summarizes current holdings of teff germplasm accession in the world. The Ethiopian genebank at the Ethiopian Biodiversity Institute alone presently holds a total of 5,169 accessions.

Following the germplasm enhancement are generation advancement and handling of segregating populations from crossing and induced mutation, observation nurseries, series of field variety trials, and ultimately variety verification trial for release. For handling such segregating populations, the breeding methods adopted are mainly modified pedigree and bulk methods; in some cases also single-seed descent methods are used (Poehlman and Davis 1995).

Breeding Strategies and Institutional Setup

When considering the vast acreage devoted to teff production in Ethiopia, and the level of investment in teff improvement research in general, the overall teff

FIGURE 3.1 Teff variety development process

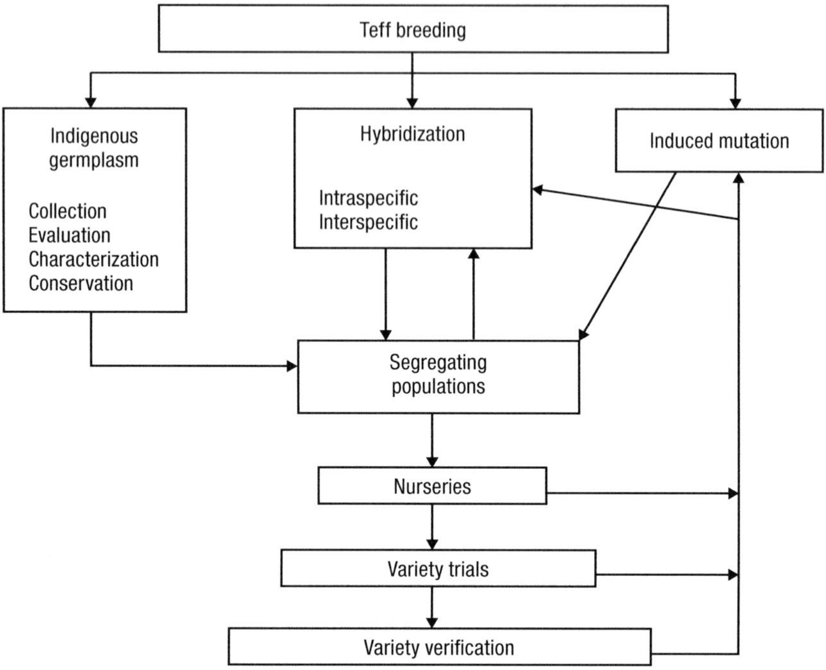

Source: Assefa et al. (2011); Assefa, Chanyalew, and Metaferia (2013a).

breeding philosophy is centered on "add a little, and it makes a difference." In other words, even if the improvement in productivity is very little, this would have a significant practical impact when multiplied by the total acreage of teff in Ethiopia. With this considered, the major strategies of the current teff breeding focus include (1) shift from wide to specific adaptation due mainly to high genotype × environment interaction while still looking for broad adaptation; (2) market orientation with respect to quality, quantity, and food security; and (3) expansion to nonconventional (new) growing areas.

The institutional setup for teff improvement in Ethiopia involves the National Agricultural Research System (NARS). The Debre Zeit Agricultural Research Center (DZARC) of the Ethiopian Institute of Agricultural Research (EIAR) forms part of the NARS and is the center of excellence for teff research. It has primary responsibilities for national coordination of the overall research endeavors, and the development and execution of country-wide teff research projects. The implementation of the research involves three institutions: (1) the Federal Research Centers of EIAR (Debre Zeit and its

TABLE 3.3 **Teff germplasm accessions in gene banks in different parts of the world**

Source and Institution	Number of samples and accessions
Ethiopia, Ethiopian Biodiversity Institute	5,169
Germany, Institute of Crop Science, Braunschweig	30
Germany, Institute for Plant Genetics and Crop Plant Research (IPK)–Genebank, Gatersleben	5
Japan, Department of Genetic Resources, International Institute of Agrobiological Resources	30
Yemen, Agricultural Research and Extension Authority	2
Russia, N.I. Vavilov All-Russian Research Institute of Plant Industry, Saint Petersburg	14
Slovak Republic, Botanical Garden of the University of Agriculture	1
South Africa, Division of Plant and Seed Control, Department of Agriculture and Technology Service, Private Bag X179, Pretoria	3
UK, Welsh Plant Breeding Station, Institute of Grassland and Environment Research	3
US, National Seed Storage Laboratory, USDA-ARS, Colorado State University, Fort Collins, Colorado	341
US, Western Region Plant Introduction Station, USDA-ARS, Washington State University, Pullman	368
Total	**5,966**

Source: Updated from Ketema (1997) and Tesema (2013).

subcenters Ambo, Assosa, Holetta, Melkassa, and Pawe); (2) centers of the Regional Agricultural Research Institutes (RARIs) such as Adet, Alamata, Areka, Axum, Bako, Mekelle, Sekota, Sinana, Sirinka; and (3) Haramaya University from the higher learning institutes (HLIs). In addition, on-farm trials are carried out on farmers' fields in different parts of the country through the various centers involved in teff research.

Achievements (Improved Teff Varieties)

To date, a total of 33 varieties have been released in Ethiopia through the National Agricultural Research System (Ethiopia, MoA 2013) (Table 3.4). Of these, 19 varieties have been released by Debre Zeit Agricultural Research Center. The remaining 14 teff varieties released were 2 by Holetta, 1 each by Melkassa and Areka, 5 by Sirinka, 3 by Adet, and 2 by Bako agricultural research centers. Of the total number of released varieties, 10 varieties were developed through hybridization, and of these, 9 were released by Debre Zeit Agricultural Research Center.

Four of the released varieties, viz. Magna (DZ-01-196), Enatite (DZ-01-354), Dukem (DZ-01-974), and Quncho (DZ-Cr-387 RIL355) are widely

TABLE 3.4 List of improved teff varieties released by Debre Zeit Agricultural Research Center, 1970–2010

Variety name	Common name	Year of release	Days to mature	Plant height (centimeters)	Seed color	Grain yield (t ha-1)	
						On-station	On-farm
A. Varieties Released by Debre Zeit Agricultural Research Center							
DZ-01-99	Asgori	1970	80–130	53–100	Brown	2.2–2.8	1.8–2.2
DZ-01-354	Enatit	1970	85–100	53–115	Pale white	2.4–3.2	2.0–2.4
DZ-01-196	Magna	1970	80–113	50–117	Very white	1.8–2.4	1.6–2.0
DZ-01–787	Wellenkomi	1978	90–130	50–110	Pale white	2.4–3.0	2.0–2.4
DZ-Cr-44	Menagesha	1982	95–140	85–110	White	1.8–2.4	1.8–2.2
DZ-Cr-82	Melko	1982	112–119	96–112	White	1.8–2.4	1.6–2.0
DZ-Cr-37	Tsedey	1984	82–90	67–92	White	1.8–2.5	1.4–2.2
DZ-Cr-255	Gibe	1993	114–126	63–116	White	2.0–2.6	1.6–2.2
DZ-Cr-358	Ziquala	1995	76–138	84–132	White	2.4–3.4	2.0–2.7
DZ-01-974	Dukem	1995	75–137	70–109	White	2.4–3.4	2.0–2.7
DZ-01-1281	Gerado	2002	73–95	83–100	White	1.7–2.4	1.6–2.2
DZ-01-1285	Koye	2002	104–118	80–92	White	1.7–2.4	1.6–2.2
DZ-01-1681	Key Tena	2002	84–93	74–85	Brown	1.7–2.4	1.6–2.2
DZ-01-899	Gimbichu	2005	118–137	46–68	Pale white	1.5–2.2	1.6–2.0
DZ-01-2675	Dega Tef	2005	112–123	47–91	Pale white	1.5–2.4	1.4–2.2
DZ-Cr-387 RIL355	Quncho	2006	86–151	72–104	Very white	2.0–3.2	1.8–2.6
Ho-Cr-136	Amarach	2006	63–87	67–81	Pale white	1.8–2.5	1.4–2.2
DZ-Cr-285 RIL295	Simada	2009	75–87	65–80	White	2.0–2.8	1.6–2.4
DZ-Cr-409 RIL 50d	Boset	2012	75–86	75–90	Very white	1.9–2.6	1.8–2.4
B. Varieties released by Holetta Agricultural Research Center							
DZ-01-2053	Holetta Key	1998/ 1999	84–112	78–112	Brown	1.7–2.4	1.5–2.2
DZ-01-1278	Ambo Toke	1999/ 2000	86–116	75–112	Brown	1.7–2.4	1.5–2.2
C. Varieties released by Melkassa Agricultural Research Center							
DZ-Cr-387 RIL127	Gemechis	2007	67–90	72–95	Very white	1.5–2.0	1.6–1.8
D. Varieties Released by Adet Agricultural Research Center							
DZ-01-1868	Yilmana	2005	98–110	89–120	Pale white	1.8–2.4	1.7–2.0
DZ-01-2423	Dima	2005	92–106	85–115	Brown	1.7–2.3	1.6–2.1
DZ-01-3186	Etsub	2008	95–105	87–112	White	1.9–2.4	1.9–2.4
E. Varieties released by Bako Agricultural Research Center							
DZ-01-1880	Guduru	2006	95–120		White	1.8–2.2	1.6–2.0
23-Tafi-Adi-72	Kena	2008	98–124		White	1.8–2.4	1.7–2.2

Variety name	Common name	Year of release	Days to mature	Plant height (centimeters)	Seed color	Grain yield (t ha-¹)	
						On-station	On-farm
F. Varieties released by Sirinka Agricultural Research Center							
DZ-01-2054	Gola	2003	82–90	65–98	Pale white	1.4–1.9	1.2–1.6
DZ-01-146	Genete	2005	75–87	67–98	Pale white	1.4–2.0	1.2–1.6
DZ-01-1821	Zobel	2005	72–87	65–95	Pale white	1.4–2.0	1.3–1.8
Acc. 205953	Mechare	2007	78–85	62–92	Pale white	1.5–2.1	1.4–1.8
DZ-CR-387 RIL273	Laketch	2009	87–92	78–95	Very white	1.7–2.2	1.8–2.0
G. Varieties released by Areka Agricultural Research Center							
PGRC/E 205396	Ajora	2004	89–96	89–98	Pale white	1.4–2.0	1.6–1.8

Source: Modified from Assefa, Chanyalew, and Metaferia (2013a).

adopted by farmers in areas with optimum rainfall in different parts of the country, while the relatively early maturing varieties of Tsedey (DZ-Cr-37), Gemechis (DZ-Cr-387 RIL127), Simada (DZ-Cr-285 RIL295), and Boset (DZ-Cr-409 RIL50d) are recommended for terminal low moisture stress areas.

Genetic Gain

Recent studies of the breeding progress in terms of genetic gain using evaluation of the 33 teff varieties released in Ethiopia since 1970 till now at Debre Zeit and Melkassa Agricultural Research Centers showed that grain yield increased from 3093.8 kilograms per hectare to 4934.4 kilograms per hectare over the past 42 years (Figure 3.2) (Dargo 2013).[2] The average annual rate of increase from 1970–2012 as estimated from the slope of the graph of the linear regression of mean grain yield on year of variety release was 21.53 kilograms per hectare with a relative genetic gain of 0.56 percent per year. Biomass yield (Figure 3.3) and grain yield per panicle also showed significant increase with respective annual genetic gains of 0.47 percent and 1.05 percent.

The linear regression indicates significant improvements in biomass production rate and grain yield per day. No marked changes were observed in phenologic traits, harvest index, plant height, panicle length, panicle weight, lodging index, and hundred seed weight during the study period. This implied that teff varieties have failed to bring substantial progress or improvements on

2 With varieties, the productivity difference is due to genetic manipulation, and hence genetic gain is used to describe the changes in productivity over time due to the genetic manipulations.

FIGURE 3.2 Relationship between mean grain yield of 33 teff varieties and year of release, expressed as number of years since 1970

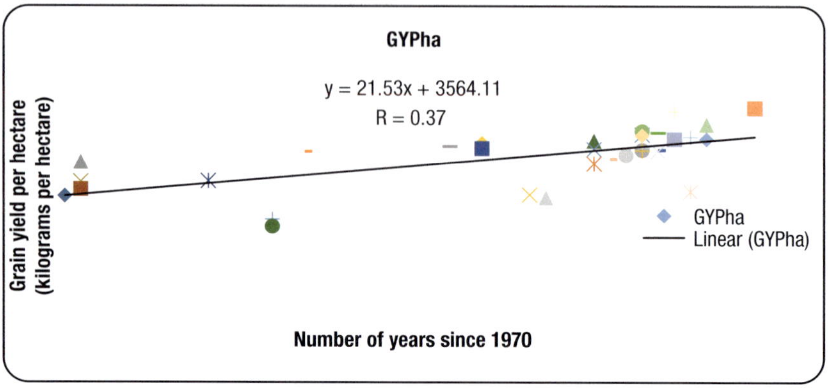

Source: Dargo (2013).
Note: GYPha = grain yield per hectare.

FIGURE 3.3 Relationship between mean biomass yield of 33 teff varieties and year of release, expressed as number of years since 1970

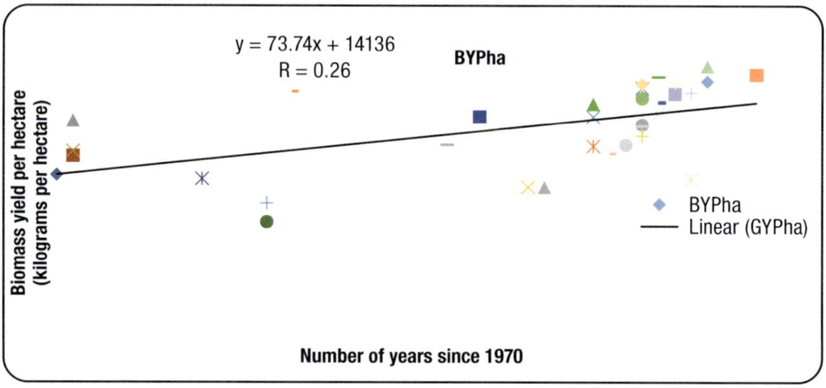

Source: Dargo (2013).
Note: BYPha = biomass yield per hectare.

these mentioned traits through the breeding efforts made over the specified years. Stepwise regression analysis revealed that most of the variation in grain yield of teff was caused by biomass yield and harvest index.

Overall, the genetic gain study revealed that the grain yield potential of teff has not reached a plateau in Ethiopia. Development of higher yielding varieties should thus continue to increase teff grain yields if past trends are indicative of the future. To see the impact in the genetic progress research of teff, it is imperative to undertake large-scale popularization of the released varieties, where the end user farmers can see the impact of such improved varieties through demonstrations and scaling-up activities, such as improved management practices.

Success Stories with the Quncho Teff Variety and Related Innovations

Before the release of the Quncho teff variety, a number of improved varieties were developed and released by the national agricultural research system. Nonetheless, the improved varieties have not been widely adopted by farmers to bring about any discernible impacts on the production and productivity of teff in Ethiopia. The slow and low rate of adoption of the improved varieties is because, among other reasons, farmers preferred the qualities of their local varieties and claimed that the improved varieties were not superior. However, the development and release of the popular Quncho teff variety in 2006 marked a breakthrough achievement in the overall development, dissemination, and adoption of improved teff technologies. This success story can be attributed to some major innovative approaches (Assefa et al. 2011; Assefa, Chanyalew, and Metaferia 2013b) as described below.

Development of the Variety

Before starting the breeding work for the development of the Quncho variety, the first step undertaken was participatory variety selection (PVS) and participatory plant breeding (PPB) to identify the varieties preferred by farmers and traits therein (Belay et al. 2006; Belay et al. 2008). The major outcomes of these studies, in addition to the yield of both grain and straw, was the overriding preferred trait of a white seed color by farmers and consumers alike. Based on this, targeted crossing was undertaken between two selected teff varieties that had been formally released to combine high yield and the farmers' and consumers' preferences.

The teff variety Quncho with the pedigree of [(974 × 196)-HT′-387 (RIL355)] was developed from the cross made by Debre Zeit Agricultural Research Center in 2000. The parental varieties DZ-01-196 (Magna) and DZ-01-974 (Dukem) are old improved varieties developed through pure-line selection and released in 1970 and 1995 respectively (Tefera and Assefa 1995; Tefera et al. 2001). The maternal (ovule) parent DZ-01-974 (Dukem) is a high-yielding variety, although farmers did not prefer this variety because

TABLE 3.5 Performance and characteristics of Quncho as compared with the parental lines and the local variety

Traits	DZ-01-974 (Dukem)	DZ-01-196 (Magna)	Quncho	Local variety
Panicle form	Very loose	Fairly loose	Very loose	Mixture
Lemma color	Yellowish-green	Yellowish-green variegated with red	Yellowish-green variegated with red	Mixture
Seed color	Pale white	Very white	Very white	Mixture
Plant height (centimeters)	107	97	102	103
Days to mature	107	97	105	118
On-station grain yield (metric tons per hectare)	2.4–3.4	1.8–2.2	2.2–2.8	1.8–2.2
On-farm grain yield (metric tons per hectare)	2.0–2.5	1.4–1.6	1.8–2.2	1.2–2.0
On-station straw yield (metric tons per hectare)	12	9.6	10.11	10.09
On-farm straw yield (metric tons per hectare)	10.00	8.10	9.10	6.18

Source: Assefa et al. (2012); Assefa, Chanyalew, and Metaferia (2013b).

of its pale white seed color fetching a low market price. The male (pollen) parent DZ-01-196 (Magna) possesses the popular very white seed color, although its productivity has been relatively low (1.6–1.8 metric tons per hectare). Subsequently, a targeted cross was made between the two varieties, with the objective of selecting recombinants combining the high yield of DZ-01-974 (Dukem) and the seed quality trait of DZ-01-196 (Magna). Rapid generation advancement up to three generations per year was made using off-season irrigation facilities.[3] Eventually, Quncho was developed as a Recombinant Inbred Line (RIL) through an F2-derived single-seed descent method. Following a series of multi-environment yield tests in various major teff-growing regions of the country, it was officially released in 2006.

The performance and distinguishing features of the teff variety Quncho, as compared with the parental and the farmers' (local) varieties, are summarized in Table 3.5. The new variety has inherited its very white seed color and also the lemma color (yellowish-green variegated with red tips and margins) from the pollen parent DZ-01-196 (Magna). It has taken its high-yield potential and panicle form (very loose) from the ovule parent DZ-01-974 (Dukem).

3 After crossing, an F1 is obtained. This has then to go through generation advancement as F2, F3, F4, and so on until homozygous lines are obtained.

Variety Branding

The variety branding by naming it Quncho has played a significant role, particularly in the popularization and promotion of the variety. The name Quncho in most Ethiopian vernaculars means "top brass," "at the helm," or "topmost."

Intensification of Seed Multiplication

To accelerate the supply of quality seeds of the Quncho variety to the ultimate users, an intensified seed multiplication scheme was followed. This new innovative and accelerated seed multiplication involved the following:

- Enhancing seed multiplication of research centers both during the off-season using irrigation facilities and during the main season.
- Enhancing on-farm seed production by strengthening the capacities of farmers through the provision of initial seeds, training, and technical support.

By using on-farm seed production, the indigenous knowledge in teff seed production and maintenance were more effectively exploited. Consequently, better quality teff seeds can be produced through such informal means, provided that the farmers are given technical support. In this respect, clustering of adjacent fields has proven effective in minimizing seed contamination and enabling the production of good quality seeds. In addition, private seed growers have been encouraged to produce teff seeds, especially that of the Quncho teff variety.

Multistakeholder Partnership Extension Approach

A new approach to demonstrate, popularize, and disseminate the Quncho teff technology was adopted. It was characterized by the following major features:

- Dissemination of technology as a package: Unlike the previous "piecemeal" approach with a single technology, the dissemination approach involved "technology as a package" with the Quncho teff variety used as the vehicle along with other associated improved management practices.[4]

4 In the improved technology package, the variety forms the central part but the package also includes improved practices involving the use of fertilizers, appropriate land preparation, time of sowing, seed rate, weed control, management of other pests, timely harvesting, and the like.

- Use of large farmers' fields: Instead of the formerly used small (10 × 10 meter) plots, large field plots of one-fourth of a hectare were used in in-farm demonstrations and scaling up of the Quncho teff technology.
- Coordination of multistakeholders' partners: These include research centers, extension agents, farmers, NGOs, farmers' associations such as farmers' cooperatives and cooperatives' unions, district administration offices, and other institutions involved in rural development.
- Revolving seed loan: In the scaling up of the technology, seeds of the variety Quncho were distributed to participating farmers on a "revolving-seed-loan" basis such that the farmers would return the same amount of seed after harvest.
- Provision of regular training: Regular training of farmers, development agents, and extension personnel on the technologies contributed immensely to the success of the demonstration and scaling up of the technology on the farmers' fields.
- Regular follow-up and supervision: In addition to training, regular input by a team of researchers and extension agents also played an important role in the rapid and effective dissemination of the technology.
- Provision of inputs and marketing options: Insofar as possible, provisions were made in terms of inputs and options for marketing of produce mainly by involving farmers' cooperatives and cooperatives' unions in the supply of such inputs as fertilizers and purchases of the produce.

As a consequence of the new extension approaches practiced since the release of the Quncho teff variety in 2006, a total of over 41,655 teff-producing farmers' households with a total area of more than 12,850 hectares directly participated in the scaling-up activities carried out through the partner research centers and the National Crop Technology Scaling-up Program (Table 3.6). This venture involved the distribution of about 385 metric tons of seed of the Quncho variety with the average yield obtained by the farmers ranging from 2.0 to 2.3 metric tons per hectare. At this juncture it is important to note that these figures do not include the dissemination of the variety made through other channels, such as horizontal farmer–farmer seed exchange and through the formal extension system of the offices of agriculture.

Recent adoption and impact assessment studies of improved teff technologies in three woredas (Minjar Shenkora, Ada, and Lume) in the central

TABLE 3.6 Summary of direct dissemination of the Quncho teff variety through center-level and national scaling-up activities, 2006–2013

Year	Number of farmers' households participated	Farm area covered (hectares)	Amount of seed distributed (metric tons)	Total grain yield (metric tons)	Average grain yield (metric tons ha-¹)
2006	300	150	4.50	300.00	2.0
2007	506	253	7.59	556.60	2.2
2008	1,060	530	15.90	1,166.00	2.2
2009	5,875	2,938	88.14	6,464.00	2.2
2010	10,113	3,029	90.87	6,967.00	2.3
2011	13,157	3,292	98.76	7,571.60	2.3
2012	9,332	2,333	69.99	5,365.90	2.3
2013	1,312	328	9.84	—	—
Total	**41,655**	**12,853**	**385.59**	—	—

Source: Assefa, Chanyalew, and Metaferia (2013b).
Note: — = data not available.

highlands of Ethiopia revealed that Quncho is reported to be the most widely adopted improved variety, followed by DZ-01-196 (Magna). Within the study area, the study showed the Quncho variety was adopted by 76 percent of the farmers while Magna was adopted by 40 percent of the respondent farmers (Figure 3.4). By comparing this result with that of a similar survey conducted in the same area during the cropping season in 2008/2009, the adoption of Quncho far exceeded expectation. For instance, its adoption rate increased from 5 percent in 2008/2009 to 76 percent in the 2011/2012 cropping season. On the contrary, the adoption rate of DZ-01-196 (Magna) dropped from 84 percent in 2008/2009 to 40 percent in 2011/2012.

In terms of intensity of adoption, which is measured by the proportion of total teff area allocated to a particular variety, Quncho comes first by covering 66 percent while DZ-01-196 (Magna) accounted for 26 percent of the total teff acreage (Figure 3.5). Similar to that of the adoption rate, the intensity of adoption for Quncho has increased from 4 percent in the 2008/2009 cropping season to 66 percent in 2011/2012. On the contrary, the adoption intensity of DZ-01-196 (Magna) has dropped from 71 percent to 26 percent in the respective cropping seasons. Figure 3.5 clearly indicates how the share of local varieties has diminished to just 5 percent.

FIGURE 3.4 Adoption of improved teff varieties, 2011/2012 cropping season

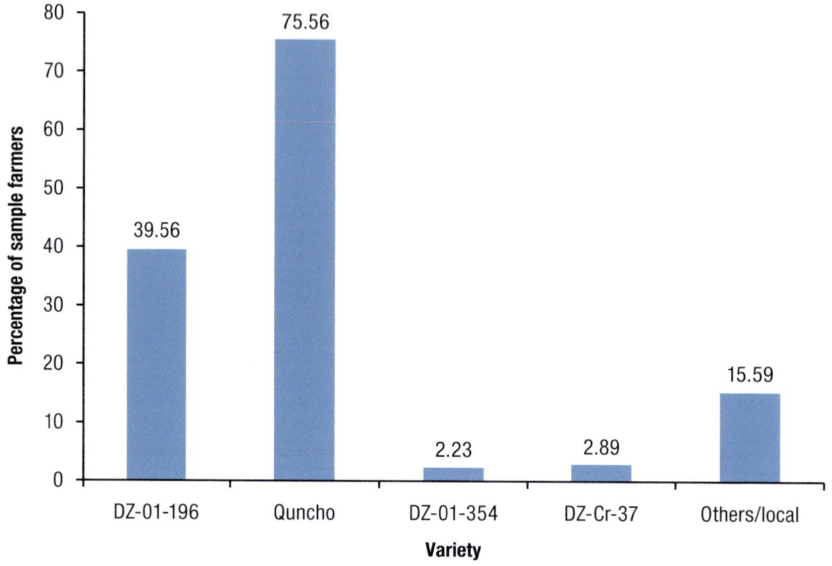

Source: Survey data, 2012.

Note: Percentages are based on multiple responses.

FIGURE 3.5 Intensity of adoption of improved teff varieties measured by the proportion of teff area covered with improved varieties, 2011/2012 cropping season

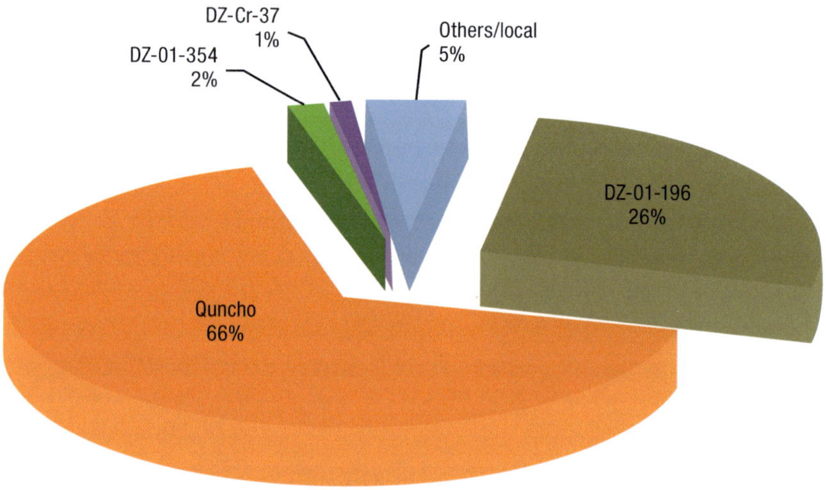

Source: Survey data, 2012.

Challenges and Opportunities

Challenges

The major challenges in teff breeding in particular, and the overall teff improvement in general, include the following:

- Lack of attention: Teff can be categorized as an orphan or a neglected crop because of its localized solitary importance in Ethiopia. Consequently, it has lacked the attention of the global scientific community as well as that of donors and has therefore remained underresearched. Unlike that of the other major world crops, no CGIAR centers or regional institutions have been established to deal with the improvement of localized crops like teff. Furthermore, the national focus has remained very limited. Even though there have been trends for improvement in crop development, teff has for a long time been omitted from Ethiopia's national research and development priority commodities, seemingly not corresponding to the actual significance of the crop in Ethiopia.
- Technical and scientific challenges: Teff improvement suffers due to a lack of studied information on the species, low productivity, the unresolved malady of lodging in teff, and the tiny seeds that render its husbandry very demanding.
- Capacity and institutional limitations: Currently, Debre Zeit Agricultural Research Center is assigned to be the "Center of Excellence" (CoE) for teff research in Ethiopia. However, there has been limited capacity both at the CoE and national level at large in terms of trained and skilled human resources, infrastructure, facilities, and financial budget. Besides, mechanisms for coordinated efforts in teff research at a countrywide level have not yet been developed.

Opportunities

Despite the challenges that require commensurate attention, there have been ample opportunities for the improvement of teff.

AVAILABILITY OF DIVERSE WEALTH OF GENETIC RESOURCES

The teff genetic resources harbor a tremendous diversity in phenologic, agronomic, and morphologic traits (Table 3.7), coupled with unexploited aspects in terms of nutritional as well as biotic and abiotic stress-tolerance traits. The wealth of diversity in the species offers ample opportunities for genetic

TABLE 3.7 Ranges of some important traits of teff

Trait	Minimum	Maximum
Days to panicle emergence	25	81
Days to mature	60	140
Grain filling period (days)	29	75
Plant height (centimeters)	20	156
Culm length (centimeters)	11	82
First culm internode length (centimeters)	2.68	8.05
Second culm internode length (centimeters)	4.15	11.45
First and second culm internode diameter (centimeters)	1.2	4.5
Panicle length (centimeters)	10	65
Peduncle length (centimeters)	5.85	42.3
Number of primary panicle branches	10	40
Number of spikelet per panicle	30	1070
Number of florets per spikelet	3	17
Grain yield per panicle (grams)	0.11	2.5
Number of tillers per plant (total)	4	22
Number of tillers per plant (fertile)	1	17
Grain yield per plant (grams)	0.54	21.9
Total phytomass per plant (grams)	4	105
Hundred kernel mass (milligrams)	18.97	33.88
Grain yield (kilograms per hectare)	1,058	4,599
Shoot phytomass yield (kilograms per hectare)	6,355	19,630
Diameter of grains (millimeters)	0.50	1.0
Harvest index (%)	5	39
Lodging index	20	100

Source: Modified from Assefa et al. (2001) and Chanyalew, Assefa, and Metaferia (2013).

improvement of the crop and to develop varieties suitable for different agro-ecologies, cropping systems, and purposes.

NEW INSIGHTS IN BREEDING AND OVERALL RESEARCH APPROACHES

The developments in agricultural sciences have opened new insights into how to tackle technical improvements by employing coordinated multifaceted strategies involving conventional breeding; modern techniques including genomics and in vitro cultures; crop, soil, and water management; food science; and mechanization. With respect to breeding in particular, the strategies to be employed involve participatory research approaches, germplasm collection/acquisition, intensification of the hybridization program through increasing the number of crosses, use of intraspecific and interspecific crossing, harnessing potentials of wide crosses (divergent crossing), and targeted crossing (that is, ideo-type crossing for lodging resistance and semi-dwarf types with reduced length of peduncles and basal culm internodes, and thick basal culm internodes).

Likewise, modern biotechnological approaches—such as in vitro culture techniques (especially DH production), molecular markers and linkage maps, QTL analysis, comparative genomics (association mapping), Targeted Induced Local Lesions IN Genomes (TILLING and ECO-TILLING), genome sequence and annotation (functional genomics), MAS, genetic transformation, and harnessing important teff genes—offer new avenues for hastening the genetic improvement of the crop.[5] Furthermore, the productivity and production of teff can be enhanced by the integration of improved management, crop protection, and farm implements and machinery. These value-added practices would be useful to enhance the utilization of the crop. Overall, the broadening of research and development endeavors in these various aspects would open further opportunities.

BRIGHTER PROSPECTS TO IMPROVE TEFF RESEARCH AND DEVELOPMENT

The long-standing belief that teff is not amenable to improvement is now redundant. For the first time in history, the Ethiopian government has realized that transformation of the Ethiopian agriculture is impossible without considering its important local crops, most notably teff. The first thing to be aligned is the national recognition of teff in the priority agricultural commodities. Tied in with the improved national attention to teff, other areas are entailed, including the development and release of the teff value-chain strategy, initiation of focus on the national teff research capability, and improvements in the seed and extension system. In addition, there has been improved international attention especially by donors—namely the McKnight Foundation Collaborative Crop Research Program—that has provided

5 TILLING and ECO-TILLING differ. TILLING involves artificial induction of mutation using mutagenic agents, preferably such chemicals as ethylmethane sulfonate (EMS), and then identifying the induced mutation (local lesion) using molecular methods. In contrast, ECO-TILLING does not involve artificial induction of mutation. It just deals with locating or identifying naturally occurring (spontaneous) mutations using molecular methods just as in the case of TILLING.

sustainable support to the national teff research project since the mid-1990s with commendable achievements.

Apart from the need for enhanced national support, the painstaking ventures of teff improvement generally require enhanced external inputs and support in terms of collaboration, technical and knowledge support, financing, and facilities. Furthermore, the increasing global interests in teff in recent years due to its gluten-free nature, status as a health and performance food, and noble stress-tolerance traits (such as drought resistance) promote attention, particularly in light of climate change.

Agronomy of Teff

Land Preparation

The minute size of teff seeds requires a very fine, flat, and smooth seedbed (Ebba 1969). Conventionally, farmers plow their teff field two to five times before sowing the seeds, depending on the soil type and weed infestation conditions. The traditional plow is called a *maresha*. It is largely used with oxen for the tillage operations, although horses or donkeys are used rarely. Despite the conventional practice, it has recently been shown that teff can be grown with reduced tillage involving pre-emergency application of Roundup at 2 liters per hectare two weeks before sowing, then practicing tillage only once at the time of sowing. Farmers in some areas also practice packing of the seedbeds before sowing using trampling with animals in the anticipation of facilitating good contact of seeds with the soil, avoiding and reducing weed infestation. However, experimental results at Debre Zeit showed that apart from facilitating germination and early stand establishment, packing did not significantly increase yields (DZARC 1989).

Planting

Conventionally, farmers sow teff by hand, broadcasting the seeds on the surface of the soil. Experimental results have indicated that sowing in rows, while it might increase productivity, has the agronomic advantages of easing up subsequent cultural operations such as weed control and harvesting and facilitating efficient use of fertilizers through application as row-side bands. However, for practical use by farmers there has to be a user-friendly solution, such as the development of appropriate smallholder row-sowing implements. Against the conventional farmers' practice of using 40–55 kilograms per hectare, the recommended seed rate with the hand broadcasting method has been

25–30 kilograms per hectare. However, the seed rate can be reduced to 7–10 kilograms per hectare provided that there are mechanisms (implements) that make it feasible for the farmers to use such reduced seed rates. Generally, teff is sown after a sufficient lapse of the onset of the rainy season to ensure the soils are sufficiently wet. The sowing time varies depending on the location, soil type, and prevailing weather conditions. For the central highland areas such as Debre Zeit, the recommended sowing time for teff is the second and the third week of July for light and black clay (vertisols) soils, respectively (Ketema 1993; Hundera, Arumuganathan, and Baenziger 2000).

Fertilizer Application

The recommended fertilizer rates for teff grown on different soil types ranges for nitrogen fertilizer from 40 kilograms per hectare nitrogen for red soils and Nitosols to 75 kilograms per hectare nitrogen for grey soils and black soils, while for phosphorus, it ranges from 50 to 60 kilograms per hectare P2O5 for the different soil types (NFIU 1993). However, the blanket fertilizer recommendation for teff for the major teff-growing areas has been 60 kilograms per hectare nitrogen and 26 kilograms per hectare P2O5 for heavy clay soils (predominantly Vertisols) and 40 kilograms per hectare nitrogen and 26 kilograms per hectare P2O5 for light soils. Commercial fertilizers in Ethiopia have so far been applied in the form of DAP (18 percent nitrogen and 46 percent P2O5) and urea (46 percent nitrogen), and accordingly the blanket recommendation mentioned above, especially for the clay soils, has for practical purposes from the size of the packaging (the least package being 50 kilograms per hectare) been approximated to 100 kilograms per hectare DAP and 100 kilograms per hectare urea.

The amount of fertilizers for teff grown on fields that have been previously used for legumes such as chickpeas can be reduced by half. Moreover, it is recommended that the DAP fertilizer is applied at the time of sowing, while the urea for supplying the remaining of the recommended nitrogen rate should be applied at about the tillering stage (four to five weeks after emergence) of the crops (Mamo, Erkossa, and Tulema 2001; Erkossa 2003).

Harvesting and Threshing

Harvesting of teff is accomplished by farmers mowing with sickles when the crops are mature and dry. The harvested crops are first piled up in the field and later transported by humans and/or using donkeys to the threshing ground areas where they are again piled into bigger piles. After preparing the threshing ground, often by coating with a thin layer of cattle dung, the crops are threshed by trampling with oxen. Winnowing to separate the seeds with the help of wind and subsequent cleaning are done manually with the use of various traditional tools (Ebba 1969).

Nevertheless, farmers in some areas have recently started using multicrop threshers and seed cleaners for threshing and seed cleaning of teff. In addition, others (like the Ethiopian Seed Enterprise) have been using combiners for harvesting and threshing of teff grains by adjusting and modifying of the drums and the seed cleaning sieves to fit to the small-seeded teff crop. Considering the difficulties entailed in teff harvesting and threshing by the smallholder farmers, the operation cannot continue to be done traditionally. It seems timely for the willing smallholder farmer to develop harvesting and threshing practices with implements for teff husbandry in Ethiopia.

Storage

Teff seeds are usually stored under ambient environmental conditions in traditional storage structures known as *gotera* or *gota* (Ebba 1969). They are also stored in farmers' houses after being packed in sacks often made of synthetic polymers. Normally teff grains can be stored for three to five years without considerable loss of viability even under traditional storage conditions, since storage pests, such as weevils, and diseases do not attack them. The only problem with the minute-size teff seeds is mechanical mixing and contamination of the pure grain at all stages of operations, starting from sowing up to the final harvesting and threshing as well as storage. The seeds can easily get dropped and missed because of their physical size.

Crop Protection (Pest Management)

Important Weeds and Their Management

Weed management has remained one of the back-breaking, labor-intensive, and time-consuming operations in teff husbandry. The major weeds of teff recorded in Ethiopia have been listed in a weed research review in Ethiopia by Fessehaie and Tadele (2001) and more recently by Zewdie and Damte (2013). Generally, annual grass weeds pose the greatest challenge because of their morphological similarity to the teff crop and their extended period of germination that is difficult to control by manual hand weeding (Fessehai and Tadele 2001). These authors, however, listed other problematic weeds in teff that include the parasitic witchweed (*Striga hermonthica* [Del.]), the introduced alien invasive weed commonly known as congress weed (*Parthenium hyterophorus* L.), field bind weed (*Convolvulus arvensis*), and other noxious weeds. The latter include weeds with the following characteristics: (1) those irritating to touch that interfere with weeding or harvesting operations, thereby increasing weeding and/or harvesting time and costs (such as *Argemone mexicana, Xanthium spinosum, X. strumarium, Oxygonum sinuatum*, and *Tribulus terristeris*); (2) those posing the biggest challenge because of their similarity to teff and extended period of germination (such as *Phalaris paradoxa* and *Setaria pumila*); (3) weeds that reduce the quality of teff grains harvested (such as *Phalaris paradoxa, Setaria pumila, Plantago lanceolata, Amaranthus* spp., *Guizotia scabra,* and *Snowdenia polystachya*); and (4) hard-to-pull-out perennial weeds (such as *Cyperus esculentus, C. rotundus*, and *Rumex bequarttii*).

While the critical period of weed completion for teff is three to four weeks and six to seven weeks postemergence of the crops, a single application of postemergence selective herbicides (such as Starane M 64 percent b EC, Derby 175 SC, Mustang, and 2,4-D Amine Salt 72 percent S) about 25 to 30 days after crop emergence has proved effective in controlling the dominant broadleaf weeds in teff, thereby giving significant yield increase. This is followed by twice hand weeding and the check with a single 2,4-D Amine Salt 72 percent SL application (Zewdie and Damte 2013). These authors also maintained that one supplementary hand weeding in addition to the single postemergence application of herbicides may be needed depending on the weed flora infestation and effectiveness of the herbicides to maximize yields.

Important Insect Pests and Their Management

More than 40 insect species have been recorded on teff. Of these, the most important, generally sporadic ones in various teff-growing areas are teff grasshopper (*Ailopus longicornis*), teff shoot fly (different species), red teff worm (*Mentaxya ignicollis*), Wello bush cricket (*Decticoides brevipennis* Ragge), termites (*Macrotermus subhyalinus* and *Odontotermus* spp.), and black teff beetle (*Erlangerius niger*) (Damte 2013).[6] In a recent review of entomological research on teff, Damte (2013) provided a list of insect species recorded on teff and further maintained that the majority of the research on teff insect pest management to date focused on the identification of appropriate insecticides to the exclusion of other management aspects such as cultural control (for example, sowing date, seed rate, fertilizer rate, teff host plant resistance), biological control (natural enemies), and ecological methods.

6 "Black teff" is an alternative name for red teff.

Important Diseases and Their Management

Teff, as compared with the other cereals, generally suffers less from disease epidemics, but the significance of diseases should not be underestimated (Amogne, Kassaye, and Bekele 2001). In a review of teff pathology research in Ethiopia, Amogne, Kassaye, and Bekele (2001) indicated that more than 24 fungal pathogens and 2 nematodes have been reported to cause diseases on teff. The authors presented a list of these diseases along with their status as either minor or major. Although most of the recorded diseases are at least sporadically economically important, the major diseases are teff rust (*Uromyces eragrostidis* Tracy), head smudge (*Heminthosporium miyakei* Nisikado), and damping-off caused by *Drechslera* spp. and *Epicoccum nigrum* Link (Eshetu 1985).

Teff rust is widely distributed in major teff-growing areas of Ethiopia. The disease, which usually appears at the post-flowering stage of the crop, was earlier reported to cause an average yield loss of 10 to 25 percent (Ebba 1969), while in more recent studies at Debre Zeit, losses were estimated at 10 to 41 percent (DZARC 1994).

Conclusion

Teff is the most important cereal in Ethiopia, and for human consumption its cultivation is almost entirely restricted to this country. This sustained cultivation of teff by Ethiopian farmers is heightened by its relative merits compared with other crops, both in husbandry and utilization aspects. The advantages of teff in farming generally relates to the broad diversity of this crop and its consequent versatility to adapt to conditions otherwise marginal for most other crops. Teff's merits also include its nutritional richness, cash crop value to farmers, and the high fodder value of its straw, as well as the preference for it in the national diet.[7]

Since 1970, a total of 33 improved teff varieties have been released to date. Of these, only 10 varieties originated from hybridization, while the rest were developed from direct mass and/or pureline selection from germplasm. Of all the varieties, 19 were released by Debre Zeit Agricultural Research Center, and the rest were released by other research centers. Nonetheless, only a

---

7 With progressive disappearance of pastures and grazing lands in the highlands, farmers increasingly rely on teff straw as dry- and wet-season supplemental fodder for their cows and working draft animals, especially oxen used for traction. Teff straw is the most preferred fodder relative to all the other cereals and is highly priced/valued by farmers, often collected and stored under high care.

limited number of these varieties have been adopted by farmers, and the varieties most widely grown currently include Quncho (DZ-Cr-387), Dukem (DZ-01-974), Magna (DZ-01-196), Tsedey (DZ-Cr-37), Etsub (DZ-01-3168), and Enatite (DZ-01-354).

The minute-size teff seeds require preparation of very fine, smooth, and flat seedbeds for planting. The issue of sowing methods and seed rates has in recent years been a major issue in teff husbandry. Although the recommended seed rate for the conventional hand broadcast sowing has been 25–30 kilograms per hectare, it has been recognized that the seed rates can be reduced to 7–10 kilograms per hectare. However, sowing in rows has also achieved substantial agronomic advantages in terms of facilitating subsequent weeding and harvesting operations and would enable efficient use of applied fertilizers. The use of both reduced seed rates and row sowing in practical teff husbandry calls for the provision of smallholder farmer-friendly farm implements.

Compared with most other major cereal crops, teff suffers less from epidemics of insect pests and disease. But, owing to its poor competitive ability with weeds, the management of weeds remains one of the most demanding cultural operations. Overall, teff as a localized crop of importance only in Ethiopia has remained an "orphan crop" that has survived without the help of scientific improvement endeavors, which are currently outstanding. With respect to donors, teff remained largely marginalized particularly until the mid-1990s, when national teff research and development started obtaining the sustained support of the McKnight Foundation Collaborative Crop Research Program. However, low productivity, lodging, the minute size of the seeds, and labor intensiveness of the cultural practices still remain the major threats of teff husbandry.

Finally, it is worth highlighting that over the past few years there has been an assertion that poor African countries with a number of neglected crops of localized importance should shift their farming systems to more productive crops of global significance. However, to date, this notion has no longer been an issue of debate, for it has been proven that agricultural development in these countries cannot be realized without due consideration of the neglected crops of supreme local importance like teff and "enset" in Ethiopia. Indeed, it has now been ascertained that even under the circumstances where the amount of effort and attention afforded to these crops is disproportionately low, the outcomes, as demonstrated by the remarkable achievement of developing and releasing the Quncho teff variety in 2006, are worth the investments. Hence, countries such as Ethiopia should "nurture" their neglected crops; indeed, the issue now is not whether to invest in these crops but rather how to bring about the required substantial improvements by using modern scientific techniques, including biotechnology that has been used extensively in other crops around the world.

References

Agren, G., and R. Gibson. 1968. *Food Composition Table for Use in Ethiopia-1.* Uppsala, Sweden: Almqvist and Wicksel Bokhandel.

Amogne, S., Z. Kassaye, and E. Bekele. 2001. "Teff Pathology Research in Ethiopia." In *Narrowing the Rift: Teff Research and Development,* edited by H. Tefera, G. Belay, and M. Sorrells, 215–222. Proceedings of the International Workshop on Teff Genetics and Improvement, October 16–19, 2000, Debre Zeit, Ethiopia.

Assefa, K. 2003. "Phenotypic and Molecular Diversity in the Ethiopian Cereal, Teff [*Eragrostis tef* (Zucc.) Trotter]: Implications on Conservation and Breeding." PhD dissertation, Swedish University of Agricultural Sciences, Alnarp, Sweden.

Assefa, K., S. Aliye, G. Belay, G. Metaferia, H. Tefera, and M. E. Sorrells. 2012. "Quncho: The First Popular Teff Variety in Ethiopia." *International Journal of Agricultural Sustainability* 9 (1): 25–34, doi:10.3763/ijas.2010.0545.

Assefa, K., S. Chanyalew, and G. Metaferia. 2013a. "Conventional and Molecular Teff Breeding." In *Achievements and Prospects of Tef Improvement,* edited by K. Assefa, S. Chanyalew, and Z. Tadele, 33–51. Proceedings of the Second International Teff Workshop, November 7–9, 2011, Debre Zeit, Ethiopia.

———. 2013b. "Quncho: The Most Outstanding Teff Variety in Ethiopia." In *Achievements and Prospects of Teff Improvement,* edited by K. Assefa, S. Chanyalew, and Z. Tadele, 325–332. Proceedings of the Second International Teff Workshop, November 7–9, 2011, Debre Zeit, Ethiopia.

Assefa, K., S. Ketema, H. Tefera, F. Hundera, and T. Kefyalew. 2001. "Genetic Diversity in Agronomic Traits of Teff." In *Narrowing the Rift: Teff Research and Development,* edited by H. Tefera, G. Belay, and M. Sorrells, 33–47. Proceedings of the International Workshop on Teff Genetics and Improvement, October 16–19, 2000, Debre Zeit, Ethiopia.

Assefa, K., H. Tefera, A. Merker, T. Kefyalew, and F. Hundera. 2001. "Variability, Heritability and Genetic Advance in Pheno-Morphic and Agronomic Traits of Tef [*Eragrostis tef* (Zucc.) Trotter] Germplasm from Eight Regions of Ethiopia." *Hereditas* 134 (2): 103–113.

Assefa, K., J. Yu, M. Zeid, G. Belay, H. Tefera, and M. E. Sorrells. 2011. "Breeding Teff [*Eragrostis tef* (Zucc.) Trotter]: Conventional and Molecular Approaches." *Plant Breeding* 130: 1–9 (review).

Ayele, M. 1999. "Genetic Diversity in Teff [*Eragrostis tef* (Zucc.) Trotter] for Osmotic Adjustment, Root Traits, and Amplified Fragment Length Polymorphism." PhD dissertation, Texas Tech University, Lubbock, Texas, USA.

Ayele, M., J. M. Dolozel, M. Van Dauren, H. Brunner, and F. J. Zapata-Arias. 1996. "Flow Cytometric Analysis of Nuclear Genome of the Ethiopian Cereal Teff [*Eragrostis tef* (Zucc.) Trotter]." *Genetica* 98: 211–215.

Ayele, M., and H. T. Nguyen. 2000. "Evaluation of Amplified Fragment Length Polymorphism Markers in Teff, *Eragrostis tef* (Zucc.) Trotter, and Related Species." *Plant Breeding* 119: 403–409.

Ayele, M., H. Tefera, K. Assefa, and H. T. Nguyen. 1999. "Genetic Characterization of Two *Eragrostis* Species Using AFLP and Morphological Traits." *Hereditas* 130: 33–40.

Bai, G., M. Ayele, H. Tefera, and H. T. Nguyen. 1999. "Amplified Fragment Length Polymorphism Analysis of Teff [*Eragrostis tef* (Zucc.) Trotter]." *Crop Science* 39: 819–824.

Belay, G., H. Tefera, A. Getachew, K. Assefa, and G. Metaferia. 2008. "Highly Client-Oriented Breeding with Farmer Participation in the Ethiopian Cereal Tef [*Eragrostis tef* (Zucc.) Trotter]." *African Journal of Agricultural Research* 3 (1): 22–28.

Belay, G., H. Tefera, B. Tadesse, G. Metaferia, D. Jarra, and T. Tadesse. 2006. "Participatory Variety Selection in the Ethiopian Cereal Teff [*Eragrostis tef* (Zucc.) Trotter]." *Experimental Agriculture* 42: 91–101.

Berhe, T. 1975. "A Breakthrough in Teff Breeding Techniques." *FAO International Bulletin on Cereal Improvement and Production* 12: 11–13.

Berhe, T., L. A. Nelson, M. R. Morris, and J. W. Schmidt. 1989a. "Inheritance of Phenotypic Traits in Teff. I. Lemma Color." *Journal of Heredity* 80: 62–65.

———. 1989b. "Inheritance of Phenotypic Traits in Teff. II. Seed Color." *Journal of Heredity* 80: 65–67.

———. 1989c. "Inheritance of Phenotypic Traits in Teff. III. Panicle Form." *Journal of Heredity* 80: 67–70.

Chanyalew, S., K. Assefa, and G. Metaferia. 2013. "Phenotypic and Molecular Diversity in Teff." In *Achievements and Prospects of Teff Improvement,* edited by K. Assefa, S. Chanyalew, and Z. Tadele, 21–31. Proceedings of the Second International Teff Workshop, November 7–9, 2011, Debre Zeit, Ethiopia.

Costanza, S. H. 1974. "Literature Review and Numerical Taxonomy of Teff *(Eragrostis tef).*" MSc thesis, University of Illinois, Urbana, IL, US.

Cufodontis, G. 1972. "Enumeratio Plantarum Aethiopiae Spermatophyta (Sequentia)." *Bulletin du Jardin Botanique de Belgique* 42 (3): 1579–1657.

Damte, T. 2013. "Insect Pest Management Research in Teff." In *Achievements and Prospects of Teff Improvement,* edited by K. Assefa, S. Chanyalew, and Z. Tadele, 171–192. Proceedings of the Second International Teff Workshop, November 7–9, 2011, Debre Zeit, Ethiopia.

Dargo, F. 2013. "Gain in Grain Yield Potential and Associated Traits of Teff [*Eragrostis tef* (Zucc.) Trotter] in Ethiopia." MSc thesis, School of Plant Sciences, School of Graduate Studies, Haramaya University, Haramaya, Ethiopia.

DZARC (Debre Zeit Agricultural Research Center). 1989. *Annual Research Progress Report for 1988/89.* Debre Zeit, Ethiopia.

———. 1994. *Annual Research Report for the Period 1991/92.* Debre Zeit, Ethiopia.

Ebba, T. 1969. *Teff (*Eragrostis tef*): The Cultivation, Usage, and Some of Its Known Diseases and Insect Pests.* Part I. Experiment Station Bulletin 60. Haile Selassie I University (HSIU), College of Agriculture, Dire Dawa, Ethiopia.

———. 1975. *Teff (*Eragrostis tef*) Cultivars: Morphology and Classification.* Experiment Station Bulletin 66. HSIU, College of Agriculture, Dire Dawa, Ethiopia.

Erkossa, T. 2003. "Some Site-Specific Soil and Water Management Technologies in the Central Highlands of Ethiopia." In *GIS for Modeling Environments in Ethiopian Agriculture,* edited by B. Alemu and A. Zelleke, 47–54. Proceedings of the Workshop, Debre Zeit, Ethiopia.

Eshetu, B. 1985. "Review of Research on Diseases of Barley, Tef and Wheat in Ethiopia." In *A Review of Crop Protection Research in Ethiopia, Proceedings of the First Crop Protection Symposium, 4-7 February, 1985, Addis Ababa,* edited by A. Tsedeke, 79-108. Addis Ababa, Ethiopia: Ethiopian Institute of Agricultural Research (EIAR).

Ethiopia, MoA (Ministry of Agriculture, Animal, and Plant Health Regulatory Directorate). 2013. *Crop Variety Register.* Issue 15. Addis Ababa.

Ethiopian Nutrition Survey. 1959. *A Report by the Inter-Departmental Committee on Nutrition for National Defense.* September. Washington, DC: US Government Printing Office.

Fessehaie, R., and Z. Tadele. 2001. "Weed Research in Teff." In *Narrowing the Rift: Teff Research and Development,* edited by H. Tefera, G. Belay, and M. Sorrells, 201–213. Proceedings of the International Workshop on Teff Genetics and Improvement, October 16–19, 2000, Debre Zeit, Ethiopia. Addis Ababa: Ethiopian Institure of Agricultural Research.

Gugsa, L., G. Belay, and S. Ketema. 2001. "The Cytogenetics of Teff." In *Narrowing the Rift: Teff Research and Development,* edited by H. Tefera, G. Belay, and M. Sorrells, 49–57. Proceedings of the International Workshop on Teff Genetics and Improvement, October 16–19, 2000, Debre Zeit, Ethiopia.

Hundera, F., K. Arumuganathan, and P. S. Baenziger. 2000. "Determination of Relative Nuclear DNA Content of Teff [*Eragrostis tef* (Zucc.) Trotter] Using Flow Cytometry." *Journal of Genetics and Breeding* 54: 165–168.

Ingram, A. L., and J. J. Doyle. 2003. "The Origin and Evolution of *Eragrostis tef* (Poaceae) and Related Polyploids: Evidence from the *Waxy* and Plastid *rps* 16." *American Journal of Botany* 90: 116–122.

Kantety, R. V., E. V. Graznak, H. Tefera, and M. E. Sorrells. 2001. "Comparative Mapping in Teff." In *Narrowing the Rift: Teff Research and Development*, edited by H. Tefera, G. Belay, and M. Sorrells, 99–107. Proceedings of the International Workshop on Teff Genetics and Improvement, October 16–19, 2000, Debre Zeit, Ethiopia.

Kebede, H., R. C. Johnson, and D. M. Ferris. 1989. "Photosynthetic Response of *Eragrostis tef* to Temperature." *Physiologia Plantarum* 77: 262–266.

Ketema, S. 1993. *Teff (Eragrostis tef): Breeding, Genetic Resources, Agronomy, Utilization, and Role in Ethiopian Agriculture*. Addis Ababa: Institute of Agricultural Research.

———. 1997. "Teff, *Eragrostis tef* (Zucc.) Trotter." *Promoting the Conservation and Use of Underutilized and Neglected Crops* 12. Gatersleben, Germany: Institute of Plant Genetics and Crop Plant Research; Rome: International Plant Genetic Resources Institute.

Mamo, T., T. Erkossa, and B. Tulema. 2001. "Soil Fertility and Plant Nutrition Research in Teff in Ethiopia." In *Narrowing the Rift: Teff Research and Development*, edited by H. Tefera, G. Belay, and M. Sorrells, 191–200. Proceedings of the International Workshop on Teff Genetics and Improvement, October 16–19, 2000, Debre Zeit, Ethiopia.

NFIU (National Fertilizer and Inputs Unit). 1993. "Agronomic Feasibility of the Proposed Recommendations and Comparison with the Previous Recommendations." NFIU General Paper 17. Addis Ababa.

Poehlman, J. M., and D. A. Sleper. 1995. *Breeding Field Crops*, 4th ed. Ames, IA, US: Iowa State University Press.

Ponti, J. A. 1978. "The Systematics of *Eragrostis tef* (Gramineae) and Related Species." PhD dissertation, University of London, UK.

Spaenij-Dekking, L., Y. Kooy-Winkelaar, and F. Koning. 2005. "The Ethiopian Cereal Teff in Celiac Disease." *New England Journal of Medicine* 353 (16): 1748–1750.

Tavassoli, A. 1986. "The Cytology of *Eragrostis tef* with Special Reference to *E. tef* and Its Relatives." PhD dissertation, University of London, UK.

Tefera, M. A., and K. Assefa. 1995. "Improved Varieties of Teff (*Eragrostis tef*) in Ethiopia." Releases of 1970–1995, Research Bulletin 1. Debre Zeit Agricultural Research Center, Alemya University of Agriculture, Debre Zeit, Ethiopia.

Tefera, H., K. Assefa, F. Hundera, T. Kefyalew, Y. Teklu, L. Gugsa, S. Ketema, and T. Adnew. 2001. "Progress of Teff Breeding Research in Ethiopia." In *Narrowing the Rift: Teff Research and Development,* edited by H. Tefera, G. Belay, and M. Sorrells, 157–163. Proceedings of the International Workshop on Teff Genetics and Improvement, Debre Zeit, Ethiopia, October 16–19, 2000.

Tefera, H., and S. Ketema. 2001. "Production and Importance of Teff." In *Narrowing the Rift: Teff Research and Development,* edited by H. Tefera, G. Belay, and M. Sorrells, 3–7. Proceedings of the International Workshop on Teff Genetics and Improvement, October 16–19, 2000, Debre Zeit, Ethiopia.

Tesema, A. 2013. "Genetic Resources of Teff in Ethiopia." In *Achievements and Prospects of Teff Improvement,* edited by K. Assefa, S. Chanyalew, and Z. Tadele, 15–20. Proceedings of the Second International Teff Workshop, November 7–9, 2011, Debre Zeit, Ethiopia.

Vavilov, N. I. 1951. *The Origin, Variation, Immunity, and Breeding of Cultivated Plants.* Translated from the Russian by K. S. Chester. New York: Ronal Press Co.

Watson, L., and M. J. Dallwitz. 1992. *The Grass Genus of the World.* Wallingford, Oxon, UK: CAB International.

Zewdie, K., and T. Damte. 2013. "Weed Research in Teff." In *Achievements and Prospects of Teff Improvement,* edited by K. Assefa, S. Chanyalew, and Z. Tadele, 199–207. Proceedings of the Second International Teff Workshop, November 7–9, 2011, Debre Zeit, Ethiopia.

Chapter 4

SEED DEMAND AND SUPPLY RESPONSES

David J. Spielman and Dawit K. Mekonnen

For centuries, efforts to improve, multiply, and distribute teff seed have relied on informal mechanisms, primarily farmers' own selection of varieties exhibiting desirable yield, taste, color, or stress-resistance characteristics, and farmer-to-farmer exchanges of seed embodying these traits. It was not until the mid-20th century that Ethiopia—like many other developing countries—developed a system based on modern science to breed improved teff cultivars, distribute improve teff seed, and accelerate the contribution of genetic gain to teff yield growth across the country's smallholder farming systems. Today, these informal mechanisms still account for up to 90 percent of seed supply, with the modern infrastructure accounting for the remainder (Bishaw, Sahlu, and Simane 2008; Sahlu, Simane, and Bishaw 2008). This suggests that there are challenges still to be overcome in enhancing teff productivity—in increasing output per area, maintaining yield gains from prior investments in research, reducing yield variability within and across seasons, and increasing tolerance and resistance to biotic and abiotic stresses.

Part of Ethiopia's challenge relates to the fact that teff is a neglected species (more pejoratively referred to as an "orphan crop"). Teff is not cultivated extensively in any other country and is thus not a destination for public investment in breeding. Teff is not a food security crop of global importance and is thus not a priority crop in the international agricultural research system—unlike rice, wheat, and maize. Teff is, in effect, unable to benefit from research spillovers from public investment in national (until recently) and international plant breeding programs, international exchanges of germplasm, and modern seed supply systems.

Nor is teff improvement a destination for private investment of any sort. Consumers of quality seed for improved teff varieties are, by and large, farmers with limited purchasing power and market access, vulnerable to both price and weather shocks that make them poor customers for most seed companies. Furthermore, because teff is a self-pollinating crop—meaning that farmers can save seed and replant it the next year without significant loss in genetic purity—private breeders and seed companies cannot appropriate the gains from investments they might make in breeding. In short, the breeding, production, and distribution of improved teff is a fairly unprofitable venture for most private companies. This is particularly the case when compared with hybrid maize, where private seed companies in Ethiopia and many other developing countries have made considerably more progress (for example, see Langyintuo et al. 2010; Morris 1998).

Yet there are other means—other strategies—through which access to improved teff varieties, quality teff seed, and the productivity benefits associated with superior genetics can be enhanced for Ethiopia's smallholders. The success of these strategies is largely determined by the institutional architecture put in place to improve, multiply, and distribute quality seed of improved teff cultivars. The strength of this architecture, in turn, depends on the extent of integration between the formal and informal seed systems as well as the roles played by the state, the private sector, and civil society actors (de Boef and Bishaw 2008). While there are lessons to be learned from successes with other self-pollinating crops such as wheat and rice (Byerlee and Dubin 2008; Dalrymple 2008), the neglected nature of teff makes for a unique case. In short, Ethiopia's challenge is to design an architecture that engages diverse actors and integrates formal and informal seed systems into a widely accessible source of continuous genetic improvement for teff.

Efforts in this direction have been pursued in Ethiopia's recent past. Projects to transition informal seed systems into more modern farmer-based seed production and marketing systems have existed in Ethiopia since the 1980s in selected areas, albeit at relatively small scales (Sahlu, Simane, and Bishaw 2008; Beshir 2005). Their contribution to genetic resource conservation, cultivar improvement, variety popularization, seed production, and seed distribution is fairly well documented (Thijssen et al. 2008). There is also an extensive literature on the contribution made by Ethiopia's formal seed system, including the contributions of public research, extension services, cooperatives, and the Ethiopian Seed Enterprise (ESE) to breeding, production, and distribution (Alemu 2010; Spielman et al. 2010; Bishaw, Sahlu, and Simane 2008).

These systems have operated both in parallel and in collaboration with a modern seed sector comprising the state's agricultural research system, extension services, area development projects, and the parastatal seed enterprise. But there are still broad policy questions about how to integrate farmer-based seed systems with the state's formal system for teff breeding, production, and distribution. Precisely what type of integrated solutions should policy makers explore, and where should they invest scarce public resources? How will these solutions address Ethiopia's goals for agricultural development and economic growth, and how will they fit into a rapidly growing agricultural sector and national economy? Which policies encourage innovation, production, and competition in a seed system that is beneficial to both farmers who cultivate teff and consumers who rely on it as a basic food staple?

This chapter examines these questions by assessing the challenges facing Ethiopia's teff seed system. Specifically, the chapter explores the demand for teff seed and the capacity of the current system to supply quality seed for improved teff cultivars in response to demand. Several recommendations are made aimed at strengthening Ethiopia's seed system and its contribution to teff productivity growth through improved genetics. First the chapter describes the data and data sources used throughout. Next the chapter characterizes teff seed demand, highlighting the heterogeneity across regions and households. Seed provisioning strategies are then examined. The chapter concludes with policy recommendations for integrating informal and formal teff seed improvement, multiplication, and distribution systems to strengthen the supply of quality seed for improved teff cultivars to Ethiopia's smallholders.

Data and Data Sources

The data presented and analyzed in this chapter are drawn from several primary and secondary sources. Official figures on seed production, distribution, and use were collected in 2012/2013 from a variety of official documents from government agencies and personal communications with government officials. Data on seed use disaggregated by crop, season, region, and landholding size were obtained from the Agricultural Sample Surveys of Ethiopia's Central Statistical Agency (CSA) from various years. Data on seed production were obtained from the ESE and the regional seed enterprises in Amhara, Oromiya, and Southern Nations, Nationalities, and Peoples' (SNNP) region. Data on seed distribution were gathered from the bureaus of agriculture in Amhara, Oromiya, Tigray, and SNNP, and the Agricultural Input and Marketing Directorate of the Ministry of Agriculture (MoA). Data on specific teff varieties and their characteristics were obtained from the Ethiopian Institute of Agricultural Research (EIAR). These data were supplemented with observations and insights from key informant interviews, recent publications in the grey and academic literature (cited throughout the chapter), and feedback from seed system actors that was provided at two stakeholder events held in 2013.[1]

Additional household data on seed use come from the Ethiopian Agricultural Transformation Agency (ATA) Baseline Survey that was conducted between June and September 2012 by EIAR and the International Food Policy Research Institute (IFPRI). The aim of this survey was to (1) provide baseline information on the livelihoods of agricultural households in Ethiopia, particularly in the 83 woredas where ATA focuses its attention, and (2) to generate information about the agricultural economy that will help the ATA design and implement its interventions. The sample covered 3,000 households across 100 woredas throughout the four main agricultural regions of Ethiopia (Amhara, Oromiya, SNNP, and Tigray). In each woreda 2 kebeles were randomly selected for inclusion in the survey sample, and within each kebele 15 households were randomly selected. Approximately two-thirds of the sampled woredas were drawn from the 83 woredas targeted by the ATA. The survey covers agricultural production and marketing, use of inputs, soil conservation, storage, livestock activities, nonfarm income, the role of cooperatives, and credit, among other topics, for the 2011 belg season and the 2011/2012 meher season. The survey also introduces a unique set of questions on the topic of seed use, purchasing, and sourcing at a crop-specific level. These questions improve the resolution and accuracy of standard questions relating to the use of improved, high-yielding, or modern seeds that generally do not provide sufficient information of what, where, and how frequently purchases are made in the formal seed market.

A few caveats are needed to fully contextualize the presentation and analysis of these data and the inferences and interpretations offered throughout this chapter. First, the data are not necessarily representative of all teff-producing areas or households in Ethiopia. Official data presented here only cover Amhara, Oromiya, SNNP, and Tigray regions because CSA data indicates that more than 99 percent of teff production in Ethiopia is concentrated in these four regions. Data from the 2012 ATA Baseline Survey offer even less coverage and are not necessarily representative of the sampled population described above because of low response rates to many questions relating to

1 "Seed Demand Assessment in the Ethiopian Formal Seed Sector Agenda: Results of the Draft Seed Demand Assessment Study in the Ethiopian Formal Seed Sector," workshop convened by the Ethiopian Agricultural Transformation Agency, Addis Ababa, January 3, 2013; "Improved Evidence towards Better Policies for the Teff Value Chain," conference organized by the Ethiopian Agricultural Transformation Agency, the Ethiopian Development Research Institute, the International Food Policy Research Institute, and the Ethiopian Institute of Agricultural Research, Addis Ababa, October 10, 2013.

teff seed and varieties. Moreover, since two-thirds of the 100 districts under study are from the high-potential woredas, it is possible that the figures provide values that are greater than the national average. What these data do provide, however, is an illustration of how higher-resolution household data can be used to better characterize the demand for seed and specific varietal traits that, in turn, can help shape policy and market responses aimed at accelerating the productivity gains associated with the cultivation of improved teff varieties in Ethiopia.

Seed Demand and the Teff Seed Market

The demand for teff seed is derived from several factors including, primarily, the demand for teff as a cereal for consumption but also several other price and nonprice determinants, such as farmers' weather expectations, farmers' preferences for particular traits in the cultivar, the price of complementary inputs such as fertilizer, and the availability of substitutes such as saved seed. To get a sense of the size and depth of the teff seed market in Ethiopia, it is necessary to first consider the official statistics from the CSA's Agricultural Sample Surveys (Table 4.1).

In the meher season of 2005/2006, 2.25 million hectares of land were under teff cultivation, accounting for 22 percent of the total area under grain cultivation. This made teff the single most important crop in Ethiopia in terms of area under cultivation. By 2012/2013, area under teff cultivation had increased by 20 percent to 2.73 million hectares and still accounted for 22 percent of total area under grain cultivation. On the intensive margin, teff yield has increased from 9.7 quintals per hectare in 2005/2006 to 13.8 quintals per hectare in 2012/2013. Area expansion coupled with yield improvements has led teff production to increase by more than 73 percent from 21.8 million quintals in 2005/2006 to 37.6 million quintals in 2012/2013. Though yield improvements of 4 quintals per hectare within a period of seven years is impressive, there is likely to be additional scope to increase yields with the use of improved teff varieties, traits, and other inputs. While the proportion of land under teff cultivation with fertilizer use has increased from 59 percent in 2005/2006 to 75 percent in 2012/2013, the corresponding proportion of land under teff cultivation with improved seed within the same period remained at about 1 percent, although this figure is slightly underestimated as we argue below.

Across this area under teff cultivation in 2012/2013, CSA figures indicate that improved seed accounted for only 1.4 percent of area under cultivation, or

TABLE 4.1 Land under teff cultivation and use of improved seed and complementary inputs in teff production during meher season, 2005/2006 and 2012/2013

	2005/2006				2012/2013			
	Tigray	Amhara	Oromia	SNNP	Tigray	Amhara	Oromia	SNNP
Area under teff cultivation (hectares)	138,346	907,057	985,666	193,193	161,798	1,090,139	1,256,565	202,376
Area under teff cultivation with improved seed (hectares)	3,458	7,664	6,304	7,286	4,545	21,132	6,832	5,771
Area under teff cultivation without improved seed (hectares)	134,654	899,182	978,880	185,831	157,253	1,068,939	1,249,732	196,604
Quantity of improved teff seed (kilograms)	159,889	259,449	366,498	394,965	223,034	635295	278,294	233,046
Quantity of indigenous teff seed (kilograms)	6,551,042	41,485,855	57,901,882	9,025,720	7,914,462	52,435,428	66,397,113	9,197,232
Seeding rate for improved teff seed (kilograms per hectare)	64	39	71	63	56	31	41	45
Seeding rate for indigenous teff seed (kilograms per hectare)	69	54	72	57	67	53	64	59
Area under teff cultivation with fertilizer use (hectares)	82,162	511,731	630,019	97,673	127,075	793,476	970,387	128,997
Area under teff cultivation with irrigation (hectares)	4,464	892	1,092	1,436	1,028	2,775	1,473	728
Teff production in quintals	1,244,213	8,658,240	10,224,520	1,454,743	2,122,235	15,281,977	17,535,597	2,515,409
Teff yield (quintals per hectare)	8.99	9.55	10.37	7.53	13.12	14.02	13.96	12.43

Source: Ethiopia, CSA (various years).

Note: SNNP = Southern Nations, Nationalities, and Peoples' region.

just over 38,000 hectares of land. This amounts to approximately 1,710 metric tons of improved teff seed. Although these figures suggest a thin market for improved teff seed in Ethiopia, they should also be treated with caution. Specifically, the way in which the question is asked of surveyed households—roughly, "Do you plant an improved or local variety of teff?"—obscures the contribution made by farmers who save seeds of improved varieties. This means that the survey is likely to capture only whether respondents had obtained (through purchase or trade) and planted seed of an improved variety in the immediate or most recent season. This also means that the survey probably does not capture whether respondents had planted seed from an improved variety that had been obtained in other prior years. Affirmative answers to both should be taken as an indication that the surveyed households are cultivating improved varieties, but it is likely that the survey only captures the current-year varietal choice. This suggests that the prevalence of improved teff cultivation is being underestimated, thereby muddling the estimation of demand for seed of improved teff varieties and thus obfuscating the market's potential viability.

To illustrate this further, the CSA figures for wheat are considered, which indicate that improved varieties accounted for 4.3 percent of area under cultivation in 2012/2013. In contrast, data from the Diffusion and Impact of Improved Varieties in Africa project (DIIVA 2013) for 2009 suggest a different figure, based on entirely different data collection methods and different definitions that aim to provide a better accounting of improved cultivar prevalence. DIIVA data indicate that through both seed purchases and saving practices, improved varieties accounted for 62 percent (based on a weighted average for both durum and spring bread wheat, which are treated separately by DIIVA).[2] In effect, CSA data are limited in what they reveal about demand for improved teff varieties or the teff seed market in general.

The question, then, is exactly how large is the market for improved teff seed? There is no easy answer, primarily because the combination of frequent seed supply shortfalls, state-run distribution channels, and state-determined seed prices obscure information on the underlying market price at any point in time. That said, a rough way of estimating market size is to consider both the frequency at which farmers purchase seed and the quantity of teff seed that is purchased by farmers in a given year. This calculation is made only for white teff since genetic improvements have been primarily introduced

2 Note that the DIIVA data are not necessarily more accurate than CSA data as they do not rely on nationally representative surveys but rather a combination of surveys and expert opinion. A more complete explanation of DIIVA's methods is in DIIVA (2013).

by Ethiopia's research system in white teff varieties and not in landraces commonly described as black, red, or mixed teff varieties.[3] Again, exercising caution in interpreting these results is encouraged because of limitations associated with the data, as detailed earlier.

This calculation is made by examining data from the 2012 ATA Baseline Survey on the share of farmers who purchased white teff seed. The data indicate that 28 percent of farmers who purchased white teff seed did so in the previous year, with another 12 percent having purchased white teff seed two years ago, 15 percent three years ago, and so on (Table 4.2). This means that in any given year, approximately 70 percent of farmers who cultivated white teff had also purchased seed within the past five years, which is the recommended seed replacement rate for teff.[4] Of those white teff farmers who purchased seed within the past five years, 34 percent did so from formal sources that have the mandate and capacity to supply improved varieties (that is, cooperatives and bureaus of agriculture), with the remaining 66 percent purchasing from other sources that have no such mandate (that is, other farmers and grain traders). This means that in any given year, 14 percent of farmers purchased seed of improved teff varieties.

Next, a few assumptions and calculations are made. First, it is assumed that white teff seed purchased from these formal sources is exclusively improved—that is, it is one of the 18 or so teff varieties released by the national agricultural research system and produced by state-owned seed enterprises. Second, it is estimated that white teff accounts for 60 percent of all area under teff cultivation, or 1,627,000 hectares of land, based on land allocation data from the 2012 ATA Baseline Survey. Third, the landholding sizes of households cultivating improved (white) teff varieties purchased from formal sources is calculated to be 0.30 hectares, which is slightly smaller than the average landholding size for all white teff farmers, which is 0.38 hectares.

With these figures in hand, an alternative estimate of the area under improved (white) teff in Ethiopia is approximately 228,000 hectares in 2011/2012. Our computation shows that 14 percent of the land under white teff is cultivated with improved seed, which is still small but much higher

3 Landraces is a term referring to indigenous farmers' varieties.

4 Note that it is not the case that this figure is skewed by some farmers (for example, larger landholders or wealthier farmers) purchasing seed more frequently than other farmers (for example, smaller landholders or poorer farmers). In general, the distribution of years since the last purchase of teff seed is consistent across these dimensions of heterogeneity (for example, landholding size and wealth) in the sampled population.

TABLE 4.2 Years since last purchase of teff seed, 2011/2012

Years since last purchase of teff seed	Red teff		White teff	
	Frequency	%	Frequency	%
1	92	15	208	28
2	68	11	90	12
3	100	16	113	15
4	74	12	88	12
5	30	5	12	2
>5	63	10	34	5
Never	183	30	186	25
Observations	**611**	**100**	**732**	**100**

Source: Authors, based on data from the Ethiopian Agricultural Transformation Agency (ATA) 2012 Baseline Survey.

than official statistics. Given an average seeding rate of 38 kilograms per hectare, this translates into a market volume of 8,664 metric tons of improved (white) teff seed. Even when accounting for regional variation in years since last purchase of teff seed or variation in seeding rates by landholding size (see Appendix Table 4.A1 and 4.A2), these rough calculations are clearly several orders of magnitude larger than CSA's figures. This suggests that the prevalence of improved teff cultivation in Ethiopia is probably more than previously estimated.

This is a useful starting point for estimating demand and market size. But for several reasons these measures are still insufficient in gauging seed system development if the primary objective is to encourage productivity growth. First, because these figures rely on seed replacement rates, they do not identify whether seed was purchased by farmers to simply refresh the quantity and quality of their seed stocks, or whether seed was purchased to obtain better cultivars with superior genetic traits. Second, because these figures simply measure the purchase of seed of an unspecified quality of what may be cultivars of an unspecified age, they obfuscate any information on the seed system's capacity to provide farmers with superior genetics or quality seed products. Third, these figures overlook the distributional dimension of who actually purchases seed and what types of farmers—measured in terms of land tenure, wealth, income, or geographic location—have access to seed embodying superior genetics. In short, a better measure of demand needs to incorporate information on specific teff varieties.

To do this, measures of varietal turnover are considered to get a sense of whether farmers are accessing superior genetics. These measures have proven useful in gauging the contribution of genetic improvement to productivity growth in rice and wheat in South Asia, both during the Green Revolution of the late 1960s and early 1970s when the shift from landraces to modern varieties resulted in a doubling of yields and output. In the subsequent decades yield growth rates stagnated with the slower shift from first-generation to newer modern varieties (Dixon and Gulliver with Gibbon 2001; Heisey et al. 1997; Heisey 1990). If a similar pattern were to prevail for teff in Ethiopia, rapid yield gains might be expected where a significant share of farmers switched from teff landraces to improved varieties, while smaller, more incremental gains might be expected in areas where improved teff cultivation is already prevalent, or where farmers have concentrated cultivation around a few high-performing cultivars such as Quncho (see Chapter 9). Necessarily, this productivity growth pattern is contingent with the development of improved varieties that are adapted to the agroecological constraints and risk preferences that shape farmers' willingness to adopt a new technology and on the provision of seed, fertilizer, credit, extension services, and other complementary inputs. This does not run counter to the prevailing focus of public policy and investment on Ethiopia's high-potential areas but does suggest the need for a higher resolution of understanding on how the largest gains are achieved in teff productivity and in the best way possible.

The importance of variety-specific information is examined by calculating the extent to which farmers are cultivating recently released teff varieties or relying instead on older varieties (Table 4.3). Despite the limited number of observations—possibly due to the inability of survey respondents and enumer ators to identify varieties by either their official or local names—it appears that DZ-CR-387 (Quncho) is relatively more prevalent than other named varieties.[5] This may suggest that some farmers are benefiting from more recent varietal releases from current research. Importantly, this also suggests that variety-specific data can be obtained with a degree of consistency and that this information can in turn be used to gauge the prevalence of more recently released improved varieties.

---

5 The 2012 ATA Baseline relied on postcoding of local names for teff varieties and matching those names with the official variety names published by EIAR. Future efforts to obtain variety-specific data would benefit from a more careful precoding of both local and official variety names.

TABLE 4.3 Area under teff cultivation by variety, 2011/2012

Variety name (number of observations)	Year of release	Variety's share of households that are cultivating a known/ named variety (%)[a]	Variety's share of area under teff cultivation (%)[a]
Quncho: DZ-CR-387 (60)	2005	2.58	3.46
Key tena: DZ-01-1681 (13)	2002	0.46	0.78
Magna: DZ-01-196 (7)	1978	0.30	0.27
Tseday: DZ-CR-37 (3)	1984	0.23	0.23
Ambo: DZ-01-1278 (1)	1999/2000	0.08	0.05
Other white teff variety (894)	—	45.30	50.00
Other red teff variety (949)	—	51.06	44.80
Unknown white or red teff varieties (7)	—	—	0.49

Source: Authors, based on data from the ATA Baseline Survey (2012).
Note: [a] Figures total to slightly more than 100 percent due to rounding; — = data not available.

Next, to get a sense of the structure of the teff seed market, the sources from which farmers procure teff seed, the distances they travel to obtain it, and the prices they pay are examined. As before, this information is drawn from the 2012 ATA Baseline Survey. Both white and red teff are included to provide insight into how these separate market segments compare. As with other data and analysis presented earlier, these investigations are interpreted with caution due to limited numbers of observations and representative data.

Sourcing strategies based on own-saved seed or farmer-to-farmer exchanges account for 88 percent of the white teff seed market and 98 percent of the red teff seed market (Table 4.4). Cooperatives and bureaus of agriculture constitute the next most important source of white teff seed, accounting for 10 percent of the market. When asked how much travel time was incurred in obtaining purchased seed using normal transportation (that is, any combination of transportation methods), farmers' responses suggest that it takes about 50 to 60 minutes to obtain seed from other farmers, cooperatives, or bureaus of agriculture, while it takes about 90 minutes to obtain seed from grain traders. The fact that distance to other farmers is more or less similar to that of cooperatives and bureaus of agriculture may suggest that farmers are likely to invest time to search for good quality seeds and traits in their surrounding villages, rather than getting any seed from a neighbor. While the absence of heterogeneity is of limited analytical relevance here (and while the analysis is limited by small sample sizes across several types of suppliers and for red teff),

TABLE 4.4 Farmers' sources of teff seed and associated travel times to purchase seed, 2011/2012

	White teff			Red teff		
Source of teff seed	Percentage of farmers (%)	Mean travel time (standard deviation)	Number of observations	Percentage of farmers (%)	Mean travel time (standard deviation)	Number of observations
Saved per self	72			86		
Other farmers	16	52.72 (63.27)	79	12	44.04 (55.62)	74
Cooperative	8	56.29 (34.43)	53	0	35 (7.071)	2
Bureau of Agriculture	2	50.74 (73.44)	13	0	30 (n.a.)	1
Grain trader	2	90.28 (72.94)	23	2	56.27 (55.74)	21
Total	**100**			**100**		

Source: Authors, based on data from the ATA Baseline Survey (2012).
Note: n.a. = not applicable.

the figures do provide a baseline that can be used to gauge future progress in improving the accessibility of quality seed or improved cultivars.[6] They also open the door to further exploration of why farmers travel so extensively to obtain teff in instances where they do not rely on own-saved seed.

Exchanges in these markets are primarily cash-based: 81 percent and 77 percent of white and red teff seed purchases, respectively, are cash transactions, while financing for credit-based transactions comprise fewer than 5 percent of all purchases. While it is possible to interpret this as a credit constraint on seed purchases, it is more likely that the use of cash is a reflection of the relatively low cost of seed acquired through both farmer-to-farmer exchanges and the public distribution networks. The average price paid for white teff was 12.1 Ethiopian birr per kilogram and for red teff was 11.4 birr per kilogram; households spent on average 187.6 birr on seed purchases (Table 4.5).

Finally, several indicators of seed quality are examined to provide a sense of how satisfied farmers are with purchased teff seed. Overall, farmers who purchase teff seed appear to be satisfied with seed quality and the timeliness of its delivery. Across all sources, there is no evidence of complaints with respect to quality attributes of seed such as timeliness, adulteration, germination, price,

6 The value of intertemporal spatial analysis is demonstrated by Ariga and Jayne (2010) in Kenya with evidence showing that travel times required to purchase synthetic fertilizer and improved maize varieties and hybrids had significantly decreased between 1997 and 2007, contributing to higher maize yields, increased farm incomes, and improved national food security.

TABLE 4.5 Seed prices and average household expenditures on teff seed, 2011/2012

Indicator	White teff (standard deviation)	Red teff (standard deviation)	Total (standard deviation)
Average seed price paid for teff seed (birr per kilogram)	12.13 (5.927)	11.40 (5.422)	11.95 (5.807)
Average household expenditure on teff seed (birr)	208.8 (178.1)	121.70 (109.1)	187.6 (168.0)
Number of observations	167	88	255

Source: Authors, based on data from the ATA Baseline Survey (2012).

TABLE 4.6 Farmer perceptions of teff seed quality, by source, 2011/2012

	Seed source			
Type of problem with seed	Other farmers (n = 181)	Cooperatives (n = 50)	Bureaus of agriculture (n = 12)	Grain traders (n = 23)
Delivered late	4%	0%	0%	0%
Mixed with other seed	1	0	0	1
Poor germination	1	0	0	0
Too expensive	0	0	11	6
Incorrect label	0	0	0	0
Other quality problem	2	1	0	1
No problem	91	98	89	92

Source: Authors, based on data from the ATA Baseline Survey (2012).

and labeling (Table 4.6). Responses to these questions are necessarily open to interpretation.

Given a choice of specific seed traits, a majority of farmers naturally expressed demand for higher-yielding teff cultivars (Table 4.7). In addition to yield improvements, farmers expressed demand for cultivars that offer improvements in grain size and tolerance to disease and drought. For white teff in particular, farmers expressed an interest in market-related traits such as color and taste that are generally rewarded by higher prices from consumers.

Considered as a whole, the data and analysis presented here paint a detailed picture of the size of the teff seed market, the frequency at which farmers purchase teff seed, the prevalence of and preferences for superior genetics embodied in seed, and the effort farmers make to obtain quality seed and traits. Although these observations should not be interpreted as conclusive market

TABLE 4.7 Farmer opinions of important varietal characteristics for teff, 2011/2012

Trait or characteristics	First most important characteristic		Second most important characteristic	
	White teff (n = 185)	Red teff (n = 85)	White teff (n = 146)	Red teff (n = 69)
Grain yield	72%	59%	16%	18%
Grain size	13	23	15	30
Disease or pest resistance	3	5	6	24
Drought resistance	4	0	17	13
Flood resistance	3	0	5	0
Low labor needs	0	1	1	1
Low input needs	0	3	5	2
Ease of processing	0	2	0	0
Market demand	3	0	13	1
Good taste	1	5	8	2
Good color	1	1	3	5
Fodder quality	0	0	1	2

Source: Authors, based on data from the ATA Baseline Survey (2012).

research and intelligence, they do suggest that the demand for quality seed for improved teff varies significantly from what might otherwise be inferred from official statistics. They also suggest that unmet demand is likely for better teff seed and traits, and that more detailed, variety-specific data can help in considering how to integrate farmer-based seed systems with the state's formal system for teff breeding, production, and distribution. This introduces the next section, which explores Ethiopia's teff seed supply system and alternative provisioning strategies.

Teff Seed Supply and Provisioning Strategies

While farmer-saved seed and farmer-to-farmer exchanges are the main sources of teff seed supply in Ethiopia, national efforts to make superior genetic material widely available rely primarily with the country's formal seed system and the organizations mandated to conduct breeding, extension, production, and distribution. This formal system is chiefly a state-led venture and is managed through the federal and regional governments' extensive infrastructure for cultivar improvement and seed supply (Figure 4.1). There are well documented

FIGURE 4.1 A schematic of the supply system for teff seed in Ethiopia

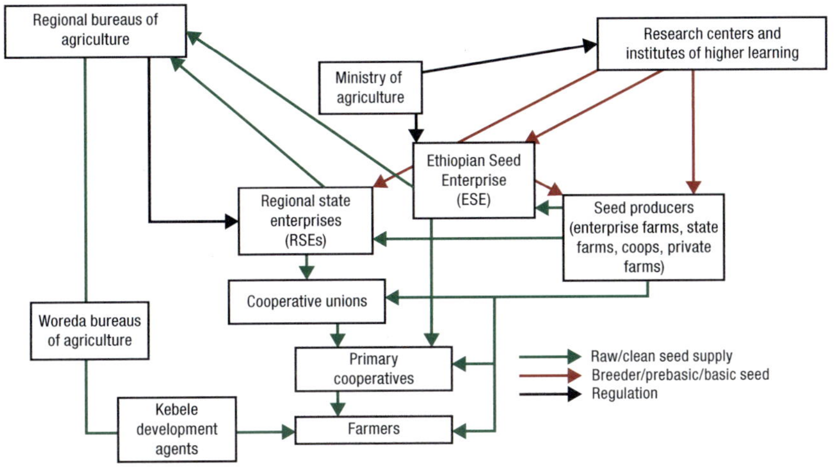

Source: Authors, adapted from Spielman, Mekonnen, and Alemu (2012).

shortcomings of the seed system, with problems related to its coverage, the timeliness of seed delivery, and the quantity and quality of seed delivered to farmers (Teklewold et al. 2012; Spielman et al. 2010; DSA 2006).

Official Ministry of Agriculture (MoA) estimates of teff seed supply suggest that shortfalls have been a common occurrence over the past two decades (Table 4.8) and that in no single year did supply exceed demand. However, these figures reflect official demand figures and production targets that are poorly grounded in reality at the farm level and thus do not provide a completely accurate record of seed supply system performance (Spielman et al. 2010; Spielman and Mekonnen 2013; Sahlu, Simane, and Bishaw 2008). Drawing on the calculations given earlier in this chapter, the actual gap between demand and supply is likely to be much higher than these figures, although the absence of significant variation in seed prices makes it difficult to arrive at any strong conclusions.

A more informative way of estimating supply and demand data is to use more detailed, variety-specific measures. Table 4.9 provides data from 2010/2011 on variety-specific seed production, variety-specific shortfalls, and a calculation of the average age of all teff varieties supplied weighted by share of teff seed supply. The key metric calculated in this analysis is the average age of teff varieties under production, weighted by each variety's share in total production. This calculation is based on an approach developed by Brennan

TABLE 4.8 Official estimates of teff seed demand, supply, and deficits, in quintals, 1995/1996–2012/2013

Year	(quintals) Demand	Supply	Deficit	Supply as a share of demand (%)
1995/1996	29,045	3,576	−25,469	12
1996/1997	32,626	2,788	−29,838	9
1997/1998	28,321	301	−28,020	1
1998/1999	2,998	2,442	−556	81
1999/2000	—	—	—	—
2000/2001	6,215	953	−5,262	15
2001/2002	508	508	0	100
2002/2003	—	—	—	—
2003/2004	32,439	1,329	−31,110	4
2004/2005	4,017	2,072	−1,945	52
2005/2006	78,389	4,197	−74,192	5
2006/2007	29,847	3,527	−26,320	12
2007/2008	29,847	6,516	−23,331	22
2008/2009	34,906	6,466	−28,440	19
2009/2010	35,984	7,872	−28,112	22
2010/2011	63,931	19,554	−44,377	31
2011/2012	89,957	43,508	−46,449	48
2012/2013	91,427	81,216	−10,211	89

Source: MoA (2012).
Note: — = data not available.

and Byerlee (1991) whereby data collected from MoA and ESE is used. The analysis showed that two teff varieties accounted for 90 percent of all production: DZ-CR-387 (Quncho), released in 2005 and accounting for 53 percent of production, and DZ-CR-37 (Tseday), released in 1984 and accounting for 37 percent of production. Shortfalls for these popular varieties are apparent.

But more important, the production-weighted average age of varieties produced by the seed supply system is 16 years. This suggests that despite the shortfalls, the seed supply system has some capacity to move superior genetic material (in the form of newly released improved teff varieties) into seed production and ultimately out to farmers. By giving more attention to the goal of maintaining a relatively low production-weighted average variety age and expanding seed production for new teff varieties, decision makers in the seed system—including policy makers at the federal and

TABLE 4.9 Seed demand and supply for selected teff seed varieties, 2010/2011

Teff variety	Year released	Variety age as of 2010/2011 (years)	Demand from the regional states (quintals)	Supply from the federal government (quintals)	Supply from the regional states (quintals)	Total seed supply (federal + regional supply) (quintals)	Deficit (quintals)	Supply as a share of demand (%)	Share of variety in total supply of teff seed (%)
DZ-CR-37 (Tseday)	1984	27	44,621	1,453	5,445	6,898	–37,723	15	37
DZ-01-196 (Magna)	1970	41	6,561	207	143	350	–6,211	5	2
DZ-CR-387 (Quncho)	2005	6	31,755	2,583	7,355	9,938	–21,817	31	53
DZ-01-354 (Enatite)	1970	41	6,971	349	250	599	–6,372	9	3
DZ-01-974 (Dukem)	1995	16	1,468	506	580	1,086	–382	74	6
DZ-01-182	—	—	50	—	—	—	–50	0	0
Lakech	—	—	1	—	—	—	–1	0	0
DZ-01-1282	2002	9	n.a.	20	n.a.	20	20	—	<1
Total	**n.a.**	**n.a.**	**91,427**	**5,118**	**13,773**	**18,891**	**–72,536**	**21**	**100**
Average age of all teff varieties supplied, weighted by share of teff seed supply (years)									16.00

Source: Authors, based on data from the Ethiopian Ministry of Agriculture (MoA) and the Ethiopian Seed Enterprise (ESE).

Note: — = data not available; n.a. = not applicable.

regional levels—would have reasonable performance metrics by which to measure progress.

However, the capacity to meet these performance metrics depends acutely on investments made by several key actors. First and foremost is the Ethiopia's research system—led by the Ethiopian Institute of Agricultural Research (EIAR)—and the Debre Zeit Agricultural Research Center (DZARC), where most teff breeding efforts are conducted. Although investment in agricultural R&D (specifically cultivar improvement) has been repeatedly demonstrated to increase productivity and reduce poverty (Evenson and Gollin 2003; Fan 2000; Fan, Hazell, and Thorat 2000; Fan and Pardey 1997), funding for DZARC and the wider research system remains insufficient relative to the needs and expectations of Ethiopia's economic development strategy. From a peak in 2001 and 2002 of approximately US$100 million (measured in constant [2005] Purchasing Power Parity–adjusted US dollars), public spending on agricultural research dropped below US$70 million by 2008 (Table 4.10). Financing has been erratic partly due to the completion of several large donor–funded projects that began in the previous decade, while structural and management challenges remain a focus of concern across the system, with consequences for teff improvement and research productivity more generally (Flaherty, Kelemework, and Kelemu 2010).

The challenges of the seed supply system do not, however, reside only at the research center level. There are also challenges in the handoff of breeding material used in seed production (that is, pre-basic and basic seed for finished varieties) to the state-owned ESE and the regional state enterprises (RSEs) in Oromia, SNNP (established in 2008), and Amhara (established in 2009). As the primary producers of certified seed for improved teff, the ESE and RSEs are responsible for managing complex operations involving seed multiplication conducted on their own production farms and through outgrowers—primarily state farms, cooperatives, and private subcontractors (Figure 4.1).

These enterprises, alongside the MoA and regional bureaus of agriculture, have consistently argued that seed supply shortfall are the result of poor quality data with which to calibrate seed production with expected demand (Teklewold et al. 2012). These data are collected by development agents (DAs) at the kebele level, compiled at woreda and then regional levels, and eventually transmitted to the ESE and RSEs as production targets. These data rarely constitute a reliable basis for making seed production decisions, but efforts to improve accuracy by further investing in the existing data collection system are probably a poor use of public resources (Spielman and Mekonnen 2013).

TABLE 4.10 Financial and human resources allocated to agricultural research in Ethiopia, 1991–2008

Year	Public-sector spending on agricultural R&D (constant [2005] US$millions PPP)	Public-sector research staff (full-time equivalent staff)	Public agricultural R&D spending as a share of agricultural GDP (%)	Public agricultural R&D spending per researcher (constant [2005] US$millions PPP)
1991	31.4	403.7	0.21	0.08
1992	23.9	397.1	0.16	0.06
1993	25.8	463.9	0.16	0.06
1994	38.0	477.9	0.26	0.08
1995	36.5	473.1	0.24	0.08
1996	38.4	534.4	0.23	0.07
1997	36.2	542.5	0.21	0.07
1998	48.4	570.2	0.32	0.08
1999	41.5	651.1	0.27	0.06
2000	49.4	750.7	0.31	0.07
2001	96.2	850.3	0.58	0.11
2002	100.5	976.2	0.65	0.10
2003	90.5	1068.1	0.63	0.08
2004	86.4	1098.1	0.51	0.08
2005	81.2	1148.5	0.4	0.07
2006	81.8	1201.5	0.35	0.07
2007	80.7	1291.0	0.32	0.06
2008	68.6	1318.3	0.27	0.05

Source: ASTI (2013).
Note: PPP = Purchasing Power Parity.

Rather, more information could be garnered from credible marketing efforts on the part of ESE and the RSEs that aim to collect more market intelligence about farmers' preferences and willingness to pay for seeds and traits.

This is where cooperatives may play a critical role. An important dimension of this seed supply system is the role of cooperatives. In many developing and industrialized countries, cooperatives and other types of farmer organizations play a central role in the production of seed for self-pollinating crops—crops that offer insufficient profit incentives to private firms. For example, Limagrain, a global supplier of wheat seed, is an agricultural cooperative owned and operated by French farmers and hosts annual sales revenues on the order of 2 billion euros over 39 countries. Some of the leading seed companies have subsidiaries with roots in farmer organizations and cooperatives that supply seed that operate in Canada, China, India, the United States, and many other countries at both national and local levels.[7]

In Ethiopia, cooperatives and cooperative unions are a central pillar of the country's rural development strategy and are being positioned to play an increasingly significant role in seed supply. At present, however, their role revolves primarily around the distribution of seed procured from ESE and the RSEs. They have limited capacity to gather market intelligence, negotiate seed supply contracts with ESE or RSEs, operate commercially oriented seed production units, or market seed at the wholesale and retails levels. The broader regulatory system also has limited capacity to credibly ensure the quality of the seed they produce and market, whether through certification or quality assured seed (the two most prevalent regulatory practices in place) or through point-of-sale monitoring or legal recourse against untruthful labeling, which are regulatory practices pursued in many other countries (Spielman and Kennedy 2016). But these are potentially the roles that cooperatives could play in a teff seed system designed to make superior genetics continuously available to Ethiopia's smallholders.

Discussion

Having described the challenges facing Ethiopia's market for teff seed and genetic improvements embodied in that seed, some of the potential solutions to improving teff breeding, production, and distribution in the country can be discussed. One critical solution is the reallocation of tasks toward those actors that have the strongest incentives to perform them. At present, the federal and regional governments assume the entire costs of seed production, marketing, promotion, and popularization, along with all the risks associated with storage losses, defaults on credit taken by cooperatives and cooperative unions for the purchase of bulk seed, and any reputational damage resulting from farmer dissatisfaction with insufficient seed supply, poor quality seed, or late seed delivery. A more effective seed system would benefit from shifting some of these costs and risks from the regional and federal governments to seed producers (cooperatives, cooperative unions, and small and medium seed enterprises)

7 In the United States, for example, legislation enacted in 1914 to create the federal-state Cooperative Extension Service required local extension agents to work through formal farmer organizations. This partnership gave birth to what became the American Farm Bureau Federation, which, in DeKalb County, IL, developed and spun off the DeKalb Agricultural Association, which eventually evolved into DeKalb, a major hybrid corn seed company that exists to this day, currently as a subsidiary of Monsanto (DCFB 2004).

and seed consumers (cooperatives, cooperative unions, and farmers). Steps in this direction would require significant changes in public policies, specifically the removal of explicit or implicit seed production targets, distribution quotas, and prices that are set by the regional bureaus of agriculture. By removing these distortionary policies, seed producers and seed consumers can more effectively negotiate over the terms of exchange and assume responsibility for production and consumption.

In effect, this suggests an opportunity to create a rudimentary market in which seed demand assessment is done by those who have the incentive to assess demand accurately, and where seed supply is carried out by those who have an incentive to provide the right quantities of quality seed delivered in a timely manner. Policies designed and implemented around this idea must necessarily be nuanced to balance market creation with the limitations in market infrastructure, equity concerns, and incentive compatibility. A rudimentary market-based design for Ethiopia's seed market, if coupled with other strategic public interventions, can improve the quantity of high-quality seed delivered to smallholders. A better seed system that is introduced in conjunction with input market reforms and stronger commodity markets can, in turn, contribute to increases in productivity and income for smallholders and reductions in the price of teff for food-insecure consumers in both urban and rural areas.

An experiment in this direction began in 2013 with the Direct Seed Marketing (DSM) initiative of the Ministry of Agriculture, ATA, and regional bureaus of agriculture, which builds on the Integrated Seed Sector Development (ISSD) project (see Benson, Spielman, and Kassa 2014). Piloted in the Amhara, Oromia, and SNNP regional states, the initiative authorized and supported a program of direct marketing of certified seed—primarily maize—by seed producers to farmers across 31 woredas and subsequently has been scaled up across a larger number of woredas. While the productivity impact of this scale-up has yet to be determined, there are some early indications of gains for seed market development. Nonetheless, translating those gains from a market for maize hybrids to a market for self-pollinating teff will be challenging.

Specifically, the architecture of a teff seed market along similar lines will require several structural reforms. First, an increase in public investment in teff breeding at DZARC and other centers is probably warranted. Second, an eventual withdrawal of ESE and RSEs from the business of producing certified teff seed could be pursued so that these enterprises could instead concentrate on producing adequate quantities of high-quality foundation seed for other seed producers. Third, stronger policy signals and public investments could be channeled toward enterprising farmers, community-based initiatives, and cooperatives to produce teff seed for onward distribution to individual farmers.

Ethiopia's cooperatives offer a real opportunity for seed system development. Cooperatives can serve as both consumers and producers of teff seed, depending on the types of farmers they serve, what crops their members produce, and what level of maturity their enterprises embody. Of course, considerable investment would be needed to strengthen their capacity to produce and market seed on a commercial basis. This necessitates investing public resources in programs designed to build farmers' technical skills and expertise in areas such as seed production operations, enterprise management, and marketing. It also requires investing public resources in systems to credibly monitor seed quality, whether based on the current seed certification system or some other standard such as quality assurances or truthful labeling of seed.

It is unlikely that cooperative seed enterprises will be able to compete against one another on the basis of superior genetics. This is because the national agricultural research system is likely to remain the sole source of improved teff varieties. However, this does not preclude cooperatives from competing on the basis of other product attributes such as timeliness of delivery, seed quality, packaging, and commission rates to distributors. If teff seed price-setting practices were withdrawn, then cooperatives could also compete on the basis of price. While further analysis, ground-truthing, and pilot evaluations are needed to determine what is possible and practical, there is already a body of evidence in Ethiopia suggesting scope for growth and expansion of cooperative seed enterprises (Thijssen et al. 2008). So long as the teff seed system is driven by farmer demand, remains flexible and responsive, and maintains open exchanges of information and materials between the national research system, extension services, seed enterprises, cooperatives, and farmers, then there are real opportunities to be seized.

Conclusion

There is probably no better time than the present to capitalize on the willingness and ability of Ethiopia's policy makers, entrepreneurs, and farmers to effect change in Ethiopia's teff seed system and accelerate the contribution of improved genetics to teff productivity growth. But it is not easy to design an architecture that integrates formal and informal seed systems and bridges the gaps between state, private, and civil society actors in the provisioning of seed. This chapter has attempted to design a road map that could strengthen

Ethiopia's teff seed system. It has illustrated how better measurement of seed demand and supply can provide information that is critical to designing seed systems that are responsive to farmers' needs and the capability of seed producers. It has described an innovative role for the public research system, state-owned seed enterprises, and cooperatives in a more robust market for teff seed. Moreover, it has provided a sense of the essential policies and investments needed to move this road map toward a reality where actions are more likely to be fulfilled. Many of the policies and investments recommended here are consistent with the strategies for agricultural development, economic growth, and poverty reduction set forth under Ethiopia's 2011–2015 Growth and Transformation Plan (GTP). They reinforce the 2013 seed sector strategy developed by the Ministry of Agriculture, the Agricultural Transformation Agency, and allied bodies of the government of Ethiopia. In addition, they build on a host of seed enterprise activities and seed sector development initiatives already occurring across Ethiopia. However, the ultimate success of these strategies, activities, and initiatives will depend on the successful introduction of an institutional architecture—the public policies and investments—that incentivize state, private, and civil society actors to play new and more effective roles in the improvement, production, and marketing of quality seed for improved teff varieties.

Appendix

TABLE 4.A1 Number of years since last purchase of seed for white teff, by region, 2011/2012

Years since last purchase of teff seed	%			
	Tigray (n = 12)	Amhara (n = 356)	Oromiya (n = 249)	SNNP (n = 41)
1	23	23	32	59
2	20	12	13	8
3	14	10	23	15
4	9	10	16	8
5	7	2	1	0
>5	18	7	1	0
Never	9	35	15	9
Observations	100	100	100	100

Source: Authors, based on data from the ATA Baseline Survey (2012).
Note: SNNP = Southern Nations, Nationalities, and Peoples' region.

TABLE 4.A2 **Teff seeding rate during the meher season, by landholding size, 2005/2006 and 2012/2013**

	2005/2006			2012/2013		
Seeding rate (kilograms per hectare)	Large farmers (> 2 hectares)	Medium farmers (0.9 to 2 hectares)	Small farmers (<0.9 hectares)	Large farmers (> 2 hectares)	Medium farmers (0.9 to 2 hectares)	Small farmers (<0.9 hectares)
Improved teff	53	54	77	31	42	54
Indigenous (local) teff	61	61	67	58	58	65

Source: Ethiopia, CSA (various years).

References

Alemu, D. 2010. *The Political Economy of Ethiopian Cereal Seed Systems: State Control, Market Liberalisation and Decentralisation*. Future Agricultures Working Paper 17. Sussex, Brighton, UK: Future Agricultures.

Ariga, J., and T. S. Jayne. 2010. "Private-sector Responses to Public Investments and Policy Reforms: The Case of Fertilizer and Maize Market Development in Kenya." Chapter 13 in *Proven Successes in Agricultural Development: A Technical Compendium to Millions Fed*, edited by D. J. Spielman and R. Pandya-Lorch, 349–380. Washington, DC: IFPRI.

ASTI (Agricultural Science and Technology Indicators Initiative). 2013. *ASTI Data Tool Queries for Ethiopia*. Washington, DC: IFPRI.

Benson, T., D. Spielman, and L. Kassa. 2014. *Direct Seed Marketing Program in Ethiopia in 2013: An Operational Evaluation to Guide Seed-sector Reform*. IFPRI Discussion Paper 1350. Washington, DC: IFPRI.

Beshir, A. 2005. "Farmer-based Seed Production an Alternative for Seed Security: The Ethiopian Experience." *Seed Info* 29: 8–10.

Bishaw, Z., Y. Sahlu, and B. Simane. 2008. "The Status of the Ethiopian Seed Industry." In *Farmers, Seeds, and Varieties: Supporting Informal Seed Supply in Ethiopia*, edited by M. H. Thijssen, Z. Bishaw, A. Beshir, and W. S. de Boef, 23–32. Wageningen, Netherlands: Wageningen International.

Brennan, J. P., and D. Byerlee. 1991. "The Rate of Crop Varietal Replacement on Farms: Measures and Empirical Results for Wheat." *Plant Varieties and Seeds* 4: 99–106.

Byerlee, D., and H. J. Dubin. 2008. "Crop Improvement in the CGIAR as a Global Success Story of Open Access and International Collaboration." *International Journal of the Commons* 4: 452–480.

Dalrymple, D. G. 2008. "International Agricultural Research as a Global Public Good: Concepts, the CGIAR Experience, and Policy Issues." *Journal of International Development* 20 (3): 347–379.

DCFB (DeKalb County Farm Bureau). 2004. "DeKalb County Farm Bureau—More Than a Century Old." Accessed March 2014. www.dekalbfarmbureau.org/about-fb/history-2/.

de Boef, W. S., and Z. Bishaw. 2008. "A System Perspective for Linking Farmers and Professionals Supporting Farmers' Practices in Seed Supply." In *Farmers, Seeds, and Varieties: Supporting Informal Seed Supply in Ethiopia*, edited by M. H. Thijssen, Z. Bishaw, A. Beshir, and W. S. de Boef, 47–54. Wageningen, Netherlands: Wageningen International.

DIIVA (Diffusion and Impact of Improved Varieties in Africa). 2013. "Ethiopia/Spring Bread Wheat Overview." Accessed March 2014. www.asti.cgiar.org/diiva/ethiopia/spring-bread-wheat.

Dixon, J., and A. Gulliver with D. Gibbon. 2001. *Farming Systems and Poverty—Improving Farmers' Livelihoods in a Changing World*. Rome: Food and Agricultural Organization of the United Nations; Washington, DC: World Bank.

DSA (Development Studies Associates). 2006. *Study on Improving the Efficiency of Input Markets*. Addis Ababa: Ministry of Agriculture and Rural Development, Ethiopia.

Ethiopia, CSA (Central Statistical Agency). Various years. *Agricultural Sample Survey. Report on Area and Production of Major Crops (Private Peasant Holdings, Meher Season)*. Addis Ababa.

Evenson, R. E, and D. Gollin. 2003. "Assessing the Impact of the Green Revolution, 1960 to 2000." *Science* 300 (5620): 758–762.

Fan, S. 2000. "Research Investment and the Economic Returns to Chinese Agricultural Research." *Journal of Productivity Analysis* 14 (2): 163–182.

Fan, S., P.B.R. Hazell, and S. Thorat. 2000. "Government Spending, Growth and Poverty in Rural India." *American Journal of Agricultural Economics* 82 (4): 1038–1051.

Fan, S., and P. G. Pardey. 1997. "Research, Productivity, and Output Growth in Chinese Agriculture." *Journal of Development Economics* 53: 115–137.

Flaherty, K., F. Kelemework, and K. Kelemu. 2010. "Ethiopia Country Note, Agricultural Science and Technology Indicators (ASTI) Initiative." Washington, DC: IFPRI/Ethiopian Institute of Agricultural Research.

Heisey, P. W., ed. 1990. *Accelerating the Transfer of Wheat Breeding Gains to Farmers: A Study of the Dynamics of Varietal Replacement in Pakistan*. Research Report no. 1. Mexico, D.F.: International Maize and Wheat Improvement Center (CIMMYT).

Heisey, P., M. Smale, D. Byerlee, and E. Souza. 1997. "Wheat Rusts and the Costs of Genetic Diversity in the Punjab of Pakistan." *American Journal of Agricultural Economics* 79: 726–737.

Langyintuo, A. S., W. Mwangi, A. O. Diallo, J. MacRobert, J. Dixon, and M. Banziger. 2010. "Challenges of the Maize Seed Industry in Eastern and Southern Africa: A Compelling Case for Private-Public Intervention to Promote Growth." *Food Policy* 35 (4): 323–331.

Morris, M. L. 1998. *Maize Seed Industries in Developing Countries*. Boulder, CO, USA: Lynne Rienner.

Sahlu, Y., B. Simane, and Z. Bishaw. 2008. "The Farmer-based Seed Production and Marketing Scheme: Lessons Learnt." In *Farmers, Seeds, and Varieties: Supporting Informal Seed Supply in Ethiopia*, edited by M. H. Thijssen, Z. Bishaw, A. Beshir, and W. S. de Boef, 33–47. Wageningen, Netherlands: Wageningen International.

Spielman, D. J., D. Byerlee, D. Alemu, and D. Kelemework. 2010. "Policies to Promote Cereal Intensification in Ethiopia: A Review of Evidence and Experience." *Food Policy* 35 (3): 185–194.

Spielman, D. J., and A. Kennedy. 2016. "Towards Better Metrics and Policymaking for Seed System Development: Insights from Asia's Seed Industry." *Agricultural Systems* 147: 111–122.

Spielman, D. J., and D. K. Mekonnen. 2013. *Transforming Demand Assessment and Supply Responses in Ethiopia's Seed System and Market*. Project report. Washington, DC: IFPRI.

Spielman, D. J., D. K. Mekonnen, and D. Alemu. 2012. "Seed, Fertilizer, and Agricultural Extension in Ethiopia." In *Food and Agriculture in Ethiopia: Progress and Policy Challenges*, edited by Paul Dorosh and Shahidur Rashid, 84–122. Philadelphia: University of Pennsylvania Press.

Teklewold, A., D. Alemu, S. Kiyoshi, and A. Kirub. 2012. *Seed Demand Assessment Practices, Challenges, and Options*. Farmer Research Groups (FRG) II Project "Empowering Farmers' Innovation" Series no. 5. Addis Ababa: Ethiopian Institute of Agricultural Research.

Thijssen, M. H., Z. Bishaw, A. Beshir, and W. S. de Boef. 2008. *Farmers, Seeds, and Varieties: Supporting Informal Seed Supply in Ethiopia*. Wageningen, Netherlands: Wageningen International.

Chapter 5

PERCEPTIONS, IMPACTS, AND REWARDS OF ROW PLANTING

Joachim Vandercasteelen, Mekdim Dereje Regassa, Bart Minten, and Alemayehu Seyoum Taffesse

Teff is Ethiopia's most important staple crop, but the crop is characterized by low yields. This low teff yield is seemingly explained by the limited knowledge about possible avenues for improving teff productivity, combined with problems inherent to teff botany. Teff research has received limited national and international attention—the latter presumably because of its localized importance in Ethiopia (Berhane et al. 2011; Fufa et al. 2011). Moreover, teff yields are low because of agronomic constraints that include lodging, low modern input use, small seeds, and high postharvest losses (Habtegebrial, Singh, and Haile 2007; Berhe et al. 2011; Fufa et al. 2011). Recently it has been argued that the traditional sowing technology is a major constraint to increasing teff productivity (Berhe et al. 2011). Farmers typically plant teff by broadcasting—that is, scattering teff seed by hand at a high seed rate. Alternative planting methods, such as row planting seeds or transplanting seedlings, in which the seed rate is reduced and more space between plants is given, are seen as being superior to traditional broadcasting (Berhe et al. 2011; Fufa et al. 2011). Experiments on these alternative planting methods in controlled settings have shown large and positive impacts on teff yields (Berhe et al. 2011; Fufa et al. 2011). As a consequence, the Ethiopian government rolled out a nationwide campaign in 2013 to promote the use of row planting, aiming to scale up its adoption to almost 2.5 million teff farmers.

However, the impacts of the widespread promotion campaign of row planting of teff in particular on land and labor productivity are unknown. This is mainly due to a lack of reliable and objective farm-level data. Moreover, no systematic effort has yet been put into examining farmers' perceptions after they experimented with the new sowing techniques. The contribution of this chapter is to analyze the impact of the promotion campaign of row planting of teff and to infer farmers' perception about the new planting technique and the promotion thereof. To do so, data were collected during the "pre-scale-up" phase of the promotion campaign in 2012/2013 by surveying farmers from 40 villages exposed to the promotion campaign. Data was collected by means of a large-scale randomized control trial (RCT), randomly assigning teff farmers to implement either row planting or broadcasting of teff seed on an experimental plot. The effect of receiving a promotion campaign for sowing teff seeds in rows, together with a reduced seed rate (this combination is referred to as row planting), was measured on teff farmers' land, as well as on labor productivity.

The promotion program of row planting was not found to significantly increase teff yields at farm level. These disappointing results conflict with the yield benefits realized in well-managed on-station research trials and on demonstration plots (ATA 2013a) and were lower than expected by farmers. Moreover, labor requirement increased when adopting row planting, and there was a substantial drop in labor productivity for row-planting farmers compared with the traditional broadcast planting. These results suggest why most farmers exposed to row planting of teff continued row planting in the year afterward, but only on a small part of their teff lands. In addition, the sensitivity of the yield findings with regard to the effects of "learning by doing" (that is, experienced farmers) were analyzed as well as examining scenarios where mechanized row planters would reduce labor requirements. In such scenarios, adopting of row planting would become more beneficial for farmers.

Reduced Seed Rate Technologies

Traditionally, farmers broadcast teff seed using a high seed rate of between 25 and 50 kilograms per hectare (ATA 2013a). It is argued that this practice reduces yield because the uneven distribution of seed increases competition between teff plants for water, light, and nutrients, and makes weeding more difficult once the plants have matured (Fufa et al. 2011). As a solution, it is recommended to reduce the seed rates and to plant in rows or, alternatively, to transplant seedlings from a nursery plot. Reducing the seed rate to 2.5–3.0 kilograms per hectare reduces competition between seedlings and allows for optimal tillering or branching out of the plants. By row planting or transplanting, land management and especially weeding can be done more easily. The incidence of lodging is also found to be reduced, as the stem of row-planted teff is better able to support the weight of the filled head of grain (Berhe et al. 2011; also see Chapter 3 in this book).

On-station agronomic research has resulted in the belief that the reduced seed rate technologies will increase teff productivity. Experiments on-station showed that when teff was planted in rows and appropriate types of fertilizer were used, teff yields were on average three times higher than yields obtained from traditional broadcasting (Berhe et al. 2011; ATA 2012). Given these positive results, programs to promote the technologies to teff farmers at a large scale were rolled out by the government (ATA 2013b). These programs, presented in the form of a technology package, were promoted to farmers. They included planting of seed or transplanting seedlings in rows, a reduction of the seed rate to 5 kilograms per hectare, a sowing depth of 2–3 centimeters, use of improved seed (Quncho variety), and the application of recommended levels of chemical fertilizer (DAP and urea).

In 2011 the Ministry of Agriculture (MoA), with the support of the Agricultural Transformation Agency (ATA), provided this package and extension to 1,400 farmers. On-farm experiments were done in 90 Farm Training Centers (FTC) at the local kebele administrative level in Ethiopia's four main teff-producing regions: Amhara, Oromia, Tigray, and the Southern Nations, Nationalities, and Peoples' (SNNP) region. The results of this promotion campaign showed an increase of 75 percent in teff yield (ATA 2013a). In 2012 this experiment was extended to almost 70,000 farmers from 1,337 FTCs. Data collected from 15,800 households that participated in this "pre-scale-up" phase indicated that teff yields had increased by 70 percent over the national average (Berhe et al. 2011; ATA 2013a). In 2013 the program was rolled out nationwide to reach 2.5 million farmers (ATA 2013a).[1]

Design of the Intervention

Design and Methodology

The experiment evaluated the impact of the "pre-scale-up" program of promotion of teff row planting implemented in 2012 through which the reduced seed rate technologies—as part of a package—were extended to a selected number of farmers. The design of the evaluation was in line with the rollout of the program by MoA in that year. However, some modifications were made to the rollout to ensure that the selection of farmers to be studied was completed

1 Overall, agronomic research tends to find positive effects of row planting (even if it is scaled up), but several small-scale trials with farmers showed lower effects that were sometimes statistically not significant. Moreover, the results from agronomic research conducted by the Ethiopian Institute of Agricultural Research (EIAR) showed that yield increases from implementing row planting were small and that changing seed rates, planting depths, and plant spacing did not affect teff yields significantly (see Chapter 3 in this book).

randomly. Furthermore, farmers that implemented the traditional broadcasting technology were included in the experiment to create an appropriate control group. The sample design followed a two-stage randomization approach. First, from the 23 Agricultural Growth Program (AGP) woredas (district-level administrative unit) in the Oromia region, 10 woredas were randomly selected (Figure 5.1).[2] Four FTCs were then randomly selected out of all FTCs within the selected woredas. From a total of 60 randomly selected farmers in each FTC, 20 farmers were randomly selected to be interviewed for the survey.[3] In the second stage, farmers were randomly allocated to treatment and control groups for the study, and 10 farmers were selected to do either row planting or broadcasting. The farmers in the sample were all progressive, so-called model farmers with whom agricultural extension agents, the development agents (DA), had worked with relatively closely.

There was close cooperation with the local DAs in each FTC for selecting, training, and assisting farmers who participated in the experiment. As the objective was to evaluate the impact of the program in the field, no additional assistance to DAs was provided, but extra training was received on the inclusion of control farmers into the study. DAs instructed all farmers to grow teff using the allocated sowing technology on a small experimental plot of 300 square meters. Farmers assigned to the row-planting treatment group received 150 grams (5 kilograms per hectare) of improved teff seed (Quncho) for free, while farmers in the control group received 900 grams (30 kilograms per hectare) of the same seed, also for free. Finally, all groups received at no cost identical fertilizer packages (3 kilograms of both urea and DAP) to ensure that the same amount of inputs was used on the designated experimental plot for each farmer involved in the study.

The selected farmers in the survey area were visited three times. First, the baseline survey of October 2012 collected data on the experimental plot characteristics and teff production for the production year of 2011/2012. Second,

---

2 AGP is a five-year program aimed at reducing poverty by increasing agricultural productivity and improving market access for smallholders in 83 woredas in Amhara, Oromia, SNNP, and Tigray (Berhane, Paulos, and Tafere 2011).

3 While randomization ensures the accuracy of the estimated effect, the precision of the estimation depends on the sample size. Vandercasteelen et al. (2016) provides a detailed explanation of the sample-size calculations and randomization approach. Ex ante power calculations showed an optimal sample size of about 570 farmers in the experiment, which allows a size effect of about 0.2 metric tons of changes in teff yield due to row planting. However, in anticipation of potential survey implementation problems, this sample size was increased to 800 farmers (that is, 20 farmers in each village).

FIGURE 5.1 **Map of the intervention woredas**

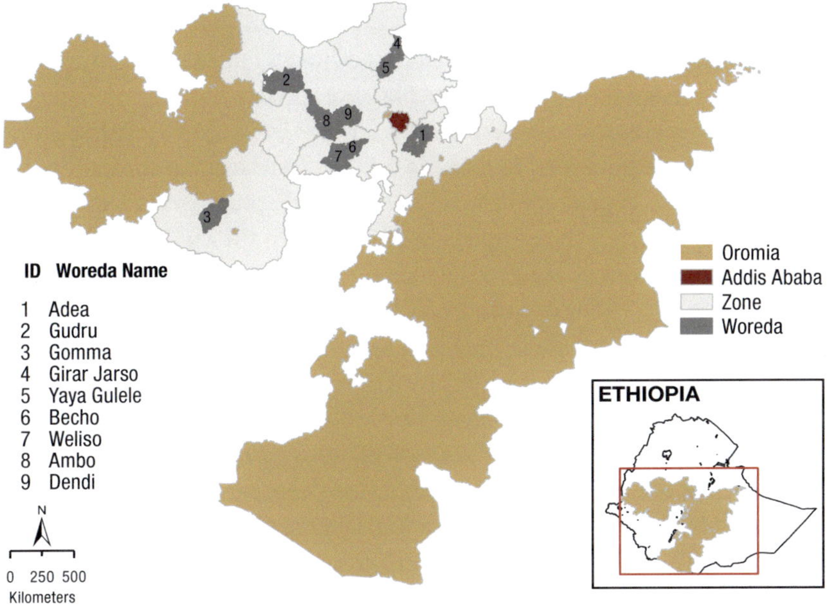

Source: Authors' illustrations, based on official maps.

Note: One of the selected woredas withdrew and is not indicated on the map.

farmers were revisited just before harvesting between November 2012 and January 2013 by enumerators from Ethiopia's Central Statistical Agency (CSA) to measure teff output from the experimental plot. Finally, an impact survey was fielded after the teff harvest in February 2013, similar to the baseline survey, with additional information collected on teff production and management practices on the experimental plot. This quantitative information was further complemented with qualitative investigations, plus a community questionnaire, administered at the same time as the impact survey, to understand the perceptions held of these new technologies by participating and nonparticipating farmers.

However, there were several issues in implementing the survey. First, one woreda did not follow the MoA's recommendations during the promotion campaign and was therefore dropped out of the experiment. Second, despite clear instructions, the assignment of farmers to the different technologies by the DAs was not implemented randomly everywhere. As a consequence, we only use the randomized data for 19 FTCs where technology assignment was done randomly.[4] Finally, in some of these "random" villages, the actual number of farmers interviewed was not equal to the target number of 20. Some of the selected farmers did not prepare their experimental plot in line with the MoA's recommendations—for example, experimental plots were too large or too small, or seed rates applied were not appropriate. The DA randomly replaced these selected farmers with other farmers from the remaining group of 40 in the village but failed to gather a total of 20 farmers in some villages. It proved difficult to engage additional broadcasting farmers in the experiment. Enumerators identified these "nonvisited" farmers in the random villages and revisited them afterward. As a consequence, the random sample consists of 537 farmers, which included both initially selected farmers (410) as well as replacement farmers (127).

Of interest in this research is the effect of implementing row planting on teff productivity for an individual farmer (*i*) in the sample. T_i is defined as the treatment variable: $T_i = 1$ for a row-planting farmer and 0 otherwise. $Y_i(T_i)$ indicates teff productivity (either land or labor) given the treatment: $Y_i(1)$ is teff productivity when a farmer implements row planting, while $Y_i(0)$ is teff productivity when the farmer uses traditional broadcasting to plant teff seed. The impact of implementing row planting on the teff productivity of the experimental plot of a farmer *i* is then the difference in teff productivity between the treatments: $\Delta_i = Y_i(1) - Y_i(0)$. This effect is measured by the Average Treatment effect on the Treated (ATT), the average gain in teff productivity a farmer realizes from using row planting for row planters:

$$E\{\Delta_i\} = E\{Y_i(1)\} - E\{Y_i(0)\}$$

In general, the yield a row-planting farmer would obtain from implementing traditional broadcasting (the counterfactual) is not observed for row-planting farmers as they were assigned to row planting only. However, the random assignment of farmers to different sowing practices and the identical input distribution implies that all farmers in the sample were statistically identical in their characteristics relevant to teff production. Hence, the observed teff productivity from traditional broadcasters could be used to identify the counterfactual of row planters. Randomization ensures that the difference in teff yield between the traditional broadcasting and row-planting farmers could be attributed solely to the sowing method. As a consequence, by taking the

4 See Vandercasteelen et al. (2013) for a complete overview of the survey implementation problems and results of analysis on nonrandomly collected data.

TABLE 5.1 Sample setup

Farmers in the sample	Broadcasting	Row planting	Total
Target of experimental sample	400	400	800
Outcome of impact survey	342	556	898
Sample of random farmers	195	342	537
Sample of random farmers with nonmissing self-reported output	193	338	531
Sample of random farmers with nonmissing crop-cut output	154	249	403

Source: Authors' calculations.

expected mean difference between the two groups, this gave an estimate of the effect of row planting on teff yield.

The implementation of row planting on the experimental plot could not be enforced, and potentially some initially assigned row-planting farmers may have shifted to the traditional broadcasting technology (or vice versa). This presents a problem in the experiment if selection occurs on the expected gains (that is, higher returns) to row planting, where adopting farmers systematically differ from those that refuse or are unable to adopt row planting. During the impact survey, careful compliance checks were made, and from the "nonvisited" farmers in the random sample, 20 farmers were identified who refused to take up the assigned technology and instead shifted to the opposite technology (18 farmers shifted from row planting to broadcasting and 2 farmers did the opposite). Even though this "one-sided noncompliance" rate is small (only 4 percent), these noncompliance issues are taken into account by comparing farmers based on their initial random assignment of (Si). The Intention-to-Treat (ITT) framework measures the effect of row planting on teff yield for those farmers who were initially selected to participate in the experiment, irrespective of the actual implementation of the assigned technology on their experimental plot. Table 5.1 gives an overview of the sample numbers that are explained in more detail below.

Characteristics of Farmers Participating in the Experiment

First, the farmers who took part in the experiment—that is, the 537 farmers, which consist of 195 control farmers and 342 treated (row-planting) farmers—are described. Table 5.2 shows the general characteristics of the interviewed farmers as well as characteristics of the experimental plots. The sample was dominated by males (99 percent) who were literate (68 percent) and on average 44 years old. The surveyed households had on average seven household members who lived half an hour away from the nearest FTC. The assigned technology was implemented on an experimental plot with an average size of 719 square meters. This is larger than the instructed size of 300 square meters because some farmers used an experimental plot that was too large. This plot was plowed on average five times and weeded twice. Most farmers did not use organic inputs, nor did they apply manure (90 percent), but all relied on the urea and DAP inorganic fertilizer that was provided for free by the DA. The teff seed provided to almost all was of the Quncho variety, obtained for free from the DA, indicating that the rollout of the distribution of that input worked well. Most farmers did not suffer from insects or other pests, plant diseases, late input supply, or problems with rain on their experimental plot.

The effect of row planting could only be directly estimated if the two groups could be shown to be balanced in the characteristics that determine teff yield (that is, education, household assets, and so on). Therefore, balancedness tests were performed by comparing the means of each variable for both groups and looking for statistically significant differences in characteristics. The balancedness property can only be tested on variables that are not affected by the treatment (that is, variables measured during the baseline) and is performed based on a regression model. In this case, the characteristics of the farmer and the experimental plot were the dependent variables and the treatment variable was the independent variable. Table 5.2 indicates that both groups of farmers were indeed similar in age, literacy, education, household size, and nonfarm income, as shown by insignificant t-values for most of the coefficients.

In Table 5.2 the difference in mean values between row planting and broadcasting farmers for variables that potentially affected the treatment status (that is, plot level variables) are reported. In general, farmers in both groups had fairly similar experimental plot characteristics, input usage (except for urea), and production practices and experienced similar shocks during the teff production period. This indicated that the only (observable) difference between both groups of farmers was the sowing technology. However, the rate of urea (grams per square meters) usage is larger for row-planting farmers, although these farmers are less likely to use herbicides compared with broadcasting farmers. Also, by design, the seed rate applied is reduced in row-planting technology. The imbalance between control and treated farmers are covered further below.

Additional qualitative information was collected from both participating and nonparticipating farmers in the experiment from all 36 villages in

TABLE 5.2 Characteristics and balancedness of control versus treated farmers

	Control (n = 195)		Treated (n = 342)
Household (head) and experimental characteristics	Mean	Difference	t-value
Age (years)	44.00	−1.04	−0.84
Gender (male = 1)	99.40	−2.79	−1.89*
Can write (yes = 1)	31.80	−6.42	−1.22
Literacy (yes = 1)	68.20	5.59	1.04
Primary education (yes = 1)	77.10	1.96	0.43
Distance to Farmer Training Center (minutes)	33.90	−0.40	−0.16
Household size (members)	7.13	−0.22	−1.06
Total agricultural assets value (ln of birr)	6.79	−0.02	−0.16
Total assets value (ln of birr)	7.25	0.09	0.44
Total land owned by household (hectares)	5.87	−0.12	−1.05
Income from other activities (yes = 1)	75.40	−7.54	−0.83
Household asked for loan (yes = 1)	14.00	4.47	1.49
Member of Iqub group (yes = 1)	35.80	0.28	0.06
Area (square meters)	719.00	−111.00	−0.99
Distance to plot from house (minutes)	11.10	0.33	0.19
Sloped plot (yes = 1)	17.30	−2.51	−0.85
High soil quality (yes = 1)	36.30	0.00	0
Number of plows (number)	4.98	−0.01	−0.06
Number of weeding (number)	1.88	0.08	0.46
Seed rate used (kilograms per hectare)	27.52	−17.00	15.30***
Organic input used (yes = 1)	11.20	−2.23	−0.71
Inorganic fertilizer used (yes = 1)	99.40	−0.28	−0.36
Manure used (yes = 1)	10.10	−3.35	−1.08
Rate of manure used (grams per square meter)	0.12	0.45	1.02
Urea used (yes = 1)	96.10	1.12	0.80
Rate of urea used (grams per square meter)	0.09	0.01	2.18**
DAP used (yes = 1)	98.90	0.00	0
Rate of DAP used (grams per square meter)	0.12	0.01	0.92
Herbicides used (yes = 1)	77.70	−8.66	−2.22**
Rate of herbicides used (100 Ethiopian birr per square meter)	0.02	0.00	−0.55
Problems of pests (yes = 1)	22.90	2.79	0.87
Problems of diseases (yes = 1)	11.20	−2.23	−0.89

(continued)

TABLE 5.2 Continued

Household (head) and experimental characteristics	Control (n = 195) Mean	Difference	Treated (n = 342) t-value
Problems of late inputs (yes = 1)	22.30	−5.59	−0.96
Days of training received on technologies (number)	2.20	−0.03	0
Visits by expert on experimental plot (number)	2.21	0.05	0

Source: Authors' calculations.

Note: Asterisks represent level of statistical significance: * (10 percent significance), ** (5 percent significance), *** (1 percent significance).

community questionnaires.[5] All of the surveyed farmers (teff farmers and community respondents) were model farmers, as they were the target of the "pre-scale-up" phase of the teff technology promotion program. Model farmers tended to be more educated and better-off farmers, making them not representative of all teff farmers in Oromia. However, this did not affect the program evaluation as these model farmers were specifically targeted by the government to adopt the new technologies first (ATA 2013c).

Regression Models

The survey design described above provided a robust framework within which the impact of row planting on teff productivity could be measured. The ITT is measured by estimating the following regression:

$$Y_i = \alpha + \beta * S_i + \varepsilon_i$$

β measures the effect of being assigned to row planting, irrespective of what technology farmers actually implemented on their experimental plot. Two robustness tests are performed to assess the sensitivity of the results. First, the characteristics in which control and treated farmers differ are included as additional control variables in the regression model. These are the variables that are significantly different as shown in Table 5.2, and include gender, seed rate, rate of urea applied, and a dummy for herbicide use. Second, as the selection of farmers to be included in the experiment was done at the village level, village fixed effects are also included in the model. By including the village dummies, this enables control for differences in village level characteristics

5 Note that the RCT used data from the 19 random FTCs, while the community questionnaire used data from all FTCs.

that might affect any teff outcome. For both models the coefficient of the ITT is only reported in the results section to ease representation.

Here, different outcomes of interest are examined. Teff yield is measured in metric tons per hectare, obtained by dividing output by area. While there is reliance on the area measured during the crop-cut survey, there are two measurements of output.[6] First, when farmers harvested and threshed output from their experimental plots, enumerators measured the teff output for the whole plot after drying using a digital balance ("yield from crop-cut"). Second, at the time of the impact survey, after the harvesting, drying, and threshing operations were completed, all farmers were asked to estimate the teff output of the experimental plot ("reported yield after harvest").[7] For both output measures, there are some missing values (see Table 5.2). For the random sample, there are six farmers for which the self-reported output is missing. There are more missing values for the crop-cut output (134), which restricts the sample to 410 farmers. In Vandercasteelen et al. (2016) the attrition in the crop-cut data is described in more detail. Additional analysis shows that attrition is not related to treatment and that our results remain once we weight the regressions with the inverse of the probability to have a nonmissing observation of crop-cut output.

Perceptions on Reduced Seed Technologies

Farmers' Perceptions

Table 5.3 shows the stated perceptions of teff farmers on broadcasting versus reduced seed rate technologies. All of these data on perceptions were inferred after farmers experimented with the new sowing technology and were collected during the impact survey. In the year the experiment was rolled out (production year 2012), traditional broadcasting was believed to yield about 0.9 metric tons per hectare and 28 bales of straw per hectare. Teff farmers believed that higher teff yields were primarily constrained by the price of

6 Area was measured during the baseline survey using ropes and tapes, and during the crop-cut survey using a compass and ropes. The two measures are strongly correlated (88 percent). Primarily the latter was used, relying only on the area measured during the baseline survey if the other area measure was missing.

7 Measurement errors might occur in area and output variables, complicating yield measures (De Groote and Traoré 2005; Carletto, Savastano, and Zezza 2013). Moreover, it is not straightforward to assess the most appropriate teff yield measure as each of these measures has its own benefits and drawbacks. See Vandercasteelen et al. (2013) for a further description of the yield measures and their correlation.

TABLE 5.3 Farmers' perception on teff production and row planting

	Number of observations	Percentage or unit stated
What is the teff yield (in metric tons per hectare) you can obtain from:		
Traditional broadcasting?	537	0.9
Broadcasting at reduced seed rate?	367	1.5
Row planting?	451	1.8
Transplanting?	165	1.8
What is the straw yield (in bales per hectare) you can obtain from:		
Traditional broadcasting?	537	28
Broadcasting at reduced seed rate?	306	27
Row planting?	448	27
Transplanting?	159	21
The most limiting factor of higher teff yields is:	537	
Price of chemical fertilizer		36
Unfavorable weather conditions		17
Declining soil quality		13
Access to improved seeds		10
Traditional sowing technique		2
The labor requirement will increase when implementing (yes = 1):	537	
Broadcasting at reduced seed rate?		12
Row planting?		95
Transplanting?		77
Are there benefits of reduced seed rate technologies (yes = 1)?	537	87
The main benefit of reduced seed rate technologies is:	466	
Saving seeds		100
Better weeding		83
Higher productivity		97

Source: Authors' calculations.

chemical fertilizer (36 percent), unfavorable weather conditions (17 percent), and declining soil quality (13 percent). Interestingly, the traditional way of sowing was generally not considered as a major limitation, but 90 percent of the teff farmers believed that the reduced seed technologies would improve teff production.[8] For those who believed these positive impacts, the new technologies were expected to save seed (100 percent), make weeding easier

8 Only 2 percent of the teff farmers responded that the sowing technique was the most important constraint on teff yields, and only 7 percent of the farmers mentioned it as one of the top three

(83 percent), and improve productivity (97 percent). Table 5.3 further reports the high yield increases expected by teff farmers when implementing row planting (93 percent higher), broadcasting at reduced seed rate (63 percent higher), and transplanting (93 percent higher).

The results reported above reflect farmers' overall beliefs on reduced teff seed rate technologies. These beliefs refer to advantages and disadvantages of reduced seed rate technologies in general and do not necessarily represent the experience of farmers on their own experimental plot. When asked about general beliefs, farmers took into account the observed results as displayed on the teff fields of other (often more successful) farmers in the village. Farmers' opinions might also be influenced by information received from extension agents, media, and training. In all instances, farmers were told that it was possible to achieve large yield increases if the reduced seed rate technologies were implemented correctly.

To induce farmers to disclose their own experiences, opinions, and implementation problems with the reduced seed rate technologies, specific perception questions about teff production on their experimental plot were asked as well (Table 5.4).[9] In this case, 87 percent of the farmers stated that teff production with row planting on their experimental plot would increase production compared with traditional broadcasting by, on average, 29 kilograms (that is, 0.7 metric tons per hectare), with all inputs (improved seed and fertilizer) being equal. While this was slightly lower than general expectations (when not referring solely to their experimental plot) of 0.9 metric tons per hectare, these numbers still illustrated the high expectations farmers had of improved teff productivity with the use of row planting. However, this also indicated that farmers had experienced lower benefits on their experimental plots personally, possibly related to implementation problems. A major concern mentioned was the increase in labor requirements associated with the use of row planting: the majority of farmers assessed the labor inputs with the planting technique to be significantly higher for men, women, and children by, on average, 1, 3, and 2 person-hours, respectively, for the experimental plot as a whole (Table 5.4).[10]

constraints, compared to 69 percent and 56 percent for the price of chemical fertilizer and unfavorable weather conditions, respectively (not reported in Table 5.3).

9 Note that these questions were only asked to farmers who had implemented the reduced seed rate technology.

10 For females, 50 percent of the farmers thought that labor input would increase (by an average of three person-hours); while for children, 62 percent of the farmers expect labor input to increase (by an average of two person-hours).

TABLE 5.4 Questions on farmers' perceptions of the effect of row planting on the experimental plot

Perceptions	Number of observations	Percentage or unit stated
Compared to traditional broadcasting and using the same seed type, inputs, etc.		
Teff production would be higher (yes = 1)?	339	87
How much (in metric tons per hectare)?	335	29
Straw production would be higher (yes = 1)?	339	55
How much (in bales per hectare)?	305	3
Compared to traditional broadcasting, labor increased (yes = 1)?	339	92
What would be the increase in labor (in hours) for:		
Male	332	1
Female	331	3
Children	326	2

Source: Authors' calculations.

Community Focus Groups' Perceptions

Given the farmers' beliefs that (1) traditional broadcasting limits teff yield and (2) reduced seed rate technologies benefit teff production, all but one community focus group expected row planting to increase teff yields (Table 5.5).[11] The sowing technique was generally not considered as a major limiting factor of teff production, but when explicitly asked whether traditional broadcasting constrained teff production, 86 percent of the community focus groups agreed that the traditional practice of broadcasting seed impeded teff productivity. When asked about the advantages of reduced seed rate technologies, all community focus groups mentioned higher teff yields, while two-thirds of the community focus groups considered the lower seed rate to be the major advantage of row planting (this was similar for broadcasting at a reduced seed rate and for transplanting).[12]

As reduced seed rate techniques are expected to bring about teff productivity benefits, community respondents were further asked to assess

11 Similar results hold for broadcasting at reduced seed rate (61 percent) and transplanting (69 percent).

12 Community respondents were asked to give the top three major advantages of the reduced seed rate technologies. A list of nine possible answers was provided: higher teff yields, higher straw yields, lower seed rate, less wastage of fertilizer, less weeding, reduced crop damage during weeding, good branching out of plants, less labor needed, and other (specify).

TABLE 5.5 Community focus groups' perception of teff production and row planting

Perceptions	Percentage or unit stated
The most limiting factor of higher teff yields is:	
Price of chemical fertilizer	47
Unfavorable weather conditions	33
Declining soil quality	3
Access to improved seeds	3
Traditional sowing technique	3
Traditional broadcasting impedes teff production	86
Teff yield would increase when using:	
Broadcasting at reduced seed rate?	61
Row planting?	97
Transplanting?	69
What is the teff yield (metric tons per hectare) you can obtain using:	
Traditional broadcasting?	0.8
Broadcasting at reduced seed rate?	1.9
Row planting?	2.0
Transplanting?	2.2
The major advantage of doing row planting (top three) is:	
Higher productivity	100
Saving seed	66
Higher straw yield	46
The major disadvantage of doing row planting (top three) is:	
Too much additional labor	100
Difficulty of doing row planting after rain	42
Sensitivity of seedlings to shortage of rains	22
Observations	**36**

Source: Authors' calculations.

the magnitude of the potential yield levels that were expected (Table 5.5). Compared with the anticipated 0.8 metric tons per hectare that could be obtained when using broadcasting, row planting was expected to increase yield on average by 136 percent to a level of 2.0 metric tons per hectare. Broadcasting at reduced seed rate was expected to increase yield by 124 percent (1.9 metric tons per hectare) and transplanting by 163 percent

(2.2 metric tons per hectare). A similar assessment was requested with respect to straw yield changes. Compared with the 28 bales of straw per hectare that could be obtained from traditional broadcasting, only transplanting was expected to decrease straw yield (by 31 percent). Teff farmers expected straw yield to be the same for broadcasting at a reduced seed rate and for row planting.

Despite the yield benefit expected by farmers, concerns were also raised about the negative effects of the new technology. The major disadvantage of both row planting and transplanting reported in all community focus groups was the large labor requirement.[13] Individual teff farmers were also asked to assess how labor needs would change when implementing the new reduced seed rate techniques (Table 5.4). Nearly all farmers feared that the labor input for row planting would increase. For example, 77 percent of the farmers thought that labor would increase significantly in the case of transplanting. Other problems mentioned by these community focus groups were the difficulty of implementing row planting after rain and the sensitivity of transplanted seedlings to a shortage of rain.

Farmers' Adoption Plans

This review of the qualitative results is concluded by examining the adoption plans with respect to row planting of farmers who implemented row planting experimental plots. Table 5.6 shows that the majority of such farmers were planning to continue to experiment with reduced seed rate technologies the year after exposure to the promotion campaign.[14] The table shows that 72 percent of the farmers reported that they planned to allocate some of their teff area to row planting, while 7 percent would implement transplanting. Farmers who were planning to implement row planting in the coming year stated that they expected higher teff yields (100 percent of the farmers), lower seed use (83 percent), and less wastage of fertilizer (30 percent) by doing so.

Yet the share of land that farmers were planning to allocate to row planting was limited. Farmers planned to plant the largest part (80 percent) of their teff

13 Community focus groups were asked to give the top three disadvantages of the reduced seed rate technology. The six possible disadvantages included too much additional labor, much harder to control the weeds, it does not give higher yields, sensitivity of seedlings to shortage of rains, difficulty of doing row planting/transplanting after rain, and other (specify).

14 Teff farmers were instructed to report the area of land they were planning to allocate to teff production in the next production season, and then they had to divide this teff production land in different parts according to the sowing technology they were planning to assign on each part. This allowed for a calculation of the average (over all teff farmers) shares of land teff farmers were going to allocate to the different sowing technologies.

TABLE 5.6 Farmers' planning strategies for the next production year

Strategies	Number of observations	Percentage
Will you allocate some part of your teff area to (yes = 1):	537	
Traditional broadcasting?		76
Broadcasting at reduced seed rate?		55
Row planting?		72
Transplanting?		7
Share of total teff production land allocated to:	526	
Traditional broadcasting?		53
Broadcasting at reduced seed rate?		27
Row planting?		19
Transplanting?		1
Total		100
The major reason for not doing row planting next year (top three) is:	155	
Too much additional labor		96
Difficulty of doing row planting after rain		25
It does not give higher yields		16
The major reason for doing row planting next year (top three) is:	378	
Higher productivity		98
Saving seed		83
Less wastage of fertilizer		30
Would you do row planting if inputs (teff seeds and fertilizer) were:	537	
Not given for free?		73
Given at a discounted price?		78
Given for free?		83
Not given for free but you had access to a row planter?		72

Source: Authors' calculations.

lands using broadcasting (that is, just over half of their teff area using traditional broadcasting and 27 percent using broadcasting at a reduced seed rate). Only 19 percent of these farmers' teff area would be allocated to row planting and 1 percent to transplanting. When all of the teff farmers that were reluctant to implement row planting or transplanting were asked why, they stated that row planting required too much additional labor, while 25 percent of the farmers responded that implementing the technology was too difficult after rainfall. These findings reinforce the conclusion of the previous section. It seems that farmers were willing to continue to experiment with row planting but only on a relatively small part of their teff land. While farmers believed in the general yield-increasing potential of row planting teff, they restricted their adoption of the planting technique to small areas.

Finally, given that inputs were provided for free during the experiment, it is possible that the composition of the provided package, or part of it, drove the decision of farmers to adopt row planting in the next year. That is, it is not certain whether it was the technology itself or the other elements in the package that caused farmers to be willing to experiment with the technology in the following year. Farmers were therefore asked if they would do row planting the year after, upon a potential change in the condition of the proposed technology package (teff seed and fertilizer) provided. If inputs were given at a discounted price or for free, more than 78 percent of the farmers indicated that they would do row planting next year (Table 5.6). If inputs were not given for free, still three-quarters of the farmers indicated that they would implement row planting the next season. Surprisingly, having access to a row-planting machine seemingly did not give an extra incentive to implement row planting. This might have been because few of the farmers had been exposed to such a machine at the time of the survey.

Impact of the Promotion Campaign of Row Planting of Teff

In the previous section, the qualitative data were reported on farmers' perceptions about the newly promoted reduced seed rate technologies for teff. This section presents the results of the quantitative analysis of the productivity impacts from being exposed to the promotion campaign.

Impact on Teff Yield

Given the widespread belief in the yield benefit of row planting, the first step in the analysis was to estimate the effect of row planting on teff yield using production data from the experimental plots. Table 5.7 reports the effect of the promotion of row planting on teff land productivity measured in the RCT. Two different yield measures are presented, the crop-cut yield and the reported yield after harvest. The third column measures the average yield attained by traditional broadcasters (the "control"), ranging between 1.10 metric tons per hectare (measured during crop-cut) and 1.13 metric tons per hectare (reported after harvest). The reported yield measure is, on average for all farmers, only 3 percent higher than the crop-cut measure of yield, possibly indicating overoptimism in output assessment by farmers. However, there is

TABLE 5.7 Effect of the promotion of row planting on teff land productivity, metric tons per hectare

Yield	Number of observations	Control (average teff yield from traditional broadcasting)	ITT	ITT with controls	ITT with village fixed effects
Yield from crop-cut	403	1.096	0.016 (0.083)	−0.092 (0.082)	−0.103 (0.062)
Yield reported after harvest	531	1.131	0.107 (0.115)	0.044 (0.137)	0.005 (0.084)

Source: Authors' calculations.

Note: ITT = yield increase obtained from row planting measured through the Intention-To-Treat (ITT) program. The column headed "ITT" reports the simple ITT coefficient of the regression of the outcome of interest on the assignment to row planting dummy. ITT with contols = adds control variables to this regression. ITT with village fixed effects = adds village fixed effects to this regression. Robust standard errors are clustered at the village level and reported in parentheses.

no evidence that row planters overestimated yields more than control farmers, as might have been done to impress enumerators or DAs.

Columns 4 through 6 report the point estimate of the treatment effect (ITT) on teff yield for the three different regression models. When focusing on the crop-cut data, the simple ITT model (column 4) shows no significant impact of the row-planting promotion program on teff yield. Implementing row planting on the experimental plot increased farmers' yield by 20 kilograms per hectare, but this effect is not statistically different from 0. The regression model that controls for the "imbalanced" characteristics between row planting and broadcasting farmers (column 5) also finds no significant impact of row planting on crop-cut yields. Similarly, the model that controls for village fixed effects (column 6) does not find significant treatment effects of row planting. In the case of reported yields just after harvest, a slightly higher effect of row planting is found, but the effect remains insignificant at the 10 percent level. Farmers who planted teff using the traditional broadcasted technique had a teff yield of 1.1 metric tons per hectare, while those who implemented row planting were able, on average, to harvest per unit area 10 percent more, resulting in a gain of 0.12 metric tons per hectare of teff. The two robustness checks in column 5 and 6 also find no significant effect of the adoption of row planting on self-reported yields.

One concern is that there are spillover effects from farmers implementing row planting (information) on the traditional broadcasting farmers. Control farmers might become aware of the agronomic benefit of using a reduced seed rate and therefore apply a lower seed rate to the traditional broadcasting sowing method. However, Table 5.3 in the previous section showed that broadcasting farmers on average applied a seed rate of 27 kilograms per hectare, which is close to the recommended "traditional" seed rate of 25 kilograms per hectare (an F-test does not indicate a significant difference). If anything, it seems that most row-planting farmers did not apply the recommended reduced seed rate of 5 kilograms per hectare. This could undermine the agronomic benefit of row planting and influence the treatment effect of row planting on teff yield. However, when controlling for the seed rate used on the experimental plot in column 5 of Table 5.7, the results are robust.

In short, no evidence is found that shows that row planting (that is, the combination of planting seeds in rows and using a reduced seed rate) improves teff yield, which is in contrast with the yield increases found in research and demonstration settings.

Impact on Labor Input and Productivity

The main complaint raised by teff farmers when implementing row planting in the qualitative section was the increased labor requirements associated with row planting teff. The impact of the adoption of row planting on labor use on the experimental plot is discussed below. "Labor requirement" is defined as total person-hours needed to grow teff on one hectare of land. This investigation of labor considers: (1) labor requirement for the different activities during teff production and (2) total labor productivity.[15] The following changes in labor input are anticipated, based on the nature of the row-planting technique: (1) Row planting requires additional tilling and farmers need to construct rows and carefully sow the seeds in them. Hence, an increase is expected in labor requirement for land preparation (small) and sowing (large). (2) Farmers were instructed to apply the fertilizer together with the seeds in the rows, and it is therefore expected that the labor requirement for applying fertilizer will increase as well. (3) The labor input for weeding is expected to decrease as row planting should make weeding easier (ATA 2012). (4) Any significant effect on the labor requirement for harvesting or threshing is not expected. (5) Depending on how the labor allocated for each of these individual activities is altered, an increase or decrease in total labor inputs is expected.

Using the detailed data collected from the experimental plots, the third column in Table 5.8 shows the labor requirement for broadcasting farmers per activity ("control") in person-hours per hectare, while (similarly to Table 5.7)

15 See Vandercasteelen et al. (2016) for a detailed impact assessment of row planting on the interhousehold and intrahousehold allocation of labor in teff production. We find that even though more labor is used from all interhousehold sources, exchange and hired labor is used relatively more, and hence households with access to exchange or hired labor seem to be in a better position to adopt row planting.

TABLE 5.8 Effect of the promotion of row planting on labor requirement and productivity

Inputs and productivity	Number of observations	Control (average teff yield from traditional broadcasting)	ITT	ITT with controls	ITT with village fixed effects
Labor input (person-hours per hectare)					
Land preparation	537	109.1	4.0 (5.8)	0.7 (5.4)	1.6 (6.4)
Planting	537	42.2	138.7*** (14.8)	138.4*** (14.1)	145.4*** (15.3)
Fertilizer application	537	14.6	40.6*** (5.8)	38.9*** (6.0)	41.6*** (5.9)
Weeding	537	265.8	34.8* (20.7)	28.8 (20.4)	37.4 (22.1)
Harvesting	537	175.7	−0.0 (9.9)	−5.2 (9.2)	−4.2 (9.5)
Threshing	537	217.2	−2.0 (12.6)	−9.6 (11.6)	−7.8 (13.6)
Total	537	884.2	255.3*** (48.7)	227.9*** (45.2)	266.0*** (50.7)
Labor productivity (kilograms per person-hour)					
Output from crop-cut	403	1.568	−0.445*** (0.130)	−0.588*** (0.137)	−0.558*** (0.098)
Output reported after harvest	531	1.643	−0.358** (0.164)	−0.373** (0.172)	−0.474** (0.121)

Source: Authors' calculations.

Note: ITT = yield increase obtained from row planting measured through the Intention-To-Treat (ITT) program. The column headed ITT reports the simple ITT coefficient of the regression of the outcome of interest on the assignment to row planting dummy; column 5 adds control variables to this regression; and column 6 adds village fixed effects to this regression. Robust standard errors are clustered at the village level and reported in parentheses. Asterisks represent level of statistical significance at 10 percent (*), 5 percent (**), and 1 percent (***).

the next columns report the ITT of row planting, measured in the three regression models. For simplicity, we only discuss the results of the simple ITT regression (column 4), but results are found to be robust in the two other regressions. As expected, there was an increase in labor input for land preparation (but not significant), especially for the sowing operation. While broadcasting one hectare of teff on average only took 42 person-hours, row planting required an additional 139 person-hours (or about 20 person-days extra per hectare). The labor requirement for applying fertilizer also increased significantly. Surprisingly, the labor requirement for weeding also increased, in contrast to expectations (that is, row planting was expected to make weeding easier). This finding may confirm statements from some farmers that high teff seeding rates help in controlling weeds. The labor input for harvesting and threshing did not change.

As a consequence of all these changes in labor inputs by activity, the total labor requirements for row planting were significantly higher than for broadcasting. The total labor input to produce a teff crop when the seed is broadcast is estimated to be 884 person-hours of labor, while implementing row planting is estimated to require an additional total labor input of 255 person-hours. This corresponds to 126 and 163 person-days per hectare, respectively, representing an increase in labor of 29 percent when row planting is used. Note that these assessments were done on a relatively small plot, and while care was taken in the data-collection process, collection of accurate labor data are notoriously difficult. Caution in interpretation of such data is therefore required.

The same procedure for assessing land productivity was used to assess the change in labor productivity using different output measurements. Labor productivity is measured as total teff output (in kilograms) divided by total labor input (in person-hours) for producing teff. This allows an estimate to be made of the effect of row planting on respectively "labor productivity from crop-cut" and "reported labor productivity after harvest" in the last two rows of Table 5.8. The ITT measured in column 3 shows that row planting has a strong and highly significant negative effect on labor productivity. Using the traditional broadcasting practice, farmers were able to produce 1.6 kilograms of teff for each person-hour of labor. When implementing row planting, this is reduced to between 1.1 and 1.3 kilograms per person-hour. Therefore, row planting is found to decrease labor productivity by between 22 and 28 percent. Similar conclusions are drawn from the regressions with controls for additional variables (column 5) or village fixed effects (column 6), and the effect of row planting is found to be even greater in magnitude.

Toward Understanding the Determinants of Farmers' Adoption of Row Planting

Cost-Benefit Analysis of Row Planting Versus Broadcasting

Farmers will switch from traditional broadcasting to row planting of teff only if the benefit of doing so outweighs the costs. Implementing row planting tends to have a positive (yet moderate) yield effect, but it also requires substantially more labor. Both effects can be combined in a simple cost-benefit-analysis (CBA) framework to analyze whether it is profitable for the farmers in this sample to adopt row planting or not. This was done by comparing profits (benefits minus costs) in each scenario. As claimed in the promotion

TABLE 5.9 Cost-benefit analysis of implementing row planting versus traditional broadcasting for teff farmers on one hectare of teff land

		Quantity		Monetary value (birr)		
Type of changes	Price (birr)	Traditional broadcasting	Change for row planting	Traditional broadcasting	Row planting	Change for row planting
Changes in benefits						
Teff output (metric tons)	10,700	1.131	0.107	12,102	13,247	1,145
Changes in costs						
Labor (person-days)						
Land preparation	28.0	15.6	0.6	430.2	445.9	−15.8
Sowing	28.0	6.0	19.8	169.4	726.2	−556.8
Applying fertilizer	27.0	2.1	5.8	55.7	210.5	−154.9
Weeding	29.0	38.0	5.0	1,097.4	1,241.0	−143.7
Harvesting	26.0	25.1	0.0	660.1	660.1	0.0
Threshing	30.0	31.0	−0.3	924.7	916.1	8.5
Seed (kilograms)						
Quncho	11.0	30.0	25.0	321.0	53.5	267.5
Total changes in cost-benefit analysis						
Difference in profits when adopting row planting (birr per hectare)						550

Source: Authors' calculations.

campaign, the benefits of row planting are increased yield and reduced seed cost, while our empirical assessment shows that labor costs are higher. It is assumed that the use of other inputs (such as fertilizer) is the same when implementing either row planting or broadcasting. The first column of Table 5.9 gives an overview of the different changes in benefits and costs that are considered in this CBA. The output is valued at the market prices of teff in Ethiopian birr.[16] Farmers using row planting and those using traditional broadcasting face different costs associated with different levels of use of labor and seed.

To measure profits in monetary values, information was collected on the input and output prices from the AGP community questionnaires for the AGP villages in Oromia. Average prices in Ethiopian birr (per unit stated) across the different villages in the AGP survey are presented in column 2. Teff prices refer to the price of one metric ton of white teff during the year prior to the survey, while wages are average daily wages for each production activity

16 In February 2013, US$1.00 = 18.40 birr.

during the same year over all villages. As prices were reported in person-days, the unit of labor input was converted into person-days (by assuming a work-day of seven hours). As no information on the price of Quncho seed was collected at the time of planting, this was estimated to be 11 birr (based on the average CSA producer price data collected at that time of year).

The changes in monetary value of teff production were calculated for both sowing technologies for one hectare of land. To do so, Table 5.9 reports the quantities of output obtained and input needed in teff production when using the traditional broadcasting and row-planting technologies, respectively. Output and labor data are the observed average values, taken from Table 5.7 and Table 5.8. The reported yield after harvest is used, along with the yield benefit measured by the simple ITT in column 3 of Table 5.7. The seed rate for farmers who broadcast is fixed at 30 kilograms per hectare and for those who use row planting at 5 kilograms per hectare. The final column of Table 5.9 then reports the difference in birr for each benefit or cost associated with teff production when row planting rather than traditional broadcasting, by multiplying prices by quantities.

The results in Table 5.9 show that, given the costs in teff production considered here, and assuming a farmer reported a yield increase of 10 percent, the adoption of row planting is profitable for teff farmers. The implementation of row planting on the experimental plot resulted in an additional profit of 550 birr in teff production. This is because the increase in the monetary value of output sales (1,145 birr) combined with seed saving (268 birr) compensates for the costs associated with the additional labor (863 birr) required when implementing row planting.

However, when this analysis is undertaken using the alternative yield data from the experimental plots that were obtained using crop-cuts, for which the average yield difference between the two planting techniques is much less, row planting is shown not to be beneficial for teff farmers. Farmers using row planting would actually incur a loss of more than 424 birr per hectare. Using the crop-cut yield data on teff output, the labor cost of row planting (816 birr) outweighs the benefits of row planting associated with slightly higher output sales (171 birr) and seed saving (268 birr). Hence, the yield increase achieved by farmers using row planting together with the labor requirements for doing so determine whether row planting is more profitable for teff farmers than the traditional broadcast method of planting. Therefore, the following sections examine two potential interventions that might make the adoption of row planting more assuredly beneficial to teff farmers by means of a sensitivity analysis of the above CBA.

Learning by Doing

When farmers adopt new technologies, it is their familiarization and learning over time that is required for such technologies to be implemented efficiently, and this ultimately leads to higher yield benefits and lower labor costs over time. This could explain why studies of various teff planting techniques in more supervised and controlled settings (McGuire 2013) found teff yield increases under row planting of at least twice those obtained when traditional broadcasting was used. In such studies, farmers were more intensively trained and assisted by private extension agents on the correct implementation of the row-planting technology. To illustrate the effects of differential yield increases because of such effects, Figure 5.2 shows a sensitivity analysis of the rewards (in birr) from changes to row planting from traditional broadcasting for different yield benefits (measured in percentage) from row planting. This analysis assumes that learning by doing does not affect labor productivity. As there is a certain degree of inaccuracy (variance) in this estimated yield effect, this also leads to a variance in expected profits. The estimated yield effect in the reported data after harvest has an estimated standard deviation of 0.075. Therefore, Figure 5.2 also shows the variance in profits for each yield increase as a vertical line (the error band).[17]

Figure 5.2 illustrates that if yield gains from row planting compared with broadcasting increase, profits per unit land will increase as well. The solid line assumes that learning increases linearly—that is, each year farmers are able to achieve the same yield gain of 10 percent. The benefits of row planting start to outweigh the costs only if the yield increases are larger than 8 percent. As described in the CBA, switching from traditional broadcasting to row planting is respectively loss making (based on the 2 percent yield increase in the crop-cut yield data) or beneficial (based on the 10 percent yield increase in the reported yield data). But if yields were to increase well beyond the break-even point of the 8 percent, implementing row planting would become considerably more profitable for teff producers. If, for example, a yield increase of 75 percent is achieved (ATA 2013b), farmers who adopted row planting could realize a profit of 8,000 birr, exceeding that which would be obtained through the traditional broadcasting technique. The dashed line in Figure 5.2 is a logarithmic curve, illustrating the case of when teff farmers learn about row

17 This error band is constructed by respectively adding and subtracting the standard error of 0.075 (per hectare more or less, which is about 6 percent) to the estimated yield effect of 10 percent and calculating the associated profits.

FIGURE 5.2 Sensitivity of profits with respect to yield improvements associated with use of new technology

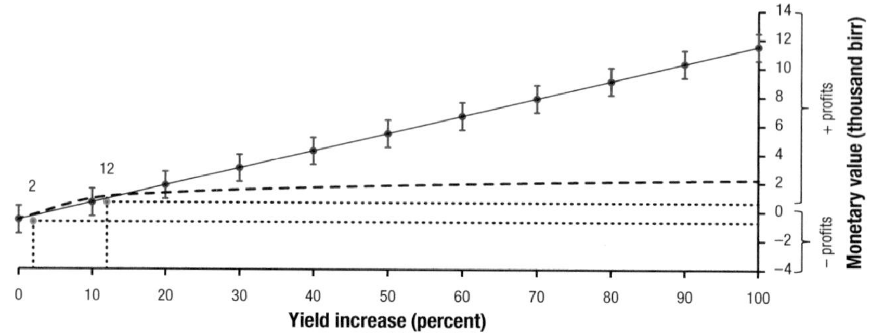

Source: Authors' calculations.

Note: Benefits to the farmer when producing teff over 1 hectare of land under row planting compared with broadcasting for different specified yield levels (given that labor productivity and seed cost remain the same). The solid line assumes linear increasing learning over time, while the dashed line assumes a logarithmic (more stagnating) pattern of learning. Vertical lines represent the yield effect as measured in the experimental plot data (crop-cuts and reported yield after harvest).

planting, implying that yield benefits decrease after a while, and the increase in monetary value slows down (around 2,000 birr).

Mechanization

A second solution to improve the profitability of row planting at farm level, given the increased requirement for labor, is to promote the mechanization of teff row sowing. Row planters are either human or animal-drawn machines that allow for opening and closing the furrows (rows), drilling the seed, and in some cases the application of fertilizer. Two types of row planters are currently being tested at the Ethiopian Institute of Agricultural Research (EIAR): the basic Type One row planter and the more advanced Type Two row planter. Both prototypes feature a dual hopper with four rows that allow for furrow opening, seeding, and furrow closing. The Type Two prototype also allows for simultaneous application of fertilizer in the furrows.

Row planters are believed to improve both the land and the labor productivity of row planting. The planters allow for a more precise adjustment for the (lower) seed rate and a uniform seed distribution, possibly leading to positive yield effects. The proper construction of furrows eases land preparation and the creation of rows as well as the sowing activity itself (Ayele 2013). Moreover, the mechanization might reduce weed infestation and drive down the cost of weeding (ATA 2013c). Temesgen (1999) found that an animal-drawn, open-furrow row planter saved labor input by one-third and by two-thirds if a closed-furrow row planter was used, while it increased yield by 30 percent.

To assess the profitability of adopting a mechanical row planter, the internal rate of return (IRR) of investment is calculated. The IRR refers to the discount rate at which the net present value (NPV) of the benefits equalize the NPV of all cost associated with adopting the mechanical row planter. The higher the IRR, the more profitable and hence the more desirable an investment in a row planter. To calculate the IRR, the benefits and costs were taken into account as presented in Table 5.9, but additionally the associated purchase costs of the row planter was factored in (the cost associated with the use of fertilizer was also included, as per agronomic recommendations). An individual farmer could choose to adopt the cheaper Type One or more expensive Type Two row planter priced at 5,000 birr and 8,000 birr, respectively. Both types are assumed to achieve (at least) the same yield increase over broadcast seeding of 2 or 10 percent—that is, the same yield increment from implementing row planting by hand.[18] As the main benefit of row planting by machine is the reduction in workload and labor cost compared with row planting by hand, the effect of the row planter on IRR is presented for different levels of labor input savings—that is, the number of person-hours that can be saved when using a mechanical row planter instead of doing row planting by hand.[19]

Figure 5.3 shows the high IRR that farmers can achieve when adopting a row planter for different labor use inputs (in percentages). Figure 5.3 distinguishes between the Type One and Type Two row planter and between the two increases in yield measured in the data.[20] Due to its lower initial cost, the Type One row planter has a higher IRR than the Type Two. If a labor input reduction of 50 percent is achieved and the row planter has a timespan of five years, the IRR for the Type One row planter is 150 percent while the IRR for

18 This is likely an underestimation of the yield effect of the row planter, as it should allow for additional yield improvements over row planting by hand. Moreover, the Type Two row planter allows for simultaneous application of seeds and fertilizer and should therefore have additional yield and labor effects. Figure 5.2 illustrates the effect of different yield levels on the profitability of a row planter, including those much higher than 2 or 10 percent. As the row planter is expected to achieve higher yield levels than 2 or 10 percent, these numbers can be interpreted as lower bounds for assessing the actual profitability of the row planters.

19 The labor-saving effect of the row planting should be expressed in constructing the rows as well as weeding and applying fertilizer. It is thereby assumed that the row planter affects both planting and land preparation and general cultivation, but not weeding, harvesting, and postharvesting. For simplicity, it is assumed that the row planter affects both activities in the same way (for example, a 10 percent increase in labor input corresponds to 30 person-hours fewer for sowing and 36 person-hours fewer for cultivation).

20 A depreciation rate of five years is assumed. Assuming a depreciation rate of ten years has a small positive effect on the IRR (about 2 percent).

FIGURE 5.3 **Sensitivity of internal rate of return (IRR) with respect to row planter type and labor-input saving when buying a row planter**

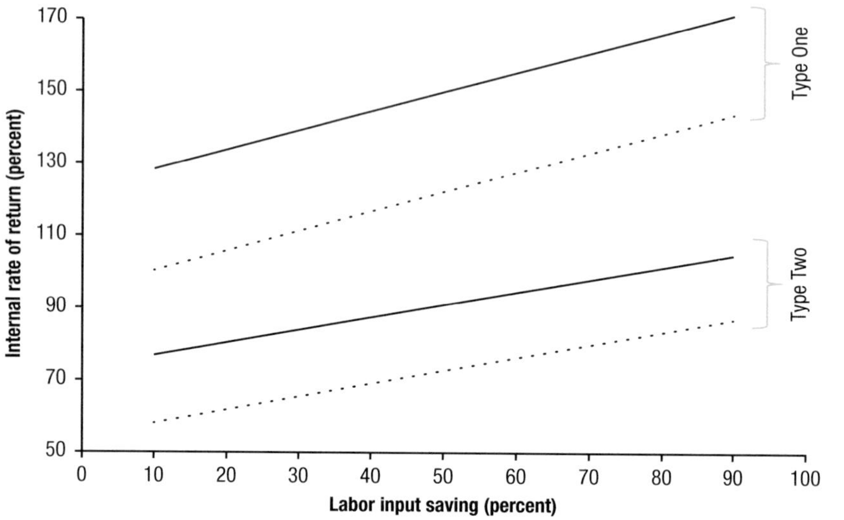

Source: Authors' calculations.

Note: IRR for the farmer when buying a Type One row planter (at 5,000 birr: above two lines) or a Type Two row planter (at 8,000 birr: below two lines) when farming 1 hectare of teff under row planting. For each type, the upper (solid) line assumes the yield increase of 10 percent measured in the reported yield data, while the lower (dashed) line assumes a yield increase of 2 percent as measured in the crop-cut yield data. Different levels of input saving are assumed as well as a depreciation rate of five years.

the Type Two row planter is 91 percent. Figure 5.3 also shows that the IRR increases if the adoption of the row planter achieves a higher reduction in labor input. Finally, the effect of higher yield levels is illustrated by comparing the IRR based on both the yield increases measured in the crop-cut and reported yield data. As expected, the higher yield increase measured in the reported data implies a higher IRR for the row planters.

An alternative solution to promote mechanical row planter adoption by farmers is to allow farmers to share a row-planting machine. Sharing a technology is an attractive possibility as it would allow the costs to decrease, such as in the case of the nondivisible row planter.[21] If farmers are assumed to adopt a row-planting machine in a group of ten persons with an average of 1 hectare of teff per farmer, and where each farmer pays an equal share in the purchase cost (that is, 10 percent of the initial purchase cost), Figure 5.4 reports that the IRR for the two row planters over different levels of labor input saving

21 The teff farmers in the sample cultivate on average half a hectare of teff land.

FIGURE 5.4 Sensitivity of internal rate of return (IRR) with respect to labor input saving when sharing a row planter

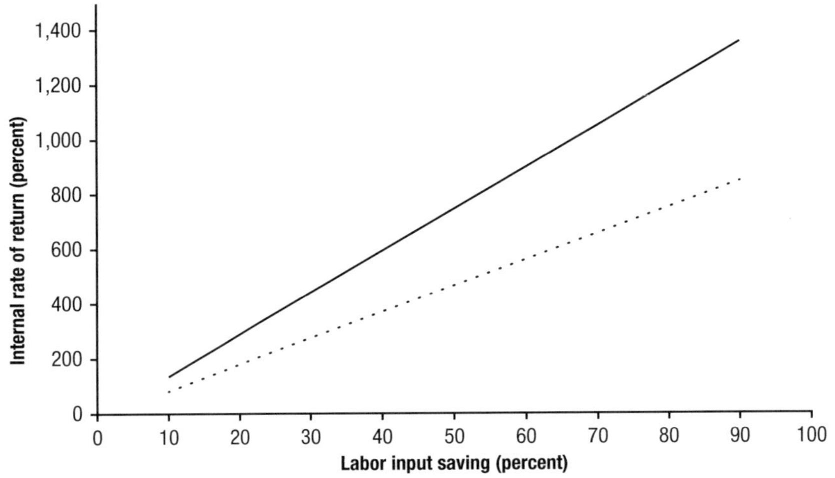

Source: Authors' calculations.

Note: IRR for the farmer when sharing a Type One row planter (initial cost of 500 birr: upper [solid] line) or Type Two row planter (initial cost of 800 birr: lower [dashed] line) with five-year depreciation for 1 hectare of teff under row planting.

changes quickly. Figure 5.4 differs from Figure 5.3 by a lower initial cost as well as an additional variable cost of renting the row planter (assuming 100 birr a day). Figure 5.4 shows that the scenario of sharing the row planter leads to much higher IRR levels and hence the row planter becomes a more profitable investment. Similarly, if half of the labor input is saved, the Type One row planter has an IRR of 911 percent; while the Type Two row planter achieves an IRR of 569 percent.

High returns are found in the adoption of row planters. While research on the field performance of the different row planter prototypes is currently under way, many challenges to adoption need to be considered. First, the row planter machine is a nondivisible and capital-intensive technology with an initial high liquidity requirement for purchase that some farmers might not be able to manage upfront. Partial adoption is impossible and, unless rental markets develop, smaller and credit-constrained farmers will be less likely to adopt the planters. Second, the suitability and performance of the row planter depends on the agroecological conditions (for example, row planters are difficult to use in vertisols), and significant research efforts toward developing suitable prototypes are required. Finally, the supply of mechanized technologies requires local production, infrastructure, and maintenance. These elements associated with the use of the row-planting machines are currently assessed as being underdeveloped in Ethiopia (Ayele 2013).

Conclusion

Given the limits on suitable arable land and a rapidly growing population, Ethiopia will need to scale up the adoption of yield-increasing technical innovations to ensure continued agricultural growth and to safeguard national food security. This study of row planting of teff in Ethiopia has sought to gain more insights into how the promotion of improved technologies can possibly increase farmers' teff production. Teff is Ethiopia's most important staple crop, but the national yield levels are low. Traditionally teff seed is broadcasted at high seed rates (typically 30 kilograms per hectare). It is believed that this impedes teff production because the uneven seed distribution makes weeding more difficult and increases competition between seedlings. By planting seed in rows at a low seed rate instead, yields have been shown to improve significantly in agronomic trials conducted on research stations. Field demonstrations of row planting showed that teff yields increased on average by 70 percent compared with the national average (ATA 2013a). As a consequence, these new technologies have been promoted to Ethiopian teff farmers on a large scale. However, there is a lack of reliable and objective data to measure the impact of widespread promotion campaigns of such improved teff technologies. The goal of this analysis was to fill this gap and provide evidence on the impact of the promotion of row planting of teff at the farm level. With quantitative and qualitative data combined, the effect of the promotion campaign on teff farmers was assessed. The main findings are as follows: First, exposed farmers were found to have a positive attitude toward row planting (and reduced seed rates in general) and believed that row planting had a large yield-increasing potential. Many plan to adopt row planting but only on a relatively small part of their plots, seemingly indicating that the farmers were concerned with the labor requirement and that more knowledge and experience was needed in implementing the technology.

Second, by implementing row planting, farmers experienced an increase in teff yield of between 2 and 10 percent, on average, but the effect is not found to be significantly different from 0. These results therefore contrast with the larger impacts measured in more controlled settings (Abayu 2012; Tolosa 2012; ATA 2013c; McGuire 2013) or with farmers' expectations. The results reported here cannot be directly compared to other sources, but they seem to be in line with farmers' perceptions in the field (K. Assefa, EIAR, personal communication, October 10, 2013). An intensive support program to significantly raise teff yields with use of the new technologies, as provided in the experimental settings, would require public resources that are not readily available. As such, the results of this impact evaluation are likely to reflect the outcome that would be achieved if a national program were to be rolled out along these lines.

The difference in magnitude of the estimated and claimed yield effect of row planting of teff is seemingly related to farmer field conditions and the design of the experiment. The high yield benefits claimed by the promotion campaign were measured at research stations or on demonstration plots, while this study's yield benefits reflect the effect of a promotion program at farm level, which considers farm-level realities and possible deficiencies in the extension program. Farmers might face different constraints in implementing new technologies on their farms than in research settings, and they might lack technical support resulting from implementation problems with the promotion campaign. The yield benefits from this study further measured the direct effect of row planting by being able to separate the sowing effect from other benefits related to the package or other factors that may have confounded the effect of row planting. In contrast with other assessments, farm-level data were further collected by independent enumerators; the row-planting treatment was randomized over similar farmers, all participating farmers received the same inputs; and safeguards were put in place to control farmers' inaccurate yield assessment, exaggerated expectations, and possible influence by extension agents and media.

Third, a substantial increase is found in labor input in the case of row planting. As expected, additional labor input is needed for sowing the seeds in rows and applying the fertilizer. The total person-hours needed to row plant 1 hectare of teff is more than one-third higher than in the case of traditional broadcasting, and it is estimated that row planting requires about 36 person-days of extra work per hectare compared to traditional broadcasting. It is also found that row planting not only increases total labor requirements but also significantly decreases labor productivity by between 22 percent and 28 percent. This implies that farmers need to invest more labor in teff production to obtain the same output that they would have got from broadcasting. This finding is crucial, as the most important yardstick for farmers' adoption is not increased land productivity but labor productivity (Moser and Barrett 2006).

Fourth, both the land and labor productivity effects have been combined in a cost-benefit analysis (CBA) for a comparison of the adoption of row planting with traditional broadcasting. As the cost of the additional labor requirement is compensated by the benefits teff farmers receive from implementing row planting, they earn 550 birr in the self-reported yield data and incur a loss of 424 birr in the crop-cut data. The CBA showed that the increase in teff yield outweighed the cost of the extra labor in the first year of adoption if yields increased by more than 8 percent and therefore made the investments worthwhile. Moreover, the results also suggested that the adoption of suitable and functional row planters had high returns to investments and that farmers with access to such row planters would be able to reduce their labor requirements for the implementation of row planting (and possibly have an additional yield-increasing effect as well).

This study points to a number of policy recommendations. First, while the agronomic superiority of the row-planting technology cannot be disproved, the results indicate that to achieve the desired adoption effects, significant effort should be put into the design and implementation of more effective promotion campaigns for such improved technologies. There is often a big gap between the supply of new technologies and their efficient adoption, since innovations spread slowly and require different management skills (Moser and Barrett 2006; Duflo, Kremer, and Robinson 2008; Collier and Dercon 2014). Farmers need to be allowed to learn, therefore continuous efforts in the extension of field assistance to farmers are needed. Correct implementation of the technology is expected to bring about larger yield increases, as illustrated by the agronomic research results in controlled settings (and the CBA). Second, it seems that the extra cost of labor requirements is not sufficiently taken into account in the current program design. The development of a suitably adapted mechanical row planter to stimulate the adoption of row planting should have large rates of return and lead to higher adoption rates. Third, on-farm constraints toward adoption should be further assessed with careful monitoring, learning, and evaluation—all of which are required to improve extension approaches for successful scaling up of adoption of the row-planting technology for teff.

References

Abayu, B. 2012. "Agronomic and Economic Effects of Blended Fertilizers under Planting Method on Yield and Yield Components of Teff in Wereda Laelay Maychew, Central Tigray, Ethiopia." Master's thesis, Mekelle University, Mekelle, Ethiopia.

ATA (Agricultural Transformation Agency). 2012. *Annual Report: Transforming Agriculture in Ethiopia*. Addis Ababa, Ethiopia.

———. 2013a. *Results of 2012 New Teff Technologies Demonstration Trials Draft Report*. Addis Ababa, Ethiopia.

———. 2013b. *Value Chain Programs: Teff.* Accessed July 15, 2013. www.ata.gov.et/programs/value-chain-programs/teff/. Addis Ababa, Ethiopia.

———. 2013c. *Working Strategy for Strengthening Ethiopia's Teff Value Chain Vision, Systemic Challenges, and Prioritized Interventions*. Addis Ababa, Ethiopia.

Ayele, S. 2013. "Improved Access and Use of Mechanization in the Teff Value Chain." Presentation made for the conference on "Improved Evidence towards Better Policies for the Teff Value Chain," Addis Ababa, Ethiopia, 2013.

Berhane, G., Z. Paulos, and K. Tafere. 2011. *Foodgrain Consumption and Calorie Intake Patterns in Ethiopia*. Ethiopia Strategy Support Paper (ESSP) II Working Paper 23. Addis Ababa, Ethiopia: International Food Policy Research Institute (IFPRI).

Berhe, T., Z. Gebretsadik, S. Edwards, and H. Araya. 2011. "Boosting Teff Productivity Using Improved Agronomic Practices and Appropriate Fertilizer." In *Achievements and Prospects of Teff Improvement,* edited by K. Assefa, T. Solomon, and Z. Chanyalew, 133–140. Proceedings of the Second International Workshop, November 7–9, 2011, Debre Zeit, Ethiopia.

Carletto, C., S. Savastano, and A. Zezza. 2013. "Fact or Artifact: The Impact of Measurement Errors on the Farm Size–Productivity Relationship." *Journal of Development Economics* 103: 254–261.

Collier, P., and S. Dercon. 2014. "African Agriculture in 50 Years: Smallholders in a Rapidly Changing World." *World Development* 63: 92–101.

De Groote, H., and O. Traoré. 2005. "The Cost of Accuracy in Crop Area Estimation." *Agricultural Systems* 84 (1): 21–38.

Duflo, E., M. Kremer, and J. Robinson. 2008. "How High Are Rates of Return to Fertilizer? Field Experiments in Evidence from Kenya." *American Economic Review* 98 (2): 482–488.

Fufa, B., B. Behute, R. Simons, and T. Berhe. 2011. "Teff Diagnostic Report: Strengthening the Teff Value Chain in Ethiopia." Addis Ababa, Ethiopia: Agricultural Transformation Agency.

Habtegebrial, K., B. R. Singh, and M. Haile. 2007. "Impact of Tillage and Nitrogen Fertilization on Yield, Nitrogen Use Efficiency of Teff (*Eragrostis tef* (Zucc.) Trotter) and Soil Properties." *Soil and Tillage Research* 94 (1): 55–63.

McGuire, T. 2013. Personal communication.

Moser, C. M., and C. B. Barrett. 2006. "The Complex Dynamics of Smallholder Technology Adoption: The Case of SRI in Madagascar." *Agricultural Economics* 35 (3): 373–388.

Temesgen, M. 1999. "Animal-drawn Implements for Improved Cultivation in Ethiopia: Participatory Development and Testing: Improving Farmers' Animal Traction." Proceedings of the Workshop of the Animal Traction Network for Eastern and Southern Africa (ATNESA), Mpumalanga, South Africa, September.

Tolosa, S. 2012. "Effects of Inorganic Fertilizer Types and Sowing Methods of Variable Seed Rates on Yield and Yield Components of Teff [*Eragrostis tef* (Zucc.) Trotter] in Ada'a Woreda, Central Ethiopia." Master's thesis, Haramaya University, Haramaya, Ethiopia.

Vandercasteelen, J., M. Dereje Regassa, B. Minten, and A. S. Taffesse. 2013. *Scaling-Up Adoption of Improved Technologies: The Impact of the Promotion of Row Planting on Farmers' Teff Yields in Ethiopia*. ESSP II Working Paper 60. Addis Ababa, Ethiopia: International Food Policy Research Institute.

———. 2016. *Perceptions, Impacts, and Rewards of Row Planting of Teff.* ESSP III Working Paper 65. Addis Ababa, Ethiopia: International Food Policy Research Institute.

Chapter 6

MARKET ACCESS, TEFF PRODUCTION, AND FERTILIZER USE OVER TIME

Mekamu Kedir Jemal, Emily Schmidt, and Helina Tilahun

This chapter aims to provide a spatial interpretation of teff production while exploring changes in infrastructure and agricultural inputs over time. Geographic overlap between transportation investments, fertilizer application, and increases in teff production provide a qualitative assessment of how road expansion, agricultural production, and agricultural inputs have changed over time in more remote areas of Ethiopia. The study covered in this chapter uses a rich set of data on agricultural indicators collected by Ethiopia's Central Statistical Agency (CSA) as well as Geographic Information Systems (GIS) data on roads, agroecologies, and other biophysical information to analyze the transformation of teff production patterns in Ethiopia since 1997.

The remainder of the chapter is as follows. The first section provides an overview of teff production in Ethiopia as well as a brief literature review of previous studies that examined the overlap of agricultural potential with regards to infrastructure development. The next section describes the data and methodology used to explore teff production, fertilizer application, and infrastructure development over time. The chapter then discusses the spatial heterogeneity of teff production patterns over time taking into account agroecological conditions, transportation infrastructure, and market access. Fertilizer application trends on teff production over time and links to major markets within the country are explored before the chapter ends with a conclusion.

Teff Production in Ethiopia

Cereals dominate crop production in Ethiopia, and teff (*Eragrostis tef*) is one of the most important crops in the country. In the meher season of 2012/2013, cereals were grown on 71 percent of the total area cultivated and made up approximately 61 percent of total agricultural production (Ethiopia, CSA 2013). Teff accounted for the largest share of cereal area and second largest share of cereal production after maize. Teff and maize comprise roughly 49 percent of area planted and half of total cereal production. Almost 28 percent of total cereal area and 19 percent of total cereal production was dedicated to teff in 2012/2013 (Ethiopia, CSA 2013).

Teff production area continues to expand, and a greater number of farmers are producing teff. Approximately 6.3 million farmers were growing teff in 2013, compared with 4.4 million farmers in 2001/2002. Similarly, teff area planted increased from 1.8 million hectares in 1997 to 2.7 million hectares in 2013 (Table 6.1). Although teff area continues to increase, the growth in production has been driven more by yield increases (that doubled) over time than area increases. This increase is due to a number of factors including relatively high market prices of teff grain and straw. In addition, teff is versatile, as it grows in a wide variety of agroclimatic conditions, including elevations from sea level to 2,800 meters above sea level (masl), under a similarly wide variety of moisture, temperature, and soil conditions. Although teff area has expanded over time, other cereal area has increased as well, and the overall area share of teff remains relatively unchanged from previous years.

Earlier studies have looked at effects of transportation infrastructure on agricultural production and input choices in Africa south of the Sahara and Ethiopia. Dorosh and Schmidt (2010) underlined the risk of constrained production due to demand constraints in terms of low population densities and large travel times to urban centers. Reducing travel time from remote rural areas expands the feasible market size. Dorosh et al. (2009) found that agricultural production is highly correlated with the amount of time it takes to reach an urban market. Research, specifically analyzing teff production in Ethiopia, reported an increasing intensification of teff production in rural areas that are well connected to cities (Minten et al. 2013a). Minten et al. (2013b) reported that teff producer prices decreased (particularly of white teff) as farmers became farther from Addis Ababa. They note that increasing investments in road infrastructure to decrease transportation costs increases the prices that farmers receive on teff.

Previous research also suggests that distance to a market affects fertilizer application choices. An earlier study by Demeke et al. (1998) underlined the need for efficient access to markets to ensure profitability of fertilizer. For example, the Value to Cost Ratio (VCR) for teff declined by 55 percent between 1992 and 1997 due to rising fertilizer prices relative to output prices. Similarly, analysis by Dorosh et al. (2010) report that adoption of high-productive and high-input technology was negatively correlated with travel time to urban centers. Yu et al. (2011) found that households in Ethiopia that adopted fertilizer tended to have better market access and improved

TABLE 6.1 Teff production characteristics

Season	Number of holders (millions)	Area (millions of hectares)	Production (millions of metric tons)	Yield (metric tons per hectare)	Total cereal area (millions of hectares)	Teff area share (%)
1997/1998	—	1.75	1.31	0.7	5.6	31.2
1998/1999	—	2.09	1.64	0.8	6.7	31.0
1999/2000	—	2.12	1.72	0.8	6.7	31.5
2000/2001	—	2.18	1.74	0.8	7.6	28.6
2001/2002	4.4	1.82	1.63	0.9	6.4	28.5
2002/2003	—	—	—	—	—	—
2003/2004	4.6	1.99	1.68	0.8	7.0	28.4
2004/2005	4.9	2.14	2.03	0.9	7.6	28.0
2005/2006	5.2	2.25	2.18	1.0	8.1	27.8
2006/2007	5.4	2.40	2.44	1.0	8.5	28.4
2007/2008	5.9	2.57	2.99	1.2	8.7	29.4
2008/2009	5.8	2.48	3.03	1.2	8.8	28.3
2009/2010	5.6	2.59	3.18	1.2	9.2	28.0
2010/2011	6.2	2.76	3.48	1.3	9.7	28.5
2011/2012	6.3	2.73	3.50	1.3	9.6	28.5
2012/2013	6.3	2.73	3.77	1.4	9.6	28.4

Source: Ethiopia, CSA (various years).
Note: — = data not available.

infrastructure (measured in terms of road density). This chapter compares teff production, area, and fertilizer application with a set of travel time models that span from 1997 to 2010 at woreda level. Using geographic information systems to explore production patterns and trends of teff, we find greater teff yields and fertilizer applications tend to be associated with better access to major roads and cities. Although improved varieties of teff seed exist within Ethiopia, under 2 percent of farmers on only 1.3 percent of teff production area are using this technology.[1] Thus the primary focus of this chapter is to

1 It is important to note, however, that low adoption of improved seed may be driven by inconsistency in the definition of improved seed application during data collection. Spielman, Kelemwork, and Alemu (2012) underline the challenge of analyzing data on improved seed given differences in application of open pollinated cereals (such as teff), which do not require purchase/application of improved seed every year.

understand the geographic patterns of teff production, fertilizer application, and transportation infrastructure over time.

Data and Methodology

A variety of spatial and tabular datasets were used to analyze teff production patterns and market access over time. Teff production, area, and fertilizer application data for the years 1997/1998, 2006/2007, and 2010/2011 were obtained from Ethiopia's Central Statistical Agency (Ethiopia, CSA 1998, 2007, 2011), published data of the Annual Agricultural Sample Survey (AgSS), as well as the Ethiopian Agricultural Sample Enumeration (EASE) (2001/2002) report. It is important to note that the AgSS is representative at the zone level, but for purposes of this study, woreda-level figures were estimated by calculating the woreda share of teff production, area, and fertilizer use for each zone recorded in the 2001/2002 census. We decided to use these AgSS data as no other datasets in Ethiopia have continuous data over time at this level of disaggregation. Woreda shares are estimated and updated for each of the analysis periods (1997/1998, 2006/2007, and 2010/2011) using AgSS data. Given that the woreda boundaries, names, and codes vary over time, a spatial database was constructed that allows for spatial consistency and comparable woreda boundaries with a unique spatial identifier following the AgSS codebook. While this method is simplistic in nature and will not capture intra-annual and interannual dynamics and determinants of production, it does provide insight into the importance of transportation infrastructure and market links on teff production patterns in the country.

In order to pair agricultural statistics with transportation infrastructure improvements, a set of travel time models were built for three study years: 1997/1998, 2006/2007, and 2010/2011.[2] The travel time models calculate time required to access the (1) nearest market and (2) paved or gravel road from any point within the country.[3] For each year considered in the analysis, a travel time grid was built by considering the transportation network (road network condition and speed limits), off-road travel time across various land cover and land use types, water bodies (rivers and lakes), and slope considered as an

2 In order to create the travel time model for 2010/2011, a variety of roads data sources were used to update the 2006 roads database, including Open Street Map (http://download.geofabrik.de/africa/ethiopia.html), Google Earth, and groundtruthing.

3 Following Schmidt and Kedir Jemal's (2009) methodology, a travel time model is constructed that calculates time required to access the nearest market (city of at least 50,000 people) from any point within the country.

impedance factor for uphill movement and an accelerator factor for downhill movement. Using GIS, the overlap between the average travel time from a woreda to the nearest city (and nearest paved and gravel road) is compared with a variety of agricultural statistics. Production patterns emerge suggesting that transportation infrastructure is vital to enhancing agricultural productivity as well as increasing agricultural input use.

Spatial Heterogeneity of Teff Production Pattern

In Ethiopia most agricultural production takes place in the Weyna Dega and Dega (highland areas between 1,500 to 2,300 and 2,300 to 3,200 meters above sea level) agroecological zones, where land productivity has traditionally coincided with the densest rural populations (Figure 6.1). The optimal growing conditions for teff corresponds to its traditional production areas: 1,800–2,100 meters above sea level, average annual rainfall of 750 to 1,000 millimeters, and an average annual temperature of 10°C to 27°C (Chamberlin and Schmidt 2012; Seyfu 1997). However, there is great variation in production and yield within this growing area.

Oromia and Amhara represent the largest teff-producing regions given that a majority of the land area in these regions are in the rainfall-sufficient highlands agroecological zone. In addition to proper growing conditions, these regions also have the most connected transportation network, linking some of the largest cities in the country (Figure 6.2). In 2010/2011, Oromia and Amhara regions comprised approximately 85 percent of the national teff production volume and 84 percent of area cultivated (Figure 6.3). The Southern Nations, Nationalities, and Peoples' (SNNP) region was the third largest teff-producing region; however, its contribution to national teff production and area coverage was considerably lower, comprising 8.5 percent and 9.6 percent in 2010/2011, respectively.

Woreda-level teff production estimates suggest that selected woredas in Amhara and Oromia account for the high production in their respective regions. A total of 23 woredas make up 25 percent of national teff production in Ethiopia (10 and 13 woredas comprise approximately 10 percent and 15 percent of national production in Amhara and Oromia, respectively). Ada'a Chukala woreda in East Shewa zone was the highest teff-producing woreda, contributing almost 3 percent to national production. The remaining top teff-producing woredas are distributed among East Gojjam, West Gojjam, North Shewa, West Shewa, North Gonder, and South Gonder zones.

FIGURE 6.1 Agroecological zones and population density

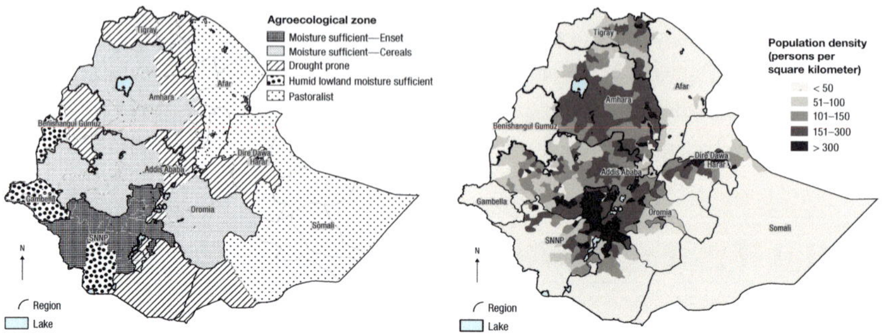

Source: Authors' calculations.

FIGURE 6.2 Roads in Ethiopia, 2010–2011

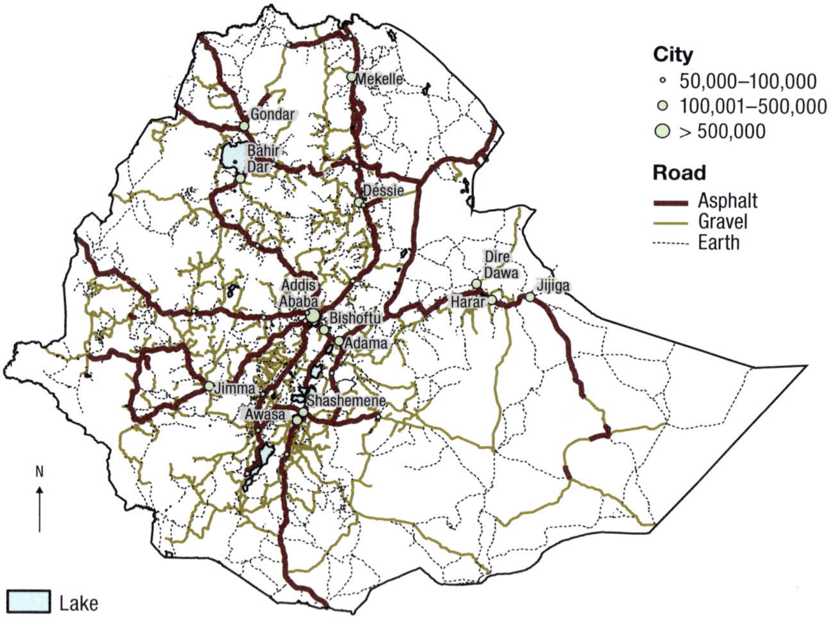

Source: Ethiopian Roads Authority, with road information updated using Open Street Map, Google Earth, and groundtruthing.

FIGURE 6.3 Production and area share of teff by region, 1997/1998–2010/2011

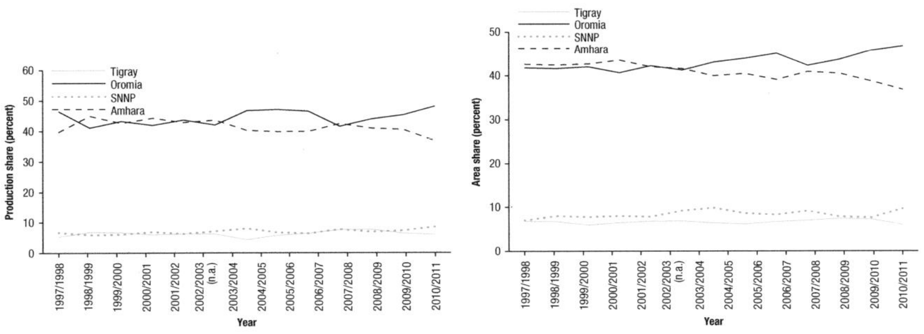

Source: Ethiopia, CSA (2015).
Note: SNNP = Southern Nations, Nationalities, and Peoples' region. n.a. = not applicable.

These high-producing areas also comprise a majority of the commercial teff surplus in the country (Figure 6.4). In total, approximately 31 percent of teff production is sold as commercial surplus (AgSS, 2010/2011). Oromia region supplies 42 percent of marketed teff, while Amhara region contributes 33 percent to overall commercial surplus. Six zones (West Shewa, East Shewa, and Arsi from Oromia region, and East Gojjam, West Gojjam, and North Shewa from Amhara region) make up more than 50 percent of commercial surplus in Ethiopia. Given the increase in urbanization (Ethiopia has grown by 3.7 percent per year on average), there is greater demand for food from urban populations (Schmidt and Kedir Jemal 2009). Mapping teff surplus by zone suggests that areas closer to urban centers with facilitated access to markets are providing the bulk share of surplus teff production.

Exploring Teff Production over Time

Between 1997/1998 and 2010/2011 the total amount of teff produced in Ethiopia almost tripled from 1.3 million metric tons to approximately 3.5 million metric tons, while total teff cultivated area grew by 58 percent. The increase in teff production and cultivated area is reflected in all major teff-producing regions (Table 6.2). The greatest change in teff production and area occurred in the SNNP region, where teff production increased from about 90,000 metric tons in 1997/1998 to approximately 300,000 metric tons in 2010/2011. Over this period, area cultivated by teff in this region grew from 123,000 hectares to 265,000 hectares. Although less teff is grown in Tigray, production increased from nearly 70,000 metric tons in 1997/1998 to over 210,000 metric tons by 2010/2011, while teff cultivated area grew by almost 39 percent.

FIGURE 6.4 Share of national teff commercial surplus by zone

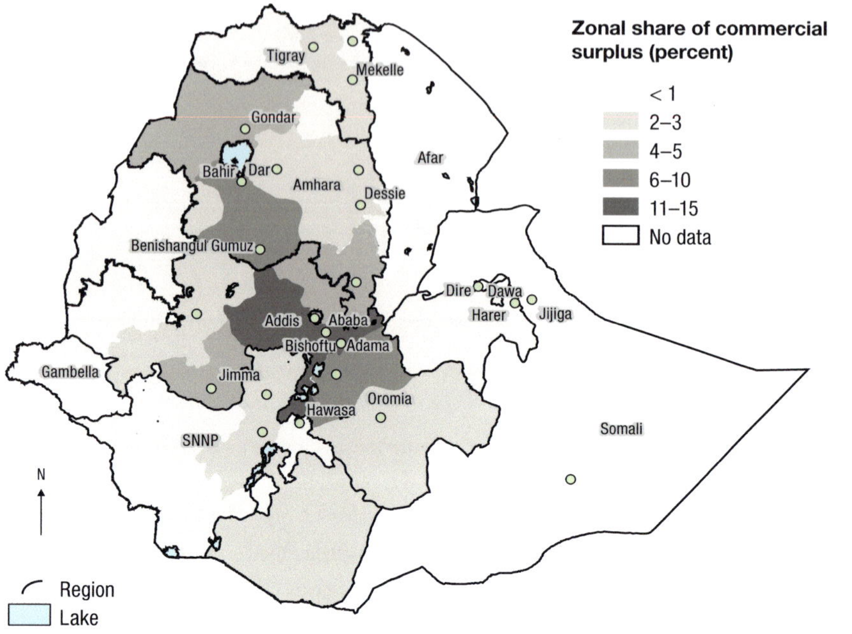

Source: Ethiopia, CSA 2011.

TABLE 6.2 Teff cultivated area and production, 1997/1998, 2006/2007, and 2010/2011

	1997/1998		2006/2007		2010/2011	
Region	Area (million hectares)	Production (million metric tons)	Area (million hectares)	Production (million metric tons)	Area (million hectares)	Production (million metric tons)
Tigray	0.12	0.07	0.16	0.16	0.17	0.21
Amhara	0.74	0.52	0.94	0.97	1.01	1.28
Oromia	0.73	0.61	1.08	1.13	1.29	1.67
Benishangul-Gumuz	0.02	0.02	0.02	0.01	0.02	0.02
SNNP	0.12	0.09	0.20	0.16	0.27	0.30
Ethiopia	**1.75**	**1.31**	**2.40**	**2.44**	**2.76**	**3.48**

Source: Ethiopia, CSA, various years.

Note: SNNP = Southern Nations, Nationalities, and Peoples' region. Area planted and production of teff were not reported or insubstantial in Addis Ababa, Somali, Afar, Gambella, Harar, and Dire Dawa.

FIGURE 6.5 Woreda-level teff production estimates, 1997/1998

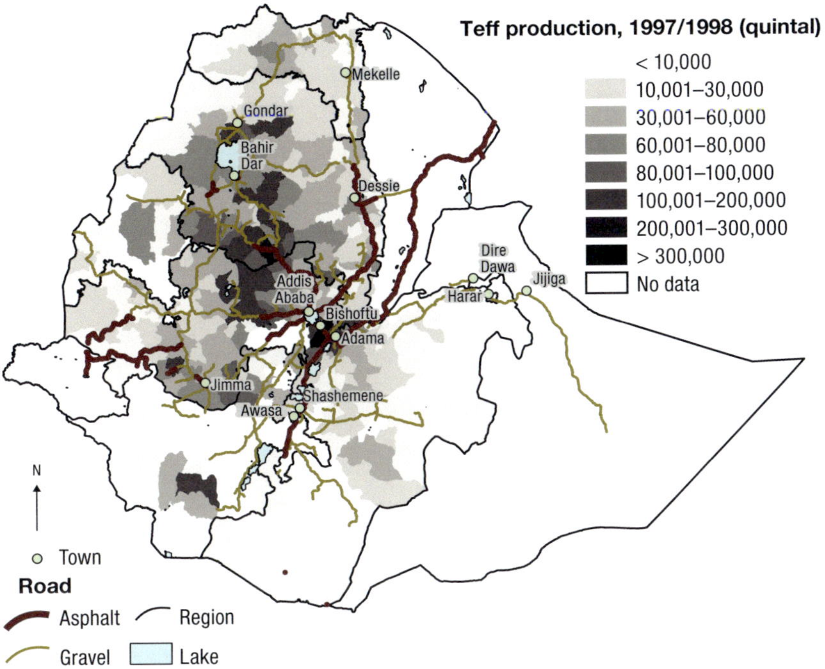

Source: Authors' calculations.

Comparing teff production in 1997/1998 with available road infrastructure at the time suggests that higher-producing areas were not only in optimal agroecological zones but were also associated along major transportation corridors (Figure 6.5). High-producing woredas in Oromia region included areas adjacent to the Addis Ababa–Adama corridor as well as the road network stretching from the capital west to Nekempte. Similarly, high-producing regions in Amhara were found along the major road stretching from Addis Ababa to Bahir Dar and Gondar.

As road infrastructure continued to expand throughout the rainfall-sufficient highland regions, teff production also expanded. Geographic comparisons of the road network and teff production suggest that greater production was reported in areas that were closer to a road. Compared to 1997/1998, in 2006/2007 there were three times more gravel roads that linked rural woredas to larger paved corridors. In addition, production increased along the major corridor that runs from Addis Ababa to Mekelle, whereby 230 more kilometers of paved roads were present in 2006/2007 compared to 1997/1998 (Figure 6.6).

FIGURE 6.6 Woreda-level teff production estimates, 2006/2007

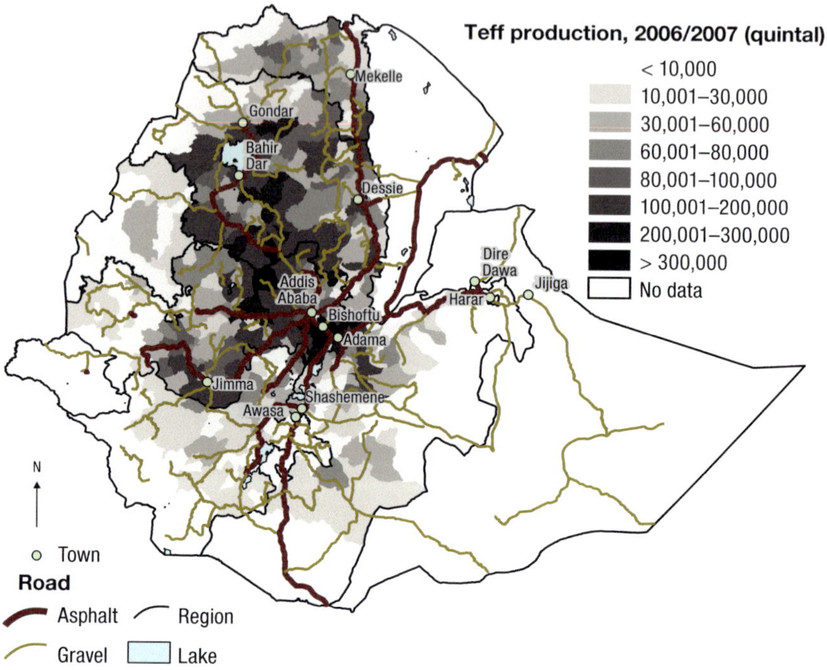

Source: Authors' calculations.

By 2010/2011 travel time to a major city decreased dramatically in the four major agricultural regions of Ethiopia (Table 6.3).[4] Whereas in 1997/1998, only 7 percent and 12 percent of teff area in Amhara and Oromia was within three hours of a major city, 37 percent and 48 percent of teff area was within three hours of a major city in Amhara and Oromia in 2010/2011, respectively. Similarly, rural populations continue to gain better access to roads (Figure 6.7). In 1997/1998, 19 percent of teff area in Amhara was within two hours of a gravel or paved road, whereas in 2010/2011, 52 percent was within two hours of a gravel or paved road. In Oromia region, 42 percent more area was within two hours of a gravel or paved road in 2010/2011 compared to 1997/1998. This expansion and improvement in road infrastructure has not only facilitated market access but has also impacted the transportation of goods and access to such services as fertilizer and agricultural extension services as well as enhanced communication and knowledge transfer.

4 A major city is defined as having at least 50,000 people.

TABLE 6.3 Travel time to a major market (% area)

Region	1997/1998		2010/2011	
	Teff area (share) under three hours	Teff area (share) over three hours	Teff area (share) under three hours	Teff area (share) over three hours
Tigray	3.3	96.7	28.9	71.1
Afar	0.0	100.0	n.a.	n.a.
Amhara	6.7	93.3	37.4	62.6
Oromia	11.7	88.3	47.9	52.1
Benishangul-Gumuz	0.0	100.0	0.0	100.0
SNNP	5.2	94.8	56.6	43.4
Ethiopia	**8.5**	**91.5**	**43.3**	**56.7**

Source: Authors' calculations; AgSS 1997/1998 and 2010/2011.

Note: n.a. = not applicable; SNNP = Southern Nations, Nationalities, and Peoples' region. Area planted of teff were not reported or insubstantial in Addis Ababa, Somali, Gambella, Harar, and Dire Dawa.

FIGURE 6.7 Woreda-level teff production estimates, 2010/2011

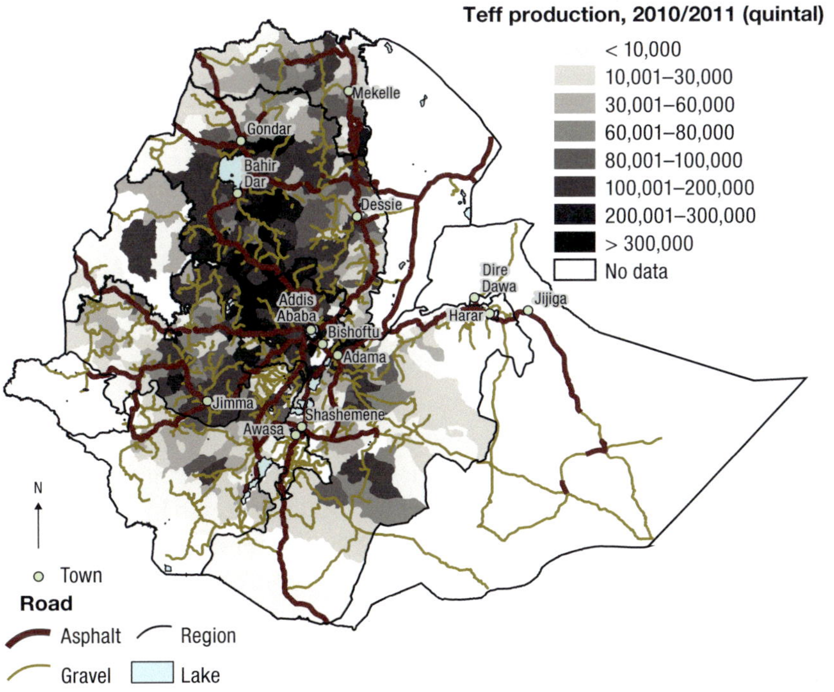

Source: Authors' calculations.

Market Access and Fertilizer Application

Although urban growth remains relatively slow in Ethiopia, investment in connective infrastructure has dramatically reduced transportation costs to market centers.[5] Given the limited infrastructure during the 1980s and early 1990s, the Ethiopian government prioritized road construction and rehabilitation investments to enhance links between markets. Beginning in 1997, a 10-year Road Sector Development Program was formulated to improve the quality and size of road infrastructure. In 1996/1997 transportation infrastructure connected Addis Ababa to a limited number of urban markets such as Bahr Dar, Dire Dawa, Jimma, and Mekelle (Figure 6.8). By 2010/2011 secondary cities linked to each other, and major corridors linking key market centers were fully constructed. Whereas in 1997/1998, only 15 percent of the population was within three hours of a market, 47 percent was within three hours of a market in 2010/2011 (Figures 6.8 and 6.9).

Fertilizer application on teff fields across the four main grain-producing regions shows a notable difference over time (Figure 6.10 and Figure 6.11). In 1997/1998 fertilizer application was concentrated in woredas near Addis Ababa and Adama as well as northern Oromia and southern Amhara near Bahir Dar. According to Minten et al. (2013a), the intensity (kilograms per hectare) of chemical fertilizer application on teff fields has increased by nearly 77 percent within the past decade. Nationally, of the total fertilizer used on teff and areas that were under fertilizer in 2010/2011, more than 85 percent was located in areas less than three hours to a road.

Taking into account only production and input use in the highland rainfall-sufficient agroecological zone where the majority of teff is grown, fertilizer application was greater in areas closer to a major city. Comparing teff production and area over time between high access areas and low access areas, it is important to note the dynamic processes occurring. Not only are road networks expanding, but more households are growing teff throughout the country. In 1997–1998 total teff production and area was greater in low-access areas accounting for 730 million kilograms and 981,000 hectares, respectively, compared to 120 million kilograms and 128,000 hectares in high-access areas.

Similarly, total quantity of fertilizer used was higher in low-access areas in 1997/1998. However, when assessing the annual growth rate of production and fertilizer use between 1997/1998 and 2010/2011, areas within three hours

5 The total share of urban residents was approximately 14.2 percent in 2007 according to the agglomeration index (Schmidt and Kedir Jemal 2009), compared with an average 30 percent urbanization rate for all of Africa south of the Sahara.

FIGURE 6.8 Travel time to a city of at least 50,000 people, 1996/1997 and 2010/2011

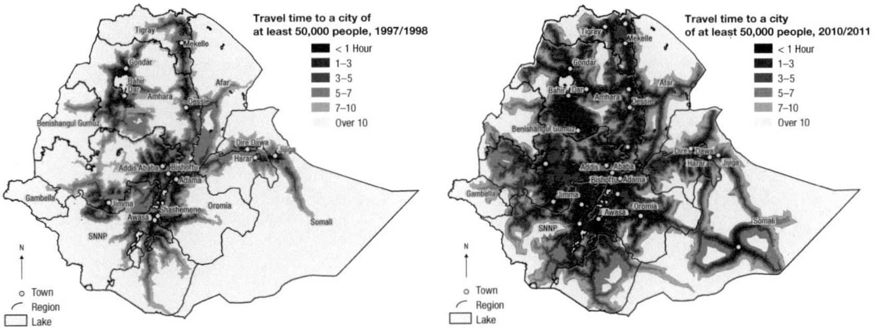

Source: Authors' calculations.

FIGURE 6.9 Percentage of population connected to a city of at least 50,000 people

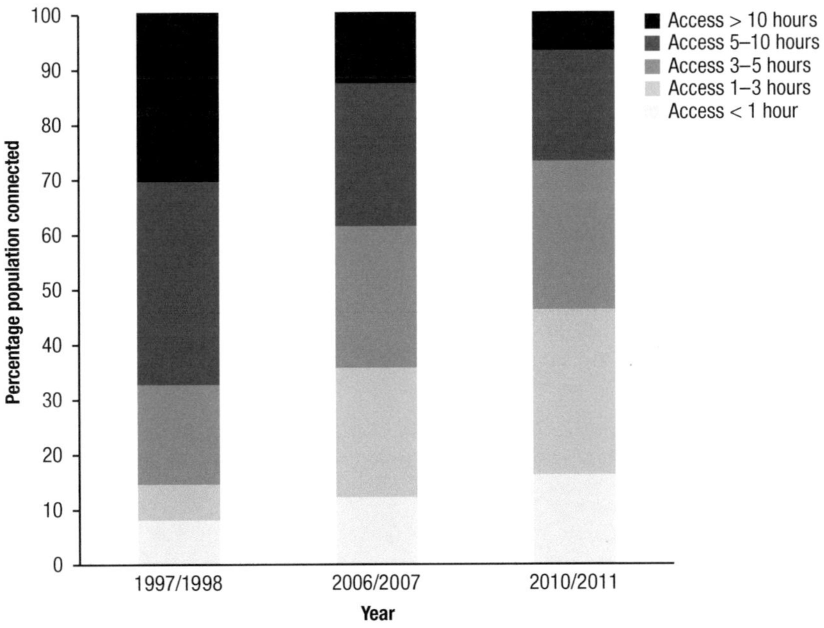

Source: Authors' calculations.

FIGURE 6.10 Average fertilizer applied on teff fields, 1997/1998 and 2006/2007

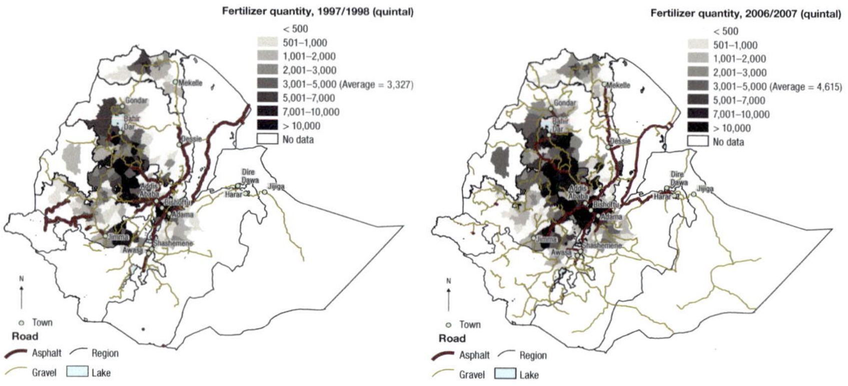

Source: Authors' calculations.

FIGURE 6.11 Fertilizer quantity applied on teff fields, 2010/2011

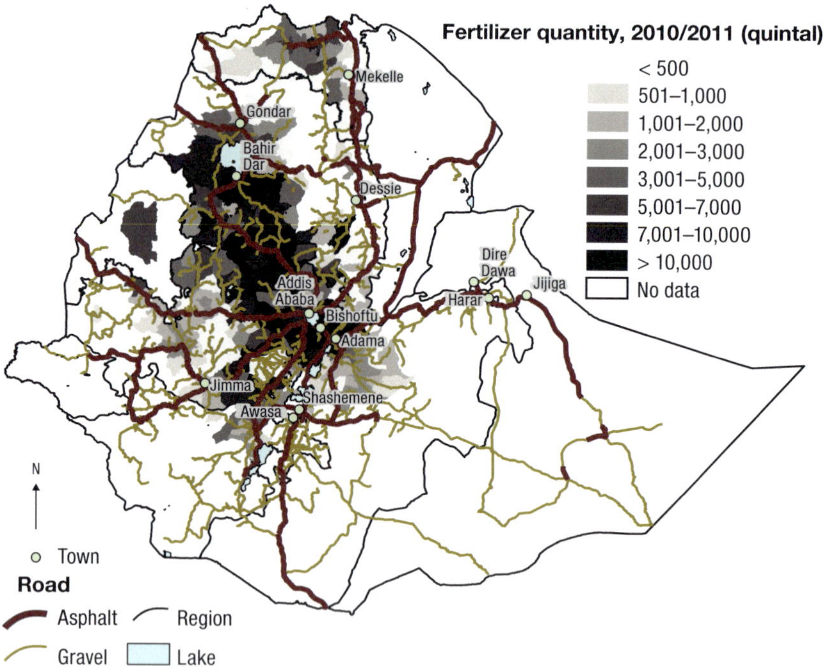

Source: Authors' calculations.

of a major city experienced large rates of growth in teff production and in fertilized area at 20 percent, respectively, per year. In low-access areas, annual growth of teff production increased by only 4 percent, and the area planted with teff decreased between 1997/1998 and 2010/2011. Although these numbers suggest a trend of greater teff production and input use along main corridors and major cities, it is important to note that these figures represent a snapshot of agricultural processes and do not take into account the portfolio of other possible agricultural enhancing investments that occurred in these areas.

Finally, focusing on intensity of fertilizer use and agricultural yields, households within three hours of a city have consistently applied more fertilizer per hectare, however not at substantially larger volume than areas that lie more than three hours from a city. This is due to several factors: first, this analysis looks at overall total values of production and input levels. In high-access areas the area dedicated to teff increased by 17 percent per year, while low-access areas did not experience considerable growth in teff area nor in fertilizer use on teff (Table 6.4). Although fertilizer use per hectare was lower in areas greater than three hours from a city, overall teff yields in low- and high-access areas were similar in 2010/2011. This suggests that other conditioning factors may have an influence on teff yields, including favorable weather patterns, political processes, and knowledge and agricultural extension campaigns to bolster teff yields (row planting, weeding, and improved seed development). Further research is needed to identify the specific determinants of yield increases in teff. It is clear that not only total production and fertilizer use is increasing throughout the primary teff-growing regions (rainfall-sufficient highlands), but yields are also increasing in both the high- and low-access areas.

Conclusion

Teff production area continues to expand and a greater number of farmers are producing teff. Oromia and Amhara represent the largest teff-producing regions given that a majority of the land area in these regions are in the rainfall-sufficient highlands agroecological zone. In addition to proper growing conditions, these regions also have the most connected transportation network, linking some of the largest cities in the country. In 2010/2011, Oromia and Amhara regions comprised approximately 85 percent of the national teff production volume and 84 percent of teff area cultivated. Access to markets has improved dramatically over time in Amhara and Oromia regions, whereby approximately 37 percent and 43 percent of the population respectively were

TABLE 6.4 Production and input use in the highland rainfall-sufficient agroecological zone, 1997/1998, 2006/2007, and 2010/2011

		Units	1997/ 1998	2006/ 2007	2010/ 2011	Annual % change (1997/1998–2010/2011)
High access (less than three hours from a city)	**Number of woredas**		**19**	**86**	**119**	
	Total teff production	kilograms (thousands)	120,103	661,175	1,270,754	19.9
	Total teff area	hectares (thousands)	128.4	609.8	982.1	16.9
	Area under fertilizer	hectares (thousands)	70.4	479.6	725.9	19.7
	Share fertilized teff area	%	54.8	78.6	73.9	2.3
	Total fertilizer on teff	kilograms (thousands)	7,940	45,008	70,181	18.2
	Fertilizer per hectare	kilograms per hectare	112.8	93.8	96.7	−1.2
	Teff yield	kilograms per hectare	935.3	1,084.20	1,293.90	2.5
Low access (more than three hours from a city)	**Number of woredas**		**189**	**171**	**132**	
	Total teff production	kilograms (thousands)	730,123	998,993	1,186,518	3.8
	Total teff area	hectares (thousands)	981	1,069	951	−0.2
	Area under fertilizer	hectares (thousands)	427	504	464	0.6
	Share fertilized teff area	%	43.5	47.2	48.8	0.9
	Total fertilizer on teff	kilograms (thousands)	40,755	39,234	39,590	−0.2
	Fertilizer per hectare	kilograms per hectare	95.4	77.8	85.4	−0.9
	Teff yield	kilograms per hectare	744.2	934.8	1,247.50	4.1

Source: Authors' calculations and Ethiopia, CSA, various years.

connected to a major city within three hours in 2010/2011 (compared to 11 percent and 13 percent in 1997/1998, respectively).

Ongoing investments in road infrastructure in the highlands have decreased transportation costs for rural farmers. Previous research suggests that improvements in market access increases the adoption of fertilizer and enhances communication and knowledge transfer, which in turn leads to improvements in agricultural production (Demeke et al. 1998; Dorosh et al. 2010; Minten et al. 2013b). GIS analysis of market access and agricultural production suggests that areas of greater teff production, teff area, and fertilizer application are closer to major roads and cities. Whereas in 1997/1998, teff was primarily grown along the transportation corridor between Addis Ababa and Bahir Dar, and Addis Ababa and Adama, teff production in 2010/2011 increased along the Mekelle, Nekempte, and Jimma corridors as well. A similar trend is observed for fertilizer use along these major roads.

Ethiopia continues to invest in road infrastructure to expand links to rural areas. Although the country has invested significantly in roads over the past several decades, it remains a country with one of the lowest road densities in the world (von Braun and Olofinbiyi 2007; Gwilliam et al. 2008), and transport costs are still relatively high compared with international standards (Minten, Stifel, and Tamru 2012). Improvements in market access will likely continue to have an effect on production patterns and input use within the country. More efficient transportation of goods, as well as enhanced communication, improved mobility of rural farmers, and facilitated access to extension agents are important elements to agricultural innovation and technical adoption. Paired with increasing demand for teff in urban areas as well as a growing urban population and relatively high market prices for teff grain suggests strong potential for further growth and geographic expansion of teff production in Ethiopia.

References

Chamberlin, J., and E. Schmidt. 2012. "Ethiopian Agriculture: A Dynamic Geographic Perspective." In *Food and Agriculture in Ethiopia: Progress and Policy Challenges*, edited by Paul Dorosh and Shahidur Rashid, 21–52. Philadelphia: University of Pennsylvania Press.

Demeke, M., V. A. Kelly, T. S. Jayne, A. Said, J. C. Le Valleé, and H. Chen. 1998. *Agricultural Market Performance and Determinants of Fertilizer Use in Ethiopia* (No. 55599). East Lansing, MI, US: Michigan State University, Department of Agricultural, Food, and Resource Economics.

Dorosh, P., and E. Schmidt. 2010. *The Rural-Urban Transformation in Ethiopia*. ESSP Working Paper 13. Washington, DC: International Food Policy Research Institute (IFPRI).

Dorosh, P., H. G. Wang, L. You, and E. Schmidt. 2010. *Crop Production and Road Connectivity in Sub-Saharan Africa: A Spatial Analysis.* Policy Research Working Paper 5385. Washington, DC: World Bank.

Ethiopia, CSA (Central Statistical Agency). 1998. *Agricultural Sample Survey 1997/1998: Report on Area and Production of Major Crops.* Addis Ababa, Ethiopia.

———. 2007. *Agricultural Sample Survey 2006/2007: Report on Area and Production of Major Crops.* Addis Ababa, Ethiopia.

———. 2011. *Agricultural Sample Survey 2010/2011: Report on Area and Production of Major Crops.* Addis Ababa, Ethiopia.

———. 2013. *Agricultural Sample Survey 2012/2013: Report on Area and Production of Major Crops.* Addis Ababa, Ethiopia.

———. 2015. *Agricultural Sample Survey: Time Series Data for National & Regional Level (from 1995/96 (1998 EC)–2014/15 (2007 EC)): Report on Area and Production of Major Crops.* Addis Ababa, Ethiopia.

Gwilliam, K., V. Foster, R. Archondo-Callao, C. Briceño-Garmendia, A. Nogales, and K. Sethi. 2008. *The Burden of Maintenance: Roads in Sub-Saharan Africa.* Background Paper 14 (Phase I). Africa Infrastructure Country Diagnostic. Washington, DC: World Bank.

Minten, B., D. Stifel, and S. Tamru. 2012. *Structural Transformation in Ethiopia: Evidence from Cereal Markets.* ESSP II Working Paper 54. Addis Ababa: IFPRI/ESSP II.

Minten, B., S. Tamru, E. Engida Legesse, and T. Kuma. 2013a. *Ethiopia's Value Chains on the Move: The Case of Teff.* ESSP II Working Paper 52. Addis Ababa: IFPRI/ESSP II.

———. 2013b. *Using Evidence in Unraveling Food Supply Chains in Ethiopia: The Supply Chain of Teff from Major Production Areas to Addis Ababa.* ESSP II Working Paper 54. Addis Ababa: IFPRI/ESSP II.

Schmidt, E., and M. Kedir Jemal. 2009. *Urbanization and Spatial Connectivity in Ethiopia: Urban Growth Analysis Using GIS.* ESSP II Working Paper 3. Addis Ababa: IFPRI/ESSP II.

Seyfu, K. 1997. "Tef (*Eragrostis tef* (Zucc.) Trotter." In *Promoting the Conservation and Use of Underutilized and Neglected Crops* 12. Gatersleben, Germany: Institute of Plant Genetics and Crop Plant Research; Rome: International Plant Genetic Resources Institute.

Spielman, D. J., D. K. Mekonnen, and D. Alemu. 2012. "Seed, Fertilizer, and Agricultural Extension in Ethiopia." In *Food and Agriculture in Ethiopia: Progress and Policy Challenges,* edited by P. Dorosh and S. Rashid, 84–122. Philadelphia: University of Pennsylvania Press.

von Braun, J., and T. Olofinbiyi. 2007. "Famine and Food Insecurity in Ethiopia." In *Case Study 7-4 of the Program: Food Policy for Developing Countries: The Role of Government in the Global Food System,* edited by P. Pinstrup-Andersen and F. Cheng. Ithaca, NY, US: Cornell University.

Yu, B., A. Nin-Pratt, J. Funes, and S. A. Gemessa. 2011. *Cereal Production and Technology Adoption in Ethiopia.* ESSP II Working Paper 31. Addis Ababa: IFPRI/ESSP II.

Chapter 7

PRODUCTIVITY AND EFFICIENCY IN HIGH-POTENTIAL AREAS

Fantu Nisrane Bachewe, Bethelhem Koru, and Alemayehu Seyoum Taffesse

A large majority of Ethiopians and those who are poor live in rural areas and derive their livelihood from agriculture. Moreover, the proportion residing in rural areas is predicted to stay high (still around 70 percent in 2040), when there is likely to be 40 percent more rural residents (UN 2014). Agriculture is dominated by smallholder households. During 2013/2014, 94 percent of the area nationwide was cultivated by smallholder farmers (Ethiopia, CSA 2005b–2014b). The average amount of land held by smallholders was about a hectare and has since declined. In addition, the number and size of households increased between 2004/2005 and 2013/2014 (Ethiopia, CSA 2005b–2014b). The facts that most Ethiopians are engaged in agriculture and the bulk of the poor reside in rural areas have provided the impetus for major policy initiatives from the government of Ethiopia that prioritize smallholder agriculture. Most notably, since the launch of the Agricultural Development Led Industrialization strategy in 1993 (Ethiopia, MoPED 1993), agriculture has become a focal point.

In the past, development economists broadly agreed on supporting smallholder agriculture owing largely to its effectiveness in poverty reduction and economic growth in a number of Asian countries during the Green Revolution (Hazell et al. 2010; Diao, Hazell, and Thurlow 2010). Smallholder agriculture is therefore mostly favored among those that give priority to poverty reduction and food security (Fan et al. 2013; FAO 2010; Bill and Melinda Gates Foundation 2011). However, such policies have increasingly been challenged in Africa on various grounds (Collier and Dercon 2009; Dercon and Zeitlin 2009). These include research findings that show medium- and large-scale farmers have superior productivity relative to smallholders (Helfand and Levine 2004; Rios and Shively 2005; Padilla-Fernandez and Nuthall 2012) and that the poor might benefit from improved labor markets generated by more efficient farms (Maertens and Swinnen 2009). Even those that promote smallholder-focused policies as key for growth and poverty reduction point to the diversity within smallholder farmers and underline the need for tailoring such policies to specific conditions (Birner and Resnick 2010; Hazell 2014) and targeting farmers with a viable future in agriculture (Fan et al. 2013).

Growth in agriculture is one of the major drivers of the remarkable growth in real gross domestic product (GDP) recorded in Ethiopia in the past decade. Official national statistics indicate that real gross and per capita GDP grew at average annual rates of 10.7 percent and 7.9 percent during the 2004/2005–2013/2014 period (National Bank of Ethiopia 2014), while World Bank data indicate slightly faster growth rates of 11 percent and 8.1 percent during 2004–2014 (World Bank 2015). During the same period, teff accounted for about a fifth of the nationwide agricultural area and was cultivated by nearly half of smallholder farmers (Ethiopia, CSA 2005a–2014a), while it contributed more than 6 percent to real GDP and growth in real GDP (Bachewe et al. 2015). With 28 percent of total teff output marketed during 2008/2009–2013/2014, it is also the most commercialized crop among cereals, with average marketed output running at 16 percent (Ethiopia, CSA 2009c–2014c).

Various staple crops dominate different parts of Ethiopia. However, teff is either the staple or among the most consumed crops in almost all parts. The share of food expenditure on teff is highest in urban areas and increased by 3.4 percent nationwide between 2005 and 2010, during which period real income increased considerably and the share of all other cereals declined (see Chapter 2). Following the increase in teff demand, which is reflected, among others, by the increase in its real price, the long-run teff supply response of households was faster than growth in its price (Bachewe and Taffesse 2015).

Teff output has grown at an average annual rate of 9.3 percent (Ethiopia, CSA 2005a–2014a) since 2005. The evidence indicates that part of the growth in teff output has been driven by increases in cultivated area (Dorosh, Robinson, and Thurlow 2015). However, it is not well understood how much rising teff yields have contributed to this output growth.

This study employs data envelopment analyses (DEA) to measure productivity of teff-producing households on a dataset collected in the baseline survey of the Agricultural Growth Program (AGP) of Ethiopia.[1] The study also conducts econometric analyses to identify the factors that influence performance in productivity. Since Sen's (1962) observation on the link between farm size and productivity, a number of studies have been conducted that

1 The AGP commenced in 2011 as a component of the government's broad effort to partly achieve the targets of GTP. It is mainly aimed at increasing smallholder productivity sustainably and value-added in agriculture (Ethiopia, MoRAD 2010).

investigate the relationship, including Barett, Bellemare, and Hou (2010); Coelli, Rahman, and Thirtle (2002); Helfand and Levine (2004); Padilla-Fernandez and Nuthall (2012); and Rios and Shively (2005). Yet, despite declining landholdings in Ethiopia and the large international literature, there is little empirical evidence on the link between farm size and productivity. This chapter investigates whether productivity improves with teff area cultivated and whether factors that influence productivity differ across scales of operation. Furthermore, relative productivity levels obtained from DEA are used to compute outputs obtainable at hypothetical levels of productivity and specialization in teff production.

This chapter has three contributions to the international literature. First, it investigates productivity issues using a recently collected large-scale dataset of farm households in Ethiopia that cultivate an important crop and uniquely integrate a number of variables. Second, the study informs the debate on the farm size–productivity relationship that is recently being revisited by development economists. Third, the study provides insights on the relationship between productivity and levels of specialization.

Works that study productivity in Ethiopia include Endale (2011); Nisrane et al. (2011); Taffesse, Dorosh, and Gemessa (2012); and Yami et al. (2013). Relative to these, the dataset used in this study is rich in details and comprises a larger number of households and a wider geographical area than most. A large number of studies employ DEA to measure productivity and use a broad range of variables to investigate factors that influence productivity and efficiency. A number of other studies focus on the effect of a specific set of factors to explain productivity, such as farm size and level of specialization. Coelli and Fleming (2004) use data from Papua New Guinea to study whether productivity improves with specialization in the type of crop and crop group produced. Helfand and Levine (2004) and Padilla-Fernandez and Nuthall (2012) use datasets from Brazil and the Philippines to study the farm size–efficiency relationship, respectively. Latruffe et al. (2005) use Polish data to investigate efficiency differences across farm sizes and levels of specialization. The analyses in this chapter use factors emphasized in the studies referred to above as well as a broad range of other variables.

Important findings of this chapter include DEA results, which indicate that an average teff farmer is only about a third as productive as farmers who are efficient in their practices, both by scale and technical efficiency. Moreover, the results of econometric analyses show that performance in productivity is positively associated with farmers' education. Households with access to financial institutions and production information (through media or extension) have higher productivity. Specialization in the production of fewer crops is positively associated with productivity. Unlike the inverse farm size–productivity hypothesis, our results indicate that largeholders are as productive as smallholders.

The remainder of the chapter is organized as follows: The next section describes the theoretical and empirical models. The two subsequent sections describe the data and discuss the results, respectively. The last section summarizes key findings and explores their policy implications.

Method of Analysis

Relative total factor productivity (TFP) and efficiency of teff farmers is measured using data envelopment analyses (DEA) that employ input and output distance functions to measure comparative performance. Output and input distance functions are defined and the empirical output distance function is specified in the first part of this section. Following this, the relative productivity and efficiency indexes are defined. Finally, the econometric model that is employed to investigate factors that explain relative TFP and efficiency is specified.

Output and Input Distance Function

Consider a production technology T that describes the relationship between an input vector $X = [x_1, x_2, \ldots, x_N]$ and an output vector $Y = [y_1, y_2, \ldots, y_M]$:

$$T = \{(X, Y): X \in \Re_+^N, Y \in \Re_+^M, X \text{ can produce } Y\}$$

Then, Färe, Grosskopf, and Lovell (1985) define an output distance function under some regularity conditions as:[2]

$$D_O^j(X_j, Y_j) = \inf_\theta\{\theta^j: (X_j, Y_j/\theta) \in T\} \text{ for all } j \in [1, 2, \ldots, J] \qquad (1)$$

where j indexes producers, in this case, farm households, and $D_O^j(.) \in (0,1)$ stands for output distance function of j. An output distance function measures efficiency by comparing output levels produced by households with those at the boundary of production possibilities. The output distance function of household j is the largest factor by which j's output can be multiplied and increased if it were to produce the optimal quantity from the inputs it is currently using. Similarly, an input distance function is defined as:

2 See Fare and Primont (1995) on regularity conditions assumed.

$$D_I^j(X_j, Y_j) = \sup_\beta\{\beta^j: (X_j/\beta, Y_j) \in T\} \text{ for all } j \in [1,2, \ldots, J] \quad (2)$$

where $D_I^j(\cdot) \geq 1$, which stands for the input distance function, is the largest factor by which household j's current input use levels can be divided and minimized if it were optimal in input use and still produce its current output levels.

DEA employs linear programming methods on input-output data to construct nonparametric piecewise linear production or input requirement frontiers. Performance of producers away from the frontier is then measured using their distance relative to those operating on the frontier or using output and input distance functions. Applied studies using DEA often employ Translog distance functions, which are also adopted in this study. The empirical output distance function of teff-producing households that use multiple inputs is defined as:

$$D_O^j(X_j, Y_j) = \alpha_0 + \alpha_1 \ln y_j + \frac{1}{2}\alpha_{1,1} \ln y_j^2 + \sum_{n=1}^{10} \beta_n \ln x_{n,j} + \frac{1}{2}\sum_{n'=1}^{10}\sum_{n=1}^{10} \beta_{n',n} \ln x_{n',j} \ln x_{n,j} + \sum_{n=1}^{10} \delta_n \ln x_{n,j} \ln y_j \quad \text{for all } j \in [1, \ldots, J] \quad (3)$$

where y_j is the quantity of teff output that household j produced using $x_{n,j}$ of input type n, with $x_{n,j} \in$ [teff area, labor, oxen, fertilizer, improved seeds, pesticides, irrigation, land quality index, rainfall, and growing degree days]. These variables are formally defined in Table 7.1.

Productivity and Efficiency Indexes

In this part the indexes used to measure performance in relative TFP and efficiency are defined. The study also uses the indexes to compute output levels that can be obtained if farmers were to operate at optimal levels and partially and fully specialize in teff production. Thus, along with the indexes, the equations used in those computations are defined.

Among classes of multifactor productivity indexes, the Färe-Primont and Lowe indexes satisfy all economically relevant axioms and tests in index number theory (O'Donnell 2011a). The study uses the Färe-Primont index because it is suitable for the input-output data used. The index defines the TFP of a multiple-input multiple-output household j as a ratio of an aggregate output and aggregate input index as:

$$TFP_j = \frac{Q_j}{I_j} \quad (4)$$

TABLE 7.1 Definition of variables used in data envelopment analyses

Variables	Definition	Aggregation
y	Teff output (kilograms)	Crop
x_1	Teff area (hectares)	Crop
x_2	Labor (sum of family and hired labor days)	Crop
x_3	Oxen used to plow land (number)	Household
x_4	Chemical fertilizer (kilograms)	Crop
x_5	Improved seeds (kilograms)	Crop
x_6	Pesticides dummy = 1 if pesticides, herbicides, and/or fungicides used	Crop
x_7	Irrigation dummy = 1 if cropland is irrigated	Crop
x_8	Land quality index = land fertility index × slope of land; where fertility ∈ [1 = infertile, 2 = semifertile, 3 = fertile] and slope ∈ [1 = steep, 2 = gentle, 3 = flat]	Crop
x_9	Total rainfall = sum of daily rainfall during May 1–October 31, 2010 (millimeters)	District
x_{10}	Growing degree days = sum of daily beneficial heat during May 1–October 31, 2010[a]	District

Source: Authors.

Note: [a] Daily beneficial heat = the contribution to yields of any given day's average temperature in excess of the lower bound of a given temperature range, generally 8°C –32°C. Growing degree days = the sum over days in the cropping season of daily beneficial heat [the excess of average daily temperature over the lower bound], multiplied by the probability of the average temperature to occur on that day in that area (see also Roberts, Schlenker, and Eyer 2013).

where $Q_j = Q(y_{m,j})$ is the aggregate output index and $y_{m,j}$ is the magnitude of type m output, such that $y_{m,j} \in Y_j = [y_{1,j} y_{2,j} \dots y_{M,j}]$. Similarly, $I_j = I(x_{n,j})$ is an aggregate input index and $x_{n,j}$ is quantity of input type n, where $x_{n,j} \in X_j = [x_{1,j} x_{2,j} \dots x_{N,j}]$. The aggregator functions $Q(.)$ and $I(.)$ are assumed to be nonnegative, nondecreasing, and linearly homogenous functions of their respective arguments (O'Donnell 2008).

Then $RTFP_{k,j}$, which denotes the TFP of j (TFPj) relative to the TFP of optimal household(s) (TFP*), is given as:

$$RTFP_{k,j} = \frac{TFP_j}{TFP^*} = \frac{Q_j/I_j}{Q_k^*/I_k^*} = \frac{Q_{k,j}}{I_{k,j}} \tag{5}$$

where k represents optimal household(s). The index at (5) can be decomposed into technical and scale efficiency indexes that obtain $RTFP_{k,j}$ multiplicatively (O'Donnell 2009 and 2011b). Figure 7.1 is used to illustrate the technical and scale efficiency components of RTFP.

Suppose household j operates at point A where it uses I_j to produce Q_j. The household at A is inferior relative to that at C, which is producing a larger

FIGURE 7.1 Output-oriented measures of technical and scale efficiency

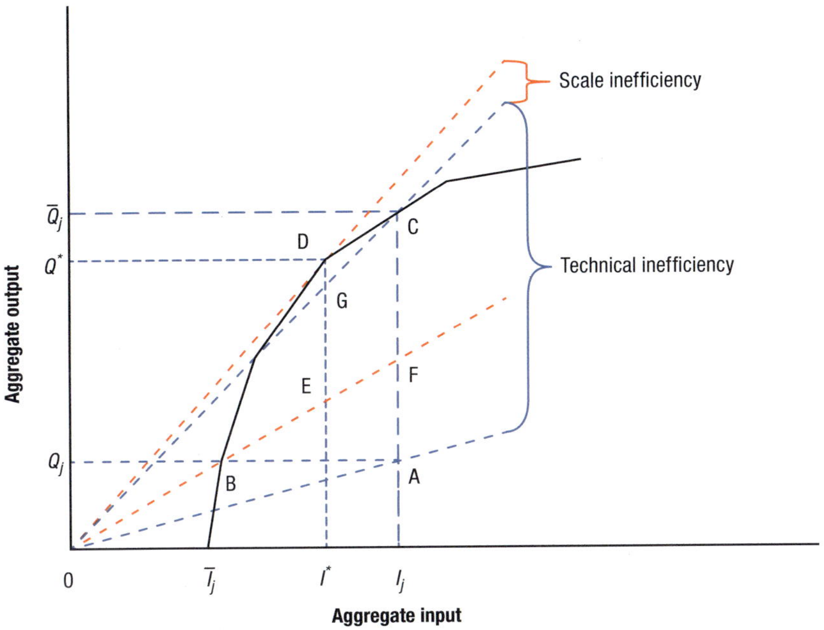

Source: Modified from Figures 1 and 2 in O'Donnell (2011b).

aggregate quantity, $\bar{Q}_j \geq Q_j$ using I_j. Then an output-oriented technical efficiency (OTE) of the household at A, relative to that at C, is given as:

$$\mathrm{OTE_j} = \frac{\mathrm{Q_j/I_j}}{\mathrm{\bar{Q}_j/I_j}} = \frac{\mathrm{TFP_j}}{\mathrm{TFP_C}} = \frac{\mathrm{Q_j}}{\mathrm{\bar{Q}_j}} = \mathrm{D_O^j(X_j, Y_j)} \leq 1 \tag{6}$$

Whereas $\bar{Q}_j$ is the aggregate output of C, it is also the maximum output A can produce if it were optimal in output-oriented technical efficiency. These magnitudes are differentiated by denoting the potential aggregate output A can produce by $\bar{Q}_j^O$, which is given as:

$$\bar{Q}_j^O = \frac{Q_j}{OTE_j} \tag{7}$$

The household at B is superior to A in input technical efficiency because it is producing Q_j using smaller aggregate input, $\bar{I}_j \leq \bar{I}_j$. Then an input-oriented technical efficiency (ITE) of A, relative to B, is:

$$ITE_j = \frac{Q_j/I_j}{Q_j/\bar{I}_j} = \frac{TFP_j}{TFP_B} = \frac{\bar{I}_j}{I_j} = D_I^j(X_j, Y_j)^{-1} \leq 1 \tag{8}$$

$\overline{Q}_j^I$ denotes the potential output the household at A can produce if it were input-efficient or, equivalently, the aggregate output the household at B can produce if it were using I_j and operating at a point such as F. This is given as:

$$\bar{Q}_j^I = TFP_B * I_j \tag{9}$$

Note that in Figure 7.1 the slope of the line that connects the origin with each point on or under the production frontier provides the TFP of the household that operates at that point. This implies that although the households at points B and C are superior to that at A, they have lower TFP relative to the household at point D, which has the maximum TFP of Q^*/I^* or the line that is tangent to point D has the maximum slope. D is superior relative to C due to output oriented scale efficiency (OSE) and relative to B in input-oriented scale efficiency (ISE).[3]

Performance in OSE and ISE of the households at C and B is given by:

$$OSE_j = \frac{\bar{Q}_j/I_j}{Q^*/I^*} = \frac{TFP_C}{TFP^*} \leq 1 \quad \text{and} \quad ISE_j = \frac{Q_j/\bar{I}_j}{Q^*/I^*} = \frac{TFP_B}{TFP^*} \leq 1 \tag{10}$$

Equation (5) can be used to compute, $\overline{Q}_j^*$, which denotes the aggregate output j could produce, if it were as productive as k, as:[4]

$$Q_j^* = TFP_k^* * I_j \tag{11}$$

The hypothetical optimal outputs given by equations (7), (9), and (11) are aggregate units. This study computes the optimal teff output in two steps. First, the factor by which aggregate output increases is computed as a ratio of optimal aggregate output and actual aggregate output. In the second step the optimal teff output is obtained by multiplying the factor calculated in the first step and household j's actual teff output. The method is justified because the output aggregator function is nondecreasing and linearly homogenous or increases at the same rate teff output increases.

3 The TFP of households are defined relative to technically and scale-efficient household(s) operating on production frontiers constructed from the dataset. Such comparisons can also be made relative to households that operate on mix-unrestricted production frontier lying above the current frontier (see O'Donnell 2008 and 2011b). The objective of comparing households within the current production possibility frontier justifies the approach used in this study.

4 Equation (11) implicitly assumes that j becomes both scale and technically efficient as k. The latter may not hold if the scale of operation of inefficient households differs from the scale at which optimal households operate. However, the assumption and consequently the computation can be justified for an average household, if increases in scale required for small inefficient farms to be optimal are equivalent to decreases in scales required for larger farms to become optimal. In this dataset aggregate input ranges between 0.76 and 14.71 for all observations, while the 35 all-rounded efficient households have aggregate inputs ranging from 1.108 to 14.34 and are well distributed across this range.

Factors Explaining Efficiency and Productivity

We use a Tobit model to study factors that are associated with teff productivity and efficiency. The empirical equation used for this purpose is given as:

$$\begin{aligned} Efficiency_j = {} & \delta_0 + \textstyle\sum_{i=1}^{4} \delta_i\, HH\ demography_{ij} + \delta_5\, Teff\ area_j + \delta_6\, Teff\ area_j^2 + \\ & \delta_7\, Land\ owned\ by\ HH_j + \delta_8\, Crop\ damage_j + \delta_9\, Partial\ Spec_j + \delta_{10}\, Full\ Spec_j + \\ & \delta_{11}\, Numb\ cash\ crops_j + \delta_{12}\, Off\_farm\ work_j + \delta_{13}\, TLU_j + \delta_{14}\, Production\ info_j + \\ & \delta_{15}\, HH\ participation_j + \delta_{16}\, Fert\ users\ in\ FA_j + \delta_{17}\, Imp\ seeds\ users\ in\ FA_j + \\ & \delta_{18}\, DA\ center\ in\ FA_j + \delta_{19}\, PAs\ in\ FA_j + \delta_{20}\, Distance\ to\ mkt_j + \delta_{21}\, red\ teff_j + \\ & \textstyle\sum_{r=A,O,S} \beta_r\ Region\ dummy_{rj} + \delta_{25}\, AGP_j + \textstyle\sum_{z=WD,D} \delta_z AEZ_{zj} + e_j \end{aligned} \quad (12)$$

In equation (12) $Efficiency_j$ stands for RTFP, OTE, OSE, ITE, and ISE, which are associated with crop-, household-, and location-specific factors. The first summation on the right includes four demographic variables: age, gender, and education of the household head, and household size. About 53 percent of the households cultivated red teff variety, which is represented by the $red\ teff_j$ dummy, while white teff is the omitted category. $Region\ dummy_{rj}$ are region dummies where r ∈ [Amhara (A), Oromiya (O), and SNNP (S)] and Tigray is omitted. Similarly, AGPj takes a value of 1 if household *j* resided in one of the 62 AGP woredas (districts). Included in the last summation are agroecologic zone (AEZ) dummies. The households surveyed lived in AEZs, locally known as Kolla, which is omitted, and Woina Dega (WD), and Dega (D).[5] The error term, e_j, is assumed to be distributed as: $e_j \sim N(0,\sigma_e^2)$. The remaining variables are defined in Table 7.2.

Data

The dataset used in this work was collected in the AGP Baseline Survey. The survey covered 93 woredas (districts) in four regions in Ethiopia: Tigray, Amhara, Oromiya, and Southern Nations, Nationalities, and Peoples' (SNNP) region (see Berhane et al. 2013 for a detailed description of the dataset). The four regions accounted for more than 90 percent of the nation's agricultural output and area during 2004 through 2013 (Ethiopia, CSA 2005a–2014a). Out of 7,928 households covered in the AGP Baseline Survey, 2,942 teff-producing households are included in this study. The data pertains to the 2010/2011 main agricultural season. We decided to rely on these AGP survey

5 This classification divides Ethiopia into five agroecologic zones (AEZs). In general, the Wurch AEZ has the highest altitude and precipitation, followed respectively by Dega, Woina Dega, Kolla, and Berha (see Ethiopia, MoA 2000). About 59 percent of households resided in Woina Dega, 25 percent in Dega, and 15 percent in Kolla; the Wurch dummy was excluded because only 1.1 percent of households resided in that AEZ.

TABLE 7.2 Definition of variables used in the econometric analyses

Variables	Definition	Aggregation
HH $demography_1$	Head gender; dummy = 1 if male	HH
HH $demography_2$	Head age in years	HH
HH $demography_3$	Head education; dummy = 1 if educated in grades 4 or higher	HH
HH $demography_4$	Household size; number of members	HH
Teff area	Teff area (hectares)	Crop
Land owned by HH	Dummy = 1 if cropland is allocated to HH by authorities, purchased, or inherited; and = 0 if rented or sharecropped	Crop
Crop damage	Total crop damage suffered due to different causes (%)	Crop
Partial spec	HH partially specializing, dummy = 1 if HH cultivates two crops	HH
Full spec	HH fully specializes, dummy = 1 if HH cultivates one crop	HH
Numb cash crops	Cash crop types grown (pulses, oilseeds, vegetables, fruits, chat, and coffee)	HH
Off-farm work	Dummy = 1 if at least one HH member is off-farm/nonfarm employed	HH
TLU	Tropical livestock units, number of livestock normalized in cattle units	HH
HH participation	Dummy = 1 if HH member/s visited DA centers, farmers' training centers, or attended community meetings	HH
Production info	Dummy = 1 if HH head obtained production information from radio, newspaper, or information board	HH
Fert users in FA	Percent in FA that use fertilizer	FA
Imp seeds users in FA	Percent in FA that use improved seeds	FA
DA center in FA	Dummy = 1 if FA has extension center where DAs provide services	FA
PAs in FA	Dummy = 1 if one or more active producers' associations in FA	FA
FIs in FA	Dummy = 1 if there exist financial institutions in FA (saving and credit or saving and loan cooperatives and banks and small microfinance institutions)	FA
Distance to market	Distance in kilometers to closest market	FA

Source: Authors.
Notes: HH = household; DA = development agents; FA = farmers' association; PA = producers' association.

data given the large sample, the geographical coverage (as a large number of teff producers were part of the sample), the detailed agricultural information, and the good quality of the data. Table 7.3 summarizes the data used in the analyses.

An average household used 0.5 hectares to grow teff and produced 3.2 quintals, and yields averaged 7.7 quintals per hectare. An average household head was 43 years old in May 2011, and about 77 percent of the households have male heads. About 43 percent of household heads are literate, and 29 percent attended grade 4 or higher. In the econometric analyses, household

TABLE 7.3 Mean value of variables

Variable	Mean	Standard deviation	Variable	Mean	Standard deviation
Output (kilograms)	320	372	Gender of head	0.77	0.42
Yields (kilograms per hectare)	769	624	Head age (years)	43	15
Teff area (hectares)	0.50	0.47	Head literate (%)	43	49
Total household area (hectares)	1.58	1.27	Head in grades 4 or higher (%)	29	46
Land owned (%)	75.1	43.3	Household size (number)	5.0	2.2
Labor (working days)	55	107	HHs with member/s employed off/nonfarm (%)	40	49
Oxen (number)	1.4	1.4	Tropical livestock units	3.7	3.9
Fertilizer (kilograms)	31	52	Obtained production information (%)	26	44
Improved seeds (kilograms)	1.0	6.5	Household member participation (%)	55	50
Pesticides (% using)	35	48	Percent in FA using fertilizer	68	33
Percentage of area irrigated	1.9	13.5	Percent in FA using improved seeds	52	32
Land quality index	6.5	2.3	FAs with extension centers (%)	90	30
Percentage of crop damaged	11	20	FAs with producers' associations (%)	24	43
Percent partially specializing	13	34	FAs with financial institutions (%)	48	50
Percent fully specializing	3.3	17.9	Distance to market (kilometers)	11.1	10.0
Cash crops cultivated (number)	1.0	1.1	Total crop season rainfall	1,497	609

Source: The authors made the calculations directly using the 2011 Agricultural Growth Program Baseline Survey data.
Note: HHs = households; FA = farmers' associations, which are the smallest administrative unit in rural Ethiopia.

heads that attended grade 4 or higher are assigned a value of 1. This follows Wier's (1999) finding that four years of schooling is the minimum threshold for education to meaningfully affect productivity.

Results and Discussion

In the first part of this section, performance in relative TFP (RTFP) and efficiency of teff producers obtained from DEA are discussed. The discussion focuses on performances of households cultivating different teff area. This is followed by a discussion of optimal output and yields computed using the performance indexes together with the assumption that all households are optimal and partially or fully specialized in teff production. DPIN 3.0, a program designed to decompose productivity and index numbers (O'Donnell 2011b), is used to compute relative TFP and efficiency indexes. Finally, results of the econometric analyses conducted to indicate the associates of relative TFP and efficiency are discussed.

Relative TFP and Efficiency

Average performance in RTFP, output-oriented technical and scale efficiency (OTE and OSE), and corresponding input-oriented measures (ITE and ISE) are summarized in Table 7.4. Average RTFP of teff production is 0.344. That is, average RTFP can potentially increase by 191 percent (= (1−0.344)/0.344). However, improvements in RTFP computed at household level indicate a potential growth of about 400 percent. The latter indicates that RTFP is skewed to lower values, which is corroborated by normality tests of RTFP. OTE and ITE averaged 0.39 and 0.64, while OSE and ISE averaged 0.91 and 0.52, respectively.

Table 7.4 also summarizes the performance indexes across three levels of specialization (measured by number of crops cultivated) and proportion of household area allocated to teff. About 77 percent of the households allocate less than half of their landholdings to grow teff, while about 84 percent grow three or more crops. About 13 percent grow two crops, 20 percent use at least half of their landholdings in teff production, and 3.2 percent specialize in teff or use all their land to grow teff.

Performance in all productivity indexes, except OSE, improves with specialization and household area sown to teff. Household landholdings are largest among those households that specialize least and smallest among those that are fully specialized. This implies that there is considerable room to increase the scale of operation as well as to specialize in fewer crops. Moreover, households that allocate half or more of their landholdings for teff, 57 percent of which grow three or more crops, cultivate larger teff area (0.77 hectares) but perform poorer in RTFP, OTE, and ITE relative to households that fully specialize in teff. The latter suggests that performance in teff productivity improves if households both specialize in fewer crops and increase their scale of teff production.

TABLE 7.4 Summary of DEA predicted relative TFP and efficiency across scale of operation and specialization

Household category (%)	Statistics	Performance in productivity/ efficiency					Land management characteristics			
		RTFP	OTE	OSE	ITE	ISE	Teff area (hectares)	Number of crops	Average area per crop (hectares)	Total household area (hectares)
All households (100)	Mean	0.34	0.39	0.91	0.64	0.52	0.50	4.22	0.40	1.58
	Standard deviation	0.23	0.27	0.15	0.19	0.26	0.47	1.85	0.31	1.27
Household area in teff										
Less than half (77.1%)	Mean	0.33	0.38	0.91	0.64	0.51	0.42	4.65	0.39	1.70
	Standard deviation	0.23	0.27	0.15	0.19	0.26	0.38	1.75	0.29	1.33
At least half (19.7%)	Mean	0.37	0.41	0.93	0.64	0.56	0.77	3.06	0.42	1.24
	Standard deviation	0.24	0.26	0.12	0.19	0.26	0.64	1.25	0.33	0.99
Number of crops cultivated										
Three or more (83.7%)	Mean	0.33	0.38	0.92	0.63	0.51	0.49	4.69	0.38	1.70
	Standard deviation	0.23	0.26	0.14	0.19	0.26	0.47	1.64	0.29	1.32
Two (13.1%)	Mean	0.39	0.45	0.89	0.72	0.53	0.52	2.0	0.51	1.02
	Standard deviation	0.24	0.27	0.16	0.20	0.25	0.44	0.00	0.36	0.73
All area in teff/ single crop (3.2%)	Mean	0.39	0.46	0.89	0.70	0.55	0.69	1.0	0.69	0.69
	Standard deviation	0.26	0.29	0.18	0.21	0.26	0.52	0.00	0.51	0.51

Source: The authors made the calculations directly using the 2011 Agricultural Growth Program Baseline Survey data.

Note: DEA = data envelopment analyses; RTFP = relative total factor productivity; OTE and OSE = output-oriented technical and scale efficiency; and ITE and ISE = input-oriented technical and scale efficiency, respectively.

Figure 7.2 depicts the productivity indexes across average teff area of nine groups of households. Seven of the nine groups constitute about 10 percent or a decile of the 2,942 observations, while households that cultivate 0.25 hectares and 0.5 hectares accounted for 18 percent and 14 percent of the total, respectively. The figure indicates that RTFP, OTE, and ISE decline with teff area up to about 0.5 hectares and increase thereafter. OSE increases up to 0.68 hectares and then declines, while the reverse holds for ITE. It appears that households gain in productivity if they allocate at least about 0.5 hectares of their landholdings for teff. In this dataset, less than 30 percent allocate half a hectare or more for teff production.

FIGURE 7.2 Relationship between teff area and relative TFP and efficiency

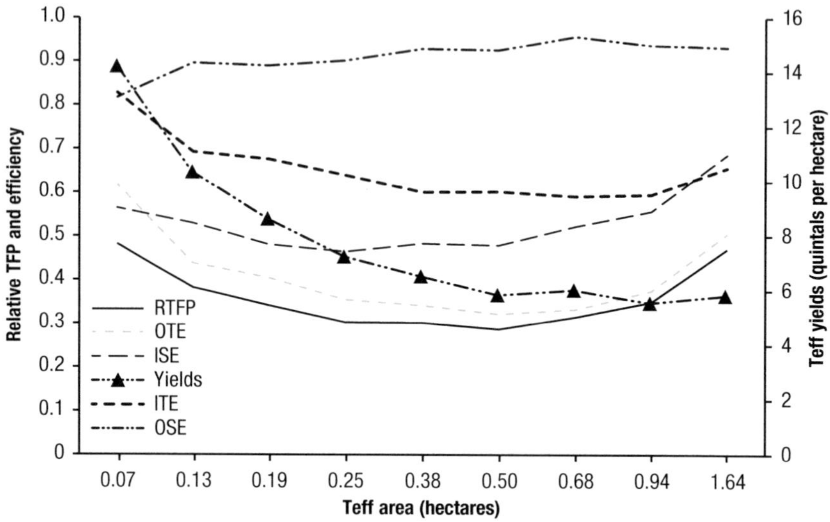

Source: The authors made the calculations directly using the 2011 Agricultural Growth Program Baseline Survey data.
Note: TFP = total factor productivity; RTFP = relative total factor productivity; OTE and OSE = output oriented technical and scale efficiency; and ITE and ISE = input oriented technical and scale efficiency, respectively.

Note that the results on teff productivity are only a partial picture of performance in overall crop productivity of the households studied, nearly 97 percent of which grow at least one other crop than teff. This implies that production decisions targeted at maximizing overall crop productivity may impact teff productivity negatively. However, Bachewe et al. (2015) find productivity levels similar to those obtained in this study using households in the AGP baseline dataset that cultivate the five most important cereal crops in Ethiopia, in terms of cropped area and number of households cultivating the crops.

Optimal Teff Output Yields

The discussion in the previous section indicates that relative TFP of an average household can potentially increase by nearly threefold if all households were optimal in RTFP, or if average RTFP equals 1. The discussion also indicates that performance in RTFP declines until about 0.5 hectares and then increases, implying that teff productivity could increase in households that use larger areas to produce teff. This study computes output and yield levels that each household could produce at hypothetically optimal levels of RTFP, OTE, and ITE—the results of which are discussed in the first part of this section. The second part discusses outputs and yields computed under the assumption that households allocate half or all of their landholdings to produce teff and become as productive as an average household that is currently using similar area to produce teff.

Scenario 1: Current Input Use and Inefficiencies Removed

Equations (11), (7), and (9) are used to compute optimal outputs that households could produce using current inputs, if inefficiencies implied by RTFP, OTE, and ITE were removed, respectively. Optimal outputs so computed are divided by teff area cultivated to obtain optimal yields. Yields and output levels computed under those assumptions are summarized in the third column of Table 7.5 ("Yields and output if fully optimal"). The first panel of the table summarizes yields. Optimal outputs of an average household are summarized in the second panel. The 2,942 households included in this study represent 3.6 million teff-producing households that resided in the districts covered by the AGP Baseline Survey. These 3.6 million households are computed using sampling weights of households included in that baseline survey. In the third panel, total teff output of the 3.6 million households is summarized.

Optimal teff yields implied by RTFP and OTE are higher than 2 metric tons per hectare or nearly three times actual yields. Optimal yields implied by ITE are lower, at about 1.2 metric tons per hectare, because households perform relatively well in ITE. Teff output could be potentially higher than 0.9 metric tons per household if all households were both technically and scale efficient. OTE and ITE implied optimal teff output averaged about 0.86 metric tons and 0.5 metric tons, respectively. The 3.6 million households in the districts surveyed cultivated 1.6 million hectares of land and produced about 1.1 million metric tons of teff. If all households were optimal in RTFP, output could increase to 3.2 million metric tons. Similarly, if output and input technical inefficiencies were removed, output could increase to 3.1 million metric tons and 1.8 million metric tons, respectively.

Scenario 2: Partial or Full Specialization in Teff Production

Gains in output that could result if households partially specialize in teff production are computed by assuming households use half of their total landholdings to produce teff.[6] Similarly, gains in output due to fully specializing

6 Households that use half of their landholdings to produce teff and the second half to grow one other crop can accurately be described as partially specializing in teff. The term describes households that use the second half of their land to grow multiple crops only loosely and can only be justified because such households use a larger proportion of their landholdings to grow teff.

TABLE 7.5 Teff output and yield at optimal productivity and at partial and full specialization in teff

Variable	Efficiency index or indicator	Yields and output if fully optimal (index = 1)	Yields and output due to: Partial specialization (teff area = half household area)	Yields and output due to: Full specialization (teff area = household area)
			First Panel	
Average teff area (hectares)	Actual or with specialization	0.50	0.79	1.58
Yields (kilograms per hectare)	Actual (current productivity)	769	769	769
	RTFP	2,259	953	1,032
	OTE	2,070	961	1,034
	ITE	1,163	825	836
			Second Panel	
Output (kilograms)	Actual or with specialization	320	554	1,058
	RTFP	925	730	1,521
	OTE	863	734	1,527
	ITE	504	608	1,182
			Third Panel	
Total area (million hectares)	Actual or with specialization	1.63	2.61	5.22
Total weighted output of 3.6 million households (thousand metric tons)	Actual or with specialization	1,099	1,933	3,745
	RTFP	3,230	2,489	5,296
	OTE	3,070	2,531	5,383
	ITE	1,825	2,155	4,264

Source: The authors made the calculations directly using the 2011 Agricultural Growth Program Baseline Survey data.
Note: RTFP = relative total factor productivity; OTE = output-oriented technical efficiency; and ITE = input-oriented technical efficiency. Output levels are computed for each household as the product of area and yields with area measured as "actual area," "area with partial specialization in teff," and "area with full specialization in teff," respectively. The figures in the Second Panel are the averages corresponding to each of these products.

in teff production are computed by assuming households use their total landholdings to produce teff.[7] These computations also use the teff area deciles described in the last section and used in Figure 7.2. Accordingly, households in the first to eighth teff area deciles are assumed to move into one of the

7 Households that currently use at least half or all of their landholdings to produce teff are considered as partially or fully specializing in teff and hence not included in computations that consider these respective scenarios.

higher (second to ninth) teff area deciles when they allocate half or all of their landholdings to produce teff. Then, gains in partial or full specialization are computed by assuming that the households:

1. Use average levels of nonland inputs used by households in the new teff area decile that they move into, and
2. Become as productive as an average household in the new area decile (in RTFP, OTE, and ITE).

Equations (11), (7), and (9) are then used to compute the new output levels implied by the new input use and RTFP, OTE, and ITE levels in the higher teff area deciles, respectively. Moreover, output levels at initial values of productivity indexes and new input use levels are also computed. The difference in the two output levels is then taken as the gain in output that results from improvements in the respective productivity index or due to partially or fully specializing in teff. Results of these computations are provided in the last two columns of Table 7.5. These computations consider only improvements in productivity that result from partially or fully specializing in teff production. The latter considerations abstract from the fact that households' current scale of production and diversification are part of the overall production decision made under existing resource constraints as well as intended to mitigate production and price shocks associated with cultivating a single or a few types of crop (Barrett, Bellemare, and Hou 2010). Nevertheless, the simple and partial exercise is worth pursuing as it adds insights into the positive relationship between productivity and teff area pointed to in the last section and further explored in the econometric analyses that follow. Furthermore, in economies with more developed markets, production and price risks are better mitigated through other tools than diversification.

The results in the fourth column of Table 7.5 indicate that average teff area will increase to nearly 0.8 hectares if all households were to use at least half of their landholdings to produce teff. At current levels of productivity, an average household could produce 5.5 quintals of teff using half of its landholdings. Teff output and yields could increase to about 7.3 quintals and 9.5 quintals per hectare due to gains in RTFP and OTE when partially specializing in teff. That is, teff output could potentially increase by over 1.7 quintals and yields by 1.8 quintals per hectare due to improvements in RTFP and OTE when partially specializing in teff. Gains implied by ITE increases are lower, at about 50 kilograms for both output and yield per hectare. The 3.6 million households in the districts surveyed would allocate 2.6 million hectares, if all of them were to partially specialize in teff. Teff output would then grow to 1.93 million metric tons at current levels of productivity. Improvements in RTFP and OTE when partially specializing in teff would increase teff output of the districts surveyed by at least 0.56 million metric tons.

If all households used their total landholdings, which averaged 1.58 hectares, to produce teff, an average household could produce 10.6 quintals at current productivity levels. Teff output of an average household could increase by at least 4.6 quintals and yields by at least 2.6 quintals per hectare due to improvements in RTFP or OTE when fully specializing in teff production. The latter implies that teff yields grow faster at full specialization than at partial specialization. If all 5.2 million hectares of land used in the main agricultural season of 2010/2011 in the districts surveyed were used to produce teff, output could increase to 3.8 million metric tons at current productivity levels. Full specialization induced improvements of RTFP and OTE could increase teff output of households in the districts surveyed by least 1.6 million metric tons, while improvements in ITE could increase teff output by 0.5 million metric tons.

Factors Associated with Efficiency and Productivity

In this section estimates of equation (12) obtained using a Tobit model are discussed. Results of the econometric analyses, which are given in Table 7.6, indicate that household size and age of the household head are not associated with teff productivity. Male headed households, which on average cultivate larger teff area, have higher scale efficiency. The education level of household heads is positively associated with performance in RTFP, OTE, and ISE.

Access to Information on Production and Services

Access to information on production from media sources is positively correlated with all productivity indexes, except OSE. Performance in most indexes is higher among households residing in kebeles (subdistricts), where government offices provide extension services and also where a higher proportion of households use improved seeds. This may indicate that households benefit from direct exposure to extension and indirect information on modern production methods. Studies that find similar results include Ajewole and Folayan (2008); Binam, Gockowski, and Nkamleu (2008); Helfand and Levine (2004); and Solís, Bravo-Ureta, and Quiroga (2007). Productivity was expected to be positively associated with attending meetings and/or visiting

TABLE 7.6 Tobit model estimates of factors associated with relative TFP and efficiency

	Dependent variable[a]				
		Output oriented		Input oriented	
Variables	Relative TFP	Technical efficiency	Scale efficiency	Technical efficiency	Scale efficiency
Household characteristics					
Gender of household head	0.424	−0.924	1.151*	−0.772	1.162
	(1.075)	(1.305)	(0.667)	(0.839)	(1.179)
Age of household head	−0.000	0.026	−0.029	0.018	−0.006
	(0.029)	(0.036)	(0.018)	(0.023)	(0.032)
Head education	1.60*	3.31***	−1.39**	0.819	2.32**
	(0.934)	(1.134)	(0.578)	(0.727)	(1.024)
Household size	0.260	0.204	0.079	−0.092	0.335
	(0.214)	(0.259)	(0.132)	(0.166)	(0.234)
Land management and risk					
Crop area	−3.14**	−9.55**	6.71**	−14.86**	7.50**
	(1.590)	(1.931)	(0.985)	(1.235)	(1.745)
Crop area squared	3.24***	4.92***	−1.49***	4.59***	0.910*
	(0.493)	(0.600)	(0.305)	(0.382)	(0.545)
Proportion of land owned	−0.479	−1.196	0.649	−1.054	−0.105
	(1.001)	(1.215)	(0.620)	(0.780)	(1.098)
Total crop damage (%)	−12.8***	−12.6***	−2.36*	−1.385	−18.4***
	(2.006)	(2.433)	(1.241)	(1.563)	(2.20)
Partially specialized	5.44***	4.12***	2.54***	1.73*	6.08***
	(1.310)	(1.594)	(0.812)	(1.031)	(1.437)
Fully specialized	7.49***	7.74***	1.55	3.54*	7.56***
	(2.345)	(2.854)	(1.459)	(1.857)	(2.576)
Number of cash crops cultivated	0.021	−0.533	1.01***	−1.21***	0.696
	(0.421)	(0.510)	(0.261)	(0.326)	(0.461)
HH member works off-farm	−0.330	−0.065	−0.668***	0.652**	−0.950**
	(0.409)	(0.497)	(0.254)	(0.319)	(0.449)
Tropical livestock units	0.123	-0.006	0.180**	−0.117	0.262**
	(0.118)	(0.144)	(0.074)	(0.092)	(0.131)
Access to information and services					
Production information	2.65***	2.91***	−0.214	1.60**	2.82**
	(0.978)	(1.188)	(0.607)	(0.763)	(1.073)

(continued)

TABLE 7.6 Continued

	Dependent variable[a]				
		Output oriented		Input oriented	
Variables	Relative TFP	Technical efficiency	Scale efficiency	Technical efficiency	Scale efficiency
Access to information and services (continued)					
Household member participation	−2.160**	−1.378	−0.505	−1.337*	−1.837*
	(0.880)	(1.068)	(0.545)	(0.685)	(0.965)
Fertilizer users in FA	0.006	−0.001	0.003	0.014	0.013
	(0.016)	(0.019)	(0.010)	(0.012)	(0.017)
Improved seeds users in FA	0.060***	0.086***	−0.013	−0.003	0.089***
	(0.017)	(0.020)	(0.010)	(0.013)	(0.018)
DA center available in FA	4.75***	4.44**	0.644	3.02***	4.10**
	(1.497)	(1.813)	(0.930)	(1.155)	(1.641)
PAs available in FA	−1.860*	−1.740	0.462	−0.544	−2.687**
	(1.010)	(1.227)	(0.626)	(0.790)	(1.107)
FIs available in FA	1.97**	2.20**	0.277	−2.34***	4.10***
	(0.894)	(1.084)	(0.553)	(0.695)	(0.980)
Distance to closest market	0.071*	0.173***	−0.116***	0.081**	0.033
	(0.043)	(0.053)	(0.027)	(0.034)	(0.048)
Constant	14.3***	29.1***	75.0***	84.8***	15.3***
	(3.468)	(4.209)	(2.148)	(2.698)	(3.804)
Log likelihood	−13,149	−13,143	−11,311	−11,437	−13,289
Number of observations	2,942				

Source: The authors made the calculations directly using the 2011 Agricultural Growth Program Baseline Survey data.

Note: Coefficients with ***, **, and * are significant at 1, 5, and 10 percent level of significance, respectively. The equations estimated are specified in equation (12) above and include region and agroecologic zone dummies. The estimates are omitted to avoid clutter. [a] The dependent variables are DEA productivity indexes expressed in percent and thus have an upper limit of 100.

farmers' training centers. Despite this expectation, households with members that participated in such events have lower RTFP and input-oriented efficiencies.

Performance in productivity was expected to be positively associated with proximity to markets, as the latter generally improves access to marketed inputs and outlets to marketed surplus. However, RTFP, OTE, and ITE of households farther from markets is higher while the reverse holds in OSE. This result is similar to the finding in Nisrane et al. (2011). The latter study argues that villages close to markets are often early-settled areas where the production potential may have diminished from years of cultivation (Nisrane et al. 2011). Moreover, households in areas closer to markets have a higher likelihood of engaging in nonfarming activities and thus less productive in teff. Relative TFP and ISE of households residing in FAs with active producers' associations are lower. This is contrary to the positive association of efficiency and membership in cooperatives that Helfand and Levine (2004) found. Households in FAs with financial institutions have higher RTFP, OTE, and ISE and lower ITE. This is similar to the findings by Solís, Bravo-Ureta, and Quiroga (2007) and Helfand and Levine (2004), which argue that access to credits impacts efficiency positively.

Land Management and Risk

The description in the previous two sections indicate that productivity generally improves with specializing in fewer crops. However, the dataset used indicates that households lack specialization. An average household cultivated 4.2 crops. Only 3 percent and 13 percent cultivated one and two crops, while 21 percent and 23 percent cultivated three and four crops, respectively. Results of the econometric analyses indicate partially specializing in teff is positively associated with performance in all five indexes, while fully specializing in teff is positively associated with four of the indexes. Moreover, where significant, estimates of the effect of full specialization are statistically significantly higher than those of partial specialization. These findings are similar to Sherlund, Barrett, and Adesina (2002), where a negative relationship between performance in efficiency and number of crops cultivated is found.

Households reported that 11 percent of their teff output was lost to damages such as bad weather, diseases, and pests (Table 7.3). The econometric analysis also indicates that households that suffered crop damages have lower productivity in all indexes, except input-technical efficiency. Households cope with variability of income generated from teff production by engaging in non-teff-production activities, such as livestock production and off-farm employment. Coelli and Fleming (2004) argue that cost efficiency improves due to gains in diversifying economies, resulting from the production of subsistence and cash crops. The results in this study indicate that both output and input scale efficiency are positively associated with the number of livestock households own, which increases households' access to plowing power. Households with members that participate in off-farm/nonfarm activities are likely to face labor constraints relative to those with no such member. Our results indicate that participation in off- or nonfarm activity is negatively associated with scale efficiency. This result is similar to the negative relationship between off-farm work and efficiency found by Coelli, Rahman, and Thirtle (2002). Moreover, Mariano, Villano, and Fleming (2011) found that efficiency of rice farmers in the Philippines declined with an increase in income generated through nonrice farming and nonfarming activities.

This study examines whether scale of operation, defined in the teff area cultivated, is related with productivity. Estimated coefficients of area and its square term imply that output and input technical efficiency decline until about 1 hectare and 1.6 hectares, respectively, and then increase. Moreover, output scale efficiency increases until 2.3 hectares before declining. Consequently, RTFP declines until 0.48 hectares and increases thereafter. The econometric analyses, which consider the effects of a number of factors other than area, implies that RTFP starts to increase at the same teff area size as implied in the descriptive analyses (Figure 7.2).

The inverse farm size–productivity relationship has been documented in a large number of studies (Barrett, Bellemare, and Hou 2010). However, most studies establish the relationship using "partial measures of productivity such as yield" and such a relationship may not hold "if a measure of total factor productivity (TFP) were used instead" (Helfand and Levine 2004, 241). The latter observation is corroborated by a number of works that study diverse countries and crop systems, which indicate a positive relationship between farm size and productivity, more specifically, between farm size and multifactor productivity measures. This includes, among others, Padilla-Fernandez and Nuthall (2012), Rios and Shively (2005), Hadley (2006), and Coelli, Rahman, and Thirtle (2002). In particular, the u-shaped efficiency-area relationship implied in the econometric analyses and depicted in Figure 7.2 is similar to that obtained in Helfand and Levine (2004) and Latruffe et al. (2005).

Bachewe et al. (2015) used the AGP Baseline Survey data to show that productivity improves with farm size among cereals producers in Ethiopia. Moreover, an inverse relationship between cereals yields and farm size was found. The data used in the current study also indicates that teff yield generally declines with cultivated area (see Figure 7.2). Bachewe et al. (2015) examine application levels and partial productivities of labor, fertilizer, and improved seeds to explain the apparently contradictory inverse farm size–yield relationship on the one hand and positive farm size–multifactor productivity relationship on the other. The study attributes the apparent contradiction, among others, to per hectare application of the three inputs, which is relatively higher among smallholders and declines with area, consequently leading to lower partial productivity of the inputs at smaller scales of operation.

This study further investigates the farm size–productivity relationship and examines whether the association of factors with productivity and efficiency differs across farm size. For this purpose the econometric analysis applied to all households and presented in Table 7.6 is conducted by dividing the households in the dataset into two groups: smallholders and medium- to largeholders (henceforth "largeholders"). Households cultivating the median teff area of 0.375 hectares or less, which constitute 51.5 percent of the total, are categorized as smallholders. Results of this analysis are provided in Appendix Table 7.A1.

When significant, almost all estimates in Appendix Table 7.A1 have implications similar to those in Table 7.6. There are two exceptions, however. Age of the household head and household size are associated with smallholders' efficiency negatively and positively, respectively, and OSE of both smallholders and largeholders is positively associated with proximity to markets. Despite the similarity in their implications, a number of the variables are associated with the productivity of either smallholders or largeholders. This includes access to media information on production, which is positively correlated with four productivity indexes of only largeholders. Similarly, off-farm employment is negatively correlated with scale efficiency of only smallholders. Four of the five performance indexes of only largeholders are negatively associated with availability of producers' associations, while only RTFP of largeholders is negatively associated with participation in meetings or visits to farmers' training centers.

The relationship between area and productivity, implied by estimates of area and area-squared, is shown to be distinct for smallholders when compared to largeholders. Accordingly, input- and output-oriented technical efficiency of largeholders increase linearly and quadratically, respectively. ISE increases until 6.25 hectares and then declines. Consequently, relative TFP of largeholders increases linearly in all teff areas. In contrast, all indexes of smallholders, except OSE, decline until teff areas ranging between 0.3 hectares and 0.38 hectares before increasing, and the reverse is true for OSE. In particular, relative TFP of smallholders declines until 0.33 hectares and increases thereafter.

Key Findings and Policy Implications

Data envelopment analysis (DEA) is employed on input-output data of teff-producing households in Ethiopia. The data used in the analyses is part of a larger dataset collected in the baseline survey of the Agricultural Growth Program and pertains to the 2010/2011 main agricultural season. The results of the DEA indicate that current relative total factor productivity levels can nearly triple with removal of inefficiencies. Performance in output-oriented technical efficiency was also considerably low. Despite differences in magnitudes, the performance measures imply a significant potential for increases in output produced on current acreage, if inefficiencies were removed. Moreover, the analyses in the chapter reveal that considerable gains in teff yields and output could be achieved by partially or fully specializing in teff production.

The econometric analyses conducted in the study indicate that relative productivity is positively associated with education, and with access to financial institutions, production information, and extension services. Off-farm income-generation activities that help reduce income variability are negatively correlated with scale efficiency. Productivity of households that specialize fully or partially in teff is higher, relative to productivity of nonspecializing households. The results also indicate that gains in scale efficiency improve productivity at lower scales of operation, while gains in technical efficiency improve productivity at larger scales. This, unlike the inverse farm size–productivity hypotheses, implies that largeholders are as productive as smallholders. The results also indicate that largeholders' productivity increases linearly with cultivated area, while smallholders' productivity first declines and then increases.

Many factors that are associated with productivity are amenable to policy targeting. These include improving access to formal education, possibly through training programs that are delivered during the off-season. Also, improved access to information on production methods and extension services are shown to be positively correlated with productivity. The decision on the type and number of crops households cultivate, and consequently the tendency to specialize depends, among others, on their subsistence requirements, profitability of the crops, risks associated with cultivating few crop types, and the size of their total land holdings. Further research is required on factors that determine levels of specialization and scale of operation in order to make more precise recommendations. However, the results in this study indicate that productivity is positively associated with both scale of operation and level of specialization. Furthermore, well-established findings in international trade and development economics imply that access to and participation in markets, along with low crop failure risks, help farmers specialize.

References

Ajewole, O., and J. Folayan. 2008. "Stochastic Frontier Analysis of Technical Efficiency in Dry Season Leaf Vegetable Production among Smallholders in Ekiti State, Nigeria." *Agricultural Journal* 3: 252–257.

Bachewe, F., G. Berhane, B. Minten, and A. S. Taffesse. 2015. *Agricultural Growth in Ethiopia (2004–2014): Evidence and Drivers.* International Food Policy Research Institute (IFPRI)/ Ethiopia Strategy Support Program (ESSP) II Working Paper 81. Addis Ababa, Ethiopia: International Food Policy Research Institute.

Bachewe, F. N., B. Koru, and A. S. Taffesse. 2015. *Cereals Productivity and Its Drivers: The Case of Ethiopia.* IFPRI/ESSP II Working Paper 74. Addis Ababa, Ethiopia: International Food Policy Research Institute.

Bachewe, F. N., and A. S. Taffesse. 2015. *Dynamic Supply Response of Farm Households in Ethiopia.* IFPRI/ESSP II Working Paper 78. Addis Ababa, Ethiopia: International Food Policy Research Institute.

Barrett, C. B., M. F. Bellemare, and J. Y. Hou. 2010. "Reconsidering Conventional Explanations of the Inverse Productivity–Size Relationship." *World Development* 38 (1): 88–97.

Berhane, G., M. Dereje Regassa, J. Hoddinott, B. Koru, F. Nisrane, F. Tadesse, A. S. Taffesse, I. Worku Hassen, and Y. Yohannes. 2013. *Agricultural Growth Program (AGP) of Ethiopia-Baseline Report 2011.* ESSP-EDRI Report. Addis Ababa, Ethiopia: International Food Policy Research Institute.

Bill and Melinda Gates Foundation. 2011. *Agricultural Development Strategy Overview.* Seattle.

Binam, J., J. Gockowski, and G. Nkamleu. 2008. "Technical Efficiency and Productivity Potential of Cocoa Farmers in West African Countries." *Developing Economies* 46 (3): 242–263.

Birner, R., and D. Resnick, 2010. "The Political Economy of Policies for Smallholder Agriculture." *World Development* 38 (10): 1442–1452.

Coelli, T., and E. Fleming. 2004. "Diversification Economies and Specialisation Efficiencies in a Mixed Food and Coffee Smallholder Farming System in Papua New Guinea." *Agricultural Economics* 31: 229–239.

Coelli, T., S. Rahman, and C. Thirtle. 2002. "Technical, Allocative, Cost, and Scale Efficiencies in Bangladesh Rice Cultivation: A Non-parametric Approach." *Journal of Agricultural Economics* 53: 607–626.

Collier, P., and S. Dercon. 2009. "African Agriculture in 50 Years: Smallholders in a Rapidly Changing World?" In *How to Feed the World in 2050: Proceedings of a Technical Meeting of Experts.* Rome: Food and Agriculture Organization (FAO) of the United Nations.

Dercon, S., and A. Zeitlin. 2009. "Rethinking Agriculture and Growth in Ethiopia: A Conceptual Discussion." Paper prepared as part of a study on Agriculture and Growth in Ethiopia. Department for International Development (DfID), London, UK.

Diao, X. 2010. "Economic Importance of Agriculture for Sustainable Development and Poverty Reduction: The Case Study of Ethiopia." Paper presented at Global Forum on Agriculture, Paris, November 29–30.

Diao, X., P. Hazell, and J. Thurlow. 2010. "The Role of Agriculture in African Development." *World Development* 38: 1375–1383.

Dorosh, P., S. Robinson, and J. Thurlow. 2015. "Implications of Agricultural Productivity Growth for Structural Change and Employment in Ethiopia." Paper presented at the EDRI-IFPRI Seminar, Addis Ababa, Ethiopia, April 9.

Endale, K. 2011. *Fertilizer Consumption and Agricultural Productivity in Ethiopia*. EDRI Research Report 3. Addis Ababa, Ethiopia: Ethiopian Development Research Institute.

Ethiopia, CSA (Central Statistical Agency). 2005a, 2006a, . . . , 2014a. *Agricultural Sample Survey: 2004/5, 2005/6, . . . , 2013/14 (1997, 1998, . . . , 2006 E.C.). Volume 1, Report on Area and Production of Crops (Private Peasant Holdings, Meher Season).* Addis Ababa, Ethiopia.

———. 2005b, 2006b, . . . , 2014b. *Agricultural Sample Survey: 2004/5, 2005/6, . . . , 2013/14 (1997, 1998, . . . , 2006 E.C.) Volume 4, Report on Land Utilization (Private Peasant Holdings, Meher Season).* Addis Ababa, Ethiopia.

———. 2009c, 2010c, . . . , 2014c. *Agricultural Sample Survey: 2008/9, 2009/10, . . . , 2013/14 (2001, 2002, . . . , 2006 E.C.) Volume 7, Report on Crop and Livestock Utilization (Private Peasant Holdings, Meher Season).* Addis Ababa, Ethiopia.

Ethiopia, MoA (Ministry of Agriculture). 2000. *Agroecological Zonations of Ethiopia*. Addis Ababa, Ethiopia.

Ethiopia, MoPED (Ministry of Planning and Economic Development). 1993. *An Economic Development Strategy for Ethiopia: A Comprehensive Guidance and a Development Strategy for the Future*. Addis Ababa, Ethiopia.

Ethiopia, MoRAD (Ministry of Agriculture and Rural Development). 2010. *Agricultural Growth Program (AGP)—Program Implementation Manual (Main Text)*. Addis Ababa, Ethiopia.

Fan, S., J. Brzeska, M. Keyzer, and A. Helsema. 2013. *From Subsistence to Profit: Transforming Smallholder Farms*. Food Policy Report. Washington, DC: IFPRI.

FAO (Food and Agricultural Organization of the United Nations). 2010. *Policies and Institutions to Support Smallholder Agriculture*. Rome: Food and Agricultural Organization.

Fare, R., S. Grosskopf, and C. A. Lovell. 1985. *The Measurement of Efficiency of Production*. Boston: Kluwer Academic Publishers.

Fare, R., and D. Primont. 1995. *Multi-Output Production and Duality: Theory and Applications.* Boston: Kluwer Academic Publishers.

Hadley, D. 2006. "Patterns in Technical Efficiency and Technical Change at the Farm-level in England and Wales, 1982–2002." *Journal of Agricultural Economics* 57: 81–100.

Hazell, P. 2014. *Is Small Farm Led Development Still a Relevant Strategy for Africa and Asia?* Accessed September 17, 2014. www.fondation-farm.org/zoe/doc/peterhazell_original_english_paper.pdf.

Hazell, P., C. Poulton, S. Wiggins, and A. Dorward. 2010. "The Future of Small Farms: Trajectories and Policy Priorities." *World Development* 38 (10): 1349–1361.

Helfand, S. M., and E. S. Levine. 2004. "Farm Size and the Determinants of Productive Efficiency in the Brazilian Center-West." *Agricultural Economics* 31: 241–249.

Latruffe, L., K. Balcombe, S. Davidova, and K. Zawalinska. 2005. "Technical and Scale Efficiency of Crop and Livestock Farms in Poland: Does Size Matter?" *Agricultural Economics* 32: 281–296.

Maertens, M., and J. Swinnen. 2009. "Trade, Standards, and Poverty: Evidence from Senegal." *World Development* 37 (1): 161–178.

Mariano, M., R. Villano, and E. Fleming. 2011. "Technical Efficiency of Rice Farms in Different Agroclimatic Zones in the Philippines: An Application of a Stochastic Metafrontier Model." *Asian Economic Journal* 25: 245–269.

NASA (National Aeronautics and Space Administration of the United States). 2014. *NASA Prediction of Worldwide Energy Resource: Climatology Resource for Agroclimatology.* Accessed July 15, 2014. http://power.larc.nasa.gov/cgi-bin/cgiwrap/solar/agro.cgi.

National Bank of Ethiopia. 2014. *Annual Report 2013–2014.* Addis Ababa, Ethiopia.

Nisrane, F., G. Berhane, S. Asrat, G. Getachew, A. S. Taffesse, and J. Hoddinott. 2011. *Sources of Inefficiency and Growth in Agricultural Output in Subsistence Agriculture: A Stochastic Frontier Analysis.* IFPRI/ESSP II Working Paper 19. Addis Ababa, Ethiopia: International Food Policy Research Institute.

O'Donnell, C. J. 2008. *An Aggregate Quantity-Price Framework for Measuring and Decomposing Productivity and Profitability Change.* Centre for Efficiency and Productivity Analysis (CEPA) Working Papers WP07/2008. University of Queensland, CEPA, Brisbane, Australia.

———. 2009. "Measuring and Decomposing Agricultural Productivity and Profitability Change." Presidential Address to the 53rd Annual Conference of the Australian Agricultural and Resource Economics Society, Cairns, Australia.

———. 2011a. *The Sources of Productivity Change in the Manufacturing Sectors of the U.S. Economy.* CEPA Working Papers WP07/2011. University of Queensland, CEPA, Brisbane, Australia.

———. 2011b. "DPIN 3.0: A Program for Decomposing Productivity Index Numbers." Mimeo, University of Queensland, CEPA, Brisbane, Australia.

Padilla-Fernandez, M. D., and P. L. Nuthall. 2012. "Farm Size and Its Effect on the Productive Efficiency of Sugarcane Farms in Central Negros, the Philippines." *Journal of ISSAAS* 18: 49–61.

Rios, A., and G. Shively. 2005. "Farm Size and Nonparametric Efficiency Measurements for Coffee Farms in Vietnam." Paper presented at the American Agricultural Economics Association Annual Meeting, Providence, RI, July 24–27, 2005.

Roberts, M., W. Schlenker, and J. Eyer. 2013. "Agronomic Weather Measures in Econometric Models of Crop Yield with Implications for Climate Change." *American Journal of Agricultural Economics* 95: 236–243.

Sen, A. K. 1962. "An Aspect of Indian Agriculture." *Economic Weekly* 14: 243–266.

Sherlund, S., C. Barrett, and A. Adesina. 2002. "Smallholder Technical Efficiency Controlling for Environmental Production Conditions." *Journal of Development Economics* 69: 85–101.

Solís, D., B. Bravo-Ureta, and R. Quiroga. 2007. "Soil Conservation and Technical Efficiency among Hillside Farmers in Central America: A Switching Regression Model." *Australian Journal of Agricultural and Resource Economics* 51: 491–510.

Taffesse, A. S., P. Dorosh, and S. A. Gemessa. 2012. "Crop Production in Ethiopia: Regional Patterns and Trends." In *Food and Agriculture in Ethiopia: Progress and Policy Challenges*, edited by P. Dorosh and S. Rashid, 53–83. Philadelphia: University of Pennsylvania Press.

UN (United Nations). 2014. *World Urbanization Prospects: The 2014 Revision, CD-ROM Edition.* Department of Economic and Social Affairs, Population Division, Washington DC.

Wier, S. 1999. "The Effects of Education on Farmer Productivity in Rural Ethiopia." Centre for the Study of African Economies (CSAE) Working Paper WPS99-7, CSAE, University of Oxford, UK.

World Bank. 2015. *World Development Indicators.* Accessed June 15, 2016. http://data.worldbank.org/country/ethiopia.

Yami, M., T. Solomon, B. Begna, F. Fufa, T. Alemu, and D. Alemu. 2013. "Source of Technical Inefficiency of Smallholder Wheat Farmers in Selected Waterlogged Areas of Ethiopia: A Translog Production Function Approach." *International Journal of Agrochemicals and Plant Protection* 1: 25–34.

Appendix

TABLE 7.A1 Tobit model estimates of factors associated with TFP and efficiency of smallholders and medium- to largeholders

	Smallholders (0.38 hectares)					Largeholders (0.40 hectares)				
		Output oriented		Input oriented			Output oriented		Input oriented	
Variables	Relative TFP	Technical efficiency	Scale efficiency	Technical efficiency	Scale efficiency	Relative TFP	Technical efficiency	Scale efficiency	Technical efficiency	Scale efficiency
Household characteristics										
Gender of household head	−0.144	−2.297	1.770*	−1.507	0.165	0.890	0.863	0.006	0.057	2.276
Age of household head	−0.006	0.027	−0.054**	0.021	−0.009	0.005	0.020	−0.006	−0.002	0.006
Head education	2.162	4.016**	−0.935	0.968	2.699*	−0.038	0.548	−0.759	−0.572	1.313
Household size	0.544*	0.515	0.077	−0.070	0.782**	0.019	−0.050	0.069	−0.030	−0.109
Land management and risk										
Crop area	−167***	−280***	72.9***	−178***	−107***	14.6***	15.4***	−0.987	1.559	19.6***
Crop area squared	254***	444***	−109***	237***	185***	−0.370	−0.278	0.166	1.20***	−1.57**
Proportion of land owned	−0.944	−1.827	1.734*	−1.291	−1.391	−0.199	−0.727	−0.058	−0.791	0.811
Percent of crop damaged	−15.5***	−14.2***	−4.36**	−3.45*	−20.1***	−8.43***	−9.24***	−0.288	1.697	−15.5***
Partially specialized	6.8***	7.4***	0.335	3.55***	6.47***	3.84**	1.249	4.20***	−0.117	5.44***
Fully specialized	7.372*	10.517**	−0.058	5.046*	6.650	5.86**	3.987	2.851**	1.630	6.52**
Number of cash crops cultivated	0.310	−0.316	1.25***	−0.918**	0.799	0.054	−0.368	0.718**	−1.29***	0.825
Household member works off-farm	−0.810	−0.638	−1.16***	0.546	−1.37**	−0.043	0.233	−0.203	0.510	−0.618
Tropical livestock units	0.243	−0.051	0.441***	−0.092	0.270	0.087	0.050	0.043	−0.119	0.280*

Access to information and services										
Production information	1.130	1.377	0.047	0.912	1.061	4.64***	4.76***	−0.226	2.48**	5.01***
Household member participation	−1.340	−0.161	−1.085	−0.871	−1.065	−2.24*	−2.065	0.255	−1.065	−2.064
Fertilizer users in FA	−0.005	−0.032	0.019	−0.022	0.015	0.016	0.002	0.016	0.044***	0.009
Improved seeds users in FA	0.076***	0.112***	−0.012	0.035**	0.081***	0.034	0.048*	−0.009	−0.044***	0.081***
DA center available in FA	4.16**	4.45*	0.118	3.245**	2.377	4.182*	3.344	1.815*	1.241	4.85**
PAs available in FA	0.868	1.208	0.755	0.578	0.278	−5.92***	−5.80***	−0.263	−2.339**	−6.58***
FIs available in FA	−1.067	−2.478	2.09**	−3.90***	0.138	5.09***	6.74***	−1.452**	−0.759	8.09***
Distance to closest market	0.034	0.107	−0.097***	0.052	0.015	−0.016	0.065	−0.090**	−0.003	−0.041
Constant	38.2***	72.0***	59.8***	108.1***	35.8***	10.4**	18.6***	82.2***	81.8***	9.85*
Log likelihood	−6,765	−6,672	−5,947	−5,704	−6,860	−6,269	−6,299	−5,156	−5,545	−6,376
Number of observations			1,516					1,426		

Source: The authors made the calculations directly using the 2011 Agricultural Growth Program Baseline Survey data.

Note: Coefficients with ***, **, and * are significant at 1, 5, and 10 percent level of significance, respectively. The dependent variables are DEA productivity indexes expressed in percent and thus have an upper limit of 100. Equations estimated including region and agroecologic zone dummies specified in equation (12). The estimates are omitted to avoid clutter.

Chapter 8

SUPPLY RESPONSE OF SMALLHOLDER HOUSEHOLDS IN ETHIOPIA

Fantu Nisrane Bachewe and Alemayehu Seyoum Taffesse

A large proportion of the poor in Africa south of the Sahara (SSA) reside in rural areas where smallholder agriculture is the dominant activity. Smallholder farms account for more than 90 percent of the cultivated area and output in Ethiopia, with about 80 percent of the total population living in rural areas (Bachewe et al. 2015). Smallholder farmer–focused policies, which derive from the Agricultural Development Led Industrialization (ADLI) framework, were predominant in Ethiopia over the past two decades. This includes the current Growth and Transformation Plan (GTP). Furthermore, considerable resources are used through a number of national and multilateral supported programs aimed at increasing smallholders' productivity and marketed supply (Ethiopia, MoA 2015). The success of such efforts crucially depends, among other factors, on how smallholders respond to changes in prices and policy interventions. This chapter examines supply responses of smallholder farmers to recent price changes.

Despite methodological differences and factors used to account for supply responses, a number of studies find that farmers in SSA respond inelastically to changes in market incentives, such as prices, and market liberalization policies.[1] The fact that the majority of smallholders in SSA produce little marketed surplus is cited as the most important factor contributing to low supply elasticities. However, Schiff and Montenegro (1997) indicate that methodological issues may have led to misleading conclusions. In the same vein, Binswanger (1990) points to the natural gestation period and the resulting fixity of inputs as an explanation for the consequent low short-run agricultural supply responses obtained in a number of studies. He also emphasized

1 Bond (1983) finds a low agricultural supply response to changes in prices in nine countries in Africa south of the Sahara. Similarly, Muchapondwa (2009) finds inelastic aggregate agricultural supply response for Zimbabwe. Studies that find low crop-specific supply responses for Africa south of the Sahara include Kavinya and Phiri (2014) and Mose, Burger, and Kuvyenhoven (2007). Furthermore, supply responses of farmers were unaffected by market liberalization policies in Uganda (Rudaheranwa et al. 2003) and in Kenya (Mose, Burger, and Kuvyenhoven 2007).

the need for distinguishing between short-run and long-run supply responses that are crucial in agriculture. Furthermore, the most important input in crop production—land—cannot be made available inelastically, making the distinction between crop-specific and aggregate output supply responses particularly important in agriculture, even in the long run. This is particularly important in Africa south of the Sahara, where the application of modern inputs is relatively low and output increases largely derive from cultivation of more land (Binswanger and Pingali 1988; Headey and Jayne 2014).

Few studies investigate agricultural supply responses in Ethiopia. Unlike findings on supply responses for other SSA countries, the studies on Ethiopia find moderately elastic supply responses. Using an aggregate dataset that extends over the 1966–1994 period, Alemu, Oosthuizen, and van Schalkwyk (2003) found elastic long-run grains supply response for both price and market liberalization. However, the same study found that short-run supply was unresponsive to changes in price in most grains. Similarly, Suleiman (2004) found elastic cereals supply response using a household level dataset that covered the 1994–2000 period. Taffesse (2003) investigated the impact of government policy on the dynamics of agricultural supply in Ethiopia during the 1980s. In particular, the study indicated that teff acreage responded negatively to the level of forced grain procurement and positively to teff prices. The period to which these studies refer was notable for the command economic system, which was replaced in the early 1990s by policies that liberalized markets. The effect on supply response of policy changes since the mid-1990s aimed at increasing smallholder farmers' productivity, and the more recent focus to increase marketed supply and value-added, as well as the fast growth in physical and communication infrastructure, have not been studied. This study attempts to fill some of this evidence gap.

This study measures output supply response to changes in crop prices and costs of production using a dataset that covers the 2004/2005–2012/2013 period. The analysis focuses on grain crops from four of the eleven regions in Ethiopia. During the period covered, grain accounted for 96 percent and 86 percent of total agricultural area and output in the country, while the four regions accounted for more than 90 percent of both area and output (Ethiopia, CSA 2005–2013). To achieve the objective stated above, a simple dynamic farm household model is developed.[2] The estimable acreage demand

2 The model is a variant of the linear rational expectations model (Sargent [1987]; Hansen and Sargent [1980]) as applied to agricultural supply response analysis (Eckstein [1984, 1985]; Tegene, Huffman, and Miranowski [1988]; and Taffesse [2003]).

equation is derived and estimated using zone-level aggregated input-output data. Estimates of acreage demand elasticities together with demand elasticities of other inputs, such as labor and fertilizer, will provide information on the importance of cultivated area vis-à-vis other inputs in output increases or supply responses—that is, whether increases in output resulted from an extensive or intensive margin. The latter, in turn, provides information not only on how farm households in Ethiopia had been coping with land scarcity in the recent past, but also indicates the extent to which efforts aimed at increasing smallholders' productivity through intensive application of modern inputs has succeeded.

There are four sections in the remainder of this chapter. Next, the empirical acreage demand equation is specified, and the long- and short-run acreage demand elasticities with respect to changes in prices and opportunity cost of teff acreage are derived. Then, the zone-level input use, output, and prices data used in the analysis are described. The subsequent section discusses the results of the analyses, and the last section concludes.

Empirical Analysis

The simple dynamic farm household model used in this study assumes that the household allocates its land to the production of two crops or groups of crops. The acreage shares of the two crops amount to 1 in each period. The production function of each crop k expresses output ($Q_{k,t+j}$) as a linear function of [lagged] acreage ($A_{k,t+j-1}$) as: $Q_{k,t+j} = y_k A_{k,t+j-1} + \varepsilon_{k,t+j}$, where k = 1, 2 denotes crops 1 and 2 and y_k is a constant. We use the quadratic cost function: $C_{k,t+j} = c_{k,t+j} A_{k,t+j-1} + \frac{b_k}{2} A^2_{k,t+j-1} + d_k A_{k,t+j-1} A_{k,t+j-2}$, where $c_{k,t+j}$ is nonland costs of production while b_k and d_k are constants. The profit function of the household is: $\pi_{t+j} = (P_{1,t+j} Q_{1,t+j} - C_{1,t+j}) + (P_{2,t+j} Q_{2,t+j} - C_{2,t+j})$, where $P_{k,t+j}$ is the price of crop k. The household first maximizes its discounted expected profits, π_{t+j}, and subsequently chooses the level of consumption and savings, subject to a budget that constrains the sum of consumption and savings in each period to be equal with the sum of profits and previous period savings augmented by interest earned (see Bachewe and Taffesse [2015] and Taffesse [2003] for further details). The profit maximization stage generates the farm household's acreage demand for crop 1. Next, the empirical acreage demand equation is derived from that, along with the implied long- and short-run acreage elasticities. The required empirical price equation is specified and the estimation procedure is described in the Appendix.

Empirical Specification

This study adopts the following acreage demand equation as the primary specification used to capture the supply response of smallholder teff producers.[3]

$$A_{1,t} = \kappa_0 + \kappa_1 A_{1,t-1} + \kappa_2 A_{1,t-2} + \kappa_3 P_{1,t} + \kappa_4 P_{1,t-1} + \kappa_5 R_{1,t} + \kappa_6 R_{1,t-1} + \varepsilon_t \quad (1)$$

Equation (1) states that current period teff acreage ($A_{1,t}$) depends on teff acreage used in the last two periods ($A_{1,t-1}$ and $A_{1,t-2}$), current and last period's teff price ($P_{1,t}$ and $P_{1,t-1}$), and current and last period's opportunity costs of cultivating teff ($R_{1,t}$ and $R_{1,t-1}$). These costs are measured as the sum of average value products of non-teff grain with yields standing for average value products. Finally, ε_t represents shocks to nonland costs of producing teff. These shocks can also be used as a means of including random errors of optimization and errors in data (Epstein and Yatchew 1985). Equation (1) is directly estimated to obtain coefficients of the acreage demand equation. The estimates are then used to compute the acreage demand elasticities, which is the primary objective of this study.

Elasticities

Equation (1) is used to derive the long- and short-run elasticities of acreage demand with respect to the market prices of teff and the opportunity costs of teff production. Accordingly, the long-run acreage demand elasticity is derived by differentiating the unconditional expectation of acreage demand, $E(A_1)$, with respect to $E(P_1)$, and weighting the result by the ratio of the unconditional means $E(P_1)$, and $E(A_1)$. That is:

$$\xi^L_{A_1,P_1} = \left(\frac{\kappa_3+\kappa_4}{1-\kappa_1-\kappa_2}\right)\frac{E(P_1)}{E(A_1)} \geq 0 \quad (2a)$$

The short-run elasticity of acreage demand with respect to period t teff price is given as:

$$\xi^S_{A_1,P_1} = \kappa_3 \frac{E(P_1)}{E(A_1)} \gtrless 0 \quad (2b)$$

3 Equation (1) represents the empirical analogue to the optimal acreage allocation rule derived from a dynamic optimization procedure. The procedure, which we briefly describe in the introduction to this section, links teff output to acreage allocation via production technology and prices in such a way that equation (1) can serve as a vehicle for analyzing the supply response of smallholder teff producers. See Bachewe and Taffesse (2015) and Taffesse (2003) for details.

Equation (2a) indicates that long-run teff acreage demand increases with a permanent increase in teff price. This is implied by the optimal acreage demand equation derived from the optimization problem (see Bachewe and Taffesse [2015] for signs of this and the remaining elasticities given by equations [2b] though [2d]). The corresponding long- and short-run acreage demand elasticities with respect to the opportunity cost of teff production are:

$$\xi^{L}_{A_1,R_1} = \left(\frac{\kappa_5+\kappa_6}{1-\kappa_1-\kappa_2}\right)\frac{E(R_1)}{E(A_1)} \leq 0 \qquad (2c)$$

$$\xi^{S}_{A_1,R_1} = \kappa_5 \frac{E(R_1)}{E(A_1)} \gtreqless 0 \qquad (2d)$$

Note that the acreage demand elasticities given in equations (2a)–(2d) are also equal to the elasticities of teff supply with respect to teff price and opportunity cost of teff production.[4]

The Data

The data on inputs, outputs, and prices used in the econometric analysis were collected by Ethiopia's Central Statistical Agency (CSA) through its Annual Agricultural Sample Surveys (AgSS).[5] Although the AgSS collects data at household level, the households sampled change from year to year. Similarly, woredas covered by the survey are also changed. However, AgSS is required to generate zonal-level representative data. It does so by selecting a representative sample of households for each zone and by covering almost all zones every year. Since this study demands observations from the same unit of analysis repeated over time, AgSS's zonal-level data are used. As the objective of the study is to look at the supply response of smallholders in Ethiopia, the AgSS data were the only data suitable for the purpose and consistently available over a long period.

Estimating acreage demand and price equations using zonally aggregated data may appear to violate the assumption that producers take market prices

---

4 This is a consequence of the linear relationship between teff acreage and teff supply, $Q_{1,t+j} = y_1 A_{1,t+j-1} + \varepsilon_{1,t+j}$. That the teff acreage and supply elasticities are equal can be shown for the long-run teff supply elasticity as:
$\xi^{L}_{Q_1,P_1} = \frac{dQ_1}{dP_1}\frac{E(P_1)}{E(Q_1)} = \frac{y_1 dA_1}{dP_1}\frac{E(P_1)}{y_1 E(A_1)} = \left(\frac{\kappa_3+\kappa_4}{1-\kappa_1-\kappa_2}\right)\frac{E(P_1)}{E(A_1)} = \xi^{L}_{A_1,P_1}$.

5 In the CSA's annual AgSS enumeration areas and farming households are taken to be the primary and secondary sampling units, respectively. CSA defines an enumeration area as a geographic area with 150–200 resident households. Kebeles constitute the smallest administrative units. The hierarchy of governance proceeds with woredas (composed of a number of kebeles), zones, regional states, and the federal government.

as given. The assumption will not hold if zones are production units because zonal supply of a given crop will influence its price. However, despite the data being zonally aggregated, the actual production units are competitive farm households, which, among other things, form expectations on prices and use the information to make production decisions. Moreover, to avoid inconsistent results, we conduct pairwise Granger causality tests between prices and outputs of teff and non-teff grains.

The results of testing the null hypothesis that output does not Granger cause prices are provided in Table 8.1. They indicate that the null hypothesis is not rejected for both teff and non-teff grains. In addition to Granger causality tests, a method proposed by Geweke (1982) for infrequent data, such as annual data, is used to test the null hypothesis: output and prices do not have instantaneous feedback. The null hypothesis is not rejected in both crop types. Given these results, we proceed with the presumption that teff and non-teff grain outputs do not affect corresponding current prices of the respective crops.

The dataset includes 21 types of grain crops, with data collected during 2004/2005–2012/2013 (1997–2005 EC) from the four major cereal-producing regions in Ethiopia.[6] The data encompassed the main agricultural season, locally known as meher. The following specific considerations influenced the choices about data. During the 2004/2005–2012/2013 period, grain accounted for an average of 82 percent of the total crop output and 93.5 percent of the area, out of which teff accounted for 21 percent (Figure 8.1). In addition to the sheer importance of grain to output and area, two more reasons justify the use of grain in the analysis. First, grain (unlike other crop categories) is cultivated in all of the administrative zones of the four regions included in the analyses. Second, nongrain crops, including fruits and other tree crops, are agroecology specific and mostly permanent crops. Supply responses of perennial crops is likely to be different to that of temporary crops.

The four important regions for crop agriculture (Amhara, Oromiya, Southern Nations, Nationalities, and Peoples' [SNNP] region, and Tigray) represent most of the country's crop agriculture. These regions on average accounted for more than 90 percent of crop output and cultivated area during the period studied. Moreover, the remaining regions lack data essential for

6 The Ethiopian calendar (EC) lags seven years and eight months behind the Gregorian calendar, with Ethiopian New Year occuring in the second week of September of the latter calendar.

TABLE 8.1 Results of pairwise Granger causality and instantaneous feedback tests of zonal crop output and prices of grains

Crop	Output does not Granger cause price	Output and price do not have instantaneous feedback
Teff	1.41	0.002
Non-teff grains (area weighted price)	2.56	0.35
Non-teff grains (mean price)	0.13	0.59

Source: Authors' analyses using Ethiopia, CSA (2005–2013) and Ethiopia, CSA (2014a, 2014b).

Note: All estimates are not significant at 10% level of significance.

FIGURE 8.1 Acreage share (%) of major crop categories, 2004/2005–2012/2013

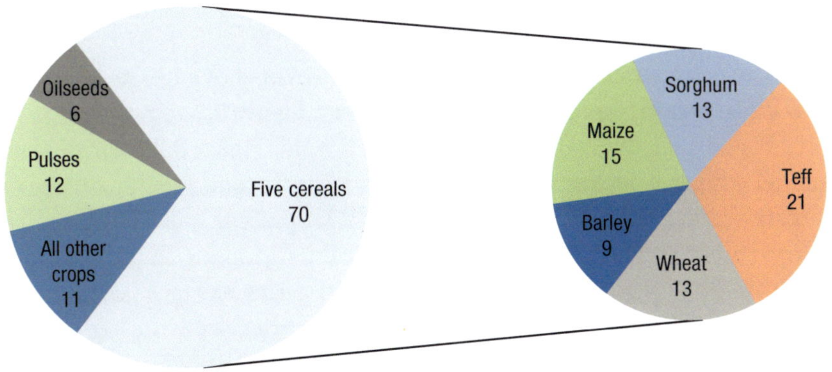

Source: Authors' computation using zone-level aggregated Ethiopia, CSA data, 2004–2012.

the analysis. Accordingly, the data used in this study covered 10, 17, 21, and 5 administrative zones from Amhara, Oromiya, SNNP, and Tigray, respectively.

Teff and Grain Acreage, Output, and Yields

In Table 8.2 the acreage shares of cereals, pulses, and oilseeds, which constitute grain crops, are summarized. In Ethiopia, cereals are the most important temporary crops followed by pulses and oilseeds. During the 2004/2005–2012/2013 period, cereals accounted for about 81 percent of the area cultivated with grain, of which 77 percent comprised the five major cereals of teff, maize, wheat, sorghum, and barley. Moreover, the area under these cereals varied only slightly between the regions, ranging from 72 percent in Tigray to

79 percent in SNNP. Although there was regional variation in acreage shares of different crops, the share of teff was the highest in Amhara and the second highest in the remaining three regions, making teff the most important crop in terms of area cultivated. During the same period, teff accounted for 23 percent and 21.5 percent of the area under grain and all crops, respectively.

Table 8.3 provides a summary of total teff output and area as well as average teff yields and prices. Accordingly, in an average year of the period covered, 2.9 million metric tons of teff was produced in the four regions, and this increased at an average annual rate of 8.3 percent. In an average year, 2.5 million hectares of land was sown with teff and growth in cultivated area averaged 3.2 percent. Teff yields averaged about 11 quintals per hectare and grew at an average annual rate of 5.3 percent.

Crop Prices

CSA collected data on monthly producer prices of about 130 items since 1995/1996 from almost all zones in the country. Figure 8.2 shows average monthly nominal and real teff prices.[7] Table 8.3 and Figure 8.2 indicate that nominal teff prices averaged about 6 birr per kilogram and grew at average monthly and annual rates of 1.7 percent and 24.4 percent respectively during the September 2004–August 2013 period. Real teff prices averaged 3.6 birr in December 2006 prices, while growth in real teff prices averaged 0.2 percent per month and 3.6 percent per year. Nominal teff prices were the highest at the end of the period considered, with the August 2013 price at approximately 12 birr per kilogram. Real prices of teff were the highest in May 2008.

Table 8.4 summarizes the data on monthly prices of all grain. Since weights or information on relative importance of crops, such as volumes of sales, are not available, the summary uses simple averages of monthly prices. Table 8.4 indicates that, on average, oilseeds sold for the highest price, with pulses second, then followed by teff as highly priced crops. Approximately half of the oilseeds produced are sold, mostly exported, which partly explains their relatively higher price. Among the cereals, teff is the most widely marketed, with 27 percent of teff output sold (Ethiopia, CSA 2014b).

7 Note that all real prices are computed as nominal prices deflated by the corresponding regional general price index.

TABLE 8.2 Mean regional acreage shares, 2004/2005–2012/2013 (%)

Crop and crop group	National	Tigray	Amhara	Oromiya	SNNP
Five cereals	76.7 (10.7)	71.7 (16.7)	73.5 (8.3)	77.8 (8.3)	78.6 (11.1)
Barley	11.1 (10.0)	16 (15.5)	12.0 (6.8)	10.8 (10.4)	9.7 (9.0)
Maize	24.9 (16.3)	9.9 (6.0)	13.8 (13.2)	28.6 (14.6)	31.1 (15.6)
Sorghum	21.9 (20.9)	35.7 (26.6)	27.3 (22.9)	18.8 (18.4)	18.3 (18.4)
Teff	28.2 (15.1)	23.1 (11.1)	33.0 (9.9)	25.5 (15.8)	29.0 (16.6)
Wheat	14.2 (12.4)	15.4 (14.5)	13.8 (8.9)	16.7 (14)	12.0 (11.6)
Other cereals	3.4 (5.4)	8.1 (7.7)	5.4 (6.5)	3.3 (4.9)	0.9 (1.5)
Pulses	15.0 (9.9)	7.2 (4.0)	15.0 (6.8)	12.0 (7.8)	20.0 (11.6)
Oilseeds	6.0 (8.3)	12.3 (16.8)	7.0 (4.8)	8.2 (7.6)	0.8 (2.3)

Source: Authors' computation using zone-level aggregated Ethiopia, CSA data, 2005–2013.

Notes: Figures in parentheses are standard deviations. Acreage shares of the groups of five cereals, other cereals, pulses, and oilseed are calculated out of the total area under grain crops, while acreage shares of barley, maize, sorghum, teff, and wheat are calculated out of the total area under the five cereals.

TABLE 8.3 Total teff output and area, and average yields and prices, 2004/2005–2012/2013

Year	Output (thousand metric tons)	Area (thousand hectares)	Yields (quintals per hectare)	Nominal price (birr per kilogram)	Real Price (December 2006 birr per kilogram)
2004/2005	2,008	2,116	8.7	2.2	2.9
2005/2006	2,168	2,232	8.3	2.6	3.2
2006/2007	2,413	2,371	8.7	3.5	3.7
2007/2008	2,970	2,543	11.5	4.9	4.2
2008/2009	3,010	2,464	11.5	7.1	4.7
2009/2010	3,161	2,569	11.5	6.1	3.5
2010/2011	3,457	2,735	11.9	6.4	3.3
2011/2012	3,473	2,706	12.1	9.2	3.7
2012/2013	3,746	2,711	12.6	11.0	3.6
Average	**2,934**	**2,494**	**10.8**	**5.9**	**3.6**

Source: Authors' computation using zone-level aggregated Ethiopia, CSA data: Ethiopia, CSA 2005–2013; Ethiopia, CSA 2014a and 2014b.

The Opportunity Cost of Teff Production

Table 8.5 reports estimates of the opportunity cost of teff acreage. This cost, represented by R_1 in equation (1), is calculated by summing the average value products of all grain crops except teff. That is,

FIGURE 8.2 Average nominal and real price of teff, 2004–2014

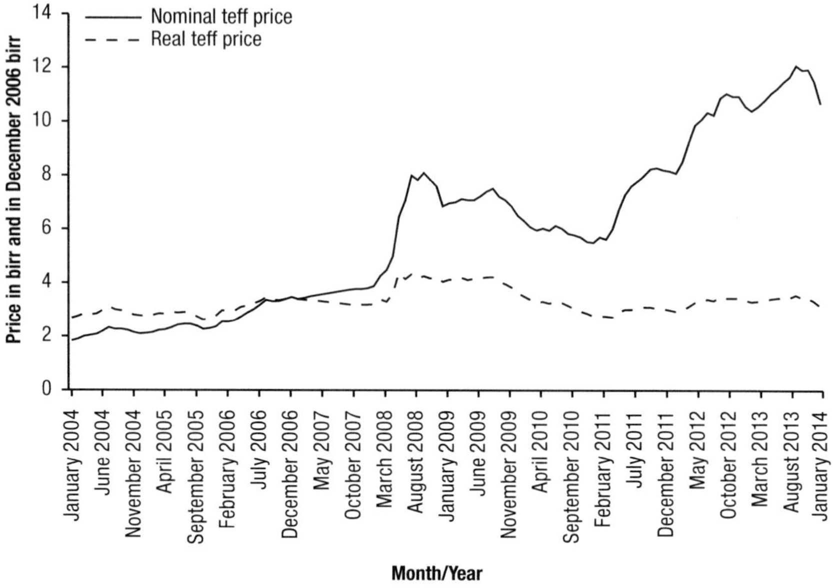

Source: Authors' computation using monthly price data (Ethiopia, CSA 2014b).

TABLE 8.4 Mean regional crop prices 2004/2005–2012/2013 (birr per kilogram)

Crop and crop group	National	Tigray	Amhara	Oromiya	SNNP
Barley	2.4 (0.6)	3.0 (0.7)	2.7 (0.5)	2.2 (0.4)	2.2 (0.4)
Maize	1.7 (0.5)	2.2 (0.5)	2.0 (0.4)	1.7 (0.4)	1.6 (0.4)
Sorghum	1.9 (0.6)	2.4 (0.6)	2.5 (0.5)	1.8 (0.5)	1.6 (0.4)
Teff	3.6 (0.7)	3.9 (0.7)	3.9 (0.6)	3.5 (0.6)	3.6 (0.6)
Wheat	2.6 (0.5)	3.0 (0.6)	2.8 (0.4)	2.5 (0.5)	2.5 (0.5)
Other cereals	2.3 (0.8)	2.9 (1.0)	3.0 (0.8)	2.0 (0.5)	2.2 (0.6)
Pulses	3.8 (1.9)	4.2 (1.2)	3.4 (1.1)	3.6 (1.4)	4.0 (2.6)
Oilseeds	4.2 (1.6)	4.5 (1.9)	4.5 (1.6)	4.1 (1.4)	4.0 (1.6)

Source: Authors' computation using monthly price data (Ethiopia, CSA 2014b).
Note: Figures in parentheses are standard deviations.

$$R_1 = \sum_{g=2}^{21} P_g y_g A_g$$

where g stands for the 21 grain types, and P_g and y_g for corresponding prices and average products of land, respectively ($g = 1$ represents teff and is not included in the summation). The respective zonal average yields are used as the measure of the average product of land. In the summation, the acreage share of crop g in total area under grains other than teff, A_g, is used to capture the relative importance of the crop in the opportunity cost of teff acreage.

During the period of study, on average, the opportunity cost of a hectare of land used in teff production was about 3,660 birr in December 2006 prices. The opportunity cost of teff acreage grew at an average annual rate of 8.5 percent. The latter includes a 37 percent rise during 2009/2010–2010/2011 and a 56 percent increase between 2005/2006 and 2006/2007. In contrast, the opportunity cost declined by 14 percent and 205 percent in the two years during 2006/2007–2008/2009, respectively. The opportunity cost of teff acreage was the highest in Tigray on average in all the years except 2005/2006 and 2006/2007, with the regional average ranging from about 4,600 birr in Tigray to the significantly lower average of about 3,100 birr in SNNP. These high opportunity costs of teff acreage in Tigray are likely to have arisen because of the high price of oilseeds and their greater acreage share in Tigray.

Results

This section covers the main findings of the analysis. Given that time-series variables were used, particularly those of price series, the first test applied is for stationarity to avoid misleading conclusions that may arise from spurious regression, which is a major concern with this type of data. Results of panel unit-root tests are given in Table 8.6. In Table 8.7 the estimated coefficients of teff price and opportunity cost equations are reported. Moreover, estimates of the teff acreage demand equation (equation [1] above) are provided in Table 8.8, while Table 8.9 summarizes the long- and short-run elasticities of acreage demand calculated using equations (2a)–(2d).

In addition to the coefficient estimates obtained from the econometric analyses, Table 8.7 and Table 8.8 report results of tests of the joint significance of all variables (χ^2-equation), the regressors excluding time dummies (χ^2-regressors), and only time-dummies (χ^2-time dummies). Under the null hypotheses the test statistics are asymptotically distributed $\chi^2(p)$, where the degrees of freedom p is equal to the number of variables whose joint significance is being tested. Also reported are the statistics from first- and

TABLE 8.5 Average regional real opportunity costs of teff acreage, 2004/2005–2012/2013

Region	2004/ 2005	2005/ 2006	2006/ 2007	2007/ 2008	2008/ 2009	2009/ 2010	2010/ 2011	2011/ 2012	2012/ 2013	Average
All regions	2,510	3,086	3,016	4,715	3,758	3,227	4,421	4,281	3,929	3,660
	(739)	(784)	(928)	(1,032)	(818)	(928)	(1,078)	(1,049)	(921)	(1,156)
Tigray	2,951	3,297	3,321	5,656	4,939	4,666	5,951	5,403	5,229	4,601
	(620)	(438)	(605)	(781)	(447)	(540)	(462)	(402)	(314)	(1,325)
Amhara	2,707	3,299	3,604	5,088	4,161	3,710	4,937	4,755	4,510	4,086
	(620)	(438)	(605)	(781)	(447)	(540)	(462)	(402)	(314)	(919)
Oromiya	2,685	3,318	3,389	5,122	3,881	3,215	4,407	4,608	4,028	3,850
	(533)	(606)	(778)	(746)	(500)	(638)	(860)	(727)	(471)	(976)
SNNP	2,171	2,747	2,360	3,984	3,185	2,666	3,822	3,524	3,263	3,080
	(798)	(974)	(890)	(980)	(796)	(819)	(918)	(1,075)	(794)	(1,065)

Source: Analyses using Ethiopia, CSA data (2005–2013).
Note: Figures in parentheses are standard deviations.

second-order serial correlation tests of residuals in the respective equations, which are given in m1 and m2 rows of the tables. The last value reported in the tables is the Sargan test of the overidentifying (moment) restrictions. Under the null hypothesis of optimal instruments the Sargan test statistic, which tests whether the overidentifying instruments are exogenous as a group, is asymptotically $\chi^2(r)$ distributed with as many degrees of freedom r as overidentifying restrictions. In the presence of heteroscedasticity, Arellano and Bond (1991) show that the one-step Sargan test overrejects the null hypotheses. As a result, the Hansen (1982) J statistic, which tests the same null hypotheses using a consistent weighting matrix, is reported. In Table 8.7 and Table 8.8 this statistic is reported as χ^2–Sargan/Hansen test.

Results of Stationarity Tests

Panel unit-root tests devised by Harris and Tzavalis (1999) and Im, Pesaran, and Shin (2003) were used as they are considered appropriate for panel data covering a short time and with a large number of observations. Table 8.6 shows the results obtained using the two panel unit-root tests with the data in levels and differences. The results provide strong evidence in favor of stationarity of teff acreage, teff price, and the opportunity cost of teff acreage. The only exception is the null hypothesis that the real teff prices series has a unit-root that is not rejected by the Harris-Tzavalis test when a trend term is

TABLE 8.6 Results of panel unit-root tests

		Im, Pesaran, and Shin		Harris and Tzavalis	
Variable	Specification	Level	Difference	Level	Difference
Teff acreage	Standard	−4.6	−9.3	−17.0	−28.1
	Demeaned	−5.1	−9.7	−16.3	−27.8
	With trend	−6.5	−9.3	−8.8	−14.8
Teff price	Standard	−4.5	−6.9	−11.3	−21.3
	Demeaned	−4.6	−9.7	−15.4	−29.1
	With trend	−3.2	−8.4	−0.9*	−11.4
Opportunity cost of teff	Standard	−6.1	−9.8	−12.9	−27.3
	Demeaned	−4.5	−9.7	−14.4	−28.6
	With trend	−6.6	−10.2	−8.1	−15.0

Source: Authors' analysis using CSA AgSS and prices data (Ethiopia, CSA 2005–2013).
Note: All coefficients are significant at 1 percent level of significance except that with *, which is not significant.

included. Given these results, it is unlikely that the relationship between the variables will be spurious.

Teff Price Equation Estimates

The results in Table 8.7 indicate that the estimate of lagged teff price satisfies the stability condition of teff price equation associated with equation (4), as discussed in the appendix to this chapter. Moreover, the positive estimate of the lagged teff price indicates that current and lagged teff prices are positively related. All three groups of variables tested for joint significance: all variables, regressors without time dummies, and time dummies, are significant. Since the first-differenced residuals are MA(1) processes, the null hypothesis of first-order serial correlation, which is shown in the m1 row, is not rejected. However, the null hypothesis of second-order serial correlation is rejected, as reported in the m2 row. The latter indicates that the estimates are consistent. The two-step Hansen test statistics is given in the χ^2–Sargan/Hansen row. The null hypothesis that the overidentifying restrictions are valid is not rejected.

Opportunity Cost of Teff Acreage

The results in Table 8.7 indicate that the estimated coefficient of lagged teff opportunity cost satisfies the stability condition of teff opportunity cost equation.[8] Moreover, the estimated coefficient implies that current and lagged teff opportunity costs are positively related. Results of tests of the joint significance of three sets of variables, serial correlation, and overidentifying restrictions of teff opportunity cost equation are qualitatively similar with that discussed above for teff price equation.

Teff Acreage Demand Equation Estimates

Parameter estimates of the teff acreage demand equation (1) are given in Table 8.8. The results indicate that the sets of variables included are jointly significant at 1 percent. Moreover, the null hypothesis that the overidentifying instruments are valid is not rejected while the null hypothesis of second-order serial correlation is rejected.

Estimated coefficients of lagged and twice lagged acreage demand variables satisfy the conditions for stationarity of the AR(2) process. Moreover, both contemporaneous and lagged teff prices are significant and positive. The estimated coefficient of lagged teff prices (Teff $price_{t-1}$) is lower than the estimate of current price (Teff $price_{t}$). This indicates that acreage responses of households to price changes decline through time. This is because previous decisions incorporate effects of price changes that already occurred, whereby acreage demand decisions in period t−1 incorporate effects of teff price in period t−1. Consistent with the theoretical model, the estimated coefficient of opportunity cost of acreage used in teff production is negative, although the estimate of its lagged term is positive.

Teff Acreage Demand Elasticities

In Table 8.9 the long- and short-run teff acreage demand elasticities with respect to (WRT) teff prices and the opportunity cost of acreage used in teff production are provided. The teff acreage demand elasticities WRT teff price in the table imply that teff acreage increases with teff price, while the elasticities WRT opportunity cost imply that teff acreage declines with an increase in teff opportunity cost. These results conform to predictions of the theoretical model.

8 The specification of empirical teff opportunity cost equation and its stability conditions are similar to the teff price equation (4) given in the appendix (see also Bachewe and Taffesse [2015]).

TABLE 8.7 Dynamic panel data estimates of teff price and opportunity cost equations

Teff price		Teff opportunity cost	
Variables	Coefficient (standard errors)	Variables	Coefficient (standard errors)
Teff price$_{t-1}$	0.417***	Opportunity cost of teff$_{t-1}$	0.413***
	(0.014)		(0.012)
Constant	2.001***	Constant	20.7***
	(0.049)		(0.383)
χ^2-equation	13,284***	χ^2-equation	12,564***
χ^2-regressors	881***	χ^2-regressors	1,275***
χ^2-time dummies	5,848***	χ^2-time dummies	6,799***
m1	−4.96***	m1	−4.43***
m2	0.94	m2	−0.43
χ^2–Sargan/Hansen test	44	χ^2–Sargan/Hansen test	45
Number of observations	424	Number of observations	424

Source: Authors' analysis using CSA prices data (Ethiopia, CSA 2005–2013).
Note: Coefficients with *** are significant at 1 percent.

TABLE 8.8 Dynamic panel data estimates of teff acreage demand equation

Variable	Coefficient	Standard error
Teff acreage$_{t-1}$	0.481***	0.032
Teff acreage$_{t-2}$	−0.096***	0.034
Teff price$_t$	0.022***	0.007
Teff price$_{t-1}$	0.017**	0.008
Opportunity cost of teff$_t$	−0.0051***	0.0004
Opportunity cost of teff$_{t-1}$	0.0034***	0.0003
Constant	0.060*	0.031
χ^2-equation	3,708***	
χ^2-regressors	1,038***	
χ^2-time dummies	424***	
m1	−4.29***	
m2	−0.98	
χ^2–Sargan/Hansen test	36	

Source: Authors' analysis using CSA AgSS and prices data (Ethiopia, CSA 2005–2013).
Note: Coefficients with ***, **, and * are significant at 1, 5, and 10 percent, respectively.

TABLE 8.9 Long-run and short-run elasticity of teff acreage demand

Elasticity	Teff price	Teff opportunity cost
Long-run teff acreage elasticity	1.067	−0.484
Short-run teff acreage elasticity	0.368	−0.871

Source: Authors' analysis using CSA AgSS and prices data (Ethiopia, CSA 2005–2013).

As expected, the long-run elasticity of acreage demand WRT teff price, about 1.07, is higher than its short-run counterpart, 0.37. The long-run teff supply elasticity implies that farmers' teff supply response increases slightly faster than a permanent growth in real teff price. Growth in teff acreage is also reinforced by the relatively slow growth in the opportunity cost of teff. Particularly, the data indicate that real teff prices grew faster than prices of 14 of the 20 non-teff grain crops. More importantly, prices grew faster in teff than in the four other cereals, which, along with teff, dominate the nationwide cultivated area. Accordingly, real teff price growth was over 2.2, 1.3, 1.4, and 2.1 times faster than growth in barley, maize, sorghum, and wheat prices, respectively.

Teff is not only a staple crop in large parts of Ethiopia; it also has been increasingly adopted in parts of the country where it was not previously cultivated, as well as in other countries. This may have contributed to the higher growth in teff price and thus for the faster growth in teff supply response. The share of teff in food expenditure is highest in urban areas and increased by 3.4 percent nationwide between 2005 and 2011, while the corresponding share of all other cereals declined (see Chapter 2). Finally, the fast growth in teff demand, combined with the limited research on teff hitherto (research that was conducted almost exclusively in Ethiopia), may have induced the recent efforts of the Ethiopian government to increase teff productivity through dissemination of high-yielding teff varieties and production methods (Bachewe et al. 2015). The resultant increases in teff productivity affect teff supply response and acreage demand positively.

The long-run and short-run acreage demand elasticities WRT teff price obtained in this study are higher than the corresponding corn acreage elasticities of 0.2 and 0.011 that Tegene, Huffman, and Miranowski (1988) compute for Iowa, US. The elasticities are close to the respective grain acreage elasticity of 0.808 and 0.274 obtained in Yu, Liu, and You (2010) for Henan province in China. In contrast, the elasticities are lower than those in Ahouissoussi, McIntosh, and Wetzstein (1995) with long- and short-run soybean acreage demand elasticity of 1.98 and 1.21 computed for Georgia, US. Moreover, the long-run and short-run soybean acreage elasticity WRT wheat price, a proxy for the opportunity cost of soybean acreage, was –1.57 and –2.11 in the latter study. In contrast, the long-run and short-run cotton acreage demand elasticities WRT the opportunity cost of cotton production in Egypt obtained in Eckstein (1984) are lower at –0.13 and –0.11, respectively.[9]

The current study employs similar theoretical and econometric methods to the work by Taffesse (2003), making comparison of results of the two studies free from methodological differences. Relative to the long-run acreage demand elasticity WRT teff price of 0.48 (Taffesse [2003]), the result from this study is considerably higher, while the short-run elasticities in the respective studies, 0.37 and 0.31, are similar. Moreover, the elasticity of acreage WRT the opportunity cost of teff acreage, again from the study by Taffesse (2003), was –0.93. This is about twice the elasticity obtained in this study, which is –0.48, whereas the short-run elasticity is considerably higher than the elasticity, –0.13, obtained in the latter study.

Unlike the period studied in this chapter, Taffesse (2003) examined the 1974–1991 period that was marked in Ethiopia with the command economic system. Consequently, the difference in the results is largely a result of the distinct economic environments that prevailed during these specific periods of study.[10] Among these differences included the abolition of the proportion/quota of grain output that farmers were required to deliver to a government agency at fixed prices. However, the difference in long-run acreage demand elasticities obtained in the two studies is large, even after accounting for the negative acreage demand elasticity of compulsorily delivered grain quota Taffesse (2003) obtained, –0.04.

The period covered witnessed more changes that positively affected agricultural supply response. Among such changes was the abolition in the early 1990s of government control of inputs and output markets. Moreover, since the mid-1990s the Ethiopian government implemented a number of

9 Three of the four studies referred to in this paragraph use the rational expectations hypothesis, as does this study, and generally use similar empirical models, particularly Eckstein (1984) and Tegene, Huffman, and Miranowski (1988). The fourth study—Yu, Liu, and You (2010)—uses a Nerlovian adaptive expectations model.

10 Indeed, Taffesse (2003) indicates that "it is reasonable to expect that the process of market liberalization, which began with the abolition of CGD (compulsory grain delivery) in 1990, stimulates greater supply responsiveness."

policy packages targeted at increasing the productivity of smallholder farmers. Agricultural supply response is also likely to be affected positively by improved integration of farmers with markets, consequential to increased road, telephone, and other infrastructure that had occurred since the mid-1990s (Bachewe et al. 2015). The country suffered frequent droughts and famines during the 1974–1991 period. More favorable weather in most surplus-producing areas of the country during most of the latter period has likely impacted supply response positively. Finally, the government's decision to allow a limited renting-in and -out of land and the consequently greater flexibility of access to cultivable land may also have boosted acreage demand elasticity.

Conclusion

Agriculture in Ethiopia is dominated by smallholder grain producers who consume most of what they produce. This study investigates the parallel characterization that smallholders respond little to changes in economic incentives, such as prices, focusing on the specific case of the responsiveness of teff supply. For this purpose, a simple dynamic model of input demand choices of a representative farm household producing two types or groups of crops under rational expectations hypothesis is developed. In the model, teff supply is a linear function of teff acreage demand. An acreage demand equation is derived and estimated using zone-level aggregated data. In addition, farmers' long- and short-run teff supply responses or acreage demand elasticities for changes in teff prices and opportunity cost of teff production are calculated.

The results indicate that teff acreage demand increases slightly faster than the permanent increase, by 100 percent, in its price that triggered the response. The acreage demand increase corresponding to an analogous change in the temporary (short-run) real teff price is lower at about 37 percent. Moreover, the results indicate that increases in the opportunity cost of teff acreage, gauged by revenue obtainable from other crops, leads to a fall in teff acreage. Teff acreage demand declines by about 50 percent and 90 percent for a 100 percent permanent and temporary increase in the real revenue per hectare obtainable in the production of non-teff grains crops, respectively. The faster growth in teff supply response that resulted from a direct impact of growth in teff price was also likely to have been reinforced by a relatively slower growth in prices of non-teff grains.

Studies of supply response in other countries obtain higher short- and long-run crop supply response elasticities than those obtained in this study.

The long-run acreage demand elasticities obtained in this study are considerably higher than that obtained by Taffesse (2003) for Ethiopia. This difference is attributable to the different economic policy regimes that prevailed in the periods of these two studies, in addition to the relatively faster growth in teff price that occurred during this same period. Moreover, policies aimed at increasing agricultural and particularly teff productivity, infrastructural development, and favorable weather are likely contributors to the faster growth in overall agricultural supply response.

References

Ahouissoussi, N. C. B., C. S. McIntosh, and E. W. Wetzstein. 1995. "Rational Expectations Estimation of Georgia Soybean Acreage Response." *Journal of Agricultural and Applied Economics* 27 (2): 500–509.

Alemu, Z. G., K. Oosthuizen, and H. D. van Schalkwyk. 2003. "Grain-Supply Response in Ethiopia: An Error Correction Approach." *Agrekon* 42 (4): 389–404.

Arellano, M., and S. Bond. 1991. "Some Tests of Specification for Panel Data: Monte Carlo Evidence and an Application to Employment Equations." *Review of Economic Studies* 58: 277–297.

Arellano, M., and O. Bover. 1995. "Another Look at the Instrumental Variable Estimation of Error-Components Models." *Journal of Econometrics* 68: 29–52.

Bachewe, F. N., G. Berhane, B. Minten, and A. S. Taffesse. 2015. *Agricultural Growth in Ethiopia (2004–2014): Evidence and Drivers.* International Food Policy Research Institute (IFPRI)/ Ethiopia Strategy Support Program (ESSP) II Working Paper 81. Addis Ababa, Ethiopia: International Food Policy Research Institute.

Bachewe, F. N., and A. S. Taffesse. 2015. *Supply Response of Smallholder Households in Ethiopia.* IFPRI/ESSP II Working Paper 74. Addis Ababa, Ethiopia: International Food Policy Research Institute.

Binswanger, H. 1990. *The Policy Response of Agriculture.* Proceedings of the World Bank Annual Conference on Development Economics, April 1989, Washington, DC.

Binswanger, H., and P. Pingali. 1988. "Technological Priorities for Farming in Sub-Saharan Africa." *World Bank Research Observer* 3 (1): 81–98.

Blundell, R., and S. Bond. 1995. *Initial Conditions and Moment Restrictions in Dynamic Panel Data Models.* Economics Discussion Paper 104. Nuffield College, Oxford, UK.

Bond, M. E. 1983. "Agricultural Response to Price in Sub-Saharan African Countries." *IMF Staff Papers* 30 (4): 512–520.

Davidson, R., and J. G. MacKinnon. 1993. *Estimation and Inference in Econometrics*. Oxford, UK: Oxford University Press.

Eckstein, Z. 1984. "A Rational Expectations Model of Agricultural Supply." *Journal of Political Economy* 92 (1): 1–19.

———. 1985. "The Dynamics of Agriculture Supply: A Reconsideration." *American Journal of Agricultural Economics* 67: 204–214.

Epstein, L. G., and A. J. Yatchew. 1985. "The Empirical Determination of Technology and Expectations: A Simplified Procedure." *Journal of Econometrics* 27: 235–258.

Ethiopia, CSA (Central Statistical Agency). 2005–2013. *Agricultural Sample Survey (Private Peasant Holdings, Meher Season)*. Addis Ababa, Ethiopia.

———. 2014a. *Producer Price Survey*. Addis Ababa, Ethiopia.

———. 2014b. *Monthly Consumer Price Index*. Addis Ababa, Ethiopia.

Ethiopia, MoA (Ministry of Agriculture). 2015. *Agriculture Joint Sector Review: Towards Supporting Agricultural Transformation in Ethiopia*. Addis Ababa, Ethiopia.

Geweke, J. 1982. "Measurement of Linear Dependence and Feedback between Multiple Time Series." *Journal of the American Statistical Association* 77: 304–313.

Hansen, L. P. 1982. "Large Sample Properties of Generalized Method of Movements Estimators." *Econometrica* 50: 1029–1054.

Hansen, L. P., and T. J. Sargent. 1980. "Formulating and Estimating Dynamic Linear Rational Expectations Models." *Journal of Economic Dynamics and Control* 2: 7–46.

Harris, R. D. F., and E. Tzavalis. 1999. "Inference for Unit Roots in Dynamic Panels where the Time Dimension Is Fixed." *Journal of Econometrics* 91: 201–226.

Headey, D., and T. S. Jayne. 2014. "Adaptation to Land Constraints: Is Africa Different?" *Food Policy* 48: 18–33.

Hsiao, C. 1986. *Analysis of Panel Data*. Cambridge, UK: Cambridge University Press.

Im, K. S., M. H. Pesaran, and Y. Shin. 2003. "Testing for Unit Roots in Heterogeneous Panels." *Journal of Econometrics* 115 (1): 53–74.

Kavinya, P., and M. A. Phiri. 2014. "Maize Hectarage Response to Price and Non-price Incentives in Malawi." *Scholarly Journal of Agricultural Science* 4 (3): 142–151.

Mose, L. O., K. Burger, and A. Kuvyenhoven. 2007. "Aggregate Supply Response to Price Incentives: The Case of Smallholder Maize Production in Kenya." *African Crop Science Conference Proceedings* 8: 1271–1275 (El-Minia, Egypt).

Muchapondwa, E. 2009. "Supply Response of Zimbabwean Agriculture: 1970–1999." *Afjare* 3 (1): 28–42.

Nickell, S. 1981. "Biases in Dynamic Models with Fixed Effects." *Econometrica* 49: 1417–1426.

Rudaheranwa, N., L. Bategeka, M. Banga, and A. Mukungu. 2003. *Supply Response of Selected Export Commodities in Uganda*. Economic Policy Research Centre (EPRC) Research Series 36. EPRC, Makerere University, Kampala, Uganda.

Sargent, T. J. 1987. *Macroeconomic Theory*. 2nd edition. Boston: Academic Press Inc.

Schiff, M., and C. Montenegro. 1997. "Aggregate Agricultural Supply Response in Developing Countries: A Survey of Selected Issues." *Economic Development and Cultural Change* 45 (2): 393–410.

Suleiman, A. 2004. *Smallholder Supply Response and Gender in Ethiopia: A Profit Function Analysis*. Sheffield Economic Research Paper 2004007. Department of Economics, University of Leicester, UK.

Taffesse, A. S. 2003. "Government Policy and Dynamic Supply Response: A Study of the Compulsory Grain Delivery System." MPRA Paper 18674. African Centre for Economic and Historical Studies, Addis Ababa, Ethiopia.

Tegene, A., W. E. Huffman, and J. A. Miranowski. 1988. "Dynamic Corn Supply Functions: A Model with Explicit Optimization." *American Journal of Agricultural Economics* 70 (1): 103–111.

Yu, B., F. Liu, and L. You. 2010. *Dynamic Agricultural Supply Response under Economic Transformation: A Case Study of Henan Province*. IFPRI Discussion Paper 987. Washington, DC: IFPRI.

Appendix

Estimation Procedure

The empirical teff acreage demand equation given in equation (1) and teff price equation are estimated using available data on the variables. Zone-level aggregated annual panel data are used, which extend over the nine-year period of 2003/2004–2011/2012. Equation (1) is restated below by introducing zone-specific effects. The resulting teff acreage demand equation is:

$$A_{1i,t} = \varkappa_1 A_{1i,t-1} + \varkappa_2 A_{1i,t-2} + \varkappa_3 P_{1i,t-1} + \varkappa_5 R_{1i,t} + \varkappa_6 R_{1i,t-1} + \eta_i^A + v_{i,t}^A \quad t \geq 3 \tag{3}$$

In equation (3) i = 1,..., 53 identifies the 53 administrative zones and t denotes the years covered in the dataset.[11] The term η_i^A stands for unobserved zone-specific effects of acreage demand. To ensure stationarity in equation (3), it is also assumed that, $\varkappa_1 + \varkappa_2 < 1, \varkappa_2 - \varkappa_1 < 1$, and $\varkappa_2 > -1$.[12]

The following teff price equation is similarly obtained from $P_{1,t} = \Theta P_{1,t-1} + u_t^P$ with $|\Theta| < 1$:

$$P_{1i,t} = \Theta P_{1i,t-1} + \eta_i^P + v_{i,t}^P \quad |\Theta| < 1, t \geq 2 \tag{4}$$

Note that, $\eta_i^A + v_{i,t}^A = \varepsilon_t$ and $\eta_i^P + v_{i,t}^P = u_t^P$ represent the "fixed effects" decomposition of the disturbance terms commonly adopted in panel data models, with $v_{i,t}^A$ and $v_{i,t}^P$ assumed to be white noise.

Equations (3) and (4) are estimated using techniques applicable to such models. Given the equations include the levels for past one or two periods (once or twice lagged levels) of the dependent variable, they must be estimated using dynamic panel data (DPD) models. Estimating the equations using ordinary least squares (OLS) or panel data methods, such as the within-groups estimator, result in biased parameter estimates (Nickell [1981] and Hsiao [1986]). OLS estimates are biased because $J_{1i,t-k}$ is correlated with $v_{i,t}^J$ through the individual specific effect, η_i^J, for $J \in (A, P)$ and k = 1, 2. The within-groups estimator, in which the variables are transformed by subtracting their time-means, the cause is the correlation between $J_{1i,t-k}$ and the time-mean of $v_{i,t}^J$.

11 Although the data extends for the 2004/2005–2012/2013 period the first two years of data are lost due to twice lagged acreage variables used in equation (3).

12 These conditions define the triangle that ensures the stationarity of an AR(2) process (Davidson and MacKinnon [1993], 343). In this regard, recall that in the present case, $|\varkappa_1| = |\lambda_1 + \rho| < 2$, and $|\varkappa_2| = |\rho\lambda_1| < 1$, since $|\lambda_1| < 1$ and $|\rho| < 1$.

Among methods developed to estimate the parameters of such models, two standard DPD models are used. The first is the linear dynamic panel-data method developed by Arellano and Bond (1991). The second method is the systems estimator that uses additional moment conditions than those used in the first.[13] This was developed by Arellano and Bover (1995) and Blundell and Bond (1995).

13 References on theoretical underpinnings of single equation dynamic panel data models include Anderson and Hsiao (1982), Arellano and Bond (1991), Arellano and Bover (1995), Blundell and Bond (1995).

Chapter 9

FARMING PRACTICES AND PRODUCTIVITY

Getu Hailu, Alfons Weersink, and Bart Minten

One of the challenges in Africa south of the Sahara is the struggle to develop sustainable agricultural production systems to cope with increasing population pressure and the associated growth in the demand for food. The Ethiopian government wants to double the production of teff to aid in the alleviation of food insecurity among the general population, which will in the process enhance the well-being of individual farm households that grow, consume, and sell teff. The increase in Ethiopian teff production over the past decade resulted primarily from an increase in the area cultivated (Demeke and Marcantonio 2013). However, since there are limits to the amount of arable land available, the desired increases in teff production will have to be met largely through increases in agricultural productivity.

Understanding the relationships between farming practices and yield increases will help in the design of programs to promote the continued and necessary increase in teff yield. For example, if the productivity difference between individual farmers is due to differences in practices employed, then one policy option is to promote the adoption of yield-enhancing technologies (Ali and Byerlee 1991). This promotion could be through modern input methods or even subsidies. This assumes that the farmers are aware of the benefits but do not use the technologies because of credit constraints or being unable to handle the uncertainty of switching practices. However, if the farmers are not using the current technology properly or are not aware of the yield-enhancing practices, there is a role for extension efforts to develop the skills and knowledge of the farmer. Either publicly funded programs or farm organizations could provide the extension education.

Information about yield-enhancing technologies, such as seed variety, is generally provided to farmers in developing countries through publicly funded agricultural extension programs (Townsend et al. 2013). Producer organizations operate as an alternative mechanism to provide technical information and may also serve to link farmers with markets for inputs and outputs.

For example, agricultural producer cooperatives provide farmers with access to inputs and output markets, whereas producer community groups provide opportunities to discuss best management practices.

In this chapter, teff production practices are described, along with their relationships with the level of land productivity of teff producers in Ethiopia. Data are used on plots of teff from a survey of 1,200 stratified randomly selected households conducted at the end of 2012. We selected this dataset as it provides high-quality data, relevant information on teff practices, and a large sample. The relationships between farming practices and teff yield are assessed through a descriptive analysis of the data and the estimation of a production function to determine teff productivity. Although input levels and characteristics of the plot and household are included as right-hand variables, the focus is on the technology employed and producer organizations used. The analysis sheds light on the relationships between farming practices and yield across plots as well as the implications for policies to improve land productivity for teff producers.

Methods and Data

Two approaches are used to examine the links between farming practices and productivity differences. First, descriptive statistics and nonparametric tests are used as a crude measure for the relationship between farming practices and the cross-sectional variations in the level and distribution of land productivity with a focus on the role of technology adoption and extension activities. Since teff yield data has a skewed distribution according to the results of the Shapiro-Francia W' test (Shapiro and Francia 1972; Royston 1983), nonparametric tests are used—that is, the Wilcoxon-Mann-Whitney and the Kruskal Wallis tests—to determine if differences in yield across factors is statistically significant in the absence of normality. To test for a possible first-degree conditional stochastic dominance in the distribution of yields between two groups (for example, cooperative members versus nonmembers), a Kolmogorov-Smirnov (KS) test is used.

Second, the following Cobb-Douglas production function is estimated by ordinary least squares (OLS),

$$y_{ijp} = \beta_0 + \beta_i + \beta x_{ijp} + \delta H_{ijp} + \gamma Plot_{ijp} + \alpha Tech_{ijp} + \tau Extension_{ijp} + \zeta Weather_{ijp} + \varepsilon_{ijp} \quad (1)$$

where i indexes household, j indexes village/district/region, and p indexes plot; y_{ijp} is the logarithm of total output for plot p from household i located in region j; β_i is a zone or kebele or household fixed effect that captures possible heterogeneity at the specified spatial level; x_{ijp} is a vector of quantity of logarithm of variable inputs; H_{ijp} is a vector of household characteristics; $Plot_{ijp}$ is a vector of plot characteristics; $Tech_{ijp}$ is a vector of technological practices adopted; $Extension_{ijp}$ is a vector of extension activities; $Weather_{ijp}$ is a vector of weather shock factors; and ε_{ijp} is an error term that summarizes the effects of unobserved plot quality variation and plot-specific production shocks on yields. β, δ, α, τ, and ζ are parameters to be estimated. Five versions of (1) are estimated: a base model without any fixed effects ($\beta_i = 0$), plus fixed effects for zone, district (woreda), village (kebele), and households.[1]

The data for the study come from a survey of 1,200 households conducted by the Economic Development Research Institute (EDRI) and International Food Policy Research Institute (IFPRI) (see Chapter 11). The main purpose of the survey was to understand the teff value chains to make recommendations to policy makers to improve the performance of value chains for farmers, wholesalers, retailers, and consumers. The survey was conducted in 2012 in sixty villages (kebele), in twenty districts (woreda), in five major teff-producing zones (regions) of Ethiopia (East Gojjam, West Gojjam, East Shewa, West Shewa, and South West Shewa). The five zones represent 38 percent of national teff area and 42 percent of the commercial surplus (Ethiopia, CSA 2012). The average (and the coefficient of variation of) altitude in meters of the five zones are 2,323 (10 percent) for East Gojjam; 2,200 (5 percent) for West Gojjam; 1,784 (24 percent) for East Shewa; 2,099 (13 percent) for West Shewa; and 2,188 (5 percent) for South West Shewa.

The detailed cross-sectional data contain household- and plot-level information on teff production. The number of teff plots per household range from 1 to 6 in the dataset with an average of 1.2. In addition to teff production on each plot, the data include information on six sets of variables identified in equation (1): (1) inputs (for example, amount of seed, labor use, number of oxen, DAP and urea fertilizer applied, and amount of herbicide applied); (2) household characteristics (for example, age, gender, and the level of education of the household head, and distance from the nearest marketplace); (3) plot characteristics (for example, plot size, soil color, slope); (4) technological practices (for example, seed variety and color, crop rotation, mobile phone

1 The fixed effect regressions estimated in this study "[are] usually called the dummy variable regression[s]" (Wooldridge 2010, 485).

ownership); (5) extension activities (for example, cooperative membership, the number of community meetings attended, the number of extension agent visits, and being a model farmer); and (6) weather shocks (for example, rainfall [timing and extent], frost).[2]

Descriptive Analysis of Teff Production

Before examining the relationships between farming practices and productivity in this section, a descriptive overview is provided of (1) the production practices of Ethiopian teff farmers, and (2) teff output and inputs. First, the statistics are presented for several parts of the production process—that is, land preparation, seed use, modern input use and teff cultivation, and harvest and postharvest practices. Then the labor allocations patterns are explored. Second, summary statistics are provided for yield and the variety of explanatory variables used in the analysis to examine yield variations.

Teff Production Practices

Most of the farmers grow teff on fragmented lands and as part of a rotation. The average number of parcels managed in the sample used is approximately four, with an average lot size of 0.48 hectares for teff. Farmers do not often plant teff two years in a row on the same plots. For the plots in the survey, in only 34 percent of the cases was teff also planted in the year prior to the survey (Table 9.1).

Plowing is one of the important land preparation practices, as the soil needs to be loose to allow the very small teff seeds to germinate. The average plot in the study sample was tilled 4.4 times (Table 9.1). In 95 percent of the cases, plowing was done by animals. In 4 percent of the cases, it was done by hand. Mechanized plowing is almost nonexistent, as it was mentioned for only 0.4 percent of the plots.[3] When animals were used, these were usually owned by the farmer himself (84 percent of the cases). Renting-in animals for plowing of teff plots in these zones is rare (4 percent).

Nutrient requirements can be provided through either organic fertilizer (that is, manure) or inorganic fertilizer. Manure use on plots for teff production is limited. Farmers stated that 89 percent of the teff plots never received

2 In many cases, "model farmers" or leader farmers are farmers chosen by extension services with the aim of working together in implementation of extension programs (Franzel et al. 2013).

3 The repeated plowing using animal traction for the preparation of fields and of trampling of fields with livestock before planting might possibly result in damaging soil structure and lead to soil erosion. The authors are, however, not aware of recent research on this issue.

TABLE 9.1 Land preparation practices employed to grow teff

	Unit	Mean (or %)	Median
Crop Rotation			
Teff was planted in prior year on plot	%	34	
Plowing			
Number of times plowed	Number	4.4	4.0
Manner that soil was plowed:			
Hoe	%	4	
Animal	%	95	
Tractor	%	0.4	
Mixed	%	0.4	
If animals used, owner of animals:			
Own	%	84	
Rented	%	4	
Sharing	%	1	
Mix	%	11	
Manure application			
Frequency of manure use:			
Every year	%	6	
Most years	%	1	
Some years	%	2	
Rarely	%	2	
Never	%	89	
Farmer used manure on the plot this year	% yes	8	
Farmer used other organic inputs this year	% yes	5	

Source: Authors' calculation using data from the 2012 teff value-chain survey conducted by the Economic Development Research Institute (EDRI) and International Food Policy Research Institute (IFPRI).

manure, while only 6 percent of the plots received it every year and 8 percent in the year prior to the survey. Only 5 percent of the plots used another organic input instead of manure. These results overall indicate that the use of organic fertilizer in teff production is low.

A wide variety of teff seeds are used. The four main color-based grades of teff are magna (very white), nech (white), sergegna (mix between white and red), key (brown/red) (see Chapter 3). In terms of market values, magna ranks first with key the least valuable. White teff seeds were used on 52 percent of the plots (Table 9.2) compared to 17 percent of magna seeds (very white).

TABLE 9.2 Input use in the production of teff by respondents

	Unit	Mean (or %)	Median
Seeds			
Color of seeds:			
Magna	%	17	
White	%	52	
Mix	%	11	
Black or red	%	20	
Variety of seeds:			
Quncho	%	19	
Other improved seeds	%	11	
Traditional	%	70	
Source of seeds:			
From own harvest	%	78	
Purchased	%	17	
For free or in barter	%	5	
If not from own harvest, source of seeds:			
Cooperative	%	19	
Other farmers	%	66	
Private trader	%	9	
Bureau of agriculture	%	6	
Seeds planted through broadcasting	%	99.5	
Quantity of seed used	kilogram per hectare	44	40
Sowed at normal time this year:			
Early	%	7	
Normal	%	85	
Late	%	9	
Late due to late access of fertilizer	% yes	3	
Late due to flooding or late rains	% yes	3	
Fertilizer			
% of plots where DAP was used	%	89	
Number of times that DAP was applied:			
Once	%	93	
More than once	%	7	
% of plots where urea was used	%	79	

	Unit	Mean (or %)	Median
Number of times that urea was applied:			
Once	%	49	
Twice	%	43	
More than twice	%	8	
Weed Control			
Number of weedings	Number	1.2	
% of plots where herbicides were used	%	65	
% of plots where pesticides were used	%	16	

Source: Authors' calculation using data from the 2012 teff value-chain survey conducted by the Economic Development Research Institute (EDRI) and International Food Policy Research Institute (IFPRI).

Sergegna (mix) and red seeds made up 11 percent and 20 percent of the plots, respectively. The high prevalence of white and magna seeds indicate the importance of consumer preferences as more white seeds are disproportionately sold than red or mixed seeds. Red or mixed seeds are often retained for home consumption (Minten et al. 2013).

Teff seeds can broadly be classified into traditional and improved varieties. In most of the cases, farmers rely on traditional seeds—as stated by the sample farmers. Of the plots, 30 percent were reported to be planted with improved seeds; 19 percent were planted with the improved Quncho ("top most") variety. Officially released in 2006, Quncho was developed by the Debre Zeit Agricultural Research Center (DZARC) from two parent materials: one high-yielding but pale color (Dukem, DZ-01-974) and the other a lower yielding but possessing a popular very white seed color (Magna, DZ-01-196) (Tefera, Belay, and Sorrells 2001). Yield performance on experimental trials with Quncho was found to be significantly higher than national average yields for teff (Assefa, Chanyalew, and Metaferia 2013). For further details, see Chapter 3. This survey was done in the most productive areas of Ethiopia (representing approximately 40 percent of national production), possibly explaining the relatively high adoption of improved seeds in this dataset.

Farmers obtained seeds from a variety of different sources including their own harvest, other farmers, cooperatives, private traders, and the Bureau of Agriculture. A full 78 percent of the seeds were obtained from their own harvest, and only 17 percent were purchased (5 percent were received for free or bartered). If the seeds were not from their own harvest, other farmers supplied seed for approximately two-thirds of the cases. Formal outlets for distribution are therefore relatively less important (that is, cooperatives 19 percent, private traders 9 percent, and Bureau of Agriculture 6 percent of the approximately one-fifth of the seeds purchased).

The government has in recent years started a program aimed at encouraging farmers to use row planting rather than broadcast seed. According to the Agricultural Transformation Agency (ATA 2013), row planting at a reduced seed rate is believed to have important positive effects on teff productivity as compared to sowing with broadcasting (ATA 2013). However, at the time of the survey, the row-planting practice had not been promoted, so the majority of the farmers practiced broadcasting for sowing. The quantities of seeds used were therefore high—that is, on average 44 kilograms per hectare, as compared to 5 kilograms per hectare seeding rate used with row planting (ATA 2013).

In terms of timing, 85 percent of the plots were sown at the normal time (typically July), 7 percent early, and 9 percent late (mostly because of late access to fertilizer [3 percent] or because of flooding or late rains [3 percent]), indicating that the survey year experienced typical growing conditions (Table 9.2).

Fertilizers and herbicides were used on a large number of the plots in the survey. The application of inorganic fertilizer is particularly widespread and is the main source of additional nutrients given the low use of organic fertilizer noted earlier. In the year prior to the survey, 89 percent of the plots received DAP and 79 percent received urea. DAP was mostly used once (at the time of planting), while urea was applied once (49 percent), twice (43 percent), or even more (8 percent). Although herbicides are often used (65 percent) to help reduce weeding efforts, manual weeding is, on average, still done once per season. The use of pesticides or other sprays is less prevalent as these were only applied on 16 percent of the teff plots. The finding that inorganic fertilizers and herbicides are often used in teff production, whereas insecticides and fungicides are not commonly used, is consistent with the analysis of Gorfu and Ahmed (n.d.).

As with most agricultural products, teff is subject to disease and weather shocks. However, it is believed that teff is more resistant to diseases than a number of other crops, which might partly explain its success in Ethiopia (Assefa, Chanyalew, and Metaferia 2013). During the cultivation period, 84 percent of the plots did not suffer from any insects, animal damage, or pests. If there were such problems, they were mostly related to cutworm, root rot, and ball worm (Table 9.3). Questions were also asked about the type of disease that affected teff on a plot. Farmers reported that 85 percent of the plots had not suffered from any diseases. Leaf rust was the most common

TABLE 9.3 Growing stresses and harvest methods on teff plots by respondents

Stresses and harvest methods	Unit	Mean (or %)	Median
Shocks and diseases			
Most important insects/animals/pests issues:			
Locust or grasshopper	%	2	
Shootfly	%	1	
Cutworm/root rot/ball worm	%	13	
None	%	84	
Most important disease issues:			
Leaf rust	%	7	
Head smudge	%	4	
Damping off	%	3	
None	%	85	
Moisture stress this year:			
Drought	%	8	
Excess moisture	%	9	
Normal	%	83	
% of plots that suffered from lodging	%	10	
Harvest and postharvest			
Length of growing period	Weeks	17	17
Time between harvesting and threshing	Days	40	30
Type of threshing floor:			
Dried cow dung	%	99.7	
Other	%	0.3	
Type of threshing used:			
Animals	%	97.3	
Humans using sticks	%	2.5	
Thresher	%	0.2	
Threshing on own or joint threshing floor:			
Own	%	59	
Joint	%	39	
Others	%	2	
Main use of straw:			
Sales	%	3	
Fodder	%	93	
Other	%	4	

Source: Authors' calculation using data from the 2012 teff value-chain survey conducted by the Economic Development Research Institute (EDRI) and International Food Policy Research Institute (IFPRI).

disease, with 7 percent of the plots reported to have been affected by this disease. Lodging is an important problem in teff cultivation and significant efforts are made in teff breeding to develop varieties with stronger stems (Assefa, Chanyalew, and Metaferia 2013). Farmers reported that 10 percent of the plots were affected by lodging during the survey year. Finally, the survey year was viewed as a "normal" cropping year in terms of the moisture content for 83 percent of the plots, with the other 8 percent of the plots suffering from drought and 9 percent from excess moisture. The lack of growing stresses in the survey year implies that the differences noted for yields in the subsequent analysis is due primarily to differences in production systems rather than the growing conditions unique to the year of the survey.

Figure 9.1 illustrates the week in which teff is planted and harvested in the five zones. Almost all of the sowing happens over a period of one month at the beginning of the rainy season (the meher), stretching from the second week of July to the first week of August. However, the harvest period is much more varied and lasts from the beginning of October to the end of January. The average length of the growing season for teff is 17 weeks (Table 9.3). However, significant variation is noted with the variation correlated with elevation (Figure 9.2). Teff that is grown in relatively lower altitudes (<2,100 meters) takes 15 weeks to mature on average as opposed to 18 weeks for teff grown at higher altitudes (>2,100 meters).

After teff is harvested, a threshing process is needed to separate teff grains from the straw. The average time between harvesting and threshing is about 40 days during which period the teff plants are left to dry. In almost all cases threshing is done on a dry threshing floor that is "polished with" cow dung and using animals (97 percent) (Table 9.3). However, some farmers thresh the teff themselves by using sticks, and a very small proportion of farmers use mechanized threshers (0.2 percent). Almost 60 percent of the farmers create their own threshing floor while 40 percent share a threshing floor with other farmers. The straw from teff is mainly used for livestock fodder, and few farmers sell the straw.

Currently little is known about the use of labor in teff production practices, but the survey provides some insights into the amount of labor used for different activities, the source of that labor, and the gender of the workers (Table 9.4). In total, about 141 person-days are spent on the production of 1 hectare of teff. The most labor-intensive activities are weeding (32 person-days), harvesting (28 person-days), and tilling (21 person-days). Postharvest activities (for example, gathering and piling), threshing and winnowing each count for about 22 person-days. Family labor makes up

FIGURE 9.1 The sowing and harvesting times of teff on the plots of survey respondents

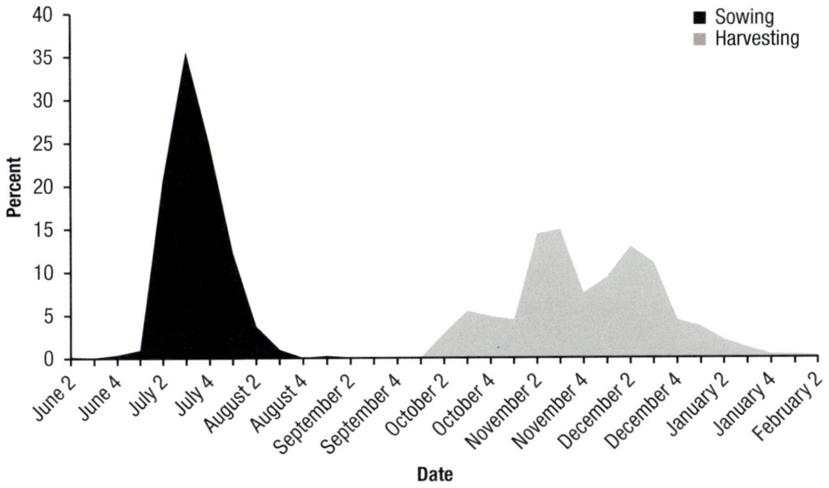

Source: Authors' calculation using data from the 2012 teff value-chain survey conducted by the Economic Development Research Institute (EDRI) and International Food Policy Research Institute (IFPRI).

Note: '2' and '4' refer to the second and fourth week of the month. 'June 2,' for example, refers to the second week in June, 'June 4,' to the fourth week in June.

FIGURE 9.2 Number of weeks between planting and harvesting by low elevation (<2,100 meters) and high elevation (>2,100 meters)

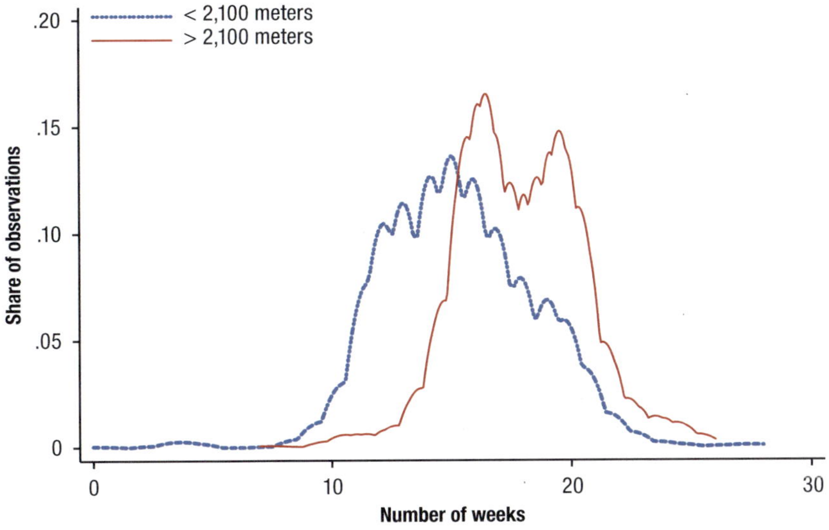

Source: Authors' calculation using data from the 2012 teff value-chain survey conducted by the Economic Development Research Institute (EDRI) and International Food Policy Research Institute (IFPRI).

TABLE 9.4 Labor use per hectare in teff production by task

	Number of person-days		Share family labor (%)			Gender (%)	
Practice	Mean	Median	Family	Hired	Exchange	Male	Female
Tilling	23.7	20.0	85	7	8	97	3
Manure and organic input use	2.3	0.0	93	4	3	71	29
Sowing and fertilizer use	7.5	4.0	86	6	7	88	12
Weeding	32.5	24.0	73	10	16	67	33
Herbicide and pesticide application	2.2	0.6	76	23	1	95	5
Harvesting	28.7	23.3	41	32	27	93	7
Postharvesting activities	21.9	16.0	69	7	24	71	29
Threshing and winnowing	21.9	16.0	57	11	32	87	13
Total	**140.6**	**112.5**	**63**	**14**	**22**	**82**	**18**

Source: Authors' calculation using data from the 2012 teff value-chain survey conducted by the Economic Development Research Institute (EDRI) and International Food Policy Research Institute (IFPRI).

63 percent of the total labor used, with hired labor accounting for 14 percent, and labor provided through a reciprocal exchange among farming families comprising the remaining 22 percent. The share of hired labor is especially high during the harvesting period, when it makes up 32 percent of total labor use. If labor supply is broken down by gender, male labor dominates teff production. Males perform 82 percent of the all the work during teff production, with tilling and harvesting almost exclusively undertaken by men. Women, however, are relatively more involved in weeding activities and make up 33 percent of all labor used for this activity.

Teff Yield and Inputs

Table 9.5 provides summary statistics for yield and the variety of explanatory variables used in the analysis to explain yield, with each given by zone. Average yield per hectare is approximately 11 quintals or 1,100 kilograms, which is lower than the 2010/2011 national average yield of 1,260 kilograms per hectare but higher than the 2004/2005 average national yield of 950 kilograms per hectare (Demeke and Marcantonio 2013). The distribution of yields across all plots is illustrated in Figure 9.3 and indicates that some plots had yields above 30 quintals per hectare. Figure 9.3 further illustrates that teff yield is lower than 1,000 kilograms per hectare for 50 percent of the sample plots, and only 10 percent of the plots have yields of 2,000 kilograms per hectare or higher. There are significant regional variations in plot productivity with

FIGURE 9.3 Distribution of teff yield per hectare across all plots for all zones

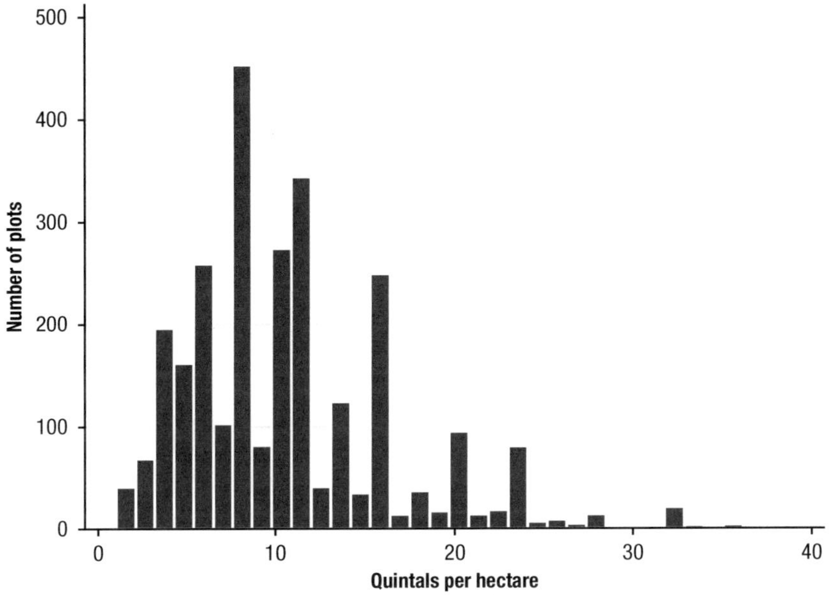

Source: Authors' calculation using data from the 2012 teff value-chain survey conducted by the Economic Development Research Institute (EDRI) and International Food Policy Research Institute (IFPRI).

average yield highest in East Gojjam (14.9 quintals per hectare) and lowest in the West Shewa and South West Shewa zones (8.9 and 8 quintals per hectare respectively) (see Table 9.5).

There are considerable differences in input use across the five zones (Table 9.5) and by yield category (Table 9.6). The average input tends to increase with yield category, particularly for yields above 14 quintals per hectare. For example, average labor use is similar at 124 person-days per hectare for the two lowest groupings with yields less than 10 quintals per hectare (that is, the first- and second-yield quartiles) and then increases to over 185 person-days per hectare used on plots with yields above 14 quintals per hectare (that is, the fourth quartile). The effect of labor on yield is similar to the effects from the other variable inputs on teff productivity.

Gender and age of the operator are similar across zones, with more than 70 percent of the plots operated by males, 28 percent by both males and females, and 2 percent by females. The average age of the operator is approximately 45 years. Education varies between regions *(text continued on page 220)*

TABLE 9.5 Descriptive statistics of variables used in the production of teff by zone

		Zones					
	Pooled Mean	East Gojjam	West Gojjam	East Shewa	West Shewa	South West Shewa	p value*
Yield (quintals per hectare)	**10.88**	**14.94**	**10.86**	**12.58**	**8.93**	**7.98**	**0.000**
Inputs							
Seed (kilograms per hectare)	45.01	33.43	45.49	59.93	49.50	38.22	0.000
Labor (person-day per hectare)	140.49	159.47	195.27	110.18	169.33	93.66	0.000
DAP (kilograms per hectare)	99.65	86.77	149.47	104.42	69.62	94.60	0.000
UREA (kilograms per hectare)	78.05	138.01	70.01	54.10	51.40	72.17	0.000
Herb (birr per hectare)	43.99	5.38	49.82	43.95	86.22	41.91	0.000
Oxen (number)	3.04	2.07	1.65	4.98	2.93	3.09	0.000
Household characteristics							
Formal education (0–14)	2.20	1.75	1.20	2.49	2.42	2.87	0.000
Adult education (0/1)	0.13	0.15	0.28	0.08	0.10	0.08	0.000
Church or mosque education (0/1)	0.02	0.06	0.07	0.00	0.00	0.00	n.a.
Household head age (in years)	45.46	43.43	45.31	46.50	45.82	46.26	0.000
Household size (number)	10.77	10.66	10.70	11.02	10.29	10.93	0.172
Plot characteristics							
Plot size (hectare)	0.48	0.31	0.27	0.64	0.52	0.59	0.000
Soil type:							
Red soil (0/1)	0.19	0.27	0.33	0.08	0.30	0.04	0.000
Brown soil (0/1)	0.20	0.14	0.22	0.30	0.17	0.16	0.000
Black soil (0/1)	0.47	0.50	0.33	0.34	0.51	0.64	0.000
Mix soil (0/1)	0.14	0.09	0.12	0.28	0.02	0.16	0.000
Plot slope:							
Meda/level (slope) (0/1)	0.82	0.85	0.81	0.84	0.64	0.93	0.000
Dagetama (nearly level) (0/1)	0.15	0.10	0.18	0.13	0.33	0.05	0.000
Gedel (0/1)	0.03	0.04	0.01	0.03	0.03	0.01	0.008
Ease of plowing (0/1)	0.81	0.79	0.75	0.85	0.79	0.84	0.000
Plowing frequency (number)	4.40	5.12	4.66	4.02	4.26	4.05	0.000
Manure (0/1)	0.08	0.09	0.08	0.02	0.16	0.04	0.000
Crop rotation (0/1)	0.63	0.66	0.57	0.57	0.92	0.52	0.000
Walking distance (minutes)	17.15	22.12	14.51	22.15	12.46	13.57	0.000
Distance to cooperative (hours)	0.99	0.86	1.29	0.82	1.19	0.89	0.000
Distance to market (hours)	1.37	1.31	1.12	1.37	1.87	1.23	0.000
Distance to all-weather road (hours)	0.90	1.23	1.16	0.51	0.91	0.77	0.000

		Zones					
	Pooled Mean	East Gojjam	West Gojjam	East Shewa	West Shewa	South West Shewa	p value*
Plot managed by:							
Male (0/1)	0.70	0.95	0.24	0.76	0.56	0.87	0.000
Female (0/1)	0.02	0.01	0.02	0.01	0.03	0.02	0.012
Female and male (0/1)	0.28	0.04	0.74	0.24	0.41	0.12	0.000
Technology							
Seed variety:							
Quncho (0/1)	0.19	0.18	0.30	0.30	0.06	0.14	0.000
Other improved (0/1)	0.11	0.10	0.00	0.08	0.05	0.25	n.a.
Traditional (0/1)	0.70	0.72	0.70	0.61	0.89	0.60	0.000
Seed color:							
Very white (magna) (0/1)	0.17	0.15	0.00	0.28	0.05	0.28	0.000
White (nech) (0/1)	0.53	0.58	0.58	0.50	0.48	0.49	0.000
Mix (sergegna) (0/1)	0.11	0.04	0.27	0.03	0.13	0.11	0.000
Red (key) (0/1)	0.20	0.23	0.15	0.19	0.34	0.11	0.000
Mobile phone ownership (0/1)	0.36	0.22	0.11	0.63	0.27	0.46	0.000
Extension and organization							
Cooperative membership (0/1)	0.64	0.77	0.67	0.50	0.53	0.74	0.000
Community meetings (0/1)	0.69	0.70	0.73	0.67	0.68	0.67	0.188
Extension with extension (0/1)	0.77	0.84	0.69	0.75	0.85	0.69	0.000
Extension by NGO (0/1)	0.04	0.02	0.03	0.02	0.05	0.06	0.000
Model farmer (0/1)	0.39	0.43	0.37	0.35	0.30	0.49	0.000
Weather shock							
Low rainfall (0/1)	0.19	0.16	0.08	0.18	0.20	0.29	0.000
High rainfall (0/1)	0.10	0.13	0.14	0.04	0.12	0.08	0.000
Less logging (0/1)	0.05	0.01	0.02	0.06	0.03	0.09	0.000
More logging (0/1)	0.10	0.09	0.10	0.11	0.13	0.07	0.003
Less frost (0/1)	0.08	0.02	0.02	0.07	0.05	0.18	0.000
More frost (0/1)	0.09	0.15	0.15	0.01	0.06	0.07	0.000
Late rain (0/1)	0.20	0.07	0.12	0.16	0.27	0.37	0.000
Early rain (0/1)	0.08	0.16	0.07	0.06	0.03	0.08	0.000
Early planting (0/1)	0.07	0.04	0.07	0.14	0.01	0.06	0.000
Late planting (0/1)	0.09	0.06	0.07	0.18	0.07	0.05	0.000
Number of plots		**569**	**451**	**600**	**494**	**646**	

Source: Authors' calculation using data from the 2012 teff value-chain survey conducted by the Economic Development Research Institute (EDRI) and International Food Policy Research Institute (IFPRI).

Note: n.a. = not applicable.

*Kruskal-Wallis equality of populations rank test p-values.

with average years of formal schooling higher in the Shewa zones. For plots with yields less than 6 quintals per hectare (that is, the first-yield quartile), the average formal level of education of the operator is 1.74 years (Table 9.6). Education level increases steadily with yield category. For operators managing plots with yields above 14 quintals per hectare, for example, the education level is 2.41 years.

The difference in yield appears to be inversely related to plot size (Table 9.6). For all plots in the sample, the average teff plot size allocated to teff production is 0.48 hectares (1.2 acres) and ranges between 0.03 and 5 hectares (12.35 acres). The average plot size tends to be larger in Shewa than in Gojjam (around 0.6 hectares versus 0.3 hectares), but yields are approximately 50 percent higher in the latter region. In general, small plots tend to have higher average land productivity, suggesting there is an inverse relationship in the average land productivity across plot size categories. This result is consistent with other studies that found an inverse relationship between plot size and productivity (for example, Assunção and Braido 2007; Barrett 1996). While smaller plots may have higher yields, there also appears to be higher variability in land productivity for smaller plots than larger ones (Figure 9.4).

The relationship between proportion of soil type (that is, color) and land productivity is statistically significant across zones (Table 9.5) and teff yield quartiles (Table 9.6). For example, plots with black soil are more prevalent in East Gojjam, West Shewa, and South West Shewa, whereas brown soil plots are more prevalent in West Gojjam and East Shewa, and the differences are statistically significant. In addition, the majority of teff plots are on flat field (meda); 88 percent of the plots in the fourth-yield quartile are on flat field, compared with 83 percent for the first quartile.

The distance of the plot to alternative site measures is generally inversely related to plot productivity. Plots closer to an all-weather road tend to have higher yields. For example, the distance from all-weather road for plots in the fourth-quartile yield category is approximately 0.78 hours (45 minutes), compared with 1.08 hours (65 minutes) for plots in the first-yield quartile. Similarly, average distance to market and to the cooperatives tends to be inversely associated with plot yield.

As noted in the previous section across the sample plots, approximately 20 percent are seeded with Quncho, 10 percent with other improved varieties, and 70 percent with traditional seed varieties. Table 9.6 shows the proportion of seed variety by yield quartile and reveals the presence of considerable differences in the proportion of seed variety by yield quartiles. For example, the proportion of Quncho seed variety is approximately *(text continued on page 223)*

TABLE 9.6 Mean values of variables used in production function by yield quartiles

	Pooled Mean	Teff yield quartiles (mean in quintals per hectare) First quartile	Second quartile	Third quartile	Fourth quartile	p value*
Yield (quintals per hectare)	**10.88**	**4.65**	**8.43**	**12.23**	**20.57**	**0.000**
Inputs						
Seed (kilograms per hectare)	45.01	41.31	45.37	47.16	47.32	0.000
Labor (person-days per hectare)	140.49	123.98	123.84	136.87	186.23	0.000
DAP (kilograms per hectare)	99.65	83.42	89.46	100.07	130.60	0.000
Urea (kilograms per hectare)	78.05	50.09	69.94	70.89	124.57	0.000
Herbicides (birr per hectare)	43.99	40.17	46.22	47.41	42.39	0.000
Oxen (number)	3.04	2.67	3.26	3.39	2.79	0.003
Household characteristics						
Formal education (0–14)	2.20	1.74	2.39	2.32	2.41	0.000
Adult education (0/1)	0.13	0.13	0.12	0.12	0.15	0.246
Church or mosque education (0/1)	0.02	0.02	0.02	0.02	0.04	0.031
Household head age (years)	45.46	47.45	45.49	44.91	43.72	0.000
Household size (number)	10.77	10.27	10.90	10.58	11.23	0.017
Plot characteristics						
Plot size (hectare)	0.48	0.55	0.52	0.49	0.35	0.000
Soil type:						
Red soil (0/1)	0.19	0.18	0.16	0.24	0.21	0.002
Brown soil (0/1)	0.20	0.15	0.22	0.23	0.19	0.000
Black soil (0/1)	0.47	0.53	0.48	0.39	0.48	0.000
Mix soil (0/1)	0.14	0.14	0.14	0.14	0.13	0.747
Slope:						
Meda/level (slope) (0/1)	0.82	0.83	0.79	0.81	0.88	0.001
Dagetama (nearly level) (0/1)	0.15	0.15	0.18	0.16	0.10	0.000
Gedel (0/1)	0.03	0.03	0.03	0.03	0.02	0.752
Ease of plowing (0/1)	0.81	0.75	0.80	0.85	0.85	0.000
Plowing frequency (#)	4.40	4.18	4.39	4.53	4.55	0.000
Manure (0/1)	0.08	0.07	0.07	0.07	0.09	0.578
Crop rotation (0/1)	0.63	0.61	0.64	0.68	0.63	0.108
Walking distance (minutes)	17.15	16.09	16.45	17.82	18.65	0.000
Distance to cooperative (hours)	0.99	1.22	0.99	0.91	0.78	0.000
Distance to market (hours)	1.37	1.59	1.41	1.36	1.11	0.000
Distance to all-weather road (hours)	0.90	1.08	0.86	0.86	0.78	0.000

(continued)

TABLE 9.6 Continued

	Pooled Mean	Teff yield quartiles (mean in quintals per hectare) First quartile	Second quartile	Third quartile	Fourth quartile	p value*
Plot managed by:						
Male (0/1)	0.70	0.68	0.70	0.71	0.72	0.488
Female (0/1)	0.02	0.03	0.02	0.01	0.00	0.001
Female and male (0/1)	0.28	0.28	0.29	0.28	0.28	0.963
Technology						
Seed variety:						
Quncho (0/1)	0.19	0.10	0.12	0.26	0.34	0.000
Other improved (0/1)	0.11	0.09	0.15	0.10	0.08	0.000
Traditional (0/1)	0.70	0.81	0.73	0.65	0.57	0.000
Seed color:						
Very white (magna) (0/1)	0.17	0.13	0.15	0.19	0.22	0.000
White (nech) (0/1)	0.53	0.44	0.54	0.56	0.57	0.000
Mix (sergegna) (0/1)	0.11	0.17	0.12	0.08	0.05	0.000
Red (key) (0/1)	0.20	0.26	0.20	0.17	0.16	0.000
Mobile phone ownership (0/1)	0.36	0.30	0.36	0.39	0.39	0.001
Extension and organization						
Cooperative membership (0/1)	0.64	0.62	0.61	0.65	0.73	0.000
Community meetings (0/1)	0.69	0.64	0.67	0.71	0.76	0.000
Extension with extension personnel (0/1)	0.77	0.68	0.76	0.79	0.84	0.000
Extension by NGO (0/1)	0.04	0.04	0.04	0.03	0.04	0.730
Model farmer (0/1)	0.39	0.35	0.38	0.43	0.44	0.002
Weather shock						
Low rainfall (0/1)	0.19	0.23	0.21	0.18	0.12	0.000
High rainfall (0/1)	0.10	0.11	0.11	0.07	0.08	0.009
Less lodging (0/1)	0.05	0.04	0.04	0.07	0.02	0.001
More lodging (0/1)	0.10	0.11	0.10	0.10	0.08	0.485
Less frost (0/1)	0.08	0.09	0.10	0.06	0.03	0.000
More frost (0/1)	0.09	0.15	0.08	0.04	0.06	0.000
Late rain (0/1)	0.20	0.28	0.25	0.16	0.10	0.000
Early rain (0/1)	0.08	0.07	0.08	0.06	0.11	0.014
Early planting (0/1)	0.07	0.06	0.07	0.07	0.07	0.634
Late planting (0/1)	0.09	0.07	0.09	0.09	0.10	0.176
Number of plots		**698**	**859**	**565**	**638**	

Source: Authors' calculation using data from the 2012 teff value-chain survey conducted by the Economic Development Research Institute (EDRI) and International Food Policy Research Institute (IFPRI).

Note: *Kruskal-Wallis equality of populations rank test p-values; First Quartile: ≤ 6 quintals per hectare; Second Quartile: 6.1–10 quintals per hectare; Third Quartile: 10.1–14 quintals per hectare; and Fourth Quartile: >14 quintals per hectare.

FIGURE 9.4 **Distribution of land productivity by plot size categories, quintals per hectare**

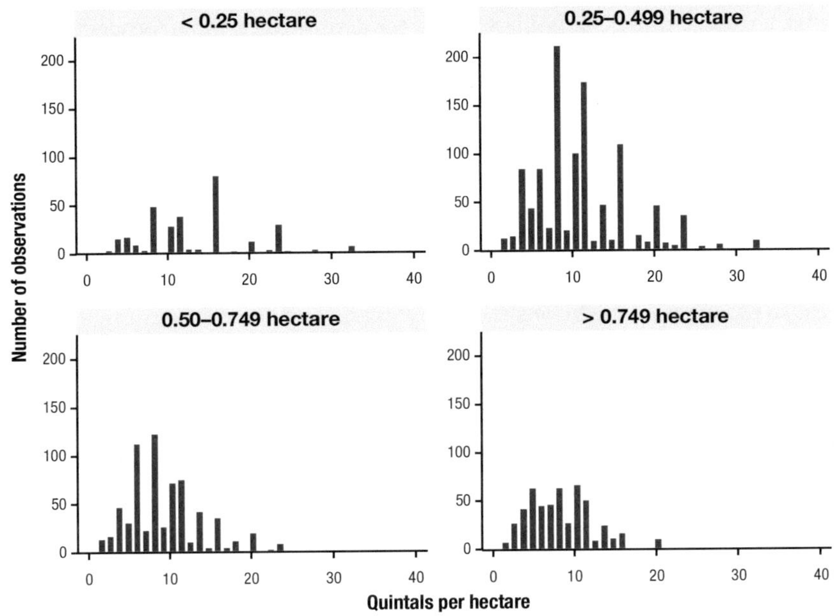

Source: Authors' calculation using data from the 2012 teff value-chain survey conducted by the Economic Development Research Institute (EDRI) and International Food Policy Research Institute (IFPRI).

34 percent for the fourth-yield quartile, compared with 10 percent for the first-yield quartile. The average yield from Quncho for all plots is 35 percent higher than with the traditional variety and the difference is statistically significant at the 1 percent significance level based on Somers' D nonparametric test. It is also found that the relative teff yield of Quncho varies across regions with the increase in yield compared with the yield from traditional seeds ranging from 46 percent for East Shewa to 8 percent for West Shewa. The Wilcoxon-Mann-Whitney nonparametric test suggests that in all zones, except for West Shewa, there is a statistically significant difference in the underlying distributions of teff yield between Quncho and traditional seed varieties. For the pooled sample, the Kolmogorov-Smirnov (KS) test suggests that the distribution of Quncho's productivity dominates the yield distribution of both the traditional and other improved seeds.

Assefa, Chanyalew, and Metaferia (2013) identify especially innovative approaches toward technology dissemination as a major reason for the success of Quncho in widespread adoption. The fundamental features of the extension approach involved the following: (1) use of technology as a package (not only was the seed variety extended but other management practices too); (2) use of large farm holders' fields for demonstration purposes; (3) coordinated multistakeholder partnership extension methods (including farmers, farmers' associations, private seed growers, governmental institutions, and NGOs); (4) revolving seed loans; and (5) regular training, follow-up, and supervision. Although these factors have contributed to widespread adoption, the success of Quncho seems also to be linked closely to the prior absence of improved teff cultivars. Quncho was, in some sense, the variety that could reinvigorate teff research. It is possible that adoption rates were so large because the market conditions were very strong and there was such a dearth of previous improved varieties.

Teff seed color and seed varieties are correlated. For example, all Quncho seed varieties are reported as very white (magna, 51 percent) or white (nech, 49 percent). Similarly, the majority of other improved seeds (94 percent) are very white (magna, 18 percent) or white (nech, 75 percent). For all varieties, very white and white color seeds tend to have higher productivity.

Cooperative members manage at least 60 percent of the plots across all zones with approximately three-quarters of the plots run by cooperative members in East Gojjam and South West Shewa (Table 9.5). While yields for cooperative members are 8 percent less than that generated by nonmembers in East Gojjam, yields are generally higher for members and up to 41 percent higher in West Gojjam (8.4 versus 11.9 quintal per hectare respectively). Cooperative membership is higher at 72 percent for plots in the fourth-yield quartile, compared with plots in the first quartile at 62 percent (Table 9.6). For the pooled sample, Somers' D nonparametric test indicates cooperative members outperform nonmembers by approximately 10 percent, and the Kolmogorov-Smirnov (KS) test suggests that the yield distribution from cooperative members dominates the yield distribution of nonmembers at a 1 percent significance level.

Extension efforts are also associated with higher yields as shown in Table 9.6. Farmers' participation in a community meeting to discuss teff-related issues results in a higher average teff yield. Further descriptive analysis indicates that relative to nonparticipants, teff productivity for participants was higher by approximately 6 percent in East Gojjam, 15 percent in West Gojjam, 17 percent in East Shewa, 7 percent in West Shewa, and 11 percent in South West Shewa. For the pooled sample, the yield on plots for those who attended a community meeting on teff was approximately 13 percent higher than for nonparticipants, indicating that the difference is statistically significant according to the Somers' D test. The Kolmogorov-Smirnov test also suggests that the yield distribution for participants dominates the distribution of productivity for nonparticipants. Average yield is also higher for plots run by farmers who had one or more extension agent visits, especially in West Gojjam. Perhaps related to extension efforts, the average productivity is found to be higher for mobile phone owners in all five zones and the differences are statistically significant for four of the five zones.

In summary, this descriptive analysis reveals (1) plots with Quncho seed variety are more productive than traditional and other improved seeds, and the magnitude varies by zone; (2) activities to enhance understanding and market access (for example, cooperative membership and participation in community meetings) increase yield; and (3) proximity to an all-weather road and the nearest agricultural cooperative has a positive effect on land productivity. However, attributing the cross-sectional differences in productivity across plots to a single factor may hide the effect of other observable and unobservable heterogeneities. For example, when examining the effect of the adoption of Quncho on plot productivity, it is important to control for differences in household- and plot-specific observable (for example, education) and unobserved factors (for example, soil quality) that may lead to higher productivity. In the next section, a teff production function is estimated that allows for the control of multiple household- and plot-specific differences simultaneously.

Associates of Teff Productivity

The estimated coefficients for five specifications of a Cobb-Douglas production function are listed in Table 9.7. The five estimations of equation (1) (described at the beginning of this chapter) represent the base model along with four fixed-effect versions: zone, woreda (district), kebele (village), and household. The vast majority of the estimated coefficients tend to be significant across the estimated models and tend to vary little in absolute terms, suggesting the estimation results are robust. Across all models, seed and labor have a statistically significant positive association with yield. The output elasticity averages approximately 0.2 for seed input across the five models. The amount of urea fertilizer applied and the number of oxen per household also tend to have a statistically significant association with yield. The output elasticity for these two inputs, however, is approximately one-tenth the elasticity for seed and labor. DAP is not shown to be significantly associated with yields. As a large number of farmers use significant amounts of DAP and urea, it is possible that estimates are done on those parts of the domain of the production function where marginal associations are relatively *(text continued on page 230)*

TABLE 9.7 Parameter estimates of teff production function

Parameter	Base		Zone fixed effect		Woreda fixed effect		Kebele fixed effect		Household fixed effect	
Inputs										
Seed	0.166***	(5.71)	0.191***	(6.46)	0.193***	(6.82)	0.183***	(6.38)	0.177***	(2.82)
Labor	0.157***	(4.27)	0.127***	(3.72)	0.116***	(3.93)	0.107***	(4.14)	0.266***	(5.42)
DAP	−0.00392	(−0.95)	0.000864	(0.21)	0.00430	(0.96)	0.00575	(1.30)	0.00158	(0.21)
Urea	0.0209***	(6.12)	0.0194***	(5.69)	0.0102***	(2.95)	0.00703**	(2.05)	−0.0000602	(−0.01)
Herb	−0.0152***	(−6.09)	0.00313	(1.09)	0.00166	(0.59)	0.00306	(1.04)	0.0107**	(2.18)
Oxen	0.0257***	(2.67)	0.0224**	(2.45)	0.0178**	(2.01)	0.0185**	(2.12)	0.132**	(2.52)
Household characteristics										
Formal education (0–14)	0.00992*	(1.88)	0.0140***	(2.75)	0.00783	(1.64)	0.00767	(1.59)		
Adult education (0/1)	−0.0354	(−0.86)	−0.0297	(−0.76)	−0.0176	(−0.51)	−0.0305	(−0.93)		
Church or mosque education (0/1)	−0.0127	(−0.14)	−0.0491	(−0.57)	−0.0848	(−1.08)	−0.0746	(−0.99)		
Household head age (years)	−0.00317***	(−3.08)	−0.00276***	(−2.76)	−0.00318***	(−3.43)	−0.00342***	(−3.65)		
Household size (number)	0.00555**	(2.42)	0.00536**	(2.49)	0.00508**	(2.57)	0.00485***	(2.68)		
Plot characteristics										
Plot size (hectares)	0.545***	(14.91)	0.549***	(15.31)	0.590***	(17.66)	0.611***	(18.66)	0.558***	(8.30)
Soil type:										
Brown soil	−0.00942	(−0.27)	0.0225	(0.63)	0.0166	(0.50)	0.0286	(0.88)	0.0156	(0.29)
Black soil	−0.0388	(−1.25)	0.00363	(0.12)	0.0473	(1.64)	0.0644**	(2.27)	0.0415	(0.90)
Mix soil	−0.0101	(−0.24)	−0.000869	(−0.02)	0.0497	(1.29)	0.0616*	(1.66)	0.0557	(0.98)

Plot slope:										
Dagetama	−0.0102	(−0.33)	−0.00939	(−0.31)	−0.0847***	(−3.07)	−0.0575**	(−2.17)	−0.0576	(−1.09)
Gedel	0.0182	(0.27)	−0.0146	(−0.23)	−0.0218	(−0.33)	0.0487	(0.74)	0.0551	(0.41)
Ease of plowing	0.104***	(3.24)	0.105***	(3.46)	0.0925***	(3.30)	0.0766***	(2.91)	0.0591	(1.28)
Frequency of plowing	0.0264***	(2.61)	0.00425	(0.40)	0.0419***	(3.77)	0.0372***	(3.37)	0.0256	(0.88)
Manure	0.0384	(1.01)	0.0393	(1.06)	0.0597*	(1.66)	0.0334	(0.90)	−0.0665	(−0.98)
Rotation	0.0631**	(2.50)	0.0532**	(2.19)	0.0517**	(2.19)	0.0503**	(2.19)	0.0326	(0.69)
Walking	−0.000278	(−0.47)	−0.00146**	(−2.58)	−0.00136***	(−2.58)	−0.00147***	(−2.72)	−0.000389	(−0.48)
Distance to cooperative (hours)	−0.0589***	(−3.09)	−0.0357*	(−1.88)	−0.0475**	(−2.53)	−0.0594***	(−3.09)		
Distance to market (hours)	−0.00672	(−0.50)	−0.0142	(−1.04)	0.0179	(1.28)	0.0441***	(2.97)		
Distance to all-weather road (hours)	−0.0106	(−0.58)	−0.0181	(−1.05)	0.00260	(0.16)	0.00633	(0.40)		
Plot managed by:										
Male	0.176**	(2.24)	0.114	(1.41)	0.102	(1.20)	0.121	(1.57)	0.382	(0.69)
Male and female	0.0584	(0.72)	0.0847	(1.02)	0.0578	(0.66)	0.0826	(1.02)	0.338	(0.59)
Technology										
Seed variety										
Quncho	0.122***	(3.51)	0.103***	(3.01)	0.127***	(3.36)	0.129***	(3.49)	0.109*	(1.89)
Other improved	0.0284	(0.69)	0.0708*	(1.76)	0.103**	(2.57)	0.100***	(2.62)	−0.00664	(−0.12)
Seed color:										
White seed	−0.0564	(−1.58)	−0.0562	(−1.61)	−0.0581*	(−1.65)	−0.0205	(−0.61)	−0.0288	(−0.56)
Mix seed	−0.227***	(−4.82)	−0.158***	(−3.32)	−0.107**	(−2.28)	−0.0822*	(−1.80)	−0.0376	(−0.52)
Red seed	−0.185***	(−4.27)	−0.174***	(−4.16)	−0.0883**	(−2.10)	−0.0568	(−1.38)	−0.0543	(−0.89)
Mobile phone	0.0232	(0.69)	0.0277	(0.86)	0.0520*	(1.80)	0.0360	(1.32)		

(continued)

TABLE 9.7 Continued

Parameter	Base		Zone fixed effect		Woreda fixed effect		Kebele fixed effect		Household fixed effect	
Extension and organization										
Cooperative	−0.0390	(−1.29)	−0.0222	(−0.73)	−0.0530*	(−1.82)	−0.0348	(−1.30)		
Community	0.0396	(1.39)	0.0453*	(1.69)	0.0438*	(1.74)	0.0345	(1.41)		
Extension	0.135***	(4.38)	0.0901***	(2.98)	0.0686**	(2.35)	0.0622**	(2.25)		
Extension–NGO	0.0241	(0.41)	0.0726	(1.27)	0.0940	(1.58)	0.0768	(1.45)		
Model farmer	0.0356	(1.18)	0.0305	(1.08)	0.0512**	(2.00)	0.0590**	(2.42)		
Weather shock										
Low rainfall	−0.0414	(−1.10)	−0.0524	(−1.47)	0.00971	(0.29)	−0.00664	(−0.21)	−0.0727	(−0.43)
High Rainfall	−0.0408	(−0.86)	−0.0386	(−0.85)	0.0284	(0.68)	0.0280	(0.75)	−0.0860	(−0.57)
Less Logging	0.0361	(0.61)	0.0743	(1.39)	0.0911*	(1.72)	0.0850*	(1.72)	0.139	(1.27)
More Logging	−0.00358	(−0.09)	0.00262	(0.07)	−0.00766	(−0.21)	0.0169	(0.51)	−0.0522	(−0.85)
Less frost	−0.192***	(−4.20)	−0.0904**	(−2.15)	−0.0676	(−1.53)	−0.0715*	(−1.70)	−0.0343	(−0.29)
More frost	−0.247***	(−4.93)	−0.232***	(−4.76)	−0.195***	(−4.35)	−0.171***	(−4.00)	−0.102	(−0.78)
Late rain	−0.123***	(−3.25)	−0.0435	(−1.22)	−0.0412	(−1.24)	−0.0534*	(−1.67)	−0.274	(−1.28)
Early rain	−0.0605	(−1.15)	−0.0819*	(−1.68)	−0.0759*	(−1.67)	−0.0719*	(−1.66)	−0.0271	(−0.14)
Early planting	0.0373	(0.83)	0.00137	(0.03)	−0.0180	(−0.42)	−0.0395	(−0.94)	−0.0294	(−0.23)
Late planting	0.0580	(1.40)	0.0264	(0.67)	0.0153	(0.39)	−0.0147	(−0.40)	−0.0265	(−0.29)

(continued)

Fixed effects										
Zone	No		Yes		No		No		No	
Woreda	No		No		Yes		No		No	
Kebele	No		No		No		Yes		No	
Household	No		No		No		No		Yes	
Constant	−0.296**	(−2.42)	0.256**	(1.99)	−0.350**	(−2.11)	−0.340**	(−2.02)	0.368	(0.62)
Observations	**2,760**		**2,760**		**2,760**		**2,760**		**2,773**	
Adjusted R^2	**0.615**		**0.651**		**0.688**		**0.712**		**0.828**	

Source: Authors' estimation using data from the 2012 teff value-chain survey conducted by the Economic Development Research Institute (EDRI) and International Food Policy Research Institute (IFPRI).

Note: t statistics in parentheses; * $p < 0.10$, ** $p < 0.05$, *** $p < 0.01$. The number of observations for the household fixed effect is higher than for the other model. This is because of missing values for some of the farmers' (for example, school) and farms' (for example, distance) characteristics.

small. The government has recently started to replace DAP with Nitrogen-phosphoric fertilizer containing sulphur (NPS), given the high deficiency of sulphur (S) in Ethiopian soils, possibly indicating its lower performance.

In addition, operator age and household size are the socioeconomic variables that have a statistically significant association with yield. While the summary statistics indicated little difference in operator age across regions (Table 9.5), younger farm managers produce higher yielding plots. In contrast, the regression analysis suggests operator's education is unrelated to teff productivity, although the summary statistics suggested otherwise. Any increases in household size are associated with a corresponding increase in teff output levels. This may be related to the labor available for production activities, which was shown to increase yield levels.

The log of plot size has a positive effect on teff output. However, increases in (logarithmic) plot size are associated with a decrease in teff yield per hectare. The average elasticity value of approximately 0.6 is statistically significant across models. This effect translates to an elasticity of −0.4 of plot size on yield per hectare, suggesting a 10 percent increase in farm size is associated with a reduction of teff yields by 4 percent.[4] A number of reasons for the inverse relationship between farm size and land productivity exist in the literature, which include labor market imperfections and opportunity costs of labor (Sen 1962), measurement errors and unobserved land quality, credit market imperfections (Assunção and Ghatak 2003), and land distribution policies and uneven off-farm work opportunities (Benjamin and Brandt 1997).

Other plot characteristics related to soil type and typography generally have no link with teff productivity. While the gentle-sloped (dagetama) and hilly (gedel) plots have lower yields than level plots, the results are generally not statistically significant, except for plots on gentle slopes. In contrast, the distance measures between the farm plot and various locations tend to have a mixed relationship with yield. For example, for the kebele fixed-effect regression, a 1-minute increase in the time it takes to a travel to the nearest marketplace is associated with 0.044 percent increases in teff yield on average. Plots owned by households that are farther away from the nearest agricultural cooperative are found to have lower productivity for the kebele fixed-effect model. The result on proximity to a marketplace contradicts the findings that relate

4 From the production function in (1), the relationship between productivity and plot size is given by $(\hat{b} - 1)$ and can be derived from the production function as follows: $ln(y) = a + bln(x)$. Subtracting $ln(x)$ from both sides and rearranging gives: $\ln\left(\frac{y}{x}\right) = \hat{a} + (\hat{b} - 1)ln(x)$. A nonlinear relationship for farm size is incorporated using quadratic logarithm of plot size. However, this effect is statistically insignificant.

to proximity to agricultural cooperatives, although the coefficient of access to market is significant for the kebele fixed-effect model only. The closer a plot is to the nearest marketplace, the lower the rate of productivity of the plot.

Proximity to a marketplace may allow farmers to participate in leisure and off-farm income-generating activities, which may provide incentive to spend less time and efforts on the farm. In this situation, distance from the marketplace may create incentives and fewer distractions from off-farm activities, thus allowing a farmer to spend more time on managing teff plots. Also, farm labor supply may be scarce for farms in close proximity to a marketplace as the labor force tends to migrate to urban areas to seek off-farm income opportunities. Furthermore, often proximity to a marketplace may not serve as a measure of remoteness, as "local markets often exist in the most remote communities, but they operate in isolation from the rest of the world" (Brooks 2012, 95). The local markets might be distant from urban centers where supplies of goods and services as well as opportunities for social interaction are concentrated.

Developments in technology result in the anticipated link with productivity. For example, from descriptive statistics, plots seeded with the Quncho seed variety produce approximately 13 percent more than plots planted with traditional varieties. Improved seed varieties, other than Quncho, yield 10 percent more than traditional seeds. The differences on the productivity benefits from new technology across the fixed-effects models highlight the importance of controlling for observed and unobserved heterogeneities across plots and households when conducting quantitative impact analysis.

Other practices considered included the use of a crop rotation. If teff was not grown on the plot in the previous year, the yield of teff is approximately 5 percent greater than on plots growing continuous teff. Owning a mobile phone leads to a 5 percent increase in teff yield for the owner, but it is only significant in one out of the four specifications used (that is, the woreda fixed-effect model). The positive yield impact from the adoption of these two practices is statistically significant and consistent with the results of previous studies such as Asfaw and Shiferaw (2010).

While the major technological practices tend to have a significant positive relationship with yield, the role of extension activities and organization on teff productivity depends on the variable considered. For example, cooperative membership generally has an unexpected negative yet statistically insignificant link with yield. In contrast, participation in a community meeting increases teff yield by 4 percent across the fixed effects and is statistically significant at the 10 percent level for zone and woreda regressions. Similarly, one or more visits by an extension agent is associated with an increase in yield by an average of 6 percent to 13 percent, depending on the model. The difference in the results for the alternative forms of extension participation may be explained by the reason that each is organized for. Cooperatives are mainly targeted at making the sector more commercial and at providing access to input and output markets, particularly fertilizer and other improved inputs. Often agricultural cooperatives do not provide technical training to their members. In contrast, the community meetings and extension visits are focused on how the operator can improve the plot's productivity for growing teff. The effect of producer cooperative membership may be reflected in the use of fertilizer and other modern inputs and distance from agricultural cooperatives. In addition, the existence of spillover effects from cooperative members to nonmembers may explain the insignificant effect of cooperative membership on productivity. Other factors that have links with plot productivity are weather shocks, such as water logging, frost, and rainfall. The only weather variables that have a consistently statistically significant relationship with yield are frost and hailstorms. As expected, a greater frequency of these events decreases plot yield.

Conclusion

There are significant variations in the productivity of plots growing teff across Ethiopia. This chapter has attempted to illustrate this variation as well as to examine the link between farming practices and these differences. The major associations for productivity differences appear to be the levels of input use, the management practices employed, the age of the operator, the ease of access to markets, and the level of engagement in extension efforts (see Chapter 7). While the links of these factors are consistent with prior expectations, the analysis does not, however, adequately consider the complexity of the system. For example, the adoption of high-yielding seed varieties (Quncho) may be the result of farmers participating in community meetings to discuss teff production and/or visits by extension agents. Conversely, the level of fertilizer use may instead be associated with the distance to travel in order to obtain this input. It is difficult to determine the direct and indirect effects of these factors, and therefore a structural equation model would be appropriate to allow for simultaneous estimation of the input factors and teff output.

While further analysis would help direct policy efforts to achieve the desired gains in teff output, the current analysis highlights that there are effective means to enhance the productivity of teff and provide encouragement to those involved with farmers who are reliant on the production and consumption of teff for their livelihoods. The findings lead therefore to a number of policy implications. First, input use, and especially improved seed varieties, is associated with improved productivity, and it appears that there are high rates to return to investments in the development of better seed varieties. The investments to Quncho development clearly illustrate this positive benefit through calculations of the rates of return. Flaherty, Kelemework, and Kelemu (2010) estimate that Ethiopia invested in 2008 US$70 million in agricultural R&D. Assuming, generously, that US$10 million would have been spent annually on teff research, and that the Quncho development was achieved after breeding investments for five years, this leads to a cumulative investment of US$50 million. The results in this chapter show that productivity of Quncho is at least 10 percent higher than other varieties. Assuming that half of the producers in Ethiopia would adopt Quncho and that prices remain unchanged, that would lead to a sustained yearly benefit of US$80 million. If these benefits were to be spread over a 20-year period, the rate of return for that investment would amount to 160 percent. Admittedly, no costs for extension efforts are included in this calculation. However, even if the investments were quadrupled to US$200 million to accommodate this, the rate of return would still be high at 40 percent.

Second, the Ethiopian government has invested heavily in the expansion of the agricultural extension system. At the end of 2010, the government had placed 45,000 extension agents in villages, compared with 2,500 and 15,000 extension agents in 1995 and 2002, respectively (Davis et al. 2010). With a target of three extension agents per kebele, Ethiopia has one of the largest extension agent–farmer ratios found in the world today (Davis et al. 2010). It seems that there is a payoff to some of these investments as shown in the higher productivity of teff that is being achieved by those farmers who have been able to participate in community meetings and had access to extension agents.

Third, remoteness is found to be an important determinant of productivity because of the lack of incentives due to lower output prices but also possibly because of the costs of getting access to modern inputs at reasonable prices (Minten et al. 2013). Reducing the costs of remoteness through the construction of rural roads, as well as increasing distribution outlets of modern inputs, is likely to have an important positive impact on teff productivity.

Fourth, teff is shown to be a labor-intensive crop with higher yields being achieved when farmers spend more time plowing and weeding. Given structural changes in the Ethiopian economy, which leads to increasing real rural wages, innovations that can initiate a reduction in these labor demands, might satisfy the increasing demands for teff at an affordable price. Further efforts to simulate greater use of mechanization for planting, threshing, and weeding might therefore be important for the sustainability of the teff sector.

References

Ali, M., and D. Byerlee. 1991. "Economic Efficiency of Small Farmers in a Changing World: A Survey of Recent Evidence." *Journal of International Development* 3 (1): 1–27.

Asfaw, S., and B. A. Shiferaw. 2010. "Agricultural Technology Adoption and Rural Poverty: Application of an Endogenous Switching Regression for Selected East African Countries." African Association of Agricultural Economists (AAAE) and Agricultural Economics Association of South Africa (AEASA).

Assefa, K., S. Chanyalew, and G. Metaferia. 2013. "Quncho: The Most Outstanding Tef Variety in Ethiopia." In *Achievements and Prospects of Tef Improvement*, edited by K. Assefa, S. Chanyalew, and Z. Tadele, 325–331. Addis Ababa: Ethiopian Institute of Agricultural Research (EIAR); Bern, Switzerland: Universitat Bern.

Assunção, J. J., and L. H. Braido. 2007. "Testing Household-Specific Explanations for the Inverse Productivity Relationship." *American Journal of Agricultural Economics* 89 (4): 980–990.

Assunção, J. J., and M. Ghatak. 2003. "Can Unobserved Heterogeneity in Farmer Ability Explain the Inverse Relationship between Farm Size and Productivity?" *Economics Letters* 80 (2): 189–194.

ATA (Agricultural Transformation Agency). 2013. "Results of 2012 New Tef Technologies Demonstration Trials Draft Report." Addis Ababa: ATA.

Barrett, C. B. 1996. "On Price Risk and the Inverse Farm Size-Productivity Relationship." *Journal of Development Economics* 51 (2): 193–215.

Benjamin, D., and L. Brandt. 1997. "Land, Factor Markets, and Inequality in Rural China: Historical Evidence." *Explorations in Economic History* 34 (4): 460–494.

Brooks, J., ed. 2012. *Agricultural Policies for Poverty Reduction*. Wallingford, UK: CABI.

Davis, K., B. Swanson, D. Amudavi, D. Mekonnen, A. Flohrs, J. Riese, C. Lamb, and E. Zerfu. 2010. *In-Depth Assessment of the Public Agricultural Extension System of Ethiopia and Recommendations for Impact*. International Food Policy Research Institute (IFPRI) Discussion Paper 1041. Washington, DC: IFPRI.

Demeke, M., and F. Di Marcantonio. 2013. *Analysis of Incentives and Disincentives for Teff in Ethiopia*. Technical notes series. Rome: Monitoring African Food and Agricultural Policies (MAFAP), Food and Agricultural Organization (FAO).

Ethiopia, CSA (Central Statistical Agency). 2012. *Agricultural Sample Survey 2011/2012: Report on Area and Production of Major Crops.* Addis Ababa, Ethiopia.

Flaherty, K., F. Kelemework, and K. Kelemu. 2010. *Ethiopia: Recent Developments in Agricultural Research.* Washington, DC: IFPRI; Addis Ababa: Ethiopian Institute of Agricultural Research (EIAR).

Franzel, S., C. Wambugu, T. Nanok, and R. Coe. 2013. *The "Model Farmer" Extension Approach Revisited: Are Expert Farmers Effective Innovators and Disseminators*? Proceedings of the International Conference on Innovations in Extension and Advisory Services: Linking Knowledge to Policy and Action, November 15–18, 2011, Nairobi, Kenya.

Gorfu, D., and E. Ahmed. n.d. *Crops and Agro-ecological Zones of Ethiopia.* Ethiopian Institute of Agricultural Research. Accessed June 11, 2014. www.prrp-ethiopia.org/index.php/component/phocadownload/category/1-public-documents?download=51:crops-and-agro-ecological-zones-total-dereje-gorfu.

Minten, B., S. Tamru, E. Engida Legesse, and K. Tadesse. 2013. *Ethiopia's Value Chains on the Move: The Case of Teff.* Ethiopia Strategy Support Program (ESSP) Working Paper 52. Addis Ababa: ESSP.

Royston, J. P. 1983. "Some Techniques for Assessing Multivarate Normality Based on the Shapiro-Wilk W." *Applied Statistics* 32 (2): 121–133.

Sen, A. K. 1962. "An Aspect of Indian Agriculture." *Economic Weekly* 14: 243–246.

Shapiro, S.S., and R. S. Francia. 1972. "An Approximate Analysis of Variance Test for Normality." *Journal of the American Statistical Association* 67 (337): 215–216.

Tefera, H., G. Belay, and M. Sorrells, eds. 2001. *Narrowing the Rift: Teff Research and Development.* Proceedings of the International Workshop on Teff Genetics and Improvement, Debre Zeit, Ethiopia, October 16–19, 2000. Addis Ababa, Ethiopia: Ethiopian Institute of Agricultural Research.

Townsend, R. F., I. Ceccacci, S. Cooke, M. Constantine, and G. Moses. 2013. *Implementing Agriculture for Development: World Bank Group Agriculture Action Plan (2013–2015).* Washington, DC: World Bank.

Wooldridge, J. M. 2010. *Econometric Analysis of Cross Section and Panel Data.* Cambridge, MA, US: MIT Press.

Chapter 10

EXPANDING TEFF PRODUCTION: ECONOMYWIDE ANALYSIS OF GROWTH AND POVERTY IMPACTS

Todd Benson, Ermias Engida Legesse, and James Thurlow

The sufficient consumption of cereals is central to the well-being of virtually all Ethiopian households. Almost two-thirds of all calories consumed come from cereal grain, while more than 40 percent of the value of the average household food basket in Ethiopia consists of cereals (Table 10.1). The diverse cropping systems of the country provide a range of cereals, with teff, wheat, maize, barley, and sorghum each having local importance in specific areas for food security. Nationally, teff, wheat, and maize, in particular, lie at the center of the increasingly vibrant agricultural output markets of Ethiopia (Minten, Stifel, and Tamru 2014). The level of annual production of these cereals is central to Ethiopia's national food security.

Given the centrality of teff, wheat, and maize to the food economy of Ethiopia, increased domestic production of the cereals can be expected to benefit both their producers and consumers and lead to positive wider economic effects. Higher productivity potentially will provide higher incomes for farmers and consequently improve the welfare of their households and enable them to further accumulate assets. Increased supply of grain will lower prices for cereal consumers and raise their overall consumption, thereby allowing them to productively reallocate economic resources that might previously have been devoted to food. More generally, increased productivity should result in greater capital investment in agriculture or in other sectors of the Ethiopian economy, propelling broader economic growth.

This chapter analyzes the economywide effects of significantly increasing the production of teff, wheat, and maize, both separately and jointly. Although our particular focus is on teff, maize and wheat are also considered closely in order to contrast the characteristics of teff and the other two cereals within the Ethiopian economy and for Ethiopian households. A detailed Computable General Equilibrium (CGE) model of the Ethiopian economy is used for this analysis. The CGE model is linked to a household survey–based

TABLE 10.1 Cereals in Ethiopia, 2004/2005—share of total calories consumed and household food expenditures (%)

	National		Rural		Urban	
Food item	Calories	Food expenditures	Calories	Food expenditures	Calories	Food expenditures
All cereals	64	41	64	43	64	27
Teff	11	9	8	8	30	17
Wheat	13	9	13	10	10	5
Maize	17	9	18	10	5	2
Other cereals	24	14	24	15	18	3
Other foods	36	59	36	57	37	73
Total	100	100	100	100	100	100

Source: Berhane et al. (2012).

microsimulation module. This enables estimation of the impact on household poverty and calorie intake of the various production scenarios run through the model. The production increases simulated in the analysis are consistent with the targets set by the Ethiopian Agricultural Transformation Agency (ATA) through their Teff, Wheat, and Maize Initiatives that began in 2012 and 2013. Accordingly, the simulation results provide additional evidence for evaluating Ethiopia's cereals investment plan and the design of broader agricultural development strategy.

Trends in Cereal Productivity and Related Economic Growth in Ethiopia

Agriculture is the major economic sector in Ethiopia, accounting for 46 percent of total gross domestic product (GDP) in 2001/2002. Within agriculture, cereal crops dominate. As shown in Table 10.2, cereal crops generated 35 percent of agricultural GDP. Over time, agriculture, and cereal crops in particular, have proven to be important sources of national economic growth. For example, the per capita GDP in Ethiopia rose from US$210 in 2001/2002 to US$438 in 2012/2013 (measured in 2010/2011 prices). Cereal crops alone accounted for more than 11 percent of this increase. Furthermore, a third of the contribution from cereal crops was due to rising teff production. Although there was equally rapid growth in maize and wheat production, these sectors are smaller than teff, so they each accounted for only a quarter of the increase in GDP per capita from rising cereals production.

TABLE 10.2 Sectoral decomposition of GDP growth in Ethiopia, 2001/2002–2012/2013 (%)

		Contribution to change in GDP, 2001/2002–2012/2013			
	Share of total GDP in 2001/2002	All sources	Overall increase in cropland	Increase in crop yields	Reallocation of cropland
Total GDP	100.0	100.0	n.a.	n.a.	n.a.
Agricultural crops	29.0	23.0	8.9	11.8	2.3
Cereals	17.0	11.4	5.2	7.2	−1.1
Teff	5.3	3.7	1.6	2.4	−0.3
Maize	3.5	2.2	1.1	1.2	−0.1
Wheat	3.3	2.3	1.0	1.3	0.0
Other cereals	4.9	3.8	2.0	2.3	−0.5
Other crops	12.0	11.6	3.7	4.5	3.4
Livestock, forestry, fishing	19.9	5.5	n.a.	n.a.	n.a.
Nonagricultural sectors	51.1	71.5	n.a.	n.a.	n.a.

Source: Diao and Thurlow (2014).
Note: n.a. = not applicable.

Table 10.2 decomposes the sources of GDP growth for crops from 2001/2002 through 2012/2013. The supply of land used for crop production in Ethiopia has grown rapidly at 4.2 percent per year. Controlling for changes in cropping patterns and yields, this land expansion was responsible for 8.9 percent of the increase in GDP per capita and about two-fifths of total crop GDP growth. During this period, there was also a significant increase in the yields of most crops. Together, rising crop yields accounted for 11.8 percent of the increase in total GDP and more than half of the increase in crop GDP. Finally, there were slight changes in the overall allocation of cropland, with a general departure from lower-value cereals toward higher-value vegetables and permanent crops, such as coffee. This land reallocation led to higher average productivity per hectare, although the contribution was somewhat marginal—that is, it generated only 2.3 percent of total GDP growth over the decade.

Crop-specific information on sources of recent production growth in Table 10.2 show that yield gains accounted for almost two-thirds of the increase in teff GDP from 2001/2002 through 2012/2013. However, the expansion of land used for cultivating teff grew more slowly than the overall supply of land. This implies that, relatively speaking, there was a general shift in cropping patterns away from growing teff, in that the share of teff land in total cropland declined slightly. Increases in maize and wheat production were from similar sources, although the relative yield gains for these two crops were somewhat smaller than for teff. Overall, it is clear that teff, maize, and wheat are central to the Ethiopian economy, both as sources of income and for economic growth. Whether these crops can continue to increase their productivity levels over the next decade is therefore of significant importance for ongoing economic development in Ethiopia.

Cereal Productivity Interventions of the Ethiopian Agricultural Transformation Agency

The government of Ethiopia, through its Agricultural Growth Program—a key element of the agricultural sector program of the country's Growth and Transformation Plans—aims to build and sustain rapid growth in crop production and productivity. It aims to do this by encouraging farmers to use the best agronomic practices and raise the availability and adoption of improved inputs, particularly seed and fertilizer. Cereals are at the center of most of these efforts. To promote increased agricultural production and catalyze agricultural transformation in the country, in 2010 the Ethiopian government established the ATA. In 2012 and 2013 the agency instituted crop-specific initiatives for teff, wheat, and maize. Under each initiative, the ATA, working through the regional Bureaus of Agriculture, makes available to farmers in the woredas (districts) targeted by the initiatives improved access to inputs, agricultural advisory services, output markets, and, in some cases, agricultural financing. These packages of improved inputs and services are expected to lead to significant sustained increases for each cereal produced in the target woredas. When the program rollout is complete, the Teff Initiative, if implemented as designed, will operate in 209 woredas, the Wheat Initiative in 95 woredas, and the Maize Initiative in 132 woredas. These target woredas are located in high-potential areas in Tigray, Amhara, Oromia, and Southern Nations, Nationalities, and Peoples' (SNNP) region.

The ATA cereal initiatives are not just about agricultural development but are designed also to advance Ethiopia further along the pathway of economic and broad social development laid out in the Growth and Transformation Plan, the country's master development framework. This is because there are strong interlinkages across agricultural subsectors, and the links between agriculture and the rest of the Ethiopian economy are strengthening, particularly between net producers and net consumers. Increasing cereal production is therefore expected to benefit not only rural farmers but also urban consumers and the overall economy.

Given this broader objective, we use an economywide CGE model to examine the likely economic impacts of successfully implementing the ATA's cereal initiatives. The model is based on a detailed social accounting matrix (SAM) for the Ethiopian economy that contains highly disaggregated information on both farm and nonfarm sectors across different agroecological regions within the country. As such, the model provides an ideal tool for evaluating economic links and how agricultural growth can contribute to broader development goals, including national economic growth and poverty reduction.

The Economywide Model for Ethiopia

To assess the economic growth, price, consumption, and distributional impacts of increased teff, wheat, and maize productivity, an economywide model is used that differentiates agricultural production in different regions of Ethiopia and a microsimulation module that captures the heterogeneity of Ethiopian households' incomes and expenditures (Diao and Thurlow 2012). The model is designed to capture trade-offs and synergies from accelerating growth in different agricultural subsectors, the economic interlinkages between agriculture and the rest of the economy, and the effects of different sources of growth on household incomes and poverty. The model is recursive dynamic and is run using annual time-steps over the 10-year period from 2006 to 2015. The model is solved as a series of equilibriums with economic actors optimizing their behavior within each time-step period—that is, there is no intertemporal or long-run optimization. Between periods the model is updated to reflect changes in population, labor supply, and exogenous technical change. Importantly, previous period investment determines the annual rate of capital accumulation, such that increases in incomes and savings will increase the subsequent supply of new capital stock.

The model identifies 69 subsectors, 24 of which are in agriculture (Table 10.3). Agricultural crops fall into five broad groups, including cereals. The cereals group is separated further into teff, barley, wheat, maize, sorghum, and millet. Most of the agricultural commodities captured by the model are not only consumed by households or exported but are also used as inputs into various processing activities in the manufacturing sector. Similarly, the agricultural subsectors in the model also use inputs from nonagricultural sectors. The model is constructed to incorporate these links between agriculture and other segments of the wider economy.

The model captures regional heterogeneity within the agricultural sector of Ethiopia's economy. Farm production is disaggregated across four rural zones,

TABLE 10.3 Subsectors in the Computable General Equilibrium model of the Ethiopian economy

Sectors or groups within sectors	Subsectors
Cereals	Teff, wheat, maize, barley, sorghum, millet
Pulses and oilseeds	Pulses, oilseeds
Horticulture	Vegetables, fruits, enset
Export crops	Cotton, sugarcane, tea, tobacco, coffee, cut flowers
Other crops	*Chat*, other crops
Livestock	Cattle, milk, poultry, animal products
Other agriculture	Fisheries, forestry
Agroprocessing	Meat, dairy, vegetable products, grain milling, milling services, sugar refining, tea processing, other food processing, beverages, tobacco processing
Other manufacturing	Textiles, yarn, fibers, lint, clothing, leather products, wood products, paper and publishing, petroleum, fertilizer, chemicals, nonmetallic minerals, metals, metal products, machinery, vehicles and transport equipment, electronic equipment, other manufacturing
Other industry	Coal, natural gas, other mining, electricity, water, construction
Services	Wholesale and retail trade, hotels and catering, transport, communications, financial services, business services, real estate, other private services, public administration, education, health

Source: Dorosh and Thurlow 2012.

as shown in Figure 10.1. These zones reflect different agroecological and climatic conditions across the country. The model is calibrated to observed cropping patterns in each of the four zones in the 2005/2006 cropping season. Representative farmers in each zone respond to changes in production technology, commodity demand, and prices by reallocating their land across different crops in order to maximize incomes. These farmers also reallocate their labor and capital between farm and nonfarm activities, including livestock and fishing, wage employment, and diversification into nonagricultural sectors, such as transport, trade, and construction. By capturing production information across subnational regions, the model is useful for capturing the growth links and income and price effects resulting from changes in productivity for teff as well as for wheat and maize.

The model endogenously estimates the impact of exogenous changes in cereal productivity on the value of household consumption, poverty, and per capita calorie consumption. There are 12 representative household groups in the model, disaggregated by the four rural zones and small or large urban centers, and by their poor or nonpoor status. In this case, "the poor" are defined

FIGURE 10.1 Rural zones in the Computable General Equilibrium model of the Ethiopian economy

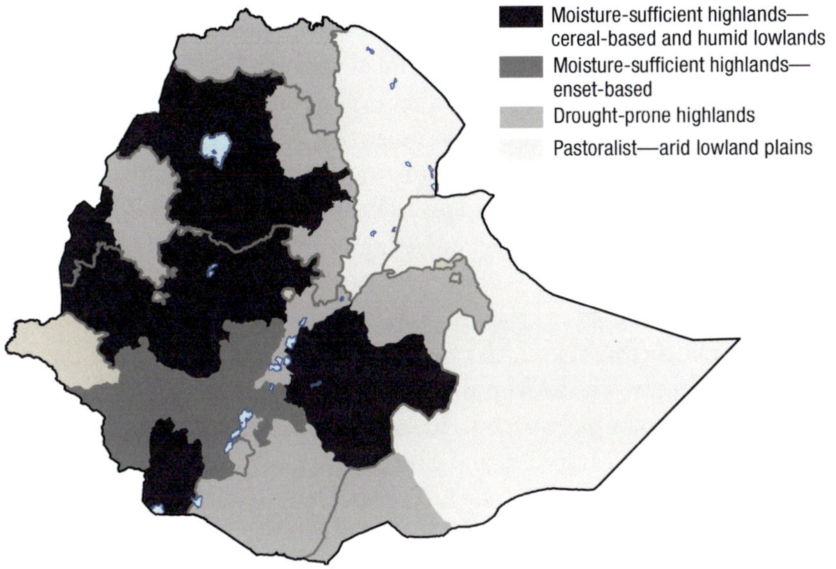

Source: Adapted from Dorosh and Thurlow (2012).

to include all households falling into the bottom two consumption quintiles (that is, the poorest 40 percent of the population).

The Ethiopia CGE model has a microsimulation component whereby each sample household in the nationally representative 2004/2005 Household Income, Consumption, and Expenditure Survey (HICES) is assigned to a corresponding representative household in the model (Arndt et al. 2012). When a model simulation is run, relative changes in *real* consumption expenditure for each of the 12 representative households in the model are passed down to their corresponding households in the household survey. The value of total real expenditures for each sample household, as captured in the survey data, is then recalculated using the modeled changes in real consumption expenditures. This new level of per capita expenditure for each survey household is compared to the separate poverty lines for rural and urban areas (in base-year prices), and standard poverty measures are recalculated. Similarly, changes in food quantity consumption patterns of survey sample households can be computed to determine changes in daily per capita calorie consumption associated with various scenarios run in the CGE model.

The model makes a number of assumptions about how the economy maintains macroeconomic balance. For the current account a flexible exchange rate maintains a fixed level of foreign savings. This means that the government cannot increase foreign debt to pay for new investments and that export earnings are needed to pay for any additional imports. For the government account, tax rates are fixed, and recurrent expenditure grows at a fixed rate. The fiscal deficit therefore adjusts to ensure that public expenditures equal receipts—any new or expanded government program will require additional revenue to finance. Investment and private consumption also are fixed shares of absorption, with private savings adjusting to ensure that savings equals investment in equilibrium.

The core dataset used to create the CGE model is the 2005/2006 social accounting matrix (SAM), which captures the economic structure of the Ethiopian economy. The SAM provides a balanced accounting of all economic transactions that take place within the economy, drawing on data from household surveys, national accounts, and a broad range of other data on production and consumption in Ethiopia. The Ethiopian Development Research Institute (EDRI) originally developed this SAM (Tebekew et al. 2009). The SAM disaggregates information on the agricultural sector by the four rural zones and includes a detailed disaggregation of household groups by those zones. Zonal-level agricultural production and area data taken from the 2005/2006 Agricultural Sample Survey were used to disaggregate production in the SAM to the subnational rural zones shown in Figure 10.1. The CGE model for Ethiopia therefore is consistent with recent agricultural production levels and yields at the level of these zones.

While most of the parameters in the CGE model are derived from the SAM, there are a number of behavioral elasticities that govern how changes in relative prices affect domestic production, foreign trade, and household consumption patterns. Household income elasticities determine how households choose to spend any additional incomes. Income elasticities used in the model were derived from econometric estimates computed from the 2004/2005 HICES (Diao et al. 2012, 137). Trade elasticities determine how readily producers respond to relative price changes in supplying domestic or export markets. Similarly, they determine the willingness and ease with which consumers switch between consuming domestically produced or imported commodities. In the absence of Ethiopia-specific estimates of trade elasticities, we use the global cross-country elasticities reported in Dimaranan (2006).

Baseline Performance of the Economywide Model for Ethiopia

The cereal production and cereal-related policy and program scenarios that were run through the CGE model involve altering parameters in the model so that it no longer reflects the production levels and economic relationships in the economy of Ethiopia as described by the 2005/2006 SAM, but reflects changes in those levels and relationships that are defined by the scenarios of interest. As the model is run over time, changes in productivity result in changes in supply, which lead to changes in product prices and, hence, demand. Movements in relative prices also cause changes in the demand for imports and supply of exports. These initial effects then prompt a range of further changes in other sectors of the economy via reallocations of land and labor from less to more economically rewarding crops. In turn, this leads to changes in noncereal crop production levels; reallocation of labor across both farm and nonfarm activities as economic actors seek to maximize returns to their labor; and changes in household expenditures and food consumption.

The supply of and demand for teff, wheat, and maize in Ethiopia in 2006, both modeled and observed, is presented in Figure 10.2. The base year for the model is 2006.[1] We see that the model reflects quite closely the observed national supply and demand conditions for these three cereals as reported in the Food Balance Sheet for Ethiopia for 2006 computed by the Food and Agriculture Organization of the United Nations (FAO 2014). The only significant difference is for teff supply, where the model estimates a supply approximately 15 percent higher than what was observed. This deviation is due to unequal supply and demand for teff in the Food Balance Sheets.

The first stage in creating the CGE model is to establish a baseline scenario for the period 2006 to 2015 that excludes the additional expansion of teff, wheat, and maize production as envisaged by the ATA under its three cereal initiatives. The supply of teff, wheat, and maize in the baseline is as shown in Figure 10.3. The purpose of the baseline scenario is not to track recent production changes or predict future growth, but rather to provide a counterfactual scenario against which the incremental benefits or losses associated with the ATA initiatives can be compared. By design, the baseline scenario is calibrated so that the year-on-year increase in the supplies of the cereal

1 When we refer to the CGE model's base year, we are referring to the information contained in the 2005/2006 SAM (which was built using official data but closely matches what appears in the FAO Food Balance Sheets).

FIGURE 10.2 Baseline teff, wheat, and maize supply and demand conditions of the Ethiopia CGE model compared to FAO crop supply and demand estimates, 2006

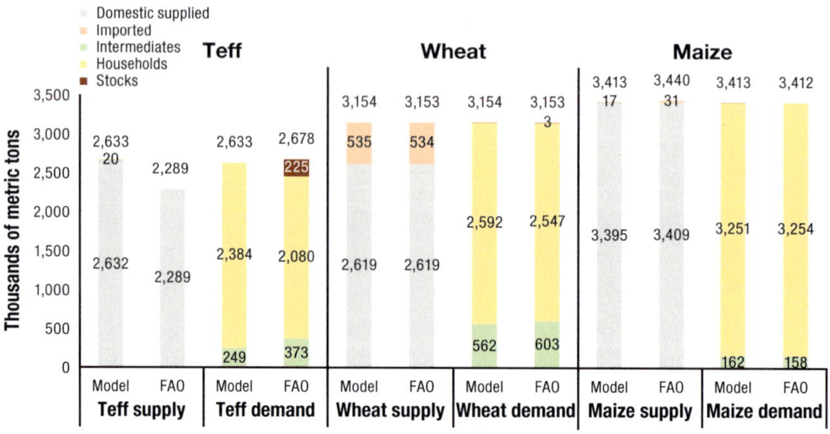

Source: Ethiopia CGE model and FAOSTAT Food Balance Sheet data (FAO 2014).

Note: CGE = computable general equilibrium; FAO = Food and Agriculture Organization of the United Nations.

crops is fairly uniform and reflects a growth rate that is slower than what has been observed in recent years. Slower growth is assumed because the ATA initiatives to be modeled are expected to contribute to maintaining recent rapid production growth in these cereals, rather than only accelerating it. As such, the annual growth in supply in the baseline scenario for teff is about 3.2 percent; for wheat, about 3.0 percent; and for maize, about 3.1 percent.

The increase in the supply of teff in the baseline is wholly from production, as there is virtually no international trade in this cereal. That of wheat is made up of both domestic production and imports, with imports making up about 18 percent of total wheat supply.[2] The supply of maize is made up primarily of domestic production, but the model does impose some small quantities of maize imports and exports—the "supplied domestically" category is the net of domestic production minus the exports imposed in the model. The total domestic maize production in 2015 predicted by the model is 4.042 million

2 For all the model scenarios that involve wheat, it is assumed that there is no difference in quality between domestic and imported wheat that would lead to differentiation between the two types of wheat in Ethiopian markets or among Ethiopian consumers. This is not likely to be the case, as imported wheat may well be better or less suited for commercial bakeries and other industrial processing than domestic wheat, or may have taste and other consumption characteristics that may make it either more or less preferred for home processing and consumption. However, the CGE model for Ethiopia does not take into account any such differences.

FIGURE 10.3 Baseline scenario between 2012 and 2015 for the national supply of teff, wheat, and maize without the ATA initiatives for each cereal, Ethiopia CGE model results

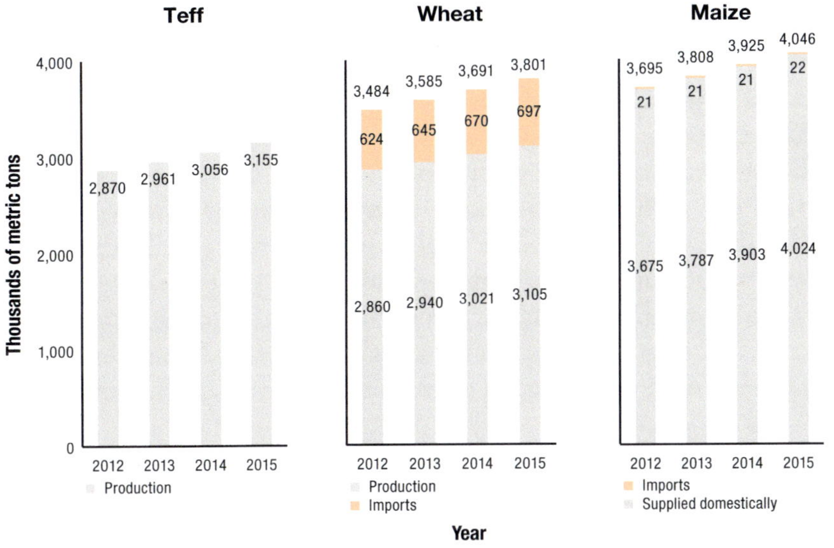

Source: Ethiopia CGE model.

Note: ATA = Ethiopian Agricultural Transformation Agency; CGE = computable general equilibrium.

metric tons, with 22,000 metric tons of maize imports and 18,000 metric tons of maize exports.

Although not presented here, similar baseline conditions are estimated by the CGE model for a range of output indicators that will be used to assess the economic effects of the productivity scenarios. These include economic growth rates, price and consumption changes, and poverty and calorie intake measures. The baseline conditions for 2015 for these variables, as predicted by the model, are the values against which the economic effects of the ATA production scenarios will be assessed.

Teff, Wheat, and Maize Production Increases

The ATA established the initiatives for teff, wheat, and maize to bring about a sharp increase in the production of the three cereals. As was noted earlier, the ATA aims to improve farmers' access to improved inputs, agricultural advisory services, output markets, and, in some cases, agricultural financing. Particularly for teff, the ATA Initiative also involved introducing farmers to promising new production techniques. These packages of inputs and services are expected to raise cereal productivity in the targeted woredas and subsequently result in the diffusion of the new technologies to other areas of the country where the cereals are produced.

The Teff Initiative began in 2012 in 158 woredas, with expansions to the initiative planned in 2013 and 2014 to reach 209 target woredas. The Wheat Initiative began in 2013 in 40 woredas and aimed to be completed in 2014 with an additional 55 woredas. The Maize Initiative was only to be launched in the 2014 season with a three-year rollout to reach 132 target woredas by the final year. Although these initiatives were introduced in a staggered fashion, the three are simulated in the analysis as if they were rolled out in parallel, starting in 2013 and with full implementation by 2015. In the design of the three initiatives, the ATA did not establish specific production increase targets in each of the target woredas. For these analyses, a relatively ambitious production increase of 25 percent in the target woredas for each initiative is used.

Simulated Production Increases

To determine the economywide effects of the ATA Teff, Wheat, and Maize Initiatives, it was first necessary to determine what a 25 percent production increase for each of the three cereals in each set of target woredas would correspond to in terms of zonal and overall national production increases. These increases were specified for each cereal across each of the four rural zones of the CGE model. To do this, woreda-level teff, wheat, and maize production data was used from the last nationally representative woreda-level agricultural production survey, the Ethiopian Agricultural Sample Enumeration (EASE) implemented by Ethiopia's Central Statistical Agency (CSA) between February 2001 and February 2002. This dataset was used to determine what share of the production of each cereal in each of the administrative zones for the EASE survey year came from the target woredas for the ATA Initiatives. These shares of administrative zone production were then applied to the most recent crop production information estimated at administrative zone level, the Agricultural Sample Survey of 2010/2011. Through this method the proportion of recent production of the cereals in those administrative zones that was accounted for by production in the target woredas of the three initiatives was determined (Ethiopia, CSA 2011). These results were then aggregated to determine changes in teff, wheat, and maize production for the country as a whole and for each of the four CGE rural zones (although the pastoralist zone has no target woredas for the ATA Initiatives) that would be attributable to 25 percent production increases for those crops in the target woredas of the three ATA Initiatives.

TABLE 10.4 Estimated national production increase for grain associated with a 25% production increase under ATA Cereals Initiatives, relative to 2010/2011 production levels

	Teff		Wheat		Maize	
25% increase in production in target woredas of the ATA Cereals Initiatives	Year-on-year national production increase (%)	Target woredas (number)	Year-on-year national production increase (%)	Target woredas (number)	Year-on-year national production increase (%)	Target woredas (number)
Year 1 (2012/2013)	15.4	158	6.6	40	8.9	69
Year 2 (2013/2014)	1.9	31	5.1	55	3.1	40
Year 3 (2014/2015)	0.8	20	n.a.	n.a.	1.5	23
Total	**18.1**	**209**	**11.7**	**95**	**13.5**	**132**

Source: Authors' calculations using Ethiopia, CSA 2006; and Ethiopia, CSA 2011.
Note: n.a. = not applicable.

As shown in Table 10.4, the 25 percent increases in teff production in the Teff Initiative target woredas should result in an estimated increase of 18.1 percent in national teff production after the initiative is fully implemented. For wheat, the corresponding figure is 11.7 percent, while for maize it is 13.5 percent. Given the dynamic nature of the Ethiopian CGE model, to define the scenario modeled for each cereal, the year-on-year production increases presented in Table 10.4, disaggregated by rural zone, were used over two (wheat) or three (teff and maize) model years as the shocks imposed on the model. This was achieved by increasing in the CGE model the productivity levels of the three cereals sectors in each of the subnational rural regions. The initial production shocks were applied in the 2013 model year. Note that the production increases are in addition to the year-on-year cereal production increases that already occur in the baseline scenario.

The scale of the Teff Initiative, with 209 target woredas, is considerably larger than that of the Wheat and Maize Initiatives, with 95 and 132 target woredas, respectively. However, given the lower yields of teff relative to wheat and maize, the impact in terms of the total increase in cereal produced under each initiative is not so different—between 430,000 and 490,000 metric tons additional cereal output is produced under each initiative. This can be seen in the results presented in Table 10.5. Ethiopia, CSA (2011) reports that the national average on-farm yields are 1,260 kilograms per hectare for teff, 1,840 kilograms per hectare for wheat, and 2,540 kilograms per hectare for maize.

Results for the Cereal Production Scenarios

The model was run for each of the three cereal production increases individually and jointly. While the production shocks are applied each year in the model, the various economic effects of the three initiatives are considered only at the end of the 2015 model year once all of the initiatives have been fully implemented. Given this staggered introduction of the initiatives, the model results reflect some second-round reallocation of land, labor, and capital due to the first-round economic effects arising from the cereal production increases. As such, the results presented here do not reflect only the immediate economic effects of increases in production of the three cereals, but they also reflect how actors in the Ethiopian economy will seek to exploit new economic opportunities that arise in consequence of those production increases and the changes in supply, demand, and prices that the increases generate.

The modeled changes in national production of the three cereals and in wheat imports due to the 25 percent increase in production in the target woredas of the ATA Initiatives are presented in Table 10.5. With the second-round economic effects of the production increases, the increases for teff and maize, when considered individually, are somewhat lower after three years of the implementation of the programs than was envisioned. For example, teff production nationally is up by 14.0 percent, rather than the 18.1 percent that was estimated from a 25 percent increase in production in the target woredas (Table 10.4). The increase in cereal productivity allows farmers to diversify into other higher-value crops—a transition that is also encouraged by declining real prices for cereals relative to other crops (Figure 10.4). The case of wheat is more complicated, because increased production displaces significant imports. Overall, domestic wheat production increases by 14.0 percent, but the total wheat available increases by only 7.2 percent, since imports drop by 22.8 percent in response to domestic wheat becoming relatively cheaper than imported wheat.

When the joint implementation of the three initiatives is modeled, cereal production overall increases by 13.5 percent nationally. Under the joint-implementation scenario, wheat imports decline relative to baseline conditions by slightly more than under the individual Wheat Initiative scenario, reflecting additional displacement of those imports from the increased production of the other cereals, which are partial substitutes for wheat. Note that the absolute increases in grain production across the three cereals are quite similar—between 430,000 metric tons and 495,000 metric tons—even though the Teff Initiative is significantly larger in scale than the other two.

TABLE 10.5 Modeled changes due to ATA Cereal Initiatives in national production and imports of grain, from the baseline scenario for 2015, in thousands of metric tons

	Baseline	Change in cereal production and imports relative to baseline by 2015			
		Teff increase only	Wheat increase only	Maize increase only	All cereal increases together
Production, all	10,302	466 (4.5%)	436 (4.2%)	488 (4.7%)	1,394 (13.5%)
Teff	3,155	440 (14.0%)	1 (0.0%)	5 (0.2%)	447 (14.2%)
Wheat	3,105	14 (0.4%)	434 (14.0%)	7 (0.2%)	456 (14.7%)
Wheat imports	697	−5 (−0.8%)	−159 (−22.8%)	−2 (−0.3%)	−165 (−23.6%)
Maize	4,042	12 (0.3%)	1 (0.0%)	476 (11.8%)	491 (12.1%)

Source: Ethiopia computable general equilibrium model.

Note: ATA = Ethiopian Agricultural Transformation Agency.

FIGURE 10.4 Modeled changes in real prices for teff, wheat, and maize, from the baseline scenario for 2015 (%)

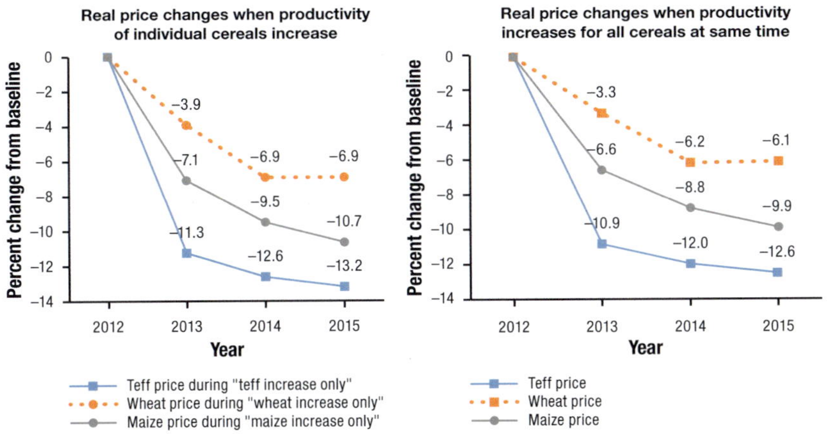

Source: Ethiopia computable general equilibrium model.

Figure 10.4 shows how the real price of the three cereals changes over the three years of implementation of the Teff and Maize Initiatives and the two years of implementation of the Wheat Initiative. The price shifts are somewhat larger when the initiatives are considered in isolation (left panel) compared to when the initiatives are considered jointly (right panel). This is partly accounted for by the higher crop incomes for producers, which arise from the broad increases in cereal production generating additional demand. This additional demand reduces the declines in prices of the cereals associated with their increased supply.[3]

The impacts of rising cereal productivity on the size of the Ethiopian economy are shown in Table 10.6. Several patterns are observed. Jointly, the increase in cereal production leads to a 1.36 percent increase in GDP for Ethiopia and a 3.07 percent increase in the size of the economy's agricultural sector. However, there is virtually no net growth in the nonagricultural sectors of the economy because of these increases in cereal productivity. This is partly a result of there being relatively little grain processing linked to domestic production that is classified as "manufacturing" in Ethiopia's national accounts. This implies that most of the milling that does take place—mainly within households—is subsumed within agricultural GDP. Moreover, increases in agricultural productivity encourage farmers to allocate more of their labor to farm rather than nonfarm activities, such that any increase in downstream processing is offset by falling nonfarm labor supplies.

Across the rural zones modeled, greatest growth is seen in the cereal-based highlands, as would be expected. However, increases in teff production also provide particular benefit to the drought-prone highlands. Maize production increases are not only important for economic growth in the cereal-based highlands, but also are the most significant contributor, from among the three cereals, to economic growth in the enset-based highlands, an area agroecologically better suited for maize production than for wheat and teff. The pastoralist zone, although no increase in cereal production was modeled in this zone,

3 The decision of consumers to source cereals from either domestic or foreign markets is an endogenous outcome in the CGE model and is based on changes in relative real cereal prices. We model the increase in production resulting from the ATA through an increase in the TFP (shift) parameter in the CES production function (this approach is consistent with the ATA's focus on raising cereal productivity). Consumers respond by sourcing a larger share of their demand from domestic producers rather than imports. This outcome from the model is what is expected following a sizable increase in cereal production, so there is no need for us to manually impose contrary consumer behavior on the model's CES Armington aggregation functions. It should be noted that imported cereal, primarily wheat, makes up a very small share of total cereal consumption in Ethiopia, so the import functions in the CGE models turn out to be much less important than domestic production and household consumption functions.

TABLE 10.6 Modeled changes in annual economic growth due to production increases in teff, wheat, and maize, from the 2015 baseline scenario (%)

		Change in GDP relative to baseline by 2015			
	Share of baseline GDP in 2015	Teff increase only	Wheat increase only	Maize increase only	All cereal increases together
Overall	**100.0**	**0.58**	**0.31**	**0.46**	**1.36**
Agriculture sector	44.5	1.31	0.70	1.05	3.07
Cereal-based highlands and humid lowlands	19.4	1.83	1.10	1.43	4.37
Enset-based highlands	5.9	0.72	0.35	1.25	2.32
Drought-prone highlands	11.4	1.59	0.69	0.96	3.25
Pastoralist–arid lowlands	3.0	0.20	−0.03	0.24	0.42
Nonagriculture	55.5	−0.01	0.01	−0.01	−0.01

Source: Ethiopia computable general equilibrium model.
Note: GDP = gross domestic product.

benefits from increased teff and maize production, likely through increased consumption made possible through reduction in the real prices of these cereals. However, production increases in wheat do not generate these positive economic effects in the pastoralist zone.

Comparing the cereals, their individual impact on economic growth primarily will be due to the production increases achieved for each and the value of that production. Although teff yields per unit area are significantly lower than are those for wheat and maize, the Teff Initiative is the largest in scale of the three initiatives. Moreover, the per unit value of teff is significantly higher than for the other two crops—the average ratio of their prices in the Addis Ababa market between 2001 and 2011 was 2.47 for teff-to-maize and 1.47 for teff-to-wheat (Minten, Stifel, and Tamru 2012). In consequence, the Teff Initiative has the largest impact on economic growth, even though the overall production increases due to each initiative are quite similar (Table 10.5).

The impact of the three cereal initiatives on household welfare and poverty are considered in Table 10.7 and Table 10.8. Household welfare is measured using the per capita real value of consumption in the CGE model. Under the ATA Initiatives, consumption increases for all households. The joint effect of the three initiatives shows that poor households in urban areas see the largest increase in their welfare, benefitting from lower cereal prices in the urban markets. Poor households in rural areas see the second highest welfare benefits, which flow both from higher incomes for cereal producers whose production levels increase and, for net rural cereal consumers, from lower prices for

TABLE 10.7 Modeled changes in household welfare (per capita real consumption) due to grain production increases, from the 2015 baseline scenario (%)

	Teff increase only	Wheat increase only	Maize increase only	All cereal increases together
All households	**0.57**	**0.21**	**0.35**	**1.13**
Rural poor	0.64	0.28	0.53	1.45
Rural nonpoor	0.46	0.22	0.37	1.05
Urban poor	1.25	0.18	0.19	1.63
Urban nonpoor	0.62	0.10	0.07	0.79

Source: Ethiopia CGE model.

TABLE 10.8 Modeled changes in poverty due to production increases in teff, wheat, and maize, from the 2015 baseline scenario

	Teff increase only	Wheat increase only	Maize increase only	All cereal increases together
Poverty headcount, % change:				
All households	−0.77	−0.50	−0.84	−2.00
Rural	−0.78	−0.53	−0.97	−2.22
Urban	−0.73	−0.31	−0.23	−0.93
Number of poor individuals	−646,000	−418,000	−708,000	−1,687,000
Depth of poverty, % change:				
All households	−0.29	−0.15	−0.28	−0.70
Rural	−0.26	−0.16	−0.31	−0.71
Urban	−0.42	-0.10	−0.12	−0.64

Source: Ethiopia CGE model with microsimulation module.

the cereals that they consume. The urban nonpoor see the lowest welfare benefits in relative terms.

When the three cereal initiatives are considered separately, the increases in teff production provide the greatest relative welfare benefits to urban households and maize production increases generate the greatest benefits to rural households, while wheat production increases deliver similar but lower levels of relative welfare benefits to households in both rural and urban areas.

By linking the results of the CGE model to information on the characteristics of sample households of the 2004/2005 HICES, the microsimulation module of the Ethiopian CGE model is used to estimate changes in the poverty measures for the Ethiopian population. Using a poverty line that is initially set at the fortieth percentile of per capita consumption of households in the 2004/2005 HICES, Table 10.8 provides insights as to what the cereal production increases will mean for the poverty status of households in Ethiopia. The poverty headcount measure—that is, the share of the population whose consumption is below the poverty line—drops under all scenarios where cereal production increases. The cereal initiatives improve the consumption of some households sufficiently such that their new level of consumption is above the poverty line. Across the three cereals, increased maize production has the greatest impact on the incidence of poverty in rural areas, while in urban areas, teff is the most important cereal in this regard.

Changes in the depth of poverty measure give insight into how the cereal initiatives affect the welfare of all of the poor, as the measure reflects the mean consumption shortfall relative to the poverty line across the whole population. The three initiatives are shown to reduce the depth of poverty in Ethiopia. However, when comparing the respective impact of the production increases of the different cereals, production increases of teff seem not to be as efficacious in reducing the depth of poverty in rural areas as they are for reducing the rural poverty headcount. This may reflect specific elements in the patterns of both teff production and teff consumption across the distribution of consumption in the rural population of Ethiopia—the poorest rural households may neither produce nor consume much teff. For maize, production increases of the cereal do not reduce the depth of poverty in urban areas to the same degree as in rural areas. However, in contrast to the relatively high impact of increased teff production on the rural poverty headcount, maize production increases lead to only a limited change in the poverty headcount in urban areas. The relative impact of wheat production increases on poverty measures in rural and urban areas is consistent across the two areas, although lower than that of the other two cereals.

The impact of the three cereal initiatives on household cereal consumption is considered in Table 10.9. The impact of the Wheat Initiative on consumption is significantly lower than for the Teff and Maize Initiatives. However, as the production increases achieved by the three initiatives are comparable (Table 10.5), the reason for the lower impact of the Wheat Initiative on overall household consumption is that much of the increased production of wheat serves to displace wheat imports.

Considering the impact of each initiative on cereal consumption, on a percentage basis the Teff Initiative increases consumption in urban centers by considerably more than it does in rural areas. For maize, as observed earlier, the opposite is the case, with a greater impact on the consumption of rural

TABLE 10.9 Modeled changes in household cereal consumption due to production increases in teff, wheat, and maize, from the 2015 baseline scenario, in thousands of metric tons

	Baseline	Teff increase only	Wheat increase only	Maize increase only	All cereal increases together
All households	9,757	423 (4.3%)	220 (2.3%)	444 (4.5%)	1,090 (11.2%)
Poor (all)	3,775	166 (4.4%)	86 (2.3%)	180 (4.8%)	434 (11.5%)
Nonpoor (all)	5,981	256 (4.3%)	134 (2.2%)	264 (4.4%)	656 (11.0%)
Rural (all)	8,534	313 (3.7%)	200 (2.3%)	428 (5.0%)	945 (11.1%)
Rural poor	3,277	123 (3.7%)	77 (2.3%)	171 (5.2%)	372 (11.4%)
Rural nonpoor	5,257	190 (3.6%)	123 (2.3%)	257 (4.9%)	572 (10.9%)
Urban (all)	1,223	110 (9.0%)	20 (1.6%)	15 (1.3%)	146 (11.9%)
Urban poor	499	44 (8.8%)	9 (1.8%)	9 (1.8%)	62 (12.5%)
Urban nonpoor	724	66 (9.1%)	11 (1.5%)	6 (0.9%)	83 (11.5%)

Source: Ethiopia CGE model.

households. For wheat, a more balanced impact on consumption is seen across the rural/urban and poor/nonpoor groups. Although the differential impacts are not large, the urban nonpoor display the greatest relative increase in overall cereal consumption with higher production of teff, while higher production of maize results in the rural poor displaying the largest percentage increase in such consumption. The modeled increase of the Maize Initiative on the cereal consumption of the poor nationwide is greater than that of the Teff Initiative, suggesting that efforts to increase national teff production are somewhat less "pro-poor" than similar efforts to increase maize production.

When the initiatives are considered jointly, it is the urban poor group that shows the largest percentage increase in cereal consumption, followed by the urban nonpoor and rural poor groups. The rural nonpoor group shows the lowest relative increase in cereal consumption under the joint initiatives scenario. Note, however, that these differences are not large.

Using the microsimulation module of the Ethiopian CGE model, changes in per capita calorie consumption of Ethiopian households resulting from the

TABLE 10.10 Modeled changes in per capita daily calorie consumption due to production increases in teff, wheat, and maize, from the 2015 baseline scenario (%)

	Calorie consumption (baseline)	Teff increase only	Wheat increase only	Maize increase only	All cereal increases together
All households	2,163	1.89	0.86	2.42	5.18
Rural (all)	2,192	1.54	0.88	2.69	5.13
Rural poor	1,374	1.64	0.79	2.97	5.42
Rural nonpoor	2,353	1.53	0.89	2.65	5.10
Urban (all)	2,021	3.79	0.70	0.94	5.45
Urban poor	1,293	3.80	0.81	1.53	6.17
Urban nonpoor	2,140	3.79	0.69	0.87	5.38

Source: Ethiopia CGE model with microsimulation module.

ATA Cereal Initiatives can be estimated, as presented in Table 10.10. These changes do not simply reflect the impact of the increased calories made available through an increase in cereal production but also changes in the composition of household food consumption baskets because of relative food price shifts that these production increases cause. Again, the Teff Initiative is seen as relatively the most important for the urban population, while the Maize Initiative is the most important for the rural population. When the initiatives are considered jointly, the relative impact on calorie consumption across the rural/urban and poor/nonpoor groups is similar to that seen in Table 10.9 on changes in cereal consumption levels—the greatest increase in calorie consumption is found among the urban poor and the lowest increase is among the rural nonpoor.

Broader Implications for Cereal Policy in Ethiopia

This analysis suggests that the impact of the cereal production increases envisioned by the Teff, Wheat, and Maize Initiatives of the ATA on the size of Ethiopia's economy are important, if not significantly transformative. If each initiative prompts a 25 percent increase in production of the cereals in question in the target woredas in which the initiatives are being implemented, this will result in a national expansion in the production of each cereal of between 430,000 metric tons and 495,000 metric tons. The increased production for each cereal alone will lead to somewhere between a 0.3 percent and 0.6 percent increase in the size of the country's economy relative to the baseline, while the increased joint production of the three cereals increases the size of total GDP by 1.4 percent (Table 10.6). While it is difficult to assign a monetary value to this expansion, it is possible to provide a broad estimate of the overall economic gain. For example, the total value of the Ethiopian economy was US$41.7 billion in 2012. As such, the 1.4 percent expansion in total GDP in the joint cereal production scenario adds about US$580 million to the Ethiopian economy. This suggests that there is a substantial economic benefit from successfully implementing the ATA cereal initiatives. However, this analysis did not consider the cost of achieving the ATA objectives. These costs, if internalized, will offset some of the economic gains (for example, raising taxes to pay for the Cereal Initiatives could reduce growth in other sectors).

It is important to note, however, that the cereal production increases simulated in the CGE model do not bring about much change in the structure of Ethiopia's economy. The change due to the ATA Cereals Initiatives in the size of the nonagriculture sectors of the economy in aggregate is virtually nil (see Table 10.6). Almost all of the economic growth associated with the production increases comes from the agricultural sector of the economy. Two factors explain this. First, as the economic returns in agriculture become more attractive due to higher productivity levels, there is likely to be a flow in factors of production out of manufacturing and services into agriculture. This will constrain continued growth in the nonagriculture sectors. Second, in compiling the national accounts for Ethiopia, most of the activities in the value chains of these cereals are defined as being within the agricultural sector. For example, teff flour is treated as an agricultural product rather than a manufactured one. As such, the value-added from processing teff is included within agricultural rather than manufacturing GDP. The only exceptions to this are the trade and transport margins associated with moving teff from farm to market—the value-added of which is assigned to the services sector.

In summary, the apparent weak links between agriculture and nonagriculture principally reflects how cereal processing is defined within Ethiopia's national accounts and competition over scarce land and labor resources between agricultural and nonagricultural activities. This suggests that if the ATA Initiatives are going to contribute to structural transformation as defined in Ethiopia's Growth and Transformation Plan, it will be necessary to extend value chains beyond the agricultural sector. For example, as the value chain of teff becomes more complex and more of the processing of teff occurs outside of the household, it is more likely that teff consumption will be reclassified as a source of manufacturing growth. Given existing value chains and prevailing definitions in national accounts, the successful implementation of the ATA Initiatives for teff, wheat, and maize will not bring about much change in the structure of the Ethiopian economy.

Concerning their impact on consumption and welfare, the simulation analysis shows that the ATA Cereal Initiatives are expected to have quite different impacts across rural and urban households and poor and nonpoor households. The insights gained from the modeling exercise are that significant increases in teff production will provide greatest benefits for urban consumers, particularly poor urban households, while the economic benefits of increases in maize production will principally flow to rural households, both poor maize consumers and maize producers. The benefits gained from increases in wheat production are distributed more evenly across all households. The reasons for this variation in the impact of the production increases of the three cereals across household groups are found in differences in the food baskets of the various groups, in relative cereal prices, and in the price elasticities of supply and demand for the cereals. Cultural factors also explain some of these patterns: teff is viewed as a superior commodity, its consumption associated among many Ethiopians with a better quality of life. Table 10.1 shows that, while urban households proportionally consume very little maize, their teff consumption is much higher than is seen in rural households. Rural and urban households, in contrast, consume wheat in almost equal proportions.

While all three cereals have their role in Ethiopia's economy and in the food baskets of Ethiopian households, one important question is from which cereal does society derive the greatest return? Using the CGE model and the data at hand, we cannot answer this question confidently and completely. However, the analysis here provides some insights into the merits of public investments in the three cereals relative to each other. It was noted that the average ratio of the prices of the cereals in the Addis Ababa market between 2001 and 2011 was 2.47 for teff-to-maize and 1.47 for teff-to-wheat (Minten, Stifel, and Tamru 2012). Similarly, the national average on-farm yields of teff are 1,260 kilograms per hectare, 1,840 kilograms per hectare for wheat, and 2,540 kilograms per hectare for maize (Ethiopia, CSA 2011)—using the average maize yield as the denominator, these correspond to ratios of the yields of the cereals nationally as 0.497 for teff-to-maize and 0.724 for teff-to-wheat. The relative market value of production per hectare for teff and wheat relative to maize can be calculated as the product of these two ratios. For teff, this is 1.23, while for wheat, it is 1.06. These results indicate that farmers who can choose between maize and the other two cereals and achieve the national average yield levels, would do better to produce teff or wheat, rather than maize, assuming the market value of that production is the principal criterion guiding their decision. Moreover, if recent increases in the average yields of teff and wheat can be sustained and exceed any increases in maize yields, these cereals will become even more financially attractive for farmers relative to maize.

However, the decision is more complicated than this analysis would suggest both at farm and at national policy levels. The significantly higher land productivity of maize will make maize a more reasonable production choice than wheat or teff for smallholders on small plots, particularly if production for own consumption is important. At a policy level the fact that maize provides more production on less land means that investments in increasing maize productivity will be strategic. The significance of this is that some of the economic objectives of Ethiopia, such as food security, can be achieved on a smaller land base with maize than would be the case with other crops, making available more land to other economic uses. Given the agroecological diversity of Ethiopia, a mix of cereals makes sense for agronomic reasons alone. However, there are also good economic reasons for maintaining a mix in cereals, both high value (like teff) and lower value (like maize).

In summary, the cereal subsector of Ethiopia's agricultural economy offers considerable scope for contributing to the economic transformation of the country. ATA's Teff, Wheat, and Maize Initiatives provide an appropriate approach to realizing some of the potential the sector has to contribute to such a transformation. Current cereal productivity levels in Ethiopia are below potential—the average wheat yields of 1,840 kilograms per hectare are only 57.9 percent of average wheat yields (3,175 kilograms per hectare) in the United States for 2013, while the average maize yield of 2,540 kilograms per hectare is only 25.5 percent of average maize yields (9,970 kilograms per hectare) of US farmers (USDA 2014). While this comparison is not wholly fair, it does demonstrate that the agronomic productivity potential of these two cereals is far from realized in Ethiopia. While judging the on-farm productivity potential for teff is more difficult than it is for the better researched maize and wheat, likely a similar story applies to teff. Ethiopian farmers can become much more productive, bringing benefits to their own households and the country as a whole.

However, policy makers should be sensitive to the possibility that there might be alternative public investments, whether in the agricultural sector or in other sectors, that would provide similar levels of economic growth, poverty reduction, and increased household consumption more efficiently at less cost. The analyses here provide no insights on this possibility. While keeping this caveat in mind, nonetheless it would appear that increasing public investments to improve productivity levels and increase overall production of cereals has considerable potential for bringing about strong economic growth in the country, particularly in the agricultural sector and across the rural economy. While the results of the modeling here do not provide any evidence of structural transformation of the economy with the level of production increases examined, it should be expected that as the agricultural sector grows through increased productivity, gradually more positive spillovers into the other sectors of the economy and strengthened links between those sectors and the agricultural sector will be observed. As such, as Ethiopia seeks sustained strong economic growth and broad poverty reduction, continued investment in raising production of cereals should be one of the principal strategies it uses to attain these objectives.

References

Arndt, C., A. Hussain, E. S. Jones, V. Nhate, F. Tarp, and J. Thurlow. 2012. "Explaining the Evolution of Poverty: The Case of Mozambique." *American Journal of Agricultural Economics* 94 (4): 854–872.

Berhane, G., L. McBride, K. T. Hirfrfot, and S. Tamru. 2012. "Patterns in Foodgrain Consumption and Calorie Intake." In *Food and Agriculture in Ethiopia: Progress and Policy Challenges*, edited by P. Dorosh and S. Rashid, 190–216. Philadelphia: University of Pennsylvania Press.

Diao, X., A. S. Taffesse, P. Dorosh, J. Thurlow, A. Nin Pratt, and B. Yu. 2012. "Ethiopia." In *Strategies and Priorities for African Agriculture: Economywide Perspectives from Country Studies*, edited by X. Diao, J. Thurlow, S. Benin, and S. Fan, 107–139. Washington, DC: International Food Policy Research Institute (IFPRI).

Diao, X., and J. Thurlow. 2012. "A Recursive Dynamic Computable General Equilibrium Model." In *Strategies and Priorities for African Agriculture: Economywide Perspectives from Country Studies*, edited by X. Diao, J. Thurlow, S. Benin, and S. Fan, 17–50. Washington, DC: IFPRI.

———. 2014. *The Economic Impact of Agricultural Research and Technology Adoption in Ethiopia, 2002–2013*. Washington, DC: IFPRI.

Dimaranan, B., ed. 2006. *Global Trade, Assistance, and Production: The GTAP 6 Database*. West Lafayette, IN, US: Center for Global Trade Analysis, Purdue University.

Dorosh, P., and J. Thurlow. 2012. "Implications of Accelerated Agricultural Growth for Household Incomes and Poverty in Ethiopia: A General Equilibrium Analysis." In *Food and Agriculture in Ethiopia: Progress and Policy Challenges*, edited by P. Dorosh and S. Rashid, 219–255. Philadelphia: University of Pennsylvania Press.

Ethiopia, CSA (Central Statistical Agency). 2006. "Area and Production of Crops and Crop Utilization." In *Ethiopian Agricultural Sample Enumeration, 2001/02 (1994 E.C.), Results at Zonal Level, Statistical Report on Socio-economic Characteristics of the Population in Agricultural Households, Land Use, and Area and Production of Crops.* Chapter 5, Multiple region-specific volumes. Addis Ababa: CSA.

———. 2011. *Agricultural Sample Survey 2010/2011 (2003 E.C.) (September–December 2010).* Volume 1, *Report on Area and Production of Major Crops (Private Peasant Holdings, Meher Season).* Addis Ababa: CSA.

FAO (Food and Agriculture Organization of the United Nations). 2014. 2014 FAOSTAT database. Accessed April 2014. http://faostat3.fao.org/faostat-gateway/go/to/download/FB/*/E.

Minten, B., D. Stifel, and S. Tamru. 2012. *Structural Transformation in Ethiopia: Evidence from Cereal Markets.* Ethiopia Strategy Support Program II (ESSP II) Working Paper 39. Addis Ababa: IFPRI.

———. 2014. "Structural Transformation of Cereal Markets in Ethiopia." *Journal of Development Studies* 50 (5): 611–629.

Tebekew, T., A. Amoge, B. Teferra, Z. Seyoum, M. Amha, H. Beyene, E. Fisseha, E. Tsehaye, H. A. Ahmed, S. Robinson, D. Willenbockel, and P. A. Dorosh. 2009. *Ethiopia: Input Output Table and Social Accounting Matrix.* Addis Ababa: Ethiopian Development Research Institute.

USDA (United States Department of Agriculture). 2014. *Crop Production: 2013 Summary.* Washington, DC: USDA.

Chapter 11

SUPPLY CHAIN FROM PRODUCTION AREAS TO ADDIS ABABA

Bart Minten, Seneshaw Tamru, Ermias Engida Legesse, and Tadesse Kuma

The importance of cities is rapidly growing. It is estimated that more than half of the world population was living in cities in 2010; this is up from 30 percent in the 1950s (UN Population Division 2010). Given this rapid urbanization, especially so in developing countries, and the increasing importance of the manufacturing and service sectors in these countries' economies, more people are making a living outside agriculture. As part of this change, many more people do not grow their own food and rely on market purchases for their food needs. This results in rapidly increasing agricultural market flows, especially from rural to urban areas, with a high number of people on the production and consumption side depending on the functioning of these value chains. This dynamic has profound implications on people's food security in developing countries.

Separate to these observed global changes in urbanization, Africa's urban population is also rapidly increasing. The urbanization rate is projected to be as high as 60 percent by 2050 (UN Population Division 2010), and there are growing concerns by local policy makers about the increasing dependence of people in African cities on imported foods.[1] This increasing dependency is often blamed on uncompetitive local value chains (for example, Rakotoarisoa, Iafrata, and Paschali 2011). However, few studies have scientifically examined the functioning of domestic food value chains in developing countries, especially so in Africa. This lack of scientific research leads to a policy debate that might not be well informed. A number of common perceptions on food value chains in developing countries exist.

---

1 Christiaensen and Devarajan (2013) found that since the mid-2000s, Africa converted from a net exporter of agricultural products to a net importer. Much of the growth in imports concerns staples for the rapidly expanding urban populations. They state that "except for wheat, which is a temperate-zone crop, these are all products in which Africa enjoys a comparative advantage" (Christiaensen and Devarajan 2013, 185).

First, it is often assumed that farmers only obtain a small share of the final retail prices. However, few systematic recent reviews based on solid surveys have been done on this issue. Ahmed (1987) compared producer shares in final retail prices in Asia and Africa in the 1980s.[2] They showed that producer shares in final consumer prices were as high as 75 to 90 percent in Asia but as low as 35 to 60 percent in Africa. Barker, Herdt, and Rose (1985) looked at the producer share of rice in Asia and found similar orders of magnitude. Gollin and Rogerson (2010) found in Uganda that farmgate prices for cassava and maize were often significantly less than half of wholesale prices, across many crops and regions. The World Bank (2008) estimates the share that farmers receive of the final retail price of maize in Ghana to be 56 percent.

Second, another perception is that these value chains are characterized by many layers of traders between producers and consumers, making the process inefficient (for example, Masters 2008; Mondal 2010; World Bank 2009). The World Bank states that "in agriculture-based and transforming countries . . . layers of intermediaries are common in the marketing of food staples and other agricultural commodities" (World Bank 2008, 119). Mattoo, Mishra, and Narain (2007) and Landes and Burfisher (2009) argued that in the case of India most agricultural trade is mediated by a large number of intermediaries. This system not only inflates prices but also takes time to move products from farmers to consumers, which leads to large transit costs. Trienekens (2011) argues that local value chains in developing countries are long in contrast with modern supermarket channels and export markets. Examples documented in Ghana (World Bank 2008) and Ethiopia (Rashid and Negassa 2011; Rashid and Minot 2010) illustrate how staple cereal chains are often long and complex.

Third, smallholder farmers are often driven to distress sales just after harvest when prices are low (Grootaert, Oh, and Swamy 2002; Prasad and Prasad 1995). This is linked to high seasonality in agricultural production in developing countries, with important vulnerability implications of producers that mostly depend on this production for their livelihood (Dercon and Krishnan 2000; Devereux, Sabates-Wheeler, and Longhurst 2012). Moreover, given farmers' vulnerable situation, traders are believed to typically prey upon them by offering exploitative interlinkage contracting where farmers are offered advances in exchange for securing supplies at low prices at harvest time (Crow

2 While producer shares are an imperfect indicator of marketing performance, this is used throughout the chapter given that it is commonly used in the debate and that there are no other easy indicators readily available.

and Murshid 1994; Bell 1988) or traders hoard agricultural products as to obtain high prices in the off-season. In some cases, it has been shown that, given imperfect credit markets and urgent liquidity needs, farmers are obliged to sell products at low prices and then they buy back the same product at high prices in the lean period (Barrett 1996; Barrett and Dorosh 1996; Stephens and Barrett 2011).

The impact of these common perceptions is not to be underestimated. Government and other stakeholders often try to intervene in these markets, assuming that they are not functioning well. The following examples illustrate this. First, cooperative marketing is often promoted on the assumption that it increases the bargaining power of farmers, solves some of the economies-of-scale issues that farmers face in the market, and thereby help to improve the prices smallholders receive for their produce (Bernard et al. 2010; CTA 2012; UK, DFID 2004). Second, modern commodity exchanges are increasingly established in Africa to improve objective grading, transparency, as well as competition in agricultural markets (Gabre-Madhin 2012). Third, credit schemes (for example, warehouse receipt systems or communal storage schemes) are being promoted to reduce the impact of distress sales (World Bank 2012; UK, DFID 2004; Alavi et al. 2012). In such schemes, farmers use their unsold produce as collateral to obtain credit to meet immediate expenditures. This enables them to retain their produce to sell later in the off-season when they can benefit from higher prices.

There are, however, issues with the evidence base on the functioning of these staple food markets. First, the common practice in food value-chain analysis is that it does not rely on representative surveys and often only uses anecdotal or qualitative evidence (for example, Webber and Labaste 2009; Nang'ole, Mithöfer, and Franzel 2011; World Bank 2009). Moreover, there is often a lack of reliable data on a larger scale in Africa (Jerven 2013), making credible inferences difficult on the state of agricultural marketing. Second, most of the recent studies on food value chains are focused on emerging high-value products, while surveys that study staple crops are often outdated (Ahmed 1987). Third, in the case that surveys were fielded, these typically focus on randomly selected farmers, who might not be representative of farmers who effectively participate in value chains of specific crops (Alavi et al. 2012; World Bank 2009) and are less important in major food supply areas.

In this chapter, the value-chain structure, price formation, and the importance of distress sales in rural–urban staple food value chains in Ethiopia are analyzed. This analysis is based on an innovative survey design involving detailed primary surveys at different levels in the value chain from major production areas to a major urban center. In particular, the focus is on the marketing of teff from the most important production zones (representing 42 percent of the commercial surplus nationally and more than 90 percent of the supply to Addis Ababa) to the biggest city in the country, Addis Ababa. This city is estimated officially to be home to four million people, although this is likely an underestimate.

In this chapter the specific areas studied are threefold. First, information on prices for a major staple in major production zones to the final terminal market are collected. Second, data on the structure of value chains is gathered by carefully investigating procurement and sales practices by these value agents. The rural–urban value chains are found to be relatively short. Consistent with this structure, the margins in these major commercial domestic staple value chains are surprisingly small, and the average share of the final retail price that the producer receives reaches about 80 percent. Third, the producer prices are found to decline over space in line with transportation costs. Also, releases by the producer of teff stocks in storage over the year is rather smooth over time, and distress sales are of minor importance.

These findings point to some important policy implications. First, given the lack of good data on food value chains and the often rapid changes that occur in such value chains globally (for example, Reardon et al. 2012), the collection of reliable primary data is essential. Such data might fuel the policy debate in order to make more informed decisions to address policies, specifically on the extent different constraints have on the functioning of these food value chains. Second, policies aimed at improving market efficiencies—such as stimulating the involvement of cooperatives in output marketing (CTA 2012), the establishment of modern exchanges (Francesconi and Heerink 2010; Gabre-Madhin 2012), or warehouse receipt systems (World Bank 2009, 2012)—should be carefully evaluated to assess where these policies are expected to improve market functioning, especially of staples, and what the expected benefits would be compared to the costs. The structure of the chapter is as follows: The data are presented first, followed by some basic descriptives of the teff value chain. Further on, the structure and price formation in the chain is explored. In the final sections the spatial and temporal concerns are discussed, followed by the conclusion.

Data

The study relies on data from major teff-producing areas and follows the value chain from there to Addis Ababa, the capital of Ethiopia. To obtain this information, two types of activities were organized. Interviews were conducted with key informants in the value chain in September and October 2012, which in turn was used to design questionnaires for each level in the value chain. Surveys using these questionnaires were fielded at the end of 2012. They were fielded upstream in the value chain with teff producers and communities, midstream with rural and urban wholesalers and truckers, and downstream with cereal shops, mills, and cooperative retail. We decided to rely on these particular datasets as no other data of this nature—where large samples of agents were interviewed along the value chain—are available in Ethiopia.

Upstream in the value chain, 1,200 teff farmers were selected, which involved several steps as follows. First, the five zones with the highest commercial surplus of teff in the country were chosen. In 2011/2012 these five zones combined represented 38 percent and 42 percent of the national teff area and commercial surplus, respectively. Second, within each production zone the woredas were ranked from smallest to largest producer (in terms of area cultivated). These woredas were then divided into two groups, the least productive (cultivating all together 50 percent of the area in the zone) and the most productive (also cultivating all together 50 percent of the area in the zone). Two woredas were randomly selected from each group. Third, a list of all the kebeles of the selected woredas was obtained. Two kebeles were randomly chosen from the top 50 percent producing kebeles and one from the low 50 percent producing kebeles. Fourth, a list of all teff producers in the preceding season in the selected kebeles was then made. They were ranked from small to large teff producers (based on the area cultivated). The farmers were then divided into two groups, the small production farmers (cultivating all together 50 percent of the area) and the large production farmers (cultivating all together 50 percent of the area). Next, 20 farmers were selected: 10 from the small production farmers and 10 from the large production farmers. In total, 240 farmers were interviewed per zone.

Midstream in the value chain, this strategy was followed. First, 40 rural wholesalers were interviewed in each rural zone. For each woreda the major trading town or temporary wholesale market used by farmers in that woreda was selected. A census of all traders in that market/town was made. As the focus of the study was to understand the value chain from rural areas to Addis Ababa, 10 traders that ship teff to Addis Ababa were randomly selected from this list in these towns/markets. Four such towns/markets were selected for each zone. Second, in Addis Ababa, 75 wholesale traders and brokers were interviewed in total. One-third was interviewed in the Ehil Beranda wholesale market and two-thirds in the Ashwa Meda market, reflecting the relative shares of teff wholesale marketing for Addis Ababa that each market handles. In Ehil Beranda, 25 wholesalers were randomly selected (13 without and 12 with shops), and 50 (25 with and 25 without shops) in Ashwa Meda. Also interviewed were 90 truck drivers transporting teff (one-third in Ehil Beranda and two-thirds in Ashwa Meda).

Downstream in the value chain, a stratified sampling scheme was adopted to select a representative sample of teff retail shops in Addis Ababa. Using the map of the city, five geographical strata were created with two neighboring similar subcities in each stratum. Then one subcity from each stratum was randomly selected, giving a total of five subcities to work with. Next, information was collected from the city's Trade and Industry Office, which provided the complete lists of teff outlets in each subcity. Following this, outlets were randomly selected for them to be interviewed. First, those surveyed were all the consumer cooperatives selling teff at the subcity level. Second, in each selected subcity, four kebeles were selected randomly, and in each of these selected kebeles, all the flour mills were surveyed and five cereal shops were randomly selected and surveyed. In total, staff at 282 retail outlets were interviewed.

Table 11.1 gives an overview of the sample and some basic characteristics of the different value-chain agents. With regard to the gender balance within the value chain, this is heavily dominated by men: 15 percent of the retail outlets are managed by women, but their contribution to other functions in the value chain midstream is limited. In fact, 95 percent of the rural wholesalers and all the truck drivers and urban wholesalers are men. Female-headed teff-farming households make up 5 percent of our sample. The level of education is slightly higher for value-chain agents midstream, with average years of education between eight and nine years, although it is lowest for the farmers at five years. The average years of experience in the teff business is around eight and ten years for all agents.

Description of the Teff Value Chain

Marketing Upstream

Table 11.2 presents some basic descriptives of teff marketing upstream (that is, by farmers). An average teff producer sold 507 kilograms in the year prior to the survey. The majority of this teff sold was white teff, which makes up two-thirds of all teff sold. The quantities of mixed and red teff sold are rather

TABLE 11.1 Sample setup and basic descriptives

Observations and variables	Unit	Mean	Median	Standard deviation
Farmers				
Number of observations		1,200	n.a.	n.a.
Gender head of household	share male	95.3	n.a.	n.a.
Level of education	years of schooling	4.6	4.0	2.9
Experience in teff business	years	9.6	10.0	1.5
Rural wholesalers				
Number of observations		205	n.a.	n.a.
Gender	share male	94.6	n.a.	n.a.
Level of education	years of schooling	7.9	9.0	3.9
Experience in teff business	years	9.5	8.0	7.8
Truck drivers				
Number of observations		90	n.a.	n.a.
Age	years	29.7	29.0	7.1
Gender	share male	100.0	n.a.	n.a.
Level of education	years of schooling	9.4	10.0	1.8
Urban wholesalers and brokers				
Number of observations		75	n.a.	n.a.
Brokers	share	65.3	n.a.	n.a.
Traders	share	64.0	n.a.	n.a.
Gender	share male	100.0	n.a.	n.a.
Level of education	years of schooling	8.7	8.0	3.4
Experience in teff business	years	8.9	7.0	6.7
Urban retailers				
Number of observations		282	n.a.	n.a.
Mills	share	83.3	n.a.	n.a.
Cereal shops	share	9.9	n.a.	n.a.
Consumer cooperatives	share	6.7	n.a.	n.a.
Gender	share male	84.7	n.a.	n.a.
Level of education	years of schooling	7.7	8.0	4.4
Experience in teff business	years	8.2	5.0	7.8

Source: Authors' calculations.
Note: n.a. = not applicable.

small.[3] Minten et al. (2013) showed that the shift from red and mixed teff to white teff varieties is a major change over the past 10 years in these production areas: 36 percent of all teff produced is sold, but there are large differences in qualities. While 58 percent of the production of magna ("superwhite") teff is sold, only 13 percent for red teff is marketed. The number of marketing transactions by these teff farmers is rather limited. The median number of transactions per year is 1 and the average is 1.75.

For each marketing transaction, farmers were asked to give details on their modalities.[4] The majority of the sales are to traders at local wholesale markets or to traders with a fixed shop, often in regional markets. Farmers traveled on average 1.5 hours to get to the place of sales. On-farm sales or sales in the village are relatively less important, in contrast with other countries in Africa (Chamberlin and Jayne 2012). Direct sales to consumers make up 7 percent of all transactions. Sales to cooperatives or government institutions (such as the Ethiopian Grain Trade Enterprise) are rather limited: they make up less than 1 percent of the sales transactions. While cooperatives are very important in input distribution in Ethiopia, they are not a significant participant in cereal output markets (Minten, Stifel, and Tamru 2012). An average sales transaction encompasses 300 kilograms of teff for a value of 3,776 birr (or about US$200). In 84 percent of the sales transactions, this was handled by a male member of the household. Interlinked transactions with traders are of very little importance upstream; 99 percent of the transactions were paid immediately and in cash. In only 2 percent of the transactions did the farmer receive an advance from the buyer.

Marketing Midstream and Downstream

Table 11.3 presents descriptives of marketing agents midstream and downstream. These agents' yearly teff turnover varies between 36 metric tons for urban retailers to almost 700 metric tons for urban wholesalers and brokers, and very few report the use of long-term storage options. The traders were asked about details on the different types of services provided to suppliers and clients. The data indicate significant transaction costs between different layers

3 The most widespread quality distinction used in the teff value chain in Ethiopia relates to the color of the grain. The distinction between magna ("superwhite"), white, mixed, and red teff is widely used and well known by farmers as well as traders, and therefore it is used as a measure for quality throughout this chapter. Teff quality is also often evaluated by origin. While the quality of teff is judged by a number of other factors—such as physical appearance, impurities, aroma, texture, and nutritional quality—these are often difficult to measure objectively.

4 In the case that farmers had more than five transactions (which was rare), they were only asked questions on the five most important ones.

TABLE 11.2 Characteristics of marketing transactions by teff farmers

Characteristics	Unit	Mean	Median	Standard deviation
Commercial surplus				
Teff sold per household, quantity	kilogram	507	250	1,130
Magna teff sold per household, quantity	kilogram	134	0	441
White teff sold per household, quantity	kilogram	318	100	1,028
Mixed teff sold per household, quantity	kilogram	22	0	128
Red teff sold per household, quantity	kilogram	33	0	149
Teff, commercial surplus for producing households	%	36	33	26
Magna teff, commercial surplus for producing households	%	58	58	26
White teff, commercial surplus for producing households	%	41	40	28
Mixed teff, commercial surplus for producing households	%	24	17	28
Red teff, commercial surplus for producing households	%	13	0	21
Characteristics of marketing transactions				
Transactions per teff farmer for producing households	number	1.75	1.00	1.52
Type of buyer:				
Farmers	%	0.6		
Farmer-assembler (farmer trader)	%	5.2		
Assemblers from outside village	%	5.5		
At wholesale market: traveling trader going to Addis Ababa	%	17.5		
At wholesale market: traveling trader going elsewhere	%	16.3		
Trader with fixed shop, selling teff to Addis Ababa	%	29.8		
Trader with fixed shop, selling teff elsewhere	%	17.4		
Consumer	%	7.0		
Other (miller, cooperative, EGTE/government)	%	0.7		
Total	%	100.0		
Sale location:				
On the farm or home	%	3.1		
Trader shop (fixed)	%	60.3		
Local (weekly) market	%	34.7		
Other (roadside, cooperative, at mill)	%	1.9		
Total	%	100.0		
Travel time between departure and arrival sales location	minutes	92.0	80.0	65.3
Time spent at location of sale before sale	hours	0.9	0.5	1.0
Total quantity sold per transaction	kilogram	299	200	685

(continued)

TABLE 11.2 Continued

Characteristics	Unit	Mean	Median	Standard deviation
Type of teff sold:				
Magna	%	22.4		
White	%	60.3		
Mix	%	7.2		
Red	%	10.2		
Total	%	100.0		
Total amount received	birr	3,776	1,800	18,082
Price received	birr per quintal	1,065	1,000	232
Person that sold the teff	% male	84.0		
Payment in cash	%	99.6		
Input advances received from buyer	% yes	1.9		
Payment in cash and immediately	%	99.1	100.0	9.1

Source: Authors' calculations.
Note: EGTE = Ethiopian Grain Trade Enterprise.

of the value chain. Weighing happens at every level, at the time of purchase as well as sales. Quality assessments are also done for each transaction. This is usually done through visual checks or by rubbing the teff. Some of the agents report to even chew the teff to determine its quality (47 percent, 28 percent, and 20 percent of the urban traders/brokers, rural traders, and retailers respectively). Family, kin, and ethnic relationship are often presumed to be important in agricultural trade (Gabre-Madhin 2001; Fafchamps and Minten 1999). Table 11.3 shows that urban brokers/traders work with a rather limited number of suppliers—7 on average over a 12-month period—and that they procure almost two-thirds of their supplies from the zones from which they originate. This suggests indeed tight, and often family, networks at that level. On the other hand, only 7 percent of the retailers work with suppliers that are originally from the same zones as theirs.

In contrast with the farm level, credit is much more prevalent in the value chain midstream and downstream. Included in the survey were questions on the importance of credit as well as cash advances. While few of the rural traders pay their suppliers on credit, this is much more important for urban wholesalers (60 percent) and urban retailers (45 percent). However, the credit provided is mostly of short duration, with average duration varying between

TABLE 11.3 Descriptives of marketing agents

		Rural traders		Urban traders and brokers		Urban retailers	
Variable	Unit	Mean	Median	Mean	Median	Mean	Median
Value assets	1,000 birr	242.4	71.5	122.4	8.9	337.4	78.7
Yearly turnover of teff	metric tons	252.6	134.3	694.1	585.0	35.9	25.0
Do storage of teff for longer than a month	share (%)	13.7		21.3			
Services for suppliers							
Picked up teff in own or rented truck	share (%)	44.9		9.3		31.1	
Teff is weighed when bought	share (%)	93.2		40.0		98.4	
Teff quality is sampled when bought	share (%)	100.0		100.0		99.3	
If yes, visually checked	share (%)	97.6		100.0		100.0	
If yes, rubbed teff by hand	share (%)	68.3		88.0		62.3	
If yes, chewed the teff	share (%)	28.3		46.7		20.4	
Bags are provided to suppliers	share (%)	23.4		1.3		23.5	
Services for clients							
Deliver to clients	share (%)	91.7		46.7		67.1	
Grade and sort to sell to clients	share (%)	85.9		90.7		-	
Teff is weighed when sold	share (%)	94.6		100.0		99.2	
Teff quality is sampled when sold	share (%)	88.3		100.0		97.1	
Provide bags to clients	share (%)	71.7		98.7		25.2	
Credit							
Suppliers that are paid on credit	share (%)	8.5	0.0	60.5	60.0	45.5	50.0
If yes, number of days before payment	number	11.1	7.0	6.7	5.0	16.6	15.0
Suppliers that were given advances	share (%)	8.7	0.0	1.1	0.0	20.9	20.0
Clients that pay on credit	share (%)	39.0	25.0	47.9	50.0	30.2	30.0
If yes, number of days before payment	number	17.7	15.0	8.0	7.0	20.5	20.0
Clients that gave advances	share (%)	2.5	0.0	0.0	0.0	4.3	5.0
Relationships							
Number of suppliers worked with in last 12 months	number			6.7	4.0		
Trader or broker is originally from Addis Ababa	share (%)			15.0			
Procurement from trader's zone of origin	share (%)			65.0	100.0		
Broker that retailer works with is from same zone	share (%)					7.2	

Source: Authors' calculations.

7 and 17 days. Advances are sometimes given to ensure teff supplies—20 percent of the urban retailers reported giving advances. However, no urban traders reported providing advances.

Structure and Price Formation

Structure of the Value Chain

To unravel the structure of the value chain, rural and urban wholesalers and urban retailers were asked from whom they obtained supplies and to whom they sold. The importance of each type of buyer and seller in total supplies was requested for each three-month period over fifteen months prior to the survey. Given that there was no clear seasonal pattern over time, Table 11.4 presents only the averages over that period.[5] The results illustrate the surprisingly short supply chain that is in place to bring teff to Addis Ababa: 85 percent of the teff supply is directly from farmers to rural traders who are based in the wholesale markets or regional towns in these five major production zones that were visited. A full 76 percent of the teff that they procured is directly sold to traders or brokers in wholesale markets in Addis Ababa; 77 percent of the sales of these urban brokers or traders goes to mills and cereal shops in town; and 86 percent of teff sold in these retail shops is directly procured by consumers.

This illustrates that the prevalent structure of the value chain from these major production zones to the urban city is rather short, from producer to regional trader to urban trader/broker to urban retailer. Commonly, three intermediaries are found between farmers and urban consumers. This finding is against conventional wisdom.[6] Notably 32 percent of the urban retailers obtain their products directly from rural areas (bypassing the urban wholesale markets), making the value chain even shorter. But the value chain can also be longer. Rural traders procure 13 percent of their produce not directly from producers but from rural assemblers or farmer-traders, and 10 percent of the urban wholesalers/brokers obtain produce not from regional traders but from other urban wholesalers/brokers.

5 No weighted averages for the turnover of the traders are shown (they would show the importance for the whole urban–rural value chain). No significant differences were noted with simple averages.

6 Fufa et al. (2011, 2) state "the teff value chain is fragmented and involves many players. Most farmers sell to assemblers individually, who then sell on to traders and wholesalers. Most teff is sold at harvest when prices are low."

TABLE 11.4 Procurement and sales patterns (averages over traders and for past 15 months)

Variable	Rural traders		Urban traders and brokers		Urban retailers	
	% bought from	% sold to	% bought from	% sold to	% bought from	% sold to
Procurement sources and sales destinations						
Farmers	84.9		4.5		9.8	
Farmer-traders or rural assemblers	13.3		2.5		4.3	
Traders in wholesale markets and wholesalers	1.3	8.1		5.8		
Cooperative unions	0.3	0.0	0.0	1.3	0.1	
Brokers		76.3				
Traders or brokers in Addis Ababa					68.3	
Mills or cereal shops		13.2				
Traders located outside Addis Ababa			83.2		17.6	
Traders in Addis Ababa			9.8			
Injera wholesalers				0.8		1.3
Injera wholesale companies				0.2		0.0
Injera retailers with fixed shops				4.4		4.8
Injera retailers without fixed shops				1.7		5.2
Institutions				1.8		0.2
Restaurants				1.4		2.1
Mills				69.8		
Cereal shops				6.8		
Consumers				5.7		85.7
Supermarkets				0.1		0.4
Others	0.2	2.4	0.0	0.3	0.0	0.4
Total	100.0	100.0	100.0	100.0	100.0	100.0
Number of observations	188	185	74	72	238	222
% sold to						
Addis Ababa		92.8		91.8		
Rural zone where trader was interviewed		4.6		n.a.		
Other zone		2.4		8.2		
% procured from						
Five major production zones				91.2		
East Gojjam				34.8		
West Gojjam				2.1		
West Shewa				44.8		

(continued)

TABLE 11.4 Continued

Variable	Rural traders		Urban traders and brokers		Urban retailers	
	% bought from	% sold to	% bought from	% sold to	% bought from	% sold to
East Shewa				2.0		
South West Shewa				7.5		
Other				8.8		

Source: Authors' calculations.
Note: n.a. = not applicable.

At the bottom of Table 11.4, the statistics on procurement areas and destination of sales are presented. From the information supplied by urban wholesale traders, 92 percent of all the teff sales was destined for Addis Ababa. In the past Addis Ababa was regarded as a clearinghouse for national cereal trade—that is, the national cereal trade went through Addis Ababa as all major traders were stationed there (Gabre-Madhin 2001). However, this role seems to have diminished. The larger agricultural marketing flows in the country, as well as improved communications, might have contributed to this change (Minten, Stifel, and Tamru 2012). Further to the investigation on procurement of teff in this survey, urban traders were also asked to indicate from which zone they procured teff. It is worth noting that the five production zones where the survey was fielded comprise 91 percent of all the teff coming to Addis Ababa.

Price Formation in the Chain

Prices were carefully collected at each stage of the value chain and for each quality of teff at the time of the survey. Information was also gathered on the origin of the teff (that is, the woreda), as that is often seen as an important associate of quality, although it is difficult to verify objectively. Farmers were asked about prices for the different qualities of teff at the time of the survey at their most common place of sale. While they might not have recently sold teff, farmers are often well aware of current prices for the major crops that they grow. In the case of traders, the prices for all qualities being sold that day or week were explored. One issue with the price collection process was that the surveys were fielded at different periods. The rural surveys were fielded in October–November 2012 (period 1), while the urban surveys were fielded in November–December 2012 (period 2). To address this problem, a daily wholesale market price survey was conducted where prices for different teff qualities and origins were carefully and consistently collected with a large number of traders in three urban wholesale markets during each of the periods. This information allowed for an adjustment in price levels between periods and for a consistent comparison.

Using the prices collected over these two periods, Table 11.5 presents two specifications to derive the price composition in these value chains. In the first specification, prices for each of four different qualities were regressed on value-chain dummies. In the second specification, the same exercise is undertaken but includes woreda dummies as additional controls for quality. Producer price locations were divided in two, depending on whether the farmer chose to report prices at the farmgate or at the rural market. The wholesale urban market price observations are split into two periods. The results in Table 11.5 show the consistency in price composition from these data. Farmgate prices in seven out of the eight specifications are lower than rural market prices, whereas rural market prices are significantly below urban wholesale prices, and urban retail prices are higher than wholesale prices during the same period.

An F-test to measure if prices changed significantly over the two periods is presented below the regression results. For the two specifications and for the four qualities, the prices decreased significantly in the second period compared to the first one, reflecting the downward price pressure from the newly arriving harvest in the second period. A common issue in price analyses in value chains is motivating traders to willingly reveal prices to outsiders, as this information would expose their profits and margins. By using the price statements by farmers in rural markets as well as procurement prices by rural traders during the same period, a comparison can be made using both sources of information. An F-test reported at the bottom of each regression shows that there is no significant difference between the prices reported by farmers and traders for seven out of the eight reported regressions (the exception is white teff in the specification without woreda controls), indicating that prices at the trader level are reasonable and seemingly well collected.

The regression results of Table 11.5 are used to construct an average price composition graph from farmer to consumer for period 1 (October–November 2012) for the four main qualities. As urban retail prices were collected later, when prices had declined, the urban distribution costs are adjusted upward for that period, assuming that absolute margins stayed similar in both periods. Information on the collected average milling and cleaning costs are added to obtain the final price formation of teff flour in retail markets. Figure 11.1 illustrates that the farmers take *(text continued on page 280)*

TABLE 11.5 Price regressions over the teff value chain (price at time of survey; in birr per quintal)

Level	Source	Time of survey	Unit	Magna		White		Mix		Red	
				Coefficient	t-value*	Coefficient	t-value*	Coefficient	t-value*	Coefficient	t-value*
Specification 1: Without woreda (community) controls											
Farmgate	Farm survey	Period 1	yes = 1	–167.2	**–8.1**	–210.1	**–13.7**	–253.2	**–5.6**	–159.3	**–5.4**
Rural market	Farm survey	Period 1	yes = 1	–146.0	**–12.2**	–166.3	**–20.2**	–159.9	**–6.1**	–126.0	**–5.3**
Rural market	Rural trader survey	Period 1	yes = 1	–143.7	**–15.8**	–141.7	**–16.0**	–128.5	**–11.5**	–128.2	**–10.5**
Urban wholesale market	Urban trader survey	Period 1	yes = 1	–2.5	–0.4	28.1	**4.6**	20.1	**2.7**	22.6	**2.3**
Urban wholesale market	Urban trader survey	Period 2	yes = 1	–68.9	**–10.3**	–46.2	**–5.3**	–60.9	**–8.6**	–123.0	**–13.5**
Urban retail (default)	Urban retailer survey	Period 2	yes = 1								
Intercept				1,598.1	**336.7**	1,516.5	**391.3**	1,389.9	**279.1**	1,173.9	**161.9**
Number of observations				859		1,386		1,042		639	
R squared				0.35		0.34		0.28		0.26	
Mean squared error (MSE)				93.28		118.34		103.13		116.31	
F-test if…				F()	Prob>F	F()	Prob>F	F()	Prob>F	F()	Prob>F
… rural market price reported by farmers is equal to reports by traders				0.03	0.87	5.20	**0.02**	1.30	0.25	0.01	0.93
… wholesale market price is equal in period 1 to period 2				101.69	**0.00**	66.78	**0.00**	113.93	**0.00**	284.64	**0.00**

Specification 2: With woreda (community) controls											
Farmgate	Farm survey	Period 1	yes = 1	–145.4	**–7.9**	–166.8	**–11.1**	–227.8	**–5.1**	–79.7	**–2.3**
Rural market	Farm survey	Period 1	yes = 1	–105.8	**–7.5**	–132.0	**–12.5**	–151.6	**–5.4**	–92.9	**–3.8**
Rural market	Rural trader survey	Period 1	yes = 1	–90.8	**–8.8**	–118.6	**–10.7**	–108.2	**–7.4**	–96.2	**–7.0**
Urban wholesale market	Urban trader survey	Period 1	yes = 1	11.0	1.5	16.3	**2.3**	1.9	**0.2**	18.0	1.5
Urban wholesale market	Urban trader survey	Period 2	yes = 1	–58.2	**–7.6**	–62.6	**–8.1**	–81.5	**–8.2**	–140.2	**–14.1**
Urban retail (default)	Urban retailer survey	Period 2	yes = 1								
Intercept				1,649.0	**224.0**	1,433.7	**204.8**	1,451.6	**51.6**	1,054.7	**30.1**
Number of observations				847		1,376		1,031		626	
R squared				0.53		0.52		0.45		0.46	
MSE				80.27		103.00		92.34		102.26	
F-test if…				F()	Prob>F	F()	Prob>F	F()	Prob>F	F()	Prob>F
… rural market price reported by farmers is equal to reports by traders				1.30	0.25	1.20	0.27	1.97	0.16	0.02	0.88
… wholesale market price is equal in period 1 to period 2				160.27	**0.00**	82.35	**0.00**	133.87	**0.00**	286.75	**0.00**

Source: Authors' calculations.

Note: * t-values in **bold** are significant at the 5 percent level.

FIGURE 11.1 Teff price structure by quality, October–November 2012

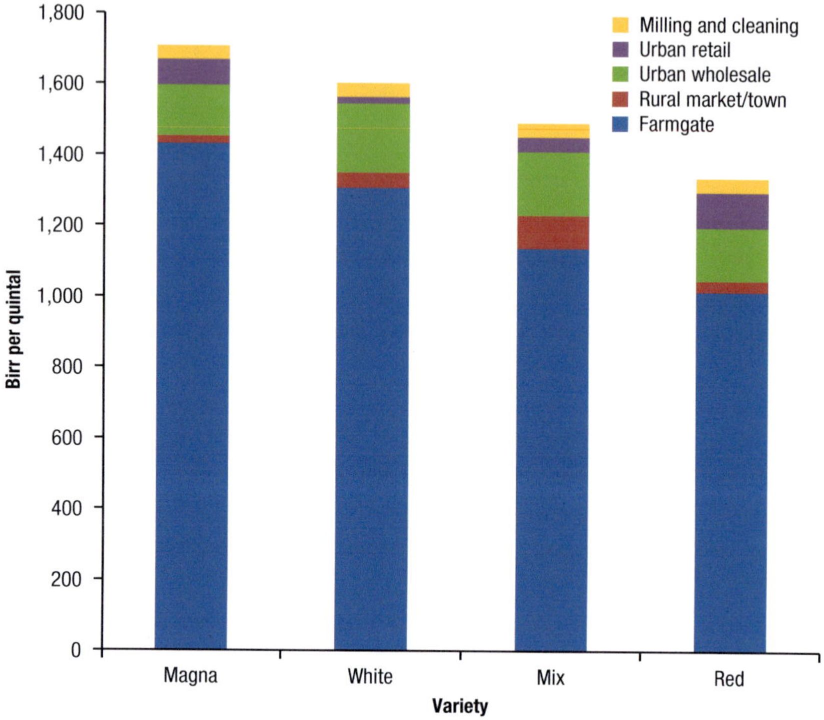

Source: Authors' calculations.

the greatest share of final retail prices of grain—an astonishing 78 percent to 86 percent, depending on the quality. The average picture described is contrary to conventional wisdom that most farmers only obtain a small share of the final retail price. The largest part of the margin between farmers and retailers is the margin between rural and urban wholesale markets. On average for the four qualities, the urban–rural wholesale margin comprises 54 percent of the total margin between farmgate prices and urban teff flour prices. The rest constitute the margin between farmgate and rural wholesale markets, between urban wholesale and retail, and for milling and cleaning—that is, 15 percent, 19 percent, and 13 percent, respectively.

This illustrates the average price composition for the period October–November 2012 when prices are relatively high (just before the new harvest). Producer shares will decrease when prices are set relatively low after the harvest period. This figure also presents an average picture for all farmers combined in the sample. Farmers who live in remote areas obviously obtain a lower share. The issues with spatial and temporal variation are discussed in more depth below.

Variation over Space

Transportation costs and remoteness matter enormously in agricultural markets in developing countries (Teravaninthon and Raballand 2009; Deichmann, Shilpi, and Vakis 2009; Fafchamps and Shilpi 2003; Gollin and Rogerson 2010; Alavi et al. 2012). For this reason the differences on how transportation costs and marketing behavior are affected spatially between Addis Ababa and rural production areas are important, particularly in understanding the link with shipping and with farmers' teff marketing. First, the transport sector is considered. To better understand how this sector for agricultural products in Ethiopia works, a survey was implemented with truck drivers who ship teff from rural areas to Addis Ababa's wholesale markets. The truck drivers were asked about themselves, the owner of the truck, and about the type of trucks used. Detailed questions were also asked about the last roundtrip (traveling from rural areas to Addis Ababa and leaving from Addis Ababa to rural areas). Table 11.6 presents some of the descriptive statistics of transport.

The average carrying capacity of a truck that ships teff to Addis Ababa is rather small—that is, 5 metric tons. This type of truck has been used for about 10 years, and its value is estimated at 0.5 million birr (or about US$25,000). In only 10 percent of cases the driver is also the owner of the truck. Drivers are paid a monthly salary as well as a daily allowance. Most of the businesses involved in the transport of teff are small, shown by the median number of trucks owned being only one.[7] The average distance covered in the last trip made by drivers in the survey was 228 kilometers. A full 20 percent of the trucks drove on nonpaved, bad quality roads during the trip, while 46 percent only drove on paved roads. The cost of transport is 18 birr per quintal per 100 kilometers (or almost US$10 per metric ton per 100 kilometers), significantly lower than recent estimates (US$24 per metric ton per 100 kilometers) on the costs from primary to terminal markets (World Bank 2012). This

7 The World Bank (2012) shows that different types of companies are active in the transport sector in Ethiopia, including private companies with large fleets, transport associations consisting of a group of private operators with a limited number of trucks, government-operated public transportation companies, and enterprises and sole proprietors that involve one or more individuals owning and operating their own trucks. The results indicate that the latter companies take care of most teff transport.

TABLE 11.6 Descriptives of transport

Variable	Unit	Mean	Median	Standard deviation
Characteristics of truck				
Carrying capacity	quintals	51.2	50.0	15.8
Age	years	9.7	7.0	14.1
Value	1,000 birr	500.0	500.0	261.9
Characteristics of truck driver				
Is also the owner	share (%)	10.7		
Is paid a fixed amount per month	% yes	98.9		
If yes, monthly salary	birr	1,183	1,000	514
Is paid a per diem	% yes	96.6		
If yes, daily per diem	birr	90.9	100.0	24.8
Characteristics of owner				
Age	years	39.6	38.5	10.6
Gender	% male	98.1		
Education	years	8.8	10.0	3.8
Trucks owned	number	1.1	1.0	0.6

may suggest that there is significant competition in these commercial agricultural areas, driving down costs compared with other areas in Ethiopia. On the trip to Addis Ababa, transporters shipped goods for two sellers and delivered goods to more than three buyers on average. In 82 percent of the cases a transport broker—a third party that is involved in searching loads for truckers and charging a commission for this service—was used to find a load. Transport charges for the return trip to rural areas are similar to traveling to Addis Ababa. However, in one-quarter of the cases the truck was idle on the return, indicating that it is often more complicated to identify goods to ship out of Addis Ababa than to Addis Ababa. The higher prices that brokers charge for finding loads for trips out of Addis Ababa seem to confirm this.

To understand how distance traveled is related with transport charges, a regression was run where these transport charges per quintal are regressed on different explanatory variables including distance but also the size of the truck, road quality, number of sellers and buyers, and the use of a broker. A quadratic term is included in the distance as to allow for potential curvature in the association with distance, as transportation costs might not increase proportionally with distance covered because of fixed costs that are incurred. Two specifications run—one including data for the trip to Addis Ababa only

Variable	Unit	Mean	Median	Standard deviation
		To Addis Ababa		
Characteristics of last trip		Mean	Median	Standard deviation
Distance	kilometers	228	254	145
Road quality:				
Only paved road	share (%)	45.6		
Drove on nonpaved road but good quality	share (%)	33.0		
Drove on nonpaved, bad quality road	share (%)	21.4		
Time for travel between departure and arrival	hours	6.8	8.0	3.7
Time for unloading/loading/searching	hours	4.7	5.0	2.7
Trucks that were idle	share (%)	0.0		
Capacity of truck used	%	94.9	100.0	13.9
Total value of good transported	1,000 birr	66.8	65.0	23.3
Transport payment	birr per quintal	41.8	40.0	19.5
Transport payment per 100 kilometers	birr per quintal	18.3	15.7	13.4
Transport payment per 100 kilometers	US$ per metric ton	9.7	8.3	7.1
Number of sellers transported for	number	2.4	2.0	5.2
Number of pickup points	number	1.8	2.0	1.0
Number of buyers delivered to	number	3.4	4.0	1.3
Number of delivery points	number	3.7	4.0	1.3
Transport broker used	% yes	82.4		
Payment to transport broker	birr	174	150	104

Source: Authors' calculations.

and a second one where data for the round trip (when mostly no teff is transported)—are added as well. The results are shown in Table 11.7. Distance and the intercept—reflecting the fixed part of the transportation cost—are the only variables that arise as significant in the regression. It is estimated that for every 100 kilometers extra traveled, transport charges go up by about 13 birr per quintal (about US$7 per metric ton per 100 kilometers).

As transportation costs go up significantly with increasing distance to Addis Ababa, this is expected to be reflected in farm prices, assuming that the costs would be transmitted to farmers. Using nonparametric regressions, Figure 11.2 shows the relationship of the reported producer prices at the time of the survey of the four main teff qualities with transportation costs to Addis Ababa. Notably overall, there are clear decreases in teff prices the farther away

TABLE 11.7 Associates of transportation costs by trucks (in birr per quintal)

		Trip to Addis Ababa only		Roundtrip	
Explanatory variables	Unit	Coefficient	t-value*	Coefficient	t-value*
Distance	100 kilometers	13.23	**6.97**	12.00	**5.33**
Distance squared	100 kilometers	−0.45	−1.63	−0.35	−1.37
Size of truck	quintals	−0.06	−0.81	−0.05	−0.96
Road quality (default only paved road):					
Drove on nonpaved road but good quality	yes = 1	−0.17	−0.05	3.99	0.84
Drove on nonpaved, bad quality road	yes = 1	3.52	1.21	2.03	0.81
Number of sellers transported for	number	0.09	0.77	0.02	0.10
Number of buyers delivered to	number	0.32	0.37	0.03	0.47
Broker used	yes = 1	3.55	1.56	−0.71	−0.22
To Addis Ababa	yes = 1			1.87	0.53
Intercept		12.68	**3.15**	16.31	**2.56**
Number of observations		101		177	
F()		47.86		44.67	
Prob>F		0.00		0.00	
R-squared		0.69		0.35	
Root Mean squared error (MSE)		11.46		19.37	

Source: Authors' calculations.
Note: * t-values in **bold** are significant at the 5 percent level.

farmers are located from the terminal market. While at the time of the survey the share of the producer price in the final retail price of the most traded teff quality (the white variety) close to the city reaches more than 90 percent, this drops to 80 percent for the most remote farmers. The only exception of the strong influence of transportation costs on producer prices is found in the case of red teff, which reveals this price drop only when the sampling is halfway through. The price increases again when farmers are farther out. It is possible that this is linked with the lower importance of red teff in the major value chain toward Addis Ababa, and price setting in these more remote environments might be driven more by localized demand and supply parameters.

The influence of transport costs on producer prices is tested further through a multivariate regression framework where other confounding factors in price formation are controlled for. Two measures of producer prices as dependent variable are relied upon. The first is the stated price by the farmer in his most common place of sale at the time of the survey. The second is the price that the farmer received in teff marketing transactions in the last

FIGURE 11.2 Producer prices of teff by transportation costs to Addis Ababa

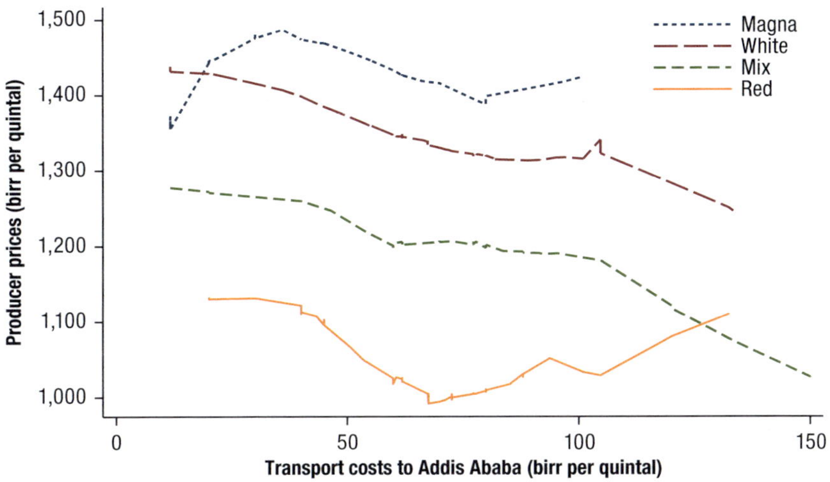

Source: Authors' calculations.

12 months prior to the survey. On top of transportation costs to Addis Ababa, in the first specification the place of sales is controlled for, and in the second regression, place of sales, quantity sold, as well as the timing of sales are controlled for.

The results of the regression are shown in Table 11.8. It is tested through an F-test if producer prices drop as fast as transportation costs to Addis Ababa increase for all specifications (the stated and the actual price for the four qualities). In all eight cases this hypothesis cannot be rejected, indicating that teff producer prices drop in line with transportation costs.[8] The results further show that prices at the farmgate are mostly lower than prices in markets. However, differences are not significant. Farmers who sell larger quantities are usually able to negotiate higher per unit prices (for example, Fafchamps and Hill 2008). The coefficients of this variable are significant in the case of the two most important qualities (white and magna). As expected, there is strong seasonality in prices, with prices significantly higher in the period just before harvest.

8 This is in contrast to results reported by Minten and Kyle (1999) in Zaire as well as Gollin and Rogerson (2010) in Uganda. They find that producer prices drop much faster, possibly linked with decreasing levels of competition and increasing risk. A specification was also tried where woreda dummies were included to additionally control for quality. In none of the cases was the F-test significant.

TABLE 11.8 Associates of teff prices (in birr per quintal)

		Magna		White		Mix		Red	
Right-hand variables	Unit	Coefficient	t-value**	Coefficient	t-value**	Coefficient	t-value**	Coefficient	t-value**
Stated price at the time of survey*									
Transport costs to Addis Ababa from kebele	birr	−0.71	−0.85	−1.75	**−2.88**	−1.18	−1.75	−1.61	**−2.03**
Farmgate	yes = 1	−31.02	−0.95	−48.68	**−2.21**	−59.54	−1.15	−0.60	−0.02
Intercept		1,488.77	**30.92**	1,467.49	**37.72**	1,304.38	**30.37**	1,141.34	19.50
Number of observations		203		565		76		121	
R-squared		0.02		0.07		0.08		0.03	
Mean squared error (MSE)		140.75		151.17		194.94		197.40	
F-test if producer prices drop as fast as…		F()	Prob>F	F()	Prob>F	F()	Prob>F	F()	Prob>F
… transport costs to Addis Ababa increase		0.12	0.73	1.52	0.22	0.07	0.79	0.59	0.45
Obtained price for transactions over the last 12 months*									
Transport costs to Addis Ababa from kebele	birr	−1.01	−1.27	−0.50	−0.87	−1.39	**−2.51**	−0.81	−1.14
Quantity	log()	18.88	**1.91**	45.23	**4.35**	11.95	0.60	−1.18	−0.06
Farmgate	yes = 1	−14.91	−0.34	−63.89	−1.47	92.42	1.09	68.07	1.05
Monthly dummies (September–October = default)									
October–November	yes = 1	−65.21	−0.95	49.65	0.97	−129.74	−1.16	−177.20	**−2.39**
November–December	yes = 1	−355.17	**−4.75**	−358.28	**−8.15**	−548.55	**−4.20**	−318.22	**−2.60**
December–January	yes = 1	−428.60	**−9.25**	−343.17	**−8.34**	−345.22	**−1.86**	−264.34	**−3.54**
January–February	yes = 1	−396.21	**−8.37**	−321.16	**−8.31**	−490.80	**−5.58**	−199.92	**−3.08**
February–March	yes = 1	−392.15	**−8.54**	−317.37	**−9.24**	−442.90	**−4.77**	−303.36	**−4.30**
March–April	yes = 1	−337.17	**−5.96**	−250.62	**−6.49**	−423.82	**−4.60**	−239.84	**−3.41**

April–May	yes = 1	–300.00	**–6.26**	–201.12	**–5.23**	–361.57	**–4.11**	–247.73	**–4.12**
May–June	yes = 1	–240.59	**–6.09**	–175.82	**–5.14**	–373.35	**–3.87**	–186.46	**–3.20**
June–July	yes = 1	–232.09	**–6.32**	–128.32	**–3.70**	–232.49	**–3.05**	–161.66	**–2.86**
July–August	yes = 1	–102.08	**–2.66**	–65.20	**–2.02**	–212.49	**–3.53**	–188.37	**–2.57**
August–September	yes = 1	–68.15	–1.71	–0.77	–0.02	–112.40	–1.65	–100.41	–1.24
Intercept		1,452.11	34.39	1,277.84	26.27	1,408.31	15.18	1,107.96	14.01
Number of observations		453		1230		166		201	
R-squared		0.33		0.3		0.33		0.15	
MSE		186.11		190.85		202.36		185.55	
F-test if producer prices drop as fast as…		F()	Prob>F	F()	Prob>F	F()	Prob>F	F()	Prob>F
… transport costs to Addis Ababa increase		0.00	0.99	0.73	0.40	0.49	0.49	0.07	0.79

Source: Authors' calculations.

Note: * Standard errors are estimated after accounting for within cluster (kebele) correlations and possible heteroskedasticity. ** t-values in **bold** are significant at the 5 percent level.

FIGURE 11.3 Commercial surplus and quantity sold to traders shipping to Addis Ababa

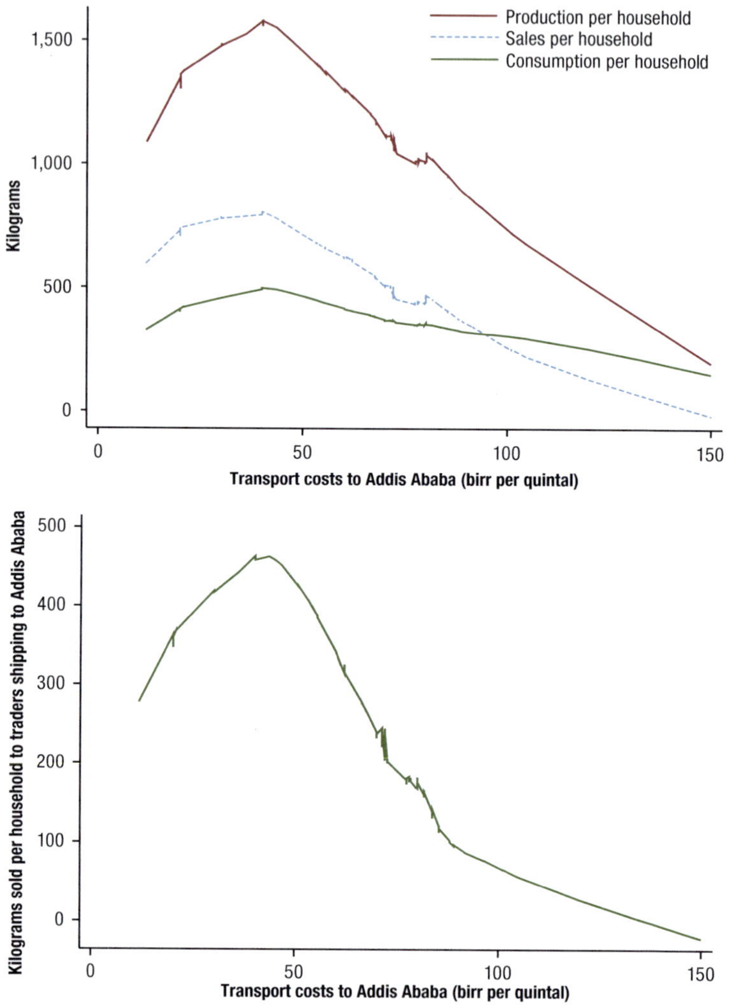

Source: Authors' calculations.

While producer prices vary over space, other production and marketing measures show strong associations across space as well. The top panel of Figure 11.3 shows how production, commercial surplus, and consumption per teff-producing household vary with transportation costs to Addis Ababa. The highest commercial surpluses are achieved by farmers that face the lowest transportation costs. Commercial surplus decreases to almost 0 for those farmers that are most remote; these farmers drop to subsistence levels. Consumption levels of teff per household show less variation over space. However, the most remote farmers have slightly lower consumption levels of teff.[9] The bottom panel of Figure 11.3 shows how the quantities of commercial surplus that are sold to traders who ship the product to Addis Ababa vary by transportation costs to Addis Ababa. As predicted, a strong relationship is apparent. For those farmers who live close to Addis Ababa, the majority of commercial surplus is sold to traders that ship to Addis Ababa. For farmers who live further out, they ship to other places or to other types of sellers or, more important, they just sell less.

Temporal Variation

Seasonality is important in most agricultural markets but especially in Ethiopia because of a short rainfall season, limited irrigation possibilities, and often the reliance on one crop a year (Dercon and Krishnan 2000; Devereux, Sabates-Wheeler, and Longhurst 2012). In this section, seasonality in price behavior and in use of production is examined, including sales. Prices were asked for from the different value-chain agents for two-month periods over the previous season. These collected prices were used as dependent variables in a regression on seasonal and on quality indicators. The results of the seasonal coefficients are shown in Figure 11.4.

The lowest prices are observed during the harvest period (December–February) and the highest toward the end of the year (August–October). Retail prices increased by 15 percent and producer prices by about 40 percent in the months of August–October compared with the harvest price. Similar seasonal price amplitudes have been found in other studies (Rashid and Negassa 2011; Minten, Stifel, and Tamru 2012), and the survey year thus illustrates a seemingly typical pattern. The share of the producer in the final retail price is significantly lower at harvest time given that retail and producer prices are significantly lower and that marketing margins do not change very much in absolute values. However, producer prices still make up 71 percent of the urban retail price during the harvest period. While urban distribution margins do not change over the year, a slight increase in margins is noted between rural markets and urban wholesale markets during the harvest season

9 Possibly illustrating the superior economic characteristics of teff as more remote households are often poorer (for example, Jacoby and Minten 2009).

FIGURE 11.4 Seasonal average teff prices in the value chain

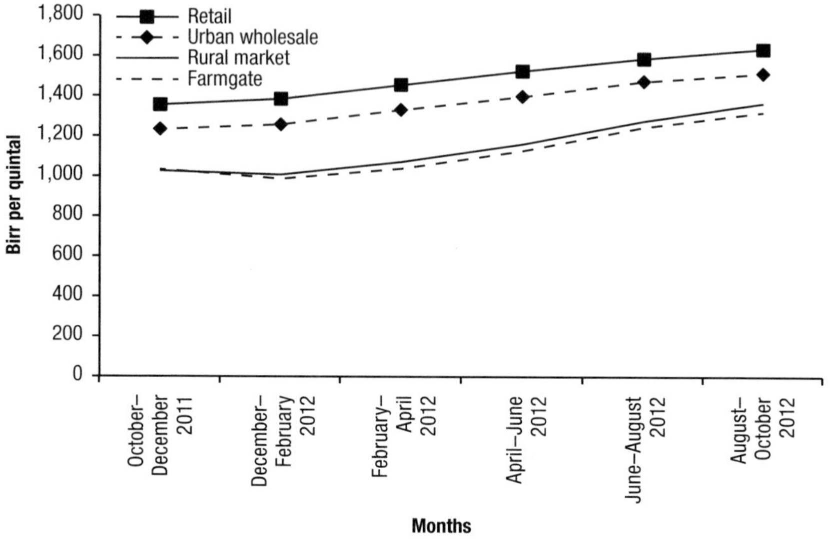

Source: Authors' calculations.

compared with the off-season period. This might be partly driven by higher transport costs during the harvest period (Minten, Stifel, and Tamru 2012).

Data were further collected on monthly storage, sales, and consumption of teff. Figure 11.5 shows how these measures change over the year. Panel A of Figure 11.5 illustrates the average smooth withdrawal of teff from peak storage after harvest (approximately 800 kilograms per household in March). This average storage level comes down to about 100 kilograms per household in November.[10] Panel B of Figure 11.5 shows monthly sales, consumption, and stock changes. Stock changes are calculated by comparing monthly changes in stock position—that is, positive values indicate a stock buildup while negative values signal stock release. Stock buildup happens during November through March. Stock withdrawal is mainly done between March and October.

The main uses of teff production are consumption and sales.[11] Teff consumption increases immediately after harvest and stays stable over the year. It

10 Teff can be stored for relatively long periods without quality loss, and the figure suggests that some farmers indeed store across years seemingly using teff as a savings device.

11 Sales and consumption are the most important uses of teff production. They make up 46 percent and 33 percent, respectively, of total use of the production in the year prior to the survey.

FIGURE 11.5 Monthly storage (A) and use (B) of teff

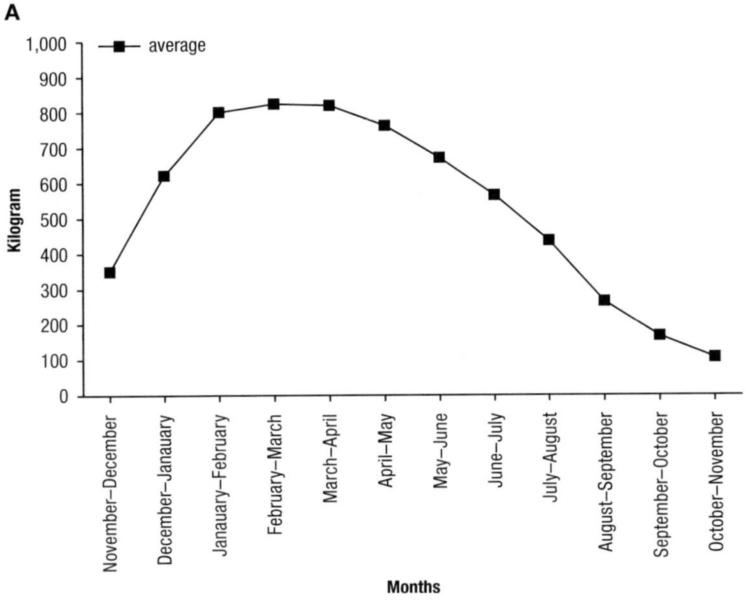

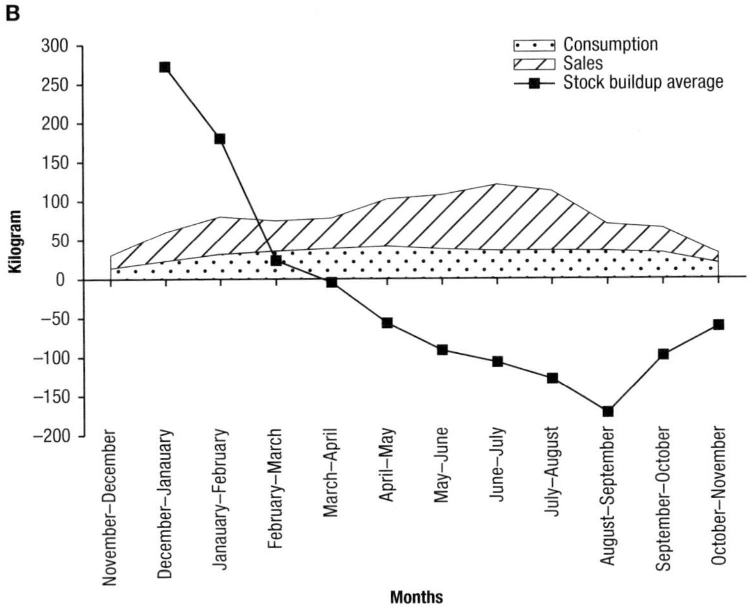

Source: Authors' calculations.

drops to half the level in the months before the harvest. As expected, there are strong seasonal patterns in the sales of teff. Surprisingly, the peak of sales in the survey data is not immediately after harvest, but it is a couple of months afterward. Stock release is highest during July through August, also during the month in which sowing of teff takes place.

Finally, the incidence of distress sales are considered at the farm. Such sales, usually immediately after harvest, are presumed to be important in these teff markets (Fufa et al. 2011).[12] Two indicators are used as a measure of distress in teff marketing. To measure this in the survey, for each sale transaction farmers were asked to indicate if they would have sold teff at that specific time if the price of teff were 10 percent lower. If they responded with "yes," a follow-up question was asked whether they would have sold at a price 50 percent lower. The positive answers to these questions are used as measures of "distress" and "extreme distress" sales respectively. Using these indicators, it is estimated that 19 percent of the transactions were sold in distress and 10 percent in extreme distress (Table 11.9).

In contrast, in 71 percent of the transactions farmers would not have accepted a lower price of that order of magnitude. It is to be noted that there might be some possible measurement issues with the implemented method for distress sales. First, there are possibly problems with recall periods as the transaction was done long before the survey was conducted and the respondent might not have been able to recollect the exact situation and circumstances of each transaction. Second, if a farmer has been pushed by circumstances to transact at an unfavorable price but is not prepared to accept an even more unfavorable price, he would have answered "no" to the question and the transaction would not be counted as a distress sale. In such a situation we would have an underestimate of distress sales. With this caveat in mind, we proceed with further analysis.

To explore what are the associates of these distress sales, a multinomial model is run with the three categorical variables (normal, distress, and extreme distress) as dependent variables and with characteristics of the transactions and of the household as explanatory variables. Distress sales show a significant seasonal pattern: they are relatively more prevalent immediately after harvest as shown by significant coefficients for the period December–January and January–February for both indicators. Extreme distress sales are

12 "[Teff] farmers usually sell their produce immediately after harvest, resulting in high supply in those seasons, thereby leading to lower farm gate prices. In almost all cases of the focus group discussions conducted, the study noted that the immediate selling behavior of farmers is the result of their immediate liquidity requirements" (Fufa et al. 2011, 26).

TABLE 11.9 Multinomial model of distress sales

Variables	Unit	Distress "would accept 10% lower price"		Extreme distress "would accept 50% lower price"	
		Share		Share	
Descriptives					
Number of transactions sold in distress	%	19.5		10.1	
Quantity of teff sold in distress	%	22.0		6.5	
Regression results*		Coefficient	t-value**	Coefficient	t-value**
Independent variables					
Characteristics of transaction					
Quantity sold (quintals)	log()	−0.030	−0.39	−0.509	**−5.07**
October–November	yes = 1	0.176	0.27	0.988	1.52
November–December	yes = 1	0.929	1.83	1.406	**2.43**
December–January	yes = 1	1.340	**3.56**	1.344	**3.01**
January–February	yes = 1	0.728	**2.01**	0.891	**2.07**
February–March	yes = 1	0.696	1.91	0.545	1.24
March–April	yes = 1	0.172	0.45	−0.177	−0.36
April–May	yes = 1	0.650	1.84	−0.564	−1.15
May–June	yes = 1	0.078	0.22	0.003	0.01
June–July	yes = 1	0.412	1.17	0.253	0.59
July–August	yes = 1	0.350	0.95	0.243	0.55
August–September	yes = 1	0.575	1.44	0.320	0.64
Characteristics of household					
Education head of household	years	−0.011	−1.15	0.017	1.46
Age head of household	years	−0.001	−0.22	0.024	**2.89**
Gender head of household	male = 1	0.443	1.43	0.899	1.90
Size of household	number	−0.088	**−2.76**	−0.007	−0.17
Share of young in household	share	0.444	1.26	−0.163	−0.36
Share of elder in household	share	1.076	1.73	0.688	0.84
Household has off-farm income	yes = 1	−0.472	**−3.13**	−0.853	**−3.88**
Land owned by household	hectares	0.029	0.74	−0.090	−1.86
Value of livestock in birr	log()	−0.070	−1.53	−0.130	**−2.30**
Value of nonland assets in birr	log()	0.004	0.07	0.006	0.07
Distance to market in minutes	log()	0.153	**2.19**	−0.087	−0.91
Transport costs to Addis Ababa	birr	0.008	**3.07**	0.008	2.46
Intercept		−2.035	**−2.52**	−2.466	−2.21

(continued)

TABLE 11.9 Continued

		Distress "would accept 10% lower price"		Extreme distress "would accept 50% lower price"	
Variables	Unit	Coefficient	t-value**	Coefficient	t-value**
Number of observations		2,042			
Wald Chi2(46)		233.35			
Prob>chi2		0.00			
Pseudo R2		0.07			

Source: Authors' calculations.
Note: * robust standard errors. ** t-values in **bold** are significant at the 5 percent level.

characterized by smaller quantities sold, and households seem to be only willing to sell in extreme distress those quantities that are required to satisfy their urgent liquidity needs. Two other variables emerge significant for both measures. First, households that have off-farm income sources are less affected by distress sales. This seems logical as they can rely on other income resources and can thus reduce pressure on sales of teff at periods of low prices. Second, more remote households are affected by more distress sales, possibly because of higher poverty levels as well as lower production levels in the more remote areas (Jacoby and Minten 2009).

Conclusion

The increasing urbanization in developing countries raises important questions on how food value chains function and on how opportunities can be harnessed from these changes to allow for better food security for people in rural areas as well as the urban poor. By examining the rural-urban value chain of teff in Ethiopia, this study offers important new insights on the marketing of this crop. Surveys were fielded at each layer of the value chain from major production areas accounting for 42 percent of national commercial surplus and for more than 90 percent of the supply to the main terminal market in Addis Ababa, the capital of Ethiopia and also its largest city. Almost 1,800 primary survey interviews in total with producers, traders, truck drivers, and retailers were conducted for this study.

These value chains are found to be relatively unsophisticated. At the farm level there are no interlinked transactions with buyers of the produce (which is often seen in other countries, especially in more developed value chains), the role of credit is minor, and most of the transactions are cash transactions.

Owing to the lack of grading and standardization along the midstream and downstream parts of the value chain, significant efforts are observed at ensuring quality and quantity at the time of each transaction. Overall, however, value chains are short and farmers obtain a relatively high share of the final retail price (on average 80 percent). The majority of the farmers would not have accepted a significantly lower price at the time of their sales, indicating that distress sales are of relatively minor importance in farmers' marketing decisions. In contrast with common perceptions, commercialization in these major teff-producing areas of Ethiopia seems fairly well organized.

The results raise questions as to why they are in contrast to conventional thinking. Several reasons can be given. First, the literature on value-chain functioning is heavily dominated by case study research (for example, Dawe et al. 2008; Hayami, Kikuchi, and Marciano 1999), which often raises questions on how representative the findings are.[13] Second, changes happen quickly in these value chains, especially in these zones where much of the teff produced is marketed, driven by improvements in transport infrastructure, better communication, and increasing demand for food choice and quality in cities (for example, Reardon et al. 2012). It is possible that research has not kept pace with these changes. Third, a relatively unsophisticated market was investigated where there is little processing or value addition. The situation might have been different with other products (Miller and Jones 2010). Fourth, as cereals were studied, the assessment of quality and quantity is relatively straightforward and losses in the value chain are relatively small. Value chains of root crops where assessments of quality and quantity are more complicated or of fruits and vegetables where perishability and losses are a significant issue might show a different structure and higher margins. Fifth, a product was studied that has a relatively high price in the urban retail market. For example, the price of teff is on average double the price of maize (Minten, Stifel, and Tamru 2012). As such, even if the maize market in Ethiopia is as efficient as it is for teff, the share of the final retail price that maize producers receive would result in lower producer share. Teff is also a major staple crop. The situation might be different for nonstaples or for products where markets are thin. Finally, the value and services that traders bring to the system are often not well recognized nor appreciated. In the face of increasing or volatile food

13 Such a case-study approach is seemingly often linked with budget and time constraints in value-chain assessments as well as with the difficulty of implementing surveys over different value-chain participants.

prices, traders are often blamed.[14] In consequence, their importance in the value chain may often be overstated.

These findings point to some important policy implications. First, given the difficulty in accurately assessing market functioning, policies aimed at improving market efficiencies—such as stimulating increasing involvement of agricultural cooperatives in output marketing, the establishment of modern exchanges, or warehouse receipt systems—should be closely examined to determine how and where these policies are expected to improve market functioning and what the expected benefits would be compared to the costs of their implementation. Second, increasing investments in road infrastructure to incorporate more remote areas and to lower transportation costs by removing barriers in investments (World Bank 2012) is shown to clearly boost the prices that farmers receive. Third, if the objective of policy makers is to reduce consumer prices in urban areas, relatively more attention should be given to lower farm production costs, given that these costs constitute the biggest part of the final retail price.

References

Ahmed, R. 1987. *Marketing and Price Incentives in African and Asian Countries: A Comparison.* Washington, DC: International Food Policy Research Institute (IFPRI).

Alavi, H., A. Htenas, R. Kopicki, A. Shepherd, and R. Clarete. 2012. *Trusting Trade and the Private Sector for Food Security in Southeast Asia.* Washington, DC: World Bank.

Barker, R., R. Herdt, and B. Rose. 1985. *The Rice Economy of Asia.* Los Banos: International Rice Research Institute.

Barrett, C. 1996. "Urban Bias in Price Risk: The Geography of Food Price Distribution in Low-income Countries." *Journal of Development Studies* 23 (6): 193–215.

Barrett, C. B., and P. Dorosh. 1996. "Farmers' Welfare and Changing Food Prices: Non-parametric Evidence from Madagascar." *American Journal of Agricultural Economics* 78 (3): 656–669.

Bell, C. 1988. "Credit Markets and Interlinked Transactions." In *Handbook of Development Economics.* Vol. 5, edited by H. Chenery and T. Srinivan, 763–830. Amsterdam: North Holland.

Bernard, T., D. J. Spielman, A. S. Taffesse, and E. Z. Gabre-Madhin. 2010. *Cooperatives for Staple Crop Marketing.* IFPRI Research Monograph 164. Washington, DC: IFPRI.

14 For example, India forbade forward trading on commodity exchanges for a number of crops to control food inflation. The increasing global volatility in food prices has been blamed as well on extensive speculation but disproven by some authors (Irwin, Sanders, and Merrin 2009).

Chamberlin, J., and T. S. Jayne. 2012. "Unpacking the Meaning of 'Market Access': Evidence from Rural Kenya." *World Development* 41: 245–264.

Christiaensen, L., and S. Devarajan. 2013. "Making the Most of Africa's Growth." *Current History* 112 (754): 181–187.

Crow, B., and K.A.S. Murshid. 1994. "Economic Returns to Social Power: Merchants' Finance and Interlinkage in the Grain Markets in Bangladesh." *World Development* 22 (7): 1011–1030.

CTA (Technical Centre for Agricultural and Rural Cooperation). 2012. *Going to Waste—Missed Opportunities in the Battle to Improve Food Security.* CTA Policy Brief 7. Brussels: CTA.

Dawe, D. C., P. F. Moya, C. B. Casiwan, and J. M. Cabling. 2008. "Rice Marketing Systems in the Philippines and Thailand: Do Large Numbers of Competitive Traders Ensure Good Performance?" *Food Policy* 33 (5): 455–463.

Deichmann, U., F. Shilpi, and R. Vakis. 2009. "Urban Proximity, Agricultural Potential, and Rural Non-farm Employment: Evidence from Bangladesh." *World Development* 37 (3): 645–660.

Dercon, S., and P. Krishnan. 2000. "Vulnerability, Seasonality, and Poverty in Ethiopia." *Journal of Development Studies* 36 (6): 25–53.

Devereux, S., R. Sabates-Wheeler, and R. Longhurst. 2012. *Seasonality, Rural Livelihoods, and Development.* New York: Earthscan.

Fafchamps, M., and R. V. Hill. 2008. "Price Transmission and Trader Entry in Domestic Commodity Markets." *Economic Development and Cultural Change* 56: 729–766.

Fafchamps, M., and B. Minten. 1999. "Relationships and Traders in Madagascar." *Journal of Development Studies* 35 (6): 1–35.

Fafchamps, M., and F. Shilpi. 2003. "The Spatial Division of Labour in Nepal." *Journal of Development Studies* 39 (6): 23–66.

Francesconi, G. N., and N. Heerink. 2010. "Ethiopian Agricultural Cooperatives in an Era of Global Commodity Exchange: Does Organizational Form Matter?" *Journal of African Economies* 20 (1): 153–177.

Fufa, B., B. Behute, R. Simons, and T. Berhe. 2011. *Strengthening the Tef Value Chain in Ethiopia.* Addis Ababa: Ethiopian Agricultural Transformation Agency (ATA).

Gabre-Madhin, E. Z. 2001. *Market Institutions, Transaction Costs, and Social Capital in the Ethiopian Grain Market.* IFPRI Research Report 124. Washington, DC: IFPRI.

———. 2012. *A Market for Abdu: Creating a Commodity Exchange in Ethiopia.* Occasional Essays Series. Washington, DC: IFPRI.

Gollin, D., and R. Rogerson. 2010. *Agriculture, Roads, and Economic Development in Uganda.* National Bureau of Economic Research Working Paper 15863. Cambridge, MA, US: National Bureau of Economic Research.

Grootaert, C., G. Oh, and A. Swamy. 2002. "Social Capital, Education, and Credit Markets: Empirical Evidence from Burkina Faso." In *Social Capital and Economic Development*, edited by J. Islam, T. Kelly, and S. Ramaswamy, 85–103. Cheltenham Glos, UK: Edward Elgar Publishing.

Hayami, Y., M. Kikuchi, and E. B. Marciano. 1999. "Middlemen and Peasants in Rice Marketing in the Philippines." *Agricultural Economics* 20 (2): 79–93.

Irwin, S. H., D. R. Sanders, and R. P. Merrin. 2009. "Devil or Angel? The Role of Speculation in the Recent Commodity Price Boom (and Bust)." *Journal of Agricultural and Applied Economics* 41: 377–391.

Jacoby, H., and B. Minten. 2009. "On Measuring the Benefits of Lower Transport Costs." *Journal of Development Economics* 89 (1): 28–38.

Jerven, M. 2013. *Poor Numbers: How We Are Misled by African Development Statistics and What to Do about It.* Ithaca, NY, US: Cornell University Press.

Landes, M. R., and M. E. Burfisher. 2009. *Growth and Equity Effects of Agricultural Marketing Efficiency Gains in India.* USDA-ERS Economic Research Report 89. Washinton, DC: United States Department of Agriculture–Economic Research Service (USDA-ERS).

Masters, A. 2008. "Unpleasant Middlemen." *Journal of Economic Behavior and Organization* 68 (1): 73–86.

Mattoo, A., D. Mishra, and A. Narain. 2007. *From Competition at Home to Competing Abroad.* Washington, DC: World Bank.

Miller, C., and L. Jones. 2010. *Agricultural Value Chain Finance: Tools and Lessons.* Warwickshire, UK: Food and Agriculture Organization (FAO) and Practical Action Publishing.

Minten, B., and S. Kyle. 1999. "The Effect of Distance and Road Quality on Food Collection, Marketing Margins, and Traders' Wages: Evidence from the Former Zaire." *Journal of Development Economics* 60 (2): 467–495.

Minten, B., D. C. Stifel, and S. Tamru. 2012. *Structural Transformation in Ethiopia: Evidence from Cereal Markets.* Ethiopia Strategy Support Program (ESSP) II Working Paper 39. Addis Ababa: IFPRI/ESSP II.

Minten, B., S. Tamru, E. Engida Legesse, and T. Kuma. 2013. *Ethiopia's Value Chains on the Move: The Case of Teff.* ESSP Working Paper 52. Addis Ababa: IFPRI/ESSP II.

Mondal, A. 2010. "The Middlemen Rule the Roost." *The Daily Star,* May 6. Accessed May 6, 2010. www.thedailystar.net/newDesign/news-details.php?nid=137151.

Nang'ole, E. M., D. Mithöfer, and S. Franzel. 2011. *Review of Guidelines and Manuals for Value Chain Analysis for Agricultural and Forest Products.* ICRAF Occasional Paper 17. Nairobi: World Agroforestry Centre (ICRAF).

Prasad, J., and A. Prasad. 1995. *Indian Agricultural Markets: Emerging Trends and Perspectives.* New Delhi, India: Mittal Publications.

Rakotoarisoa, M., M. Iafrata, and M. Paschali. 2011. *Why Has Africa Become a Net Food Importer? Explaining Africa's Agricultural and Food Trade Deficit.* Rome: Food and Agriculture Organization of the United Nations.

Rashid, S., and N. Minot. 2010. "Are Staple Food Markets in Africa Efficient? Spatial Price Analyses and Beyond." Paper presented at the Comesa Policy Seminar "Food Price Variability: Causes, Consequences, and Policy Options," January 25–26, Maputo, Mozambique.

Rashid, S., and A. Negassa. 2011. *Policies and Performance of Ethiopian Cereal Markets.* ESSP II Working Paper 21. Addis Ababa: IFPRI/ESSP II.

Reardon, T., K. Chen, B. Minten, and L. Adriano. 2012. *The Quiet Revolution in Staple Food Value Chains. Enter the Dragon, the Elephant, and the Tiger.* Mandaluyong City, Philippines: Asian Development Bank and IFPRI.

Stephens, E. C., and C. B. Barrett. 2011. "Incomplete Credit Markets and Commodity Market Behavior." *Journal of Agricultural Economics* 62 (1): 1–24.

Teravaninthon, S., and G. Raballand. 2009. *Transport Prices and Costs in Africa: A Review of the International Corridors.* Washington, DC: World Bank.

Trienekens, J. H. 2011. "Agricultural Value Chains in Developing Countries: A Framework for Analysis." *International Food and Agribusiness Management Review* 14 (2): 51–82.

UK (United Kingdom), DFID (Department for International Development). 2004. "Rethinking Tropical Agricultural Commodities." Accessed March 10, 2015. http://dfid-agriculture-consultation.nri.org/summaries/wp10.pdf.

UN (United Nations) Population Division. 2010. *World Urbanization Prospects: The 2009 Revision.* New York: UN Population Division.

Webber, M., and P. Labaste. 2009. *Building Competitiveness in Africa's Agriculture: A Guide to Value Chain Concepts and Applications.* Washington, DC: World Bank.

World Bank. 2008. *World Development Report 2008: Agriculture for Development.* Washington, DC: World Bank.

———. 2009. *Eastern Africa: A Study of the Regional Maize Market and Marketing Costs.* Report number 49831-ET. Washington, DC: World Bank.

———. 2012. *Agribusiness Indicators: Ethiopia.* Report 68237-ET. Washington, DC: World Bank.

Chapter 12

STRUCTURAL TRANSFORMATION OF TEFF MARKETS

Bart Minten, David Stifel, and Seneshaw Tamru

Since the beginning of the 2000s, important changes have occurred in Ethiopia's economy.[1] In this chapter, the extent to which these changes have affected teff markets are assessed using primary data collected from wholesale markets and secondary data on teff prices and margins, obtained from Ethiopia's Central Statistical Agency (CSA) and the Ethiopian Grain Trade Enterprise (EGTE). Five possible reasons are considered for teff market transformation and for the changes in teff price margins over the period 2001–2011.[2] This study period has been influenced by changes in five factors that may have affected how teff markets function. First, fast economic and income growth is changing food demand. Second, urbanization is leading to larger rural–urban food and teff marketing flows. Third, investments in road infrastructure and a better organized transport sector have led to significant declines in real transportation costs. Fourth, the widespread availability of mobile phones has improved access to price information for a large number of players in the commercial food circuit and has led, for some, to a different way of sealing commercial deals. Fifth, increased adoption of modern inputs and better access to extension agents are likely to have contributed to an increase in teff supply.

Price data collected since 2001 at wholesale and retail levels show that these changes are associated with significant declines in real margins of teff prices between supplying and receiving markets over time, in real teff milling margins, as well as in retail margins. Teff prices are found to have increased over the period, although these price levels were affected differently in different markets. Price integration and price co-movements between wholesale

1 This chapter is based on Minten, Tamru, and Stifel (2014). This is reprinted by permission of the publisher (Taylor & Francis Ltd, www.tandfonline.com).

2 One important caveat of this analysis is that the markets that are analyzed, and for which there exists consistent price series data, mostly serve regional centers. It is quite possible that rural markets are more dysfunctional and responsible for famines in rural areas (for papers on famines and market behavior, see, for example, Rivers et al. 1976; Shin 2010; Ravallion 1987; Drèze and Sen 1989).

markets have also improved significantly over the period studied. The teff marketing system thus appears to have markedly transformed in Ethiopia to the benefit of producers and consumers alike.

The structure of the chapter is as follows: First, the data and the methods used are discussed. The next section considers the changes that are likely to have contributed to structural transformation in the country. Then, spatial price variation, price integration, quality price premia, processing margins, and retail margins are explored, before the chapter concludes.

Data and Methodology

Two main datasets are used for the analysis in this chapter, using both primary and secondary data.[3] The EGTE, a grain procurement arm of the government, gathers prices of teff in 66 major wholesale markets in the country. Prices are collected during the early morning, late morning, and afternoon on major market days, and simple averages of these prices over the course of a month are reported as monthly prices. The price information is collected, not by requesting price levels from traders, but by noting the prices through observation of actual transactions. Producer, wholesale, and retail prices are all collected; however, only wholesale and retail prices at 12 selected markets are publicly available.[4] The EGTE data are our preferred source of data given the high quality of the prices that are collected, the consistent methodology used over time, and the geographical spread of the markets surveyed.

A survey was also conducted in 25 major teff wholesale markets in Ethiopia during the beginning of 2012. The objective of this survey was to gather information about changes that had taken place in these markets over the past 10 years. Almost all major cities, as well as the most important production

3 Primary: data were collected by the authors themselves; secondary: data were collected by a third party.

4 "Producer prices" are defined as those prices that are received by producers at the wholesale market; "wholesale prices" are the prices that wholesalers obtain when they sell in large bulks; "retail prices" are prices on the wholesale market or in nearby markets obtained by traders that sell in small quantities to consumers. These price data were electronically gathered and are thus used in the analysis. Because the weights of individual cereals in the national Consumer Price Index (CPI) are relatively low, and due to a lack of any reasonable alternative, this national CPI as constructed by Ethiopia's Central Statistical Agency (CSA) is relied upon to deflate prices. A de-seasonalized index is used. To construct such a de-seasonalized index, a 12-month moving average is calculated and the constructed series is used as the deflator.

areas, were included in this survey.[5] Focus groups, comprising those involved in transporting goods, and key informants for teff in the selected wholesale markets, provided input to the survey. The respondents within the focus groups had significant experience in teff trade in each market (as there were many recall questions). Questions were asked about the extent of changes in transport costs and travel times between different wholesale markets, changes in access to and the spread of mobile phones and the use of mobile phones in teff trade, and changes in the size of the market.[6]

Several aspects of teff price behavior are examined in the section that follows. First, the quality premia and spatial margins are analyzed. The EGTE wholesale price series is used as left-hand variables, and regression models are estimated that include on the right-hand temporal, spatial, and quality variables as explanatory variables. The year-month fixed effects are used to control for all potential temporal variation.[7] These controls allow for a better estimate of the coefficients of interest—that is, of quality and location. In estimating the standard errors, clustering by quarter is allowed, and therefore dependence between months is controlled for. The regression used is as follows:

$$\text{Log (real price of teff)} = f(\text{year*month, market location, quality}) \qquad (1)$$

Second, the processing and retail margins are studied. To do this, the wholesale prices are combined with two other datasets. For the analysis of processing margins, teff flour price data collected by the CSA in retail markets are merged with the wholesale teff market prices. The prices are retained only for these markets and for those periods that are common to both datasets. For the analysis of the retail margins, the wholesale prices are merged with the prices collected by EGTE at the retail level. Unfortunately, these retail price data

5 Of the 13 cities with a population more than 100,000, two of these cities were not part of the EGTE price series—that is, Harar and Awassa.

6 While the focus group interviews were carefully fielded and therefore provide a good indication of changes over time, the methods used within the focus group interview are disposed to measurement error and are especially so in the case of recall questions. Consequently, the statistical techniques, which are based on sampling to test differences over time from the recall data, are unreliable.

7 Most of the agricultural seasons in the highlands of Ethiopia (where the majority of the analyzed markets are located) are similar, with harvests occurring at the same time. Taffesse, Dorosh, and Gemessa (2013), for example, show that 97 percent of all agricultural production in the country occurs during the meher season and that the belg season is of minor importance. Therefore, this does not include additional market-month interactions in the regression as this would also limit the scope of the spatial price analysis.

only exist up to the end of 2009, and thus the analysis is limited to the 2001–2009 period. A similar method is followed as described above and the estimated regression is as follows:

Log (real price of teff) = f(year*month, market location, quality, grain/flour, retail/wholesale) (2)

A major objective of the study is to evaluate the structural transformation of these markets. To understand if a structural break in these time series occurred over the decade 2001–2011, the different variables are set to interact with a time dummy for the second part of the period studied (2006–2011). The significance of these coefficients is then assessed and a comparison is made with the coefficients in the first part of the decade (2001–2005) through an F-test. If a significant difference is detected, a structural break in the market is assumed over the decade. The results of these tests are shown for spatial variation, quality premia, retail margins, and processing margins.

Third, the extent to which teff markets in Ethiopia are integrated is assessed. Following Van Campenhout (2007), the use of threshold autoregressive (TAR) modeling allows estimates to be generated that incorporate thresholds and adjustment parameters to vary over time as follows:

$$\Delta d_t = \begin{cases} \rho_{out} d_{t-1} + \rho'_{out} t.d_{t-1} + \varepsilon_t & : d_{t-1} > \theta_t \\ \varepsilon_t & : -\theta_t \le d_{t-1} \le \theta_t \\ \rho_{out} d_{t-1} + \rho'_{out} t.d_{t-1} + \varepsilon_t & : d_{t-1} < -\theta_t \end{cases}, \qquad (3)$$

where d_t is the difference between the teff price in Addis Ababa and the regional wholesale market of interest (that is, $d_t = p_{t,A} - p_{t,r}$, where $p_{t,A}$ is the market price in Addis Ababa and $p_{t,r}$ is the market price in regional markets at time t), $\Delta d_t = d_t - d_{t-1}$, ε_t is the estimated residual, t denotes the time trend, θ is an approximation for transaction costs, and ρ_{out} is the adjustment factor for prices outside of the transaction cost band (that is, −θ to θ).

Possible Reasons for Structural Transformation in Teff Markets

Over the period studied, a number of structural changes have occurred in the overall economy as well as in Ethiopia's food economy—on top of the changes in the international food markets (Headey, Malaiyandi, and Fan 2010)—that have affected teff markets and price formation in the country. Given data constraints, it is impossible to estimate the exact effects of the changes of these different factors on teff price formation and market transformation, but it seems clear that they have all had some impact.[8] These changes include economic and income growth, urbanization and commercial surplus, transport and communication infrastructure, agricultural technologies, and extension. The following section elaborates on each of these.

Economic and Income Growth

Since 2004, Ethiopia has been one of the world's fastest growing economies, which is a remarkable achievement for a non-oil-exporting African country. While growth of the GDP, which is measured in constant market prices, was negative in the beginning of the decade, it escalated from 2004 on and has stayed in double digits ever since. It remains unclear how the benefits of economic growth were distributed among Ethiopia's population, but the consequence of such growth rates leads to significantly different consumption patterns for the beneficiaries of this growth. This has important implications for food markets.

To understand how food markets have been affected, two effects of GDP growth are distinguished: (1) how the incomes of consumers are affected, and (2) how consumers change their consumption patterns because of increases in income. First, evidence from national household surveys suggests that consumption expenditures are increasing and that poverty levels are decreasing. Real per adult equivalent consumption in 2004/2005 (1,542 birr at 1995/1996 constant prices) was 16 percent higher than the previous five years and 17 percent higher than ten years earlier (Ethiopia, MoFED 2008). Kuma (2010) finds similar results in urban areas, where consumption expenditures grew by almost 15 percent between 1994 and 2004. Analysis of the most recent national household data shows that poverty declined between 2004/2005 and 2010/2011 from 38.7 percent to 29.6 percent, indicating further welfare improvements over the period considered (Ethiopia, MoFED 2012). Although welfare has improved, it is important to note that poverty and livelihood resilience still remains a big challenge, especially in rural areas, and that per capita income growth has started from a very low base. Ethiopia still often suffers from major and variable food shortages—often linked with droughts—and the country continues to be an importer of food.

8 For a discussion of market transformation and its drivers, see, for example, Reardon and Timmer (2007) and Minot and Roy (2007).

Second, as incomes grow, consumption patterns are likely to change as households consume more high-quality foods relative to lower-quality foods (as shown in Chapter 2). An indicator that this is taking place in Ethiopia in the presence of income growth is that income elasticities of demand for meat, fruits, and vegetables are estimated to be considerably higher than for most cereals. Even among cereals, however, some (for example, teff) have high demand elasticities while others (such as sorghum and maize) have low elasticities (Tafere, Taffesse, and Tamru 2010). As such, it is not surprising that urban consumption patterns over the decade have increasingly included more teff, milk and milk products, meat, and fruit (Kuma 2010).

Urbanization and the Increase in Commercial Surplus

Although it started from a low base, Ethiopia has experienced rapid urbanization over the past couple of decades (Schmidt and Kedir Jemal 2009). This trend is important for agricultural markets in particular since urban populations typically do not grow their own food. Instead, they rely on markets for their food needs. As a consequence of these growing urban areas, there is an increasing flow of agricultural commercial surplus within the country.[9] Based on data from the national census in 2007, Schmidt and Kedir Jemal (2009) estimated that 14.2 percent of the Ethiopian population lived in urban areas and that urban centers have grown by up to 3.7 percent per year on average. Using these growth rates, the urban population grew by 44 percent, or by 3.7 million people over the period 2001–2011. To put that number in perspective, consider the following: Assuming that the average urban consumption level of teff was as high as was estimated in the national household survey (HICES) of 2004/2005 (that is, 61.4 kilograms per capita), and that the urban population relied completely on production shipped in from rural areas, commercial flows of teff increased by about 237,000 metric tons between 2001 and 2011. This is equivalent to an additional 30,000 truckloads of teff (of 7.5 metric tons in a widely used Isuzu FSR truck) between rural and urban areas over the decade, or 300 additional trucks per year (assuming 100 return journeys per truck). According to official statistics published by the CSA,

9 While urbanization has led to increased rural-market flows, higher population growth in rural areas has also led to increased demand for marketed food in rural areas. Using the census data of 1994 and 2007, Schmidt and Kedir Jemal (2009) estimate that the absolute growth of the rural population (13.7 million) was twice as high as the urban population (6.7 million). However, given that most household food consumption in rural areas was of food produced by the rural household, it is unlikely that rural population growth has had as much of an impact on food marketing flows as has increasing urbanization, as city dwellers typically depend completely on purchased food.

there was indeed a large increase in the commercial quantities of teff traded in the country over the period studied. The commercial surplus for teff increased by an estimated 117 percent over this 10-year period.[10]

Focus group participants in the wholesale market survey were asked about level and trends with respect to numbers of traders and brokers in the markets and of cereal trucks arriving in these markets. These numbers confirm that the commercial surplus has rapidly increased over the decade. For example, significantly more trade is reported on average in these markets over time. The reported number of trucks increased over 10 years by almost 70 percent and by almost 80 percent in the lean and peak periods, respectively. These growth rates are faster than the urban population growth rates in the country (Schmidt and Kedir Jemal 2009). This possibly indicates higher consumption levels of teff in the cities over time, more trade between rural areas that might pass through these urban wholesale markets, and shifts from other means of transportation to trucks. The focus groups' assessment of trends in the number of teff traders and brokers that operate on these markets also indicates considerable growth over time. With the number of teff traders perceived to be growing by more than 300 percent over the period studied, and the number of brokers rising by more than 50 percent, competition appears to have become keener and turnover per trader and broker lower.

Roads and Transportation Costs

Several factors have contributed to changes in transportation costs over the period studied. Some of these factors include changes in the road network and investments in road infrastructure improvements, increases in fuel costs, and changes in the types of trucks plying the roads. These are reviewed in turn.

First, since coming to power at the beginning of the 1990s, the Ethiopian government has embarked on a large road investment program, and the current level of infrastructure development in the country is unprecedented. For example, all-weather surfaced roads are in the process of being built or have already been built between the capitals of all regions. Furthermore, the total length of all-weather surfaced roads tripled in fewer than 15 years, from an estimated 32,900 kilometers in 2000 to 99,500 kilometers in 2013. This type of road development has important effects on the connectivity of agricultural markets in the country. Based on interviews with transporters in the wholesale market survey who were questioned about travel times between different

10 Comparing CSA data on production and percentage sold in 2012/2013 with 10 years earlier.

wholesale markets in the country and the Addis Ababa wholesale market, transport times have fallen on average by 20 percent over the period studied, from 10 hours to 8 hours.[11]

Second, fuel prices have risen considerably over time. Until October 2008 the Ethiopian government subsidized fuel prices.[12] But with the abolition of fuel subsidies, combined with the increase in international fuel prices, real fuel prices increased significantly. CSA retail price data indicate that the real price of diesel at the beginning of the 2000s was 60 percent lower than in 2010. Given that fuel is an important determinant of transport costs, this undoubtedly contributed to relatively higher transport costs over time.

Third, the increase in the number of larger capacity trucks plying the roads is putting downward pressure on transportation costs. This follows because the bigger the truck, the lower the per unit transport costs. As increasing quantities of food are being shipped between markets, it is becoming easier to fill larger loads in bigger trucks, and consequently there are greater incentives to enter into food trade with larger trucks. The wholesale market survey data indicate that this is occurring. Over time, the importance of larger trucks (mostly Isuzu FSR; able to carry about 7 to 8 metric tons) has grown compared to smaller ones (regular Isuzu; carrying about 5 to 6 metric tons). The share of FSR trucks in the total number of trucks transporting cereals grew from about 15 percent in 2001 to 33 percent in 2011. The use of trailer trucks, able to transport 20 metric tons, is still limited and its share stayed constant over time. Overall these trailer trucks make up 13 percent of the trucks that transport cereals (they are more important for longer distance journeys).[13]

---

11 This trend is consistent with estimates taken from the 1983 and 2007 population censuses. Because of improved infrastructure and of urbanization, the population census data show the percentage of people who were connected with cities increased dramatically over the twenty-three-year period between 1983 and 2007. According to Schmidt and Kedir Jemal (2009), the percentage of the population that lives further than 10 hours away from a city (more than 50,000 people) decreased from 40 percent in 1984 to 12 percent in 2007. Given that a number of large construction projects have continued since the 2007 census, it is safe to assume that this trend has only continued.

12 Ethiopia froze fuel prices between August 2006 and January 2008; it had decreased the price of gasoline in February 2007. In October 2008 it eliminated fuel price subsidies altogether (Kojima 2009).

13 However, given that they are able to transport between twice and four times the load of the smaller trucks, their share of the total quantity of cereal transported is significantly higher than 13 percent. While increasing competition in the transport sector is hard to measure, one rough indicator is the increasing number of trucks imported into the country each year. Comtrade data (data on international trade are collected by the UN and can be downloaded from http://comtrade.un.org/), for instance, show that the number of trucks imported in the country doubled between 2001 and 2011. This increase is greater than observed in the wholesale markets. These imports thus illustrate not only the important increases in commercialization in the country but likely also reflect other important changes, such as in the construction sector.

Collectively, these three factors are likely to have affected transportation costs between wholesale markets in Ethiopia. To assess this, participants in the transporter focus groups were asked to estimate travel costs from 2001 to 2011 for those trips that were commonly taken from the market where they were interviewed. To allow for comparison over time, these prices were deflated by the CPI.[14] The results from recall data from focus group interviews indicate that the mean and median of transport costs fell significantly throughout the decade.[15] The improvements in roads and the shift to bigger and cheaper trucks appear to have outweighed the rise of fuel prices and have resulted in significantly lower real transportation costs between markets in the country.

Access to Mobile Phones

Mobile phones have become widely available in Ethiopia, enabling traders and farmers to exchange information easily. The widespread availability of mobile phones in rural areas of developing countries has led to a number of beneficial effects on farmers and on the trade environment in general (for example, Aker and Fafchamps 2014; Jensen 2007). These effects may also benefit Ethiopian farmers and traders given that at the time of the wholesale survey in early 2012, almost all traders and brokers in the survey used mobile phones in their business. Figure 12.1 shows how cell phone coverage changed over time in the teff wholesale markets in the survey. In 2000 only the Addis Ababa market had cell phone coverage but that quickly changed, and by 2005 there was almost universal coverage of these rural wholesale markets. Figure 12.1 further shows that cell phone usage rates increased to 100 percent for teff traders in the various markets within an average of only four to five years after the introduction of coverage.

To understand the impact of this rapid spread of cell phones on teff trade, the focus groups were questioned further. First, to better understand their access to communication technology over time, focus groups were asked to assess the percentage of teff traders and brokers who had access to fixed phones (land lines) before mobile phones became available. The results reported in Table 12.1 indicate that a large majority of these traders and

14 For those trips where no complete time series could be collected from the group over the whole 10 years, the rest of the series was deleted. Thus there ended up being 204 consistent price series of transport costs between wholesale markets.

15 This is estimated by focus groups to be about 50 percent, although this is admittedly a very rough estimate given that recall error for cost estimates is likely to be large in the presence of high inflation.

FIGURE 12.1 Mobile phone use by teff traders on wholesale markets, cumulative percentage over markets, 2000–2011

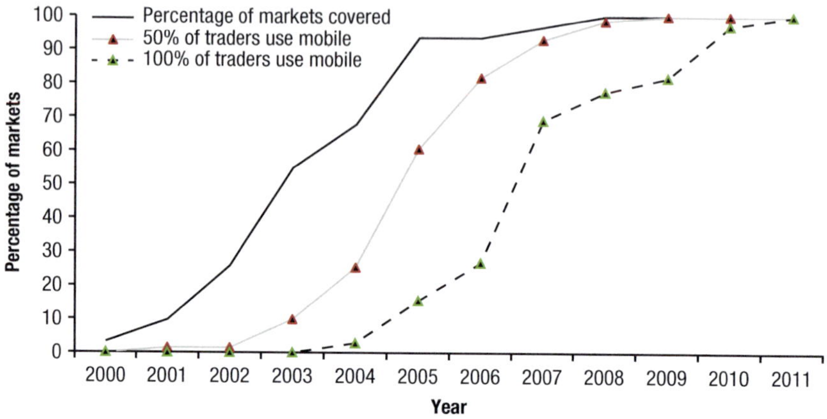

Source: Authors' compilation from focus group interviews.

brokers previously had some form of access to fixed phones (for example, at home, on the market, or at another location), and 39 percent of the traders reported having a fixed phone at home before gaining access to mobile phones, indicating that mobile phones did not fill a complete communication void as experienced in other countries.

Second, while telephone communications existed prior to the introduction of mobile phones, mobile phone technology has improved the ease of access to communications as evidenced by the frequency of phone use. According to the focus groups, an average teff broker now makes 31 business calls per day during the peak trading period, while traders make 24. This is roughly three to six times more than the number of calls made using fixed lines before the introduction of mobile phones. It is also worth noting that the number of calls made with mobile phones drops off significantly in the lean period, reflecting the important seasonality in traders' and brokers' teff business activities.

Third, questions regarding the purpose for using mobile and fixed-line phones indicate that 83 percent of teff traders and 57 percent of brokers use mobile phones to transmit prices, compared to 43 percent and 13 percent respectively who did so previously with fixed lines (Table 12.1). Furthermore, 41 percent of the traders and 40 percent of the brokers use the mobile phones to request traders or farmers to come with their teff to the market as they inform them they should be able to find buyers that day. Fewer use phones to agree on prices with sellers and buyers. In Ethiopia standards are often

TABLE 12.1 Use of mobile phones by traders and brokers (%)

	Percentage of traders and brokers			
Use of phone	Mean	Median	Mean	Median
Percentage of traders and brokers who had access to a fixed phone	*now*		*before*	
Traders				
at home			39	40
on the market			21	10
at another location			68	90
Brokers				
at home			11	2
on the market			0	0
at another location			63	90
Estimated number of phone calls per trader per day related to his trade business	*by mobile phone*		*by fixed phone*	
Traders				
in the peak period	24	25	7	5
in the lean period	8	10	3	2
Brokers				
in the peak period	31	30	6	5
in the lean period	13	10	2	2
Use of phone	*"Are mobile phones used to"?*		*"Were fixed phones used to"?*	
Traders				
"inform/transmit prices"	83	90	43	50
"agree on prices (plus quantity/quality) with sellers"	29	15	6	0
"request a showup (quantity requested but without price agreements) with sellers"	40	25	14	0
"agree on deals (prices and quantity) with transporters"	40	35	4	0
"agree on prices (plus quantity/quality) with buyers"	46	50	14	5
"request a showup (quantity requested but without price agreements) with buyers"	41	40	23	10
"follow-up payments with buyers/sellers"	75	100	34	25
Brokers				
"inform/transmit prices"	57	75	15	5
"agree on prices (plus quantity/quality) with sellers"	18	0	0	0
"request a showup (quantity requested but without price agreements) with sellers"	35	0	12	0
"agree on deals (prices and quantity) with transporters"	39	25	5	0

(continued)

TABLE 12.1 Continued

Use of phone	Percentage of traders and brokers			
	Mean	Median	Mean	Median
Use of phone	*"Are mobile phones used to"?*		*"Were fixed phones used to"?*	
Brokers				
"agree on prices (plus quantity/quality) with buyers"	15	0	2	0
"request a showup (quantity requested but without price agreements) with buyers"	40	10	14	0
"follow-up payments with buyers/sellers"	47	30	17	0
Number of observations	25		25	

Source: Authors' compilation from focus group interviews.

lacking, and as a result, it is likely that buyers may wish to inspect the produce personally before sealing a deal. A large majority of traders use phones to follow up on payments of traders and buyers. This number is much lower for brokers, possibly because their transactions are less likely to involve extending credit. Compared to the situation before mobile phones were introduced, it is clear that more information is obtained and more deals are struck by phone. Indeed, more than twice as many teff traders and brokers use their mobile phones today for conveying price information and for making deals with sellers, buyers, and transporters than did so with fixed-line phones when these were the only available method in telecommunications.

Finally, focus group participants were asked subjective questions about how the situation in teff trade has changed since mobile phones were introduced. While it is highly unlikely that mobile phones were the sole cause of the changes reported by the focus groups, the spread of mobile phones likely did contribute in some way. Most of the teff traders and brokers report interacting with more sellers, buyers, and transport brokers before making deals. Since physical location of the market matters less with mobile phone technology, traders and brokers appear to be bypassing wholesale markets in rural areas and in Addis Ababa. While the wholesale markets are not completely bypassed, the focus groups report that in rural areas this is occurring to a greater or less extent in 100 percent of the markets for traders and 82 percent for brokers. Furthermore, 60 percent of the trader and 64 percent of the broker focus groups report bypassing the Addis Ababa wholesale market. The traditional role that Addis Ababa has played as a clearinghouse in the teff trade in Ethiopia primarily because of its central geographical location and the lack of alternative roads (Gabre-Madhin 2001a) may therefore slowly be changing because of easier access to information and because of the improved road network.

Agricultural Technology and Agricultural Extension

A number of changes have taken place over the period studied that have led to increases in agricultural production. While part of the increased production appears to be driven by the expansion of cultivated land (Taffesse, Dorosh, and Gemessa 2013), and while the adoption of improved agricultural technologies in the country is rather low, there are some indicators that bode well for increased productivity. Foremost among these are the increasing availability and adoption of improved modern technologies and the widespread placement of extension agents. Undeniably, those in better-connected areas have greater access to these technologies and services (Minten et al. 2013).

First, although adoption rates for improved cereal seeds are low (as shown in official statistics), these rates are underestimated, and adoption has seemingly improved over the period studied (Spielman, Kelemwork, and Alemu 2011). Improved seeds have primarily been used with the cereals maize and wheat (Spielman, Kelemwork, and Alemu 2011), although the adoption of an improved teff (Quncho) seed variety accelerated in the latter part of the decade (Minten et al. 2013). Second, fertilizer consumption in Ethiopia grew from 140,000 metric tons in the early 1990s to about 650,000 metric tons in 2012, and the fertilized area dedicated to cereal production more than doubled over the decade (Rashid et al. 2013).

Third, the Ethiopian government has invested heavily in the expansion of the agricultural extension system. At the end of 2010, the government had placed 45,000 extension agents in villages. This compares to 2,500 and 15,000 extension agents in 1995 and 2002, respectively (Davis et al. 2010). With a target of three extension agents per kebele, Ethiopia has one of the largest extension agent–farmer ratios found in the world today (Davis et al. 2010).[16]

The details, shown in Table 12.2, provide a summary of the possible covariates of structural transformation in Ethiopia's cereal markets and how they changed over the period studied. In all cases, important changes are noticeable.

---

16 While there are questions on the efficacy of this system (Davis et al. 2010), evaluations have shown that access to extension did positively affect agricultural yields (Dercon et al. 2009) and adoption of improved technologies (Krishnan and Patnam 2012).

TABLE 12.2 Changes in structural factors over 2001–2011

Driver	Number of observations	Average 2001–2005	Average 2006–2011
1. Economic growth			
GDP per capita (constant 2005 US$, PPP)	10	6.7	10.6
2. Urbanization/commercial surplus*			
Cereal trucks per week arriving			
in peak period	31	37	50
in lean period	31	15	21
3. Roads and transportation costs**			
Time taken to travel between markets (hours)	205	9.6	8.4
Real transportation costs between cereal wholesale markets (constant 2010 costs; birr/quintals per trip)	205	128	79
4. Mobile phones***			
Share of markets (%) where at the end of the period			
100% of teff traders are using mobile phones	25	12	100
50% of teff traders are using mobile phones	25	60	100
100% of teff brokers are using mobile phones	17	6	100
50% of teff brokers are using mobile phones	17	29	100
5. Agricultural technology			
Share of cereal land with improved seeds (%)	10	5	5
Share of fertilized cereal land (%)	10	47	51

Source: Authors' compilation from World Bank macroeconomic data (1); focus group discussions (2, 3, 4); CSA Agricultural Sample Surveys (5).

Note: * = 31 observations reflecting the 31 markets visited; ** = the 205 observations reflect the major effective product flows of the 31 surveyed wholesale markets with the other major wholesale markets (time and costs were only asked for those markets where there was an effective flow); *** = 25 teff wholesale market focus groups.

In short, the changes in the overall and agricultural economy are likely to manifest themselves in a number of predicted outcomes in teff markets. For example, increasing urbanization, increasing supply, and income growth is likely to lead to more quantities traded and greater economies of scale and thus lower margins. In addition, access to better price information should lead to a more efficient marketing system and consequently decrease overall margins. Finally, changes in food consumption patterns (see Chapter 2) due to income growth may be reflected in higher-quality premia, if such changes in the supply of high-quality products do not keep pace with the growing demand for these products. The next section addresses these questions, analyzing in particular spatial price variation, spatial market integration, quality premia, and margins (processing and retail) in teff markets.

Price Behavior

Spatial Price Variation

Ethiopia is characterized by a very diverse agroecology that results in different agricultural production and consumption patterns across the country and in spatial specialization (Chamberlin and Schmidt 2011; Ethiopia, CSA, EDRI, and IFPRI 2006). To better understand the spatial flows of teff in Ethiopia, the focus groups in the wholesale markets were asked questions about trucks arriving in and departing from their markets and about the types of loads carried. Using this information, it is possible to identify areas in Ethiopia that supply and receive teff. The supply base for teff is more diverse than for other cereals, but most of the demand comes from Addis Ababa, Dire Dawa, and Mekelle—three of the most important cities in the country.

To test the degree to which these flows are reflected in wholesale market price differences, the prices of produce from different markets to the Addis Ababa market (the default market) are compared using the model described in equation (1) at the beginning of this chapter. Since the dependent variable (real price of teff in market *j*) is expressed in logs, the reported coefficients for the market dummies in Table 12.3 show the relative difference in real prices compared to the Addis Ababa market (the left-out category). In a second specification the analysis period is effectively split into two parts (2001–2005 and 2006–2011). This is done by including a dummy for the latter period separately and interacting it with all of the other coefficients in the model. The Addis Ababa market in the first and second period are therefore the default markets. The structural change is tested by comparing price differences in the first period to those in the second period (significant changes are highlighted in gray in Table 12.3). In particular, it is the price changes that are of interest from the major supplying areas—with the price of the Ambo market taken as an indicator for these—to the other markets. Significant changes at the 5 percent level over the period are shaded in Table 12.3.

Three salient points arise from the results in Table 12.3. First, although Addis Ababa is Ethiopia's biggest city, teff prices are not always at their highest there. For example, prices tend to be higher in teff deficit areas such as the eastern city of Dire Dawa, where the prices of teff are 12 percent higher than

TABLE 12.3 Regional wholesale price differences compared to Addis Ababa (results of coefficients of regression)

†	Market	Dummy time interaction	Teff Coefficient	Teff t-value
1	Ambo	none	**−0.05**	−5.61
	Assela	none	**0.02**	3.17
	Bale Robe	none	**0.08**	4.77
	Dessie	none	**0.04**	3.13
	Dire Dawa	none	**0.12**	7.49
	Gondar	none	0.00	0.29
	Jimma	none	**−0.04**	−3.35
	Mekelle	none	**0.08**	7.58
	Nazreth	none	0.00	0.28
	Nekemt	none	**−0.14**	−16.96
	Shashemene	none	−0.01	−0.48
2	Ambo	2001–2005	**−0.06**	−5.27
	Assela	2001–2005	**0.03**	2.51
	Bale Robe	2001–2005	0.03	1.18
	Dessie	2001–2005	**0.09**	3.97
	Dire Dawa	2001–2005	**0.18**	7.13
	Gondar	2001–2005	**0.08**	7.91
	Jimma	2001–2005	**−0.04**	−3.74

in Addis Ababa (see the first section of Table 12.3). In the northern cities of Mekelle and Dessie, teff is also significantly more expensive than in Addis Ababa.[17] Teff prices in major supply areas—such as Ambo—tend to be lower than in Addis Ababa.

Second, there are substantial changes in the relative ratios between the first and second halves of the decade (see the second section of Table 12.3), possibly reflecting the effective changes in transport costs between wholesale markets. Differences in teff prices relative to the major supply area declined significantly within 5 of the 11 markets. For two major demand "sinks," Mekelle and Dire Dawa (after Addis Ababa, these are the country's two biggest cities), price

17 Mekelle is the capital of Tigray region. Tigray is among the poorest and most vulnerable regions in the country, together with the pastoralist regions (Ethiopia, MoFED 2012). Dessie is the capital of the South Wollo zone. The population in this zone has been hit hard by several famines in the past (Graham, Rashid, and Malek 2012).

†	Market	Dummy time interaction	Teff	
			Coefficient	t-value
	Mekelle	2001–2005	**0.13**	13.38
	Nazreth	2001–2005	**0.02**	2.05
	Nekemt	2001–2005	**−0.17**	−13.01
	Shashemene	2001–2005	−0.03	−1.60
	Ambo	2006–2011	**−0.04**	−3.16
	Assela	2006–2011	**0.02**	2.01
	Bale Robe	2006–2011	**0.12**	6.03
	Dessie	2006–2011	0.00	0.34
	Dire Dawa	2006–2011	**0.07**	6.30
	Gondar	2006–2011	**−0.05**	−4.08
	Jimma	2006–2011	−0.04	−1.92
	Mekelle	2006–2011	**0.04**	3.52
	Nazreth	2006–2011	−0.01	−1.47
	Nekemt	2006–2011	**−0.12**	−13.54
	Shashemene	2006–2011	0.01	0.92

Source: Authors' calculations.

Note: † = model specification; Addis Ababa is the default market in all specifications; shaded values represent statistically significant differences at the 5 percent level between the 2001–2005 and 2005–2011 periods from that market to major supplying areas, which coefficients are underlined (teff; Ambo); shaded values indicate statistically significant differences at the 5 percent level between the 2001–2005 and 2005–2011 periods for the price differences between the supplying regions and the Addis Ababa (default) market; coefficients in **bold** are significant at the 5 percent level; robust white standard errors to within cluster (by quarter) correlation.

differences relative to Addis Ababa fell. Similar changes occurred between supply areas and Addis Ababa with respect to these price differences (see the Ambo market with a negative coefficient in Table 12.3) but to a lesser extent. Despite a lack of infrastructure improvements in some of the supplying areas, decreases in price differences are occurring, such as in Nekemt, where this difference has fallen significantly.

Third, the variation in price differences among the wholesale markets with respect to the Addis Ababa markets declined over time. The difference between the highest and the lowest price differences in the first half of the decade compared with the second half declined by 11 percentage points.

Spatial Price Integration

The degree to which cereal prices move together across markets throughout Ethiopia (that is, how well they are integrated) provides a measure of how well

TABLE 12.4 Degree of market integration of Addis Ababa with other teff wholesale markets, 2001–2011

Integration variables	Year	White teff	Mixed teff	Red teff
Total market pairs		6	6	6
% integrated markets	2001	50	50	50
	2011	83	100	100
Number of pairs where coefficient time trend is significant at 5% level		2	3	3
Half-life of adjustment to price changes (in weeks)	2001	4	12	9
	2011	3	6	7
Transaction cost (% average price)	2001	9	8	15
	2011	8	7	8

Source: Authors' calculations.

these markets function. Thus the integration of wholesale markets is analyzed by studying various market pairs for teff using the TAR model described in equation (3). In particular, Addis Ababa is paired with the five most important regional teff wholesale markets for each of the three teff qualities, thus reflecting major teff flows in the country.[18] Three important results stem from this market integration analysis (Table 12.4). First, there has been an improvement in market integration over the decade studied. In the aggregate, significantly more markets were integrated in 2011 than in 2001.[19] Furthermore, all of the most important markets for mixed teff and red teff were well integrated at the end of 2011, while only half were in 2001. Of the regional white teff markets, 83 percent were integrated with respect to the Addis Ababa market in 2011, compared with 50 percent in 2001.

Second, the speed of price adjustments has also improved considerably. This is illustrated in the average half-life of adjustment to price changes that declined significantly in 2011 compared with 2001. In other words, it now takes less time for teff prices between wholesale markets to adjust halfway

18 In the TAR model, unit root behavior in the transaction cost band is imposed by setting $\rho_{in} = 0$. This reduces the estimated model inside the band (if $-\theta_t \leq d_{t-1} \leq \theta_t$) from $\Delta d_t = \rho_{in} d_{t-1} + \varepsilon_t$ to $\Delta d_t = \varepsilon_t$. Consistent with the TAR model's requirement, all the markets considered for all categories of cereals are tested for a unit root and only those that are nonstationary in level terms and stationary in the price differences for any market pair were considered for the analysis.

19 A market pair is considered integrated when the price adjustment in one market in response to a shock in the other is statistically significant in the TAR model. It is considered well integrated when the estimated adjustment parameter is not statistically different from −1 (that is, prices in the two markets move in step with each other).

from deviations in long-run equilibrium prices than it did in 2001. Third, the transaction costs between markets estimated in the TAR model (that is, the thresholds) fell. Certainly the declines have sometimes been substantial, averaging nearly 50 percent for red teff between 2001 and 2011.[20] These declines have been slightly lower for other types of teff.

Quality Premia

When consumers become wealthier, they demand more high-quality food products. This often implies an increase in *willingness-to-pay* for quality for such products (for example, Vandeplas and Minten 2011). To gauge whether this is occurring in Ethiopia, the EGTE wholesale market price data are used to examine the levels of and trends in quality premia at the national level and in Addis Ababa. The color of the teff grain provides a measure of quality, and this is the only quality information available in the data. Although color is often only one characteristic of teff quality, Bekele and Ayele (2006) and Minten et al. (2013) find that it is an especially important associate of quality premia paid in the Ethiopian marketplace.

The results of the regression analysis on price premia (from equation [1]) and their evolution over time in Table 12.5 illustrate two points. First, quality premia do exist in the Ethiopian markets in that white cereals all command a premium over mixed-quality teff or red teff. These premia are as high as 27 percent for white teff over red teff in the national market. The price premia paid in Addis Ababa are generally higher than in other markets. Second, the quality premia change surprisingly little over time. In none of the cases are the changes between the first and second halves of the decade 2001–2010 significant. Moreover, the quality premia paid by consumers are stable or declining.

Processing Margins

Part of the supply chain that affects the transmission of prices from producers to consumers is the processing sector. To analyze how processing and milling margins have changed as part of the structural transformation of teff markets in Ethiopia, the prices of milled products such as flour are compared to the wholesale grain prices as described in the data and methodology section.

20 Unfortunately, no data are available on observed transaction costs between these markets. In the focus group interviews, respondents were asked about average transportation costs over the past year. From this, transportation costs (an important part of the transaction costs) as a share of average annual prices in Addis Ababa at the time of the survey are found to be as high as 7 percent for white teff, 8 percent for mixed teff, and 9 percent for red teff. These numbers are close to the transaction costs estimates from the price integration model (based on weekly data) and suggest that the results of the model are mostly consistent with these data.

TABLE 12.5 Quality premia of teff

	Compared to	Overall		Period 2001–2005		Period 2006–2010		F-test structural change	
		Coefficient	t-value	Coefficient	t-value	Coefficient	t-value	F-value	Prob>F
All markets									
Mixed teff	White teff	**−0.12**	−18.57	**−0.12**	−11.20	**−0.12**	−15.20	0.00	0.99
Red teff	White teff	**−0.27**	−24.52	**−0.28**	−14.27	**−0.26**	−22.42	1.14	0.29
Addis Ababa									
Mixed teff	White teff	**−0.11**	−9.43	**−0.12**	−6.58	**−0.11**	−6.80	0.36	0.55
Red teff	White teff	**−0.32**	−17.54	**−0.33**	−10.13	**−0.32**	−15.15	0.16	0.69

Source: Authors' calculations.

Note: Coefficients in **bold** are significant at the 5 percent level; robust white standard errors to within cluster (by quarter) correlation.

To test the extent to which prices of processed products changed over time relative to raw materials, changes in processing margins are examined. The model described in equation (2) is applied using retail price data for the Addis Ababa market as well as for all wholesale markets. Through this analysis flour margins are found to be declining over time (Table 12.6). This result may reflect an improvement in the milling sector.

Furthermore, changes in the milling sector are confirmed by secondary data from the Addis Ababa Trade and Industry Office Database. For example, the number of mills in the capital city increased substantially over the decade studied. While there was on average less than one mill per ward (kebele) in the middle of the decade, by 2011 there were five. Although part of this increase is probably due to a more formal approach within the milling sector, and consequently those informal mills are now being recorded in the data, this is however unlikely to explain the entire increase. A consequence of this growing number of mills may be an increase in competition and a relative reduction in milling costs. Retail data collected by CSA endorse this since the real price charged for milling cereals at the end of 2010 was 50 percent lower than it was a decade earlier.

Retail Margins

The final link in the supply chain affecting the transmission of prices from producers to consumers is at the retail level. To estimate the changes that have taken place at this level, retail margins are analyzed by using data collected by EGTE on retail pricing and merging these data with their wholesale price series. These retail price data are collected from traders who operate in or close

TABLE 12.6 Premium of flour over teff grain (measured as prices of teff flour retail to teff grain wholesale)

	Overall		Period 2001–2005		Period 2006–2010		F-test structural change	
	Coefficient	t-value	Coefficient	t-value	Coefficient	t-value	F-value	Prob>F
All markets								
Teff	**0.22**	13.62	**0.29**	19.76	**0.15**	7.90	**44.43**	0.00
Addis Ababa								
Teff	**0.31**	13.15	**0.37**	12.61	**0.24**	7.46	**10.89**	0.00

Source: Authors' calculations.

Note: Coefficients in **bold** are significant at the 5 percent level; robust white standard errors to within cluster (by quarter) correlation.

to the wholesale market and who sell directly to consumers. In many cases, however, these retail traders are also involved in wholesale activities.

There are two caveats with respect to the EGTE retail price data that deserve highlighting before examining the results. First, these retail data are only available through the end of 2009. Therefore, the retail margin analysis is limited to comparisons between the periods 2001–2005 and 2006–2009. Second, the retail data collected are not representative of the entire retail sector within the cities. This is because the data are only collected for those particular retail agents near to or in the wholesale markets. As such, they do not include retailers far away from wholesale markets, nor do they include the amalgam of retailers who supply cereals through their shops or supermarkets or especially through small mills. Nonetheless, despite these shortcomings, the data provide indications about the sizes of retail margins and how they evolve over time.

Three relevant findings emerge from the teff retail margin regressions in Table 12.7 for Addis Ababa and for all the markets for which the data were available. First, retail margins in Addis Ababa are significantly higher than in the rest of the country. This is not surprising, however, given the higher retail costs associated with a large city the size of Addis Ababa (for example, real estate costs and higher labor costs).[21] Second, retail margins have generally fallen over time. In the cases tested, the decline is significant. Furthermore, teff margins declined significantly in Addis Ababa. Indeed, the average retail margin fell by half in the capital city.

21 For example, Ethiopia, MoFED (2012) shows that nonfarm prices in Addis Ababa (mostly rent) are significantly higher than in the rest of the country.

TABLE 12.7 Retail margins for teff, 2001–2005 and 2006–2009

	Overall		Period 2001–2005		Period 2006–2009		F-test structural change	
	Coefficient	t-value	Coefficient	t-value	Coefficient	t-value	F-value	Prob>F
All markets	**0.016**	14.71	**0.018**	12.69	**0.014**	9.41	**4.12**	0.05
Addis Ababa	**0.043**	10.62	**0.056**	10.64	**0.028**	13.11	**24.52**	0.00

Source: Authors' calculations.

Note: Coefficients in **bold** are significant at the 5 percent level; robust white standard errors to within cluster (by quarter) correlation.

Conclusion

The structural transformational changes taking place in teff markets is associated with many possible reasons. In this chapter these changes as well as the changes themselves in terms of teff price behavior have been examined. A wholesale market survey was fielded at the beginning of 2012 and monthly price data were collected in major wholesale markets by the EGTE throughout the country. A number of findings come out of this analysis. First, quality premia among teff are found to exist, but these premia changed little over time. Second, the spatial variation in teff prices among wholesale markets and the margins between supplying and receiving markets have decreased significantly over time. Third, markets are becoming more spatially integrated as prices move together and co-vary among more markets since price adjustments take less time to establish. Fourth, retail and milling margins declined by half. Such price changes have been noted for most other major cereals in Ethiopia (Minten, Stifel, and Tamru 2012).

While better road conditions, declining transportation costs, and smaller marketing margins generally result in a more efficient agricultural economy, change inevitably results in both winners and losers. The winners are the suppliers in major production zones as they receive higher prices on average, while urban consumers in the big cities also benefit from the lower prices that result from lower margins. The losers are likely to be the net consumers residing near to or in the supplying areas as they might now be faced with higher prices. Furthermore, producers who reside close to the consuming areas may be worse off as they now face relatively lower prices. Nonetheless, the net gain for the economy as a whole from such market improvements is likely to be substantial (for example, Gardner 1975). Moreover, despite the high increase in the nominal commodity prices that could have benefited the net-sellers, the real prices for teff have not changed much (see Chapter 8). The same case exists for most other staples (Minten, Stifel, and Tamru 2012). Increases in prices may hurt the net-buyers, many in rural areas and almost all consumers in urban areas, but especially the poor or families around the poverty line.

While these findings are overall encouraging for Ethiopia, there is still significant room for market improvement. First, despite the large sums of money invested in road improvements, Ethiopia started from a low base and still has one of the lowest road densities in the world (von Braun and Olofinbiyi 2007). Second, even when roads are constructed, transport costs are still relatively high compared with some other countries, and further measures are needed to reduce transportation costs (Teravaninthon and Raballand 2009). Third, while access to information is now widely available for traders and brokers, the use of mobile phones by farmers is still one of the lowest in Africa (Nakasone, Torero, and Minten 2014). Fourth, although modern input adoption has improved considerably, adoption levels, especially of improved seeds, are still low often because of the lack of supply.

References

Aker, J. C., and M. Fafchamps. 2014. "Mobile Phone Coverage and Producer Markets: Evidence from West Africa." *World Bank Economic Review* 29 (2): 262–292.

Bekele, A., and G. Ayele. 2006. *Market Price Index for Quality Characteristics of Teff: A Hedonic Price Analysis of Six Markets in the Eastern Shewa*. Addis Ababa: Ethiopian Development Research Institute (EDRI).

Chamberlin, J., and E. Schmidt. 2011. *Ethiopian Agriculture: A Dynamic Geographic Perspective.* Ethiopia Strategy Support Program (ESSP) II Working Paper 17. Addis Ababa: International Food Policy Research Institute (IFPRI)/ESSP II.

Davis, K., B. Swanson, D. Amudavi, D. Mekonnen, A. Flohrs, J. Riese, C. Lamb, and E. Zerfu. 2010. *In-Depth Assessment of the Public Agricultural Extension System of Ethiopia and Recommendations for Impact.* IFPRI Discussion Paper 1041. Washington, DC: IFPRI.

Dercon, S., D. O. Gilligan, J. Hoddinott, and T. Woldehanna. 2009. "The Impact of Agricultural Extension and Roads on Poverty and Consumption Growth in Fifteen Ethiopian Villages." *American Journal of Agricultural Economics* 91 (4): 1007–1021.

Drèze, J., and A. Sen. 1989. *Hunger and Public Action.* Oxford, UK: Clarendon Press.

Ethiopia, CSA (Central Statistical Agency), EDRI (Ethiopian Development Research Institute), and IFPRI (International Food Policy Research Institute). 2006. *Atlas of the Ethiopian Rural Economy.* Addis Ababa, Ethiopia: CSA, EDRI, and IFPRI.

Ethiopia, MoFED (Ministry of Finance and Economic Development). 2008. *Dynamics of Growth and Poverty in Ethiopia (1995/96–2004/05)*. Photocopy. Addis Ababa.

———. 2012. *Ethiopia's Progress towards Eradicating Poverty: An Interim Report on Poverty Analysis Study (2010/2011)*. Addis Ababa.

Gabre-Madhin, E. Z. 2001a. *Market Institutions, Transaction Costs, and Social Capital in the Ethiopian Grain Market*. IFPRI Research Report 124. Washington, DC: IFPRI.

Gardner, B. L. 1975. "The Farm-Retail Spread in a Competitive Food Industry." *American Journal of Agricultural Economics* 57 (3): 399–409.

Graham, J., S. Rashid, and M. Malek. 2012. "Disaster Response and Emergency Risk Management in Ethiopia." In *Food and Agriculture in Ethiopia: Progress and Policy Challenges*, edited by P. Dorosh and S. Rashid. Philadelphia: University of Pennsylvania Press.

Headey, D., S. Malaiyandi, and S. Fan. 2010. "Navigating the Perfect Storm: Reflections on the Food, Energy, and Financial Crises." *Agricultural Economics* 41 (s1): 217–228.

Jensen, R. 2007. "The Digital Provide: Information (Technology), Market Performance, and Welfare in the South Indian Fisheries Sector." *Quarterly Journal of Economics* 127 (3): 879–924.

Kojima, M. 2009. *Government Response to Oil Supply Volatility*. Extractive Industries for Development Series 10. Washington, DC: World Bank.

Krishnan, P., and M. Patnam. 2012. *Neighbours and Extension Agents in Ethiopia: Who Matters More for Technology Diffusion?* IGC Working Paper 12/0159. London: International Growth Centre.

Kuma, T. 2010. *Analyzing Changes in Food Consumption Patterns in Urban Ethiopia*. EDRI Working Paper 2. Addis Ababa: Ethiopian Development Research Institute.

Minot, N., and D. Roy. 2007. *Impact of High-Value Agriculture and Modern Marketing Channels on Poverty: An Analytical Framework*. Photocopy. Washington, DC: IFPRI.

Minten, B., D. Stifel, and S. Tamru. 2012. *Structural Transformation in Ethiopia: Evidence from Cereal Markets*. ESSP II Working Paper 39. Addis Ababa: IFPRI/ESSP II.

Minten, B., S. Tamru, E. Engida Legesse, and T. Kuma. 2013. *Ethiopia's Value Chains on the Move: The Case of Teff.* ESSP II Working Paper 52. Addis Ababa: IFPRI/ESSP II.

Minten, B., S. Tamru, and D. Stifel. 2014. "Structural Transformation in Cereal Markets in Ethiopia." *Journal of Development Studies* 50 (5): 611–629.

Nakasone, E., M. Torero, and B. Minten. 2014. "The Power of Information: The ICT Revolution in Agricultural Development." *Annual Review of Resource Economics* 6: 533–550.

Rashid, S., N. Tefera, N. Minot, and G. Ayele. 2013. "Can Modern Input Use Be Promoted without Subsidies? An Analysis of Fertilizers in Ethiopia." *Agricultural Economics* 44 (6): 595–611.

Ravallion, M. 1987. *Markets and Famines*. Oxford, UK: Clarendon Press.

Reardon, T., and C. P. Timmer. 2007. "Transformation of Markets for Agricultural Output in Developing Countries since 1950: How Has Thinking Changed?" In *Handbook of Agricultural Economics*. Vol. 3, edited by R. E. Evenson and P. Pingali. Amsterdam: Elsevier Press.

Rivers, J., J. Holt, J. Seaman, and M. Bowden. 1976. "Lessons from Epidemiology from the Ethiopian Famines." *Annals de la Societé. Belge Médicale Tropicale* 56 (4–5): 345–357.

Schmidt, E., and M. Kedir Jemal. 2009. *Urbanization and Spatial Connectivity in Ethiopia: Urban Growth Analysis Using GIS*. ESSP II Working Paper 3. Addis Ababa: IFPRI/ESSP II.

Shin, M. 2010. "A Geospatial Analysis of Market Integration: The Case of the 2004/05 Food Crisis in Niger." *Food Security* 2: 261–269.

Spielman, D. J., D. Kelemwork, and D. Alemu. 2011. *Seed, Fertilizer, and Agricultural Extension in Ethiopia*. ESSP II Working Paper 20. Addis Ababa: IFPRI/ESSP II.

Tafere, K., A. S. Taffesse, and S. Tamru. 2010. *Food Demand Elasticities in Ethiopia: Estimates Using Household Income, Consumption and Expenditure (HICE) Survey Data*. ESSP II Working Paper 11. Addis Ababa: IFPRI/ESSP II.

Taffesse, A. S., P. Dorosh, and S. A. Gemessa. 2013. "Crop Production in Ethiopia: Regional Patterns and Trends." In *Food and Agriculture in Ethiopia: Progress and Policy Challenges*, edited by P. Dorosh and S. Rashid, 89–129. Philadelphia: University of Pennsylvania Press.

Teravaninthon, S., and G. Raballand. 2009. *Transport Prices and Costs in Africa: A Review of the International Corridors*. Washington, DC: World Bank.

Van Campenhout, B. 2007. "Modeling Trends in Food Market Integration: Methods and an Application to Tanzanian Maize Markets." *Food Policy* 32: 112–127.

Vandeplas, A., and B. Minten. 2011. *Food Quality in Domestic Markets of Developing Economies: A Comparative Study of Two Countries*. LICOS Discussion Papers 28911. Leuven, Belgium: LICOS–Centre for Institutions and Economic Performance, K.U. Leuven.

von Braun, J., and T. Olofinbiyi. 2007. "Famine and Food Insecurity in Ethiopia." In *Case Study 7-4 of the Program: Food Policy for Developing Countries: The Role of Government in the Global Food System*, edited by P. Pinstrup-Andersen and F. Cheng. Ithaca, NY, US: Cornell University.

Chapter 13

DYNAMICS IN TEFF VALUE CHAINS

Bart Minten, Seneshaw Tamru, Ermias Engida Legesse, and Tadesse Kuma

The purpose of this chapter is to understand the changes that have been happening in the teff value chain in Ethiopia based on carefully fielded primary stacked surveys at different layers in the value chain.[1] This chapter uses the same data as in Chapter 11 and takes a dynamic angle on the teff sector, as was presented in Chapter 12. However, the scope of the analysis is much broader than in the previous market-focused chapter. In this chapter the dynamics are examined in detail, focusing closely on what exactly has been happening, beyond output markets, in technology adoption upstream in the value chain and downstream, at service delivery, competition, mixing teff with other cereals in the preparation of injera, and changes in the food service industry.

Since 2001, very rapid changes have been seen in various stages of the teff value chain. Upstream, quick adoption of new varieties is found, though from a low starting point, as well as an increasing use of chemical fertilizer, especially by those farmers living close to urban centers. Downstream, the milling sector is being transformed toward one-stop shops that provide different additional services and more efficient processing systems, as illustrated by the declining milling margins. Quality requirements are transforming throughout the chain, with an increasing trade in more expensive teff varieties. There is a notable smaller share of marketing costs in the final retail price, which indicates improvements in marketing efficiency. These rapid changes in the teff value chain seem to be driven by a number of factors, including public investments in agriculture (especially agricultural extension), income growth, urbanization, and improved communication and transport infrastructure.

1 This chapter is based on Minten et al. (2016). This is reprinted by permission of the publisher (Taylor & Francis Ltd, www.tandfonline.com).

Data and Methodology

This chapter focuses on how the teff value chain is transforming. To develop a better understanding, data are used from major teff-producing areas and follow the value chain from these teff-producing areas to Addis Ababa, the capital of Ethiopia and, along with its metropolitan area, home to approximately 4 million people. To gather this information, interviews were conducted with key informants in the value chain in September and October 2012. This information was used to design questionnaires for each level in the value chain. These questionnaires were then fielded at the end of 2012 (November and December). The instruments deployed included surveys upstream in the value chain with 1,200 teff producers and communities, midstream with rural and urban wholesalers and truckers, and downstream with cereal shops, mills, and cooperative retail. A detailed overview of the dataset is given in Chapter 11. We rely on these datasets for this chapter given the high quality of the data collected, the specific information on teff, and the recall questions over a longer period that were included in these different instruments that allow us to assess dynamism in this sector.

An important factor in any food market is quality. The most widespread distinguishing quality property used in the teff value chain in Ethiopia relates to the color of the grain (see Chapter 3 for more details). The distinction between magna ("superwhite"), white, mixed, and red teff is widely used and well known by farmers as well as by traders, and therefore this color differentiator will be used as a measure for quality throughout this chapter. The quality of teff is often evaluated by its origin, and by a number of other factors too, such as physical appearance, impurities, aroma, texture, and nutritional quality, although these are often difficult to measure objectively.

Teff Upstream in the Value Chain

Changes

Table 13.1 shows the self-reported changes during 2001–2011 for the farmers who were part of the survey. Tillage frequency per season is on average high (4.4 times). As teff seeds are small, germination is hard in unbroken soil. Farmers have not changed their tilling behavior over time, despite recommendations by Ethiopia's Ministry of Agriculture to reduce tilling as well as a number of extension efforts for the no-tilling method (an improved method to better preserve soil structure). Broadcasting is the common method used for teff sowing. Seed rates with this method are high—on average between

TABLE 13.1 Changes in production practices, 2001–2011

Production practices	Unit	Number of observations	10 years prior to survey*	At time of survey	T-test**	
					t-value	Pr(|T|>|t|)
Traditional production factors						
Number of tillings	number	1,200	4.0	4.4	11.78	**0.00**
Seed use:						
Red or black teff	kilograms per hectare	380	46.9	48.7	3.92	**0.00**
Mixed teff	kilograms per hectare	141	44.3	45.0	1.91	**0.06**
White teff	kilograms per hectare	593	44.4	43.0	−0.60	0.55
Magna teff	kilograms per hectare	91	44.4	41.9	−0.24	0.81
Number of weedings	number	1,199	1.5	1.3	−7.87	**0.00**
Modern inputs						
Adoption of improved seed	share (%)	1,199	6.5	35.2	−21.22	**0.00**
Use of chemical fertilizer:						
DAP	kilograms per hectare	1,128	50.6	87.9	21.26	**0.00**
urea	kilograms per hectare	1,121	35.0	63.8	18.31	**0.00**
Adoption of herbicides	share (%)	1,197	31.0	62.9	−22.52	**0.00**
Adoption of pesticides	share (%)	1,197	3.9	11.5	−9.28	**0.00**
Type of teff						
Farmers' interviews:						
Red teff	share (%)	1,200	36.0	19.7	−16.28	**0.00**
Mixed teff	share (%)	1,200	15.8	10.7	−6.20	**0.00**
White teff	share (%)	1,200	42.6	54.9	10.54	**0.00**
Magna teff	share (%)	1,200	5.6	14.7	10.68	**0.00**
Community focus group interviews:						
Red teff	share (%)	60	32.7	14.4	−6.28	**0.00**
Mixed teff	share (%)	60	31.8	21.6	−3.77	**0.00**
White teff	share (%)	60	26.5	40.2	3.62	**0.00**
Magna teff	share (%)	60	7.7	24.3	5.97	**0.00**

Source: Authors' calculations.

Note: * As correct weighing factors for the situation 10 years prior to the survey are unknown, the extrapolation factors at the time of the survey were used for 10 years prior to the survey as a best approximation. ** Significant values at the 5 percent level are highlighted in **bold**.

40 kilograms and 50 kilograms per hectare—and they have changed little over time. If anything, an increase of seed rates over time is seen. Teff weeding is a laborious task that is critical for teff productivity. A slight but significant decline has been found following the increased use of herbicide. Overall, little change is found over time in these production practices.

The second part of Table 13.1 reviews modern input use. The increasing use of herbicide (usually the 2-4-D herbicide) has helped to control the development of broadleaf weeds. A significant change in the number of teff farmers using herbicides has occurred, rising from 31 percent 10 years earlier to 63 percent at the time of the survey (Fufa et al. 2011). Pesticide use increased from 4 percent of the farmers to 11 percent. Ten years prior to the survey, 7 percent of teff farmers used improved teff seeds.[2] This had increased to 35 percent of the farmers at the time of the survey. The use of chemical fertilizer increased from 51 kilograms of DAP and 35 kilograms of urea per hectare 10 years before the survey to 88 and 64 kilograms, respectively, at the time of the survey, on average almost a doubling of the amount of fertilizer used.

Over time, large changes in the type of teff produced are observed—in particular, an increasing importance of magna and white teff at the expense of red and mixed teff. Reports from the farmers suggest that magna and white teff combined made up 49 percent 10 years before the survey. This had increased at the time of the interview to 70 percent, an increase of 21 percent. The share of red teff in production declined from 36 percent of total production to 20 percent. Similar changes were noted in focus group interviews at the kebele level (the bottom of Table 13.1). The majority of the red teff was grown for own consumption, explaining the lower shares of red teff in the commercial surplus compared to the production by farmers. The move away from growing red and mixed toward white and magna teff is significant in all cases, as shown by a t-test.

There are several reasons for the decline in the importance of red teff over time. First, the prices for red teff are significantly lower than for white teff, providing farmers an incentive to focus on white teff to increase their income. These higher prices of white teff seem to be driven by a number of factors, including lower conversion ratios of red teff for the production of injera.[3] Other factors include the longer shelf life of white teff injera (as confirmed by

2 This is in the perception of farmers, as it is often not clear after a couple of generations if varieties are improved or not.

3 Key informants indicated that 500 injeras can be made from 1 quintal of red teff. This compares to 600 to 700 injeras from white teff.

the majority of mills), indicating possible higher premiums for this trait, and the preferences of urban consumers for white teff if incomes allow.[4] Second, while red teff traditionally used to have higher productivity than white teff, this is now changing as high-performing white varieties (especially Quncho) have recently become available. However, only very few improved red varieties are currently available (Fufa et al. 2011).

Adoption of Modern Inputs

With more modern inputs used in farming practices, more in-depth analysis is being undertaken to help improve understanding of this visible change. The adoption of improved seeds has spread quickly over the 10-year period studied, but it is especially the Quncho (DZ-Cr-387) variety that is now widely adopted in these major teff production zones.[5] The quick spread of Quncho is remarkable given that the variety was only released recently. The first farmers in the survey zone only adopted Quncho in 2010, three years prior to the survey. Teff farmers were questioned about their adoption of Quncho (Table 13.2), and 32 percent of the teff farmers stated that they used Quncho at some point. For those who used it, it was currently being used on 83 percent of the white teff area. There was a multitude of stated reasons for the adoption of Quncho, including higher yields, lower seed rates, longer straw, and stronger stem. As Quncho is a white teff, it fetches a significantly higher price than mixed or red teff, making it attractive for the farmer. The major reasons given for not using Quncho or improved seed at all, or for using less improved seed than desired, is the lack of supply. This is in contrast with chemical fertilizer, where a lack of cash is the most common constraint (Table 13.2).

Figure 13.1 shows how the adoption of modern inputs varies over the distance to Addis Ababa. Both panels show a clear spatial pattern. Households that are located near Addis Ababa are more readily adopting Quncho. While more than 40 percent of the teff area is planted with Quncho for close-by areas, this drops to almost 0 for the areas farthest out. This distance association likely indicates better access to improved varieties as well as better incentives for the adoption of such varieties. Figure 13.1 also shows the stated

4 There is, however, an increasing perception with richer customers that red teff has major health benefits (presumably because of higher iron content), and 65 percent of the retailers "agreed" or "strongly agreed" with the statement that "red teff is increasingly being bought by rich consumers who are concerned about their health."

5 Quncho is a combination of the magna quality DZ-01-196 and the white quality DZ-01-974. It seems to have been successful because it combines the preferred magna characteristics of the DZ-01-196 and better yield performance of DZ-01-974 (Fufa et al. 2011).

TABLE 13.2 Statistics for takeup of Quncho and chemical fertilizer, 2001–2011

Quncho statistics	Unit	Chemical fertilizer	Improved teff seed
Household ever used Quncho	%	n.a.	32
If yes:			
Household used Quncho in 2011/2012 (meher/belg 2011/2012)	%	n.a.	76
Number of years since the household used Quncho	number	n.a.	2
Part of white teff area where the household uses Quncho	%	n.a.	83
Perceived advantages of Quncho compared to other white teff varieties:			
Higher yield	%	n.a.	89
Lower seed rates	%	n.a.	83
Better price	%	n.a.	91
Straw is longer; there is more fodder	%	n.a.	89
Stem is stronger; there is less lodging*	%	n.a.	87
Household used modern inputs in meher/belg 2011/2012	%	93	34
For nonusers:			
Major reason for not using modern inputs:			
No need because soil is good enough	%	22	0
I don't know how to best apply them	%	4	17
I was unable to find them	%	2	34
The quality of modern inputs is not good	%	0	3
There is too much hassle/transaction costs to obtain modern inputs	%	1	4
Modern inputs are too expensive	%	9	7
I lack the money at the time of need	%	33	12
Lack of transportation	%	0	0
I am happy with the traditional seeds	%	n.a.	15
Other	%	29	1
Farmers tried to buy modern inputs but could not obtain them	% yes	13	18
For users:			
Farmer was able to buy as many modern inputs as desired	% yes	69	75
Reason for not buying as many modern inputs as desired			
I was unable to find more	%	10	65
There is too much hassle/transaction costs to obtain modern inputs	%	5	19
I lacked the money at the time of purchase	%	85	16
Lack of transportation	%	0	0
Other	%	0	0

Source: Authors' calculations.

Note: n.a. = not applicable. * Lodging is the falling over of the plant stem at maturity, as it cannot support the weight of the grain formed.

FIGURE 13.1 Chemical fertilizer use and Quncho adoption by distance to Addis Ababa

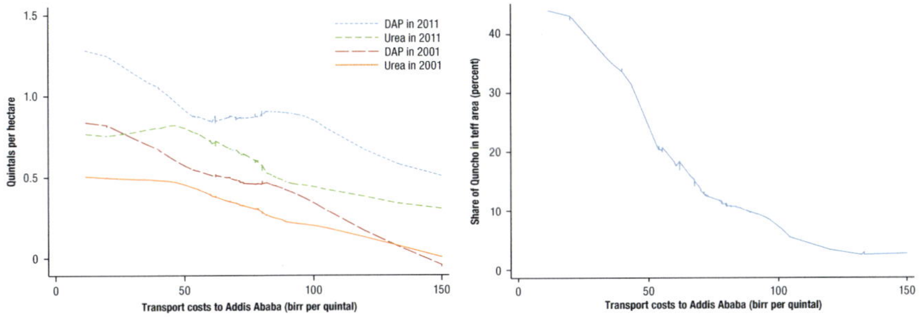

Source: Authors' calculations.

changes in adoption of chemical fertilizer per hectare and shows how more fertilizer use is especially prevalent in areas closer to Addis Ababa, indicating most intensification of agriculture—as measured through the increasing use of chemical fertilizers—is taking place in these well-connected areas. Such patterns are also seen in other settings (Reardon et al. 2012; Wiggins 2000).[6] The increasing use of fertilizer seems driven by the better access to fertilizers, incentives (through the higher relative prices of teff over time [Minten, Stifel, and Tamru 2012]), and the better knowledge of its use through efforts of extension agents (see later in the chapter).

To further understand what factors are driving adoption of modern inputs, a double hurdle regression model (Cragg 1971) is run. Modern input adoption at the plot level is used as a dependent variable along with plot and household characteristics and independent variables such as transport costs to the major market (that is, Addis Ababa) and to cooperatives. In such a setup, the "first hurdle" is used to estimate the factors associated with modern input use on a specific plot, while the "second hurdle" analyzes associates of the quantities of modern inputs used conditional on being used.[7] Table 13.3 illustrates the associates of the adoption of these new technologies.

The results of this model show that distance to Addis Ababa affects both the choice to adopt chemical fertilizers and improved seed as well as the

6 While the recommended rate of fertilizer use in teff production is 100 kilograms of DAP and 100 kilograms of urea per hectare (Kenea, Ayele, and Negatu 2001), a minority of farmers do this in practice.

7 Ricker-Gilbert, Jayne, and Chirwa (2011) argue that this is often the most appropriate way to model modern input use in Africa, especially given the large number of farmers who do not use modern inputs and consequently given the importance of modeling nonusers correctly in such situations.

TABLE 13.3 Associates of Quncho and fertilizer adoption, 2011

		Chemical fertilizer		Quncho	
	Unit	Coefficients	z-value*	Coefficients	z-value*
Use (yes/no) of modern inputs					
Transport costs to/from Addis Ababa	log(birr)	−0.51	**−3.04**	−0.95	**−9.88**
Distance to nearest cooperative	log(minutes)	−0.20	**−2.68**	−0.13	**−2.45**
Characteristics of plot					
Altitude	meters	0.00	**6.48**	0.00	1.48
Share red soil	share	−0.25	−1.17	−0.29	**−1.73**
Share brown soil	share	−0.16	−0.75	0.02	0.11
Share black soil	share	−0.12	−0.58	−0.14	−0.78
Share flat land	share	0.01	0.02	0.62	1.72
Share slightly sloped land	share	−0.59	**−1.69**	0.04	0.10
Characteristics of household					
Gender of head of household	male = 1	−0.44	−1.61	−0.02	−0.10
Age of head of household in years	years	0.00	0.21	0.00	0.15
Education of head of household	years	0.02	**1.94**	0.01	**1.83**
Size of household	number	0.00	−0.11	−0.03	−1.35
Household owns a mobile phone	yes = 1	0.68	**3.94**	0.37	**3.56**
Household owns a donkey	yes = 1	0.67	**5.39**	0.31	**2.95**
Total land owned	hectares	−0.01	−0.20	−0.12	**−3.60**
Household received visit of extension agent in past two years	yes = 1	0.06	0.46	0.33	**2.98**
Household is a member of the cooperative	yes = 1	0.19	1.53	0.21	**2.14**
Household is a model farmer	yes = 1	−0.05	−0.35	0.18	**1.78**
Intercept		0.96	0.97	2.18	**2.99**
Quantity used of modern inputs (kilogram for fertilizer; % of teff area for Quncho)					
Transport costs to/from Addis Ababa	log(birr)	−49.52	**−4.91**	0.52	0.14
Distance to nearest cooperative	log(minutes)	−16.31	**−2.87**	−2.35	−0.99
Characteristics of plot					
Altitude	meters	0.13	**6.02**	−0.01	−1.14
Share red soil	share	−20.25	−1.03	18.22	**2.12**
Share brown soil	share	50.26	**2.58**	4.52	0.58
Share black soil	share	16.17	0.93	−9.63	−1.38
Share flat land	share	81.80	**2.26**	−12.76	−0.82
Share slightly sloped land	share	45.20	1.19	−7.83	−0.46

	Unit	Chemical fertilizer		Quncho	
		Coefficients	z-value*	Coefficients	z-value*
Characteristics of household					
Gender of head of household	male = 1	−20.73	−0.96	0.39	0.05
Age of head of household in years	years	0.83	**2.21**	0.31	**2.04**
Education of head of household	years	0.37	0.47	0.25	0.88
Size of household	number	−7.70	**−3.25**	−0.60	−0.63
Household owns a mobile phone	yes = 1	5.86	0.51	−0.79	−0.20
Household owns a donkey	yes = 1	42.09	**3.67**	−4.91	−1.04
Total land owned	hectares	−25.37	**−6.21**	−3.35	**−2.34**
Household received visit of extension agent in past two years	yes = 1	15.71	1.36	5.91	1.21
Household is a member of the cooperative	yes = 1	31.29	**2.90**	−2.22	−0.54
Household is a model farmer	yes = 1	22.04	**2.03**	−16.74	**−4.11**
Intercept		52.16	0.67	116.06	**3.81**
Sigma		125.14	**28.19**	28.23	**21.73**
Number of observations		1,197		1,199	
Wald chi2()		125.95		217.64	
Prob>chi2		0.00		0.00	
Average partial effect, APE (100 iterations)					
Transport costs to/from Addis Ababa	log(birr)	−38.29	**−6.06**	−17.26	**−7.98**
Distance to nearest cooperative	log(minutes)	−13.16	**−4.06**	−2.99	**−3.07**

Source: Authors' calculations.
Note: * z-values of coefficients that are significant at the 5 percent level are in **bold**.

quantity of chemical fertilizer applied. However, it does not significantly affect the quantity used of improved teff seed. To assess the magnitude of these effects, at the bottom of Table 13.3 the average partial effects (APE) of transport costs to Addis Ababa is recorded. These reflect the overall—including both the first and second hurdles—link with modern input use.[8] The highly significant result of 38 for the unconditional APE of transport costs on chemical fertilizer use indicates that a doubling of the transport costs to Addis Ababa reduces the fertilizer use by 38 kilograms per hectare. In the case of Quncho teff seeds, the share of the area planted declines by 17 percent, with a doubling of the transport costs to Addis Ababa. These links of transport costs from urban centers with the adoption of modern inputs are thus substantial.

8 Standard errors for the unconditional APE were obtained from bootstrapping the model with 100 repetitions.

Similar results are found for distances to cooperative unions, the often exclusive distributors of modern inputs. A doubling of the distance to cooperative unions reduces the fertilizer use by 13 kilograms per hectare and the share of teff area planted with Quncho by 3 percent.

Teff Downstream in the Value Chain

Service Delivery and Competition

Retailing of teff in Addis Ababa is mostly done by mills: they account for 70 percent of all the teff sold in Addis Ababa, while cereal shops and consumer cooperatives make up the remaining 18 percent and 9 percent respectively (Woldu et al. 2013). Over the period studied, several changes occurred in the procurement, processing, and milling of teff in Addis Ababa. First, traditionally mills only ground the teff grain; households typically would buy teff from a cereal shop or a market, take the teff home for cleaning, get the teff milled at the mill, and then prepare the injera at home (as is still commonly the case in smaller and less-developed towns as well as in rural areas). This traditional pattern has changed in Addis Ababa, with mills increasingly becoming one-stop shops. Most of them are now delivering different services, including sales of a wide range of cereals (and sometimes other products), cleaning of these cereals, plus transport services. In Table 13.4 unweighted averages are presented for the retail shops in the panel survey—that is, those that existed at the beginning of the period studied—as well as weighted averages for the complete sample at the time of the survey. Conversely, over time a large number of cereal shops have started adding milling and cleaning to the services they offer consumers.

Second, there seems to be increasing competition between retail outlets. Retail outlets were asked to estimate the number of mills and cereal shops that existed in the kebele ten years before and at the time of the survey. A significant increase is seen, from six to ten mills and three to four cereal shops per kebele (Table 13.4). While 30 percent of the retail shops stated that queuing was a problem 10 years prior to the survey, often because of the lack of mills, only 17 percent of the retail shops indicated that this was a problem at the time of the survey. The increasing competition is further confirmed through qualitative statements, with the majority of the urban retailers responding "strongly agreed" or "agreed" to the statement that the competition between mills has increased over time. The rapid emergence of teff retail shops is further illustrated by analyzing their start-up dates, with 50 percent of the mills being established five years previously.

Third, some retailers procure teff directly from rural areas and thereby cut out urban wholesale markets. However, this phenomenon is still rather rare. Using unweighted averages of the panel retail shops, it is estimated that 83 percent of the teff supplies are obtained on urban wholesale markets and few changes are seen over time. Direct rural procurement is especially undertaken by the larger retailers, as shown in the weighted averages of the procurement sources (Table 13.4). Using this latter method, it is estimated that 27 percent of the teff sold in Addis Ababa does not go through the urban wholesale markets. The investments in shop premises, mills, and stocks of cereals illustrate that some upscaling has been occurring in the downstream portion of the teff value chain, requiring relatively heavy capital investments for some retailers. The significance of these investments by retailers is shown in Table 13.1 (earlier in the chapter), by the higher value of their assets relative to those of other agents in the value chain.

Mixing with Other Cereals

Teff is often and increasingly mixed with other cereals for the preparation of injera. The proportions of mixing with other cereals seem driven by preferences (often linked to the origin of consumers), prices of other cereals, as well as by changing conversion rates from flour to injera when mixed.[9] As seen in Table 13.4, mixing of teff with other cereals is on the rise. For example, while 22 percent of urban customers mixed teff with sorghum 10 years prior to the survey, this had increased to 26 percent at the time of the survey. Increases in the proportion of customers mixing teff with rice and with maize are equally seen as well: from 8 percent to 21 percent in the case of rice and from 8 percent to 12 percent in the case of maize. This mixing seems to explain the strong correlation of teff prices with other cereal prices that is typically seen as customers seemingly readily substitute in other cereals depending on relative price changes (Rashid 2011).

Table 13.5 shows to what extent poor consumers—as subjectively defined by the retail shop owner—consume different types of teff compared to the rich. While the rich consume almost exclusively *(text continued on page 340)*

9 While the chapter authors are not aware of any research on this, this seems to be the common perception, as 60 percent of the retailers "agreed" or "strongly agreed" that "One can get more injera out of a quintal if teff is mixed with other cereals; the conversion rate is higher if teff is mixed with other cereals."

TABLE 13.4 Operational changes of the teff retail outlets since 2001

		Panel—unweighted			Paired T-test**		Full sample		Unpaired T-test**	
					10 years ago versus now				10 years ago versus now	
	Unit	Number of observations	10 years prior to survey	At survey	t-value	Pr(|T|>|t|)	Number of observations	At survey (weighted)	t-value	Pr(|T|>|t|)
Technology and products sold per outlet										
Number of milling machines per outlet	number	100	3.1	3.3	4.42	**0.00**	256	2.8	−0.60	0.55
Number of crops sold in outlet	number	106	6.2	7.4	4.45	**0.00**	280	8.2	2.66	**0.00**
Services*										
Share of customers that get home delivery	%	74	59.6	66.9	2.81	**0.01**	266	64.0	0.22	0.82
Share of customers that clean at home	%	96	29.9	21.2	−3.69	**0.00**	250	15.6	−3.18	**0.00**
Share of customers that only come for milling	%	93	30.1	25.4	−2.55	**0.01**	245	17.6	−2.21	**0.02**
Competition										
Number of mills in the kebele	number	92	6.1	9.7	8.14	**0.00**	250	9.0	5.04	**0.00**
Number of cereal shops in the kebele	number	75	2.9	3.6	2.36	**0.02**	202	5.0	2.05	**0.04**
Often queuing of consumers	%	102	30.3	16.7	−3.28	**0.00**	271	17.5	−4.45	**0.00**
Procurement (share)*										
In Addis Ababa	%	103	82.1	83.3	0.66	0.51	270	72.7	0.53	0.59
Outside Addis Ababa on temporary markets	%	104	11.8	10.0	−1.26	0.21	270	10.2	−1.45	0.15
Outside Addis Ababa not on temporary markets	%	103	6.0	6.4	0.35	0.72	270	17.2	1.08	0.28
% of teff consumers that mix teff with										
Sorghum	%	101	22.1	25.5	1.40	0.16	269	25.2	1.52	0.13
Rice	%	101	8.0	21.2	6.61	**0.00**	269	20.1	6.10	**0.00**

Wheat	%	101	1.1	0.1	−1.83	0.07	269	0.3	−2.01	**0.04**
Maize	%	102	8.5	12.1	2.17	**0.03**	269	11.1	1.98	**0.04**
Other cereals	%	102	1.6	1.4	−0.96	0.34	269	1.4	0.21	0.83

Source: Authors' calculations.

Note: * In full sample means, weighted by turnover of the retailer and therefore indicating shares for Addis Ababa. ** Significant values at the 5 percent level are highlighted in **bold**.

TABLE 13.5 Mixing teff with other cereals, 2011/2012

		Consumers			Injera sellers	
	Unit	Poorest	Middle income	Richest	With fixed shops	Without fixed shops
Number of observations	number	275	274	251	79	86
Type of teff bought*						
Magna	%	3	11	58	9	2
White	%	12	50	31	47	21
Mix	%	62	32	4	42	75
Red	%	23	7	6	2	2
Total	%	100	100	100	100	100
Share of customers that mix teff with other cereals*	%	55	39	14	76	74
Typical composition of flour bought*						
Teff	%	76	84	93	77	77
Sorghum	%	14	4	0	11	15
Rice	%	1	8	4	10	6
Maize	%	6	2	0	3	2
Wheat	%	0	0	0	0	0
Other	%	3	2	2	0	0
Total	%	100	100	100	100	100

Source: Authors' calculations.
Note: * weighted by turnover of the retailer and therefore indicating shares for Addis Ababa.

magna and white teff, the poor almost only eat red and mixed teff (see Chapter 2). The influence of income on mixing teff with other cereals is further shown by starkly different mixing patterns of rich versus poor customers. First, poor consumers mix teff more readily with other cereals: 55 percent of poor consumers mix cereals, compared with rich consumers, of whom only 14 percent mix teff with other cereals. Second, when cereals are mixed by richer and middle-income consumers, they mostly do so with rice, which has a price similar to white teff. This combination improves the whiteness and the flexibility of injera. Poorer consumers mix teff mostly with the cheaper sorghum and maize.

Foodservice Industry

The foodservice sector is defined as those businesses, institutions, and companies responsible for any meal prepared outside the home. In the foodservice industry the injera sellers are especially important, as reported by urban retailers and wholesalers. While they represented about 15 percent and 8 percent—using unweighted averages—of sales 10 years prior to the survey, they now make up about 13 percent and 9 percent of total sales of retailers and wholesalers, respectively, indicating a slight shift in their procurement to wholesale markets (Table 13.6). It is estimated that about 20 percent of the teff sold in Addis Ababa is currently being marketed as prepared injera by injera sellers and that this share has changed little over time. Direct procurement from retailers by restaurants (4.5 percent), institutions (such as schools, universities, jails, army, and so on) (0.4 percent), and supermarkets (0.6 percent) is relatively less important. Table 13.6 further shows how the mills have become increasingly important over time, and how the share of customers who buy directly from wholesale markets has declined over the period 2001–2011, further confirming the increasing role of mills as one-stop retail shops.

Four different categories of injera sellers can be distinguished—that is, formal large injera wholesale companies (that usually sell branded products), informal injera wholesalers (that sell to schools and restaurants, for example), injera retailers with fixed shops (baltena shops—local shops that sell different kinds of traditional flour products, based on milled spices, pulses, cereals, and others), and injera retailers without fixed shops (microsellers or gulits). The injera retailers are the most important of all injera sellers, representing almost 90 percent of all injera sellers who buy cereals from retail shops. Injera sellers have different procurement patterns than direct consumers as they visit teff retail shops more frequently, negotiate lower prices, access credit more often, and more regularly mix teff with other cereals (Table 13.5).[10] The share of the large injera wholesale companies selling branded products is still rather small.

In short, in these urban settings and downstream in the value chain, an increasing willingness to pay for convenience is noted, in particular by the emergence of one-stop retail shops as well by the presence of a sizable food-service sector. Also, a diverse range of products is being offered, with innovative mixes of teff and other cereals being tried out. Below, the changes in marketing margins are further explored between the different layers in the value chain.

---

10 The table shows that injera sellers mix teff with other cereals in similar proportions to that of the poorest consumers. It is unclear how injera sellers market their product—for example, as unmixed teff injeras or as a mixed product. Further research is required.

TABLE 13.6 Share of customers of urban wholesalers and retailers, 2011/2012

	Panel—unweighted			Paired T-test**		Full sample		Unpaired T-test**	
				10 years ago versus now				10 years ago versus now	
	Number of observations	10 years prior to survey (%)	At survey (%)	t-value	Pr (|T|>|t|)	Number of observations	At survey (weighted) (%)	t-value	Pr (|T|>|t|)
Type of customers for wholesalers (share)									
Wholesalers	33	11.7	9.3	−0.92	0.36	75	6.9	−1.24	0.22
Mills	33	51.5	59.6	1.61	0.11	75	69.0	2.39	**0.02**
Cereal shops	33	8.5	8.6	0.05	0.96	75	8.2	−0.09	0.92
Cooperatives	33	1.4	2.6	1.38	0.17	75	1.4	0.03	0.97
Consumers	33	13.0	5.9	−2.56	**0.01**	75	4.1	−3.25	**0.00**
Injera wholesalers	33	2.0	2.4	0.54	0.59	75	1.2	−0.78	0.44
Injera wholesale companies	33	0.7	1.1	0.44	0.66	75	0.6	−0.15	0.88
Injera retailers with fixed shops	33	4.9	4.7	−0.33	0.74	75	4.7	−0.05	0.96
Injera retailers without shops	33	0.9	0.7	−0.30	0.76	75	1.7	0.51	0.61
Institutions	32	3.3	2.8	−0.53	0.60	75	2.3	−0.42	0.67
Restaurants	33	1.8	2.2	0.35	0.72	75	1.0	−0.90	0.37
Supermarkets	33	0.2	0.2	0.00	n.a.	75	0.1	−0.59	0.55
Others	33	0.0	0.0	0.00	n.a.	75	0.3	0.66	0.50
Total	33	100.0	100.0			75	100.0		
Type of customers for retailers (share)*									
Consumers	103	80.4	82.5	1.46	0.14	277	81.2	2.58	**0.01**
Injera wholesalers	103	0.8	1.2	0.79	0.43	277	2.2	0.45	0.65
Injera wholesale companies	103	0.3	0.0	−1.15	0.25	277	0.1	−1.41	0.16
Injera retailers with fixed shops	103	4.7	4.8	0.05	0.96	277	4.4	−1.71	0.09
Injera retailers without shops	103	8.7	7.0	−2.28	**0.02**	277	5.3	−2.10	**0.04**
Institutions	103	0.7	0.4	−1.04	0.30	277	0.4	−1.13	0.26
Restaurants	103	1.9	2.1	0.29	0.77	277	4.5	−0.87	0.37
Supermarkets	103	0.0	0.0	0.00	n.a.	277	0.6	0.86	0.39
Others	103	0.0	0.2	1.00	0.32	277	0.7	0.27	0.79
Total	103	100.0	100.0			277	100.0		

Source: Authors' calculations.

Note: n.a. = not applicable; * in full sample means, weighed by turnover of the retailer and therefore indicating shares for Addis Ababa; ** significant values at the 5 percent level are highlighted in **bold**.

Marketing Margins

Monthly price series for teff have been collected over the period studied by Ethiopia's Central Statistical Agency (CSA) at the retail, producer, and milling level and by the Ethiopian Grain Trading Enterprise (EGTE) at the wholesale level. By comparing these prices, the evolution of urban-rural marketing, urban distribution, and processing margins over time can be analyzed. The increasing competition between mills, as mentioned by retailers, seems to have led to a significant reduction of the ratio of milling charges over teff retail prices over the period 2001–2012 (Figure 13.2). These margins have dropped on average to half the level of 10 years earlier.

By comparing wholesale to retail prices in Addis Ababa, a decrease of the share of urban retailers is observed in the final retail price over time (Figure 13.3). This was using producer price data from those five major production zones that were part of the producer survey. The share of urban retailers in final retail prices (using linear trend lines) declined from between 13 percent and 15 percent in 2001 to between 7 percent and 11 percent in 2011, depending on the type of teff. Using data from the trend line, the share of the producer in the final retail prices increased from a level of between 74 percent and 78 percent in 2001 to between 76 percent and 86 percent in 2011. Despite having the highest prices, white teff shows the lowest producer-to-retail ratio, indicating significantly higher marketing costs than other types of teff. Moreover, large variability of these margins is seen over time with a significant decrease in shares of wholesale and producer in final retail prices in 2009 and 2010. It is not immediately clear what has been driving this variability and these differences between different types of teff, thus further research appears necessary. Overall, despite large variability, the shares of urban-rural marketing, urban distribution, and milling in final retail prices have declined significantly over the 10-year period.

Drivers for Change

From these investigations both notable and important changes have occurred in the teff value chain over the years. A number of drivers can be linked to this agricultural and food market transformation (for example, Reardon and Timmer 2007; Minot and Roy 2007). First, the public sector has played an active role at improving the delivery of modern agricultural inputs. In particular, the government has invested especially heavily in developing the spatial reach of agricultural extension in the country—Ethiopia now has one of

FIGURE 13.2 The ratio of milling charges over (white) teff retail prices in Addis Ababa, 2001–2012

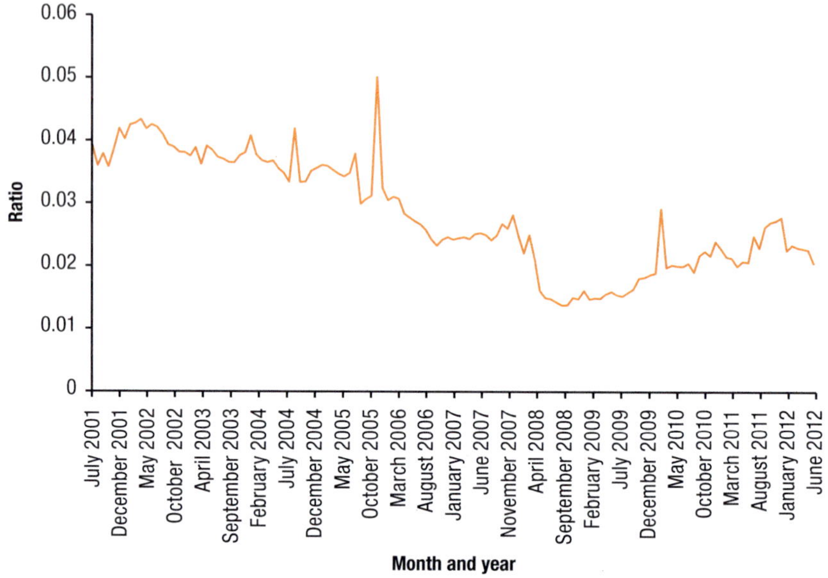

Source: Authors' calculations.

the lowest farmers-to-extension agent ratios in the world (Davis et al. 2010). The wide access to extension agents is illustrated in Table 13.7. Almost three-quarters of the surveyed farmers were visited by an extension agent in the two years prior to the survey, and a large share of farmers have been exposed to individual and community meetings, visits of demonstration plots, and visits to the government's office of agriculture to discuss teff-related issues over the twelve-month period before the survey. As a result, a high percentage of farmers became aware of recommended fertilizer use (50 percent) and improved technologies in teff (Table 13.7). Fertilizer delivery also has improved, and there are now fewer complaints about the lack of fertilizer, especially so in the more accessible zones, compared with 10 years earlier. The government has also invested in research and development. However, investments toward the development of better teff varieties have been limited. For example, Flaherty, Kelemework, and Kelemu (2010) show that investments in agricultural R&D declined by about 30 percent between 2002 and 2008. This study also found that the staff engaged in agricultural research in Ethiopia is among the least qualified in Africa, as measured in terms of postgraduate degrees.

FIGURE 13.3 Share of producer and wholesale in final retail prices of teff in Addis Ababa (12-month moving average), 2002–2011

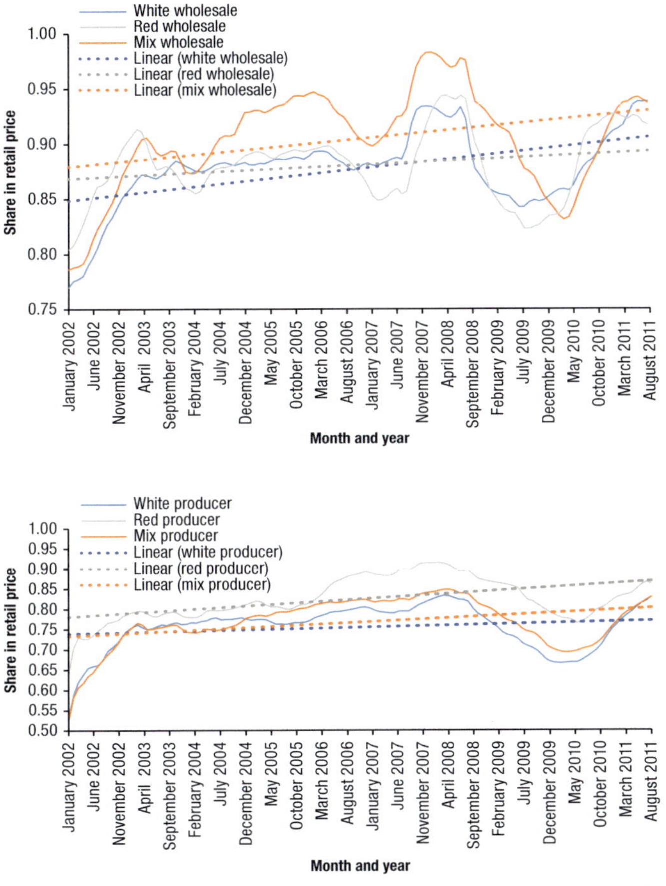

Source: Authors' calculations.

Second, during the period 2001–2011 improved road and communication infrastructure has been provided (Chapter 12). Improved infrastructure has resulted in significant declines in transport costs and better connectivity of rural to urban areas (Schmidt and Kedir Jemal 2009). The increasing spread of mobile phones has presumably also led to important efficiency gains, as seen in a number of other countries (for example, Aker and Fafchamps 2011; Jensen 2007). While mobile phone connection only became available in Addis Ababa in the beginning of the 2000s, cell phone coverage is now widespread in rural areas. Consequently, the cell phone has been adopted by a large

TABLE 13.7 Use of agricultural extension, 2011/2012

	Unit	Mean (%)	Median	Standard deviation
Contact extension agents				
Received a visit of an agricultural extension agent in the past two years	share (%)	74.4	n.a.	n.a.
Type of organization that provided the extension service:				
NGO	share (%)	4.7	n.a.	n.a.
Government	share (%)	95.3	n.a.	n.a.
Private	share (%)	0.0	n.a.	n.a.
Other	share (%)	0.0	n.a.	n.a.
In past 12 months				
Number of times that farmer talked individually with extension agent on teff issues	number	2.3	2.00	4.0
Number of times that farmer participated in a community meeting to discuss teff issues	number	2.2	1.00	3.1
Farmer visited a demonstration plot of teff	share (%)	35.3	n.a.	n.a.
Farmer visited a government office of agriculture and discussed teff issues	share (%)	27.1	n.a.	n.a.
Farmer awareness of technologies				
Farmer knows the recommended fertilizer use on teff plots	share (%)	50.4	n.a.	n.a.
Farmers is aware of:				
broadcasting at lower seed rates	share (%)	91.5	n.a.	n.a.
row planting of teff	share (%)	77.9	n.a.	n.a.
transplanting of teff	share (%)	39.3	n.a.	n.a.
0 tillage of teff soils	share (%)	10.4	n.a.	n.a.

Source: Authors' calculations.
Note: n.a. = not applicable.

number of value-chain agents with important implications for the way business is done in teff value chains.

Table 13.8 shows the extent to which telephones are now used in the teff value chain. Mobile phone penetration is quickly increasing with farmers in Ethiopia. However, it still remains low, with only 27 percent of the farming households in the survey area reporting that they own a phone. It is estimated that in 12 percent of the teff transactions undertaken by farmers, a phone was used to contact traders beforehand, and in 71 percent of these cases a price was agreed with the trader by phone. However, phone use is much more widespread with wholesalers and retailers. Almost all of the traders and retailers report

TABLE 13.8 Farmers' use of (fixed and mobile) phones, 2011/2012

	Unit	Farmers	Rural traders	Urban traders	Urban retailers
Owners of a phone	share (%)	27	100	100	98
Year since they own a phone	year	n.a.	2006	2007	2008
Used mobile phone in the last marketing transaction	share (%)	12	n.a.	97	56
If yes, agreed on a price with the trader by phone in the last transaction	share (%)	71	n.a.	52	32
Before using a mobile phone, they used a fixed phone	share (%)	n.a.	n.a.	43	28
Use of mobile phone:					
Use it to inform himself or transmit teff prices	share (%)	n.a.	99	100	73
Agree on prices (plus quantity/quality) with teff suppliers by phone	share (%)	n.a.	52	85	40
If yes, % of suppliers	share (%)	n.a.	38	74	64
Request a showup (without price agreements) with suppliers by phone	share (%)	n.a.	35	36	10
If yes, % of suppliers	share (%)	n.a.	35	67	57
Follow up on payments with teff suppliers by phone	share (%)	n.a.	34	88	54
If yes, % of suppliers	share (%)	n.a.	40	74	78
Agree on prices (plus quantity/quality) with teff clients per phone	share (%)	n.a.	86	68	34
If yes, % of clients	share (%)	n.a.	80	54	30
Follow up on payments with teff clients by phone	share (%)	n.a.	87	95	40
If yes, % of clients	share (%)	n.a.	81	62	48

Source: Authors' calculations.
Note: n.a. = not applicable.

owning a phone and using it actively to conduct their business: 97 percent of the urban traders report having used a mobile phone in their last marketing transaction. This contrasts with only 56 percent of urban retailers. Table 13.8 illustrates that mobile phones are intensively used by these traders to obtain information about prices, to complete trade deals, and to follow up on payments.

Third, the urbanization and economically superior characteristics of teff have augmented demand in Addis Ababa, leading to economies of scale such as the use of larger trucks and therefore relatively lower transport costs (Minten, Stifel, and Tamru 2012). Assuming that the average urban consumption level of teff is as high as estimated in the national household survey (HICES) of 2004/2005, this implies a flow of approximately 250,000 metric tons of teff into Addis Ababa in 2012, for an approximate value of US$165 million—using the 2012 mixed teff wholesale prices of approximately 1,200 birr per quintal. With high population growth in urban areas (World Bank 2015) an increase in the quantity of teff traded to Addis Ababa is estimated at approximately 45 percent over the period 2001–2011. Unfortunately, however, no good data are available on this change. By assuming that average income grew by 30 percent over the period 2001–2011, this would have added another 32 percent to urban teff demand, using estimated income elasticities. Both factors combined have thus led to important changes for marketed teff surplus to Addis Ababa, possibly almost a doubling over the 10-year period studied.

Fourth, economic and income growth is often linked with higher opportunity costs of time, especially for women. As each step involved in the purchase of teff and the preparation of injera requires significant effort and time, this higher opportunity cost leads to increasing demand for prepared products in such settings (Kennedy and Reardon 1994; Reardon and Timmer 2007; Minot and Roy 2007) and gives an impetus toward the further take-off of ready-to-eat products delivered by the foodservice industry.

Conclusion

Important changes have occurred in the teff value chain during the 10-year period studied, both at the production level and on the consumption side. Modern inputs are increasingly adopted in teff production. Quality and convenience demands are on the rise among teff consumers, and the teff marketing system is becoming more efficient. The changes upstream have especially transpired in those areas that are reasonably well connected to the city, illustrating the importance of market access and demand as drivers for rural and agricultural transformation (Wiggins 2000). Even though changes are happening, the transformation of the teff production and marketing systems is still at an early stage of agricultural development (for example, Reardon and Timmer 2007). At the production level, the number of farmers who use improved varieties is still low, the quantities of chemical fertilizers that are being used are still below the recommended levels, and mechanization, which is quickly happening in other emerging economies (for example, Yang et al. 2013; Binswanger 1986), is still mostly absent (see Chapter 6). In addition, very little vertical integration is observed as well as minimal coordination mechanisms between teff production and marketing. Midstream and downstream of the value chain, little evidence of upscaling of trade is seen, nor of modern retail or of branding, which are typically observable as agricultural market development gets under way (Reardon et al. 2012).

Despite the progress, there still exists a number of constraints that need to be addressed to facilitate further transformation in the upstream production portion of the teff value chain in Ethiopia. First, while the Quncho variety has quickly taken off, there is still plenty of room to further stimulate the development of the teff sector. For example, a major problem in teff cultivation is the problem of lodging of the crop, but lodging resistant varieties have not yet been developed. There has also been little attention in current breeding programs focused on taste preferences and downstream requirements (as, for example, shown in complaints on the drying out disadvantages of injera made with the improved white teff variety Quncho) as well as disease- and pest-resistant varieties. Furthermore, teff breeding has until now focused on conventional cross-breeding and selection techniques. More sophisticated breeding techniques that allow for a faster selection process are currently available and should best be employed to enhance availability of a larger portfolio of improved teff varieties to farmers (see Chapter 3).[11]

Second, besides improved seed development, little is currently known on the potential of other technologies to improve teff productivity. For example, studies at the farm level have been implemented to evaluate the potential of row planting and transplanting toward better productivity of teff (see Chapter 5).[12] On-station trials have also shown high responses to fertilizers that contain zinc and copper (Tareke 2011) as well as a good effect of minimal tillage methods (Habtegebriel, Singh, and Haile 2007), but no research beyond experimental settings has been conducted.

Third, despite the large importance of teff in the local food sector of Ethiopia, investments in research toward the development of improved agronomic practices have not been at appropriate levels.[13] The neglect of teff in

---

11 These include a technique of doubling the chromosome number of gametes at the first generation after crossing (known as gynogenesis based doubled haploid production) (Tareke 2011).

12 By reducing the high seeding rates common currently in teff production, by improving weeding practices, and thus by enhancing the nutrient uptake of teff plants, these technologies show great promise. However, they are currently underevaluated. On-station research indicates that the shift from broadcasting to row planting can reduce seeding rates by 90 percent. Lower planting densities result in increased tillering, much stronger stems, and increased grain yields (Tareke 2010).

13 This is illustrated by the fact that teff is not one of the targeted value chains in the government's Agricultural Growth Program (AGP)—the largest current investment program in the high-potential areas in the country. A number of reasons explain this. Attention on studies of teff by Ethiopian agricultural researchers was discouraged locally during the Derg period in the 1970s

research and development illustrates the importance of demand analysis and priority setting toward appropriate investments in agronomic R&D. Given the consumption patterns in Ethiopia, as well as high economic growth, it was and is expected that there will be a rapid increase in demand for teff and thus the payoffs to public investments in research and development to improve teff production in Ethiopia is likely to be high.

Fourth, while large investments in road improvements were made in the period 2001–2011—Ethiopia started from a low base—the country still has one of the lowest road densities in the world (von Braun and Olofinbiyi 2007). Similarly, while access to information is now widely available for traders and brokers, through the rapid development of the mobile phone network in the country over the past 10 years, penetration and use of mobile phones by Ethiopian farmers is still one of the lowest in Africa. Further investments in this area would thus be welcome. In this study, urban demand has been clearly shown to be a major factor driving rural change. While urbanization has been increasing in Ethiopia, the proportion of the Ethiopian population that resides in urban centers is still one of the lowest in Africa, possibly linked to rural land tenure rules that make rural-urban migration cumbersome.

Fifth, quality demands for teff are on the rise. However, uncertainty on quality rewards for sellers, as well as on the exact quality demands required from buyers, exists at all levels. This is shown by the lack of trust exhibited by farmers of teff traders, the difficulty of finding quality teff in urban areas unless retailers visit teff production zones individually and link directly with producers, and the mixing of teff with other cereals of which consumers are often not aware. Improved branding practices or vertical coordination could possibly take care of such coordination problems. It is thus expected that such practices will increase over time. This will especially be the case when consumers are willing to pay for assured quality teff and teff products, as branded products usually are significantly more expensive (Reardon et al. 2012; Minten, Reardon, and Sutradhar 2010). Further stimulation to expand a private modern retail sector—that is currently hardly involved in cereal trade (Woldu et al. 2013)—might possibly lead to better coordination toward quality assurance for teff consumers.

and 1980s (Tareke 2011). Internationally, teff does not fit well within the agricultural research priorities of the international agricultural research institutes of CGIAR. The CGIAR institutes' work is typically closely linked with the NARS (National Agricultural Research System) in the development of better varieties and technologies and have seen significant successes over time (Spielman and Pandya-Lorch 2009). However, CGIAR research focuses on crops grown in a large number of countries. Consequently, to date, teff has been the subject of almost no research by the CGIAR.

References

Aker, J. C., and M. Fafchamps. 2011. *Mobile Phones and Farmers' Welfare in Niger*. Berkeley, CA, US: University of California Press.

Binswanger, H. P . 1986. "Agricultural Mechanization: A Comparative Historical Perspective." *World Bank Research Observer* 1 (1): 27–56.

Davis, K., B. Swanson, D. Amudavi, D. Mekonnen, A. Flohrs, J. Riese, C. Lamb, and E. Zerfu. 2010. *In-depth Assessment of the Public Agricultural Extension System of Ethiopia and Recommendations for Impact*. IFPRI Discussion Paper 1041. Washington, DC: International Food Policy Research Institute.

Flaherty, K., F. Kelemework, and K. Kelemu. 2010. *Ethiopia: Recent Developments in Agricultural Research*. Washington, DC: IFPRI; Addis Ababa: Ethiopian Institute of Agricultural Research.

Fufa, B., B. Behute, R. Simons, and T. Berhe. 2011. "Strengthening the Tef Value Chain in Ethiopia." Mimeo, Agricultural Transformation Agency (ATA), Addis Ababa, Ethiopia.

Habtegebrial, K., B. R. Singh, and M. Haile. 2007. "Impact of Tillage and Nitrogen Fertilizer on Yields, Nitrogen Use Efficiency of Teff (*Eragrostis tef* (Zucc.) Trotter) and Soil Properties." *Soil and Tillage Research* 94: 55–63.

Jensen, R. 2007. "The Digital Provide: Information (Technology), Market Performance, and Welfare in the South Indian Fisheries Sector." *Quarterly Journal of Economics* 127 (3): 879–924.

Kenea, Y., G. Ayele, and W. Negatu. 2001. "Farming Research on Teff: Small Holders Production Practices." In *Narrowing the Rift: Teff Research and Development*, edited by H. Tefera, G. Belay, and M. Sorrels, 9–23. Addis Ababa: Ethiopian Agricultural Research Organization (EARO).

Kennedy, E., and T. Reardon. 1994. "Shift to Non-traditional Grains in the Diets of East and West Africa: Role of Women's Opportunity Cost of Time." *Food Policy* 19 (1): 45–56.

Minot, N., and D. Roy. 2007. "Impact of High-Value Agriculture and Modern Marketing Channels on Poverty: An Analytical Framework." Mimeo, IFPRI, Washington, DC.

Minten, B., T. Reardon, and R. Sutradhar. 2010. "Food Prices and Modern Retail: The Case of Delhi." *World Development* 38 (12): 1775–1787.

Minten, B., D. C. Stifel, and S. Tamru. 2012. *Structural Transformation in Ethiopia: Evidence from Cereal Markets*. ESSP II Working Paper 39. Addis Ababa: IFPRI/ESSP II.

Minten, B., S. Tamru, E. Engida Legesse, and K. Tadesse. 2016. "Transforming Staple Food Value Chains in Africa: The Case of Teff in Ethiopia." *Journal of Development Studies* 52 (5): 627–645.

Rashid, S. 2011. *Intercommodity Price Transmission and Food Price Policies: An Analysis of Ethiopian Cereal Markets.* IFPRI Discussion Paper 1079. Washington, DC: IFPRI.

Reardon, T., K. Chen, B. Minten, and L. Adriano. 2012. *The Quiet Revolution in Staple Food Value Chains: Enter the Dragon, the Elephant, and the Tiger.* Mandaluyong City, Philippines: Asian Development Bank (ADB); Washington, DC: IFPRI.

Reardon, T., and C. P. Timmer. 2007. "Transformation of Markets for Agricultural Output in Developing Countries since 1950: How Has Thinking Changed?" In *Handbook of Agricultural Economics,* vol. 3, edited by R. E. Evenson and P. Pingali, 2808–2855. Amsterdam: Elsevier Press.

Ricker-Gilbert, J., T. S. Jayne, and E. Chirwa. 2011. "Subsidies and Crowding Out: A Double-Hurdle Model of Fertilizer Demand in Malawi." *American Journal of Agricultural Economics* 93 (1): 26–42.

Schmidt, E., and M. Kedir Jemal. 2009. *Urbanization and Spatial Connectivity in Ethiopia: Urban Growth Analysis Using GIS.* Ethiopia Strategy Support Program (ESSP) II Working Paper 3. Addis Ababa: IFPRI/ESSP II.

Spielman, D., and R. Pandya-Lorch. 2009. *Millions Fed: Proven Successes in Agricultural Development.* Washington, DC: IFPRI.

Tareke, B. 2010. "Implementation of Modern Improvement Techniques to Boost the Productivity of Teff in Ethiopia." Mimeo, research proposal for submission to USAID/Ethiopia.

———. 2011. "Teff Breeding Concept Note." Addis Ababa: Agricultural Transformation Agency.

von Braun, J., and T. Olofinbiyi. 2007. "Famine and Food Insecurity in Ethiopia." In *Case Study 7-4 of the Program: Food Policy for Developing Countries: The Role of Government in the Global Food System*, edited by P. Pinstrup-Andersen and F. Cheng. Ithaca, NY, US: Cornell University.

Wiggins, S. 2000. "Interpreting Changes from the 1970s to the 1990s in African Agriculture through Village Studies." *World Development* 28 (4): 631–662.

Woldu, T., G. Abebe, I. Lamoot, and B. Minten. 2013. *Urban Food Retail in Africa: The Case of Addis Ababa, Ethiopia.* ESSP Working Paper 50. Addis Ababa: IFPRI/ESSP II.

World Bank. 2015. *Ethiopia Urbanization Review: Urban Institutions for a Middle-Income Ethiopia.* Washington, DC: World Bank.

Yang, J., Z. Huang, X. Zhang, and T. Reardon. 2013. "The Rapid Rise of Cross-Regional Agricultural Mechanization Services in China." *American Journal of Agricultural Economics* 95 (5): 1245–1251.

Chapter 14

TEFF CONSUMPTION IN URBAN ETHIOPIA

Yonas Alem and Måns Söderbom

The proportion of households regularly consuming teff constitutes 66 percent of the whole Ethiopian population (Berhane, Paulos, and Tafere 2011).[1] The figure reaches as high as 89 percent in Ethiopia's major urban areas (EUSS 2009). Teff appears in different colors (superwhite, white, mixed, and red), and these are used as indicators of quality and hence market value by producers, traders, and consumers (Minten et al. 2013). As discussed in this chapter, despite the rapid food price inflation Ethiopia experienced during 2004 through 2009, the quantity of teff consumed by households in urban Ethiopia changed very little, suggesting that price inelasticity of demand exists for teff.

Although teff is consumed by a large proportion of urban Ethiopian households, little is known about teff consumption patterns, the nutritional contribution that it provides in the diet of urban Ethiopians, and the socioeconomic characteristics of urban households that consume teff. This chapter uses unique household-level data—the Ethiopian Urban Socio-economic Survey (EUSS)—collected in 2000, 2004, and 2009 to explore the trends and correlates of teff consumption in urban Ethiopia. The relatively long panel data that is available spans a decade. Consequently, it provides established information to investigate trends in teff consumption over time and to estimate the role of the different correlates relatively accurately. Analysis of the patterns and correlates of teff consumption, covered in this chapter, potentially provide important information to build understanding and knowledge of the food culture of Ethiopia's urban population and to investigate the scope for interventions that aim at reducing food poverty.

1 The 2008/2009 household survey was funded by Sida through the Environmental Economics Unit (EEU) of the Department of Economics, University of Gothenburg, Sweden. Alem gratefully acknowledges financial support from the Gothenburg Center of Globalization and Development. Söderbom gratefully acknowledges financial support from Sida Sarec. The views expressed in this chapter are entirely those of the authors.

Following a brief description of the EUSS panel on which this analysis is based, this chapter investigates the role of teff in the total household food consumption basket in urban Ethiopia. Further on, the chapter presents a descriptive analysis of the patterns of teff consumption, disaggregating household teff consumption by time, place of residence, and income group. The chapter then continues to analyze the correlates of teff consumption using alternative linear panel data models. The chapter concludes with a discussion about the importance of interventions that could alter the consumption basket of the average urban Ethiopian household to reduce food poverty.

Data and Descriptive Statistics

Data Description

The research covered in this chapter uses three rounds of the EUSS—a panel dataset collected in 2000, 2004, and 2008/2009.[2] The first two rounds were collected by the Department of Economics of Addis Ababa University in collaboration with the Department of Economics, University of Gothenburg, Sweden. Originally, the survey covered seven major cities in Ethiopia—the capital Addis Ababa, Awassa, Bahir Dar, Dessie, Dire Dawa, Jimma, and Mekelle—which were believed to represent the major socioeconomic characteristics of the Ethiopian urban population. The sample of approximately 1,500 households were allocated to each city in proportion to the population size of each specific city. Once the sample size for each city was determined, the allocated sample size was distributed over all woredas (districts) in each city. Households were then selected randomly from half of the kebeles (the lowest administrative units) in each woreda, using the registration for residences available at the urban administrative units.

The final round of the survey was conducted by the authors from a subsample of the original sample covering four cities—Addis Ababa, Awassa, Dessie, and Mekelle—comprising 709 households in late 2008 and early 2009.[3] The cities were selected carefully to represent the country's major urban areas and to link with the original sample. All panel households in the three smaller cities and about 350 in the capital Addis Ababa were surveyed following

2 Data was also collected from these cities in 1994, 1995, and 1997. However, the data required extensive cleaning. As a result, it was decided to use the three rounds from 2000 on. Refer to Bigsten and Shimeles (2008) for details on sampling.

3 Other cities were not included in this round because of resource constraint.

the sampling procedure discussed in the preceding paragraph. Of the 709 households surveyed in the 2009 round, 128 were new households randomly included in the survey to check how representative the panel households were, which were formed back in 1994. Alem and Söderbom (2012) investigated this and did not find a statistically significant difference in welfare among the panel and the new households, which implies that the panel data represents urban Ethiopia reasonably well.

In addition, given the fact that the number of households surveyed in 2009 had to be reduced, having concern about the possibility of attrition bias was entirely feasible. Using attrition probits and BGLW (Becketti, Gould, Lillard, and Welch) tests, Alem (2015) undertakes a thorough investigation of the possible impact of attrition bias.[4] The conclusion of this investigation suggests that the data attrition does not result in a statistically significant bias in the sample. The dataset is comprehensive and documents information on household living conditions, income, expenditure, demographics, health, educational status, occupation, asset ownership, and other variables at the household and individual levels. In addition, the 2009 round includes new sections on shocks and coping mechanisms, government support and institutions. We decided to use these data for this analysis given that these data are of very high quality, that they were the only panel data in urban areas at the time of the writing of this chapter, and that detailed consumption information on teff was contained in the survey instruments.

Descriptive Statistics

This section presents some key descriptive statistics related to teff consumption in urban Ethiopia. The EUSS collected comprehensive information on both food and nonfood purchases and consumption in a monthly and weekly basis. Food items were purchased both in standard units and local units. Fortunately, about 98 percent of teff in urban Ethiopia was purchased in standard units (kilograms and quintals). Quantities of other food items (such as vegetables and spices, which were purchased in local units) were converted into standard units using carefully constructed conversion units. In order to be able to compare monetary values over time and across cities, all nominal expenditures were converted into real values using reliable price indexes constructed from the survey. The values of consumption of the different food items were thus adjusted for both spatial and temporal price differences using

4 Attrition bias in this context is possibly the result of the reduction in the sample size of the number of households surveyed in 2009.

1994 prices of the capital Addis Ababa as the base year price. To compute average values per household, the household size was taken into account for economies of scale and of differences in needs. These computations used adult equivalent units (AEU) based on Dercon and Krishnan (1998).[5]

Figures 14.1 and 14.2 show the share of real per capita expenditure for teff and other food items respectively. The importance of teff in the average urban Ethiopian food basket is clearly evident from both figures. On average, teff constituted 29 percent of total household food expenditure over the period under analysis. When compared to rural households, this figure is only 6 percent (Berhane, Paulos, and Tafere 2011). The budget share of teff in urban Ethiopia actually remained the same during 2000 and 2004; however, the figure increased to about 32 percent in 2009—the period in which Ethiopia experienced rapid but inflationary economic growth. Figure 14.2 further displays the budget share of other food items. The figure also confirms the importance of teff as the dominant cereal and food item for the average urban Ethiopian household. The budget share of all food items shows that there is little change over the 2000–2009 period. Wheat follows teff by comprising about 6 percent of the budget share of food, while maize represents only about 2 percent. Households spend about 33 percent of their food budget on other food items, such as spices, sugar, and edible oil; 13 percent on animal products, such as butter and meat products; 10 percent on fruits and vegetables; and 8 percent on pulses, such as lentils, beans, and chickpeas. Urban Ethiopian households on average spend about 71 percent of their total budget on food. This illustrates how low the level of standard of living is within urban Ethiopia.

The actual amount of teff purchase by year on a per capita basis is presented in Figure 14.3. Teff purchase remained much the same over the decade under analysis. Households purchased about 9.2 kilograms of teff in per adult equivalent terms per month in both 2000 and 2009. According to the results shown in Figure 14.4, the nominal price of teff nearly tripled between 2000 and 2009. The real price of teff remained unchanged during 2000 through 2004, but it increased by about 24 percent between 2004 and 2009 (from 2.42 per kilogram to 3.18 per kilogram). This provides *(text continues on page 359)*

5 It is to be noted that injera purchases were not accounted for in this teff consumption analysis. Although caution in interpretation is warranted, we believe that this was the most appropriate way for our analysis for two reasons. First, teff is still mostly bought in grain form and while the situation is quickly changing (Minten et al. 2016), injera markets at the time of the surveys were still relatively less important. Second, as it is not clear how much teff went into injera (given the mixing with different cereals), converting the purchased injera to teff is not straightforward and therefore prone to measurement error.

FIGURE 14.1 Budget share of teff in total food expenditure, 2000–2009

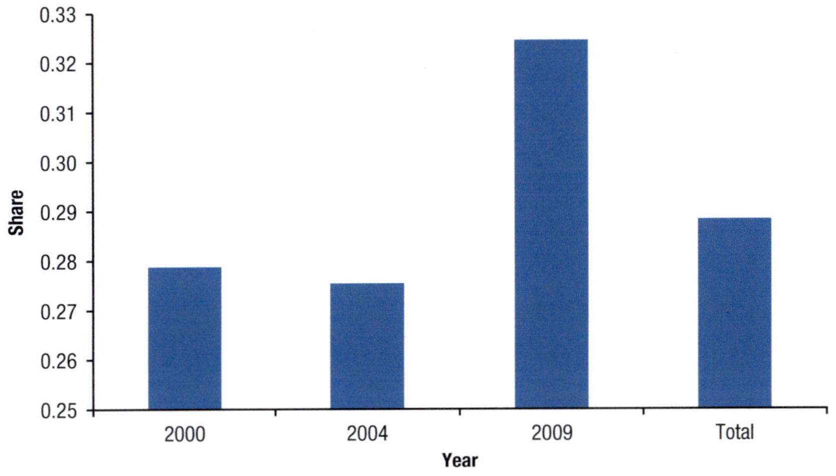

Source: Authors' calculations from EUSS 2000–2009.

FIGURE 14.2 Budget share of different food items in total food expenditure, 2000–2009

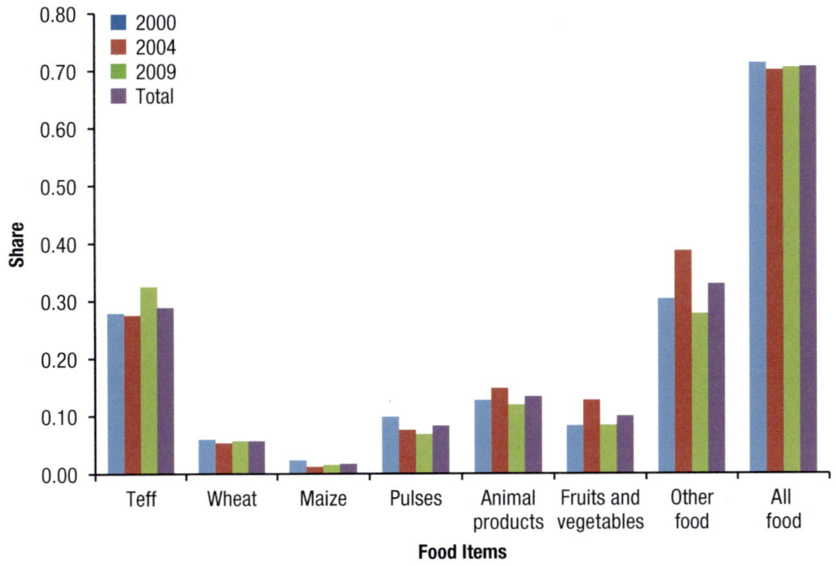

Source: Authors' calculations from EUSS 2000–2009.

FIGURE 14.3 Quantity of teff purchase per month in adult equivalent units (AEU), 2000–2009 (kilograms)

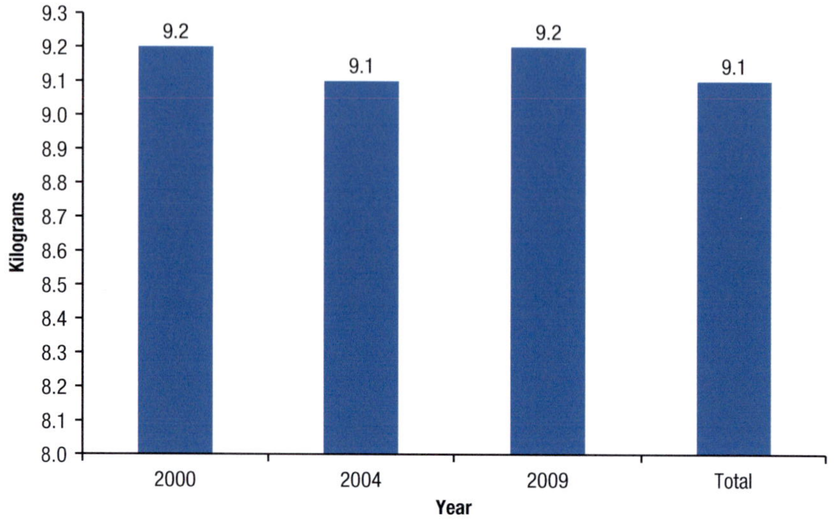

Source: Authors' calculations from EUSS 2000–2009.

FIGURE 14.4 Average price of teff, 2000–2009 (birr per kilogram)

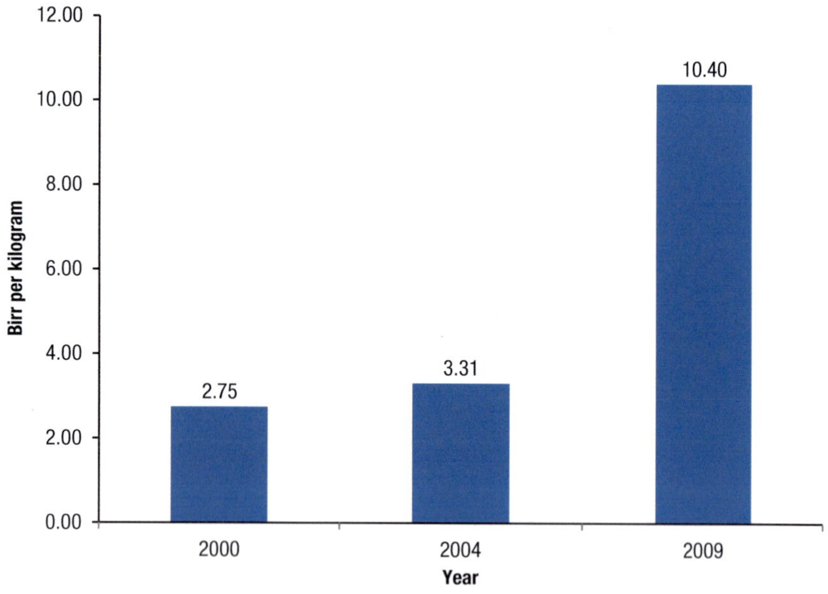

Source: Authors' calculations from EUSS 2000–2009.

FIGURE 14.5 Quantity of teff purchased per month in kilograms by city, in adult equivalent units (AEU)

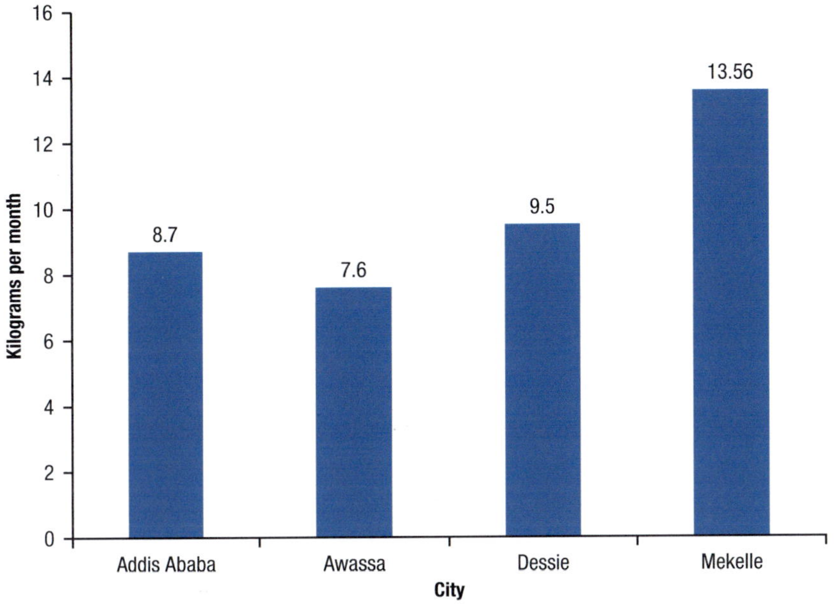

Source: Authors' calculations from EUSS 2000–2009.

suggestive evidence that teff is a price-inelastic food item with little change in quantity consumed even when price increases significantly. The teff consumption pattern appears to differ by city as well, as Figure 14.5 illustrates. Households in Mekelle on average purchased (consumed) 13.56 kilograms of teff per month in terms of per adult equivalent units. This represents, for example, 55 percent more consumption than households in Addis Ababa, and 78 percent more than households in Awassa. This probably indicates the diversity of food items consumed by households in Addis Ababa and Awassa.

Finally, as seen in Figures 14.6 and 14.7, teff purchase notably varies across income groups measured by per capita consumption expenditures. Figure 14.6 shows that the poorest 20 percent of households on average consume about 4.4 kilograms of teff per capita per month, while the households in the top 20 percent of the income distribution consume about 14.37 kilograms per capita per month. This provides some evidence that teff is an economically superior staple whose demand increases with income. The high price of teff, which on average is more than twice the price of maize (the cheapest cereal), partly explains the lower consumption by the poorest section of the urban

FIGURE 14.6 Teff purchase per adult equivalent units (AEU) by income group (kilograms)

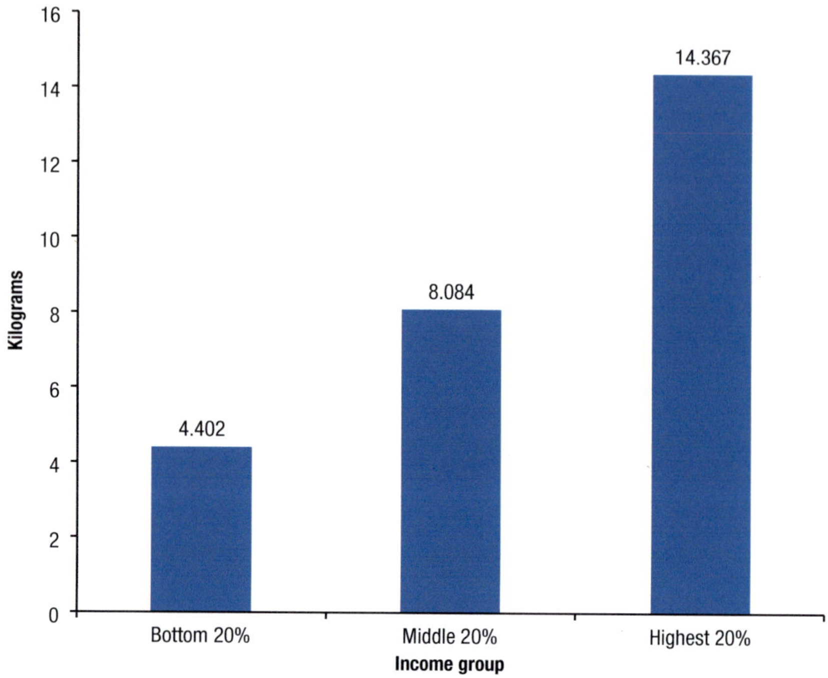

Source: Authors' calculations from EUSS 2000–2009.

community (Minten, Stifel, and Tamru 2012). It is, however, evident from Figure 14.7 that although the top 20 percent of households consume more than three times those of the bottom 20 percent, the proportion of food budget that is allocated to teff is far lower than the bottom 20 percent. This is probably due to the fact that the richest 20 percent of households consume other food items and nonfood items more proportionately.

Econometric Results

To investigate the different correlates of teff consumption during the period under analysis, a linear model of per capita teff consumption is run, specified as

$$f_{it} = x_{it}\beta + c_i + u_{it} \qquad (1)$$

where f_{it} is monthly per capita teff consumption in kilograms; x_{it} is a vector of explanatory variables; c_i is a term capturing unobserved household

FIGURE 14.7 Teff budget shares by income group (%)

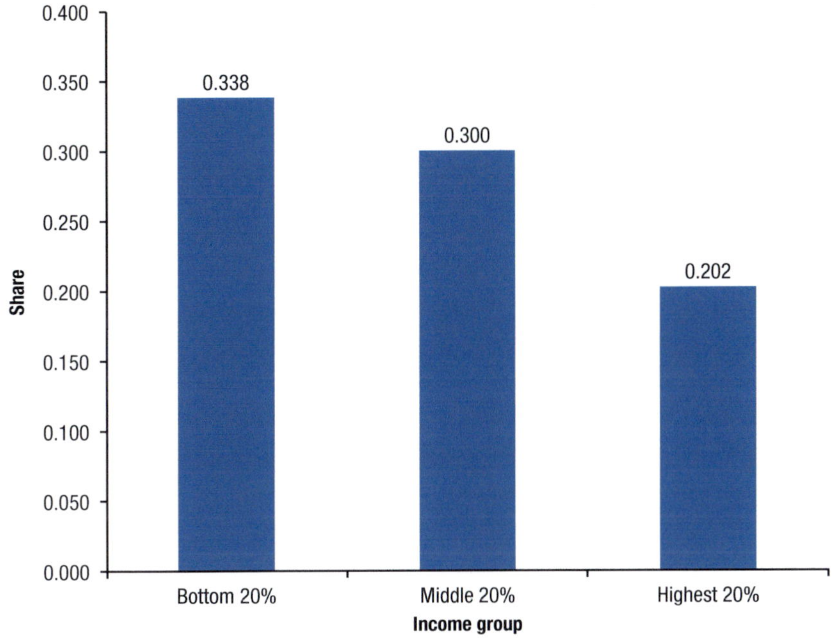

Source: Authors' calculations from EUSS 2000–2009.

heterogeneity; and u_{it} is a normally and independently distributed mean 0 error term. The subscripts $_i$ and $_t$ refer to households and time periods, respectively. The fundamental problem that one faces in estimating equation (1) using Ordinary Least Square (OLS) is the possible correlation between x_{it} and c_i. If such a correlation does not exist, that is, if $E(x_{it}c_i) = 0$, OLS would be consistent. However, with this assumption fulfilled, the random effects model, which works in a Generalized Least Square (GLS) framework and which exploits the correlation of $\varepsilon_{it} = c_i + u_{it}$ over time, would yield a more efficient estimator of the parameters in β. If, however, x_{it} and c_i are correlated, which is often the case in applied research, one could use the fixed effects model, which enables estimation through a "within" transformation. One limitation of this estimator, however, is that the coefficients of the time-invariant observable variables cannot be identified, as they are dropped through the "within" transformation. The model provides the most robust parameter estimates if the interest is on the time-varying variables (Wooldridge 2010). If one needs to identify the coefficients of the time-invariant variables, the most appropriate estimator would be the Hausman-Taylor two-stage estimator. The model is specified as

$$f_{it} = x'_{1it}\beta_1 + x'_{2it}\beta_2 + w'_{1i}\gamma_1 + w'_{2i}\gamma_2 + c_i + u_{it} \qquad (2)$$

where the x variables are time-varying and the w variables are time-invariant. The variables with index 1 are assumed to be uncorrelated to both the unobserved household heterogeneity term c_i and the random error term u_{it}, while the ones with index 2 are correlated with c_i but not with u_{it}. Hausman and Taylor show that equation (2) can be estimated by instrumental variables using the variables in the model itself. x'_{1it} and w'_{1i} instrument themselves, x'_{2it} will be instrumented by $x'_{2it} - x'_{2i}$ that is, by its deviations from the individual means, and w'_{2i} will be instrumented by x'_{1i}. Identification requires that the number of variables in x'_{1it} is at least as large as that in w'_{2i} (Wooldridge 2010).

Teff consumption by households in urban Ethiopia is assumed to depend on a number of household-level variables such as income (proxied by consumption expenditure), household head characteristics, and other household members' characteristics.[6] The consumption measure that is used comprises both food and nonfood components. The nonfood part of consumption includes expenditures on items such as clothing, footwear, energy, personal care, utilities, health, and education. Total household consumption expenditure has also been adjusted for spatial and temporal price differences using carefully constructed price indexes from the survey. To take account of differences in needs and economies of scale in consumption, the aggregate consumption by standard adult equivalent units was divided.[7] Finally, because three rounds of panel data from four cities were used, the household fixed effects (time-invariant unobservables), city, and time fixed effects were controlled.[8] The specific variables used in the regressions are presented in Table 14.1.

Table 14.2 presents estimation results for teff consumption regressions from alternative linear panel data models for households in urban Ethiopia. To test for the robustness of the different correlates of teff consumption, the regression using four alternative econometric specifications are estimated: pooled Ordinary Least Squares (OLS), random *(text continues on page 365)*

---

6 Consumption is very often used as a proxy for income in the context of developing countries. This is mainly because income is often underreported and in many cases volatile and difficult to remember, while consumption is relatively stable and is smoothed using various consumption smoothing mechanisms. See Deaton (1997) and Deaton and Grosh (2000) for further discussion.

7 See Alem and Söderbom (2012) for details on computation of consumption.

8 It is to be noted that when households changed cities, they were not part of the panel anymore.

TABLE 14.1 Descriptive statistics of variables

Variable	Mean	Standard deviation
Monthly teff per capita in kilograms	9.14	7.94
Real monthly teff expenditure per adult equivalent unit (AEU)	24.05	21.96
Real monthly food consumption expenditure per AEU	97.62	102.89
Real monthly total consumption expenditure per AEU	154.52	183.07
Share of food in total consumption expenditure	0.71	0.14
Age of head	50.95	14.00
Head, male	0.54	0.50
Head, primary schooling complete	0.30	0.46
Head, secondary schooling complete	0.37	0.48
Head, tertiary schooling complete	0.08	0.27
Head, employer/own-account worker	0.24	0.42
Head, civil sector worker	0.13	0.34
Head, public sector worker	0.05	0.21
Head, private sector worker	0.10	0.30
Head, casual worker	0.10	0.30
Number of own-account members	0.18	0.50
Number of civil sector worker members	0.14	0.43
Number of public sector worker members	0.08	0.31
Number of private sector worker members	0.41	0.77
Number of casual worker members	0.16	0.52
Number of unemployed members	0.56	0.98
Number of out-of-labor-force members	1.55	1.40
Number of children members	1.50	1.45
Number of elderly members	0.05	0.23
Addis Ababa	0.71	0.45
Awassa	0.10	0.30
Dessie	0.09	0.29
Mekelle	0.10	0.29
Number of observations	2,979	

Source: Authors' compilation from EUSS 2004–2009.

TABLE 14.2 Teff consumption regressions

	Ordinary Least Squares (OLS)		Fixed effect (FE)		Hausman-Taylor (HT)	
Variables	Coefficient	Standard error	Coefficient	Standard error	Coefficient	Standard error
Real consumption/adult equivalent units (log)	0.477***	0.024	0.351***	0.036	0.390***	0.033
Age of head	0.030***	0.007	0.026**	0.009	0.027***	0.007
Age of head squared	−0.023***	0.006	−0.021*	0.009	−0.022***	0.006
Head, male	−0.066*	0.034	0.104	0.071	−0.028	0.037
Head, primary schooling complete	0.073	0.042	−0.012	0.058	−0.001	0.056
Head, secondary schooling complete	0.099*	0.042	−0.022	0.062	0.029	0.059
Head, tertiary schooling complete	−0.096	0.065	−0.105	0.099	−0.018	0.092
Head, employer/own-account worker	−0.100*	0.042	0.043	0.067	−0.076	0.042
Head, civil sector worker	0.171***	0.046	0.057	0.093	0.152**	0.055
Head, public sector worker	0.170**	0.059	0.183	0.117	0.176*	0.075
Head, private sector worker	0.046	0.052	−0.05	0.087	0.017	0.057
Head, casual worker	−0.169**	0.062	−0.021	0.087	−0.164**	0.058
Number of own-account members	−0.085**	0.030	−0.015	0.043	−0.071*	0.029
Number of civil sector worker members	0.043	0.024	−0.014	0.047	0.037	0.035
Number of public sector worker members	0.032	0.043	−0.067	0.066	0.019	0.046
Number of private sector worker members	0.022	0.016	−0.013	0.030	0.023	0.019
Number of casual worker members	−0.089**	0.028	−0.064	0.041	−0.096***	0.029
Number of unemployed members	0.047***	0.013	−0.013	0.025	0.03	0.016
Number of out-of-labor-force members	0.035**	0.012	−0.008	0.018	0.024*	0.012
Number of children members	0.013	0.011	0.01	0.020	0.004	0.012
Number of elderly members	−0.049	0.060	−0.092	0.094	−0.064	0.062
Addis Ababa	−0.342***	0.057	—	—	−0.340***	0.061
Awassa	−0.533***	0.072	—	—	−0.514***	0.080
Dessie	−0.162*	0.066	—	—	−0.179*	0.079
Year 2004	−0.021	0.034	0.032	0.038	−0.022	0.032

	Ordinary Least Squares (OLS)		Fixed effect (FE)		Hausman-Taylor (HT)	
Variables	Coefficient	Standard error	Coefficient	Standard error	Coefficient	Standard error
Year 2009	−0.124**	0.042	−0.104*	0.049	−0.138***	0.038
Intercept	−0.843***	0.223	−0.352	0.322	−0.279	0.266
Number of observations	2,921		2,921		2,921	
R-squared	0.24					
Rho			0.51		0.300	

Source: Authors' estimation from EUSS 2000–2009.

Note: OLS = Ordinary Least Square estimator with robust standard errors. FE = linear fixed effects estimator. HT = Hausman-Taylor two-stage estimator. Significance at the 1 percent, 5 percent, 10 percent level is indicated by ***, **, *, respectively; — = data not available.

effects, fixed effects (FE), and Hausman-Taylor (HT) models. The robust Hausman test rejected the random effects estimator and consequently these results are not discussed. However, the fixed effects regression drops time-invariant variables from the regression. The focus is therefore on comparing regression results from the OLS and Hausman-Taylor models.

Consistent with the descriptive statistics presented in Figure 14.6, all the regression results show that economic status, proxied by the log of real per capita consumption expenditure is an important correlate of teff consumption in urban Ethiopia. OLS results suggest that a 1 percent increase in per capita consumption expenditure is associated with 0.48 percent increase in teff consumption. However, the role of consumption expenditure declines when household fixed effects are controlled. According to the fixed effects and Hausman-Taylor models, a 1 percent increase in per capita consumption expenditure is associated with a 0.35 percent and 0.39 percent increase in teff consumption, respectively. This highlights the importance of controlling for household fixed effects and the advantage of having panel data. The results from all the regressions clearly show that teff is a normal food item, whereby consumption increases as income increases.

Turning attention to the role of household head variables, it is established that age, gender, and educational and labor market characteristics of heads affect teff consumption. However, only age of head and labor market status have statistically significant associations with teff consumption in the Hausman-Taylor model. Teff consumption is positively correlated with being headed by a civil and public sector worker individual, while it is negatively correlated with being headed by a casual worker individual. The positive association of being headed by a civil or public sector worker with teff consumption is consistent with the negative association of being headed by these types of individuals with consumption poverty as documented by previous studies (for example, Alem 2015; Bigsten and Shimeles 2008). Household heads working in these sectors have relatively stable income streams and better access to savings and credit that enables a higher consumption, which includes teff, in the household. Teff consumption, however, is negatively correlated with a household headed by a casual worker individual. Casual workers depend on unstable and volatile income, which makes them vulnerable to poverty and shocks (Alem and Söderbom 2012). It is therefore not surprising that these households consume relatively less teff—a high-priced commodity that is consumed by the relatively well-off urban Ethiopian society.

Other characteristics pertaining to household members are also important correlates of teff consumption. Households with more own-account (self-employed) members and casual workers consume less teff, while those with more members out of the labor force consume more teff.[9] Casual workers depend on unstable and volatile sources of income for their livelihood, and about 67 percent of own-account worker household members in urban Ethiopia are engaged in low-paying and unstable jobs, such as petty trading and preparing and selling food and drinks. Given that teff is consumed by the relatively well-off households, it is therefore not surprising that households with members categorized as casual or own-account workers consume less teff. Alem (2015) shows that these types of households are highly likely to be in consumption poverty, but Alem, Köhlin, and Stage (2014) document that these types of households are less likely to feel "poor" although they are more likely to be in consumption poverty.

Finally, the spatial difference in teff consumption displayed in Figure 14.5 is also clearly evident in the regression results reported in Table 14.2. Compared with households residing in Mekelle (the reference group), households in all the three cities consume less teff in per capita terms. This may be because the city of Mekelle is located in the far north of Ethiopia, while the other cities are relatively close to the capital Addis Ababa, which gives them better access to more diversified food products and food culture. The coefficients on the time dummies indicate a slight temporal variation in teff consumption by urban Ethiopian households. Compared to 2000 (the base year),

9 This group constitutes household members such as housewives and pensioners that are not a part of the labor force and earn income from other sources such as international remittances and house rents.

teff consumption in 2009 declined by 13.8 percent. Ethiopia experienced the highest rate of food price inflation in its history in 2008. The average price of food in the summer of 2008 was 92 percent higher than the price of food in the summer of 2007 (Ethiopia, CSA 2008, 2009). The marginal decline in quantity of teff purchased in 2009 is therefore not surprising.[10]

Conclusion

Comprising a third of the total food budget, teff plays a significant role in the average urban Ethiopian household's diet. This chapter used a rich panel dataset—the Ethiopian Urban Socio-economic Survey—spanning the decade 2000–2009 to investigate the trends and correlates of teff consumption. Both descriptive and econometric analysis were used on the three rounds of panel data, then estimated alternative linear panel data models that control for time-invariant unobserved household heterogeneity. The results show that teff is consumed largely by the well-off households and its purchase seems to increase with income. Households headed by individuals with better labor market status seem to consume relatively more teff than those with poor labor market status, such as casual workers.

There seems to be a strong taste for teff among consumers in urban Ethiopia. Teff consumption barely changed during the period under analysis. Descriptive statistics show that urban Ethiopian households on average consumed 9.2 kilograms of teff per month both in 2000 and 2009, the period in which the price of teff increased nearly threefold. This fact indicates that households continued to rely on teff as a main source of carbohydrate in their diet even though the price of teff increased rapidly over this period and that teff consumption appears to be price-inelastic. Teff flour is considered to be nutritionally rich and healthy with similar amounts of protein and fiber as whole wheat flour, yet it provides more nutritional substances such as iron and is gluten-free (Baye 2014). As a result, relying on teff as a main staple may not be necessarily bad. However, given the fact that the proportion of urban households below the absolute poverty line is around 28 percent (Alem 2015), bringing more diversity to the average urban Ethiopian household's staple

10 The 13.8 percent decline in the quantity of per capita teff consumed by households displayed by the coefficient for the 2009 dummy does seem a bit contradictory with the descriptive statistics presented in Figure 14.3, which shows no change in the quantity of teff consumed. The coefficient for the 2009 dummy became significant once this was controlled for real per capita consumption expenditure, which is a measure of the economic status of households. In fact, given the fact that the price of teff increased by almost 280 percent during 2000–2009, the 13.8 percent decline in quantity purchased and consumed does not appear to be substantial.

basket through cheaper cereals would help improve calorific intake and reduce food poverty.

References

Alem, Y. 2015. "Poverty Dynamics and Intra-Household Heterogeneity in Occupations: Evidence from Urban Ethiopia." *Oxford Development Studies* 43 (1): 20–43.

Alem, Y., G. Köhlin, and J. Stage. 2014. "The Persistence of Subjective Poverty in Urban Ethiopia." *World Development* 56: 51–61.

Alem, Y., and M. Söderbom. 2012. "Household-Level Consumption in Urban Ethiopia: The Effects of a Large Food Price Shock." *World Development* 40: 146–162.

Baye, K. 2014. *Teff: Nutrient Composition and Health Benefits.* Ethiopia Strategy Support Program (ESSP) II Working Paper 67. Addis Ababa: International Food Policy Research Institute (IFPRI).

Berhane, G., Z. Paulos, and K. Tafere. 2011. *Foodgrain Consumption and Calorie Intake Patterns in Ethiopia.* ESSP II Working Paper 23. Addis Ababa: IFPRI/ESSP II.

Bigsten, A., and A. Shimeles. 2008. "Poverty Transition and Persistence in Ethiopia." *World Development* 36 (9): 1559–1584.

Deaton, A. 1997. *The Analysis of Household Surveys: A Microeconomic Approach to Development Policy.* Baltimore: Johns Hopkins University Press.

Deaton, A., and M. Grosh. 2000. "Consumption." In *Designing Household Survey Questionnaires for Developing Countries: Lessons from 15 Years of the Living Standards Measurement Study*, edited by M. Grosh and P. Glewwe, 91–133. Oxford, UK: Oxford University Press.

Dercon, S., and P. Krishnan. 1998. *Changes in Poverty in Rural Ethiopia 1989–1995: Measurement, Robustness Tests, and Decomposition.* CSAE working paper series 98.19-7, Centre for the Study of African Economies (CSAE), Oxford, United Kingdom.

Ethiopia, CSA (Central Statistics Agency). 2008. Country and Regional Level Consumer Price Indices, September 2008. Addis Ababa, Ethiopia.

———. 2009. Country and Regional Level Consumer Price Indices, August 2009. Addis Ababa.

EUSS (Ethiopian Urban Socio-economic Survey). 2000, 2004, 2009. Addis Ababa University, Addis Ababa; University of Gothenburg, Sweden.

Minten, B., T. Assefa, G. Abebe, E. Engida Legesse, and S. Tamru. 2016. *Food Processing, Transformation, and Job Creation: The Case of Ethiopia's Enjera Markets.* ESSP Working Paper 96. Addis Ababa: IFPRI/ESSP.

Minten, B., D. C. Stifel, and S. Tamru. 2012. *Structural Transformation in Ethiopia: Evidence from Cereal Markets.* ESSP II Working Paper 39. Addis Ababa: IFPRI/ESSP II.

Minten, B., S. Tamru, E. Engida Legesse, and T. Kuma. 2013. *Ethiopia's Value Chains on the Move: The Case of Teff.* ESSP II Working Paper 52. Addis Ababa, Ethiopia: International Food Policy Research Institute.

Wooldridge, J. M. 2010. *Econometric Analysis of Cross Section and Panel Data.* Cambridge, MA, US: MIT Press.

Chapter 15

NUTRIENT COMPOSITION AND HEALTH BENEFITS

Kaleab Baye

Teff (*Eragrostis tef*) is an ancient tropical cereal that has its center of origin and diversity in the northern Ethiopian highlands from where it is believed to have been domesticated (Ketema 1997a and 1997b; Demissie 2001). Teff is an underused cereal crop worldwide, whereas in Ethiopia, it is a major food grain, mainly used to make injera, a traditional fermented Ethiopian pancake. In other countries, like Australia, South Africa, and the United States, it is principally used as a forage crop for animal feed. Relative to more common cereals like wheat, rice, and maize, little is known about the nutritional composition and potential health benefits of teff. This, along with technological limitations in processing teff, has long restricted its more widespread consumption from its center of origin, Ethiopia. Although teff is the preferred grain for making the staple injera (Yetneberk, Rooney, and Taylor 2005), the limited information available to the general public and the lack of global interest in teff has prolonged thinking by Ethiopians that their grain is of inferior nutritional quality. However, the recent recognition that teff is gluten-free has spurred global research interest by nutritionists and food scientists. Consequently, studies on the nutritional composition of teff and its processing qualities have grown, and the development of new teff-based products has accelerated.

This chapter looks at the physical and chemical characteristics of teff and its nutrient composition. The use of teff and teff-based products for human nutrition in Ethiopia are described, along with the food-processing challenges impeding teff's worldwide consumption. Recent research advances to solve these challenges are discussed. Finally, the potential health benefits that could be associated with higher consumption of teff are highlighted.

Physical Characteristics of Teff Grain

Teff is possibly the smallest cereal grain with an average length of about 1 millimeter (Table 15.1) (Umeta and Parker 1996; Lacey and Llewellyn 2005;

TABLE 15.1 Teff grain characteristics

Average of 12 teff varieties
Length (millimeters) = 1.17
Width (millimeters) = 0.61
Percentage of sample that passes through sieves of different mesh size:
710 microns – 1.1
600 microns – 52.7
300 microns – 45.3
250 microns – 0.1
Thousand kernel weight (g) = 0.264

Source: Bultosa 2007.

Bultosa 2007; Adebowale et al. 2011). The average thousand kernel weight of 12 teff varieties tested by Bultosa (2007) was 0.264 grams. The minuteness of teff grains has nutritional and technological implications. For instance, as teff grains are difficult to decorticate, the cereal is consumed as a whole grain, improving nutrient intake for consumers.

The color of teff can vary from white (ivory) to dark brown (black) depending on the variety. In Ethiopia three major categories can be identified: white (nech), red (quey), and mixed (sergegna). It is also common for wholesalers to further subdivide white teff into very white (magna) and white (nech). However, given that these classifications are imprecise and subjective, what may be referred to as magna by some may be considered nech by others. White teff generally grows only in the Ethiopian highlands and require relatively good growing conditions. This, along with its higher consumer preference, may justify why white teff is the most expensive type of teff. However, in recent years, red teff, which is believed to be more nutritious, is gaining popularity among health-conscious consumers in Ethiopia.

Nutritional Composition of Teff Grain

Carbohydrates

Carbohydrates are the major source of energy for human nutrition and play an important role in metabolism and homeostasis. Based on the molecular size and degree of polymerization, carbohydrates can be classified into sugars, oligosaccharides, starch (amylose, amylopectin), and nonstarch polysaccharides.

Complex carbohydrates make up 80 percent of the teff grain. It has a starch content of approximately 73 percent, making teff a starchy cereal. The amylose content of 13 teff varieties tested ranged from 20 percent to 26 percent, comparable to other grains, such as sorghum (Bultosa 2007). The extent to which carbohydrate is digested and absorbed in the small intestine determines its health effect. Rapidly digested and absorbed carbohydrates (glycemic carbohydrates) have greater impact on blood glucose levels, as they lead to greater metabolic perturbation (Lafiandra, Riccardi, and Shewry 2014). Such perturbations have been associated with metabolic diseases such as type-2 diabetes and cardiovascular diseases (Ludwig 2002). Hence, from a health standpoint, slowly digesting carbohydrates are preferred over rapidly digesting ones.

The rate of carbohydrate digestion of a food can be characterized by its glycemic index (GI) (Harris and Geor 2009).[1] The GI of a food depends on endogenous factors of the food matrix, such as starch susceptibility to α-amylase, protein and lipid content, and the macroscopic structure of the food (Fardet et al. 2006). Starch susceptibility to α-amylase is in turn determined by its structure, encapsulation, crystal structure, degree of gelatinization, the proportion of damaged granules as well as the retrogradation of the starch granules (Fardet et al. 2006). Using a scanning electron microscope (SEM), the size of teff starch was found to be 2–6 μm (Bultosa, Hall, and Taylor 2002; Wolter et al. 2013). This makes teff starch granules smaller than those of wheat (A type 20–35 μm), sorghum (20 μm), and maize (20 μm) (Delcour et al. 2010). Given their larger surface area, smaller starch granules are more susceptible to enzymatic attack (Tester, Karkalas, and Qi 2004). Nonetheless, in comparison to wheat, which has larger starch granules, the in vitro starch digestibility of teff was found to be significantly lower (Wolter et al. 2013).

In line with this, the predicted glycemic index of teff (74) was significantly lower than that of white wheat (100) but comparable to that of sorghum (72) and oats (71) (Wolter et al. 2013). This somewhat lower GI for teff than expected may be explained by its amylose content, lower starch damage, and the possible formation of amylose-lipid complexes that can hinder enzymatic access and thus starch digestibility (Singh, Dartois, and Kaur 2010; Wolter et al. 2013). In addition, the high gelatinization temperature of teff (68–80°C)

1 The glycemic index (GI) is a measure of how carbohydrate-containing foods raise blood glucose. Foods are ranked based on how they compare to a reference food, either glucose or white bread, which has a GI of 100. The consumption of high GI foods leads to a rapid and large release of glucose into the blood.

(Bultosa 2007; Wolter et al. 2013) can hinder gelatinization and thus decrease susceptibility to enzymatic attack by α-amylase (Fardet et al. 2006).

Protein

The average crude protein content of teff is 11 percent, similar to other more common cereals such as wheat (Table 15.2). Teff's fractional protein composition suggests that glutelins (45 percent) and albumins (37 percent) are the major protein storages, while prolamins are a minor constituent (about 12 percent) (Bekele et al. 1995; Tatham et al. 1996). In contrast, more recent studies report that prolamins are the major protein storages in teff (Adebowale et al. 2011). The different methods of extraction between these studies may explain the contradictory findings. By examining the amino acid profile, the higher contents of glutamine, alanine, leucine, and proline and the relatively lower content of lysine further suggests that prolamins are the major storage proteins (Adebowale et al. 2011). Teff's amino acid composition is well balanced (Table 15.2). A relatively high concentration of lysine, a major limiting amino acid in cereals, is found in teff. Similarly, compared with other cereals, higher contents of isoleucine, leucine, valine, tyrosine, threonine, methionine, phenylalanine, arginine, alanine, and histidine are found in teff.

Another important feature of teff is that it has no gluten (Hopman et al. 2008). Spaenij-Dekking, Kooy-Winkelaar, and Koning (2005) investigated the presence or absence of gluten in pepsin and trypsin digests of 14 teff varieties. The digests were analyzed for the presence of T-cell–stimulatory epitopes.[2] In contrast to known gluten-containing cereals, no T-cell stimulatory epitopes were detected in the protein digests of all the teff varieties assayed, thus confirming the absence of gluten in teff. This makes teff a valuable ingredient for functional foods destined for celiac patients who are gluten intolerant.

Fat

Cereals are not the best source of fat, but as they are often consumed in large quantities, cereals can contribute a significant amount of essential fatty acids to the diet (Michaelsen et al. 2011). Fatty acids are potentially beneficial to growth, development, and long-term health. Consequently, there has been significant interest in recent years in their inclusion in diets. For instance,

2 T-cell stimulatory epitopes are defined as peptide sequences that, in association with proteins on antigen-presenting cells (APC), are required for recognition by specific T-cells.

TABLE 15.2 Macro, amino acid, and fatty acid composition of teff grain compared with maize, sorghum, wheat, and rice

	Teff	Maize	Sorghum	Wheat	Rice
Energy (kcal)	357	375	370	359	357
Starch (%)	73	72	63	71	64
Crude protein (%)	11	8–11	8.3	11.7	7.3
Amino acid (g / 16 g N)					
Lysine	3.7	3.6	0.3	2.1	3.7
Isoleucine	4.1	3.8	0.7	3.7	4.5
Leucine	8.5	13.8	2.1	7.0	8.2
Valine	5.5	5.0	0.8	4.1	6.0
Phenylalanine	5.7	5.1	0.9	4.9	5.5
Tyrosine	3.8	3.3	0.7	2.3	5.2
Tryptophan	1.3	0.6	0.2	1.1	1.2
Threonine	4.3	3.2	0.5	2.7	3.7
Histidine	3.2	3.0	0.4	2.1	2.3
Arginine	5.2	4.3	0.6	3.5	8.5
Methionine	4.1	2.2	0.3	1.5	2.7
Cystine	2.5	2.2	0.3	2.4	1.8
Asparagine	6.4	—	—	5.1	9.0
Serine	4.1	4.0	0.8	5.0	5.0
Glutamine + Glutamic Acid	21.8	19.7*	—	29.5	17.0
Proline	8.2	9.2	1.3	10.2	5.0
Glycine	3.1	3.8	0.5	4.0	4.5
Alanine	10.1	8.0	1.6	3.6	5.5
Crude fat (%)	2.5	4.9	3.9	2	2.2
Total polyunsaturated fatty acids	1.1	1.8	1.4	0.5	0.8
Linoleic acid (LA)	0.9	1.7	1.3	0.5	0.78
α-linoleic acid (ALA)	0.14	0.05	0.07	0.03	0.03
LA:ALA ratio	7:1	34:1	20:1	17:1	26:1
Crude fiber (%)	3.0	—	0.6	2.0	0.6–1.0
Total dietary fiber	4.5	2.6	—	—	—
Soluble dietary fiber	0.9	0.6	—	—	—
Ash (%)	2.8	1.4	1.6	1.6	1.4

Source: Agren and Gibson 1968; Bultosa and Taylor 2004; FAO 1992; Gebhardt et al. 2006; Gebremariam, Zarnkow, and Becker 2012; Hager and Arendt 2013; Juliano 1993; Ketema 1997a and 1997b; Khoi et al. 1987; Mbuya, Nkongolo, and Kalonji-Mbuyi 2011; Michaelsen et al. 2011; Mossé, Huet, and Baudet 1985; Shoup et al. 1969; and Wolter et al. 2013.

Note: *Glutamic acid only; — = data not available.

increased intake of n-3 fatty acids (α-linoleic acid) were found to reduce biological markers associated with cardiovascular disease, cancer, inflammatory and autoimmune diseases, among others (Simopoulos 2001).

The crude fat content of teff is higher than that of wheat and rice, but lower than maize and sorghum (Table 15.2). Rice, wheat, and maize contain negligible amounts of linoleic acid (LA) and only traces of α-linoleic acid (ALA). Furthermore, these widespread cereals are consumed after decortication and further refining, which reduces their amount of crude fat and n-6 and n-3 poly-unsaturated fatty acids. By maintaining whole grains, as in the case of teff, this provides a better source of fatty acids than refined ones. Teff grains are rich in unsaturated fatty acids, predominantly oleic acid (32.4 percent) and linoleic acids (23.8 percent) (El-Alfy, Ezzat, and Sleem 2012). Although a clear consensus has not been reached on the optimal ratio between LA and ALA fatty acids, the Codex standards for infant formula recommends an LA-to-ALA ratio in the range of 5 to 15 (Koletzko et al. 2005). In this regard, the LA-to-ALA ratio of 7:1 for teff can be considered favorable and is comparable to legumes that are good sources of fatty acids, such as soybean.

Fiber

The American Association of Cereal Chemists defines dietary fiber as the "edible parts of plant or analogous carbohydrates resistant to digestion and absorption in the human small intestine with complete or partial fermentation in the large intestine" (DeVries 2003). The most recent Codex definition further added that dietary fibers should have "proven physiologic effects of benefit to health" (Cummings et al. 2009). Some of these physiologic effects include fecal bulking (laxation), lowering blood glucose levels after eating, and lowering plasma LDL-cholesterol (Champ et al. 2003). The crude fiber, total, and soluble dietary fiber content of teff is several folds higher than that found in wheat, sorghum, rice, and maize (Table 15.2). There may be several reasons for this. First, whole grains have higher fiber content than decorticated ones. Second, small grains have a relatively high proportion of bran, which is high in fiber (Bultosa 2007). Therefore, higher dietary fiber intake and the associated health benefits are expected with increased consumption of teff.

Minerals

The difference in mineral content between and within teff varieties is wide ranging. Red teff has a higher iron and calcium content than mixed or white teff (Abebe et al. 2007), while white teff has a higher copper content than red

TABLE 15.3 Mineral content of teff grain compared with other cereals (milligrams per 100 grams)

Minerals	White teff	Red teff	Mixed teff	Maize	Sorghum	Wheat	Rice
Iron	9.5–37.7	11.6– >150	11.5– >150	3.6–4.8	3.5–4.1	3.7	1.5
Zinc	2.4–6.8	2.3–6.7	3.8–3.9	2.6–4.6	1.4–1.7	1.7	2.2
Calcium	17–124	18–178	78.8–147	16	5.0–5.8	15.2–39.5	23
Copper	2.5–5.3	1.1–3.6	1.6	1.3	0.41	0.23	0.16

Source: Abebe et al. 2007; Baye et al. 2014; Gebremariam, Zarnkow, and Becker 2012; Kebede 2009; and USDA 2013.

and mixed teff (Table 15.3). Ketema (1997a and 1997b) analyzed 12 genotypes of teff grown in different agroecologic settings and 5 varieties grown in a greenhouse in Great Britain and reported that genetic and environmental factors affect the iron content of teff. This may partly explain the high variability in the mineral content reported in different studies.

Notwithstanding the differences described in Table 15.3, teff has a higher iron, calcium, and copper content than other common cereals (Mengesha 1966). The zinc content of teff is also higher than that of sorghum and wheat. However, the very high mineral content of teff (that is, iron) has been contested and in many instances attributed to soil contamination (Ketema 1997a and 1997b; Abebe et al. 2007). For example, Hallberg and Björn-Rasmussen (1981) reported that teff's iron content is not different from other cereals by showing that iron content drops from 39.7 milligrams per 100 grams to 3.5 milligrams per 100 grams when grains are washed with dilute hydrochloric acid. However, washing with acid is likely to lead to loss of acid-labile intrinsic iron and thus may underestimate the iron content. For instance, Areda et al. (1993) reported that acid-washing of teff grains led to a 50 percent greater loss of iron than washings with de-ionized water. Comparing uncontaminated teff to barley, wheat, maize, and sorghum, Mengesha (1966) reported that teff is superior in its mineral content, particularly in calcium and iron. More recently, Baye et al. (2014) examined the content of iron, zinc, and calcium in teff, barley, wheat, and sorghum before and after washing with de-ionized water. Mengesha (1966) found that washing the grain significantly decreased the iron content as well as the variability between replicates. Despite this decrease, the variability between replicates for teff remained relatively high, suggesting that soil contamination in teff is relatively high compared with other cereals.

The mineral contamination of teff is probably due to its small size, which suggests increased contact with soil over a larger area (Baye et al. 2014). The contamination of cereal grains in Ethiopia, particularly in teff, has often been associated with traditional methods of threshing grain under the hooves of cattle (Bezwoda et al. 1979). More recently, Ambaw (2013) compared the iron content of the same teff variety after laboratory (manually) and traditional threshing. Traditional threshing led to 30 percent to 38 percent increase in iron content, mainly due to soil contamination. The iron content of the lab-threshed teff was 16 milligrams per 100 grams dry matter, which was still higher than what is found in many cereals. This suggests that although the intrinsic iron content of teff may not be as high as previously thought, teff is still a better source of iron than other cereals like wheat, barley, sorghum, and maize.

In contrast to iron, Baye et al. (2014) showed that under the same conditions the values reported for calcium and zinc are consistent and are less affected by washing. This suggests that soil contamination contributes little to the content of these minerals in teff.

Phytochemicals in Teff

For minerals to be used for normal metabolic functions (bioavailable), they need to be absorbed through the small intestine (Fairweather-Tait 2002). The bioavailability of minerals depends on subject/host and dietary factors (Hurrell and Egli 2010). Among dietary factors, phytochemicals, such as polyphenols and phytates, constitute major mineral absorption inhibitors and hence were, for a long time, referred to as "antinutritional factors." However, in recent years the recognition of their health-promoting effects including antidiabetic, anticancer, and antioxidative (Shamsuddin 1995) properties made the term "antinutritional factor" obsolete (Schlemmer et al. 2009).

Phytates

Phytates are a common constituent of cereals and legumes (Schlemmer et al. 2009). It is the primary form of phosphorus storage in seeds and accounts for 60 percent to 90 percent of the total phosphorus. It can constitute as much as 1.5 percent of the dry weight of cereals (Loewus 2002; Bohn, Meyer, and Rasmussen 2008). Teff contains high amounts of phytate (Table 15.4) with a wide range of variability, probably due to differences in varieties and growing conditions. Teff's phytate content is comparable to values reported for whole grain cereals (Schlemmer et al. 2009). Such high values in phytate are likely to impair the absorption of iron and zinc (Hurrell and Egli 2010). The mechanism by which phytate inhibits mineral absorption is based on the formation of insoluble phytate-mineral or peptide-mineral-phytate complexes in

TABLE 15.4 Phytochemical composition of teff grain

Phytochemicals	Quantity
Phytate (milligrams per 100 grams dry matter)	682–1,374
Tannin (milligrams catechol equivalent per 100 grams dry matter)	16
Total polyphenols (milligrams gallic acid equivalent per 100 grams dry matter)	140
Iron-binding phenolics	
Galloyls (milligrams tannic acid equivalent per 100 grams dry matter)	210
Catechols (milligrams catechin equivalent per 100 grams dry matter)	200
Phenolic acids (μg per milligrams)	
Protocatechuic	25.5
Gentisic	15
p-OH Benzoic	—
Vanillic	54.8
Caffeic	3.9
Syringic	14.9
Coumaric	36.9
Ferulic	285.9
Cinnamic	46

Source: Abebe et al. 2007; Baye 2013; Baye et al. 2014; Dykes and Rooney 2006; McDonough, Rooney, and Derna-Saldivar 2000; and Umeta, West, and Fufa 2005.

Note: Most analyses did not use the same method and thus comparison among cereals would be misleading; — = data not available.

the gastrointestinal tract (Weaver and Kannan 2002). Furthermore, phytates form complexes with endogenously secreted minerals such as zinc (Sandström 1997; Manary et al. 2002) and calcium (Morris and Ellis 1985), making these minerals unavailable for reabsorption into the body.

Phytate can be degraded by endogenous phytases, which can be activated by food-processing techniques like soaking, fermentation, and germination and to a lesser extent during cooking. For instance, fermentation of injera has been shown to result in phytate degradation through the activation of endogenous phytases (Umeta, West, and Fufa 2005; Baye, Mouquet-Rivier et al. 2013; Baye et al. 2014). However, the application of exogenous commercial enzymes can be more effective in degrading phytates (Troesch et al. 2009; Baye, Guyot et al. 2013). On a positive side, phytates have been shown to prevent kidney stones by serving as crystallization inhibitor of calcium salts in biological fluids (Curhan et al. 2004). They also have glucose-lowering (Lee et al. 2005, 2006) and anticancer properties (Singh, Agarwal, and Agarwal 2003). Given these positive effects of phytates, it remains unknown as to whether there is an optimal concentration of phytate where the beneficial effects can be appreciated with little or no compromise to mineral bioavailability. Further investigations are needed to find more conclusive results.

Polyphenols

Polyphenols are secondary metabolites of plants involved in the defense against pathogens or ultraviolet radiation (Manach et al. 2004). Polyphenols similarly protect cell constituents against oxidative damage, limiting the risk of diseases associated with oxidative stress (Scalbert et al. 2005). Baye (2013) reported the total polyphenol content of teff, wheat, barley, and sorghum whole grains using the modified Folin-Ciocalteu's method. Red sorghum has the highest content of total polyphenols expressed as gallic acid equivalents (GAE) per 100 grams of flour (1,607 milligrams), followed by barley (310 milligrams), wheat (143 milligrams), teff (140 milligrams), and white sorghum (81 milligrams). However, only one variety of teff, sergegna, was analyzed; thus, to what extent varietal differences in teff influence polyphenol contents remains to be investigated.

Polyphenols can hamper iron absorption from plant-based foods (Hurrell and Egli 2010). Consequently, reducing polyphenol contents in predominantly plant-based diets has been encouraged (Matuschek and Svanberg 2002). The iron-binding properties of polyphenols are associated, however, with the catechol (ortho-dihydroxy benzene) and galloyl (trihydroxy-benzene) functional groups. Hence, not all polyphenols possess inhibitory effects (Brune, Rossander, and Hallberg 1989). The galloyl content of teff was similar to that of wheat, white sorghum, and barley, whereas the catechol content was comparable to that of barley but higher than that of wheat and white sorghum (Baye 2013).

The polyphenol profile of teff was reported by McDonough, Rooney, and Derna-Saldivar (2000) (Table 15.4). Ferulic acid is the major constituent of phenolic acid in teff. Vanillic, cinnamic, and coumaric are also important constituents of the phenolic acids. These major constituents of phenolic acids in teff do not have galloyl and catechol functional groups and thus are less likely to hamper iron absorption. This suggests that it may be possible to benefit from the antioxidative properties of the polyphenols in teff while not compromising on iron bioavailability. Indeed, Alaunyte et al. (2012) showed that by supplementing wheat bread with 30 percent teff flour, it was possible to significantly increase the total antioxidant capacity from 1.4 to 2.4 mM trolox equivalent antioxidant capacity (TEAC) per 100 grams.

In summary, compared with grain of other more common cereals, teff is superior in its nutrient composition. Its starch is slowly digestible and consequently has a low GI; it has a favorable amino acid composition and contains no gluten. Teff is also a good source of unsaturated fatty acids and has a favorable LA-to-ALA composition. Teff is high in minerals, especially iron and calcium. Furthermore, the high dietary fiber along with the relatively good concentration in phytochemicals makes teff a good contender for a functional food for health promotion and disease prevention. Nevertheless, the use of teff for human consumption is limited to only a few countries in the world (Ethiopia and Eritrea).

Use of Teff for Human Consumption

Teff is cultivated in a few countries such as South Africa, India, the United States, Eritrea, and Ethiopia, but it is primarily used for human consumption only in the latter two. Although teff has been used for food in Ethiopia for many centuries, it is only recently that its use as a food ingredient has gained interest in other parts of the world. As technological challenges are overcome in processing teff to make bread and other food products, demand for teff is likely to increase globally.

Forms of Consumption

Teff is mainly used for the making of injera. Injera is made by mixing cereal flour with water to make dough and then triggering the fermentation process by inoculating with ersho, a starter obtained from previous fermentations (Baye, Mouquet-Rivier et al. 2013). The fermentation lasts on average two to three days, after which the dough is thinned into a batter before steam baking. Teff is the preferred grain for making injera, primarily for its better sensory attributes (taste, color, smell) and shelf life (Zegeye 1997; Yetneberk et al. 2004). Besides the ability to easily roll injera, softness is an important quality attribute since this allows easy wrapping of the sauces (wot) consumed with it. In this regard, the superiority of teff was demonstrated by the minimal force required to bend fresh, 24-hour- and 48-hour-stored injera relative to injera made from other grain (Yetneberk et al. 2004). Similarly, incorporating teff flour into the sorghum flour has been shown to improve the sensory attributes of sorghum in injera (Yetneberk, Rooney, and Taylor 2005). Moreover, blending teff with wheat, as is often observed in less-privileged households (Piccinin 2002), has been found to be nutritionally beneficial, as it allows higher phytate degradation due to the higher endogenous phytase activity in wheat (Egli et al.

2004; Good 2009). Although used to a much lesser extent than for injera, teff can also be used for the making of porridges, unleavened breads (kitta), gruels (atmit), and traditional alcoholic beverages like tella and arake (Gebremariam, Zarnkow, and Becker 2012).

Teff: A Future Global Food

There has been a growing global interest in the use of teff as a food ingredient.[3] This interest is mainly attributed to the growing Ethiopian diaspora community but also to teff being gluten-free and thus a candidate ingredient for food products destined for people with celiac disease (Hager et al. 2013; Wolter et al. 2013). The relatively high nutrient content (that is, minerals) of teff is also likely to be well suited for celiac patients who usually suffer from mineral malabsorption (García-Manzanares and Lucendo 2011).

The incorporation of whole grains in bread making is often challenging. This is further complicated when gluten-free ingredients are used, since gluten plays an essential role in producing leavened bread with a fine open structure (García-Manzanares and Lucendo 2011). In relation to this, the addition of teff flour to bread dough in higher quantities has been shown to negatively affect the sensory properties of the bread. For instance, the replacement of wheat flour with greater than 10 percent teff flour has been associated with lower sensory scores, lower specific volumes, and higher crumb firmness than wheat bread (Ben-Fayed, Ainsworth, and Stojceska 2008; Mohammed, Mustafa, and Osman 2009).[4]

The use of enzymes provides an alternative strategy to improve the texture and sensory properties of teff-enriched breads. Alaunyte et al. (2012) have shown that the application of a combination of enzymes, including xylanases, amylase, glucose oxidase, and lipase improved the quality of teff-enriched breads. In contrast, treatment with glucose oxidase or protease did not show any improvement in the sensory and textural attributes of teff breads (Renzetti and Arendt 2009). This suggests that the type, dose, and combination of the enzymes used determine their effects on the quality

3 For a discussion of injera exports from Ethiopia, see Chapter 2. No data are available on teff exports given that there is still an export ban in place (except for a limited number of commercial farmers who have recently been granted an exemption).

4 Sensory evaluation consists in giving scores for sensory attributes such as taste, color, mouthfeel, odor, and texture. The scores are given using hedonic scales with a maximum score of 5, 7, or 9. Specific volume and crumb hardness are among the major sensory attributes for bread.

of teff-enriched breads. Further studies are needed to determine the optimal doses and conditions needed to improve the processing and sensory attributes of teff-enriched breads. Another alternative is to use hydrocolloids such as xanthan gum and hydroxypropylmethylcellulose (HPMC). Hager and Arendt (2013) have shown that the addition of HPMC in gluten-free cereals, including teff, reduced crumb hardness, whereas xanthan increased it. Further research in this regard is needed to determine optimal water and hydrocolloid addition levels.

Although the addition of enzymes and hydrocolloids can improve the sensory attributes of teff-enriched or teff-based breads, there is a growing interest in reducing the use of food additives. A good alternative is sourdough technology, which can lead to improvements in the texture and shelf life of breads (Arendt, Ryan, and Dal Bello 2007; Schober, Bean, and Boyle 2007; Moore, Dal Bello, and Arendt 2008). However, much work is needed to evaluate the robustness of this approach, particularly for teff-enriched or teff-based breads. The possibility of using teff for food products other than bread has begun to be evaluated. Coleman et al. (2013) confirmed the suitability of teff flours for biscuits and cake making. Similarly, studies evaluating the possibility of using teff in pasta formulations (Hager et al. 2013), beer making (Gebremariam, Zarnkow, and Becker 2012), and gel-like food formulation (Abebe and Ronda 2014) have shown promising results. These efforts show that teff can be used in various products familiar to Western culture, especially in the formulation of gluten-free products.

Health Benefits of Teff and Teff-Based Products

Iron Deficiency

Iron-deficiency is the most widespread micronutrient deficiency globally, affecting more than 2 billion people (Zimmermann and Hurrell 2007). Growth retardation, impaired mental and psychomotor development, child and maternal morbidity and mortality, and decreased immunity and work performance are among the adverse effects of iron deficiency (Georgieff 2011). The etiology of iron deficiency includes diseases that induce excessive loss or cause malabsorption of dietary iron, low intakes of bioavailable iron, or increased requirements due to physiologic status (for example, pregnancy, infants, and young children) (Pasricha et al. 2013).

Inadequate iron intake is common in low- and middle-income countries, particularly among infants and young children (Gibson et al. 2010) and pregnant women (Clark 2008). Food fortification and nutritional supplements may constitute effective strategies to prevent iron deficiency (Stoltzfus 2011). However, these strategies are not without side effects, especially when applied to environments where malaria and infections are prevalent (Sazawal et al. 2006; Zimmermann et al. 2010). Therefore, adjusting iron intakes with iron-rich foods may be preferred. Teff can be a good alternative (Gebre-Medhin et al. 1976; Adish et al. 1999). Alaunyte et al. (2012) showed that by supplementing wheat bread with 30 percent teff flour, the iron content of the bread more than doubled. By assuming an average daily consumption of 200 grams of teff-enriched bread, it is possible to cover between 42 and 81 percent and 72 and 138 percent of daily intake requirements for iron in women and men, respectively (Alaunyte et al. 2012).

The bioavailability of iron in teff is likely to vary depending on processing. For instance, during the fermentation of injera, significant decreases in phytate content results in an ideal phytate-to-iron molar ratio (Umeta, West, and Fufa 2005; Baye et al. 2014). Given that part of the iron in teff has been attributed to soil contamination, to what extent molar ratios accurately predict iron bioavailability has been questioned (Baye et al. 2014). However, Bokhari et al. (2012) showed that consumption of 30 percent teff-enriched wheat breads can help maintain serum iron levels in pregnant women. The study also suggested that degradation of phytates may lead to better iron bioavailability. Given the high iron content of teff and its potential contribution to food-based approaches to improve nutrition, further investigations on the iron bioavailability of teff are required.[5] Indeed, if the bioavailability of iron in teff can be confirmed, teff can be a very good ingredient for celiac patients not only due to the absence of gluten but also for its high iron content.

Celiac Disease

Worldwide, 0.6 percent to 1.0 percent of the population is affected by celiac disease (CD) (Gujral, Freeman, and Thomson 2012). The prevalence of the disease in populations at risk of CD is as follows: 3 to 6 percent in type 1 diabetic patients, up to 20 percent in first-degree relatives, 10 to 15 percent in those with symptomatic iron-deficiency anemia (IDA), 3 to 6 percent in those with asymptomatic IDA, and 1 to 3 percent in individuals with

---

5 Food-based approaches are strategies to prevent and control micronutrient deficiencies. They consist of dietary improvement or fortification using inorganic forms of vitamins and minerals. Dietary improvement includes strategies like food-to-food fortification, dietary diversity, and household processing with the aim of improving the micronutrient content.

osteoporosis (Dubé et al. 2005). CD is caused by aberrant T-cell responses to glutens and gluten-like proteins found in wheat, barley, rye, and possibly oats (Vader et al. 2003; Arentz-Hansen et al. 2004). The symptoms include diarrhea, abdominal pain, and disturbances in nutrient absorption caused by histological alterations of the small bowel. Extraintestinal complications such as osteoporosis, infertility, and cancer have also been reported (Alaedini and Green 2005).

The only treatment for those with CD available to date is to follow a strict gluten-free diet (Fasano and Catassi 2001). This in practice is difficult given the abundance of food products containing wheat or other gluten-containing cereals. Consequently, inadequate intakes of essential nutrients such as folate and vitamin B12 (Hallert et al. 2002), calcium, iron, and fiber have been observed in those with CD (Thompson et al. 2005). Also, a higher percentage of energy intake in such patients was found to be from fat instead of carbohydrates. This has a negative impact on their nutritional status (Bardella et al. 2000). Therefore, nutrient-dense gluten-free alternatives are needed.

Teff, as discussed in previous sections, contains a good amount of minerals, fiber, and phytochemicals. Compared with gluten-free cereals and pseudocereals such as quinoa, amaranth, buckwheat, maize, brown rice, and sorghum, teff is more nutrient-dense (Alvarez-Jubete, Arendt, and Gallagher 2010; Gebremariam, Zarnkow, and Becker 2012). Furthermore, the low glycemic index of teff may help maintain good glycemic control. This is very important given the high incidence of diabetes in those with CD (Viljamaa et al. 2005).

Diabetes

The global incidence of diabetes is increasing alarmingly and has become a major public health problem (Danaei et al. 2011). In 2010 an estimated 285 million people worldwide were diabetic—a figure projected to rise to 439 million by 2030 (Shaw, Sicree, and Zimmet 2010). The socioeconomic and health implication of this disease, particularly in low- and middle-income countries, are enormous. The onset and progression of diabetes can be prevented by modifying lifestyle factors, of which diet constitutes a great part (Hu 2011). Several features of teff suggest that its consumption may prevent or control diabetes. Diets high in whole grains have been associated with a 20 to 30 percent reduction in the risk of developing type-2 diabetes (Hu 2011). Given that teff is consumed as a whole grain, similar effects can be expected from the consumption of teff. Although the mechanism by which whole grains help in the prevention of type-2 diabetes is not clearly elucidated, it is thought to be through the synergistic effects of the essential macronutrients and micronutrients as well as phytonutrients (Jonnalagadda et al. 2011).

Among macronutrients, the type of carbohydrate and its digestibility play a central role in glucose levels after eating and hence on the risk to diabetes (Sheard et al. 2004). Relative to wheat, teff has a low glycemic index and thus is better suited for diabetic patients (Wolter et al. 2013). In addition, the relatively high dietary fiber in teff relative to other common cereals can decrease fasting blood glucose levels and thus contribute to the prevention and management of diabetes (Post et al. 2012). The conditions of impaired antioxidant status and inflammation have been linked to the development of insulin resistance and type-2 diabetes (Wellen and Hotamisligil 2005; Folli et al. 2011). In this regard, the high phytate and polyphenol content in teff (Abebe et al. 2007; Baye et al. 2014) and the associated antioxidative property is likely to prevent and control diabetes (Lee et al. 2006; Munir et al. 2013). However, while studies to evaluate the antidiabetic property of teff consumption are of interest, so far such studies are very limited.

Conclusion

Teff, perhaps the world's smallest cereal grain, is composed of complex carbohydrates with slowly digestible starch. It has a similar protein content to other more common cereals like wheat but contains no gluten. Teff's amino acid composition is well balanced and contains relatively higher concentrations of lysine than what is commonly found in other cereals. Teff is a comparatively good source of essential fatty acids, fiber, minerals (especially calcium and iron), and phytochemicals, such as polyphenols and phytates. Despite having a very good nutrient profile, teff's consumption is limited to Ethiopia and Eritrea. The limited knowledge of teff's nutrient composition along with processing challenges faced in making teff-based food products adapted for international consumers has restrained its global use for human consumption.

However, in the recent past studies on the nutritional composition of teff and its processing quality and development of new teff-based food products have grown. These studies have confirmed the excellent nutrient composition of teff and demonstrated that through the use of enzymes, hydrocolloids, or sourdough fermentation that it may be possible to overcome food-processing challenges faced when using teff as an ingredient for bread making. Further research should investigate the variation in nutrient composition across teff varieties, the role of teff consumption on the management and prevention of diabetes, and the human absorption (bioavailability) of iron in teff and how it can contribute to the prevention of iron deficiency. Along with the possible health benefits in managing celiac disease, and a possible solution in preventing and controlling iron deficiency and diabetes, these all indicate the potential of teff to be a future global functional food for health promotion and disease prevention.

References

Abebe, Y., A. Bogale, K. Michael Hambidge, B. J. Stoecker, K. Bailey, and R. S. Gibson. 2007. "Phytate, Zinc, Iron, and Calcium Content of Selected Raw and Prepared Foods Consumed in Rural Sidama, Southern Ethiopia, and Implications for Bioavailability." *Journal of Food Composition and Analysis* 20 (3): 161–168.

Abebe, W., and F. Ronda. 2014. "Rheological and Textural Properties of Teff [*Eragrostis tef* (Zucc.) Trotter] Grain Flour Gels." *Journal of Cereal Science* 60 (1): 122–130.

Adebowale, A. A., M. Naushad Emmambux, M. Beukes, and J. Taylor. 2011. "Fractionation and Characterization of Teff Proteins." *Journal of Cereal Science* 54 (3): 380–386.

Adish, A. A., S. A. Esrey, T. W. Gyorkos, and T. Johns. 1999. "Risk Factors for Iron Deficiency Anaemia in Preschool Children in Northern Ethiopia." *Public Health Nutrition* 2 (3): 243–252.

Agren, G., and R. S. Gibson. 1968. *Food Composition Table for Use in Ethiopia*. Stockholm, Sweden: Swedish International Development Authority; Addis Ababa: Ethiopian Nutrition Institute.

Alaedini, A., and P.H.R. Green. 2005. "Narrative Review: Celiac Disease: Understanding a Complex Autoimmune Disorder." *Annals of Internal Medicine* 142 (4): 289–298.

Alaunyte, I., V. Stojceska, A. Plunkett, P. Ainsworth, and E. Derbyshire. 2012. "Improving the Quality of Nutrient-Rich Teff (*Eragrostis tef*) Breads by Combination of Enzymes in Straight Dough and Sourdough Breadmaking." *Journal of Cereal Science* 55 (1): 22–30.

Alvarez-Jubete, L., E. K. Arendt, and E. Gallagher. 2010. "Nutritive Value of Pseudocereals and Their Increasing Use as Functional Gluten-Free Ingredients." *Trends in Food Science and Technology* 21 (2): 106–113.

Ambaw, A. 2013. "Determination of Iron Fractions of Laboratory Threshed and Field Threshed Teff Injera." Addis Ababa University, Addis Ababa.

Areda, A., S. Ketema, J. Ingram, and R. H. Davis. 1993. "The Iron Content of Teff [*Eragrostis tef* (Zucc.) Trotter] and Its Controversy." *SINET: An Ethiopian Journal of Science* 16: 5–13.

Arendt, E. K., L. A. Ryan, and F. D. Bello. 2007. "Impact of Sourdough on the Texture of Bread." *Food Microbiology* 24 (2): 165–174.

Arentz-Hansen, H., B. Fleckenstein, Ø. Molberg, H. Scott, F. Koning, G. Jung, P. Roepstorff, K.E.A. Lundin, and L. M. Sollid. 2004. "The Molecular Basis for Oat Intolerance in Patients with Celiac Disease." *PLoS Medicine* 1 (1): e1.

Bardella, M. T., C. Fredella, L. Prampolini, N. Molteni, A. M. Giunta, and P. A. Bianchi. 2000. "Body Composition and Dietary Intakes in Adult Celiac Disease Patients Consuming a Strict Gluten-Free Diet." *American Journal of Clinical Nutrition* 72 (4): 937–939.

Baye, K. 2013. "Food-Based Strategies to Enhance Iron and Zinc Bioavailability of Complementary Foods Consumed by Young Children in Ethiopia." PhD dissertation, University of Montpellier, Montpellier, France.

Baye, K., J. Guyot, C. Icard-Verniere, and C. Mouquet-Rivier. 2013. "Nutrient Intakes from Complementary Foods Consumed by Young Children (Aged 12–23 Months) from North Wollo, Northern Ethiopia: The Need for Agro-Ecologically Adapted Interventions." *Public Health Nutrition* 16 (10): 1741–1750.

Baye, K., C. Mouquet-Rivier, C. Icard-Vernière, C. Picq, and J. Guyot. 2014. "Changes in Mineral Absorption Inhibitors Consequent to Fermentation of Ethiopian Injera: Implications for Predicted Iron Bioavailability and Bioaccessibility." *International Journal of Food Science and Technology* 49 (1): 174–180.

Baye, K., C. Mouquet-Rivier, C. Icard-Vernière, I. Rochette, and J. Guyot. 2013. "Influence of Flour Blend Composition on Fermentation Kinetics and Phytate Hydrolysis of Sourdough Used to Make Injera." *Food Chemistry* 138 (1): 430–436.

Bekele, E., R. J. Fido, A. S. Tatham, and P. R. Shewry. 1995. "Heterogeneity and Polymorphism of Seed Proteins in Teff (*Eragrostis tef*)." *Hereditas* 122 (1): 67–72.

Ben-Fayed, E., P. Ainsworth, and V. Stojceska. 2008. "The Incorporation of Teff (*Eragrostis tef*) in Bread-Making Technology." *Cereal Food World* 53: A84.

Bezwoda, W. R., T. H. Bothwell, J. D. Torrance, A. P. MacPhail, R. W. Charlton, G. Kay, and J. Levin. 1979. "The Relationship between Marrow Iron Stores, Plasma Ferritin Concentrations and Iron Absorption." *Scandinavian Journal of Haematology* 22 (2): 113–120.

Bohn, L., A. S. Meyer, and S. K. Rasmussen. 2008. "Phytate: Impact on Environment and Human Nutrition: A Challenge for Molecular Breeding." *Journal of Zhejiang University-Science B* 9 (3): 165–191.

Bokhari, F., E. Derbyshire, W. Li, C. S. Brennan, and V. Stojceska. 2012. "A Study to Establish Whether Food-Based Approaches Can Improve Serum Iron Levels in Child-Bearing Aged Women." *Journal of Human Nutrition and Dietetics* 25 (1): 95–100.

Brune, M., L. Rossander, and L. Hallberg. 1989. "Iron Absorption and Phenolic Compounds: Importance of Different Phenolic Structures." *European Journal of Clinical Nutrition* 43 (8): 547–557.

Bultosa, G. 2007. "Physicochemical Characteristics of Grain and Flour in 13 Tef [*Eragrostis tef* (Zucc.) Trotter] Grain Varieties." *Journal of Applied Science Research* 3 (12): 2042–2051.

Bultosa, G., A. N. Hall, and J. Taylor. 2002. "Physico-Chemical Characterization of Grain Tef [*Eragrostis tef* (Zucc.) Trotter] Starch." *Starch-Stärke* 54 (10): 461–468.

Bultosa, G., and J.R.N. Taylor. 2004. "Teff." In *Encyclopaedia of Grain Science*, edited by H. Corke, C. E. Walker, and C. Wrigley, 281–289. Waltham, MA, US: Academic Press.

Champ, M., A. Langkilde, F. Brouns, B. Kettlitz, and Y. L. Bail Collet. 2003. "Advances in Dietary Fibre Characterisation. 1. Definition of Dietary Fibre, Physiological Relevance, Health Benefits and Analytical Aspects." *Nutrition Research Reviews* 16 (1): 71–82.

Clark, S. F. 2008. "Iron Deficiency Anemia." *Nutrition in Clinical Practice* 23 (2): 128–141.

Coleman, J., A. O. Abaye, W. Barbeau, and W. Thomason. 2013. "The Suitability of Teff Flour in Bread, Layer Cakes, Cookies, and Biscuits." *International Journal of Food Sciences and Nutrition* 64 (7): 877–881.

Cummings, J. H, J. I. Mann, C. Nishida, and H. H. Vorster. 2009. "Dietary Fibre: An Agreed Definition." *The Lancet* 373 (9661): 365–366.

Curhan, G. C., W. C. Willett, E. L. Knight, and M. J. Stampfer. 2004. "Dietary Factors and the Risk of Incident Kidney Stones in Younger Women: Nurses' Health Study II." *Archives of Internal Medicine* 164 (8): 885–891.

Danaei, G., M. M. Finucane, Y. Lu, G. M. Singh, M. J. Cowan, C. J. Paciorek, J. K. Lin, et al. 2011. "National, Regional, and Global Trends in Fasting Plasma Glucose and Diabetes Prevalence since 1980: Systematic Analysis of Health Examination Surveys and Epidemiological Studies with 370 Country-Years and 2–7 Million Participants." *The Lancet* 378 (9785): 31–40.

Delcour, J. A., C. Bruneel, L. J. Derde, S. V. Gomand, B. Pareyt, J. A. Putseys, E. Wilderjans, and L. Lamberts. 2010. "Fate of Starch in Food Processing: From Raw Materials to Final Food Products." *Food Science and Technology* 1: 87–111.

Demissie, A. 2000. "Teff Genetic Resources in Ethiopia." In *Narrowing the Rift: Tef Research and Development*. Proceedings of the International Workshop on Tef Genetics and Improvement, Debre Zeit, Ethiopia, October 16–19.

DeVries, J. W. 2003. "On Defining Dietary Fibre." *Proceedings of the Nutrition Society* 62 (1): 37–43.

Dubé, C., A. Rostom, R. Sy, A. Cranney, N. Saloojee, C. Garritty, M. Sampson, et al. 2005. "The Prevalence of Celiac Disease in Average-Risk and at-Risk Western European Populations: A Systematic Review." *Gastroenterology* 128 (4) Supplement 1: S57–S67.

Dykes, L., and L. W. Rooney. 2006. "Sorghum and Millet Phenols and Antioxidants." *Journal of Cereal Science* 44 (3): 236–251.

Egli, I., L. Davidsson, C. Zeder, T. Walczyk, and R. Hurrell. 2004. "Dephytinization of a Complementary Food Based on Wheat and Soy Increases Zinc, but Not Copper, Apparent Absorption in Adults." *Journal of Nutrition* 134 (5): 1077–1080.

El-Alfy, T. S., S. M. Ezzat, and A. A. Sleem. 2012. "Chemical and Biological Study of the Seeds of *Eragrostis tef* (Zucc.) Trotter." *Natural Product Research* 26 (7): 619–629.

Fairweather-Tait, S. J. 2002. "Bioavailability of Trace Elements in Human Diet." *Trace Elements in Man and Animals* 10: 255–260.

FAO (Food and Agriculture Organization of the United Nations). 1992. *Maize in Human Nutrition*. Rome: FAO.

Fardet, A., F. Leenhardt, D. Lioger, A. Scalbert, and C. Rémésy. 2006. "Parameters Controlling the Glycaemic Response to Breads." *Nutrition Research Reviews* 19 (1): 18–25.

Fasano, A., and C. Catassi. 2001. "Current Approaches to Diagnosis and Treatment of Celiac Disease: An Evolving Spectrum." *Gastroenterology* 120 (3): 636–651.

Folli, F., D. Corradi, P. Fanti, A. Davalli, A. Paez, A. Giaccari, C. Perego, and G. Muscogiuri. 2011. "The Role of Oxidative Stress in the Pathogenesis of Type 2 Diabetes Mellitus Micro- and Macrovascular Complications: Avenues for a Mechanistic-Based Therapeutic Approach." *Current Diabetes Reviews* 7 (5): 313–324.

García-Manzanares, Á., and A. J. Lucendo. 2011. "Nutritional and Dietary Aspects of Celiac Disease." *Nutrition in Clinical Practice* 26 (2): 163–173.

Gebhardt, S. E., R. L. Cutrufelli, J. C. Howe, D. B. Haytowitz, P. R. Pehrsson, L. E. Lemar, G. T. Holcomb, M. A. Stup, R. G. Thomas, J. Exler, B. A. Showell, and J. M. Holden. 2006. USDA National Nutrient Database for Standard Reference, Release 19. Accessed September 21, 2017. www.ars.usda.gov/nutrientdata.

Gebremariam, M. M., M. Zarnkow, and T. Becker. 2012. "Teff (*Eragrostis tef*) as a Raw Material for Malting, Brewing, and Manufacturing of Gluten-Free Foods and Beverages: A Review." *Journal of Food Science and Technology* 1–15.

Gebre-Medhin, M., A. Killander, B. Vahlquist, and E. Wuhib. 1976. "Rarity of Anaemia of Pregnancy in Ethiopia." *Scandinavian Journal of Haematology* 16 (3): 168–175.

Georgieff, M. K. 2011. "Long-Term Brain and Behavioral Consequences of Early Iron Deficiency." *Nutrition Reviews* 69 (S1): S43–S48.

Gibson, R. S., K. B. Bailey, M. Gibbs, and E. L. Ferguson. 2010. "A Review of Phytate, Iron, Zinc, and Calcium Concentrations in Plant-Based Complementary Foods Used in Low-Income Countries and Implications for Bioavailability." *Food and Nutrition Bulletin* 31 (Supplement 2): 134–146.

Good, S. 2009. "Animal Source Foods and Nutrition During Early Life: An Evaluation of the Possible Link between Livestock Keeping, Food Intake, and Nutritional Status of Young Children in Ethiopia." ETH Zurich.

Gujral, N., H. J. Freeman, and A.B.R. Thomson. 2012. "Celiac Disease: Prevalence, Diagnosis, Pathogenesis and Treatment." *World Journal of Gastroenterology: WJG* 18 (42): 6036.

Hager, A., and E. K. Arendt. 2013. "Influence of Hydroxypropylmethylcellulose (Hpmc), Xanthan Gum and Their Combination on Loaf Specific Volume, Crumb Hardness and Crumb Grain Characteristics of Gluten-Free Breads Based on Rice, Maize, Teff, and Buckwheat." *Food Hydrocolloids* 32 (1): 195–203.

Hager, A., M. Czerny, J. Bez, E. Zannini, and E. K. Arendt. 2013. "Starch Properties, *in Vitro* Digestibility and Sensory Evaluation of Fresh Egg Pasta Produced from Oat, Teff, and Wheat Flour." *Journal of Cereal Science* 58 (1): 156–163.

Hallberg, L., and E. Björn-Rasmussen. 1981. "Measurement of Iron Absorption from Meals Contaminated with Iron." *American Journal of Clinical Nutrition* 34 (12): 2808–2815.

Hallert, C., C. Grant, S. Grehn, C. Grännö, S. Hulten, G. Midhagen, M. Ström, H. Svensson, and T. Valdimarsson. 2002. "Evidence of Poor Vitamin Status in Coeliac Patients on a Gluten-Free Diet for 10 Years." *Alimentary Pharmacology and Therapeutics* 16 (7): 1333–1339.

Harris, P., and R. J. Geor. 2009. "Primer on Dietary Carbohydrates and Utility of the Glycemic Index in Equine Nutrition." *Veterinary Clinics of North America: Equine Practice* 25 (1): 23–37.

Helbing, J. 2009. *Konfokale laser scanning-mikroskopie und rasterelektronenmikroskopie zur beobachtung der mälzung verschiedener zerealien und pseudozerealien*. Munich, Germany: Technische Universität München.

Hopman, E., L. Dekking, M. Blokland, M. Wuisman, W. Zuijderduin, F. Koning, and J. Schweizer. 2008. "Teff in the Diet of Celiac Patients in the Netherlands." *Scandinavian Journal of Gastroenterology* 43 (3): 277–282.

Hu, F. B. 2011. "Globalization of Diabetes: The Role of Diet, Lifestyle, and Genes." *Diabetes Care* 34 (6): 1249–1257.

Hurrell, R., and I. Egli. 2010. "Iron Bioavailability and Dietary Reference Values." *American Journal of Clinical Nutrition* 91 (5): 1461S–1467S.

Jonnalagadda, S. S., L. Harnack, R. H. Liu, N. McKeown, C. Seal, S. Liu, and G. C. Fahey. 2011. "Putting the Whole Grain Puzzle Together: Health Benefits Associated with Whole Grains—Summary of American Society for Nutrition 2010 Satellite Symposium." *Journal of Nutrition* 141 (5): 1011S–1022S.

Juliano, B. O. 1993. *Rice in Human Nutrition*. Los Baños, Laguna, Philippines: International Rice Research Institute.

Kebede, Z. 2009. "Levels of Essential Elements in Three Teff [*Eragrostis tef* (Zucc.)Trotter] Varieties." Addis Ababa University, Addis Ababa.

Ketema, S. 1997a. *Tef-Eragrostis tef* (Zucc.). Vol. 12. Rome: Bioversity International.

———. 1997b. "*Tef, Eragrostis tef* (Zucc.) Trotter: Promoting the Conservation and Use of Underutilized and Neglected Crops 12." Institute of Plant Genetics and Crop Plant Research, Gatersleben; International Plant Genetic Resources Institute, Rome.

Khoi, B. H., L. D. Dien, R. Lásztity, and A. Salgó. 1987. "The Protein and the Amino Acid Composition of Some Rice and Maize Varieties Grown in North Vietnam." *Journal of the Science of Food and Agriculture* 39 (2): 137–143.

Koletzko, B., S. Baker, G. Cleghorn, U. F. Neto, S. Gopalan, O. Hernell, Q. S. Hock, et al. 2005. "Global Standard for the Composition of Infant Formula: Recommendations of an Espghan Coordinated International Expert Group." *Journal of Pediatric Gastroenterology and Nutrition* 41 (5): 584–599.

Lacey, T., and C. Llewellyn. 2005. "*Eragrostis tef* as a Specialised Niche Crop." *Government of Western Australia, Department of Agriculture Farmnote* 42.

Lafiandra, D., G. Riccardi, and P. R. Shewry. 2014. "Improving Cereal Grain Carbohydrates for Diet and Health." *Journal of Cereal Science* 59 (3): 312–326.

Lee, S., H. Park, S. Y. Cho, H. Jung, S. M. Cho, Y. Cho, and H. S. Lillehoj. 2005. "Effects of Dietary Phytic Acid on Serum and Hepatic Lipid Levels in Diabetic Kk Mice." *Nutrition Research* 25 (9): 869–876.

Lee, S., H. Park, H. Chun, S. Y. Cho, S. M. Cho, and H. S. Lillehoj. 2006. "Dietary Phytic Acid Lowers the Blood Glucose Level in Diabetic Kk Mice." *Nutrition Research* 26 (9): 474–479.

Loewus, F. A. 2002. *Biosynthesis of Phytate in Food Grains and Seeds*. Boca Raton, FL, US: CRC Press.

Ludwig, D. S. 2002. "The Glycemic Index: Physiological Mechanisms Relating to Obesity, Diabetes, and Cardiovascular Disease." *Journal of the American Medical Association* 287 (18): 2414–2423.

Manach, C., A. Scalbert, C. Morand, C. Rémésy, and L. Jiménez. 2004. "Polyphenols: Food Sources and Bioavailability." *American Journal of Clinical Nutrition* 79 (5): 727–747.

Manary, M. J., C. Hotz, N. F. Krebs, R. S. Gibson, J. E. Westcott, R. L. Broadhead, and K. M. Hambidge. 2002. "Zinc Homeostasis in Malawian Children Consuming a High-Phytate, Maize-Based Diet." *American Journal of Clinical Nutrition* 75 (6): 1057–1061.

Matuschek, E., and U. Svanberg. 2002. "Oxidation of Polyphenols and the Effect on in Vitro Iron Accessibility in a Model Food System." *Journal of Food Science* 67 (1): 420–424.

Mbuya, K., K. Nkongolo, and A. Kalonji-Mbuyi. 2011. "Nutritional Analysis of Quality Protein Maize Varieties Selected for Agronomic Characteristics in a Breeding Program." *International Journal of Plant Breeding and Genetics* 5 (4): 317–327.

McDonough, C. M., L. W. Rooney, and S. O. Serna-Saldivar. 2000. "The Millets." In *Food Science and Technology,* 177–202. New York: Marcel Dekker.

Mengesha, M. H. 1966. "Chemical Composition of Teff (*Eragrostis tef*) Compared with That of Wheat, Barley, and Grain Sorghum." *Economic Botany* 20 (3): 268–273.

Michaelsen, K. F., K. G. Dewey, A. B. Perez-Exposito, M. Nurhasan, L. Lauritzen, and N. Roos. 2011. "Food Sources and Intake of N-6 and N-3 Fatty Acids in Low-Income Countries with Emphasis on Infants, Young Children (6–24 Months), and Pregnant and Lactating Women." *Maternal and Child Nutrition* 7 (S2): 124–140.

Mohammed, M. I., A. I. Mustafa, and G.A.M. Osman. 2009. "Evaluation of Wheat Breads Supplemented with Teff (*Eragrostis tef* (Zucc.) Trotter) Grain Flour." *Australian Journal of Crop Science* 3 (4): 207–212.

Moore, M. M., F. D. Bello, and E. K. Arendt. 2008. "Sourdough Fermented by Lactobacillus Plantarum Fst 1.7 Improves the Quality and Shelf Life of Gluten-Free Bread." *European Food Research and Technology* 226 (6): 1309–1316.

Morris, E. R., and R. Ellis. 1985. "Bioavailability of Dietary Calcium." In *Nutritional Bioavailabilty of Calcium,* 63–72. Washington, DC: American Chemical Society.

Mossé, J., J. C. Huet, and J. Baudet. 1985. "The Amino Acid Composition of Wheat Grain as a Function of Nitrogen Content." *Journal of Cereal Science* 3 (2): 115–130.

Munir, K. M., S. Chandrasekaran, F. Gao, and M. J. Quon. 2013. "Mechanisms for Food Polyphenols to Ameliorate Insulin Resistance and Endothelial Dysfunction: Therapeutic Implications for Diabetes and Its Cardiovascular Complications." *American Journal of Physiology-Endocrinology and Metabolism* 305 (6): E679–E686.

Pasricha, S., H. Drakesmith, J. Black, D. Hipgrave, and B. Biggs. 2013. "Control of Iron Deficiency Anemia in Low- and Middle-Income Countries." *Blood* 121 (14): 2607–2617.

Piccinin, D. 2002. *More about Ethiopian Food: Teff.* EthnoMed: Ethiopian Food. https://ethnomed.org/clinical/nutrition/more-about-ethiopian-food-teff.

Post, R. E., A. G. Mainous, D. E. King, and K. N. Simpson. 2012. "Dietary Fiber for the Treatment of Type 2 Diabetes Mellitus: A Meta-Analysis." *Journal of the American Board of Family Medicine* 25 (1): 16–23.

Renzetti, S., and E. K. Arendt. 2009. "Effects of Oxidase and Protease Treatments on the Breadmaking Functionality of a Range of Gluten-Free Flours." *European Food Research and Technology* 229 (2): 307–317.

Sandström, B. 1997. "Bioavailability of Zinc." *European Journal of Clinical Nutrition* 51: S17.

Sazawal, S., R. E. Black, M. Ramsan, H. M Chwaya, R. J. Stoltzfus, A. Dutta, U. Dhingra, et al. 2006. "Effects of Routine Prophylactic Supplementation with Iron and Folic Acid on Admission to Hospital and Mortality in Preschool Children in a High Malaria Transmission Setting: Community-Based, Randomised, Placebo-Controlled Trial." *The Lancet* 367 (9505): 133–143.

Scalbert, A., C. Manach, C. Morand, C. Rémésy, and L. Jiménez. 2005. "Dietary Polyphenols and the Prevention of Diseases." *Critical Reviews in Food Science and Nutrition* 45 (4): 287–306.

Schlemmer, U., W. Frølich, R. M. Prieto, and F. Grases. 2009. "Phytate in Foods and Significance for Humans: Food Sources, Intake, Processing, Bioavailability, Protective Role, and Analysis." *Molecular Nutrition and Food Research* 53 (S2): S330–S375.

Schober, T. J., S. R. Bean, and D. L. Boyle. 2007. "Gluten-Free Sorghum Bread Improved by Sourdough Fermentation: Biochemical, Rheological, and Microstructural Background." *Journal of Agricultural and Food Chemistry* 55 (13): 5137–5146.

Shamsuddin, A. M. 1995. "Inositol Phosphates Have Novel Anticancer Function." *Journal of Nutrition* 125 (3) supplement: 725S–732S.

Shaw, J. E., R. A. Sicree, and P. Z. Zimmet. 2010. "Global Estimates of the Prevalence of Diabetes for 2010 and 2030." *Diabetes Research and Clinical Practice* 87 (1): 4–14.

Sheard, N. F., N. G. Clark, J. C. Brand-Miller, M. J. Franz, F. X. Pi-Sunyer, E. Mayer-Davis, K. Kulkarni, and P. Geil. 2004. "Dietary Carbohydrate (Amount and Type) in the Prevention and Management of Diabetes: A Statement by the American Diabetes Association." *Diabetes Care* 27 (9): 2266–2271.

Shoup, F. K., C. W. Deyoe, J. Campbell, and D. B. Parrish. 1969. "Amino Acid Composition and Nutritional Value of Milled Sorghum Grain Products." *Cereal Chemistry* 46 (2): 164–171.

Simopoulos, A. P. 2001. "N-3 Fatty Acids and Human Health: Defining Strategies for Public Policy." *Lipids* 36 (1): S83–S89.

Singh, J., A. Dartois, and L. Kaur. 2010. "Starch Digestibility in Food Matrix: A Review." *Trends in Food Science and Technology* 21 (4): 168–180.

Singh, R. P., C. Agarwal, and R. Agarwal. 2003. "Inositol Hexaphosphate Inhibits Growth, and Induces G1 Arrest and Apoptotic Death of Prostate Carcinoma Du145 Cells: Modulation of Cdki-Cdk-Cyclin and Prb-Related Protein-E2f Complexes." *Carcinogenesis* 24 (3): 555–563.

Spaenij-Dekking, L., Y. Kooy-Winkelaar, and F. Koning. 2005. "The Ethiopian Cereal Teff in Celiac Disease." *New England Journal of Medicine* 353 (16): 1748–1749.

Stoltzfus, R. J. 2011. "Iron Interventions for Women and Children in Low-Income Countries." *Journal of Nutrition* 141 (4): 756S–762S.

Tatham, A. S., R. J. Fido, C. M. Moore, D. D. Kasarda, D. D. Kuzmicky, J. N. Keen, and P. R. Shewry. 1996. "Characterisation of the Major Prolamins of Teff (*Eragrostis tef*) and Finger Millet (*Eleusine coracana*)." *Journal of Cereal Science* 24 (1): 65–71.

Tester, R. F., J. Karkalas, and X. Qi. 2004. "Starch Structure and Digestibility Enzyme-Substrate Relationship." *World's Poultry Science Journal* 60 (2): 186–195.

Thompson, T., M. Dennis, L. A. Higgins, A. R. Lee, and M. K. Sharrett. 2005. "Gluten-Free Diet Survey: Are Americans with Coeliac Disease Consuming Recommended Amounts of Fibre, Iron, Calcium, and Grain Foods?" *Journal of Human Nutrition and Dietetics* 18 (3): 163–169.

Troesch, B., I. Egli, C. Zeder, R. F. Hurrell, S. D. Pee, and M. B. Zimmermann. 2009. "Optimization of a Phytase-Containing Micronutrient Powder with Low Amounts of Highly Bioavailable Iron for In-Home Fortification of Complementary Foods." *American Journal of Clinical Nutrition* 89 (2): 539–544.

Umeta, M., and M. L. Parker. 1996. "Microscopic Studies of the Major Macro-Components of Seeds, Dough and Injera from Teff (*Eragrostis tef*)." *SINET: Ethiopian Journal of Science* 19 (1): 141–148.

Umeta, M., C. E. West, and H. Fufa. 2005. "Content of Zinc, Iron, Calcium and Their Absorption Inhibitors in Foods Commonly Consumed in Ethiopia." *Journal of Food Composition and Analysis* 18 (8): 803–817.

USDA (United States Department of Agriculture). 2013. National nutrient database for standard reference. Accessed February 2014. www.nal.usda.gov/fnic/foodcomp.

Vader, L. W., D. T. Stepniak, E. M. Bunnik, Y. Kooy, W. D. Haan, J. W. Drijfhout, P.A.V. Veelen, and F. Koning. 2003. "Characterization of Cereal Toxicity for Celiac Disease Patients Based on Protein Homology in Grains." *Gastroenterology* 125 (4): 1105–1113.

Viljamaa, M., K. Kaukinen, H. Huhtala, S. Kyrönpalo, M. Rasmussen, and P. Collin. 2005. "Coeliac Disease, Autoimmune Diseases, and Gluten Exposure." *Scandinavian Journal of Gastroenterology* 40 (4): 437–443.

Weaver, C. M., and S. Kannan. 2002. "Phytate and Mineral Bioavailability." *Food Phytates* 2002: 211–23.

Wellen, K. E., and G. S. Hotamisligil. 2005. "Inflammation, Stress, and Diabetes." *Journal of Clinical Investigation* 115 (5): 1111–1119.

Wolter, A., A. Hager, E. Zannini, and E. K. Arendt. " 2013. *In Vitro* Starch Digestibility and Predicted Glycaemic Indexes of Buckwheat, Oat, Quinoa, Sorghum, Teff, and Commercial Gluten-Free Bread." *Journal of Cereal Science* 58 (3): 431–436.

Yetneberk, S., H. L. de Kock, L. W. Rooney, and J. R. N. Taylor. 2004. "Effects of Sorghum Cultivar on Injera Quality." *Cereal Chemistry* 81 (3): 314–321.

Yetneberk, S., L. W. Rooney, and J. Taylor. 2005. "Improving the Quality of Sorghum Injera by Decortication and Compositing with Teff." *Journal of the Science of Food and Agriculture* 85 (8): 1252–1258.

Zegeye, A. 1997. "Acceptability of Injera with Stewed Chicken." *Food Quality and Preference* 8 (4): 293–295.

Zimmerman, M. B., C. Chassard, F. Rohner, E. K. N'Goran, C. Nindjin, A. Dostal, J. Utzinger, et al. 2010. "The Effects of Iron Fortification on the Gut Microbiota in African Children: A Randomized Controlled Trial in Cote D'Ivoire." *American Journal of Clinical Nutrition* 92 (6): 1406–1415.

Zimmermann, M. B., and R. F. Hurrell. 2007. "Nutritional Iron Deficiency." *The Lancet* 370 (9586): 511–520.

Chapter 16

CONCLUSION

Bart Minten, Alemayehu Seyoum Taffesse, and Petra Brown

By any measure, teff is an important crop in Ethiopia. It is estimated that one-fifth of all land under cultivation in the country, approximately 2.7 million hectares, is used to grow teff. However, while teff has been grown and consumed in Ethiopia for centuries, relatively little is known about the economics of teff production and the postfarm teff value chain that supplies this staple to millions. This is set to change with more time and effort being devoted to building the value chains surrounding its production, marketing, and consumption in various ways. People in government, agriculture, health, research, and other areas are becoming more aware that by increasing teff productivity through research, application, and training, this drive could turn around the lives of many poor people in rural communities.

Ethiopia's economy is transforming, people's incomes are increasing, and as consumers purchase more preferred foods, they consume more teff. But such demands come at a price. There is pressure on the government and other stakeholders to change agricultural and food policies and their implementation, as well as pressure on the smallholding traditional farmers to modify their practices to adapt to a changing consumption pattern, with new farming techniques that increase yield and minimize waste. Teff is emerging to become a crop that is more productive and renowned for its gluten-free and rich nutrient constitution. This "orphan crop" is receiving more attention after decades of relative neglect, and this first book on the teff economy represents the beginning of greater insight into the economic fundamentals of the value chain of this tiny grain. The important consequence and possibility of teff for Ethiopia's economy, and further afield, deserve broader recognition.

Although unique, teff has been subject to many misconceptions. Even from the early years in primary school education, Ethiopian children were raised with the notion that teff was of low nutritional value and that it was the food of the well-to-do or the rich. Moreover, it was considered a low-yield crop with little potential for technological manipulation. Fortunately, growing scientific understanding and empirical evidence have eroded these misconceptions.

Nevertheless, the price of teff is still prohibitive for most lower-income households although it offers, as a cash crop, an important source of income for agricultural households.

Past food security policies in Ethiopia seem to have been influenced by certain characteristics of teff. First, the environmental impact of teff-based farming systems, especially in terms of low productivity, were considered not suitable for ensuring food security for a fast-growing population. The land preparation techniques therefore require significant improvement to attain sustainable teff production. Second, given the low yields, the calorie output per hectare is limited compared with other crops, and this constitutes a considerable constraint with the increasing scarcity of land in the mid-altitude ecozones of the highlands where teff is well adapted to the conditions. Therefore, expansion of teff at the expense of other higher-yield crops like maize, wheat, sorghum, and enset that consequently generate more calories will pose significant challenges in terms of meeting food security and food self-sufficiency nationally, especially for poor families who cannot afford to farm or purchase this crop. A key policy challenge is finding ways to promote production and consumption of teff, while maintaining the mixed farming systems that combine these other crops as well as legumes and livestock.

Teff's productive potential has intensified significantly, albeit from a low base, over recent years with a combination of better seeds and improved farming practices. Farmers' yields still remain relatively low though. In parallel, the rising domestic and potential international demand can only be met via considerable growth in teff production. The dilemma continues as to how much exposure to international trade this "hidden food source" can carry in light of the impact this could have on domestic teff prices and Ethiopian consumers. Nevertheless, the time is ripe for the emergence of teff from what was once thought "a threat to food security that should be abandoned" to a crop that deserves more recognition locally and globally. It is hoped that this book contributes toward that recognition.

A Transforming Teff Economy

Based on emerging patterns in teff production, marketing, and consumption as described throughout this book, the overall shift within the teff sector is driven by changes in technology, urbanization, and behavior, among others. The teff value chain is on the move; and through identifying the working practices, processes, and drivers from upstream through downstream in the value chain, key revelations about teff are brought to attention. The following highlights the key findings and discussions within the three domains referred to in the introduction—production, marketing, and consumption. The concluding part of this chapter covers the policy implications with due consideration of the challenges faced in developing the teff economy in Ethiopia.

Production

Teff is Ethiopia's most important cereal crop in both area and value. Teff production in 2013/2014 was valued at approximately US$2.5 billion, significantly higher than any other single crop in the country. The value of its commercial surplus was as high as US$750 million, equal to the value of commercial surplus of all other cereals in the country combined. Teff provides comparable calorific value to other cereals as well as considerable nutrient content and is gluten-free. It plays a complex and significant role in the diets of the Ethiopian consumer. Consumption of teff and its different qualities—white, mixed, and red—are linked to the budgetary constraints of consumers. The budget share of teff grows with income since it is a more preferred cereal. This growth is agumented by two price-related facts. First, teff prices are high compared with other cereals. Second, the highly preferred and expensive white teff varieties are consumed more by richer consumers than red varieties (Chapter 3). Both lead to growing expenditure on teff consumption as household income rises.

It was not until the mid-20th century that modern science was introduced to programs to improve teff cultivars, distribute improved teff seed, and accelerate the contribution of genetic gain to teff yield growth across the country's smallholder farming systems (Chapter 4). Teff breeding has, until now, focused on conventional cross-breeding and selection techniques. With more sophisticated techniques available, a faster selection process is possible to deliver a larger portfolio of improved teff varieties to farmers (Chapters 3 and 13). While the Quncho variety has been successful, there remains room to further breeding programs that address, for example, consumers' preferences as well as disease and pest resistance (Chapters 3, 13, and 14).

In this regard, it is not easy to design an architecture that integrates formal and informal seed systems and bridges gaps between state, private, and civil society actors in the provision of seed (Chapter 4). Nevertheless, creating better ways to measure seed demand and supply could provide the critical information to designing seed systems that are responsive to farmers' needs and the capability of seed producers. A market-based design in which seed demand assessments are conducted by those who have greater incentives to engage in delivering seed quality and quantity would, if coupled with other strategic public interventions, improve supply to smallholders (Chapter 4). Building on policy initiatives already in place, any structural reform needs to raise practical and flexible collaboration between essential actors to expand seed enterprises.

Bridging the gap between formal and informal systems as described above presents parallels with traditional and modern practices in farming. There is often a big gap between the supply of new technologies and their efficient adoption, since innovations spread slowly and require different management skills (Moser and Barrett 2003; Duflo, Kremer, and Robinson 2008; Collier and Dercon 2011). The design and implementation of a promotional campaign for adopting improved technologies (described in Chapter 5) shows the challenges in the adoption of row planting to increase teff yields. Like most improved land management technologies (for example, Moser and Barrett 2003), labor requirement showed an increase from traditional broadcasting to organized row planting. In addition, other changes such as the time and effort for learning new methods by farmers, and the engagement from extension workers, are illustrated. Using cost-benefit analyses, teff yield gain was shown to outweigh the extra labor cost, if yields increased by more than 8 percent, making the investment worthwhile. Moreover, the use of a mechanical row planter demonstrated high returns and could also stimulate higher adoption rates (Chapter 5).

Many factors influencing teff productivity are analyzed in this book. In Chapter 6 the spatial patterns that emerge from examining the road infrastructure, the connectivity between the regions, and access to markets suggest that areas of greater teff production and fertilizer application are closer to major roads and cities. This pattern is much broader than the production corridors between Addis Ababa and two other cities—Bahir Dar and Adama—that existed almost 20 years ago. However, continued investment in road infrastructure to expand road links to rural areas and improve communications, and the resultant improvements in market access, are likely to be associated with improved production patterns and input use (Demeke et al. 1998; Dorosh et al. 2010; Minten, Koru, and Stifel 2013). Relatedly, productivity is shown to improve with both scale of operation and level of specialization (Chapter 7). Teff-producing households are more productive with better levels of education and with greater access to financial institutions, production information, and extension services. Access to and participation in markets, along with low risks of crop failure, help farmers specialize to become more efficient and productive. However, specialization depends on many factors and may not be appropriate for all households because of the risks associated with cultivating fewer crops (Chapter 7).

Some believe that smallholders respond little to changes in economic incentives. Using dynamic models, the association of price with the amount of land farmers cultivate with teff (teff acreage demand) was examined in Chapter 8. The results show that teff acreage demand rises both in the short run and long run in response to increases in teff price. Moreover, increases in the opportunity cost to farmers, as a result of a potentially greater revenue attained from other crops, led to a fall in teff acreage allocation. Overall, teff was found to be sensitive to market changes even over a short period and teff supply is price elastic. Indeed, a comparison of these estimated elasticities with those obtained by a previous study using the same approach but with data from a different period illustrates the importance of government policies to agricultural supply response (Taffesse 2003) (Chapter 8).

A number of further insights regarding productivity growth come from analysis covering the major teff production zones (Chapter 9). First, the levels of input use exhibit high rates of return to investments in the development of better seed varieties such as Quncho. Second, that farmers with access to extension services achieve higher productivity suggests that the investments made by the government to expand the agricultural extension system have paid off (Davis et al. 2010). Third, remoteness is associated with decreased productivity due to lower output prices and possibly restricted access to modern inputs at reasonable prices. Reducing the costs of remoteness by building roads and increasing distribution outlets therefore has a positive association with teff productivity (Minten et al. 2013b). Finally, teff is a labor-intensive crop producing higher yields when farmers spend more time plowing and weeding.

A large fraction of Ethiopia's economic growth comes from the agricultural sector. Having explored teff productivity from different angles, the question remains as to what impact an expansion of teff and cereal production might have on Ethiopia's economy. In Chapter 10 the effects of changes in production of teff, wheat, and maize in particular on the Ethiopian economy are analyzed using Computable General Equilibrium (CGE) modeling. This chapter considers the impacts of the government's Cereal Initiative, which promotes growth in the production of these three cereals. The analysis generates insights on the merits of such investments.

The results show that increasing teff production generates greater benefits for urban consumers, particularly for urban poor households. This impact is lower with growth in the output of the other two cereals. Demand factors explain some of the consumption patterns observed—teff is viewed as a superior commodity and its consumption is associated with a better quality of life.

Nevertheless, maize provides more production on less land, which has strategic significance regarding the productivity decision. Furthermore, the market value of production is an important criterion guiding farmers' decisions on which crops to cultivate (Chapters 8 and 10). Given the agroecological diversity of Ethiopia, though, a mix of cereals makes sense for agroeconomic reasons alone (Chapters 7 and 10).

The cereal subsector has already made and continues to offer a large contribution to potential economic transformation through agronomic productivity. Should the value chain become more complex with more of the processing of teff occurring outside the household, it is likely that teff consumption may be reclassified as a source of manufacturing growth rather than agricultural growth, as it is currently classified based on the prevailing definitions in the national accounts. This would then result in a shift in the economic structure with respect to the compilation of the national accounts. Through increased productivity and the extension of these value chains beyond the agricultural sector, gradually more positive spillovers into other sectors of the economy and stronger links will become established (Chapter 10).

Marketing

Teff value chains are found to be relatively unsophisticated, short, and in contrast with common perception, fairly well organized (Chapter 11). At the farm level there are no interlinked transactions with buyers of the produce (which is often seen in other countries, especially in more developed value chains), the role of credit is minor, and most of the transactions are cash transactions. Farmers obtain a relatively high share of the final retail price (on average 80 percent), and the importance of distress sales is low. During 2001–2011, changes in the market structure of teff seem to have been linked with economic growth, urbanization, improved roads (and consequently decreased transport costs and possibly competition in better and bigger fleets), greater access to information and communications technology (mobile phones are universally used by brokers and traders, striking deals and bypassing wholesale markets entirely), and better agricultural technology adoption. These changes in teff markets have given rise to predicted outcomes of considerable market improvements. For example, increasing urbanization, increased supply, and income growth have led to more quantities traded and greater economies of scale and thus to lower margins overall. In addition, access to better price information has contributed to a more efficient marketing system and consequently lower overall margins (Chapter 12).

While better road conditions, declining transportation costs, and smaller marketing margins generally result in a more efficient agricultural economy, change inevitably results in both winners and losers along the value chain. Nonetheless, the net gain for the economy as a whole is likely to be substantial, yet there is still significant room for improvement. The transformation of the teff production and marketing systems is shown to be still at an early stage of agricultural development (for example, Reardon and Timmer 2007) (Chapter 13). At the production level the number of farmers who use improved varieties is still low, the quantities of chemical fertilizers that are being used are still below the recommended levels, and mechanization, which is happening quickly in other emerging economies, is still mostly absent (Chapter 6). In addition, very little vertical integration is observed as well as minimal coordination mechanisms between teff production and marketing. Midstream and downstream of the value chain, little evidence of upscaling of trade is seen nor of modern retail or of branding. Typically, these can be observed as agricultural market development gets under way (Reardon et al. 2012).

However, despite this seemingly negative picture, modern inputs are increasingly adopted in teff production. Quality and convenience demands are on the rise among teff consumers, and the teff marketing system is becoming more efficient. All these changes have resulted from exposure to the increasing availability of improved varieties and chemical fertilizer, a better extension system in rural areas, and conversely the increasing downstream demand for commercial teff, which is driven by growing incomes, urbanization, and high income elasticities for teff. The changes upstream have especially transpired in those areas that are reasonably well connected to the city, illustrating the importance of market access and demand for rural and agricultural transformation (Chapter 13).

Consumption

Comprising a third of the country's total food budget, teff plays a significant role in the average urban Ethiopian household's diet. Teff is consumed largely by the well-off households and its purchase increases with income. Households headed by individuals with better labor market status also seem to consume relatively more teff than those with poor labor market status, such as casual workers (Chapter 14). Over the period of study covered in Chapter 14, the consumption of teff barely changed, yet the price increased by nearly threefold. This indicates that some households continue to rely on teff as a main source of carbohydrate in their diet, irrespective of the price increase (see Chapter 10). However, given the fact that around 28 percent of urban households fall below the absolute poverty line (Alem 2014), there is some concern that the high prices of teff are excluding the poor, who seem to resort to cheaper cereals in their food baskets (Chapter 14).

Teff appears in different colors (super white, white, mixed, and red), and these are used as indicators of quality and hence market value by producers, traders, and consumers (Minten et al. 2013a) (Chapters 3 and 14). In addition, there is variation in nutrient composition across teff varieties, which warrants further research (Chapter 15). Teff flour is considered to be nutritionally rich and healthy with similar amount of protein and fiber as whole wheat flour, yet it provides more nutritional substances such as iron and is gluten-free (Baye 2014). Despite having a very good nutrient profile, teff's consumption is limited to Ethiopia and Eritrea. Knowledge about teff seems a well-kept secret. Limited awareness of its rich nutritional profile, along with the challenges faced in making teff-based food products for domestic and international consumers, has restrained its advantage as a global food source for human consumption. However, studies on the excellent nutritional composition of teff and its potential to create teff-based food products have grown (Chapter 15).

The role of teff consumption on the management and prevention of diabetes, and the human absorption (bioavailability) of iron in teff and how it can contribute to the prevention of iron deficiency, has generated great international interest. Moreover, there are the possible health benefits in managing celiac disease linked to gluten. Obviously, all these areas pertaining to health benefits require further investigation. Nevertheless, all point to the potential of teff to be a future global functional food for health promotion and disease prevention (Chapter 15).

Implications

This book describes and documents major changes that are occurring throughout the teff value chain. However, transformation of teff production and marketing systems in Ethiopia are yet to reach the level to which the country aspires. Despite the progress, a number of constraints still apply and need to be addressed by policy and other interventions to facilitate further transformation. Table 16.1 describes the principal challenges faced by producing and marketing teff in Ethiopia, along with those factors or actions that could help mitigate these challenges.

TABLE 16.1 Challenges for policy changes and proposed actions

Challenge	Response
Improving productivity and resilience	Invest in basic research and researchers
	Invest in a breeding program that addresses multiple traits
	Consider climate change in technology development
Selecting and scaling-up new technologies	Consider gender impacts
	Improve monitoring and evaluation of uptake of improved technologies
	Conduct rigorous and regular evaluation of outcomes
Establishing fit-for-purpose distribution systems	Experiment with alternative input delivery mechanisms involving different arrangements, actors, and payment modalities
	Improve market efficiencies by stimulating involvement of cooperatives
Managing labor demand and postharvest operations	Provide sturdy, multipurpose, cheap mechanized planters and harvesters
	Invest in storage technology
Extending markets	Devote time for study and exploration of output options and to mitigate marketing challenges
	Promote appropriate deepening of credit, insurance, and labor markets

Source: Authors.

Challenge 1. Improving Productivity and Resilience

Over time, there have been relatively few investments in Ethiopia toward improving teff productivity, and expenditures for R&D in this area have not been at appropriate levels (Flaherty, Kelemework, and Kelemu 2010). Given the size of the sector in the country, the beneficial attributes of teff, the increasing urban demand for the crop, and the relatively low yields, as well as the growing challenges of climate change, it seems that increased investments toward the development of appropriate technologies that can assure a resilient teff sector would be beneficial for Ethiopia.

As shown in Chapter 9, the returns gained from successful developments in improved seeds have been very high, and there is still significant room for growth given the low investments of the past. Further strengthening of agricultural research and extension can lead to higher generation and adoption rates of improved, high-performing, and resilient seeds, and thus it is likely to deliver large payoffs. To stimulate adoption, better supply and marketing conditions are required. On the supply side, although the public sector plays an important role, channeling more resources into the development of improved seeds at local research centers would reap higher returns (Alston et al. 2000). So would a more active role from the private sector. Moreover, a more vibrant seed sector with better marketing, distribution, and information provision on improved seeds is critical.

Climate change is expected to have a significant impact on Ethiopian agriculture in the decades ahead. It is estimated that the shifting rainfall patterns and increasing temperatures will lead to large crop yield decreases (Robinson, Strzepek, and Cervigni 2013). Moreover, the incidences of unexpected weather shocks are projected to increase. Incorporating climate change and developing more teff seeds adapted to weather stress and shocks will therefore become increasingly important to assure resilience of the sector.

Challenge 2. Selecting and Scaling-up New Technologies

Once promising improved technologies have been developed and tested in research settings, there is need for careful on-farm trials that are subject to rigorous impact evaluations before the scale-up process. Often important lessons can be learned from such impact evaluations that allow fine-tuning of technologies, extension packages, and messages, which in turn lead to more successful scaling-up of improved and adapted technologies. It is also important to ensure that appropriate monitoring and evaluation schemes are in place at the national level. This would assure that appropriate lessons are learned on adoption and disadoption of new technologies, and which policy instruments (for example, access to credit, extension, distribution, and incentives) can be better tailored to improve uptake of superior technologies.

Challenge 3. Establishing Fit-for-purpose Distribution Systems

Intensification of teff production will need to receive even more attention in the future since land constraints have increasingly become binding (Headey, Dereje Regassa, and Taffesse 2014). There will be a need for more widespread adoption of modern inputs and improved technologies. Two modern inputs—chemical fertilizer and improved seeds—widely used in teff production and delivered through extensive national distribution systems are important. Chemical fertilizer use stays central to the government effort to increase agricultural productivity overall. It has therefore initiated a unique soil-mapping exercise in the country to adjust fertilizer packages to specific soil conditions. This is a promising development that might address soil deficiencies in the country more appropriately. However, prices of chemical fertilizers are sometimes out of reach for poor farmers or simply not available at all to them. Moreover, the distribution system of improved teff seeds could be improved. As illustrated throughout this book, the accessibility of good distribution systems, whether for seed or for fertilizer, is crucial to encouraging the adoption of these inputs. Therefore, alternative and more inclusive distribution systems of these modern inputs should be considered.

Challenge 4. Managing Labor Demand and Postharvest Operations

The increasing transformation of Ethiopia's economy is leading to higher real wages in rural areas (Bachewe et al. 2015). These higher rural wages will provide the impetus and incentives for innovative labor-reducing technologies (Ruttan and Hayami 1984). This trend can already be seen by the increasing adoption of herbicides, a substitute for weeding labor, in commercial teff areas, but it will also drive the demand for more mechanization, especially for those activities where there is a peak demand for labor, such as during planting and harvesting periods. Mechanization in teff production and postharvest activities is currently low. Making sure that sturdy multipurpose mechanized planters and harvesters, and spare parts, at affordable prices will be available to alleviate that constraint is an important further challenge for sustained higher teff productivity.

Investments will be required to fund new off-farm technologies, such as storage and processing, which might help to satisfy the rapidly increasing urban demand. It seems that current storage is mostly carried out at the farm level, but the rather often rudimentary storage in these settings might need to be upgraded to reduce storage losses and smooth out teff supply over the year. The milling sector might also see a drive toward upgrading and modernization, as seen in other countries driven by the requirements of more demanding consumers (Reardon et al. 2014).

Challenge 5. Extending Markets

As the Ethiopian population is becoming richer and more urbanized, this will lead to changing demands for foods, different consumption baskets, and a transformed agricultural sector overall (Worku Hassen et al. 2016). The teff sector is a case in point, although it has to be recognized that there will be a significant part of the population that remains relatively poor and that will likely not be involved in shaping future teff markets, given the high income elasticity of teff. It seems there will be an increasing willingness-to-pay for quality and convenience teff food products by these relatively better-off consumers, likely leading to two major changes in future market demand. First, it is expected that demand for teff flour and injera will grow fast, given the increasing opportunity costs, especially for women who will increasingly demand convenient and ready-to-use products. We are therefore likely to see a movement away from the purchase of unprocessed teff grains. Second, adulteration has been reported to be a major issue in urban teff markets. Hence, branded teff products with ensured quality characteristics might likely take off in a market where quality matters, and where consumers are willing to pay for such characteristics. Further stimulation to expand a private modern retail sector—that is currently hardly involved in teff trade—might possibly lead to better coordination toward quality assurance for teff consumers.

Further exploring the appropriate role of farmer unions and cooperatives in output marketing would be useful. It is assumed that cooperatives can play an important role in improving the access of smallholders to markets (Bernard et al. 2010; Francesconi and Heerink 2010). However, while these cooperatives have been successful in the marketing of some crops, their importance in cereal—and teff—markets is less pronounced, given that coordination of output sales by cooperatives is more complicated in such situations.[1] International experience has shown that the role of cooperatives is especially successful in cases of export crops or perishable products (such as dairy), where good coordination between small farmers is a precondition for successful development of value chains (for example, Cunningham 2009). For these reasons the role of cooperatives and farming organizations has seemingly been less important until now in the case of teff.

Moreover, the increasing focus on gluten-free food products in international markets will lead to a surge in demand in the near future within these markets (Research and Markets 2014). Given the unique gluten-free property of teff, positioning Ethiopia in a situation where it can take full advantage of these emerging opportunities would be beneficial for Ethiopia's teff export performance. However, it will need to build up supply chains that can reliably and sustainably deliver quality products in sufficient quantities. Developing an export sector such as this for teff might therefore demand considerable time and effort, especially given the limited expertise and experience in this

---

1 Based on a large-scale survey of farmers and cooperatives in 2005/2006, Bernard et al. (2010) show that only a limited number of farmers participate in cooperatives, even when cooperatives were established in their villages. Especially the smallest farmers tended to not use cooperatives. Similar results are cited in this book about teff (see Chapter 11).

area and considering that cereal export bans have been in place for a number of years, which have restricted exposure to market opportunities.

The dilemma, however, is how small-scale Ethiopian teff farmers may benefit from such export opportunities and the effect that such rapid growth in the export sector may have on domestic consumption (especially for the poor from the high prices of teff). It seems that there could be comparative advantages for potential new entrants and/or companies to rapidly increase production and tap into the expanding export market. Rapid growth in supplying the export market can seemingly be facilitated under situations where tradeoffs with domestic consumption are limited, and agronomic and climatic conditions would be permissive to increase yields. With this in mind, the government is therefore currently looking at stimulating large-scale commercial farming in less land-constrained settings of Ethiopia, with a focus on these export markets.

These efforts should be complemented by those that aim to strengthen credit, insurance, and labor markets. The demand for improved credit and insurance services is likely to rise, not only reflecting the needs of an increasingly more complex teff value chain but also in response to the challenges of climate change. Experimentation with different modalities of provision, such as index insurance and innovative input credit schemes, should continue and be scaled up as appropriate. Similarly, labor markets have to develop further to more efficiently address the expansion of wage labor and the reallocation that will occur due to greater prevalence of modern techniques of production and concomitant growth in agricultural labor productivity. In this regard, further exploring traditional seasonal agricultural labor flows can provide useful insights.

This book has systematically established the considerable benefits and the even greater potential of teff in Ethiopia. In parallel, it has highlighted that the realization of this potential requires further public sector leadership and investment as well as noticeable expansion in private sector participation, in part promoted by a more active public policy and public-private partnership. These efforts, this book also underscores, need to be undergirded by rigorous evidence on and deepening understanding about the challenges and their solutions.

References

Alem, Y. 2015. "Poverty Dynamics and Intra-Household Heterogeneity in Occupations: Evidence from Urban Ethiopia." *Oxford Development Studies* 43 (1): 20–43.

Alston, J. M., C. Chan-Kang, M. C. Marra, P. G. Pardey, and T. J. Wyatt. 2000. "A Meta-analysis of Rates of Return to Agricultural R&D: Ex pede Herculem?" Research Report 113. Washington, DC: International Food Policy Research Institute (IFPRI).

Bachewe, F., G. Berhane, B. Minten, and A. S. Taffesse. 2015. *Agricultural Growth in Ethiopia (2004–2014): Evidence and Drivers.* Ethiopia Strategy Support Program (ESSP) discussion paper. Addis Ababa: IFPRI and Ethiopia Development Research Institute.

Baye, K. 2014. *Teff: Nutrient Composition and Health Benefits.* ESSP II Working Paper 67. Addis Ababa: IFPRI.

Bernard, T., D. J. Spielman, A. S. Taffesse, and E. Z. Gabre-Madhin. 2010. *Cooperatives for Staple Crop Marketing.* IFPRI Research Monograph 164. Washington, DC: IFPRI.

Collier, P., and S. Dercon. 2014. "African Agriculture in 50 Years: Smallholders in a Rapidly Changing World?" *World Development* 63: 92–101.

Cunningham, K. 2009. *Rural and Urban Linkages: Operation Flood's Role in India's Dairy Development.* IFPRI Discussion Paper 924. Washington, DC: IFPRI.

Davis, K., B. Swanson, D. Amudavi, D. Mekonnen, A. Flohrs, J. Riese, C. Lamb, and E. Zerfu. 2010. *In-depth Assessment of the Public Agricultural Extension System of Ethiopia and Recommendations for Impact.* IFPRI discussion paper 1041. Washington, DC: IFPRI.

Demeke, M., V. Kelly, T. S. Jayne, A. Said, J.-C. Le Valleé, and H. Chen. 1998. *Agricultural Market Performance and Determinants of Fertilizer Use in Ethiopia.* Grain Market Research Project Working Paper 10. Addis Ababa, Ethiopia: Ministry of Economic Development and Cooperation.

Dorosh, P., H. G. Wang, L. You, and E. Schmidt. 2010. *Crop Production and Road Connectivity in Sub-Saharan Africa: A Spatial Analysis.* Policy Research Working Paper 5385. Washington, DC: World Bank.

Duflo, E., M. Kremer, and J. Robinson. 2008. "How High Are Rates of Return to Fertilizer? Field Experiments in Evidence from Kenya." *American Economic Review* 98 (2): 482–488.

Flaherty, K., F. Kelemework, and K. Kelemu. 2010. *Ethiopia: Recent Developments in Agricultural Research.* Washington, DC: IFPRI; Addis Ababa: Ethiopian Institute of Agricultural Research.

Francesconi, G. N., and N. Heerink. 2010. "Ethiopian Agricultural Cooperatives in an Era of Global Commodity Exchange: Does Organizational Form Matter?" *Journal of African Economies* 20 (1): 153–177.

Headey, D., M. Dereje Regassa, and A. S. Taffesse. 2014. "Land Constraints and Agricultural Intensification in Ethiopia: A Village-Level Analysis of High-Potential Areas." *Food Policy* 48: 129–141.

Minten, B., B. Koru, and D. Stifel. 2013. "The Last Mile(s) in Modern Input Distribution: Pricing, Profitability, and Adoption." *Agricultural Economics* 44 (6): 629–646.

Minten, B., S. Tamru, E. Engida Legesse, and T. Kuma. 2013a. *Ethiopia's Value Chains on the Move: The Case of Teff.* ESSP II Working Paper 52. Addis Ababa: IFPRI/ESSP II.

———. 2013b. *Using Evidence in Unraveling Food Supply Chains in Ethiopia: The Supply Chain of Teff from Major Production Areas to Addis Ababa.* ESSP II Working Paper 54. Addis Ababa: IFPRI/ESSP II.

Moser, C. M., and C. B. Barrett. 2003. "The Disappointing Adoption Dynamics of a Yield-Increasing, Low External-Input Technology: The Case of SRI in Madagascar." *Agricultural Systems* 76 (3): 1085–1100.

Reardon, T., K. Chen, B. Minten, and L. Adriano. 2012. *The Quiet Revolution in Staple Food Value Chains: Enter the Dragon, the Elephant, and the Tiger.* Mandaluyong City, Philippines: Asian Development Bank (ADB); Washington, DC: IFPRI.

Reardon, T., K. Chen, B. Minten, L. Adriano, T. A. Dao, J. Wang, and S. Das Gupta. 2014. "The Quiet Revolution in Asia's Rice Value Chains." *Annals of the New York Academy of Sciences* 1331: 106–118.

Reardon, T., and C. P. Timmer. 2007. "Transformation of Markets for Agricultural Output in Developing Countries since 1950: How Has Thinking Changed?" In *Handbook of Agricultural Economics.* Vol. 3, edited by R. E. Evenson and P. Pingali, 2808–2855. Amsterdam: Elsevier Press.

Research and Markets. 2014. "Global Gluten-Free Food Market 2014–2018." Ireland.

Robinson, S., K. Strzepek, and R. Cervigni. 2013. *The Cost of Adapting to Climate Change in Ethiopia: Sector-Wise and Macro-Economic Estimates.* ESSP II (ESSP) Working Paper 53. Addis Ababa: ESSP.

Ruttan, V. W., and Y. Hayami. 1984. "Toward a Theory of Induced Institutional Innovation." *Journal of Development Studies* 20 (4): 203–223.

Taffesse, A. S. 2003. "Government Policy and Dynamic Supply Response: A Study of the Compulsory Grain Delivery System." MPRA Paper 18674. African Centre for Economic and Historical Studies.

Worku Hassen, I., M. Dereje Regassa, B. Minten, and K. Hirvonen. 2016. *Diet Transformation in Africa: The Case of Ethiopia.* ESSP Working Paper 87. Addis Ababa: ESSP.

Contributors

Yonas Alem (yonas.alem@economics.gu.se) is a researcher at the Gothenburg Centre for Globalization and Development, Department of Economics, University of Gothenburg, Sweden.

Kebebew Assefa (kebebew.assefa@yahoo.com) is a senior researcher at the Debre Zeit Agricultural Research Center, Ethiopian Institute of Agricultural Research (EIAR).

Fantu Nisrane Bachewe (F.Bachewe@cgiar.org) is a research coordinator in the Development Strategy and Governance Division and Ethiopia Strategy Support Program of the International Food Policy Research Institute (IFPRI), Addis Ababa.

Kaleab Baye (kaleabbaye@gmail.com) is affiliated with the Center for Food Science, College of Natural Sciences, Addis Ababa University, Ethiopia.

Todd Benson (T.Benson@cgiar.org) is a senior research fellow in the Development Strategy and Governance Division of IFPRI, Washington, DC.

Guush Berhane (guush.berhane@cgiar.org) is a research fellow, Development Strategy and Governance Division and Ethiopia Strategy Support Program of IFPRI, Addis Ababa.

Petra Brown (petrabrown@hotmail.co.uk) is a collaborator with the Development Strategy and Governance Division and Ethiopia Strategy Support Program of IFPRI, Addis Ababa.

Solomon Chanyalew (solchk2@gmail.com) is a director at the Debre Zeit Agricultural Research Center, EIAR.

Mekdim Dereje Regassa (mekdimdereje@gmail.com) was a research assistant in the Ethiopia Strategy Support Program of the Ethiopian Development Research Institute (EDRI), Addis Ababa, at the time he contributed to this work. He is currently a PhD candidate at Bonn University, Germany.

Ermias Engida Legesse (ermiasengida@gmail.com) was a research assistant in the Ethiopia Strategy Support Program of EDRI, Addis Ababa, at the time he contributed to this work. He is currently a PhD candidate at the Institute for Food and Resource Economics, Bonn University, Germany.

Getu Hailu (ghailu@uoguelph.ca) is an associate professor in the Department of Food, Agricultural, and Resource Economics (FARE) of the University of Guelph, Ontario, Canada.

Mekamu Kedir Jemal (m.kedirjemal@cgiar.org) is a research analyst in the Development Strategy and Governance Division of IFPRI, Washington, DC.

Bethelhem Koru (betiye97@yahoo.com) is a research assistant in the Ethiopia Strategy Support Program of EDRI, Addis Ababa.

Tadesse Kuma (kwtadesse@yahoo.com) is a researcher at EDRI, Addis Ababa.

Dawit Kelemework Mekonnen (d.mekonnen@cgiar.org) was a PhD candidate in the Department of Agricultural and Applied Economics at the University of Georgia, Athens, US, at the time he contributed to this work. He is currently a research fellow in the Environment and Production Technology Division of IFPRI, Washington, DC.

Bart Minten (b.minten@cgiar.org) is a program leader and senior research fellow in the Development Strategy and Governance Division and Ethiopia Strategy Support Program of IFPRI, Addis Ababa.

Emily Schmidt (E.Schmidt@cgiar.org) is a research fellow, Development Strategy and Governance Division of IFPRI, Washington, DC.

Måns Söderbom (mans.soderbom@economics.gu.se) is a professor of economics at the Department of Economics of the School of Business, Economics and Law, University of Gothenburg, Sweden.

David J. Spielman (d.spielman@cgiar.org) is a senior research fellow in the Environment and Production Technology Division of IFPRI, Washington, DC.

David Stifel (stifeld@lafayette.edu) is a chair, International Affairs Program, and professor in the Department of Economics of Lafayette College, Easton, PA, US.

Alemayehu Seyoum Taffesse (A.SeyoumTaffesse@cgiar.org) is a senior research fellow in the Development Strategy and Governance Division and Ethiopia Strategy Support Program of IFPRI, Addis Ababa.

Seneshaw Tamru (seni2y@yahoo.com) is a PhD student at LICOS—Centre for Institutions and Economic Performance, University of Leuven, Belgium.

James Thurlow (J.Thurlow@cgiar.org) is a senior research fellow in the Development Strategy and Governance Division of IFPRI, Washington, DC.

Helina Tilahun (helinatilahun@yahoo.com) is a GIS analyst, Ethiopia Strategy Support Program of EDRI, Addis Ababa.

Joachim Vandercasteelen (Joachim.Vandercasteelen@kuleuven.be) is a post-doctoral fellow at LICOS—Centre for Institutions and Economic Performance, University of Leuven, Belgium.

Alfons Weersink (aweersin@uoguelph.ca) is a professor in the Department of FARE of the University of Guelph, Ontario, Canada.

Ibrahim Worku Hassen (ibra1612@yahoo.com) was a research assistant in the Ethiopia Strategy Support Program of EDRI, Addis Ababa, at the time he contributed to this work. He is currently a master's candidate at the Kennedy School of Government, Harvard University, Cambridge, MA, US.

Index

Page numbers for entries occurring in figures are followed by an *f*; those for entries in notes, by an *n*; and those for entries in tables, by a *t*.

Made in the USA
Las Vegas, NV
03 November 2026

57424840R00266